Cornelius Brown

The Annals of Newark-Upon-Trent

Comprising the history, curiosities, and antiquities of the borough. Illustrated with engravings and autographs, and with 9 photos. by the Woodbury permanent process, from original drawings by George Sheppard

Cornelius Brown

The Annals of Newark-Upon-Trent

Comprising the history, curiosities, and antiquities of the borough. Illustrated with engravings and autographs, and with 9 photos. by the Woodbury permanent process, from original drawings by George Sheppard

ISBN/EAN: 9783337012168

Printed in Europe, USA, Canada, Australia, Japan

Cover: Foto ©ninafisch / pixelio.de

More available books at **www.hansebooks.com**

THE ANNALS

OF

NEWARK-UPON-TRENT

COMPRISING THE

History, Curiosities, and Antiquities of the Borough

BY

CORNELIUS BROWN

FELLOW OF THE ROYAL SOCIETY OF LITERATURE, JOINT-PROPRIETOR OF THE 'NEWARK ADVERTISER,' EDITOR OF 'NOTES ABOUT NOTTS, HISTORICAL AND ANTIQUARIAN'

ILLUSTRATED WITH ENGRAVINGS AND AUTOGRAPHS

AND WITH

NINE PHOTOGRAPHS BY THE WOODBURY PERMANENT PROCESS

FROM ORIGINAL DRAWINGS BY MR. GEORGE SHEPPARD, BOROUGH SURVEYOR

LONDON
H. SOTHERAN & CO., 36 PICCADILLY AND 136 STRAND
NEWARK: S. WHILES, 30 AND 31 STODMAN STREET
MDCCCLXXIX

[Entered at Stationers' Hall.]

PREFACE.

AMONGST the interesting old towns which have a history that is worth narrating the Borough of Newark-upon-Trent, once dignified by the title of "The Key of the North," may fairly claim a worthy place. Commanding in its situation on the Great North Road, and possessed of a formidable fortress, it fell to the lot of Newark to be actively concerned in events of great national importance. If we glance over the record of olden times what a list of memorable scenes is brought vividly before us!— fierce troops contending for the possession of the much-coveted castle; King John, harassed in mind and diseased in body, borne on a litter through the streets, and ending his days within the castle walls; excited messengers rushing in to inform the townsmen that a terrible battle had been fought at Stoke, and that the adherents of the impostor Simnel had been struck down until their blood flowed in a crimson stream to the Trent; Cardinal Wolsey, when fickle fortune had ceased to smile upon him, passing through, gloomy and sorrowful, with a limited retinue to seek repose at his "poore house" at Southwell; Lord Shrewsbury marching with the troops of his royal master Henry VIII. to disperse the York and Lincoln rebels, with whom the Vicar of Newark had lucklessly cast in his lot; Lord Suffolk and the regiments under him sent on a similar errand, confident in the belief that ere long the discontented ones would find to their sorrow that "oon payr of light legges wilbe worth five payre of handes;" Lord Clinton, with the forces of "good Queen Bess," on their way to encounter the rebellious partisans of the rich Duke of Norfolk; the first James, proceeding from Scotland to the English throne, loyally entertained by the townsmen, and specially gratified with the eloquent Latin oration of Alderman Twentyman; Charles the First, as the storm-clouds gathered, calling the knights, gentlemen, and freeholders of the county around him to express his confidence in their devotion; a loyal garrison, encouraged by the king-loving people, successfully resisting besieging forces; Queen Henrietta, "generallissimo" over several thousand troops, heartily cheered as she marches on her way to join the king; sturdy Cavaliers issuing stealthily forth to attack the county town; the garrison again in action repelling the combined efforts of determined foes; Prince Rupert charging impetuously down Beacon Hill, and, with a shout "for God and for the king," driving the enemy within the shelter of their works at the Spital; the Parliamentarians marching discontentedly away, and returning again for a third unsuccessful effort; tired, dust-covered, almost broken-hearted troops from the fatal field of Naseby seeking the succour which Newark afforded; the defeated monarch on his weary wanderings supping at the Friary; Prince Rupert running the gauntlet that he may give the king his own account of the loss of Bristol; Scotch and English forces quartered thickly round the town making unavailing efforts to effect its capture; a messenger from the king, now a prisoner with the Scotch at Kelham, bidding the gallant governor to surrender; deputations of undaunted townspeople urging his lordship to "trust God and sally;" elated Parliamentarians taking possession after the "brave old rugged boys with iron faces" have marched sadly away; and then a mixed gathering of destructive spirits demolishing with pick and spade the fine old castle. But the stirring events of olden times are far from constituting all that is noteworthy in the history of Newark. In more recent and more peaceful days the celebrated David Hartley might have been seen teaching in the Grammar School and writing medical treatises; Dr. Stukely, the antiquary, hunting for information whilst visiting his friends; Bishop Warburton, the learned author of *The Divine Legation of Moses*, and the friend of Pope, rambling in early life through the meadows and lanes around Newark, "the unthinking place of his nativity;" Byron, passing from the Clinton Arms to Ridge's shop to inspect the proof-sheets of his first poetic effusions; Sadler, author and orator, busy canvassing for votes; Wilde and Thesiger, two Lord Chancellors in embryo, fighting a stubborn political battle on which great things depended; and Gladstone making his first bow as a politician before the "worthy and independent electors" of the borough.

These, strung together in the briefest form, are a few of the memorable scenes and notable incidents which Newark has witnessed, and it will readily be conceded that the career of a town which possesses such reminiscences is well worth describing. In the belief that a volume which would embody a careful record of the doings of byegone days, with an account of the objects of historical interest that remain in the borough, would be acceptable to the public, I determined, when I became connected with Newark, that I would make an effort to produce one. About five years ago I entered upon the somewhat laborious but congenial task, and since then it has occupied such portions of time as I could spare from the pursuit of an always anxious and often arduous profession. I do not feel disposed to trouble the reader with a dry list of the numerous sources to which I have gone for information. No one can pretend to do justice to the history of an old town without referring to some hundreds of books, documents, and newspaper files, the bare enumeration of which would be of no interest to the general reader, and of no value to the experienced antiquary, who is already familiar with the best means of obtaining serviceable material. It would be ungracious of me, however, not to say that I have derived assistance from the labours of Mr. Dickinson, whose History of the Borough, published sixty years since, contains the fruits of much industry and care; and that the *Calendars of State Papers*, the *Reports of the Royal Commission on Historical Manuscripts*, and the various Rolls issued by official authority, have opened out to me rich treasures of information about Newark that have not hitherto been referred to or collected. I have quoted many of the authorities in the footnotes, and others are referred to incidentally in the body of the work. Perhaps it will suffice if I add further that wherever I have thought I could glean anything useful and reliable I have willingly and cheerfully gone, and that if I have left any source unvisited or unused it has not been for want of the will to take advantage of it.

Having said this much of the nature of the work, and of the field from which I have tried to reap a harvest of useful details, it becomes a pleasing duty to unburden myself, as far as possible, of a heavy load of obligation. There are few writers of local history who have met with more courteous and efficient assistance than myself; and the ready aid which it has been my good fortune to meet with has not only lightened my labours, but has been an invaluable encouragement and support. To the Right Hon. W. E. Gladstone, M.P., I am indebted for the revision and improvement of those pages which refer to his first candidature and subsequent connection with Newark; to the Right Rev. the Bishop-Suffragan of Nottingham (Dr. Trollope) I owe my hearty thanks for the readily-accorded permission to embody valuable papers written by him, descriptive of the Castle and the Parish Church; and to Captain A. E. Lawson Lowe, F.S.A., I am under much obligation for his interesting and carefully prepared Notes on important families who have been connected with Newark. I desire also to tender my thanks to the Worshipful the Mayor (Mr. Alderman Pratt), for permission to examine the Corporation Minute-Book and Papers; to the Vicar (the Rev. Dr. Pearson), for giving me access to the Parish Registers; to the Town-Clerk (Mr. Godfrey Tallents), for his readiness to place any Records in his office at my service; to Mr. W. Stevenson of Hull for his thoughtful Paper on the Antiquity of the Borough: to Mr. C. J. Ridge for information concerning the first editions of Byron's Poems; to Mr. R. F. Sketchley, B.A., of South Kensington Museum, Mr. Edward Marshall of Leicester, and Mr. W. H. Stevenson of Hull, for useful References and Extracts; to Mr. J. P. Briscoe, the Chief Librarian of the Nottingham Free Libraries, for the careful preparation from the proof-sheets of the Index to this volume; to the Librarians of the various Libraries to which I have resorted, for their unvarying courtesy; to the numerous Correspondents who have communicated with me; and to the Subscribers, whose support has obliterated financial anxiety. As will be seen from the title page, the Illustrations which are introduced in the volume are taken from drawings placed at my disposal by Mr. George Sheppard, Borough Surveyor. Their excellence is beyond question, and they will be a standing testimony to his artistic skill. It only remains for me to add the expression of my earnest hope that the book will be found satisfactory, and that it may prove a useful addition to local literature. I trust the narrative form in which the information is presented will tend to remove from it any imputation of dryness or dulness, and that readers will have the pleasure of finding, as they peruse these pages, that there is much to interest and something to edify in the Annals of Newark.

CORNELIUS BROWN.

NEWARK, *May* 1879.

LIST OF ILLUSTRATIONS.

Photographs.

Newark Parish Church, Exterior	*Frontispiece.*
The Fleming Brass	*Facing Page* 22
The "Dance of Death"	38
Original Grant of Arms	78
The Beaumont Cross	118
Newark Castle	176
Parish Church before its Restoration	210
East End of the Church	256
Interior of the Church as it is	308

Engravings and Autographs.

Facsimile of Signature of Magnus	*Page* 50
Monastic Seal found at the Friary	,, 63
Common Seal of the Town	,, 78
Facsimile of Signature of Dr. John Moseley	,, 108
,, ,, Hercules Clay	,, 135
The Governor's House, Stodman Street	,, 149
Facsimile of Signature of William Baker, Mayor	,, 162
Siege Coins struck at the Castle	,, 167
Portrait of Bishop Warburton	,, 227
,, Mr. M. T. Sadler	,, 265
,, Sergeant Wilde	,, 266
,, Mr. W. E. Gladstone	,, 289

ANNALS OF NEWARK-UPON-TRENT.

IN the charter of Charles the First, conferring valuable rights and serviceable privileges on the inhabitants of Newark, the town is described in complimentary language as being "ancient and populous." It is probable that a critic disposed to question the strict applicability of such definitions would have no trouble in advancing reasons why the term "populous" should not have been employed. Against the use of the word "ancient," however, it would be more difficult to raise substantial objections. The name Newark or New-wark is regarded as implying that there had previously been an old work in existence,[1] though it cannot, we fear, be definitely decided when the borough was founded or under what designation it was known before the name of Newark came into general use. Authentic references begin during the Anglo-Saxon Government. In the time of Edward the Confessor, Leofric, the famous Earl of Mercia, possessed the manor of Newark. Evidence prior to this record is naturally slender. The particulars which we have been able to obtain will be fully presented, together with the inferences to be drawn therefrom. We are aware from incontestable proofs that the town was familiar to the Saxons under the name of Newark. Was it, however, of Roman origin? If so, what designation did it bear? To a consideration of these points we invite attention, though we cannot but regret with an eminent historian that "the history of remote ages should always be so much involved in obscurity, uncertainty, and contradiction."[2]

In a treatise corrected for publication in 1734,[3] and dedicated to the Rev. W. Warburton, afterwards Bishop of Gloucester, who was a native of Newark, Dr. Stukely, the well-known antiquary, enters at some length into an inquiry as to the origin of the borough. He expresses himself satisfied from deliberation and examination that the town was a Roman city. He has no doubt it was built to protect the navigation of the Trent, and that what is now the castle was then a large granary, like the castle of Colchester, and the white tower of London. Many coins have been found in Newark, which were struck on the erection of buildings of

---

[1] Aldwark (Oldwork), says an antiquary, means the old Roman city repaired, and Newark, upon the same principle of construction, implies a new city built on the ruins of the old (?).
[2] Hume, chapter I.
[3] Quoted by Dickinson in his *History of Newark*, published in 1819.

this kind, with the inscription, *Providentiæ Aug.* For the purpose of security, the Romans surrounded their cities with walls. Dr. Stukely is satisfied that Newark was surrounded with a wall of Roman construction, at least on three sides, the castle and the river guarding the fourth. There were three gates: one stood at the junction of Castlegate with Northgate, and was not taken down until 1762. Another stood in the middle of a narrow street leading out of the market-place, known for many years as the Dry Bridge. This was called the Eastgate, and was taken down in the year 1784. The Doctor admits that the arches were not of Roman origin, but says they appeared to be composed in a great measure of Roman materials. A ditch existed contiguous to the wall, but building and modern improvements have obliterated it. A street close to the wall which guarded the south side of the town was known in Dr. Stukely's time as Potter's ditch. It then became Potter dike, but a banking-house being established there, it changed its name to Lombard Street, by which designation it is now known.

The next evidence that can be adduced is the finding of various Roman remains. Many years ago, a gentleman digging to plant some trees by the side of the Fossroad (which, running from Leicester to Lincoln, passes through Newark), discovered four urns lying in a straight line and at equal distances. They were soon broken in pieces by the workmen, imagining to find treasure therein; in one of them was only a rude piece of brass about the bulk of a small walnut, half melted down, with a bit of bone and some ashes sticking on the surface thereof amidst a quantity of burnt bones and ashes. In the others were square earthen beads, which seemed to be British, and a small brass Lar about an inch and a half long, but much consumed by rust. Of Roman coins considerable numbers have been found.

Dr. Stukely says, "I have in my possession one of Cneius Piso (mint-master to Augustus), consul two years before the time of our Saviour's birth, two very large ones of Trajan, one of Adrian, one of Verus, a Magnentius, having on the reverse the monogram of Christ, one of Antoninus Pius, and many of inferior size and value of later emperors. There have been found also the following:—a silver Domitian, reverse Minerva; a silver Volusenus, reverse Hygeia; a base silver Posthumus, a large and fine brass Diva Faustina, reverse Augusta S.C.; an Antoninus Pius, reverse Britannia. A Mr. Jno. Herring of Newark, who has been industrious in collecting coins found there, has a large Faustina, a Nero, a large Trajan of Corinthian brass with a Victory on the reverse, standing behind the emperor crowning him with the inscription, S.P.Q.R. *optimo principi.* He has also a very large medal, much defaced, some coins of Carausius, some of Aurelian, Gallienus, and Constantius. No foundations are ever dug about the town, but some of these coins are found; indeed, the ordinary ones are so common that the tradesmen of the place pass them for halfpence. I believe the Roman city was built here in the latter days of the empire; certainly after the construction of the Fosseway which passes through it." In another article the Doctor expresses his belief that the town was raised from neighbouring Roman cities, and was walled about with their remains. Horsley entertains a similar opinion, for in his observations on the sixth Iter of Antoninus we read, "I make no doubt but that this large town has arisen out of the ruins of Ad Pontem on the one side, and Crococalano on the other."

Having in this way laid it down as a self-evident truth that Newark had a Roman birth, Dr. Stukely inquires what name it possessed at its first erection. He inclines to think that it was *Eltavona*. The learned Mr. Baxter has placed it, he says, almost beyond controversy that the Roman name of the river Trent was *Tavus*, whence he calls Stafford, seated at the head of the river, *Trajectus ad Tavum*, *Ael* or *El* in old Celtic signifying supercilium. The two together give us the word Eltavum, or, according to other pronunciation, *Eltavon*. "Perhaps, however," writes the Doctor, "we need not go even so far as this for an etymology to support my conjecture of this place having been the *Eltavona* of the Romans. The river Davon (now pronounced Devon) or Tavon, runs under the castle walls of the town. Here the British built a fortification which took its name from the river on which it was erected. The Romans built this city, according to their usual custom, on the site of the British oppidum, and in part continued its name. Being destroyed by the Scots and Picts after the departure of the Romans, when the Saxons repaired, or rather rebuilt, it, not knowing its former name, they called it by that of one of the tributary streams on which it stands, the Snid or Snite, adding to it the termination *cester* to express its having been a Roman station. Thus the *Ael Tavum* of the Britons became the *Eltavona* of the Romans, and in course of time the *Sidnacester* of the Saxons." Now Sidnacester was an episcopal see of the Mercians: no less than nine bishops sat there successively, and it was consequently a place of considerable importance. To define its situation has been always a matter of great difficulty. Dr. Stukely boldly claims the distinction for Newark. He argues that it can only be sought for in *Provinciâ Lindissi*, that it must have been on the borders of the Mercian, and near to the Northumbrian, kingdom, and that it must have been a Roman city fenced about with a wall and ditch, for to such places the name cester was affixed by the Saxons.[1] Now the province of Lindsay did extend to the Trent as far as Newark,[2] and the country lying about Newark, between the Trent and the Witham, was the frontier between the Northumbrian and Mercian kings, and often contested by them. Under these circumstances Dr. Stukely thinks there need be little difficulty in identifying Newark as Sidnacester.

We have ventured thus far to advert to the treatise of an eminent antiquary in favour of the Roman origin of Newark, inasmuch as it includes the best arguments that can be used in proof of its ancient importance. The additional inquiries we have made enable us to supplement the learned Doctor's evidence in several particulars. Since the date of his comments, interesting antiquities have been brought

---

[1] It is tolerably certain that the Roman towns, or the sites upon which they stood in Saxon times, were called, in the case of important towns, "cesters," from the Latin *castra* (A.S. *ceaster*) a camp or fortified place; and in the case of secondary towns, "boros," from the Saxon *burh*, a town.

[2] Peck's *Annals*.

to light. In a little pamphlet [1] issued in the year 1847 we have a very intelligent account of the discovery of urns in Newark. The writer says:—

> Sepulchral urns were found by the side of the present Nottingham road, formerly the old Fosse-way of the Romans. Some workmen were employed in excavating foundations for a house, in 1836, on the premises of Mr. R. Norton, situated at the extremity of the town, in the direction before stated. After they had got a little beneath the surface of the ground, their progress was arrested by striking their implements against some earthen vessels, which they had hopes might have contained some hidden treasure; several of these were speedily reduced to fragments against a neighbouring wall, when, to the no small disappointment of these ruthless beings, nothing presented itself, save the dishonours of the grave—dust and mouldy bones.
>
> Urns to the amount of fifteen or sixteen were taken out in a tolerable state of preservation; but three or four times that number were broken and destroyed in digging, and many, I have no doubt, are still remaining in the ground. Mr. Norton very politely gave me every information in his power, and afterwards wrote me to this effect:—"*Newark, 24th Oct. 1837.* Sir—Since you were here, I have sunk a saw-pit, about 24 ft. long, 4 ft. wide, and 6 ft. deep: in digging out the earth and gravel we found many urns; they appear to have been placed in regular order, so much so, that before we had finished the work, we could guess, within a few inches, where we should find them. * * * Some years ago in building houses in our neighbourhood, a little nearer the town, several urns were discovered."
>
> I (continues Mr. Milner) was informed the whole of them were placed in an upright position in the ground, and within about 2 ft. or 2 ft. 6 inches from the surface; each contained calcined human bones; one alone, of which a drawing is preserved, contained, in addition to the dust and bones, these relics, now in possession of the author, viz. — a pair of tweezers about three inches long and with one of the arms missing—most probably broken off for want of care, in removal from the urn; a pair of scissors of iron much oxydised, likely to be of British manufacture, as Strabo mentions "sheeres" in enumerating articles of iron exported by the ancient Britons; these tell us that the urn contained the ashes of a female, as distinctly as the flint arrow-heads indicate the character of the huntsman; and the spear-head and battle-axe, that of the warrior. Combs in ivory and in wood, tweezers and scissors in bronze, are enumerated amongst other articles that have been found with the female mummies of Egypt. Several of the urns were made of clay, worked by hand, and simply dried in the sun; these were ornamented by indentures of various fashions, made in the moist clay, or by figures drawn in a rough manner, with a pointed instrument; whilst others were of a more regular form, much harder in structure, from having apparently undergone the application of the fire (probably that of the funeral pile) and seemed in other respects more nearly to correspond with the coarser description of Roman pottery.
>
> From the above circumstances, we are inclined to the opinion that these sepulchral urns may be reckoned as belonging to the Romanised British Period; the absence of flint or stone weapons proves, according to the rules laid down by Sir R. C. Hoare—and few have given more attention to these matters than that distinguished antiquary—that they belong to a later period than what is denominated the Celtic era. The situation in which they were found, viz., within a short distance of a Roman road, and at a convenient space beyond the boundary of one of their stations, together with the immense number of urns in the ground without any appearance of tumulus or barrow, seem to favour the opinion that this spot may have been used as an ordinary Roman cemetery. The pottery appears to resemble British rather than Roman manufacture—here we may probably have both, as it was not by any means unusual for the Romans to establish stations on the site of towns deserted by the vanquished Britons; hence these very urns may one day prove the town of Newark to be of greater antiquity than is generally supposed, as some of them may belong to the Celtic, whilst others to the Romanised British Period.

---

[1] *Cemetery Burial; or, Sepulture Ancient and Modern,* by George Milner.

In addition to the urns which have been turned up from time to time in Newark, human bones, Roman coins, and earthen vessels have been discovered at Balderton.

Such is the evidence that exists, and the arguments which, so far as we are aware, can be adduced in proof of the Roman origin of the town. The investigation would be incomplete, however, did we not give the facts on the other side. It must be borne in mind that there is no station to be found on the celebrated Itinerary of Antoninus which can be supposed to represent Newark. The ancient Fosseway which lies between Leicestershire and Lincoln enters the county near Willoughby on the Wolds, and at Newark runs along Castlegate, where it is crossed by the great north road from London to York. On this Fosseway there are marked in Iter VI. the following stations:—Vernometum, Margidunum, Ad Pontem, and Crococalanum. The first-named place was Willoughby, the second East Bridgford, the third is stated to be Farndon,[1] and the fourth was Brough, below Newark. There is thus no mention of a station on the site which Newark at present occupies, however eligible such a site may seem. For the other objections that can be raised, and arguments that can be advanced, we are indebted to Mr. William Stevenson of Hull (late of Nottingham), whose extensive acquaintance with local antiquarian subjects entitles his views to a respectful deference. In answer to a letter wherein we had explained the reasons to be urged in support of Dr. Stukely's theories, Mr. Stevenson writes:—

Camden was of opinion Sidnacester was somewhere between Gainsborough and Lincoln, and Gibson fixes it at Stow, which was an ancient place of ecclesiastical note, and is still an archdeaconry. There is no evidence of Newark being an episcopal see, nor of its pre-eminence in any way. Gibson gives proof of the boundary of the see of "Lindissi" Bede. This word occurs in a Latin document, quoted by Camden as "Lindissar" which is evidently the Latinised form of "Lindsey," the ancient name of Lincolnshire, and means the *land or islands in the lakes or waters.*

I think it is clear you must give Sidnacester up to Lincolnshire; I adhere to my view of *Ad pontem* being a ferry or crossing of the Trent at Farndon. It was a branch Roman road crossing the Trent and coursing up the valley of the Greet to Mansfield, where it joined the Roman road from Derby to Bawtry.* * *

Newark implies in its name a fortified place, *i.e.* Wark or defence, but the prefix "New" is, I think, fatal to its being Roman. The application of the term is perhaps more Danish than Saxon: opinions of antiquarians are tending to the belief that the Danes played a more important part in Mercia (the Marches) than has been generally accepted. It is certain that the Danes erected the earthworks in Southwark (London) and called them the Southworks (south fortifications). The fact of the town being walled counts for nothing; works of this character would not date nearer the Norman Conquest than one century, prior to which the defences would be of earth and stakes or trees. The evidence of Roman work in the building of the gates, might be Norman. There has been great confusion on this point; architects half a century ago called early Norman buildings Saxon, and the peculiar masonry practised by the Romans and known as *herring-bone masonry*, was practised by the Saxons under the Normans. There is a deal of it in the Castle walls of Lincoln, which are Norman, but it has often been taken for Roman work. I opine that the Roman work alluded to in the gates of Newark was something of this kind, and that it has wrongly been referred to the Romans: I have somewhere

---

[1] *Monumenta Historica Britannica*; Brewer's *Historical Letters*; and Dr. Smith's Map of Roman Britain.

read that Newark was built from the ruins of Aldwark, *Margidunum*, but I doubt if wrought stone or bricks were used in these guard stations on the military roads.

Roman coins, Roman interments, and remains such as are found at Newark and Balderton may be accounted for,—1st, from the Roman road passing through the site of Newark, where coins may have been lost or buried; 2d, from interments being made on the roadside, which was customary; 3d, from the probability of a Roman villa or other residence being fixed at Balderton, off the line of the road.

I have tried to trace the antiquity of Newark from its being situate on the great north road, but I am of opinion that this great road has been made out of a series of small local roads. I cannot get at the age of the bridges of Newark, Kelham, and Muskham, but they do not carry either the sense or association of a bridge, or a wauth or ferry in their names; hence I think that the bridge at Nottingham was the first and oldest bridge, and the great north road of ancient times, as noted in the Doomsday Survey, went through Nottingham, Ollerton, and Blyth instead of the later one through Newark and Retford. We know that the road passing through Retford is comparatively modern, and that it formerly went from Newark to West Drayton, but was diverted to Retford to avoid the open forest, which was dangerous to travel through. I mention this to show that for centuries there has been a diversion of the north road from the line of Nottingham and the great street now called Blyth Lane.

In looking over the village names on the north road I find no evidence of Roman towns or stations, or of ancient or important roads. Nor do I think that Newark would be selected as the site of a Roman town, seeing it is not on the river Trent, and there is no ancient evidence of artificial connection with the Trent as it now exists. I think it was a point selected by the Saxons to form a stronghold when they were pushing their conquests from the south to the north. When there intrenched, they would have two rivers between themselves and their enemies. I also think it was a place seized and held by the Danes who marched up the valley of the Trent, say on the Fosseway, from their fleets riding in the Trent near Gainsborough, and that it would be made strong as a place of shelter and retreat if they had to fall back upon their fleet, in case of reverses at Nottingham or other midland places. The town was a considerable place at the time of the Conquest, and was held of sufficient note shortly afterwards to become the seat or stronghold of the then military bishop of Lincoln. I think that Kelham bridge is older than Muskham bridge, and that it was erected about the time of the castle, and that this bridge would draw the north traffic from Nottingham, where it would go *via* Ollerton to Worksop. It is a well-known fact that the destruction of bridges in early times caused the decay of important towns, and that prosperity dawned upon insignificant ones situate on the line of some other and probably newer bridge. I think after Newark had ceased to be a military position, in Saxon and Danish times, it would get a new life from the fact of a bridge being built over the Trent at Kelham and a great northern road formed or founded through Newark.

If you take the Ordnance Map and leave the Fosseway out of the question, you may trace what I consider an old British road from the Nottingham Trent Bridge, through Radcliff, Bridgeford, Kneeton, Stoke, Farndon, Newark (*via* Beaumont's Cross), Winthorpe, and so on to Gainsborough, and along the Trent Bank to the mouth of the river. Between Kneeton, Stoke, Farndon, and Newark, this road is partly lost and partly merged into the severe line of the Fosseway, and I attribute the fact of this partial loss to the subsequent influence of the Fosseway. I take this to be a far older highway than the Fosseway, from the fact that all the villages are situate on it, and none of them are on the Fosseway. It is very strange that there is scarcely a village on the lines of the Roman roads in Notts and Lincolnshire. Newark I take to be on this old way and not on the Fosseway, but there is no doubt that it has been drawn towards the Fosseway from the influence of the castle and the water navigation. You may glean from this that I admit the possibility of the site of Newark, in the neighbourhood of Beaumont Cross, being a British settlement or town, and like the other residential spots on this old line of road, existing contemporary with the Roman occupation of this country. If you take the map again, you will find a mass of roads from the south and east and north-east, all making for some point in this particular neighbourhood. They do not make for the Fosseroad, nor do they, as a system, fit in with it. The Fosseway appears something like a modern railway, cut through the country in a straight line, regardless of other and older roads. I think the convergence of all these roads to this particular spot implies a place of very ancient importance. I take this arrangement of roads to be the natural development of a system of ancient roads, converging to a given spot on the British roadway, skirting the south bank of the Trent.

I cannot account for the convergence of these roads on the hypothesis of a bridge crossing the Trent at this point, hence they can only be accounted for as bearing to some important town. Taking this view, we have a British town existing during the Roman occupation—a town, the buildings of which were not Roman but British, and of a simple pastoral nature or character. The Fosseway would pass to the north-west of this town, and it might in some degree receive a Roman population, but I take it to have been clear from the military character imparted to the great road, and not situate at the proper distance from either Leicester or Lincoln, to admit of being chosen as a station or halting-place. It would, no doubt, possess a British name, but that name is lost and it was re-named "Newark" by the Saxons who, not caring about measured distance points on this great road, would select the spot for defensive purposes, from the fact that it was a town of some importance, and a place worth fortifying against the British or Romano-British people. This view would account for Roman coins being found thereabout, and for interments in the Roman fashion. I do not admit for a moment that it was a Roman town, that is a town founded, built, or kept up by the Romans, or one that would act any part in the working of their roads for military purposes, as entering into the compilation of any iters of such roads. I do not even claim that it was at that time situate on that great road, which it would most assuredly be, had it been of Roman origin or foundation.

I may note in conclusion, that the remarkable old road called 'Sewsterne Lane,' which branches off from the Roman Road (Ermine Street), near the town of Witham, and runs in the direction of Newark, is engrossing considerable attention. For many miles of its course it forms the boundary of the counties of Lincoln and Leicester, which proves its antiquity. Dr. Smith in his map of Roman Britain, claims it as a Roman way, but instead of continuing it on to Newark, where it appears to fit in with the road, *via* Kelham, Ollerton, and Worksop, to York, he diverts it to cross the Trent at Farndon (*ad pontem*), and terminates it at Mansfield. If further investigation should prove that 'Sewsterne Lane,' as a Roman way, ran *via* Shire Bridge and Balderton to Newark, it would mark the site of the town at the intersection of two Roman roads, and thus clearly account for the presence of Roman remains at Balderton."

Having thus given in regard to the disputed origin of the town what we may venture to call both sides of the question, we advance with pleasure from the region of argument and inference to that of historical fact. Before doing so, however, we may interpose an interesting tradition of the visit to this district of the energetic missionary bishop Paulinus about the year 637. Paulinus had been sent from Rome to assist in the conversion of the Britons, and in the discharge of his duty he visited Southwell and Newark; at the former place he resided some time, and is said to have laid the foundation of the Collegiate Church. At Newark multitudes flocked to hear him, and, converted to Christianity by his powerful oratory, were, with the aid of his deacon James, baptized in the Trent, which at that time ran in closer proximity to the town. It is during the Saxon Heptarchy that we come upon the first authentic historical records. Newark formed part of the kingdom of Mercia, and gave its name to the Wapentake which is still styled the Newark Hundred. By the Danes it was ransacked if not destroyed, but on the accession of Edward the Confessor (1041) it was entirely rebuilt, receiving its present name of New-wark or

THE REFERENCES IN DOOMSDAY BOOK.

Newark. On the division of the kingdom into separate districts, each under the governance of an Earl, the powerful Earl of Mercia, Leofric, had the manor of Newark in his possession. He did not, however, retain it for his own private use. In conjunction with his wife, the celebrated Countess Godiva, sister of Therald de Burgenhall, Sheriff of Lincolnshire, he gave Newark, together with the manor of Fledborough (then called Flatburch), to the monastery of Stow, near Lincoln. The Earl's agreement with Wulwi Bishop of Lincoln, was "that the monastery of Stow should have priests and service in the same manner as St. Paul's Church in London; that lands given should be appropriated to provide food and raiment for the brethren or friars; saving to the bishop himself, for his table all those things which Ætheric and Ædnoth, his predecessors, bishops of Lincoln, used to have, and his right to two parts of all things coming to that monastery, the remaining third being the property of the priests."[1] The munificence of the gift attracted the attention of the nobility, and it reached even the ears of the king. On the formal consecration of the manors of Newark and Fledborough to religious purposes—a ceremony which included placing the title-deeds on the altar of the principal church—the King and his Queen Edytha attended together with many nobles of their court, and freely testified their assent to the gift.[2] It was also ratified by William the Conqueror.

The next authentic reference to Newark occurs in *Doomsday Book*. The entry in that famous survey shows that Godiva, the Countess, paid the Dane-geld (the public tax of that time) for the manor of Newark with the two Berues, Baldertune and Farendune, or seven carucats and two bovats of land.[3] The land of it, in her own time, in King Edward the Confessor's survey had been returned as twenty-six carucats. Bishop Remigius of Lincoln had in demesne seven car., and fifty-six burgesses, forty-two villains, four bordars, having twenty car. (or plough lands) and a half. There were ten churches and eight priests, having five car. There were seven French or freemen (Franci homines) having five carucats and a half. There was one mill 5s. 4d. and one piscary or fishery. To "Newerche" lay all the customs of the king and Earl of that wapentac. Thoroton adds that in King Edward the Confessor's time the rent of it was £50; in the latter end of the Conqueror's it was but £34. It had soc in Balderton, Chelintone, Scirestone, Elvestone, Stoches, Holton, Cotintone, Barnebye, Wymunthorpe, Scorveley, Greton, Spaldford, Tomeshay, Wiggesley, Hardebye, and Cotum—as the names of the villages were written in those days. The entry relative to the churches and priests is, to say the least of it, rather confusing. The town was either larger than it is now, or the people were so regular in their attendance at church as to need great accommodation, or the churches were very small, or else the word church cannot be literally translated. Mr. Dickinson fancies it may mean altars, which were probably numerous in those days; and Thoroton conjectures that they were not all in the town but in the soc.

---

[1] Thoroton's *Antiquities*.   [2] *Mong. Angl.* vol. i. p. 263.
[3] A carucat was about a hundred and twenty acres of land, and a bovat an oxgate, or as much as a one-ox team could plough in a year.

ST. LEONARD'S HOSPITAL FOUNDED.

It was to the association of the borough with the Bishops of Lincoln that the castle owed its importance, if not its origin. Some historians have fancied that its foundation may be dated as far back as the reign of Egbert. Dr. Stukely considers it existed in Roman times, and Mr. Dickinson mentions it as having been improved by Leofric before he gave the manor to the monastery of Stow. Whether there is any ground for these conclusions or not, it is certain that its conversion into a powerful and important edifice was due to Alexander, Bishop of Lincoln, who was consecrated in 1123. His lordship, who is renowned in monkish annals for his munificence and liberality, is stated to have commenced the work a few years after his elevation to the bishopric, and to have obtained a royal charter for the establishment of a mint there. When he had completed the castles of Newark and Sleaford, at a vast expense, he proceeded with the erection of monasteries and the founding of hospitals.

At Newark he founded a hospital which he dedicated to St. Leonard. The charter of foundation is preserved in the registry of Lincoln cathedral in an ancient book entitled *Libellus de chartis Pensionum*. In 1350 a license was granted from John Synwell, Bishop of Lincoln, to Thomas de Sibthorpe, parson of Beckingham, of one messuage, in Middlegate, in Newark, held of him the said bishop as of the hospital of St. Leonard, extra Northgate, to Robert de Aryngton, Robert Leef, and Robert de Stokum, perpetual chauntry priests in the church of Newarke, to pray for the souls of William Saucimer, and Matilda, his wife; and Master William de Glenham; as also for those of the said Thomas de Sibthorpe, and Isabella Durant. This to be for the habitation of the said priests non-obstante Mortmain act, saving to the hospital of St. Leonard the accustomed rents and services. On the feast of St. Barnabas following, there was a grant from the said Thomas de Sibthorpe of the before-mentioned premises for the purposes specified in the license. Testibus Thomas Adam, Constabul de Castello de Newarke, Alan Fleming, Robert de Caldwell, Johan de Staunton, Johan Grym. In 1417, Philip, Bishop of Lincoln, by an instrument under his episcopal seal, confirmed by the dean and chapter, decreed that there should be one master of the hospital who should have rule of the same, and two poor men kept in the hospital, with one chaplain to perform divine service to them,[1] which chaplain and poor men should be received into the hospital and maintained with the priest's rents and profits of the same, the residue being devoted to the master's use, to repairing the building and the places belonging to it, and to the supporting of other charges. Amongst the commissioners' certificates of the reign of Edward VI.,[2] we find one, not hitherto published, relating to the value of St. Leonard's hospital. It will be seen that it makes the mistake of describing the place as founded by Bishop Philip, whereas he simply confirmed the original foundation.

[1] Dickinson.   [2] In the Augmentation Office.

ST. LEONARD'S HOSPITAL ENDOWMENT.

Sec. 12. No. 29.

THE PARISH OF ST. LEONARD, NEAR NEWARK.

The Hospital of St. Leonard near Newark, founded by Philip, sometime Bp. of Lincoln, for a Priest daily to serve Divine service there; and to find 3 poor Bedemen to serve God, and also that they shall maintain hospitality as appeareth by the foundation of the same dated 1417 doth appear. £27 : 11 : 9.

£22 : 12 : 2 Clear besides 13s. for rents resolute to divers persons, which revenue has been employed as well for the salary and living of the said Priest 100s. : and 3 poor Bedemen £3 : 18 : 10 there ; and also in the mayntenance of hospitality as for the reparations, sustentations and mayntenance of such necessary reparations and other charges as to the same is incident.

The said Hospital is a parish Church of itself having all sacramentals and sacraments therein ministered and observed.

The said Hospital is not void, but full, having a mansion house thereunto belonging.

There hath been no more land nor yearly profits belonging to the same since the time above said, more than is before specified. £1 : 12 : 6. As particulars doth appear by an Indenture hereunto annexed.

There hath been no Hospital nor other like promotions there dissolved, purchased or by any other means obtained without the King's license since the time aforesaid.

Another hospital, dedicated to St. Leonard, existed in the parish of Stoke, but was suppressed in the reign of Queen Elizabeth, and the site with the lands granted to John Marsh and Francis Grensham. Thoroton confounds the two places in his *Antiquities*, and speaks thus of the hospital *of Stoke*, evidently meaning the hospital of Newark :—" This place (Newark) was usually divided into the borough of Newark and Northgate, at the further end whereof from the town stood a fair house belonging to the hospital of St. Leonard *of Stoke*, commonly called the Spittle, which Sir Robert Constable had by lease, the interest whereof his son Henry Constable had, and from him it came to William Cecil, Esq., late Earl of Exeter, who built a goodly house there, which, after his decease, was, by Act of Parliament 17th of Charles I., exchanged from the hospital for lands of better value, and settled upon his widow, Elizabeth, Countess Dowager of Exeter, and her heirs." In the Act it was provided that the Countess should, within the space of three years, build a house of brick or stone to be covered with tile or slate, consisting of eight rooms, viz., four low rooms and four chambers over the same, for the receipt of master, chaplain, and two poor men, in or near Newark, "together with the enclosing of an acre of ground with a brick or stone wall to make there an orchard and garden." The hospital is now endowed with property in Newark, Girton, Balderton, Claypole, and Elston, let mostly on leases, some of which are beginning to fall in. The rents and reserved rents amount to £96 : 11 : 8 half-yearly. Of this sum £17 : 6 : 8 half-yearly is paid to the chaplain, the Rev. Joshua Brook of Car Colston, and two poor men, residing in the hospital, have 7s. per week each, in addition to which coats are provided for them. The residue, after payment of incidental expenses, is devoted to defraying the costs incurred in the Court of Chancery, and is paid in accordance with an order of the Court.

An old historian, quoted by Camden, says, Bishop Alexander founded these religious houses to "wipe off the stain" of making castles, and to obviate the reflection that such buildings were ill fitting the character of a bishop. What the object of establishing the monasteries may have been we do not stay to inquire. Of the reason for creating the castles substantial there can be little room for doubt. Before the structure at Newark was completed, the difficulties between King Stephen and the powerful amongst his subjects had commenced. The barons consented to yield him allegiance, but they demanded as a part of the price of their loyalty the right to erect and fortify castles. To this the king had no alternative but to submit, and 126 new castles arose. From these centres of strength issued unfeeling troops who plundered all around. Of the sufferings of the common people, the chroniclers give graphic descriptions. One writes:—"They (from the castles) seized those whom they supposed to have any goods, labouring men and women, and threw them into prison for their gold and silver, and inflicted on them unutterable tortures. Some they hanged up by the feet, and smoked with foul smoke; some by the thumbs, or by the beard, and put weights to their feet. They put them into dungeons with adders, snakes, and toads; many thousands they wore out with hunger. They burned all the towns; thou mightest go a day's journey, and not find a man sitting in a town, or an acre of land tilled. Wretched men starved of hunger; to till the ground was to plough the sea."[1] Sensible of the mischiefs attending the numerous citadels that had sprung up, the king determined to gain possession of them, and to begin with capturing those belonging to the clergy, who, by their functions, seemed less entitled than the barons to such military securities. Taking advantage of an affray which had arisen in court between the retinue of the Bishop of Salisbury and that of the Earl of Brittany, he seized both that prelate and the Bishop of Lincoln, and threw them into prison at Devizes, where they were kept on bread and water until they had surrendered their fortresses to the Crown. When the Bishop of Lincoln had consented to yield the stongholds which had cost him so much, the king's forces proceeded with him to Newark to take possession of the castle. A messenger was sent to the governor demanding its surrender, but with an obstinacy which, as the sequel will show, characterised some of his brave successors, he refused to deliver it up without an order from the bishop in person. In reply, the prelate informed his faithful vassal that the king had vowed not to let him have either meat or drink until the place was in his hands. The castle was thereupon surrendered, and his Majesty marched off with the captive bishop to Sleaford, to take charge of the castle there.

Henry, Bishop of Winchester, resolved to vindicate the clerical privileges which he alleged had been violated by these proceedings. He assembled a synod at Westminster, and complained of the impiety of Stephen's measures. The synod forwarded a summons to the king, charging him to appear before them; and Stephen, instead of resenting the indignity, sent Aubrey de Vere to plead his cause. De Vere accused the two prelates (Lincoln and Salisbury) of treason and sedition; but the synod refused to try the cause until the castles, including the castle of Newark,

---

[1] See *Chron. Sax.* p. 238.

of which they had been dispossessed were restored to them.[1] The Bishop of Salisbury declared that he would appeal to the Pope, but Stephen and his partisans, intimating that if needs be they would employ violence, prevented the adoption of such a proceeding. While the quarrel was in progress the Empress Matilda, daughter of Henry I., landed in England with Robert, Earl of Gloucester, and a retinue of a hundred and forty knights. Many of the barons declared for her, and Ralph, Earl of Chester, acting in her interest, surprised and seized the castle of Lincoln. The citizens invited Stephen to their aid, and he marched with a large force to recover the castle by assault or famine. The Earl of Gloucester hastened to assist his friends, and after ransacking Nottingham, proceeded (doubtless through Newark) to Lincoln. A battle ensued in which the king's forces were defeated, and Stephen himself, after displaying great valour, was borne down by numbers and taken prisoner (1141). Some years after a compromise was effected, it being agreed that Stephen should possess the crown during his lifetime, and that Henry, son of Matilda, should succeed on his demise. Stephen in this way retained in peace his possessions and his power.

Deprived of Newark Castle, the successor of Alexander in the see of Lincoln (Robert de Chesney, who was promoted to the see in the twelfth year of Stephen's reign, resolved to build himself a palace. Accordingly he erected one at Lincoln, and purchased a house near the Temple at London, which he settled on the see for the accommodation of those who should come after him. Having founded the priory of St. Catherine near Lincoln, he endowed it, among other things, with "the mother church of Newark, with the houses and land lying on the north-east part of the said mother church, with four bovats of land in the fields of the same, with the dwelling-houses and twenty acres of land in the heath, with a dwelling-house (belonging to the church) and two bovats of land in the fields, with two messuages in the borough, with the chapel of the apostles Philip and James founded in the castle of the same town and anciently given to the mother church, with the tenth penny of the whole toll of the borough of Newark, except the fairs, and four shillings, out of land which one Malger then held in Newark." [2]

In the eighteenth year of Henry II., who succeeded Stephen, a decree was issued by Pope Alexander ordering the clergy and laity of Nottinghamshire to attend at the church of St. Mary at Southwell in solemn procession with a pentecostal offering from every parish and hamlet in the county. The amount contributed at one time by Newark was 13s. 4d. It is, we are told, but a little more than a century since the corporation of Nottingham relinquished the practice of a personal compliance with the requirements of the decree.

In 1185 a hospital granted to the Knights Templars for the use of sick persons was founded at Newark. The site of the hospital cannot be accurately ascertained. In Mr. Dickinson's time a chapel remained dedicated to St. John of Jerusalem, the patron of the order according to their last institution, and this is believed to be the

[1] William of Malmesbury.   [2] Thoroton.

most probable situation. It was, when Mr. Dickinson wrote, divided into several apartments which served for offices to some of the dwelling-houses on the north side of Stodman Street. A small portion of it was exposed to view at the west end of the Town Hall, between that and the shambles. The head of the patron saint, of almost colossal size, well cut in stone, was at the time to be seen in the end of the chapel. It is believed that on the dissolution of the Knights Templars in 1312 the property was settled on their kindred order, St. John of Jerusalem, and the knights of that order may have built the chapel after they succeeded to the revenues. Tradition attributes the destruction of the monastery to fire during the civil wars.

We pass over the reign of Richard I., whose crusading exploits are interwoven with the history of the Holy Land, and come to the last days of King John before we meet with further references to the borough. The times were then troublous. The nation was unsettled—Magna Charta notwithstanding. The king could not be relied upon. He could be either blunt and unapproachable, or servile and fawning. Inwardly, no doubt, he did not relish that bulwark of liberty which had been wrung from him at the point of the sword. He signed it with seeming willingness, but regarded it with regret and vexation. As soon as the opportunity offered he appealed to the Pope. A bull was obtained declaring the charter unjust, and prohibiting the barons from enforcing its provisions. Foreign forces arrived simultaneously with the papal mandate, and John, thus doubly fortified, recalled the liberties that had been granted. With his army he marched through the country from Dover to Berwick, laying the provinces waste on either side. In their dilemma the barons invited over Prince Lewis, the eldest son of Philip of France. On his arrival John's foreign troops deserted him. They had been drawn mostly from the French provinces, and they did not care to serve against the heir to their own monarchy. The king's forces were further weakened by the withdrawal of several powerful noblemen and their adherents, and one by one the great castles were wrested from the monarch's control. Under the command of Gilbert de Gaunt, the barons seized upon the castle of Newark (1215). The garrison offered a brave resistance, but were overpowered.

The condition of affairs at this time was deplorable. The kingdom, says an old writer, "was made the stage of all the miseries of rapine and cruelty. Two armies were in it on foot at once, each of them seeking to prey on the other, and both on the country." In the midst of this turmoil and distress the king resolved to make a bold stroke for fortune. Assembling a considerable army, he set forward to meet, and if possible to crush, the barons. All his hopes, however, were blighted by an occurrence as unexpected as it was disastrous.

Passing from Lynn, in Norfolk, his road lay along the sea-shore. At high water, the pathway was covered by the sea, and it happened to be during such a period that John commenced his journey. The king and his suite, travelling farther round, passed the sands in safety ; but the rank and file of the army, in ignorance of their danger, took no heed of the course they were pursuing. With considerable rapidity the waves approached, and the rise in the water was so sudden and so extensive that it swept away all the baggage, carriages, treasure, and regalia; weakening the royal forces when they most needed strength. As Shakspeare makes Philip the Bastard say, in describing the extent of the disaster :—

> Half my power this night,
> Passing these flats, are taken by the tide;
> These Lincoln washes have devoured them.[1]

It was fortunate for the king that the barons, on hearing of the approach of the royal forces, had left Newark, for it was to this town John directed his weary steps; and when he reached the Castle he was more fit for the bedroom than the battle-field. A sickness, under which he was suffering prior to the loss of his goods, was considerably aggravated by the catastrophe. His mind was wearied and troubled, and his body weak with the fatigue of a long march. When he came to rest his tired limbs within the Castle, his condition was alarming. His followers did all they could to cheer the drooping spirits of their royal master. Their efforts, however, were futile. Dysentery, from which he had previously suffered at Sleaford, set in with great violence.

It was accompanied by fever, which is said to have attacked him first at Swines-head Abbey, where he had lodged for the night. Feeling death imminent, he took steps to secure the succession of the crown to his son Prince Henry, and then sought for religious aid from the Abbot of Croxton. Committing his soul to God and his body to the keeping of St. Wulstan at Worcester, he breathed his last on the 18th of October 1216, three days after his arrival at Newark. The room in which he is believed to have died is in the north-east angle of the castle, and is still pointed out to interested visitors.

In giving this account of the king's death, we discard altogether the various unauthenticated tales that have been told. Some state that a surfeit of peaches and new ale laid him on his deathbed, whilst others assert that he was poisoned;[2] but for the latter allegation especially, there seems to be no foundation whatever. One writer says a cowl of a monk was, in the superstitious days of John, reckoned a sure defence against the attacks of evil spirits. John therefore, conscious of his enormous crimes, desired he might be wrapped in one when he was dead, which was accordingly done. There are other stories extant, but they are scarcely worth reproducing. The will of his Majesty was made at Newark, and it is a very brief one, simply conferring general powers upon his executors, and giving directions as to the burial of his body. It is in Latin, and runs as follows :—

I, John, King of England, Lord of Ireland, Duke of Normandy and Aquitaine, Count of Anjou, being afflicted with a grievous sickness which, having not sufficient strength to bear, it behoveth me to provide for all mine by making my will concerning my affairs. I commit the lawful administration and

---

[1] *King John*, Act 5, Scene 6.
[2] "The King, I fear, is poisoned by a monk."—Shakspeare's *King John*. In the same play the scene of the king's death is laid at Swineshead Abbey.

distribution of my will to the trust and direction of my faithful counsellors, without whose advice even when in health I would in no wise direct, but particularly at the present instant; and that what they shall honestly direct and order concerning my affairs may be lawful and binding, as well in making satisfaction to God and Holy Church for all indignities offered, damages sustained, and injuries brought upon it by any means; as in giving succour to the land of Jerusalem, in procuring aid to my sons for the purpose of seeking and maintaining their inheritance, and in remunerating those who have faithfully served us; in making distribution to the poor, and to religious houses for the salvation of my soul. And I pray that he who shall give advice and assistance in fulfilling my Will may possess the grace and favour of God; but he who shall disturb its administration and order may incur the curse and indignation of almighty God, of the blessed Mary, and of all the saints IMPRIMIS; therefore I will that my body shall be buried in the church of Saint Mary and Wulstan of Worcester. And I appoint as such administrators and distributors Lord G., by the grace of God titular Cardinal of the Church of Saint Martin, Legate of the holy church; Lord Peter, Bishop of Winchester; Lord Richard, Bishop of Chichester; Lord Silvester, Bishop of Worcester; William Mareshall, Earl of Pembroke; Robert, Earl of West Chester; William, Earl Ferrars; W. Browne; Walter de Lacy; John de Monemut; Savery de Maleo; Faulk de Brent.

An historian says it was evidently compiled with great haste, the word "imprimis" at the end showing clearly that fuller instructions to his executors were intended to follow, had they not been prevented by the precipitate approach of death. Stowe mentions that immediately upon his Majesty's decease, his attendants, after taking all that was about him, fled, not leaving so much of anything worth the carriage as would cover his dead carcase. However this may be, it is clear that the body was decently removed under the direction of the Abbot of Croxton, and was buried in Worcester Cathedral.

It was at the tender age of ten years that Henry III. came to the throne, and in consideration of his youth the management of his affairs was entrusted to the Earl of Pembroke. The renewal and confirmation of the great charter gave general satisfaction, and, supplemented by an appeal from Pembroke, served to draw many of the rebellious barons to the side of the young monarch. Prince Lewis made an effort to obtain power, but after several disasters, deemed it prudent to conclude a peace with Pembroke, and to quit the kingdom. The war was thus at an end, to the great gratification of the vast majority of the people. There were some, however, who had become so accustomed to excitement and tumult, and had profited so largely by the opportunities for plunder which were afforded, that they did not relish a return to peaceful pursuits. A number of these, including several of the English nobility, accordingly proceeded to Newark, and took possession of the castle. The particulars of the event and of the siege which followed are given in the chronicle of Roger de Wendover. He writes:—"King Henry spent Christmas (A.D. 1218) at Northampton, where Falcasius supplied all the necessaries for the royal festival. At that time there were many nobles in England whose chief pleasure had been, during the late war, to live by plunder; and now, even after peace had been made and granted to all, they could not keep their hands from pillage; the main incentors of this being William, Earl of Albemarle, Falcasius and his castellan, Robert de Vipont, Brian de l'Isle, Hugh de Baliol, Phillip Marci, and Robert Gangi, and many others, who in defiance of the king's prohibition, and against the will of the owners, presumed to hold in their own hands the castles of some of the bishops and nobles, with their lands and other appurtenances. This Robert de Gangi, even after several remonstrances from the king, refused to deliver up to Hugh, Bishop of Lincoln, the castle of Newark, with the town and other appurtenances, which belonged of right to the bishop. From this circumstance the Grand Marshall, in anger, raised a large army by the king's order, and, accompanied by the king himself, approached in a hostile manner the said castle, and when they had advanced near to the castle they sent soldiers in advance that they might prevent the garrison from leaving the castle, lest, as they had often done, they should rush out and burn the town. When Robert and his comrades heard that this army was come, they sallied forth upon them from the castle, but were forced to retire into the castle by the king's troops, where William de Diva, a knight of the household of Hugh, Bishop of Lincoln, was killed as he was following them up in their retreat to the castle, and several others were wounded; the king and the marshal were much annoyed at this, and ordered their engines [of war] to be placed around the castle, that they might batter the walls with continued assaults from their petrariæ. The siege lasted for nearly eight days, during which time the friends of the said Robert treated for peace with the Bishop of Lincoln, and finally the two parties came to this understanding, with the consent of the king, namely,—That the bishop should pay to Robert de Gangi for the munitions which were in the castle, a hundred pounds sterling; and thus the siege being raised, every one returned to his home."[1]

As the king grew to man's estate it became evident that he was totally unqualified for his position. To maintain authority over the fractious barons firmness and vigour were requisite, and the king possessed neither of these qualities. Unfortunately for his popularity with the English people, he chose foreigners for his bosom friends. He looked out for men of other nationalities who were calculated to please him most, and heaped honours upon them with a lavish hand. Amongst those who were the subjects of the monarch's extraordinary bounty was a Simon De Montford, a foreigner of noble extraction, having his title from a place near Paris. He found such favour in the sight of the king that he elevated him to the dignity of Earl of Leicester, and gave him in marriage the hand of his own sister, the Dowager Countess of Pembroke. De Montford was not without some local associations. Having bound himself to allow the newly-wedded couple £400 a year, Henry gave him in part payment the manor of Gunthorpe, a village between Newark and Nottingham, with the soc and all appurtenances.

It was not to be expected that so great a favouritism could be one of long duration. The king overdid it, and a surfeit ensued. Tired of De Montford, he began to treat him with studied coldness, and a feeling of estrangement grew rapidly between them. The great charter having been repeatedly violated, a cry arose for

---

[1] From the *Chronicle of Roger de Wendover*, edited by Coxe for the English Historical Society, 5 vols. 1841-4. Roger de Wendover was a monk of St. Albans and prior of Belvoir.

its ratification. The king yielded, and it was read aloud to him in the presence of all the barons, the prelates and abbots standing by with burning tapers in their hands (1255). The ceremony was made as solemn and as striking as possible. The king said, " So help me God, I will keep all these articles inviolate." The prelates declared that whoever broke the provisions of the charter would be excommunicated, and they wound up the last act in the play by throwing their tapers on the ground and exclaiming with more vehemence than charity, " May the soul of every one who incurs this sentence so stink and corrupt in hell."[1]

The play, as we have called it, was nothing more than a farce. The king cared no more for the ceremony than the ceremony cared for him. He was completely in the hands of his favourites, blown hither and thither by the breath from their mouths like a straw by the east wind. The charter was soon broken, and the barons felt that decisive action was again necessary. By this time De Montford was at their head. With his aid the representative system of government was established. The freeholders received votes, and four knights were ordered to be elected from each county, to state the grievances, if any, under which their constituencies laboured. In this way the power of the people grew, and when civil war became imperative, the king found himself confronted by a powerful opposition. At the battle of Lewes (1264) his Majesty and prince Edward were taken prisoners, and were kept for some time in the priory of Lenton, near Nottingham. Many of the flower of the country perished in the struggle, and as some on both sides came from Notts, we have reason to conclude that Newark was not without its representatives in the terrible conflict. In the following year the fortunes of war changed. The barons were defeated, De Montford slain, and peace restored. Quietude succeeded, like the calm after a storm. The king reigned until 1272, and then expired, having been monarch for no less than fifty-six years.

We come now to the reigns of the Edwards and to the local events happening during their rule. On the demise of Henry III. Edward I. ascended the throne. In 1286, the fifteenth year of this king's reign, the Abbot of Peterborough and the Bishop of Lincoln became involved in a singular controversy. The Bishop complained that the Abbot had set up a *gallows* at Collingham, and there hanged a thief, to the derogation of the liberty of his wapentake of Newark, which the prelate held of the grant of the king's predecessors ; to which the Abbot answered that the king's father, in the thirty-seventh year of his reign, granted to him and his successors infangtheof and outfangtheof (the right to try and execute criminals) in all his hundreds and demesnes, and so he avowed his gallows ; and complained against the Bishop that he took two horses and six cows at Newark, and drove them to his pond for pound. After some controversy the Abbot, having failed to prove his right to *hang men* at Collingham (which enviable privilege it appeared only pertained to the Bishop of Lincoln) was compelled to pull down his gallows and submit.

[1] M. Paris and others.

ORIGIN OF THE BEAUMONT CROSS.

In 1290 the town would doubtless feel deeply concerned in the death of Queen Eleanor, happening as it did within so short a distance of the borough. Her Majesty, whilst accompanying her husband on a northern journey to attend a conference at Berwick, was taken ill, and died at Harby. A local writer says: "She died on the 27th November, at the house of Richard de Weston, where the body was embalmed, the viscera being conveyed to, and deposited in, the Lady Chapel, at Lincoln, the heart to the now destroyed Church of the Friars' Preachers, London (somewhere near the site of Printing House Square), and the body to London, where it yet lies in the Abbey of Westminster. The viscera deposited at Lincoln was covered by a cenotaph, and metal images were upon or about it, if there was not, as some archæologists suppose, an effigy of the Queen upon it, in stone or brass gilt. All seem to have been destroyed in the civil war, when Cromwell's troopers turned the Minster into a stable, and modern barbarians have even rooted up the viscera to make room for a Moses Ferry, LL.D., Prebendary of the Church, and his wife, whose remains are deposited there. The house, church, etc., of the Friars' Preachers, where the heart was deposited, were granted by Edward VI. to Sir Thomas Carwarden, who destroyed everything, and all is, and has been, long built over. Edward, following the example of the King of France, ordered crosses to be erected where the corpse of the queen rested for the night on its way to London, although there does not appear to have been one at Harby; the first being at Lincoln, and Robert de Stow, 'Cemetarius,' the builder." Beaumont's Cross, at Newark, was supposed to have been erected at this period, but Mr. Dickinson effectually disposes of the supposition. No mention is made of Newark as being one of the places through which the corpse passed, and the structure of the cross is totally different to that of the crosses erected by order of the king. The more probable conjecture is that it was erected to the memory of Lord Beaumont, who was killed at the battle of Towton in the reign of Edward IV. Dr. Stukely says, "the tradition of the place is that the cross was built by the Duchess of Norfolk." It appears that John Lord Beaumont married as his second wife a Duchess of Norfolk, his first having been Elizabeth, daughter and heiress of the Lord Bardolph. The family burying-place was at Dunnington, in the county of Suffolk, the road to which would naturally be through Newark. Putting these circumstances together, and bearing in mind the name it has always borne, Mr. Dickinson considers that "there is little room for doubt respecting the age, design, and appropriation of this beautiful piece of antiquity."

Mr. Shilton[1] considers that the extreme lightness and delicacy of the architecture would lead to the conclusion that it was not erected on a solemn but on a festive occasion. "A few flashy inhabitants," he writes, "styling themselves the *Beau monde*, in a fit of puerile ostentation and at a little expense, might erect this elegant *morceau* in commemoration of their taste."[2] The weight of evidence, however,

---
[1] *History of the Borough*, 1829.
[2] In a schedule of Brown's Property, dated 1532, that part of the town where the cross stands was called Beamond.

is in favour of the tradition which Dr. Stukely mentions and Mr. Dickinson adopts. Captain Lowe, F.S.A., who has inquired carefully into the subject, tells us he has no doubt that Thoroton is quite correct in his statements as to the marriage of John, Viscount Beaumont with Katherine, Duchess of Norfolk. "That nobleman," he says, "who was the sixth Lord Beaumont, was created a viscount in 1440. He was twice married. His first wife was Elizabeth, only daughter and heiress of Sir William Philip (who in right of his wife was created Lord Bardolph by Henry VI.) and by that lady he had one son, who died without issue in 1507, and one daughter. His second wife was Katherine, Duchess of Norfolk, and by her he had no issue. That lady was a daughter of Ralph, Earl of Westmoreland, and her first husband was John, eighth Lord Mowbray, who was restored to the dignity of Duke of Norfolk in 1424. The duke died in 1432, and his widow afterwards married Thomas Strangways, Esq., and after his death she became the second wife of the above-named Viscount Beaumont. She survived him also, and was married for the fourth time to Sir John Widvile. It is thus very probable that the tradition mentioned by Stukely that the Beaumond or Beaumont Cross at Newark was built by a Duchess of Norfolk is substantially correct, for there can be no doubt but that Katherine, Duchess of Norfolk, was the second wife of Viscount Beaumont, and likewise that she survived him. The cross may, therefore, probably be a memorial of her husband; but it is not very easy to see why such a monument should be erected at Newark. The suggestion that Lord Beaumont's body was carried through Newark on the way from Towton Field to the burial-place of his family in Suffolk might have been feasible enough; but it happens, unfortunately for this supposition, that the first Viscount Beaumont was not at Towton Field, having been killed at the battle of Northampton in 1459. The style of the cross is undoubtedly that of the latter half of the fifteenth century; and the facts being as I have stated, there does not appear any more probable conjecture than that the cross commemorates the first Viscount Beaumont. Why it was erected at Newark has yet to be discovered." We may add that the following inscriptions in brass are on two sides of the pedestal:—(1) Repaired and ornamented 1778 at the expense of Charles Mellish, Esquire, Recorder; (2) This cross, erected in the reign of Edward the Fourth, was repaired and beautified from the town estates A.D. MDCCCI. The modern additions consist of the heavy top or covering of stone and the vane. They will be observed on reference to the illustration which we give elsewhere.

It is a noticeable circumstance that, as far back as the reign under notice, the principal streets of Newark bore much the same designations as they do now. That this was the case is manifest from old deeds and records. For instance, in the 26th of Edward I., John Durant of Newark gave to Hugh de Shelton, son of Robert de Flintham, a messuage in *Balterton Gate*. In the same year William de Scampton granted to Rodger de Montfort and Margaret, his wife, all his right to a messuage in *Barnby Gate*. The name Middle Gate was mentioned in a deed of the reign of Edward

III. Castle Gate is doubtless almost as ancient as the castle itself. Carter Gate was known by that name in the time of Richard II. North Gate is so named in a deed of the time of Henry VIII., as is also Miln Gate. Stodemere Street is mentioned in a document of Edward the Third's reign. Other names mentioned in old documents, such as Delholm Way, Cooke's Row, and Coddington Lane, are extinct, but the principal streets have clearly borne their existing names with but slight alteration for centuries.

In the year 1295 one Henry de Newark, Dean of York, was chosen archbishop of that province. War existing at the time of his appointment, he did not venture, according to custom, to go to Rome for his pall. He was confirmed in his office in his own church by Papal Bull two years afterwards. He was a canon of Southwell, and the fact of his name being attached to deeds conveying land to the church at Muskham leads to the belief that he was a prebend of that place. In 1301 Walter de Coddington was instituted vicar of Newark. As an illustration of the value of money about this period we may mention that, during the Scottish wars, the Bishop of St. Andrews was taken prisoner and confined in Nottingham Castle. On account of the dignity of his station, there was granted to him for his maintenance, an allowance of 6d. per day, to which was added 3d. for a servant man, 1½d. for a footboy, and 1½d. for a chaplain. By what possible calculation the value of the services rendered by the two last individuals were equalised, it is impossible to say.

The second Edward succeeded his father in 1307, and amongst the events of his reign was a serious famine which happened in 1316, and from which Newark severely suffered in common with the rest of the country. For three years the seasons had been most unpropitious, and victuals became so scarce that dogs and cats were destroyed for the purposes of food. Some terrible accounts are given of the fearful distress which prevailed. It is said that children were stolen and eaten, and other acts of cannibalism were of frequent occurrence. A pestilence followed, and its list of victims was about as long as that produced by the famine. The social condition of the country is thus described:—"The kingdom continued greatly infested with robbers, who were still further increased by the famine which obliged the nobility to dismiss many of their retainers. They met in troops like armies and overran the country. Two cardinals, notwithstanding the numerous train which attended them, were robbed and despoiled of their goods and equipages when they travelled on the highway."[1]

A license is mentioned as having been granted to the parishioners of Newark in 1312 to remove a Chapel which stood in the churchyard. The Chapel in question appears to have been built by Henry Murdac, who was Archbishop of York between 1147 and 1153.

Newark had about this period three vicars in rapid succession, namely, William de Lincoln in 1320, Galfridus de Wilford in 1321, and Francis Roslyn in 1322.

In 1341, the 14th year of Edward the Third's reign, two tofts in the parish of

[1] *Hume*, vol. iii. p. 59; *Ypod Neust*, p. 503.

Newark, together with the Talbot public-house, the Manor of North Muskham, and the appurtenances of all kinds, were granted by Henry de Edwinstowe and Robert, his brother, to the prior and religious men of the parish of Newstead to support two priests. In referring to this matter, Bailey, in his *Annals of Nottingham*, says:—
"It is a curious circumstance in the history of public-houses, or inns, for the accommodation of travellers, etc., that the 'Talbot' should have continued an inn down to the present. But, remarkable as this is,—considering the great changes which property of almost every description has undergone during the last five hundred years—it is not unique in Newark. The 'Saracens Head,' which was an inn at the same period, still continues so occupied. Two or three other public-houses in the borough of Newark, as 'The White Hart,'[1] 'The Dragon,' and 'The Swan and Salmon,' are also of great antiquity, having been established, each, from three to four centuries." The Manor of North Muskham is described as having "passed" two years later to the Prior of Newstead, but this must have been a confirmation of a previous gift, with additional provisions. The additions were that the prior should find two chaplains daily to celebrate in Edwinstowe Church, in honour of the Virgin Mary, to whom the Church is dedicated, and for the souls of Henry and Robert de Edwinstowe, their relatives, and friends. Besides the manor, in the liberality of their souls, the Edwinstowe gentlemen gave half a pound of pepper, a commodity that is often identified with charitable bequests made in former times.

On the 25th of May 1349, according to the abstract of the foundation deed as given in Torres' *Collectanea*, at York, "Alan Flemyng of Newark, founded in the Chapel of Corpus Christi, within the Church of Newark, a chauntry for one secular chaplain to celebrate for the souls of William de la Zouch, Archbishop of York, of himself, the said Alan Flemyng, and Alice, his wife, and of others his friends; and for his support appointed five marks of silver to be yearly paid by the Prior and Convent of Shelford. The patronage after the death of the said Alan, to be in the vicar of Newark, and four faithful men in name of the parishioners thereof." The endowment was increased by himself before his death, or by some benefactor afterwards; for in the account of this chauntry in the *Valor Ecclesiasticus*, besides the five marks from Shelford, the chaplain had another pension of one mark from Thurgarton Priory, and was in receipt also of certain rents from tenements in Newark.

That the Fleming family were intimately associated with Newark, is evidenced by the large marble slab and elaborate brass within the parish church, the latter of so curious a character as to be an object of much interest. The brass is justly described as one of the most splendid remaining in the kingdom, and in fact on the continent. It was removed from its original position on the floor of the south-west transept in 1823, by the churchwardens, and fixed in an elevated position on the back of the reredos in the lady chapel. The stone, a blue-grey marble slab measuring 9 ft. 10 in. by 6 ft. 3 in., on which it was fixed, was also removed at the same time, and now covers a modern family vault in the nave of the church. During the restoration of

[1] The White Hart was the badge of Richard II.

DESCRIPTION OF THE FLEMING BRASS.

the sacred edifice in 1852-5 a splendid new reredos was erected from a design by Mr. Scott, of much lower dimensions than formerly. The brass was then taken back to the south transept, and fixed on the west wall over the place it originally occupied. Its dimensions are 9 ft. 3 in. by 5 ft. 7 in.

The following graphic description of the brass was written by the late Mr. E. J. Willson, of Lincoln:—"The portrait of Alan Fleming reposes within a gorgeous tabernacle of architectural design. Various smaller figures are placed in niches at the sides and upon the canopy, and a double border of tendrils and leaves encircles the whole composition, including the epitaph. Such is the outline of the design, but the elegant taste and minute care displayed in filling up every part with appropriate enrichment, are beyond the power of verbal description. Some parts are nearly worn out, and require explanation, which the Lynn and St. Alban's brasses enable us to give. The background to the principal figure is diapered with architectural tracery, filled up with an animal in every compartment. At the bottom a hunting match is exhibited in the centre, and on one side a mock tournament performed by animals; on the other, animals ludicrously dancing, etc. Immediately over the head of the deceased was a small figure denoting the disembodied spirit held in the bosom of its Divine Creator; who was represented in the likeness of an ancient man, as in the vision of the Prophet Daniel. On each side were angels offering incense or playing upon musical instruments. In the other niches were saints holding scrolls inscribed with sentences of prayer or instruments of their martyrdom. On each hand of the deceased are six of his friends, three men and three women, standing in pairs. The countenance of Alan Fleming appears young. He is placed in the pious attitude invariably observed in old monuments, and holds in his uplifted hand a scroll inscribed with the pathetic prayer, 'Miserere mei, Domine Deus meus.' His head rests upon a pillow richly flowered, supported by two angels. Under his feet is a lion, in allusion to a passage in one of the Psalms. It is remarkable that there is no shield nor armorial bearing of any sort; such distinctions being regarded as inappropriate to the peaceful followers of commerce. The inscription on the verge is in Latin, of which the following is a translation:— 'Here lieth Alan Fleming, who died in the year of the Lord 1361, on the day of St. Helena. Whose soul, through the mercy of God, rest in peace. Amen. I believe that my Redeemer liveth, and that in the last day I shall rise from the earth, and shall again be clothed with my skin, and in my flesh shall see God my Saviour whom I myself shall see, and mine eyes shall behold, and not another. This, my hope, is laid up in my bosom.' The Scripture text is taken from the 19th chapter of the book of Job, according to the Latin Vulgate version. On three of the small compartments inserted between the words of the inscription, appear what seems to be the engraver's personal device or cipher. It would probably be in vain to inquire who the excellent artist could be, but from the peculiar style of some of the architectural details, I am inclined to think he was a native of Flanders or Germany. Whoever he was, he has left a splendid proof of his skill, as well as of the munificent encouragement of the arts in his days."

The name of Fleming appears as a witness to the confirmation of a grant of premises, belonging to St. Leonards, on St. Bartholomew's day, 1350; and there was also in the church Fleming's chauntry, as we have already mentioned. An entry at the beginning of one of the parish registers says, "The Bishop Fleming built this church A.D. 1303." A more recent hand has struck out "built," and written "consecrated," changing also the date into 1373. There is a tradition that Alan Fleming was the founder of the original church, and that he was the brother of the Bishop Hugh Fleming. The story, however, is unreliable, inasmuch as there was no Bishop of Lincoln of that name. There was a Bishop Richard Fleming, but he was not consecrated until 1420. Various members of the family resided in Newark after the death of Alan, and their names frequently occur as witnesses to deeds. Thos. Fleming appears in that capacity on the 1st Richard II., 1377, and Arnold, Ralph, and John, severally surnamed Fleming, signed other deeds between the last mentioned period and the reign of Henry V.

From 1349 to 1370 there resided in Newark one John Arderne, a surgeon of considerable eminence. He showed remarkable skill in curing the plague, and removed to London, where he exercised the healing art in such a way as greatly to increase his income and his reputation. He made several improvements and inventions in surgery, and is described as the earliest to introduce a rational practice into England. He looked sharply after his fees, stipulating with the patients as to the sums he should receive, and taking security for payment of the money. Amongst the Sloane MSS. (563 f. 124), is a "Treatise on the Fistula in ano," by John Arderne, of Newark, in which the writer thus quaintly speaks of his success:—

"Johan Arderne fro the first pestelence that was in the yere of our Lord 1349, duelled in Newerke, in Notinghamschire, unto the yere of our Lord 1370, and ther I heled many men of fistula inano; of which the first was Sir Adam Everyngham of Laxton in the Clay byside Tukkesford, whiche Sir Adam forsothe was in Gascone with Sir Henry, that tyme named herle of Derby, and after was made Duke of Lancastre, a noble and worthy lord. The forsaid Sir Adam forsoth soufferend fistulam inano, made for to aske counsell at alle the lechez and corurgienz that he myght fynd in Gascone, at Burdeux, at Briggerac, Tolows, and Neyybon, and Peyters, and many other placez, and alle forsoke hym for uncurable; whiche y-se and y-herde, the forsaid Adam hastied for to torne home to his contree, and when he come home he did of al his knyghtly clothings, and cladde mournyng clothes in purpose of abydyng, dissolvyng, or lesyng of his body beyng nyz to him. At the laste I forsaid Johan Arderne y-sozt, and covenant y-made, come to hyme and did my cure to hym, and, our Lorde beyng mene, I heled hym perfitely within halfe a yere, and afterward hole and sound, he ledde a glad life 30 yere and more. For which cure I gate myche honour and lovyng thurz alle Ynglond; and the forsaid Duke of Lancastre and many other gentilez wondred thereof. Afte[r]ward I cured Hugon Derlyng of Fowich of Balne by Snaythe. Afterward I cured Johan Schefeld of Rightwelle, aside Tekille."

Both before and after the plague the wars in which the country had engaged commanded general attention. The ambition of Edward led him to undertake a conflict with France. He aimed at uniting in his person the sovereignty of the two countries, and with that object in view, extensive preparations were made. A series of remarkable successes aroused the enthusiasm of every part of the nation, and formed the subject of conversation and the theme of song. At Crecy the English bowmen, many of whom came from the Midland districts, gained a crushing victory, and a multitude of princes and nobles became the captives of the conquerors. During the absence of the king and his son in connection with these conflicts, the Scotch king, David the Second, marched upon England, seeking to take advantage of the unprotected state of the country. With an army of sixty thousand men at his back he made himself sure of a speedy victory. In these expectations, however, he was signally disappointed. England, unguarded as she was, was not to be easily subdued. With a courage worthy of a warrior the queen stepped into the arena, and people rushed forward to serve under her banner. The feeling conveyed in the words still current in South Notts that "Ere the Scots should cross the Trent, many a batch of arrows should be spent," was felt as strongly in those days as in years after. The Scotch forces were encountered at Nevil's Cross, and completely routed (17th Oct. 1346). King David was discovered on the field of battle severely cut about the head and legs, and with two spears dangling from his body. Pain and sorrow goaded him to desperation. When called upon by Squire Copeland to yield, he indignantly refused, and with a smart blow knocked out two of Copeland's teeth. The squire and his men, in the long run, proved too much for him, and he was led in captivity from the scene of the conflict. Copeland received a large grant of land for his services, and the Scotch monarch, after being taken to London, was transferred to Nottingham, where he remained for several years. The famous battle of Poictiers in 1356, ended in the capture of the French king, who was sent, in 1359, to Somerton Castle at Navenby, a few miles from Newark. Some interesting particulars of his stay there are given in Chambers' *Book of Days* (vol. i. p. 489). We read that—

Previous to this coming into Lincolnshire, in accordance with an edict of Edward III., John had been forced to dismiss forty-two of his attendants; he still, however, retained about the same number around his person. Among these were two chaplains, a secretary, a clerk of the chapel, a physician, a maître d'hôtel, three pages, four valets, three wardrobe men, three furriers, six grooms, two cooks, a fruiterer, a spice-man, a barber, and a washer, besides some higher officers, and a person bearing the exalted name of 'Le roy de Menestereulx,' who appears to have been a maker of musical instruments and clocks, as well as a minstrel; and last, but not least, 'Maître Jean le Fol.' The Somerton Castle furniture being utterly insufficient, for such a vast increase of inmates, the captive king added a number of tables, chairs, forms, and trestles, besides fittings for the stables, and stores of fire-wood and turf. He also fitted up his own chamber, that of the Prince Philip, and of M. Jean le Fol, besides the chapel, with hangings, curtains, cushions, ornamental coffers, sconces, etc., the furniture of each of these filling a separate waggon when the king left Somerton. Large consignments of good Bordeaux wines were transmitted from France to the port of Boston, for the captive king's use, as much as 140 tuns being sent at one time as a present, intended partly for his own use, and partly as a means of raising money to keep up his royal state. One of the costly items in the king's expenditure was sugar, together with spices bought in London, Lincoln, and Boston, immense quantities of which we may infer were used in the form of confectionery.

In the article of dress John was most prodigal. In less than five months he ordered eight complete suits, besides one received as a present from the Countess of Boulogne, and many separate articles. One ordered for Easter was trimmed with miniver; another for Whitsuntide, of rosy scarlet, lined with blue taffeta. The fur and trimmings of these robes formed a most costly additional item, there having been paid to William, a furrier of Lincoln, £17 : 3 : 9 for 800 miniver skins, and 850 ditto of 'gris,' also £8 : 10s. to Thornsten, a furrier of London, for 600 additional miniver skins, and 300 of 'gris,' all for one set of robes. Thus 2550 skins, at a cost of £25 : 13 : 9, were used in this suit, and the charge for making it up was £6 : 8s. Indeed, so large were the requirements of the captive king and his household in this particular, that a regular tailoring establishment was set up in Lincoln by his order, over which one M. Tassin presided.

The pastimes he indulged in were novel-reading, music, chess, and backgammon. He paid for writing materials in Lincolnshire three shillings to three shillings and sixpence for one dozen parchments, sixpence to ninepence for a quire of paper, one shilling for an envelope with its silver binder, and fourpence for a bottle of ink.

One very marked trait in King John's character was his love of almsgiving. His charitable gifts, great and small, public and private, flowed in a ceaseless stream, when a captive in adversity no less than when on the throne of prosperity. Wherever he was, he made a small daily offering to the curate of the parish, besides presenting larger sums on the festivals of the Church. For instance, he gave to the humble Curé of Boby (Boothby) a sum equal to 12s., for masses offered by him at Christmas; 8s. at the Epiphany; and 4s. 4d. at Candlemas. The religious orders also received large sums at his hands; on each of the four mendicant societies of Lincoln he bestowed fifteen escus or £10. On his way from London to Somerton, he offered at Grantham five nobles (£1 : 13 : 4) gave five more nobles to the preaching friars of Stamford, and the same sum to the shrine of St. Albans. In fact, wherever he went, churches, convents, shrines, recluses, and the poor and unfortunate, were constant recipients of his bounty. On the 21st of March 1360 King John was removed from Somerton, and lodged in the Tower of London, the journey occupying seven days. Two months after (May 19), he was released on signing an agreement to pay to England 3,000,000 of gold crowns (or £1,500,000) for his ransom.

With two captive kings in the country at once, English military glory was at its height. Rejoicings took place in most towns, but they were not of long duration. The cloud rapidly succeeded the sunshine. One by one the provinces that had been won fell from Edward's grasp, until all that remained to him of French territory consisted of Calais, Bordeaux, and Bayonne. The latter days of the king were not enviable. His proud spirit was broken by grief at the loss of the Black Prince (1376), and his reputation became slurred by his association with Dame Pierce. Frequent demands were made upon the Commons for the supply of money to defray the expenses of the wars. On the assembling of one of the Parliaments, when the king desired financial aid, instead of acceding to his request, the Commons drew up a list of complaints charging the king's officers with fraud, and requesting that Dame Alice Pierce, the king's mistress, should be banished from his presence. There were good grounds for the indictment which the Commons framed against their ruler. The behaviour of Dame Pierce had been of a most extraordinary character. It was no uncommon thing for her to sit in courts of justice by the side of judges, and dictate to them in a most insolent manner. In eloquent terms Peter de la Mare, the Speaker of the House, protested against her conduct; but his earnest representations and arguments were in vain. Some obnoxious persons were removed, but Dame Pierce was retained, and as a punishment to Peter de la Mare for his intrepidity and presumption, he was ordered to be confined for life in Nottingham or Newark Castle. Nottingham historians say it was Nottingham, and other authorities mention Newark. The unjust sentence was not carried into effect, for, after an imprisonment of two years, Richard II. set the Right Hon. gentleman at liberty. Though it is doubtful whether Peter de la Mare was imprisoned at Newark, it is not altogether improbable that the Castle may have been in use as a State prison at this period. The building was without doubt in the control of the king, but after this time royalty does not appear to have exercised any proprietorial right in it, until the reign of Edward the Sixth—the Bishops of Lincoln being the guardians of the whole of the manor, soc, or wapentake.

We give the following references to documents in the Patent Rolls relating to Newark and, for the most part, bearing date Edward III.

393a. Newark villa De mercato ibidem tenendo in die Mercurij. Dorso Clausarum A°. 3 E. 3. m. 4.

395a. Newark. Pro mes. et di. acr. terre ibidem conc Cantarie in eadem villa Pat. 26. E. 3. ps. 2. m. 43, et Cantaria in ecclesia beate Mar. Magdalene ibidem et ten ibidem et in, Balderton, Barneby, Houghton, Kelme, ffarnedon, Muskham, Codington, et Northgate, Pat. 39 E. 3. ps. 1. m. 21. Et p Cantaria fac in ecclesia beate Marie Magdalene in Newark et pro ten in eadem villa Pat. 14 H. 4. ps—m. 21.

Ibidem. Newark. Pro Cantaria in honorem Sce. Trin ibidem fundanda vocata ffosters Chantry et pro terris perquirendis ad valorem 12 marcaru Pat. 29 H. 6. ps. 2. m 18. et p. ten. ibidem a°. 30° ps 1. m. 15, et pro Cantaria in ecclesia pochiali ibidem et redd in Nembo Segbrok et Casthorp Pat. 3 R. 2 ps. 1. m. 12 et A° 4 ps. 2. m. 11.

Ibidem. Newark Pro Cantaria fac. ad altare Sce Katerine in ecclia pochiali ibidem Pat. 15 E. 3 ps. 2. m. 16. et al Cantaria ad altare Corporis Christi ibidem. Et pro Cantaria Corporis Christi ibidem fundanda confirm. Pat. 23 E. 3. ps. 1. m. 12. et Newark ecclesia confirm Cantarie ibidem p Matild. Saucemere Pat. 21 E 3. ps. 1. m. 31.

401a. Newark Prior. Assisa versus ipsum de ten. in Wolking p. Petr. Rutele Pat. 2 E. 1. m. 16. Dorso.

402a. Newark. Hospitale Sci Leonardi de 2 mes. 20 ac. terre ibidem et in Balderton et Horton perquirendis de W. Durant pro Cantaria fac ibidem Pat. 5 Edw. 2. ps 1. m. 7.

404a. Newark. Hospitale Sci Leonardi percipere consuevit 20 quartia frum 20 quarteria siliginis singulis Annis de granario Episcopi Linc. in castro de Newark. Claus. 15 E. 2. m. 9.

404b. Newark. Hospitale Sci Leonardi ibidem ad Regis collationem ptinet ratione Episcopatus Linc & 3 Pat. 16. E. 2 ps. 1. m. 2.

407b. Newark. De Cantaria fundanda in ecclesia poch. ibidem et terr &c. ad valorem 6 marcarum p annum conc. p Simonem de Bottesford Pat. 1. E. 3. ps. 2. m. 20.

On the Issue Roll, under date 50th Edward III., is the following entry:—

20th November.—To John Vendour of Newark, coming by command of the Council from Lincoln, to bring Sir William de Cantelupe, knight, to the Tower of London, upon suspicion had against him for the death of Nicholas de Cantelupe, his brother, slain; and there safely and securely to keep him in the King's prison until otherwise respecting the same William it should be ordered by the King and his Council. In money paid, etc., in discharge of 100 shillings, which the Lord the King commanded to be paid him for the wages and expenses of himself and his men going with him and his retinue, for the safe custody of the aforesaid William.

During the reign of Richard II., son of the Black Prince, there is no event of a local nature on record. In 1404, the fifth year of Henry IV., Henry de Codyngton parson of Bottesford, founded a chauntry at the altar of St. Peter, in the parish of Codyngton, for one priest to pray for him while he lived, and for his soul after his decease; and for the soul of John de Codyngton, late parson of Adesham, and of their fathers and mothers, brothers, sisters, and benefactors, to which he gave five messuages, three tofts, and one hundred and seventy-one acres of land, with the appurtenances, in Codyngton and Holme, by Muskham. It appears that John Ashwell was the first priest nominated by the founder, whose successors, after the death of the said Henry de Codyngton, were to be named by the Prior of Thurgarton. The lands were, in the 6th year of the reign of Edward VI., granted to Sir Edward Bray and others; and afterwards (6th June, 44 Q. Elizabeth) to Thomas Pocklington and his heirs, being at the estimated value in those days of 67s. 4d. per annum.

A good deal of attention was directed at this time, to certain wells which existed in the county, and which were believed to possess medicinal virtues. On St. Ann's Well-road at Nottingham, there was a spring famous for healing disorders of the eyes, which was visited by a great number of people suffering from diseases in the visual organs. The person seeking relief had to use the waters and to leave the piece of cloth employed in washing the eyes exposed upon a hawthorn bush which overhung the spring. Southwell, according to Bailey's *Annals*, is believed to have taken its name from one of these springs. There were three in existence, the "Lord's well," on the south-east side of the town, famous for the cure of rheumatism; the "Holy well," near the cloister leading to the chapter-house, and the "Lady's well," dedicated to the Virgin Mary. The latter was, we believe, under the walls of the choir, and was filled up in consequence of a clergyman who was returning home at night, falling accidentally into it and being drowned. At Westhorpe there was a well dedicated to St. Catherine, and a chapel stood near, where visitors who had used the waters might say their prayers and deposit gifts in acknowledgment of the benefits received. One of the most famous of the holy wells, however, was the well of St. Catherine, at Newark, which long retained a good deal of celebrity. It was situate near the Sconce Hills, and the water was remarkably transparent and pure. There is a singular tradition in reference to the origin of the well, which is worth repeating. It professes to be copied from an ancient legend in the possession of the Bettison family, and is as follows:—

> Near unto the fortified place called our Lady the Queen's Sconce, and betwixt that and the river Davon, is a famous well, in the waters of which, by the help of the holy Saint Catherine and the blessing of our lady the Virgin, divers leprous persons have been purged of their judgements. The auncient ballad, the which hath remayned even to our time, setteth forth with great trouth the intendment of these Kings, to the manifestation of God's justice. Two valourous knights, Sir Everard Bevorcotes and Sir Guy Saucimer by name, wooed a fair maid, the daughter of Alan De Caldwell,

named Isabell. They were loving companions, and they both served their suite so stoutly that the maid was hard pressed to make her choice, so even did they carry themselves in her eyes. Sir Everard finally prevailed, but lest, peradventure, Sir Guy should discover her preference, he never came to her till after eventide, and departed again before midnight. Howbeit, Sir Guy discovered the cheat which was passed upon him, and waylaid the knight, whom, nothing fearing, he slew, on Saint Catherine's eve, and he fell covered with blood on the spot: sithence has arisen a fair stream of water, for no sooner had the body of Sir Everard touched the ground, but it gushed out in a pure fountain, and hath flowed plentifully to these times.

Sir Guy, in melancholy mood, travelled to Nottingham, but the memory of his misdeeds followed him, and vexed him so sore that he was fain to go into foreign parts, where he was punished by God's righteous judgement with leprous sores, so that nothing gave him any ease. Meanwhile the fair Isabell dyed of grief. Sir Guy hearing thereof, could find no rest day nor night, wherefore, taking the habit of a pilgrim, he was returning to England sick at heart and sore pressed with disease, when about eventide he laid himself down on a bed of dry leaves in the forest of St. Avold. Here, as doubtless the Saint herself had ordayned, he fell in a sound sleep, when the holy Catherine appeared to him as in a dream, and told him that in the place where Sir Everard had whilom fallen by his hand was the only water that could cleanse his grievous sore. Full of repentance, and emboldened by this manifestation of the Saint's intercession, he straitway hied to England, and having received absolution from Holy Church, he took the habit of a hermit and journeyed to Newerck, where he built himself a narrow cell, hard by the place where he slew Sir Everard. But he had not long tarried when the waters of Davon overflowed, and he was necessitated to pass over to the other side of the waye, about a furlong to the north-east, where was another clear spring of pure water. Here, with his own hands, he builded himself an abiding-place with a chapel, and graved the image of Saint Catherine, also the death of Sir Everard, over the altar. He also inclosed the spring with a wall of stone curiously carved to imitate one belonging to some holy fathers, where he had quenched his thirst nigh to the place where Saint Catherine vouchsafed to appear to him.[1] Here he lived a sad and godly life, being much venerated by all hereabouts, and known by the name of St. Guthred, the reason whereof doth not appear. He died well stricken in age, being eighty-seven years and some months old, on All Hallow's Day, in the seventeenth year of our late soverain Lord Henry of Bullinbrook. His name was had in remembrance by his posterity, one of whom, William Sauciner, founded a chauntry in the church of Newerck, and endowed the priest thereof with lands in Baldertune, to pray for the soul of Sir Guy, as also for those of his father Adam, and of Alicia his mother. The hermitage hath lately fallen to decay, and a goodly house hath been builded where it stood, but the chapel with the grave of the hermit were fair to be seen even till of late time, and the well still aboundeth with wholesome and pleasant water.

A ballad is attached, but is in many parts illegible. Eleven verses are preserved intact, and portions of several others. They describe the fight between Sir Guy and Sir Everard, and state that at the outset the latter had the advantage. He with heavy strokes gave his antagonist a "woeful overthrow," but Sir Guy having recovered himself, pierced his adversary to the heart. Sir Everard gasped out a few words, telling his opponent to fly, and bidding him farewell, and then expired. Sir Guy went to a foreign land, and returned in penitence, as mentioned in the tale.

[1] It is a noticeable fact that there was a well (now covered over) in the middle part of the old hall in Millgate, occupied for about forty-two years by the late Dr. Waterworth. Alluding to this well, Mr. Dickinson says it is a furlong north-east from the other, precisely as described in the legend, and used to contain beautifully clear water; whilst the walls were of stone, most curiously, though not very scientifically, wrought.

ENDOWMENT OF THE CHURCH.

An endowment of the parish church took place in the year 1428. The document, which is of course in Latin and of considerable length, is by John, archbishop "primate of England and legate of the apostolic see," and is dated from the palace of Suthwell (Southwell) the last day of the month of September. It commences by stating that the parish church of Newark, with its rights and appurtenances, had been "from formerly" incorporated, annexed, united, and appropriated to all the religious men, the prior and convent of the house or priory of St. Katherine, without the walls of Lincoln, of the order of St. Gilbert. To them the profits had lawfully accrued, and by them a vicar had been appointed, who had been paid such portions of the rents or dues as the canons directed. But amongst the churches of the diocese that of Newark, being one of the larger and on which a greater care of souls depended, it was right that the vicar should be provided with a competent stipend for his maintenance, and to defray the expenses incumbent upon him. A portion of the profits, called the first-fruits, were by express consent to be dedicated to the use of "that religious man Walter Iklingham, prior of the house or convent of St. Katherine," and to Nicholas Feriby, the vicar, for a "lawful and reasonable profit." The document then proceeds:—

We likewise appoint and ordain that the said present vicar and each of his successors shall have for his own habitation the house or place of his aforesaid vicarage, with all its buildings and the garden adjoining and to the same belonging, which house or place of residence the said present vicar now occupies, and which is to be repaired and at all times maintained at the cost of the said vicar for the time being and his successors; except the principal chamber on the west side of the hall of the said habitation, with two chambers to the said principal chamber annexed, together with a stable and repository for the tenths, and also two granaries of which one roofed with lead is situated on the north side of the said parish church, and the other situated contiguous to the north gate of the said mansion. And also with the houses and tenements without the aforesaid gate, all which buildings, etc., we reserve for the use, utility, and advantage of the said prior and convent aforesaid; the whole to be for ever kept up and repaired at the costs and expenses of the said prior and convent.

Also, we decree and ordain that the said present vicar and his successors shall have and receive all obventions which shall arise within the jurisdiction of the said parish church of Newark, or of whatsoever kind shall arise in future. Also, all mortuaries whatsoever, and also the tenth of all young fit to be eaten. Also of all fowls, of the goats, of the cocks, of the pasturage, of the doves, of the lambs, of the bees, of the honey and wax, of the hemp, flax, mills, fisheries, and other tenths and obventions. And all dues to the said church and all emoluments whatsoever to the same church belonging; all lands of the same church with the tenths arising from the same. And all the tenths of hay, wool, and land, within the bounds and limits of the same parish, wherever now due or to become due; except only such lands and tenths so excepted as we decree ought to belong for ever to the prior and convent of the Priory of Saint Katharine aforesaid.

Moreover, we will and ordain that the aforesaid vicar who now is, and all his successors for the time being, shall pay, or cause payment to be made, to the before mentioned prior and convent twenty marks yearly on the feast of Easter, or within one month then next immediately ensuing. For which payment well and faithfully to be made, we will and ordain that the said Nicholas, the present vicar, within six days next after the day of the date of these presents, and his successors on their admission, be bound by the bond of an oath, and also under the penalties of suspension from divine matters, and sequestration of the profits belonging to the vicar. Which penalty the vicar, or vicars, not making payment, shall incur by such omission, we will in no wise to be relaxed until the Prior and Convent aforesaid shall be fully satisfied for such payment, and their damages and expenses on that account.

We furthermore ordain that all ordinary and extraordinary burdens in any wise belonging to the said church of Newark aforesaid, are to be borne by the said vicar and his successors; except the expense of repairing the chancel and of the payment of the tenth or tenths, or any other part of the same, to the king already granted, or hereafter to be granted. Which burdens we will and decree that the said Prior and Convent, and their successors, do acknowledge and bear. Also, that when the before mentioned Prior and Convent shall be commanded, by virtue of a decree made before this, or ordain or depute any brother of the said Prior to celebrate mass of the Blessed Virgin in the parish church of Newark aforesaid, at the express consent of the Prior, Convent, and Vicar aforesaid, we order and decree that whatsoever brother of this Order appointed, or at all times hereafter to be appointed, to celebrate such mass, according as leave is given, he shall have a chamber, meat, and drink, for himself, fit for his dignity, at the cost of such vicar for the time being; but all other things necessary for the said Brother the said Prior and Convent and their successors shall be at the expense of, as before, this between the said Prior and Convent and the Brother of the said Order appointed, or to be appointed, for the celebration of the said mass, who may be agreed to be fit for the services aforesaid. Nevertheless we declare, decree, and ordain a stipend for the honourable and sufficient maintenance of the vicar, now incumbent, and his successors, and fit and competent for the support of the expenses of the incumbents, with the payments imposed upon and assigned to them. And we will and do judicially pronounce that the aforesaid decree, of us ratified and confirmed in every respect, be observed and kept for ever by these presents; saving always, all things by law and custom belonging to us of our church of York.

The names of the gentry of the county returned to the commissioners in 1434 included the following:—Richardi Caxton de Tuxford, Johannes White de Colyngam, Richardi Walfeld de Newerk, Roberti Kelom de Newerk, Wilhelmi Skrymshire de Muskham, Roberti Garnon de Muskham, Johannes Kelom de Kelom, Rob. Darley de Thorp, Thom. Columboli de Thorp, Johan Spondon de Newerk, Johan Dennett de Newerk, Hugonis Garnon de Muskham.

We are not aware that Newark was the scene of any of the earlier battles between the partisans of the rival houses of York and Lancaster, which made the period we have now to notice a sadly memorable one in English history. The Yorkists, we know, came no nearer with the main body of their army than Nottingham until years after the first outbreak of the struggle. At Nottingham, the young and aspiring Edward, Duke of York, first rallied his forces, and the castle was held in his interest during the greater portion of the wars. No mention, however, is made of Newark, and we are left in the dark as to whether or no it sent a contingent to participate in the various engagements. That the town, having within it so important a military stronghold as the castle, would feel deeply interested in the events that were transpiring, there need be no question. We may venture also to conclude that it would side with the reigning dynasty, and whilst Nottingham gave in an adhesion to Edward, the red rose of the Lancastrians would be popular in Newark. In confirmation of this view we may mention that one of the neighbouring nobility, Thomas Lord Roos, Lord of Orston, along with many others, was deprived of his estates by an act of attainder, passed in the first year of the reign of the victorious Edward, in consequence of his known attachment to the house of Lancaster.

Bailey tells us that the estates of numerous noblemen were vested in the Crown, "though their only crime appears to have been a constant and loyal devotion to a sovereign to whom themselves, along with the Parliament whose votes now sanctioned these extreme proceedings, had previously tendered their allegiance."

Edward having overcome King Henry at Mortimer's Cross in 1461, ascended the throne as Edward IV., but he was not permitted to hold his position unchallenged, though he had dealt his adversary a severe blow. Three weeks after his coronation he had to fight the battle of Towton; and in 1464 another fierce contest took place at Hexham. A few years later the tide of popular feeling set in strongly against him, and the Lancastrians enlisted numerous adherents to their cause. Hearing in 1470 that a powerful body of the supporters of the red rose had assembled in the neighbourhood of Doncaster, Edward started for that town, passing on his way through Grantham and Newark.

Amongst the Paston letters is one addressed to John Paston by a correspondent signing himself "For Truth." It is No. 36 in Fenn's second volume; No. 638, vol. ii., in Gairdner's edition, and is as follows, save that we have reduced the ancient to the modern spelling :—

"To my cousin, J. Paston.—The King came to Grantham, and there tarried Thursday all day: and there was headed Sir Thomas Delalaunde, and one John Neille, a great captain; and upon the Monday next after that at Doncaster, and there was headed Sir Robert Wellys and another great captain; and then the King had word that the Duke of Clarence and the Earl of Warwick was at Esterfield [Chesterfield] xx mile from Doncaster.

"And upon Tuesday, at IX of the bell, the King took the field and mustered his people; and it was said that were never seen in England so many goodly men, and so well arrayed in a field. And my Lord was worshipfully accompanied, no lord there so well; wherefore the King gave my Lord a great thank.

"And then the Duke of Clarence and the Earl of Warwick heard that the King was coming to themward incontinent, they departed and went to Manchester in Lancashire, hoping to have had help and succour of the Lord Stanley; but in conclusion, there they had little favour, as it was informed the King; and so men say they went westward, and some deem to London. And when the King heard they were departed and gone, he went to York, and came thither the Thursday next after, and there came in to him all the gentlemen of the shire: and upon our Lady Day [he] made Percy Earl of Northumberland, and he that was Earl before Marquis Muntakew. And [so] the king is purposed to come southward. God send him god speed."

The letter is written on Tuesday, March 27, 1470, and taking this as a clue we find the king tarrying at Grantham Thursday, March 15, and Newark on the 16th, and probably on the 17th. He reached Doncaster on Monday, March 19, and being in doubt how Clarence and Warwick would receive his summons, the next morning (Tuesday, March 20) he mustered his army and advanced with the whole, or with part, of his force to Rotherham. There he heard of the departure of the rebels for Manchester, and reconnoitred the country with a view to following them. That night (March 20) the king slept in Rotherham, and finding no inducement to march direct to Manchester, next day he turned towards York, reaching the city on Thursday, March 22.

In October he deemed it prudent to withdraw into Holland, and Henry, with the aid of the Earl of Warwick, was released from the tower where he had been confined. Early, however, in the following year Edward, who had secured aid from his brother-in-law, the Duke of Burgundy, landed at Ravenspur. After his landing with 500 men, and having obtained of Richmond, afterwards Duke of York, and the Lord Rivers, almost as many more, his little army, in his march to London, came to Nottingham, where he hoped to increase it. This succeeded to his wishes, for soon after his arrival there, Sir William Parr and Sir James Harrington, with 600 men well armed and appointed, and shortly after Sir Thomas Burgh and Sir Thomas Montgomery, with another considerable body of men, joined him, upon which he caused himself to be proclaimed by the name of King Edward IV., and having been informed that a considerable Lancastrian force, under the Duke of Exeter, the Earl of Oxford, and the Lord Bardolph, were lodged at Newark, he, with his whole army, marched against them. The Duke of Exeter, hearing of his coming, did not think fit to meet him, but retired at night; whereupon Edward, having notice of it, returned to Nottingham, and from hence began his march towards the Earl of Warwick, who had gone into Warwickshire to levy forces for King Henry. The contending armies met at Barnet in Hertfordshire (April 14, 1471), and the battle resulted in the total defeat of Henry's adherents.

Edward continued to reign until 1483, when he was removed by death. His infant sons, Edward V. and a younger brother, having been cruelly assassinated, Richard III. came to the throne. Richard was several times at Nottingham, and in 1485 he held his court there, when the nobility and gentry from this and other parts of the country attended and acknowledged their allegiance. Hearing that an insurrection had broken out in favour of the House of Lancaster, and that the Earl of Richmond was at Shrewsbury, at the head of the insurgents, he called his army together, and they marched out of Nottingham five abreast, with the king, on a white horse, at their head. Two days after they came up with Richmond's forces at Market Bosworth, in Leicestershire, and a great battle ensued. The royal forces were completely routed, the king, whilst aiming a blow at Richmond, was killed, and his crown was subsequently found in a hawthorn bush close by. Many of the Nottingham gentry, including Sir Gervase Clifton, were slain, and Richmond succeeded to the throne as Henry VII. (A.D. 1485). For some time quiet prevailed, but it was of brief duration. Plots were laid to disturb the tranquillity, and several small risings, which were rapidly suppressed, indicated the existence of a feeling of discontent. At this juncture a person named Simnel was introduced as the Earl of Warwick, and the rightful heir to the throne. Nothing could have exceeded the audacity of the imposture, but it succeeded so well that the king grew alarmed. The Earl of Lincoln with 2000 troops joined Simnel at Dublin, and the two with their united forces landed subsequently at the Pyle of Fowdrey in Lancashire. Hastily collecting an army, his Majesty marched to meet them, intending to do battle at Newark. The two armies, however, met at Stoke. As the conflict that ensued forms one of the most interesting historical events with which the neighbourhood of Newark is associated, we must describe in detail the engagement, and speak more fully of the circumstances out of which it arose.

There can be no doubt that, so far, many historians have failed to attach to the battle of Stoke, the importance which it possessed from a national point of view. It has been regarded simply as the overthrow of a casual rebellion; whereas, it was not only the utter annihilation of a deeply laid plot, but the last occasion where the hatred between the Houses of York and Lancaster ended in the destruction of life. It was in reality, if not in name, the last of the Wars of the Roses. As we have already indicated, the bad feeling which had produced a disastrous civil war was not wholly allayed by the accession to the throne of Henry VII., nor did the king act in a way calculated to secure its extinction. His marriage with the Lady Elizabeth was a conciliatory step, but he deprived it of its proper influence by the indifference which he showed towards his wife. It was only a dread of disaffection which induced him to consent to her coronation; an event that did not take place until two years after their marriage, and a year after a son and heir had been born. The people favourable to the Plantagenets objected to conduct of this kind, and it served to fan a fire which might otherwise have smouldered and died away.

It was whilst the discontentment was rife that a wily priest, Richard Simon, determined to take advantage of it. Engaging the youth, Lambert Simnel, he arranged with him to play the part first of Richard, Duke of York, second son of Edward IV., murdered in the Tower, and subsequently the Earl of Warwick, son of the Duke of Clarence, and then a close prisoner in the Tower of London. The lad entered with spirit into the imposture, and profited so much by the tuition he received as to learn how to conduct himself with princely dignity. Thinking Ireland the best place to commence operations, Simon went thither with his scholar, and presented him to the Earl Kildare as the rightful heir to the throne. With great solemnity the counterfeit Plantagenet was brought to the Castle of Dublin, and there, saluted and honoured as a king, "the boy in all respects becoming it well, and doing nothing that did bewry the baseness of his condition." The Earl of Lincoln, though aware of the imposition, was not averse to it. He was glad to find the feeling on behalf of the Plantagenets still a living reality, and he was well aware that if success attended the efforts of Simon, it would be easy to put away the false youth, and to introduce the true. With this view he sailed to Flanders, to consult with Lord Lovel, who was staying there, and it was resolved, with the connivance of the Duchess of Burgundy, to send to Ireland a regiment consisting of 2000 Germans, under the command of Martin Swartz. Upon the arrival of these troops a council

F

of war was held, and the party decided to proceed to England, and to commence military operations without delay. Crossing the Channel, the rebels, led by the Earl of Lincoln, the Earl of Kildare, Lord Lovel, and Capt. Swartz, landed at Fowdrey, in Lancashire, and were there joined by Sir Thomas Broughton, at the head of a small English force. From Fowdrey the army proceeded as far as York, but being refused admission into that city, they hurried towards Newark, desiring to intercept the king's forces as soon as possible. Moreover, two of the noblemen in command had influences in the district which were expected to operate favourably in securing recruits. Lord Lovel was lord of the manor of Stoke Bardolph, and the Earl of Lincoln had numerous tenants and vassals in Lincolnshire,[1] from amongst whom he could doubtless have drawn assistance.

It was on the evening of Friday, the 15th of June 1487, that the rebels reached Stoke, and took up a position on the hills close by. The king meanwhile had been made fully acquainted with the proceeding, and seeing that a conflict was imperative, had gathered together a large force of stalwart men. Starting from Kenilworth, he proceeded through Coventry, Leicester, Loughborough, Bunny, and Ratcliffe. At the latter place we are informed on the authority of one of the heralds who chronicled the incidents of the march,[2] "There was a great skyre whiche causede many cowards to flee; but the Erle of Oxenforde, and all the nobles in the forward with hym, were some in a good array and in a fayr-bataile, and so was the king, and al the very men that ther were. And in this estiye I hard of no man of worship that fledde but raskells." The king started for Stoke the next morning. This is how the chronicler narrates it: "On the morne whiche was Saturday, the king erley arros and harde 2 masses whereof the Lorde John Fox, Bishop of Excester, sung the ton, and the king had 5 goode and true men of the village of Ratcliffe whiche shewede his grace the best way for to conduyt his hooste to Newark, whiche knew welle the countrey, and shewede wher wer marres and wher was the river of Trente, and wher wer villages or grovys for bushment; or strayt weyes that the king might conduyt his hooste better, of which guides the king gave 2 to the Erle of Oxenforde to conduyt the forwarde and the remanent retynd at his pleasures. And so in good order and array before 9 of the clock, *besides* a village called Stoke a large mile out of Newark, his forarde recountrede his enemyes and rebells."

There is a noticeable discrepancy between this account and that of several of the old historians, inasmuch as the latter represent the king's forces to have reached Newark before the arrival of the rebels, and to have turned back in order to intercept them. Hall, who flourished in the reign of Henry VIII., says that the king came the night before he fought, to Newark, and there "approached nere hys enemyes soner than they loked for him." He adds, that after tarrying a short time in the town, his Majesty pitched his tent near Stoke, where the rebels shortly afterwards

---

[1] This can be verified by a reference to the Act of Provision for Edmund de la Pole, the Earl of Lincoln's brother, *Rotul. Parl.*, part iii. 2, Henry VII.

[2] From a MS. in the Cottonian Library, 4 Lel. Col., p. 210.

arrived. Holinshead[1] speaks of the rebels taking their way from York to Newark. King Henry, understanding which way they took, came the night before the battle to Newark, and going three miles off, near to Stoke, waited their approach. The position chosen by the king as the site of his encampment in Stoke field was on and around a little eminence where the toll-bar recently stood. The Earl of Lincoln, by the advice of Martin Swartz, pitched his tent on the brow of the hill above, west of the Fosseway, and between the windmills in Stoke and Elston fields, on a spot commanding the level ground below, formerly, in part, of a marshy character, and lying on the edge of the Trent.

Both armies passed the night in their respective quarters quietly, but fully prepared for the now inevitable fight on the next day, Saturday, June 16. When the morning dawned, the king drew up his army in three lines, placing his best men in the van, which was supported by wings. He earnestly addressed them, and created three of the captains knights bannerets—viz., Gilbert Talbot, John Cheney, and William Stow. The van then advanced towards the enemy with loud shouts, and trumpets sounding as a challenge to the Earl's forces to do battle in the plain. In answer to the king's challenge, the Earl's men poured into the plain of Stoke and Elston fields. The combatants met on the south or south-east of the village of Stoke, on a spot now partly occupied by Sir Henry Bromley's garden.

The best description of the engagement itself is that given by Holinshead. After stating how that the parties met on a fair plain, "meete for the hayle of suche a conflict," he tells us that the Earl addressed his troops, desiring them to remember his honour, and their own lives. And so he writes, "Both the armies ioyned and fought verye earnestly in so muche that the Almaynes, beeing tryed and experte menne of warres ware in all thynges, as well in strength as pollicie, egall and matches to the Englishmenne. But as for Martine Sward, theyre coronell, fewe of the Englishmen, either in valyaunt courage or strength, and nymblenesse of bodye was to hym; the Irishmen, although they foughte manfully and stucke to it valiantly, yet because they were, after the manner of their countrey almost naked, without anoe conuenable furniture of armour, they were stricken down and slayn lyke dull and brute beastes. Which was a great discouragement to the residue of the companie. Thus they fought for a space so sore and egrely on both partes that no man coulde well judge to whom the victorie was lyke to enclyne. But at length the kings forwarde beyng full of people, and well fortyfyed wyth winges, whiche only both began and continued the fight; set upon the aduersaries with such force and violence, that first they oppressed and killed such capitaynes as one by one resisted their mighte and puissaunce. And after that, put all the other to flyghte, the which were eyther apprehended as prisoners in their running away or else slayne and broghte into confusion in a small momente. But when the battayle was ended, and fought out to the extremetie, then it wel appered, what hyghe prowes, what manfull stomackes, what hardie and courageous heartes rested in the king's aduersaries. For there the

---

[1] *Vide* Holinshead's *Chronicles*.

chief captaine the Earle of Lincolne, and the Lord Lovell, Sir Thomas Broughton, Martin Swarde, and the Lord Gerardine, captain of the Irishmen, were slaine and found dead in the verie places which they hadde chosen alyve to fight in, not giving one foote of grounde to theyr adversaries. Howbeit some affirme, that the Lord Lovell tooke his horse, and would have fledde over Trente, but was not able to recover the further side, for the highnesse of the banke, and so was drowned in the river. There were killed at that battaile with theyr five captains before rehersed of that partie about foure thousand. Of the king's part ther wer not half of them which fought in the forwarde, and gave the aisef, slayn or hurt."

The total loss of life has been estimated at 7000 men, 4000 of whom were rebels, and 3000 Royalists. The conflict was, without doubt, one of the most desperate that has ever been fought in this country. The combatants were powerful, brave, and determined; on the one side flushed with loyalty and hope, and on the other incited by the knowledge that defeat meant ruin or death. For above an hour the result was doubtful. The rebels fought with the vigour of desperation, and the Royalists with the energy of a cooler courage. At one period it was likely that the swift, eager rush of the rebel forces would carry all before it. This opinion was so strong and well grounded that many fled into the adjacent villages, and reported that the king's troops were overthrown. His Majesty, however, met with better success, and the tale-bearers were subsequently fined for their pains. As a last effort, for so it proved, the rebels turned their whole strength upon the van of the king's army. Rallying his forces round that centre, the attack was repelled and the rebel soldiers forced down the ravine leading to Stoke Marsh, and Fiskerton Ford. The slaughter in this locality must have been tremendous; for a thick stream of blood flowed down the road, giving to the spot the name of the Red Gutter, a cognomen that clung to it for many years after. Earl Lincoln, Captain Swartz, and many other of the leading personages were slain, and the impostor and his tutor made prisoners. The tutor was consigned to a dungeon for the remainder of his days, but the young Simnel obtained employment as turnspit in the king's kitchen, and was subsequently advanced to the office of Falconer, an appointment that he retained to his death. After the battle the king proceeded to Lincoln, where some of the prisoners who had been captured were executed, and others set at liberty. What became of Francis, Viscount Lovel, the lord of the manor of Stoke Bardolph, and the possessor of other considerable estates in this county, must remain a matter of conjecture. Three theories have been broached; one, that he was slain during the engagement; another, that in endeavouring to escape across the Trent, he and his horse were drowned; and a third, that he made his way to a secret cave, where he was waited upon by an old and faithful servant. The place was made secure from observation, and its security proved fatal to the Viscount, for, the servant by some mischance leaving him, he miserably perished for want of food. A circumstance that happened three centuries later is recorded in verification of the last-named theory. On making alterations about 1708, at Minster Lovel, in

Oxfordshire, formerly the property of Lord Lovel, the skeleton of a man was discovered in a large vault underground. He was attired in rich clothes, seated in a chair, and having a table before him with writing materials thereon. In another part of the room lay a cap much mouldered and decayed.[1]

One of the most able and valiant of the commanders for the king was Sir John Markham, of Cotham, a descendant of an ancient family, taking their surname from East Markham in this county. He displayed unusual skill in directing the operations of the forces, and was of great service in securing a victory. In military matters he was a man of great power, but, according to Dugdale, he had an "unrulie spirit." Quarrelling with the people of Long Bennington as to the boundaries of their lordship, which adjoined his property, he gathered together a small force, and falling upon the villagers, who were engaged setting out their bounds, killed several of them on the spot, and the rest were driven away. Some have it (says Thoroton) that he also hanged the parish priest, who had kindly offered himself as a mediator between the enraged knight and the people. To avoid punishment for these crimes he was compelled to flee from home, and he remained secreted at a place called Cressy Hall, until the influence of his friends secured for him a free pardon from the king. Memorials of the Markham family exist in the parish church of Newark. Mr. Dickinson says, "The choir is bounded on the south and north sides by two handsome chauntry chapels, in both of which it seems there were formerly altar tombs. They were dedicated to the two Markhams, father and son, the former of whom became connected with Newark by the intermarriage of his ancestor, Lord Chief-Justice Markham, with the heiress of the Leekes, of this place, and of Cotham in its vicinity.[2] These chapels are profusely ornamented, besides the arms of Markham, with those of Leekes, Meering, Bosome, and other families, from whom the Markhams were descended, or with whom they had connected themselves in marriage. That on the south side is of considerable dimensions, in the most beautiful style of Gothic architecture, and extremely curious on account of some of its decorations, which remain to this day. There are two paintings which fill two compartments of the ornamental stonework, one of which represents a man dressed in gorgeous apparel, like royal robes, a head-dress ornamented by jewels and a plume. The other is a whole-length figure of a skeleton (supposed to be intended for a representation of Death) in an attitude somewhat like that of dancing with a red rose in his right hand. What allegorical or hieroglyphical allusion may be concealed under these representations it may perhaps not be easy to decide with certainty. Death appears to be menacing the king-like figure, 'grinning horribly a ghastly smile,' and upbraiding him with something to which the rose appears to bear a reference. The white rose, we know, during the contests between the houses of York and Lancaster, was the emblem or signal of the former family, while the red rose was that of the Lancastrian faction. This tomb and chapel having been erected to the

---

[1] *Vide* a letter given in Banks' *Dormant and Extinct Baronetage*, 321, from Wm. Cowper, Esq., Clerk of the Parliament.

[2] It will be seen from the particulars given on p. 40 that Mr. Dickinson is in error in this respect.

memory of Sir Robert Markham, probably by his son John, who took an active part in the contests between the rival houses, the most probable conjecture seems to be that the king-like figure is intended to represent the impostor Lambert Simnel, the pretended Earl of Warwick, who, about the period when Sir Robert Markham died, contended for the possession of the crown with King Henry VII. in the famous battle of Stoke." Sir Robert, who died in 1496, was a warm supporter of the side of the white rose, and for his services was rewarded at the coronation of Edward IV. by being created a Knight of the Bath. He had two sons, John who succeeded him, and Robert, who married Elizabeth, daughter of Sir William Mering of Mering. Over the chauntry chapel, at the south-west corner of the choir, there used to be an arch of freestone, and on the side of that, "orate pro animi Roberti Markham armigeri et Elizabethæ uxoris ejus." On the outside of the tracery are several coats of arms, coarsely cut, Markham quartering Lecke, etc., impaling Mering, Burdon, Bozome, etc. The theory advanced by Mr. Dickinson as to the meaning of the paintings is ingenious, but the foundation on which it is established is somewhat shaken when we call to mind the fact that "the Dance of Death," of which the skeleton figure is undoubtedly a partial representation, was a favourite subject during the fourteenth and fifteenth centuries. In St. Paul's, London, and in the Church of the Holy Innocents, Paris, full illustrations of the dance were in existence, and consisted of a long procession of figures, each led by a skeleton towards the grave where the dance terminated. The number of characters varied from twenty-six to thirty-eight, and at Newark there was room for twenty-four, allowing two panels for each group. An excellent letter on the subject appeared in the *Gentleman's Magazine* in 1846. The writer (Mr. J. C. Robinson) after describing the exact position of the painting, which occupies the two lower panels towards the east of the southern or sedilia screens, and faces the aisle, says:—

> The date of the screens, as well as the rood loft and stalls, I have no hesitation in referring to a period not earlier than the reign of Henry the Eighth (about 1520), an opinion which is confirmed by the costume of the figure in the painting. The picture appears to be in oil, and its style much resembles that of painted glass, as the figures have the same hard decisive outline absolutely necessary for effective glass painting, but which is unnatural on any other than a transparent ground. Though very rude in design, there is yet a considerable degree of expression in the symbolical meaning of the group; the action of the skeleton, holding in one hand a flower, and with the other pointing to the grave beneath, together with its ghastly grin, and the solemn measure of the ghostly dance, is very significant, while the earnest, thoughtful countenance of the gaily dressed figure, whose hand mechanically rests on the contents of the purse at his girdle, coupled with the apparent unconscious action of the legs joining in the dance, suggest the idea of the rich man busied in the multifarious pleasures and employments of life, and giving little heed to the warnings of mortality. There is a sort of dreamy earnestness and mystery in the composition, to be found nowhere but in Catholic art, and which is to a certain extent visible even in its rudest and least refined productions.
>
> The Dance of Death, as must be well known to most of your readers, was a favourite subject during the 14th and 15th centuries; and the earliest allusion, according to Warton, seems to be in Piers Plowman's Vision, written about 1350. Warton is of opinion that the pictorial representation was founded upon a kind of spiritual masquerade, anciently enacted by the ecclesiastics in the churches

of France; but I am not aware that this ceremony, which seems to have been allied to that of the lay bishop and feast of asses, was ever actually performed in the English churches. The first painting on the subject on record was at Minden, in Westphalia, as early as 1384. The next was a celebrated one at the Holy Innocents, in Paris, in the century succeeding, and from which Lydgate translated the verses accompanying, at the request of the chaplain of St. Paul's, London, who caused them to be inscribed under a Dance of Death, executed at the expense of one Jenkin, a carpenter, on the walls of the cloister, somewhere about the year 1430, and which Drydale (History of St. Paul's) says was an imitation of that in the cloister of the Holy Innocents. These paintings at Paris and at St. Paul's appear to have consisted of a long procession of figures, each led by a skeleton towards the grave, where the dance ended: whereas the Newark one was evidently in single groups similar to those in the "Imagines mortes," erroneously attributed to Holbein, the woodcuts to which must have been executed as early as 1520 or 1530. The number of characters presented at St. Paul's was 38, at Lubeck 26, and in the earliest edition of the "Imagines mortes" 43; whilst the Newark screen contains 48 panels, which, allowing two panels for each group or character, gives 24 as the original number of subjects.

An editorial note was appended, and it was as follows:—

In answer to an expression of doubt on our part that there was really an entire Dance of Death at Newark, but possibly only this one picture, which is paralleled by that of "Death and the Gallant," in the Hungerford chapel at Salisbury cathedral, our correspondent has favoured us with the following additional remarks: In reply to your inquiry, I beg to state that the painting of which I sent you a drawing is all that remains at Newark, and that there are no vestiges of any others, the rest of the divisions being quite open; nor is there, I believe, any rebate or other contrivance in the interior side of the mullion to receive a panel, as would have been expected; but this appears to be the same in the divisions which contain the paintings, as the inlaid panel comes fair with the commencement of the hollow mould or level of the mullion, without any set off or distinction between the mullion and the panel. One of the principal circumstances that induced me to think there had been other paintings is the fact of there being so many divisions precisely similar to each other, and without either cusps or tracery of any kind, together with the unsymmetrical position of the remaining painting at the extreme corner of the screen. The surface of the screens beneath the string-course is also panelled, which panels are cusped, and contain shields bearing the arms of Markham, Meering, Bosom, and other neighbouring families. I have referred to Dickinson's *History of Newark*, and he is of opinion that the parcloses were chauntries, or sepulchral chapels of the Markham family. He also says that one of them—the north one—formerly contained an altar tomb. They may have been enclosures for sepulchre or sacella, but that they ever were chauntries containing an altar is, I think, very unlikely, as they have no piscinas; neither would there have been convenient space for the priest to perform mass, as the enclosures are not above at most 4 ft. 6 in. to 5 ft. wide in the interior; besides the two altars would have flanked the high altar within a few feet on either side. I think there is very little doubt that my view of the chapel on the south side being intended to receive the wooden sedilia for the service of the high altar is the correct one, as both of them have a wide four-centred arch, which is quite open to the choir; besides there are no sedilia remaining in the church. If there has been a series of paintings, which I still feel inclined to think more than probable, we may easily account for their removal by the fact that the choir would have been considerably darkened had they existed; for the obscurity of the centre division of the church on account of the great elevation and small dimensions of the clerestory windows has often been complained of; and the present paintings, from their position, would intercept scarcely any light.

We have reproduced the greater part of Mr. Robinson's communication because it is evidently the production of a man who has paid a good deal of attention to

THE FAMILY OF MARKHAM.

the subject, and is competent to express an opinion. The date of the painting and its nature would lead to the belief that a full illustration of the Dance was contemplated; but whether it was ever completed, and occupied the other panels, or whether the design was laid aside, must remain a matter of conjecture.

Thus far we have but referred incidentally to the Markhams. To most readers, however, somewhat fuller particulars of so important a family cannot fail to be highly interesting. For the details which follow we are indebted to Capt. A. E. Lawson Lowe, F.S.A. He writes:—

Sir John Markham, of East Markham, puisne judge of Common Pleas from 1396 to 1406, and remarkable as having prepared the instrument for the deposition of King Richard II., was the son of Sir Robert Markham, a king's serjeant, by Isabel, daughter of Sir John de Caunton. He was twice married—first to Elizabeth, daughter and co-heiress of Sir Roger de Cressy, of Hodsock, by whom he acquired Cressy Hall, Risegate, and a fourth part of the manor of Braytoft, in Lincolnshire; and secondly to Milicent, daughter and heiress of Sir John de Bekering, and widow of Sir Nicholas de Burdon, who was killed at the battle of Shrewsbury in 1403. Sir John Markham died on St. Silvester's Day (December 31), 1409, and was buried in the chancel at East Markham. By his first wife he had a son, Sir Robert Markham, of East Markham, Sheriff of the counties of Nottingham and Derby in 1434, who married Elizabeth, sole daughter and heiress of Sir Nicholas de Burdon, whose widow became his father's second wife. By his second marriage Sir John Markham had a son of his own name, who settled at Sedgebrooke, in Lincolnshire, and was Lord Chief-Justice of the King's Bench from 1462 to 1471. This second Sir John Markham, who was created a Knight of the Bath, together with his nephew, Sir Robert, at the coronation of King Edward IV., died in 1481, having married Margaret, second daughter and co-heiress of Simon Leeke, Esq., of Cotham, near Newark, and was ancestor of the Markhams of Sedgebrooke. One of his descendants, Sir Robert Markham of Sedgebrooke, was created a baronet by King Charles I., August 15, 1642, and served that monarch at the siege of Newark. Sir Robert Markham, of East Markham (the eldest son of the first-named Sir John), was the father of another Sir Robert Markham, who was made a Knight of the Bath at the coronation of King Edward IV., as already mentioned. This Sir Robert was High Sheriff of Lincolnshire in 1477, and of Nottinghamshire and Derbyshire in 1481. Joane, his wife, was the sole daughter and heiress of Sir Giles Daubeny, by Mary, eldest daughter and co-heiress of Simon Leeke, Esq., and through this marriage the Cotham estates passed into the hands of the Markham family. Sir Robert Markham died in 1496, and was buried near the high altar in Newark church. He left two sons, namely, Sir John, who succeeded his father in the enjoyment of the family estates, and Robert, who married Elizabeth, daughter of Sir William Mering, of Mering, and who, there is reason to believe, was also buried at Newark. The elder son, Sir John Markham of Cotham, was a commander at the battle of Stoke, which was fought within a mile or so of his father's mansion at Cotham in 1487. He was High Sheriff of the counties of Nottingham and Derby in 1519 and again in 1526. Thoroton says of him, that he was "an unruly-spirited man," and having been outlawed for hanging the priest of Long Bennington, he was compelled to live in obscurity for several years, but was eventually pardoned by King Henry VII., whose mother interceded for him. His death occurred in 1536. By Alice, his wife, daughter of Sir William Skipwith, of Ormesby, in Lincolnshire, he had a son, Sir John Markham, Lieutenant of the Tower of London, who was High Sheriff of Lincolnshire in 1533, and of Nottinghamshire and Derbyshire in 1539, and knight of the shire for Nottinghamshire in 1546 and 1558. He was thrice married—first to Anne, daughter of Sir George Nevile, by Mary, daughter of Sir Henry Fitz Lewes and of Elizabeth, daughter and co-heiress of Edmund Beaufort, second Duke of Somerset; secondly, to Margery, daughter of Sir Ralph Langford; and thirdly, to Anne, daughter and co-heiress of John Strelley, Esq., of Strelley, and widow of Sir Richard Stanhope, of Rampton. By his first wife Sir John Markham had a son, John, who resided at Syreston; he married Katherine, daughter of Sir Anthony Babington, of Kingston, but died in his father's lifetime, leaving an only son, Robert Markham, Esq., of Cotham, who was born at Syreston in 1536, and inherited the family estates upon the death of his grandfather, Sir John Markham, in 1564. He was knight of the shire for Nottinghamshire in 1571, and served as High Sheriff in 1571 and again in 1573. It was this member of the family who was referred to by Queen Elizabeth in her famous distich on her four Nottinghamshire courtiers :

"Gervase the gentle, Stanhope the stout ;
Markham the lion, and Sutton the lout."

f By Mary, his first wife, the daughter of Sir Francis Leeke, of Sutton Scarsdale in Derbyshire, he had, with other issue, a son, Robert, who succeeded to the estates upon the death of his father in 1606. He was subsequently knighted by king James I., and is styled by Thoroton "a fatal unthrift and destroyer of this eminent family." How far Sir Robert Markham may have deserved this character we are unable to judge. It is certain that the Cotham estates were sold by him, together with all the other landed property which he possessed, but there is evidence that his father was in embarrassed circumstances, and the estates may possibly have been hopelessly encumbered when they descended to him. Sir Robert was twice married, and a monument to his first wife, Ann, daughter of Sir John Warburton, of Arley, in Cheshire (who died in 1601), yet remains on the north side of the chancel at Cotham. Francis Markham, a younger brother of Sir Robert, was an author of some repute in his day, whilst Gervase Markham, another brother, was even better known for his literary productions. Godfrey Markham, another brother, served in the royalist army, and was killed in a sortie at the siege of Newark in 1646. It may be observed *en passant* that William Markham, D.D., Bishop of Chester from 1771 to 1776, and Archbishop of York from the last-named year until 1807, claimed descent from Daniel Markham, the third son of the last Sir John Markham of Cotham. It has already been noted that Sir John Markham, Lieutenant of the Tower of London, was thrice married. By his second wife he had a son, Robert, who was blind, and who represented the town of Nottingham in Parliament, and died unmarried. By his third wife Sir John had two sons, namely, William, likewise representative in Parliament for the town of Nottingham, who left no male issue, and Thomas, who settled at Ollerton, and was ancestor of the Markhams of that place. This Thomas Markham was High Steward of Mansfield, Ranger of Sherwood Forest, Standard-bearer to Queen Elizabeth's band of gentlemen pensioners, and High Sheriff of Nottinghamshire in 1577. He married Mary, sole daughter and heiress of Ryce Griffin, Esq., of Braybroke and Dingley, in Northamptonshire, by whom he had seven sons, several of whom became Roman Catholics, for which their father humbly apologised to William, first Lord Burghley, in letters dated 1592 and 1594. His grandson, Thomas Markham, Esq., was Lieut. Colonel of Horse in the Royalist army, and was slain in the battle of Winceby, in Lincolnshire, in 1644. This last-named branch bore the ancient arms of Markham— viz., *Azure* on a chief *or*, a demi lion rampant issuant *gules*, differenced with a bordure *argent*.

In 1487 the erection of the chancel of Newark church was commenced at the joint expense of the prior and convent of St. Catherine, near Lincoln, and certain individuals of the town of Newark. The deed in which the agreement for this object is recorded, recognises the church as being newly rebuilt, and that the completion of the chancel should be fully effected within the space of fourteen years from the date of the document.

The disputes and faction fights between the rival houses of Lancaster and York began gradually to diminish after the battle of Stoke field. The king, Henry VII., became settled on the throne when the lingering affection for the white rose which caused people to cluster round the impostor Simnel had died away, and thenceforward he devoted himself to the advancement of his foreign influence, and the amassing of money. A marriage between the Scotch king, James IV., and Margaret, Henry's eldest daughter, allayed for a time the enmity which kept bubbling up hot and strong between England and Scotland, and laid the foundation for that union of the two crowns which became effected a century later. Various accounts are given of his Majesty's attempts at extortion, and he seems to have been as cute and bold at obtaining money as he was in influencing matrimonial alliances. His career, however, was drawing to a close. In 1509, after several attacks of gout, consumption set in, and the king succumbed to a greater enemy than any of the Yorkists.

By a codicil to his will he gave £200 to the convent "that by his succour and aid was newly begun in the town of Newark." We are told that not many years ago a long chapel-like building of stone with a large Gothic window was standing in what was then known as Osmundthrope, near the road, midway between North Gate and Appleton Gate. It has been conjectured by some that this may have been the site of the convent to which the king refers.

During the earlier years of the reign of Henry VIII. we find few local references, but they subsequently become somewhat numerous. On the 31st July 1521 John Smythe, at one time vicar of Newark, made his will. After many bequests, he proceeds, " Also I will that Sir Roger Walhed, my executor, shall cause to be made the whole half-part of the stalls on the right side of the choir (in the parish church) in honour of St. Mary Magdalene, at a cost of £25." He directs his body to be buried in the chancel, under the middle stone between the sepulchre of his father on the right hand and his mother on the left, at the entrance of the choir, and near the vicar's stall. The brass plate still remains, recording his death a fortnight after the date of his will, namely, on the 14th of August, 1521. The inscription runs thus:—" Here lies Mr. John Smythe, LL.B., formerly vicar of Newark, in the year of his vicarage 44 ; Prebendary of Wynchester and Rector of Kelham, who died the 14th day of the month of August, in the year of our Lord, 1521 ; on whose soul God have mercy."

At this period, as had been the case from early times, there was a right of sanctuary attached to churches ; the right is defined by Blackstone in the following terms :—" It is to be observed that if a person accused of any crime (except treason wherein the crown, and sacrilege, wherein the church was too nearly concerned) had fled to any church or churchyard, and within forty days after, went in sackcloth, and confessed himself guilty before the coroner, and declared all the particular circumstances of the offence ; and thereupon took the oath in that case provided—viz., that he abjured the realm and would depart from thence forthwith, at the part that should be assigned him, and would never return without leave from the King ; he by this means saved his life, if he observed the conditions of the oath, by going with a cross in his hand and with all convenient speed to the port assigned, and embarking. For if, during this forty days' privilege of sanctuary, or on his road to the seaside, he was apprehended and arraigned in any court for this felony, he might plead right of sanctuary, and had a right to be remanded if taken out against his will." In minor matters this right of sanctuary attached to churches generally, but for the protection of murderers there were higher sanctuaries, where a *frith* or *fridstool* was erected near the altar. There are two of these stools in existence at the present time; one at Hexham and another in Beverley Minster.

In the British Museum there is a register of the persons who sought the sanctuary at Beverley, with the crimes that had caused them to flee to this city of refuge. One entry states that on the 10th December, in the fifteenth of the reign of Henry VIII. (1524) Christopher Thomlynson, late of Newark, in the county of Nottingham, glover, came to the liberty and sanctuary of St. John of Beverley, because he was attached for buying of a man unknown, three ells of woollen cloth suspected, and afterwards the said Christopher was led to *the King's prison at Nottingham;* and then and there Thomas Clarke of Newark aforesaid, mercer, became the surety and pledge of the said Christopher, and afterwards the said Christopher feloniously fled from the custody of the said Thomas Clarke, etc., and for other causes touching the safety of his body; and he was admitted and sworn. A copy of the oath the fugitives took who fled to Beverley has been preserved, and it does not seem in this instance to have involved a promise to leave the country, as was the case in many to which Blackstone refers. The bailiff of the Archbishop of York, by whom the oath was administered, was directed to inquire of the refugee "what man he had killed, and wherewith, and both their names, and then make him lay his hand on the book, the bailiff saying, 'Sir, take hede on your oth, ye shal be treu and fayhtful to my lord archbishop of York, lord off this towne, to the provest of the same, to the chanons of this chirch, and all other ministers thereof. Also ye shall bere gude hert to the baillie and XII governors of this town, to all burges' and comyners of the same. Also ye shall bere no poynted wapen, dagger, knyfe, ne none other wapen ayents the kynge's pece. Also ye shal be redy at all your power if there be any debate or stryf or od so than (sudden) case of fyre within the town, to help to s'cess (suppress?) it. Also ye shal be redy at the obite of King Adelstan, at the dirige, and the messe at such time as it is done at the warnying of the belman of the town, and do your dewte in ryngying, and for to offer at the messe on the morne, so help you God and these holy evangelistes,' and then gar (make) hym kysse the book."

Similar privileges to those which attached to Beverley Minster, were conferred at a very early period upon the Collegiate Church at Southwell. In the year 1106 it was ordered, both by royal and ecclesiastical authority, that "neither the king's officer nor any other should have law nor take distress there, till the canon of that prebend was first required. And if any person whatsoever shall take and detain any man, though guilty, and convict of any crime or wickedness whatever, from within the porch, he shall be adjudged to make amends by six hundredths; if from within the church by twelve; if from within the choir by eighteen; every hundredth containing six pounds (of silver) and for every the said faults, or any, shall be enjoined penance as for sacrilege. But if any should be so mad and instigated by the devil as to presume to take one from the stone chair by the altar, called the Chair of Peace, for so wicked a sacrilege no judgment or sum of money can atone." Whether Southwell Church had lost its privileges in the days of Henry VIII. we cannot say, but if it had not, Christopher Thomlynson of Newark must have had an especial desire to leave the county, or he would not have travelled all the way to Beverley when there was an equally safe sanctuary within a few miles of his home.

Of the restrictions put upon trade we have a curious illustration in the following entry, copied from the records of the city of Lincoln, under date 26th September 1527. At a common council it was agreed "y^t wher Thomas Clerk of Newark hath boght and ingrosyd mytch corne in ye cuntrey, wherby scarsenes of corne is by the same, wherfor all sutch corne as y^t he and other bryngyth through ye citie schalbe restreynyd and tarye here to be sold in ye markyt to serve ye people with."

In 1530 Cardinal Wolsey, who had wielded so remarkable a power in the nation, came into the district, but his stay was one of brief duration. It appears that when his power began to diminish, as his favour with the monarch grew less, he bethought himself of the palace of Southwell, towards the enlargement and completion of which he had been a liberal contributor, and thither he retired in the summer of 1530 to seek that rest which he was unable elsewhere to obtain.[1] On his way to Southwell he visited Newark, and spent some time at the castle, another place that had commended itself to him as a pleasant and commodious residence. At the latter end of September he proceeded from Southwell to Scrooby, intending to visit York, but on the way he was arrested for high treason, and commanded to proceed to London with all speed. The shock, acting upon a frame which ill health had somewhat shaken, made the fallen prelate seriously ill of dysentery, and by the time he reached Leicester, riding on a mule and followed by a small band of attendants, he presented a pitiable spectacle of suffering and misery. Alighting at the abbey, he was taken inside, and in a short time he breathed his last.

The year following Wolsey's wretched death an indenture was created, bearing date the 21st February (1531), by which Mr. Thomas Magnus, with whom Wolsey had often had occasion to correspond on State business, divested himself of all ownership in his extensive estates, and secured them for the lasting benefit of the town of Newark. Before detailing the nature of so noble a gift, we must say something of the remarkable, and in many respects distinguished, career of the giver. As to the date and place of his birth, and the social position of his parents, there is some doubt. Dr. Fuller, in his account of the worthies of the county, tells us, that Thomas

[1] Two letters from Wolsey, dated from "my poore house at Suthwell" (August 1530), are amongst the *State Papers*.

Magnus was "an exposed child, left by his mother (nobody knows who) in the parish church of Newark, and being found in the way by some Yorkshire clothiers in the dark of the morning, they had compassion upon the babe, and being unwilling to leave it yet exposed, agreed among themselves to pay for its nursing and education (which would come to a little among many), and first of all had him baptized at Newark by the name of Thomas, giving his surname *Amang-us*—*i.e.*, to be maintained *among us*." The story is romantic, and would vest the biography of Magnus with a touch of even deeper interest, could it be substantiated by anything more reliable than common tradition. A reference to the will, however, destroys the foundation of the tale, seeing that Magnus therein refers to his father and mother, and directs an obit to be kept in the church for the repose of their souls. The accounts given by other authorities state that Magnus was the son of a publican at Newark, in humble circumstances, at whose house certain Yorkshire clothiers who visited Lincolnshire for the purpose of purchasing wool were in the habit of calling. These tradesmen observed the unusual tact and sprightliness of the child, and resolved to carry him home with them to Yorkshire, where he could be educated at a cheap rate, and more thoroughly fitted for the after business of life than he could possibly be by remaining at home. The parents, realising the advantages which their son would possess, yielded to the suggestion of the clothiers, under whose kindly care young Magnus received a sound education, and gave evidence of the possession of those graces and talents which distinguished him so much in after life. When he returned to his native town he was a youth of great promise, intelligent, courteous, and of noble appearance.

Fortunately for Magnus, his qualities of mind and body did not pass unnoticed by those in authority. A Mr. Robert Brown, Receiver to Cardinal Wolsey, and to Longland, Bishop of Lincoln, had his attention drawn to the youth, and took so genuine an interest in his welfare as to recommend him to the Cardinal, when the latter was on a visit to Southwell. The prelate, who, whatever his defects in the shape of cupidity and over-reaching ambition, was not deficient in shrewdness, speedily recognised in Mr. Magnus the existence of a superior intellect, and being favourably impressed, as well by his address as by his abilities, took him at once into his service and his confidence. For some time Mr. Magnus was permitted to pursue his studies, which he doubtless did with industry and success, and at the conclusion of his university career he was recommended to the king, from whom he obtained the office of chaplain. Whilst acting in this capacity he was employed in several important embassies. On one occasion, at a period when Wolsey was striving to obtain the help of the Emperor Charles V. in his struggle for the Papacy, Mr. Magnus was selected by him to visit that monarch, and to solicit his powerful intervention in the Cardinal's behalf. Whatever the result of the mission may have been, it is evident Wolsey was well satisfied with the promptitude and ability of Mr. Magnus, who continued to grow in the favour of his superiors, and the respect of his equals. Evidence that the Cardinal approved of the efficiency and energy of Magnus is not far to seek. The death of James IV. of Scotland, who fell in the battle of Flodden Field, left the English king the sole monarch of influence and power in Great Britain, and the jealousies of the two great rival continental potentates, the Emperor and Francis I. of France, caused the approving smile of Henry to be courted by both. Henry was, in fact, at that period, in the dignified position of "arbiter of peace throughout Europe."

In this situation, at once responsible and critical, the king took upon himself, with but little reason, to declare war against France (1522). It then became necessary to watch carefully the progress of Scotland, and to see what negotiations would take place between France and the Scottish Court. To exercise this watchful spirit, some person was needed as accredited agent at the Court of Scotland, who should officiate as ambassador extraordinary, carefully note the progress of affairs, and promptly transmit to his royal master intelligence of everything which threatened the predominance of English influence. It will readily be conceived that to select a suitable person to fill so important a position was a matter of the gravest difficulty and concern. As a writer well puts it, when illustrating the importance of the task, "an ambitious woman—for such the Scotch Queen-mother undoubtedly was,—an exasperated and degraded husband, and a profligate and aspiring paramour, were to be so influenced as to make their different propensities, even their very vices, co-operate in the same general purpose, the placing of all these various characters under the control of England."[1] There was but one person who seemed to possess the requisite tact and talent for this difficult duty, and that was Mr. Magnus.

Before describing the progress of his important mission, it becomes necessary to note that on the death of James IV. his wife Margaret, to whose marriage we alluded in a previous page,[2] had with the assistance of English influence become Regent. About a year after she had assumed this dignified and responsible position, she married the Earl of Angus, a proceeding which gave rise to much dissatisfaction, and resulted in her banishment from the country. The Duke of Albany took upon himself the duties of the office from which Margaret had been expelled, but Henry VIII. was entirely averse to him, and he was compelled to retire. Margaret and her husband having returned, the Government was administered by a congress of deputies, with Angus at their head. After various changes, which we need not recapitulate, Albany, in October 1523, brought over 6000 French soldiers, and was joined by many of his adherents in Scotland. At the head of this force he proposed attacking the Earl of Surrey, who had the chief command of the English forces in the north. The Earl prepared to meet him. Lords Dorset, Latimer, Northumberland, Clifford, and Darcy, and the gentlemen of Yorkshire hastened to the rescue. In Lancashire, Cheshire, Nottingham, and Derby, large bodies of troops were raised. A repetition of Flodden Field was expected, and the English looked for a battle so decisive that it should discourage the Scots for a long time

---

[1] *Bailey*, vol. i. p. 390. [2] *Ante*, p. 42.

to come: "Of likelihood" wrote Lord Surrey to Wolsey, "no man living shall ever see the Scots attempt to invade this realm if they be well resisted now."

The Scotch army came down the Tweed, and Albany fixed his camp opposite Werk Castle, which Surrey had lately repaired. He sent over some troops to attack the garrison, but they were vigorously repulsed. Albany's heart thereupon failed him, and after a while he left Scotland, and a government was established in the name of James V. Mr. Froude calls the castle that of Newark, and it appears to be so described in the letters of the Earl of Surrey.[1] It must not, however, be confused with Newark-upon-Trent. Meanwhile, Margaret had transferred her affections from her husband, and had commenced an intrigue with Lord Methuen. She threatened that if the Earl of Angus returned to her, she would join the faction of France, and she kept her word, for when Angus made his appearance, she released the prelates who had been imprisoned for their French tendencies, and despatched David Beton to Paris as an accredited ambassador.

It was in the midst of this unhappy condition of affairs, that Magnus was sent to make his observations and reports, and to act as the exponent of the English king's desires. One of his first efforts was to reconcile Margaret with her husband. With that object in view, he visited Edinburgh about the end of October 1524, and on the 1st of November was admitted to an interview. In the opening conversation she expressed herself in moderate terms, and Magnus had hopes of success. The day following, however, he recognised the hopelessness of his mission: writing to Cardinal Wolsey, he says,[2] she would listen to no advice except it was approved by Methuen. "He keepeth," wrote Magnus, "as is said, all the seals, and ordereth all causes in such a manner as is without any other counsel, either of wisdom, honour, or reputation." Methuen was devoted to the Earl of Arran and Archbishop Beton, and Arran and the archbishop were devoted to France. Margaret was thus wholly committed to the faction, averse to her brother and to England. Henry was extremely angry, and described her as "rather like an unnatural and transformed person, than like a noble princess or a woman of wisdom or honour." On the 26th of November Angus and his followers scaled the walls of Edinburgh; and Magnus, fearing that Margaret would order the Castle guns to be fired on her husband's followers, hastened to her to counsel calmness and moderation. When he reached Holyrood he found the palace in confusion; he pushed his way into the queen's presence, but she ordered him to retire, and not to meddle in matters of no concern to him. Directly after one of the guns was fired, and several persons were killed. At dark, Angus withdrew to Dalkeith, and civil war seemed imminent. To rid herself of Angus, her husband, Margaret sued for a divorce, putting forth the extraordinary plea, that on the date of her second marriage, her first husband was alive, having escaped the dangers of Flodden Field. Writing to Wolsey, Magnus says,[3] "The queen's grace sueth for a divorce between her said grace and the Earl

---

[1] *Vide State Papers*, vol. iv. p. 52. [2] *State Papers*, vol. iv. p. 215.
[3] *State Papers*, vol. iv. p. 385.

of Angus, surmitting her cause to be that she was married to the said Earl, the late King of Scots, her husband being alive, and that the same king was living three years after the Field of Flodden." Her statement was accepted as the ground of a suit, but before it was proceeded with a conference took place as to the mode of government, which resulted in the establishment of a council of eight, under the nominal presidency of the queen.

A formal peace not having been concluded between England and Scotland since the rupture in 1523, negotiations were opened with the new council. Magnus brought forward the English proposals with what he terms his "four reasonings,"[1] he dwelt "upon the nigh marching together of the two realms within one isle, and of one speech and language," upon "the proximity of blood between the king's Highness of England and the young king, his tender nephew;" upon "the said young king's possibility of inheritance to the two crowns," and "upon the great likelihood he had to be preferred before all others to the marriage of the lady princess (Princess Mary), if favourably and in loving manner his grace could and would use him towards the king his uncle." Having urged these points, Magnus desired the council to agree to a perpetual peace with England in which France should not be comprehended. The council replied that they desired security before committing the country to such a treaty. There must be a formal betrothal between the young king and the Princess Mary, and then the whole realm of Scotland was minded and inclined utterly to abandon France, and wholly to be conjoined with England. As three years must elapse before James was of age to sign a legal contract, a treaty of peace until that time was concluded, James telling Magnus that he wished he was in England with the king his uncle.[2] So far, matters had progressed fairly, but directly the peace was agreed upon, Magnus found himself an object of popular disfavour. It happened that the weather was wet and the harvest threatened. A rumour was forthwith diligently circulated that Magnus was an enchanter who, having in former years blighted the vines of France and Flanders, was now overlooking Scotland with an evil eye. As he walked through Edinburgh the women cursed him and his servants openly to their faces. Under these circumstances, he desired to be permitted to return from "a cumbrous country, where ever was suspicion without trust, disdain, slander, malice, and cruelty without virtue, or dread of God or man." We append the full text of the letter,[3] giving also a facsimile of his signature:—

> PLEAS it Your Grace to be advertissed. Of late I received a lettre from my Lorde Dacre, dated at Hontingdon the 3de day of this moneth whereby amongges other thingges I conceved his Lordship desired to be advertissed of noumber and names of suche personnages, as shulde be commissioners for the partye of Scotland to mete with the Kinge our Maister's Commissioners, and of the place where our assemble shulde bee; requryng the same mooste effectually to bee at Baruick, or elles our furst meting to be wythynne the realme and grounde of Einglande. Soe it is, that the Chaunceler and other

---

[1] Letter from Magnus to Wolsey, *State Papers*, vol. iv. p. 335.
[2] *Vide* Froude's *History*.
[3] *State Papers*, vol. iv., Part IV., Hen. VIII., p. 404.

the Lords here doe lye in sondrey contreys, oone farre frome an other; and specially the Erle of Anguisshe hath bene frome the yong Kinges Grace here upon 14 dayes, aboute his oune affaires and busyness; soe that for ordouring of causes there hath bene noone other person present aboute the said yonge Kinge but only the Archebussop of Glasco, with other mean personages. Howe be it, it is appoynted and determyned nowe, and also autorised by commission, that thErle of Anguisshe, thAbbott of Holy Roodhouse, or in his roomme thAbbott of Arbrooth, and Mr. Adam Otterbourne the Kinges Advocate, or in his place Sir William Scotte, bye cause dyverse thaym be sekelewe, as the said Abbot of Holy Roodehouse and Mr. Adam shall geve meteing to the Kinge our said maisters, to treat commyn and speke for the concluding of the peas, lately determynned here to be had, for three yeare; as afore with the further circumstances hath bene declared and sygnyfyed to your said Grace bye my former letteres.

And albe it, upon suche conciderations as of late I mentioned to youre said Grace by my laste letteres, our repairing hyder and meteing at this the Toune of Edinburgh hath specially bene required, and grete instaunce meanes and devices motionned for the same intent and purpoos; yet nevertheless it is determynned that the said Commissioners come to Barwik, and remayne there duringe the tyme our assemble and meteing, assyned and appointed to be the sext daye of October next coming, and the said Commissioners to repaire thider under the noumber of an hundreth or 120 personnes.

Theffecte of thaire articles, as farre as in any wise I cann conceve, notwithstanding the matier afore mooved unto me openly in the Parliament, as hath bene mentionned unto youre said Grace, shall only reste in effecte for a peas for thre yeres, with the generall comprehension, and that Scotlande may aide and assiste France with men, horse and harnes in the meanetyme if the same be required, And as is said the same was agreede unto at the last being and assembling of the commissioners at Barwik. The poore effect of my former letters concidered with these premises, it may therefore like your said Grace to directe unto me and to other the Commissioners the Kinges high pleasure and youres, if any thing be further to be doon and executed.

Of late the Chancellor wrote to the Archbussop of Glasco, and shewed that for somyche as the Ambassodour of France had contynued here upon 8 or 9 days, that therefore it was convenient that the Kings Grace shulde geve unto him presence and receive his lettres and wrytynges; shewing to the said Ambassadour, that at the conveynyng and assembling of the Concill he shulde have further audience and annswer concerning the cause of his messuage, Whiche presence was given, and like annsuer made on Sonday the 10th daye of the monthe, at whiche tyme the Erle of Anguissh not being present there were Sondry lettres delyvered from Madame, the Ffrenche Kings moder, and from the duke of Albeny. The contynue of the said Dukes lettre to the yong King purpoorted amongst other thynges that whereas his Grace had written and sent to the said Duke requiring him to comme hider for the better ordouring of this realme, he shewed and made answer that at this time he had grete affayres and busyness in hand concerying the Kinge his masters cause, nevertheless if he mought knowe it were the Kinges expreste pleasure to have his comyng hider, he wolde prepare and order hym to be at the King's commandment and pleasure ymmediately upon the delivery of the said lettres, afore all suche prenence as was at that tyme, the yonge King called me unto hym and shewed unto me the matiers were to little effecte or purpoos. Howe be it, at that tyme his Grace had no perfite intelligence of the Duke of Albany's letter, but as soon as his grace was perfitely advertissed of the contynue thereof, thenne being paste in to his Privea Chamber. His said Grace was not a little mooved, and said as I am credible infourmed, He never sent for the said Duke nor never was agreeable consenting mynded nor privea that he shulde be sent fore, and said his frends shulde faill hym, if the said Duke attempted or approached to come into this his realme withoute his speciall lisece, but His Grace woold lay his sworde upon his face. The next day after being Monday, his said Grace being somedall greved and stirred at this matier remooved sodainly from hennes to Dakheath 4 myles from this towne, purpoosly to avoid from his presence the said French Ambassodour, came

H

not again till 8 days after, And thus as yet, there is noone other spede geven to the Ffrenchse ambassadour.

The Archebussop of Saint Andrew's contynueth at Domefarmeling, notwithstanding sondery messages made and sent unto his Lordeship, for his repayring and coming hider for ordouring of the Frenchse causes, as yet being dormaunt; and woll not come hider till ageinst our meteing at Barwik.

Sethenne my last writing unto your said Grace, here hath been right ragious wynds with exceeding rayn, wete weder, and grete waters to the dangerous getting and yinnyng of thair corne in these partes.

Whereupon there is an open slannder and murmour raised upon me, not oonly in this toune of Edinburgh, but throwoe a great part of the realme, surmitting that I shulde be the occasion thereof; and that I have doon in Ffrance, Flaunders and other countreys, where I never was nor without the relame of Einglande but here in Scotlande, I woll not departe froome hennes, till I shall procure all this realm to a distraction, booth in their cornes, frutes and otherwise, as is saide Chaunced, by my meanes, oone yere of the vynes in France, Insomuche that I nor my servants couthe nor mought passe of late in the stretes naither to or from the Courte, but openly many women banned, cursed, waried, and gave me and mine the mooste grevous maledictions that couthe be to our faces.

Whereupon there or nigh about half score of them women, taken and putte in prison and as yet doe remayn there for condign punytion, and to be example to other like offenders. And also the Freeres Observauntes have preeched soore ageinste thaym that furst procured and contynueth this false untrue and detestable saying and oppinyon. This ungracious demeandour hath bene putte in execution here, for the moost parte alle by wemen. The begynners thereof canne not be knowne but it is supposed to be by Frenshe men, or by some other favouring thair causes, not being content with this peas and the maner thereof to be concluded; nor that Englisshemenn doe coome at alle tymes, att thair pleasures, and whenne they luste to the King presence, and seeing the Frenshe not entertainted as they have bene of late. To long is it fatigate and weary youre Grace with the ongacious Sondery oppnyons that have bene here of late against me; whereof there is no grate marvail, for here is not dread of Justiss, nor correction to bee doone aither by oone parsonne or by other; which appeareth by Sondrey Hainous murdours lately commytted openly withynne the towne of Edinbroo. Theffecte of my laste letter with these premisses remembered, I trust the Kings Highness and youre said Grace after the peas concluded, woll not have myne aboode to be contyned in the combros Contrey wherever is suspicion withoute truste: disdayn, slander, malice and cruelety, withoute vertue, drede of God or Manne. And yette I canne not conjecture that any noble personne should be fawty or culpable touching any parte of the said Slaunder; whiche is thinge to all sad, wise, discrete personnages incredible. Notwithstanding here is muche devision, debate and discention, charite ofte putte aparte and excluded. Here ar many stoppages made by such as are named to be commissioners, touching thair going Forward, oonless provision be maide forr thair costs and charges, as I conceve at thair laste being at Barwik goode rewardes were geven to Sondery personnes specially to those as were the principle for autorite, wisdom and polecy, and as had the wayes for conveying of causes. I putt this matier in youre gracious remembrance, to thentent the Kings High pleasure and youres may be had and knowne in that behalfe; whyche for so much as shall be in my poore powere and parte, shall be accomplisshed, As knoweth God who ever moore have your Grace in His mooste blessed governance. At Edinburgh the 25 day of September.

Youre umost hehumble preyst and bedesman T. Magnus.

Superscribed unto My Lorde Legate's good Grace.

Magnus appears to have left Edinburgh at the end of January, and to have removed to Berwick. Following the dates of his numerous letters which are preserved amongst the *Cottonian MSS.*,[1] we find he left Berwick in March and went to York. From that city he writes to Wolsey, under date March 26 (1526) reporting the desire of James V. to quit the borders. Margaret, he says, leaves the court, and Angus has all the influence. The year following he was still concerned with Scotch affairs, which were far from settled. On August 30 (1527) he wrote to Wolsey from Sheriff Hooton that the young James V. is unwilling to continue in the custody of Angus, and in September he describes the situation of Angus as being dangerous. The revolution and overthrow of Angus followed in 1528. Angus defended himself at Tantallon, and Magnus, in a letter of November 14, relates to Wolsey the attempt made upon that place by Margaret's friends, and the particulars of negotiations at Berwick. Henry VIII. appears to have mediated in favour of Angus, and Magnus writes to Queen Margaret from Berwick, November 18, desiring her to intercede. She replied to this letter, giving reasons why she could not do so, and eventually Angus retired into Gaul. On December 6 King James wrote to Dr. Magnus, thanking him for his zeal. In January 1529 Magnus had an audience of the Scotch king, and he reports particulars of the same to Wolsey from Berwick, under date February 13. He says:—" The 19th daye of January the said King of Scotts came to Edinburgh, and the nexte daye after I had presence, and was accompanyed unto his grace by the Busshop of Galawaye and the Abbot of Arbrooth, being Privea Seale. And after due salutation, and showing that, for somyche as I was at the Bordours, and not farre from Edinburgh, the pleasure of the Kingges Highnes my Soveraigne Lord was that, or and afore I shulde retourne southwards I shulde viset and see the prosperous estate of the said yong King, to thentent that thereupon at my repaire and commyng into Englande I mooght make due reaporte unto the Kingges Highnes his dereste uncle, not only touching the waxing and furnisshing of his noble personage, but also of other his qualities and vertuous procedingges; and thereupon deliverede the Kingges said mooste honourable letters and youres, which the saide yong King recieved right joyously, and with good countenance, demanding and inquiering for the proosperous estate and welfare of his dereste uncle the Kingges Highnes, and of your Grace. After the said letters were redde, and somdeall conscidered by the said King and his counsaill, His Grace saying that I was right hartely welcom desired me to have pacience for a daye or twayne to thentent that he mought be the better advised of the effecte, purpoorte, and contynue of the said letters, and thenne his grace shewed he wolde be gladde to here my credence at large. Two days after, accompanyed as afore I was sent foore to come unto the Kingges presence, at whiche tyme his Grace said to all his Lordes that for somyche as I was his oolde acquayntaunce he woolde use me famylierly, and soe caused me to passe with His said Grace unto his privea chamber noone other being present but we twayne."

[1] *Caligula*, B. 1, 2, 3, 6, 7 and 8.

THE GRAMMAR AND SONG SCHOOLS FOUNDED.

In 1531 rumours being in circulation that King James was about to contract a foreign marriage, he writes to Magnus from Peebles (January 29) to contradict the statement. In 1532 war broke out, and Magnus's services were again called into requisition. On July 1 (1533) he and three other commissioners took steps to obtain a truce, and in May 1534 peace was signed. It is evident from this that he had not given up the discharge of important functions (as has been erroneously supposed) when he found time to devote attention to the foundation and endowment of the Newark Grammar and Song Schools. He had a residence at Sibthorpe, and it may have been whilst on a visit to that village to seek a little rest and quiet, that he prepared those generous schemes which will make his name familiar as a household word in Newark for all time.

The deed establishing the schools of grammar and of song is dated the 21st of February, in the 23d year of the reign of King Henry VIII. (1531). A year previously, namely on June 20, 1530, Magnus had by deed poll conveyed to trustees to carry out the purposes of his will, a number of houses, a fishery, and many acres of land at Everton; also land at Sandwath, near York, at Folkingham, Walcottys, Boylby, and Aslowby, in the county of Lincoln. By another deed poll dated February 24, 1530, he left two houses, two gardens, and an acre of pasture in Newark; and by a further deed, dated December 5 of the same year, he conveyed land in Mattersey, Barmby, and Ranby, for a similar purpose to the one above mentioned. The language in which the deeds are drawn up implies that the trustees of the properties are "to have and to hold to them and their heirs to the use of the said Thomas Magnus and his heirs, and to perform his last will thereof made." Mr. Burnaby, to whom the town was indebted, in 1855, for the careful preparation of an interesting pamphlet, giving particulars of the estate, says:—"It appears by the three feoffments of Mr. Magnus, and likewise by his recital of them in his deed, that his original intention was to give his charities by his will, and consequently not to take effect until after his decease; yet by his said deed, which was a year after the date of his last feoffment, he declares the use of his feoffments, gives away the estates from himself, and settles them in immediate possession for the benefit of his charities." The indenture establishing the Grammar and Song Schools is a document of great interest; but it has been so frequently described, it is unnecessary to do more than give a brief outline of it.

After reciting the properties to be used for the purposes of his will, and mentioning their yearly value, which at that period, strange to say, only amounted to £42 : 8 : 4, the Doctor directs that £18, "parcell of the Yssues, Revenues, and Profitts of the saide Landys, Tenements, and Heredytaments, shall yerely be payde, and ymployde to and for the Exhibition and fiyndyn of two seculer honest Prests, wherof the one Prest shall have sufficient Connyng and Lernyng to teche Gramer and the other Prest Connyng and Lernyng to teche playne Song, pryk Song, descant, and to play at the Organs; and the said two Prests frely shall teche and instruct all Persons and Chyldren that wyll, at Newarke aforsaid, come to Scoole with theym, and shall be dysposed to lerne Gramer, pryke Song, playne Song, or descant. That is to saye, the one of the same Prests to teche Gramer, and the other playne Song, pryk Song, and descant." The document goes on to direct what salaries are to be paid, and what orders and directions are to be observed by the masters. Six children are to be taught to sing and play at the organs, and the selection of them is left to the Song schoolmaster, who is not to show favour or affection in his choice, but to single out such as shall seem to him "apte in Age and their Breste for syngyng." They are each to receive yearly towards their meat, drink, and clothing, 26s. 8d.; parcel of the said sum to be "employed upon cloth" for a gown for each child, made after "chapel facyon;" and further, the said children shall have "their Heere of theire Heds long, and not polled, honestly and clene kept by the master of the said Song Scoole." Besides the pleasing duty of supervising the toilet and conduct of the lads, Mr. Magnus makes other directions for the master's guidance. Both the song school-master and the master of the grammar school are directed to pray daily for the "soule of the late King of moost and blessed memory Kyng Henry the VII., and Qneene Elizabeth his Wife; the prosperous Estate of the Kyng's Majestie King Henry the VIII., my moost dread Soverayne Liege Lord and master; the Queen's Grace and my Lord Prince," and moreover for the souls of Thomas Magnus, John Magnus, his father, Alice his (Thomas's) mother, Johanne, Elizabeth, and Kateryne, his sisters. One would have thought that this list would have been sufficient; but Mr. Magnus was too large-hearted to wish prayers only for royalty and for his own family. The priests are to include in their petitions appeals for all his other "benefactours, Famyliers, and for the estate of the Inhabitantys of the said Town and Parysshe of Newark,' and of all who should then or hereafter be connected with the property which he was disposing of with so charitable a heart. Directions are given for the attendance at church of those concerned in the benefactions; also for the appointment of a receiver, who should pay the rents to the church masters.

The sum of £2 per annum is left for an obit in the parish church, with placebo and dirige for the soul of the said Thomas Magnus, his father, mother, and benefactors; 2s. 4d. of it to the vicar for executing the dirge; 6d. to each of the parish priests and chauntry priests who shall attend the same; and 4d. to every other priest, so as the number present do not exceed 24; to each of the parish clerks 4d.; to each of the six children 2d.; 2s. to the aldermen of Trinity Guild, being present at the said obit and offering, 2d.; to the wife of the said alderman (if he be married) in like manner 1s. 4d.; to the alderman of Mary Magdalen Guild, offering one penny at the said obit, 1s. 4d.; and to his wife offering the same 1s.; and similar payments to the aldermen of Our Lady's Guild and of Corpus Christi Guild, and to their wives. 2s. 8d. is left for wax to be used at the dirige, and the usual recompense for ringing the bells was to be given to the bellman. £2 per annum was to be paid to the alderman of Trinity Guild for his expenses in the said office; and 40s. per annum to each of the chauntry priests for their commons. The statutes against mortmain and superstitious uses, and the separation of the last monarch of the Tudor line from the communion of Rome, rendered many of these applications in course of time impossible.

The dissolution of the guilds and the appointment of a corporation for the government of the town under another title and vested with different powers, rendered their authority over the distribution of the charities doubtful. But had the difficulties on any of these accounts been less than they were, the lapse of two centuries had occasioned such a difference in the value of money, and had seen such an advance in the rents of the estates bequeathed by Magnus, that the interference of some superintending authority to direct the application of the surplus, and to arrange the distribution of the original income, was become absolutely necessary. Accordingly, in 1736 an application was made to the Court of Chancery by two of the churchwardens and some of the inhabitants of the town. Lord Talbot, who then sat on the Chancery bench, after comparing all such parts of Magnus's bequests as were not become impossible by the changes which had taken place in Church and State, referred it to one of the Masters of the Court to say in what manner the surplus of the estate might be best applied for the benefit of the town, and most in conformity with the charitable intentions of the donor. The master made his report, to which the corporation took several exceptions.

The cause came on again to be heard before Lord Chancellor Hardwick, in 1738, when his lordship made a voluminous decree, the principal directions being as follows:—(1.) That a receiver of the estates shall be chosen by the vicar, mayor, senior alderman, and four churchwardens; (2.) That such receiver shall pay the rents to the churchwardens within eight days after his receipt of the same; (3.) That he shall pass his accounts annually on the 7th of January, before the vicar, mayor, senior alderman, and four churchwardens; (4.) The churchwardens to pay £20 to the grammar schoolmaster, £17 to the song schoolmaster, £8 to the six singing boys, £2 to the mayor at Michaelmas, £2 to the town-clerk, and besides his reasonable expenses, 13s. 4d. to the receiver on passing his accounts; and to the vicar, mayor, churchwardens, and senior alderman, being present, 2s. each; (5.) The surplus arising from the rents of the estates after these applications, to be put into an iron chest till it amounts to £40; and (6.) So often as it shall amount to that sum, to be applied by the before mentioned trustees, or a majority of them, in works for the common good and weal of the town, in such manner as shall be most agreeable to the intentions of the donor. On the rents increasing, the salaries of the masters, boys, and receiver, were to be raised, etc. In 1830 the question of the disposition of the funds again came before the Court.

By an order, dated 1st April in that year, on the petition of the mayor and alderman of the borough, the then present mayor, first senior alderman, vicar, and four churchwardens, it was referred to John Edward Dowdeswell, Esq., one of the masters in chancery, to approve of a proper scheme or plan for the increase of the salaries, and for the application of the surplus rents and profits of the Magnus estates. The master's report is dated 24th March 1834, and the principal provisions are these:—(1.) That the grammar schoolmaster shall have a salary of £220 per annum; that a schoolroom be erected for teaching English, writing, and arithmetic; and that an additional usher be appointed by the master for teaching English, writing, and arithmetic, at a salary of £60; (2.) That an usher, or assistant master be appointed, who shall be a member of one of the universities, at a salary of £60; (3.) That the song schoolmaster shall have a salary of £105; (4.) That six choristers be paid £10 per annum each; (5.) That six low boys, or assistant choristers, be paid £4 each; (6.) The parish clerk £50 per annum; (7.) The sexton £20 per annum; (8.) The head verger £10 per annum; (9.) The three other vergers

PRESENT DISTRIBUTION OF THE CHARITY.

£5 : 5s. per annum, each ; (10.) Another verger, and for cleaning the church £9 per annum ; (11.) To the receiver £1 per cent per annum ; (12.) To the town-clerk as auditor, £10 ; (13.) To the mayor £50 ; (14.) For his officers £44 : 14 : 6 ; (15.) To support the national schools the annual sum of £150 ; (16.) To the dispensary annually, £150. Then follow provisions for £100 per annum to be paid to the churchwardens for repairs of the church ; and for the establishment of a Fabric Fund. The mode of letting the estates is prescribed, also the mode of executing church repairs. The accounts are to be printed, and two exhibitions of £80 per year established ; and the residue or surplus rents are to be applied in beautifying the church, or in some other good work or works, for the common good and weal of the town.

By a decree, dated December 26, the master's report was confirmed, and it was referred back to him to settle the mode in which the exhibitions should be founded, and to tax the costs. The exact manner in which the funds of the Magnus estates are at present appropriated will be gathered from the following statement, showing the expenditure from January 1877 to January 1878. The receipts amounted to £2508 : 8 : 8.

			£	s.	d.
To the Master of the Grammar School, a year's Salary			220	0	0
,, the two Ushers, ditto			120	0	0
,, the Song School Master, ditto			105	0	0
,, the Newark Urban Sanitary Authority, year's payment			290	0	0
,, the Subscription Schools, ditto			150	0	0
,, the Newark Dispensary, ditto			150	0	0
,, the Mayor of Newark, one year's allowance			50	0	0
,, ditto, for his Officers, half-year			44	14	6
,, the Fund for the Fabric of the Church			100	0	0
,, the Exhibition Account			160	0	0
,, the Everton Schools, one year's Subscription			5	0	0
,, Churchwardens for year's Salary for Choristers			60	0	0
,, ditto	ditto	Lowboys	24	0	0
,, ditto	ditto	Sexton	20	0	0
,, ditto	ditto	Parish Clerk	50	0	0
,, ditto	ditto	Vergers	34	15	0
,, ditto, for dinners			10	0	0
,, ditto for Warming the Church			16	3	6
,, ditto, for Church Repairs to be applied with consent of the Vicar			100	0	0
,, Receiver, one per cent on Receipts			23	13	2
,, Tenants' dinners, chaise hire, etc., at rent audit and for journey of the Trustees to Bilborough and Everton			40	3	6
,, Clerk of Trustees, one year's Salary			10	0	0
,, Assessments under the Everton Drainage Act			146	17	2
,, River Idle Assessment			9	2	1
,, James Knight, year's Interest			6	7	6
	Carry forward		£1945	16	5

Brought forward		£1945 16 5
To John Bradley, year's Interest		11 5 0
„ Court Generous Briton, ditto		13 10 0
„ Insurance on Farm Buildings and other Property against Fire		16 10 11
„ the Churchwardens for general out-goings of the Church and Estate		348 0 8
„ the Town Clerk as auditor		10 0 0
„ Duke of Newcastle chief rent		0 3 8
„ the Trustees on passing Accounts		0 12 0
„ the general body of Mr. Magnus's Trustees, the sum of twenty pounds, to meet the expenses of an Examiner or Examiners, to conduct a general examination of the Scholars of the Grammar School before the commencement of Midsummer Term, and to report thereon to the general body of the Trustees		20 0 0
Arrears		142 10 0
Total		£2508 8 8

After the generous deeds of gift, by which Mr. Magnus has placed the town of Newark under lasting obligations to him, he lived about nineteen years. In 1540, when the clergy of the provinces of Canterbury and York declared their opinion that the king's marriage with Anne of Cleves was void, Mr. Magnus was one of those who signed the document. The signature is, "T. Magnus, Archedeaconis, Estriding." In 1545 the king, "desiring the guidance and good government of the people, and the speedy and indifferent administration of justice," continued the services of his honourable council, called the King's Council in the northern parts. Magnus was a member of this council. It was ordered that they should appoint their own times of meeting, and that the president should have £300 a year towards the furniture and the diets of himself and the rest of the councillors, with such number of servants as should be allowed. Mr. Magnus and every esquire were to have seats in the hall with the president, and to have three servants each in attendance. One month in the year they were to sit at York, another at Newcastle, a third at Hull, and a fourth at "Durisme," and to keep in every one of the said places a gaol-delivery, referring any abstruse questions of law that might arise to the judges at Westminster. On the 22d of December 1546 they reported that they had held a gaol-delivery in York, when twelve persons were executed for felony. Magnus signed the report in common with the rest of the council, but we do not again meet with his signature to any record of the council's proceedings. The various offices which Magnus held were as follows:—Canon of Windsor, 1520-47; receiver of the court of wards, 1523; king's chaplain, 1524; and master of St. Leonard's Hospital at York, 1530. In addition to holding these offices he was, as we have shown, archdeacon of the East Riding, ambassador to Scotland, and a member of the northern council. He died in 1550, and was buried at the parish church of Seassay, in the North Riding of the county of York. Upon a gravestone in the middle of the chancel was inscribed in brass the following : "Here lyeth Mr. Thomas Magnus, archdeacon of the East Rydeing in the Metropolitan Church of York, and parson of this church, which died the 18th day of August, anno domini 1550, whose soule God pardon." In Tonge's *Visitation of Yorkshire* in 1530, as published by the Surtees Society in their vol. xli. p. 59, we read: "These be the armes of the Right worshipful Mr. Magnus, *arms* Bendy of six, vert and gules, on a fess or a lion passant between two cinquefoils gules. Motto, 'As God wyll'" (written above the arms). In an editorial note, Mr. W. Hylton Dyer Longstaffe, F.S.A., says that the windows of the old church of Seassay contained his rebus, an *Agnus Dei*, with M thereupon. Above was the motto in the text, and the herbage was full of columbines. The same flower and the *Agnus Dei* alternately occur on the curves of his gravestone at the same church.

> "The columbine in tawny often taken,
> Is then ascribed to such as are forsaken."[1]

The person to whom, as we have shown, Magnus owed his introduction to Cardinal Wolsey was Robert Brown, and there seems to have been much in common in the disposition of the two worthies. Both were animated with the same generous spirit. The date of Magnus's benefaction was 1531, and a year only had elapsed ere his friend followed suit. In a deed dated the 4th of September 1532, Brown entrusted to eighteen persons his estates in Newark, Balderton, and Coddington, for the performance of his last will and testament. The will prescribes the uses to which the receipts of the property are to be put, and are about as liberal-minded as any we have ever read. The good of the town is the main object aimed at, and the receipts are accordingly left to the vicar of Newark, and in his default, to the alderman of Trinity Guild, "that the same may be employed and spent to the use of the commonwealth of the town of Newark, whether it shall be to the support of the Church there, or any good works to be done in the town, as mending of highways, as shall be thought expedient from time to time." The trustees discharged the duty assigned to them until 1551, when they relegated their power over the property to other parties, who, in turn, vested it in the aldermen and their successors for ever. The ordinary yearly income of the charity now amounts to about £237, varying a little, according to the receipts from the shambles. The net proceeds are applied in accordance with a decree of the Court of Chancery, made in 1738. The sum of £90 goes to the urban sanitary authority, and the rest is devoted to purposes for the "good and weal of the town." In 1876 £50 was granted towards the new mission rooms in Balderton Gate, and various other serviceable public objects have benefited, and continue to benefit by the charity. A tomb in the parish church exists to the memory of this generous benefactor. It bears an inscription in Latin, which runs as follows :—" Here lies Robert Brown, Esq., and Agnes, his wife, late alderman of the guild of the Holy Trinity, of this church, constable of the Castle, principal steward of the liberty of this town, and also receiver as well of Thomas Wolsey, Cardinal of York, as of John Longland, Lord Bishop of

[1] Browne's *Britannia's Pastorals*, temp. 1613.

Lincoln, and further also, Sheriff of the County of Nottingham and Derby, and moreover, Custos Rotulorum as well in the county of Nottingham as in the parts of Kesteven, in the county of Lincoln, which said Robert died the 10th day of the month of December, in the year of our Lord 1532. Upon whose soul may God have mercy." In the spring of 1817 (or 1819), the tablet was removed from its original position in the Trinity Chapel, above the north-east corner of the south transept, to the south-west corner of the aisle, where some years afterwards it was found, from its close proximity to the wall, to be in a very damp state ; it was, therefore, again removed by the churchwardens, for the time being, on the 4th of March 1832, and placed in "The Ladye Chapel," or eastern aisle, under the large east window, having first being carefully cleaned, the decayed parts restored in composition to match the original stone, a grey or *Derbyshire marble*, the arms newly painted, and the whole of the tomb varnished, and raised on a plinth, where it at present remains.

With Henry VIII. on the throne, uniting in his person the claims of the rival houses of York and Lancaster, any remaining sparks of that fierce fire of hatred which had split the country into bitter factions had ere this been thoroughly extinguished. But though there was no rivalry to excite hostility and provoke disturbance, events occurred which aroused in some classes a feeling of discontent. The suppression of the abbeys and other similar institutions excited the displeasure of many of the country gentlemen, who missed the various conveniences with which those institutions had furnished them. Amongst the commons the introduction of large grazing farms was a step regarded with general disfavour. The demand for English wool in Flanders had increased largely, and owners of property found it to their advantage to turn their corn land into pasture, breaking up the farms, enclosing the commons, and becoming graziers on a gigantic scale. The statutes prohibiting enclosures remained unenforced especially in the northern counties, and the small farmers and petty copyholders, hitherto thriving and independent, found themselves turned out of their farms and deprived of the resources of the commons.[1] At this time (1536) when, to quote again Mr. Froude, "a deep and angry spirit of discontent had arisen which could be stirred easily into mutiny," three commissions were issued by the Crown, one to levy a subsidy, a second to carry out in regard to monasteries the Act of Suppression, and a third to examine the character and qualifications of the clergy, and eject summarily all inefficient persons from their offices and emoluments. A rumour was diligently circulated that many of the parish churches were to be destroyed, and rebellion against such proceedings began to be openly talked about and encouraged. Lord Hussey in his castle at Sleaford told a gentleman of the county that "the world would never mend until they fought for it."[2] And in September, when Heneage, one of the examiners under the clerical commission, proceeded to Louth, the alarm bell was rung, the inhabitants armed themselves with bills and staves, and Heneage was

---

[1] *Vide* Froude's *History*.   [2] Deposition of Thomas Brian, *Rolls House MSS.*

ROYAL FORCES IN THE TOWN.

compelled by the excited multitude, upon pain of death, to swear fealty to the commons, to the king, to the commonwealth, and to the Holy (Roman) Church. From Louth the excitement spread hastily throughout Lincolnshire. The chancellor of the Bishop of Lincoln was murdered near Horncastle, Bishop Longland's palace near Lincoln was plundered and the city occupied with armed bodies of insurgents. The king, on hearing of the rebellion, directed Lord Hussey and Lord Shrewsbury to raise forces for its suppression. The former made no effort; the latter took up a position at Nottingham with between three and four thousand men. Meanwhile the rebels for want of provisions began to disperse, and as they were separating the king's message arrived in answer to their demands. They had complained of the suppression of monasteries, of evil counsellors, of persons meanly born raised to dignity, of the danger to which the jewels and plate of their parochial churches were exposed; and they prayed the king to consult the nobility of the realm concerning the redress of these grievances. His Majesty replied that the suppression of the abbeys was by Act of Parliament, and in consequence of their notorious vice, and the subsidy was granted by Parliament, and should be paid. He advised them to surrender their leaders and disperse to their homes. A little while after the royal army entered Lincoln the ringleaders were surrendered and the commotion came to an end.

The discontent, however, was not allayed. Robert Aske, a barrister, going to London was stopped in Lincolnshire by rebels, and induced to take the command of a new gathering of excited men. The Percies joined the insurgents, and with a powerful army Aske marched to York. The monks and nuns who had been dispossessed were invited to return to their houses, and orders were issued by Aske commanding all lords, knights, and gentlemen in the northern counties to repair to his presence. Lord Darcy of Templehurst, who had been written to by the king to take steps to check the outbreak, had shut himself up in Pomfret Castle in company with Mr. Magnus (the benefactor of Newark of whom we have already spoken), Sir Robert Constable, Lord Neville, and Sir Nicholas Babthorpe. This proceeding aroused the king's displeasure, and his Majesty wrote to Lord Darcy saying, if what he heard was true, negligence had been manifested. In reply Lord Darcy professed inability to help himself, and declared that Pomfret was defenceless. "The commons," he said, "do stop the passage so straitly that no victual can come to us. The castle is in danger to be taken, or we to lose our lives." By this time Lord Shrewsbury having been supplied with arms and money, had gathered additional recruits, and had taken up his quarters at Newark. He and his colleagues wrote from Newark to Lord Darcy as follows:—" My very good lord, in a right hearty manner we commend us unto you, advertising you that this day in the morning the king's highness sent unto the Earl of Shrewsbury a commission to be his lieutenant northwards, with divers letters wherein we are commanded to stay here & not march forwards towards the north till such time as we know the rebels in Lincolnshire to be appeased; & that done we intend (God willing) with all diligence & celerity, to go forward towards the rebels in Yorkshire for the suppression & convincement of them with such number of men as we have. And in the meantime, till our coming unto you, we desire you to do as much as you may to stay the passages there; and as touching our said coming hitherwards, you shall be informed by our letters from time to time accordingly; and thus the Holy Trinity keep you in good health. From Newark the 17th day of October.—Yours assured, G. SHREWSBURY, THOMAS RUTLAND, G. HUNTINGDON; to my very good lord, my Lord Darcy.[1]

Before Lord Shrewsbury could reach Pomfret, however, Aske arrived there, and threatened to storm the castle. Lord Darcy surrendered, and his lordship, Mr. Magnus, and every other man within the castle walls, was compelled to take the oath which Aske and his friends administered. Lord Shrewsbury, advancing towards Pomfret, found that the rebels had secured the passages of the Don. In haste the Duke of Norfolk and the Marquis of Exeter were despatched to his assistance, and the forces of these two noblemen were expected to unite at Newark. In his letter to the Duke of Suffolk and others[2] (dated Oct. 24, 1536) the king states that he has received a letter from the Duke of Norfolk, declaring himself to abide at Newark, and that Lord Exeter could not reach the town until the next day, "whereupon," continued his Majesty, "remembering as well that Doncastre is thirty myles from Newark, which, with the bandes of our said cousin of Norfolk, canne not be passed in any short tyme as that, in cace it shuld fortun our said cousin of Shrewsbury, eyther being pressed therunto by the rebells, or elles thinking himself to have some great advauntage to give the onsett of them, and in such an adventure to have the worse (which God defende) then it would be necessary for the sure stopping of the passages to keep the rebels on that side the Trent, to have the aid and assistance of the Duke of Suffolk." The duke, therefore, is directed to leave some forces under an efficient commander at Lincoln and thereabouts, and to repair himself unto such places as shall be thought fit for the sure keeping of the passages. Lord Suffolk appears to have proceeded to Newark in accordance with this instruction, for Wrothesley writes to Cromwell[3] saying that letters had been received from Lord Suffolk, who was at Newark, declaring all to be well there. The town of Louth had "come in" to the number of two hundred, and were not only newly sworn to their allegiance, but had presented to the Earl of Shrewsbury, the lord lieutenant, the names of fifteen persons who were the great movers in the matter. He goes on to say that two hundred rebels had entered Hull, but it appeared they had all fallen to talking, and if this were so it would not be long ere "oon payr of light legges wilbe worth five payre of handes to them." Lord Norfolk would join Lord Shrewsbury; a special commandment had been sent unto him to see the passages at Nottingham and Newark surely fortified, so that the rebels might certainly be kept on that side, and so enforced shortly to "disperkle" or to "eate their fyngers."

[1] *Rolls House MSS.*, Series 282. [2] *State Papers*, vol. i. p. 492.
[3] From Cromwell's correspondence in the Chapter House, bundle W.

The Marquis of Exeter, says Mr. Froude, never passed Newark. "He seems to have been recalled and sent down into Devonshire to raise the musters in his own county." With the men under his command, the Duke of Norfolk joined Lord Shrewsbury at Doncaster on the 25th, but the united armies did not exceed 8000 men; great caution was therefore requisite, and the king wrote urging Norfolk to be careful, and to avoid a battle unless with a certainty of victory. "The chances of war," said the king, "being so uncertain, many times devices meant for the best purposes turning to evil happs and notable misfortunes," it would be better, rather than run any risk, for the duke to fall back on the line of the Trent, fortify Newark and Nottingham, and wait his own arrival, until (using the king's own words) "with our army royal, which we do put in arediness, we shall repair unto you, and so with God's help shall be able to bear down the traitors before us." On the day that Norfolk and Shrewsbury met, the rebels in great strength started from Pomfret to Doncaster. Aske, at their head, advised the opening up of negotiations, and on the 26th a conference was held on the bridge at Doncaster. A truce was arranged until the king could be communicated with, both parties hoping to gain by delay. We need not follow the course of the negotiations farther than to state that at the request of the king, Aske went to see him, explained the nature and origin of the insurrection, and received in return an assurance from his Majesty that a parliament should be held at York to take the subjects into consideration. In April 1537 Aske, Lord Darcy, and Sir Robert Constable were arrested. In May Lord Hussey of Sleaford was executed. Lord Darcy shared the same fate in June. In July Constable was hanged in chains at Hull, and Aske, after being drawn through the streets of York on a hurdle, was hanged from the top of a tower. In this way the rebellion came to an abortive termination.

The Lancaster Herald, who had reported an interview he had with Aske at Pomfret, in the presence of Lord Darcy, Mr. Magnus, and others, was indicted at York in July 1538 for comforting and encouraging the rebels. At the same time charges were preferred against the vicar of Newark, Henry Lytherland, and a monk named Moreby. Brief references to the trials occur in the *State Papers*, from which it appears that all three were convicted of high treason and sentenced to death. Bishop Holgate writing to Cromwell says,[1] that at the gaol-delivery eighteen were executed, fifteen for felonies, robberies, and burglaries, and three for high treason—viz., Thomas Mylnar, otherwise called the Lancaster Herald, Henry Lytherland, vicar of Newark, and the monk of Fountayns (Moreby). He states that Christopher Eystcoyst, a young gentleman of Marcheland in Yorkshire, and Mr. Candysche, a priest of Lincolnshire, gave evidence against the vicar of Newark. "For," he continues, "immedyaltely off the receyt off Milner and the vicar off Newarke, we send to Mr. Candysche to cum to the Assys at York, and to bryng hys prest wythe him; and he accorddynglye cum thyddyr, and servyd the kynge vere diligentlye. And when the vicar was condemnyd off hys arrenmentt, we all by our

[1] *State Papers*, vol. v. p. 139.

lettures dyssyrd Mr. Candysche, and on Mr. Dalison off Lincolnschyre, to tayke an inventore off all such guddes as was off layt the vicar of Newarkes, othyr att Lincoln or in ony othyr plays; to farthyr off the kynges plesur or youres were knowne for orderyng off the same guddes." What part the unfortunate vicar had taken in the rebellion does not appear, but it may be that he joined the rebels at Lincoln, seeing that mention is made of some of his goods being there. There is no reference to lead us to conclude that Newark itself participated in the outbreak, and the passing of the royal troops through the borough without let or hindrance, and the frequent presence of the principal commanders on the king's side, would render such a proceeding very improbable. Mr. Christopher Eystcoyst seems to have been very busy. He is described by Bishop Holgate as having acted with diligence, and the bishop recommends that he should be thanked for his efforts as an encouragement to others to follow in his footsteps. Christopher Jenny, sergeant-at-law, and subsequently judge of the Common Pleas, also sends Cromwell a brief notice of the trials,[1] adding that the Lancaster Herald, after his condemnation, used himself like a good Christian man. Both he and Lytherland made requests concerning the disposal of their goods, and in reference to the payment of their debts. "We caused them," says Jenny, "to write severall bookes of remembrance with theire owne handes, which I doo sende unto your lordship herein enclosed."

There are few monarchs whose names are so associated with local history as Henry the Eighth. The transfers of property that took place through the stripping of the monasteries, the quantity of land that was handed over by Wolsey and the king to their favourites, and the number of manors that changed hands in various parts of the country, causes His Majesty's name to occur in numerous documents. There are many that could be mentioned in reference to this county. In 1522 the manor of Kneesal, previously the property of Edmund, Duke of Buckingham, was granted to Lord Hussey and his heirs. His lordship, as we have shown, was attainted of high treason seventeen years after, and the manor passed (3rd Edward VI.) to the then Lord High Admiral of England, Lord Clinton and Say. It is now belonging principally to the Earl Manvers. In 1536 the manor of Stoke Bardolph was bestowed on Lady Anne Stanhope, and in the year following the king granted the house and site of the Abbey of Rufford to Sir John Markham. A deed preserved in the archives of the Mayor and Corporation relates the conveyance of a house in Castle Gate in the reign of Henry VIII., and speaks of it as being bounded on the south by the Swan and Salmon Inn. The other boundaries mentioned are, on the north, a house and yard, next the Castle of the Bishop of Lincoln, on the west the river, and on the east the King's highway. We copy the following additional particulars of grants of property from the Patent Rolls:—

Patent Roll, 34 Hen. VIII., Part 5.

Grant to the Dean and Chapter of Westminster of certain Messuages, lands, and tenements, parcel of Mountgrace.

---

[1] *State Papers*, vol. v. p. 560.

THE TRANSFERS OF PROPERTY.

Patent Roll, 37 Hen. VIII., P. 4.

Grant to John Bellow and John Broxholme, in consideration of certain sums of money.

Ten acres of land in Newark and Hawton, possessions of the late Monastery of Newborough, Lincoln. Several Messuages in Newark belonging to Newborough.

A close of land in Newark, possessions of the Priory of St. Catherine, Lincoln, City.

Farms in Newark and Carleton-Moreland, Lincoln, late of the Priory of Semperingham, Lincoln, belonging.

Patent Roll, 38 Hen. VIII., Part 2.

Grant to William Ramesden and Richard Vavasor for certain money.

Several Rents, tenements, and Messuages *in Stocke*, near Newark, parcel of the late Preceptory of Eagle.

Particulars for Grants to Richard Androys. Request to purchase 35 Hen. VIII. (Sec. 3).

Lands in the Town of Newark, late of the Austin Friars and Woods.

Particulars for Grants to Trinity College, Camb., 38 H.n. VIII. (Sec. 2).

The Rectory of Newark.

N.B.—The pen has been drawn through Newark entry.

No Grant can be found on the Patent Rolls for the above "Particulars;" so that it is presumed that no Grant was subsequently made after the date of the Particulars.

Amongst the religious houses dissolved during the reign was a large establishment of friars in Newark of the order of St. Augustin. On the Patent Roll, 35th Henry VIII., part 3, we find the particulars of the possessions of the friars in Newark entered as follows:—"Demesne lands in the tenure of Sir John Markham: mansion-house 10s.; cemetery 1s., one rood; a garden east of the mansion 1s., one rood; pasture 3s., one acre two roods east of the church; a hop yard, north of the church, half an acre, 1s.; garden and two orchards, one acre, 3s; within the church walls, 1s.—total value 20s." The possessions were granted to Richard Androys and his heirs. The Friary passed from him to Sir John Markham, the tenant, and was subsequently in the occupation first of Sir Francis Leeke, and then of Lord Deyncourt and his sons, by one of whom (the Earl of Scarsdale) it was sold to Mr. Matthew Jenison, who was knighted by Queen Anne, and of whom we shall have more to say in subsequent pages. Sir Matthew Jenison is said to have mortgaged it to Sir Francis Willoughby of Wollaton, and at a later period he made an absolute conveyance of it to Thomas Baron Middleton, brother and successor of Sir Francis. It remained with the Middleton family until 1867, when it was sold by auction (February 28), along with other property in Newark, and was purchased for £3500 by Mr. Henry Branston, an alderman and justice of the peace for the borough. Mr. Branston has since spent a considerable sum in improving the property and in adapting it to the purposes of a modern family residence. In the vast vaults that were underneath the Friary much treasure was deposited for security during the civil wars. The monastic seal, a Madonna and child, was found some years ago, and when Lord Middleton occupied the place several skeletons were discovered underneath the hall

floor. The origin of the Austin Friars is very uncertain. They were brought into England in 1250.[1] For their habit they had a white garment and scapulary when they were in the house and in the choir; and when they went abroad they had over the former a sort of cowl and a large hood, both black, which were girt with a black leather thong.[2] If one of them so attired could revisit the town, we fancy he would soon find himself the "observed of all observers." As an illustration of the tenure of land at this period, we may mention that there was a recovery (32 Henry VIII.) wherein Thomas Rooper and William Wright Clark claimed against Francis Lecke Esq. the manor of Elston, with the appurtenances and three mess., two cottages, one dovecote, one hundred acres of land, forty of meadow, forty of pasture, 8s. rent, and the rent of 1lb. of common seed, two pair of gloves, *and a steel needle*, in Elston, Thorpe, and Stoke, by Newarke.

An influential personage, who took a large share in the work of the Reformation, which characterised the reign, was Archbishop Cranmer, a Nottinghamshire man. He was the son of Thomas Cranmer, Esq., of Aslacton (now spelt Aslockton), a pleasant village within easy distance of Newark. He was born in the year 1489, and received his early education at the village school. At the age of fourteen he became a student of Jesus' College, Cambridge, and subsequently a fellow. The last-named position he is stated to have forfeited through marrying the relation of an innkeeper's wife in the city;[3] but on the death of the lady he was re-admitted to the fellowship. He was made Doctor of Divinity in 1523, and received the appointment of theological lecturer and examiner, a post for which his abilities as a divine made him eminently qualified. His advancement into royal favour was brought about in a singular manner. To avoid the plague, which made its appearance in Cambridge, he retired to Waltham Abbey, then the residence of an intimate friend, and whilst sojourning there in easy quietude, he came in contact with Fox, almoner to Henry VIII., and Gardiner, the secretary. The conversation turned on the subject of the king's marriage with Catherine, the king having found it extremely difficult to discover a pretext for a divorce. Cranmer, abandoning all the various points that had been raised, suggested that the controversy should be reduced to the simple question, "May a man marry his brother's wife or no?" and submitted to the universities of Europe for their decision. When Henry was informed of this he exclaimed, "That is it! This fellow alone has got the sow by the right ear;" whereupon he sent for Cranmer to court, made him one of his chaplains, and directed him to write in defence of the divorce.[4]

After a work had been issued, elaborately arguing the point, Cranmer was despatched abroad to controvert the assertions of foreign divines, and on his return was created Archbishop of Canterbury. This was in March 1533, and in May following he pronounced a divorce between the king and queen, and performed the marriage

---

[1] Dugd. *Warw.* p. 1086. Edit. 1730, from Matt. *Westm. sub anno* 1250.   [2] Dugd. *Monasticon.*
[3] "He visited his wife at the inn, which gave rise to slanderous reports."—*Vide Writings and Disputes of Cranmer*, edited for the Parker Society. 1844.   [4] *Hume*, vol. iv. p. 378.

ceremony between his Majesty and Anne Boleyn. From this period he was thoroughly established in the king's favour, and he used the mighty influence he possessed to further the cause of Protestantism and to cripple the influence of the Pope. In view of his approaching death, Henry appointed Cranmer one of the executors of his will, and he had granted to him by Edward, the rectories of Whatton and Aslockton, near Newark, together with certain lands in the county of York.

Henry Holbeach, Bishop of Lincoln, conveyed, among other alienations of his see at the commencement of Edward's reign, the castle and manor of Newark to the Crown.[1] In return for this concession, the see of Lincoln had granted to it the reversion of the rectory of Worksop, and all the tithes of corn, hay, etc., in the hamlets of Sloswick, Kilton, Reton, Scofton, Clumber, and Osberton, and all other hamlets within the parish of Worksop to the said rectory belonging, and also a rent of £35, reserved upon the demise made to William Chastelyn, merchant of London, to hold to him and his successor in pure and perpetual alms.[2]

This transfer of the castle was a matter of some moment, but a much more notable event took place shortly afterwards. The town was incorporated in 1549 (3 Edward VI.), and the municipal authority was vested in an alderman and twelve assistants. The first alderman was Anthony Forster, and one was elected each year until 1625, when a Mayoralty was created. Prior to the incorporation, the principal bodies in the town were the guilds of the merchants and traders. Their foundation is believed to have been of Saxon origin, and to have been brought about as follows :—It was the custom for every freeman of fourteen years old to find sureties for his keeping the peace or be committed to prison. The neighbours in each district, to the number of ten families, entered into an association, and became bound for each other, either to produce any of their members who had violated the laws, or to make satisfaction to the party who had sustained the injury. After the Norman conquest these guilds began to assume a form of more authority, and to receive instruments of incorporation from the Crown.[3] In Newark there were four or five of these guilds, and, like the churches and religious houses, each had its patron saint. There were the guilds of the Holy Trinity, the Virgin Mary, Holy Richard de Newark, and St. Peter, and each had a head or chief called the alderman of the guild. The incorporation of the borough rendered them unnecessary.

In 1552 Sir John Loude gave by deed or will to the then alderman and assistants and their successors, two tenements in Milnegate of 20s. per annum, and £20 in gold for the use of the town. A reference to the gift occurs in the avowal of the mayor and aldermen of Newark in Chancery, sworn May 28, 1733, relative to the charitable donations of the town. In the report issued in 1829, the commissioners say, "It does not appear what became of these tenements; none such are now held by the corporation."

An account of the various chauntries remaining in existence was taken in the

[1] Thoroton. [2] Bailey. [3] Anderson, *Hist. Commercial.*

reign of Edward VI.[1] The commissioners inquired who founded each chauntry? what was its yearly value? did it possess any plate or ornaments? and other similar particulars. In the Augmentation office, we find the certificates relating to Nottinghamshire, and the majority refer to Newark; the number of chauntries at the parish church having been very considerable, and far exceeding the number at any other church in the county. We give the substance of the certificates so far as they relate to Newark.

CHAUNTRY CERTIFICATES, Notts, Roll 13, Sec. 11.

No. 14.

The chauntry of Saint Nicholas, in the parish of St. Mary Magdeleine, in Newark, founded by one Robt. de l'osto of Newark, and Maud his wife, for one priest to pray for their souls and their predecessors', successors', fathers' and mothers' (souls), at the altar of Saint Nicholas, in the said church, for ever, as appointed by the foundation thereof to the commissioners showed. £5 : 16 : 2½.

£5 : 13 : 5, over and besides six shillings and sevenpence for rent resolute to divers persons, as appeareth by a rental, which revenues hath been employed in the living of Hugh White, chauntry priest there.

The said chauntry is no parish church, but within the parish church of Mary Magdeliene in Newark, having an alter to say mass there, which is a great parish.

The said chauntry is not void, and hath no mansion house but one little chamber within the mansion house of other his brethren, to him appointed by the consent of his said brotherhood.

No. 15.

The chauntry at the alter of St. James in Newark, being founded by one William (? William Grenefield, sometime Archbishop of York, and William Dyrrante and Isabell his wife, deceased, for one priest to say mass, and otherwise daily to pray for their souls, and for all Christian souls, as appeareth by the foundation thereof; to the commissioners showed. £4 : 18 : 4.

£4 : 15 : 8 clear, besides 3s. 4d. paid in rent resolute to the Bishop of Lincoln, which is received and is yearly paid unto the chauntry there by the receiver of the revenue of the late monastery of St. Katherin by Lincoln, and is employed to the living of John Dicson, incumbent there.

The said chauntry is no parish church, but within the said parish church of Newark, having an alter there to celebrate according to his foundation. The said chantery is not void, and as for his mansion or dwelling-room, he hath commonly with his brethren there.

No. 16.

The chauntry of Magdelen Sawsemer in Newark aforesaid, founded by one Maude Sawsemer for one priest daily to say mass and other service at the alter of Saint Lawrence in Newark, and to pray for her soul and all Christian souls, as appeareth by the foundation of great "ancienty." £4 : 12 : 8.

£4 : 9s. clear, with £4 : 6 : 8 paid to the chauntry priest there yearly for ever, out of the revenues of the late monastery of Wellow, in the country of Lincoln, besides sevenpence in rent resolute to the

---

[1] The commissioners were appointed by virtue of an Act passed in 1547, which provided that the lands and profits of chauntries should be given to the king. The commissioners were instructed to make full inquiries relative to such lands and profits; and power was given them to assign a yearly pension to any priest whose salary the king was entitled to by this Act.—*Vide Statutes at Large*, vol. ii. p. 207.

bishop of Lincoln, as appeareth as well by his foundation as by a decree out of the Court of Augmentation, and is employed to the living of John Houis, now chauntry priest there.

The said chauntry is not a parish church, but within the parish church of Newark, having an alter there to celebrate according to his foundation.

The said chauntry is not void, and as for mansion or dwelling-place, he hath none otherwise than a chamber within the house, called the Chauntry House, like other of his brotherhood. There hath been no more land or yearly profits belonging to the same since the time above said more than is before specified.

£2 : 16s. (in goods), as well for this chauntry as for the Morrow Mass Chauntry, as appeareth by a particular inventory hereunto annexed.

No. 17.

The chauntry of Sawsemer called the Morrow Mass Chauntry, being founded by William Sawsemer, parishioner in Newark, to the intent and for one priest to celebrate daily morrow Mass at four of the clock in the morning, for ever, at the alter of Saint Lawrence in Mary Magdelen Church, there praying for the souls of the said founder, his parents and friends, and all Christian souls, as appeareth by the foundation, dated 1326, to the commissioners showed. £4 : 10 : 4¼.

£4 : 10 : 4 clear, besides 7d. in rent resolute to the Bishop of Lincoln, and with £4 : 8s. is paid yearly by the king's majesty's receiver of the revenues of the late Priory of St. Catherine by Lincoln, and is employed to the living of John Crosten, now incumbent there.

The said chauntry is no parish church, but within the parish church of Mary Magdelen in Newark aforesaid.

The said chauntry is not void, having no mansion house, but a chamber and a parlour within the old Chauntry House at Newark, amongst other brotherhood.

The goods and ornaments thereof are answered next before by John Houis, another chauntry priest of Sawsemer.

No. 18.

The chauntry of St. Catherine, founded within the parish of Mary Magdelen in Newark by William Wansey and others of that name, for one priest to pray for their souls and all Christians', without any foundation showed to the commissioner. £4 : 3 : 4.

£4 clear, which is yearly paid out of the revenues late surrendered to the monastery of Thurgarton, and is employed to the living of William Gilbert, now priest there ; the said chauntry is no parish church, but within the parish church of St. Mary Magdelen in Newark aforesaid.

The said chauntry is not void, having no mansion, but only a chamber with the residue of his brethern there.

No. 19.

The chauntry of Corpus Christi in the church of Mary Magdelen, founded by one Alan Flemynge for one convenient priest, not otherwise beneficed, daily to celebrate divine service to the honour of God for all Christian souls, without composition, showed to the commissioners. £5 : 7 : 6¼.

£5 : 5 : 4 clear, besides six shillings in rent resolute to the Bishop of Lincoln, with £4 yearly received of the revenues of the late monastery Shelford, £3 : 6 : 8, Thurgarton, 13s 4d., which is employed to the living of Sir William Moulton,[1] chauntry priest there, and for the keeping of an obit 4s., for the founder.

The said chauntry is no parish church, but within the parish of Mary Magdelen in Newark aforesaid.

---

[1] Clergymen used to have the title of Sir instead of Reverend. Thus, in the "Merry Wives of Windsor," we have Sir Hugh Evans, a priest.

The said chauntry is not void, having no other mansion but with the other brethern within the house there called the Chauntry House.

There hath been no more land nor yearly profits belonging to the same since the time aforesaid, more than is before specified. £3 : 11s., as appeareth by a particular inventory for the goods of three chauntries celebrated at the alter of Corpus Christi in Newark, as well by the said William Moulton as by William Skelton and Edmund Medcalfe.

No. 20.

The Chauntry of Corpus Christi, in the church of Mary Magdalen in Newark, founded by one Isabell Caldwell, to the intent that one convenient priest, not being otherwise beneficed, be presented by the ordinary of the diocese, to the intent that he should daily celebrate mass at the alter of Corpus Christi; there for the soul of the said founder, and all Christian souls, as by the foundation thereof doth appear. £4 : 3 : 8½.

£4 clear, which is paid of the revenue of the late monastery of Thurgarton, and is employed to the living of William Skelton, now chauntry priest there.

The said chauntry is no parish church, but within the parish church of Mary Magdelen in Newark aforesaid.

The said chauntry is not void, and hath no mansion, but only a chamber within the house there, called the Chauntry House, amongst the other of his like bretheren.

No. 21.

The chauntry of Corpus Christi, in the parish church of Mary Magdalen in Newark, founded by one Robert Caldwell, for a priest not otherwise beneficed to celebrate daily mass of Corpus Christi, and to pray for all Christian souls, as by the foundation thereof doth appear. £4 : 3 : 8.

£4 clear, which is yearly received of the Earl of Shrewsbury out of his revenues, sometime belonging to the late monastry of Rufford, which is employed to the living of Edmund Medcalfe, now chauntry priest there.

The said chauntry is no parish church, but within the parish church of Mary Magdalen in Newark aforesaid.

The said chauntry is not void, and hath no mansion, but only a chamber within the house there, called the Chauntry House, amongst the other of his like bretheren.

No. 22.

The chauntry in Newark, founded by one Sir William Newark, sometime Archdeacon of Huntington, to celebrate divine service daily in the church of Newark, and to pray for his soul and all Christian souls, as by the certificate of William Wyse, chauntry priest, there doth appear £4 : 3 : 8.

£4 : 2 : 4 clear, with £4 received yearly of the parson of Fullingham and his successors, and besides twenty-one pence for rents resolute, which revenues are employed to the living of William Wyse, chauntry priest there.

The said chauntry is no parish church, but hath one alter in the parish church of Newark, to celebrate, according to his foundation, the said chauntry.

The said chauntry is not void, having no mansion, but only a chamber within the house there, called the Chauntry House, like as other the brotherhood hath.

There is neither plate, goods, jewels, nor ornaments belonging to the same, but he borrows all that he occupies of the church wardens there.

No. 23.

The chauntry of the Blessed Trinity of the Church of St. Mary Magdelen in Newark aforesaid, founded by one Robert Caldewell to the intent that a convenient priest, not otherwise beneficed, should daily fore ever celebrate mass at the alter of the Holy Trinity there, and minister other services to the honour of God. And to pray as well for founders and all persons living, as for all Christian souls, as by the said foundation doth appear. £6 : 4 : 10.

£5 : 6 : 8 clear which is paid to him yearly by the King's Majesty's receiver of the revenues of the late monastery of Newborough for ever, and is employed to the living of Stephen Bently, chauntry priest there.

The said chauntry is no parish church, but is celebrated within the parish of Mary Magdelen in Newark aforesaid.

The said chauntry is not void, and hath no mansion, but one little chamber within the common house there, called the Chauntry House, amongst other of his brethren there.

No. 24.

The chauntries of All Saints and the nativity of our Lady in the Church of St. Mary Magdelen in Newark, founded by Symone Surfleet, Roger Beircy, William Wakebryde, and William Fryn, in consideration that Newark is a great town, and a thorowfare, and the vicar and his parish priest were not sufficient to find the cure to the intent that two chauntry priests should say Mass, Mattyns, and other divine service, and to pray for the founders' souls, and all Christian souls, as by the foundation and the king's licence to the commissioners showed doth appear. £19 : 7 : 9.

£15 : 9 : 2 clear, besides £1 : 7 : 6 in rents resolute to divers persons, and which revenues have been employed to the living of Richard Hopkins and William Ersbey, chauntry priests there, and also for the reparations of the cottage belonging to the same.

The said chauntry is no parish church, but within the parish of Mary Magdalen, in Newark aforesaid.

The said chauntry hath not been void, and hath no mansion, but two little chambers within the common house there, called the Chauntry House, amongst other of the brethren there.

No. 25.

The Chauntry called Foster's Chauntry founded by John Burton, some time Vicar of Newark, Thomas Foster, priest, Thomas Haystan, John Clerke, and William Boston, by the licence of King Henry VI. in the 30th year of his reign; whereof the copy was showed to the commissioners, being founded to the intent that one priest, not otherwise beneficed, should be bound to daily service and to celebrate mass at the Trinity alter there, and to pray for the founders' souls; and for the brotherhood and systers of Trinity Guild, as well quick and dead, and all Christian souls. £5 : 10 : 4½.

£4 : 14 : 10 clear, besides 10s. 2d. in rents resolute to the Bishop of Lincoln, which revenue been employed to the living of John Euston, chauntry priest there.

The said chauntry is no parish church, but within the parish church of Newark aforesaid.

It is not void, and has no mansion, but a chamber in the common house amongst other of the brethren.

Nothing here (in the shape of goods), forasmuch as he hath a chalice and other ornaments in common with Thomas Thornton, and Hugo Young, serving at the same alter which he afterwards charged.

No. 26.

The chauntry of the Holy Trinity, within the parish of Newark, founded there for ever for a priest to celebrate daily mass for the brotherhood and sisters of Trinity Guild, and specially to pray for the souls of Edward, late King of England after the conquest the third, and for Isabella his mother, and Phillipa his wife, as appeareth by the foundation thereof showed to the commissioners. Three pounds eight shillings and one farthing.

Six pounds ten shillings and fivepence clear, beside fourteen shillings and three pence in rent resolute to divers persons, which revenues have been employed to the living of Thomas Thornton, chauntry priest there.

The said chauntry is no parish church, but is celebrated within the parish church of Newark aforesaid.

The said chauntry is not void, and it hath no mansion, but a chamber in the common house amongst other of his brethren.

Five pounds eleven shillings and sixpence for the goods and ornaments belonging to the Trinity altar, which are in common betwixt John Euston, Thomas Thornton, and Hugh Young, chauntry priests there.

No. 27.

The chauntry in the church of Newark founded by John Leke, Richard Saywell, Thomas Fanor, and Roger Gell, of the same town (Newark), for a priest to continually keep the quire at Matting, Mass, and Evening Song, and one day in the week to say mass of requiem, one in the week of our Lady, and every Sunday of Blessed Trinity, and yearly to celebrate one trendall of masses for the founder's soul, and of all Christians as appointed by the foundation thereof. Eight pounds seventeen shillings and eightpence half-penny.

Eight pounds thirteen shillings and eightpence farthing, clear value, beside eight shillings and sevenpence three farthings in rent resolute to sundry persons, which revenue hath been employed to the living of Knight Young, chauntry priest there.

The said chauntry is no parish church, but is celebrated within the parish church of Newark aforesaid.

The said chauntry is not void, and hath no mansion but a chamber within the common house amongst other of his brotherhood there.

Nothing (as to goods), for as much as the same has been answered above, within the sum of £5 : 11 : 6, the goods being in common betwixt John Euston, Thomas Thornton, and Hugh Young, chauntry priest there.

No. 28.

The common mansion house of all the chauntry priests in Newark aforesaid, founded by one Alice Fleming, widow, to the intent that they should converse and associate together, as by the licence of King Edward the third doth appear. In consideration whereof they be bound to do yearly one obit with dirige and mass, and requiem for the soul of Alice Fleming, her husband, and for all Christian souls. Nothing for that is supposed and particularly charged in the King's Majesty record of the tenths in the several chauntries abovesaid.

Four pounds eight shillings and eightpence, besides three shillings and tenpence in rents resolute to the Bishop of Lincoln, with 40 shillings for the mansion house, and 48 shillings for a certain house which is employed amongst all the said chauntry priests in common.

The common mansion house being rated at 40 shillings by year is not void, but full as particular in every chauntrie in Newark may appear.

Particulars of the chauntries are also to be found amongst the corporation papers, and in the records at York. The above certificates, however, seem to us to give the details in the most complete and reliable form. Referring to the subject at a meeting of the Lincoln Diocesan Architectural Society, held in Newark in 1855, the Rev. J. F. Dimock says:—"This number of chauntries in a parish church, founded as they would be, and all were, by inhabitants of the place, strikes me as very remarkable. Compare similar churches in two or three other important towns. At Nottingham, as we learn from the *Valor Ecclesiasticus*, there was one chauntry, at St. Mary's; none in either of the other churches. At Mansfield but one, at Louth one, at St. Michael's, Coventry, four, at Trinity Church three; at Grantham, however, there were eight, while at Boston, then a town of far more relative importance than at present, and one of the most wealthy and important seaports in the kingdom, but twelve chauntry priests are recorded. We might, I believe, search through all England, and should find few, indeed, if any, parish churches which could boast such an array of chauntries as Newark possessed in the fourteenth and fifteenth centuries, and this affords, it seems to me, a convincing proof of the great wealth and prosperity of the town in those days, and a proof as well, we may add, of the piety and devotion of the citizens; for, however much of error we may believe to have been involved in these foundations, yet they were then an ordinary mode in which Christians expressed their love of their brethren, and their zeal for the glory of God. But my main reason for mentioning these chauntries is the relation which they bear to the fabric of the church. The number of priests daily officiating, the number of altars which were required, demanded a large space: a large number of chambers would in fact render a large church indispensable, and the same wealth, and piety, and zeal, which led to those foundations, led also, as a matter of course, to the long-drawn aisles and spacious transepts, the almost cathedral-like proportions of the church, which no longer indeed resounds with requiems for the dead, but where the living, we will hope, still worship God no less earnestly than their fathers before them." We extract the following particulars of endowments from the chancery records:—

CHANCERY RECORDS—GUILDS AND CHAUNTRIES, Notts, File 5.

No. 33.

Licence in Mortmain of Edward III. to make the Abbey of Rufford pay and endow a chauntry priest at the altar of Corpus Christi in Newark Church to pray daily for the souls of all the members of the guild there.

A deed dated at Rufford Chapter House, 10 May 24 Edward III., whereby the abbot gives 6 marks of silver for ever out of Park Lache to the above chaplain.

A deed of Robert de Caldecot of Newark, dated 7th November 1351, giving six marks for the endowment of the guild or chauntry of Corpus Christi. A confirmation by the Archbishop of York of the above gifts dated at Carwood 29 Nov. 1351.

No. 33 b.

A deed dated 2d April 1351, from Robert de Clascton, prior of Thurgarton, granting six marks of silver out of lands in Thurgarton and Crophill Butler, etc., to the chaplain of Corpus Christi chauntry in the parish church of St. Mary Magdalen, Newark.

A confirmation by Edward III., dated 1st June in the 25th year of his reign, of the above grant by the prior.

No. 34.

Licence in Mortmain by Richard II., dated 8th May at Nottingham, granting permission to Simon de Bottesford to give lands for the endowment of a chaplain at the altar of the Holy Trinity in Newark.

Deed of Simon de Bottesford giving 6 marks to celebrate at the altar daily for the king's safety and his mother Isabella, dated at the feast of St. Barnabas.

PENSIONS TO CHAUNTRY PRIESTS.

A confirmation of the gift by William Archbishop of York dated at Thorp near York, 18th May 1339.

A confirmation by the King Edward III. dated at Northampton 20th March in the 8th year of his reign.

A confirmation by Pope Benedict to the chaplain of the Holy Trinity altar, date 3d May in the 7th year of his pontificate.

No. 35.

A writ of Edward III., dated 15 July in the 36th year of his reign, to the escheator of the County of Notts, authorising the conveyance of lands in Mortmain for the endowment of two chaplains for the chauntry of the Blessed Virgin Mary in Newark church, and further directing an inquisition to be held.

The inquisition at length with return of the Jurors.

Deed of Simon de Surslect, dated 2d Oct. 1367, giving 34 houses, 10 acres of meadow, and 50 acres of land, with 5 marks of rent, all in Newark for the support of the chaplains.

Confirmation by John, Archbishop of York, of the above gift, dated at Thorp near York, 1367.

The following pensions appear to have been granted to the incumbents of chauntries in Newark on the occasion of the demolition of the chauntries :—

AUGMENTATION COURT-PENSIONS TO INCUMBENTS OF CHAUNTRIES IN NEWARK.

Name of Chauntry Priest.	Name of Chauntry.	Amount of Pension.
Richard Hopkins	All Saints	£6 0 0
William Ersbey	All Saints	6 0 0
Thomas Thornton	Holy Trinity	5 0 0
John Euston	Holy Trinity	4 0 0
Edward Medcalf	Corpus Christi	3 12 0
William Skeiton	Corpus Christi	3 11 0
John Askew	Matilda Sauemers	3 10 0
John Crosten	William Sauemers	4 0 0
William Gilbert	St. Catherine	3 11 0
Peter Hugett	St. Nicholas	4 0 0
Hugh White	St. Nicholas	4 0 0
William Wise	St. Mary Magdelen	3 14 0
Stephen Bently	Holy Trinity	4 0 0
William Moulton	Corpus Christi	4 0 0
		£58 18 0

The chauntry house so frequently referred to stands in Appleton Gate, and is stated to have been an establishment of Observant friars,[1] and to have been founded

[1] The Observants were a branch of the Franciscan friars, brought to England by Edward IV.

by King Henry VII. about the year 1499.[1] In Dodsworth's MSS.[2] occurs a mention of "Gabriel, fader of the Observant friers at Newark," and in Willis's *Abbeys*[3] it is stated that Gabriel was warden of the Observants here.[4] It seems clear, however, from the certificate given on a preceding page,[5] that the chauntry house was founded by Alice Fleming for the use of the chauntry priests; and this statement is fully borne out by the numerous references to the place which occur in the other certificates, and which indicate plainly that the priests had rooms allotted to them, and occupied the mansion in common. We must look elsewhere for the site of the convent of the Observants founded by Henry VII., and it may have been the old chapel-like building that existed in Osmundthorpe to which allusion has already been made (p. 42). If this was the convent to which Henry VII. left £200 in a codicil to his will, as tradition affirms, it would undoubtedly be the place which the Observants occupied. This conjecture is strengthened by the fact that in the above-named codicil no less than five bequests to other houses of Observant friars almost immediately precede that of £200 to the newly-founded "convent" at Newark.

The chauntry house, the common abode of the chauntry priests, passed into the possession of the Leekes. Of this important family, and of the subsequent owners of the chauntry house, we have been supplied with an account by Captain A. E. Lawson Lowe. He says:—"Sir Francis Leeke of Sutton Scarsdale, in Derbyshire, appears to have possessed both the friary and the chauntry house at Newark as early as the year 1605. This Sir Francis Leeke was twice married. His first wife was Frances, daughter and co-heiress of Robert Swift, Esq., by whom he had a son of his own name, who was created a baronet, May 22, 1611, and raised to the peerage in 1624 as Baron Deincourt of Sutton Scarsdale, and further advanced in 1645 as Earl of Scarsdale. This nobleman was a devoted Royalist, and is said to have felt the execution of King Charles the First so deeply that he clothed himself in sackcloth, and causing his grave to be dug some years before his death, laid himself therein every Friday for divine meditation and prayer. He died in 1655, leaving by Anne, his wife, the daughter of Sir Edward Carey of Berkhamstead, in Hertfordshire, a son, Nicholas, who succeeded as second Earl of Scarsdale, and sold the friary estate to Matthew Jenison not long after his father's death. By his second wife, Mary, daughter of John Egioke, Esq., of Egioke, in Worcestershire, Sir Francis Leeke had a son, William, upon whom he appears to have settled the chauntry house in his lifetime, for the inquisition taken after his death, in 1629, only refers to the friary. His widow subsequently became the third wife of Sir Gervase Clifton, Bart., of Clifton, and died in 1631. William Leeke, Esq., of the chauntry house, was twice married, and died intestate in 1641. His first wife was a daughter of Sir

---

[1] *Collect. Anglo. Minorit.*, P. I. p. 211; P. II. p. 39. Mr. Dickinson says the chauntry house was occupied by Observant friars, but that the house founded by Henry VII. was not the chauntry house (*ante*, p. 42).
[2] Vol. xcix. fol. 200.   [3] Vol. ii. p. 168.
[4] There is also a reference in MS. Cole, Brit. Mus., vol. xxvii., fol. 78b.
[5] Certificate No. 28, p. 70.

Guy Palmes of Ashwell, in Rutland, and his second wife was a daughter of (William ?) Orme of Elston, near Newark. Sir Francis Leeke, the eldest son of William Leeke by his first marriage, was created a baronet December 15, 1663, in reward, it is said, for the vigilance which he displayed in apprehending Colonel Hutchinson, the regicide, on the 11th of October in that year. In 1672 he obtained the appointment of governor of the Blockhouse at Gravesend, previous to which he appears to have resided at the chauntry house. By his will, dated at Milton-next-Gravesend, October 2, 1679, he settled the chauntry house upon his only son, Francis, and his heirs male, failing which he gave it to his (testator's) four daughters in equal proportions. His will was duly proved, November 10, 1679, by Dame Frances Leeke, his widow. That lady was a daughter of Sir William Thorold, Bart., of Marston, in Lincolnshire, and after her husband's decease she appears to have resided in Park Place, St. James's, Westminster. She made her will September 23, 1690, and it was proved January 13, 1693-4, by Anne, wife of Robert Vyner, the eldest of her three surviving daughters. In this will no mention whatever is made of the estate at Newark, but there are legacies of £100 to the poor of that town, and £200 to purchase communion plate for the use of the church there. Her only son, Sir Francis Leeke, Bart., who succeeded to his father's appointments,[1] and who describes himself in his will, dated June 15, 1681, as 'Govern' of His Majestie's fforts of Gravesend and Tilbury,' thereby gave all his lands, tenements, and hereditaments whatever, to his uncle, Clifton Leeke, Esq., to whom probate of the same was granted, May 10, 1682. This Clifton Leeke was the second surviving son of William Leeke, Esq., and died unmarried. By his will, dated March 13, 1682-3, he left, amongst numerous legacies, the sum of £20 to the poor of Newark, and the whole residue of his estate, real and personal, he devised to his nephew, Drewell Leeke, who appears to have been the only child of Nicholas Leeke of Hedley, in Yorkshire (the son of William Leeke, Esq., by his second marriage); and probate of the will of Clifton Leeke was duly granted to him, May 4, 1683. Drewell Leeke is described as 'of the parish of Saint Clement-Danes,' and appears to have died without issue, intestate, and in embarrassed circumstances, administration of his personal effects being granted, January 15, 1688-9, to his principal creditor, George Hudson.

"It is somewhat doubtful who was the next possessor of the chauntry house. John Odingsells Leeke, the son of John Leeke, Esq., of Epperston, by Elizabeth, daughter and sole heiress of Emanuel Odingsells, Esq., of that place, would ultimately, if not immediately, succeed to the real estate of his first cousin, the above-named Drewell Leeke. This gentleman, who was born in 1672, practised as an attorney at Epperston in 1703, and again, as such, at Wirksworth, in Derbyshire, in 1726. Between these years the chauntry house is said to have been sold to Samuel Foster, Esq., of Woodborough, and there is every probability that he

---

[1] Pocock's *Hist. of Gravesend*, p. 170.

purchased it from John Odingsells Leeke. Actual proof of this is wanting.[1] There seems, however, to be no foundation for the statement made by Dickinson, that the chauntry house passed by the marriage of an heiress of this branch of the Leekes with William Snell (mayor of Newark in 1701), into the family of the latter, and that it was sold after her decease. Indeed, the monumental inscription in Newark church, to Mary, wife of Mr. William Snell, who died September 9, 1701, records her maiden name as Mason, and her connection with the Leeke family would seem to be altogether fallacious. Samuel Foster, the purchaser of the chauntry house, appears to have almost, if not entirely, reconstructed the fabric sometime previous to the year 1725, and the armorial bearings of his family formerly adorned the principal front, but were superseded by those of the Sikes family (which still remain) some time after the transfer of the property in 1783. Robert Foster, Esq. (the son of the above-named Samuel Foster), was high sheriff of the county in 1769, and in 1783 he sold the property to Joseph Sikes, Esq., an alderman of Newark, who filled the office of mayor in 1756 and 1767, and again in 1780. This gentleman died in 1798, leaving an only son, the Reverend Joseph Sikes, LL.B., who died unmarried in 1857, having devised his estates at Newark and elsewhere to Mr. Francis Baines, who assumed the name and arms of Sikes by royal license in 1857. He died in 1870, and his widow is the present possessor of the chauntry house."

On the Patents Rolls are the following grants of land, made during the reign of Edward VI.

Patent Roll. 1 Edw. VI. Part 5.

Grant of the Bishop of Lincoln of the Borough, hundred, tolls, Wappentiq, and Castle of Newark, in exchange for other property.

3 Edw. VI. Part 4.

Grant to Brooke and Mohidrip (? Medhop), for a money payment, of messuages, lands, and tenements, in Pavement Street and in Northgate.

3 Edw. VI. Part 6.

Grant to Thomas Marshe for a money payment of seven cottages in several tenures, late of the property of the common mansion house of the chantry priests.

3 Edw. VI. Part 11.

Grant to Breton and Ambrose, for a money payment, of farms and tenements in Middlegate, late of the chantry at the altar of All Saints, the Holy Trinity, and the altar of St. Mary, Newark.

7 Edw. VI. Part 7.

Grant to Philpot and[2]   , for a money payment, of six cottages and rents belonging to the priorate of Brodholm and priory of Worksop; a toft of lands in Balderton Gate, belonging to Croxton; tenements in Castle Gate belonging to Kirkston; tenements and rents belonging to a Chantry.

---

[1] *Vide Herald and Genealogist*, vol. vii. pp. 495, 496, 497, 498, 499, where numerous additional particulars of considerable interest are to be found.   [2] Name illegible.

On the demise of Edward VI. in 1553, the people declared in favour of Mary. The nobility clustered around her to support her claim, and she was acknowledged Queen by general assent. Being a Roman Catholic she used her power to undo the work of the Reformation, and to re-introduce papal influence and authority. Cranmer and scores of others were arrested and burnt at the stake for their adherence to the Protestant faith. Soon after her accession, the behaviour of Mary to her sister Elizabeth was characterised by unwarrantable harshness. The attachment of Elizabeth to the reformed religion offended Mary's bigotry, and when the Earl of Devonshire, who had been suggested as a suitable husband for her Majesty, preferred the youth and agreeable conversation of Elizabeth to all the power and grandeur of her sister, the Queen's resentment, excited by pride, no longer knew any bounds.[1] The misfortunes of Elizabeth were shared by those about her, and, at the instigation of Bishop Gardiner, several of them were committed to the Tower. Amongst the devoted ladies who were accused of heretical opinions and sent to prison was Isabella Markham, daughter of Sir John Markham, and thus a descendant of the ancient family of Markham, to whose connection with Newark allusion has already been made. Sir John, who was Lieutenant of the Tower of London, and whose country seat was at Cotham, was thrice married, and Isabella was the youngest daughter by his last wife Anne, relict of Sir Richard Stanhope, daughter and co-heir of John Strelley, Esq. of Strelley, who was descended from Walter de Stradlegh in the time of Henry I. Isabella, who appears to have been possessed of high personal attractions, won the admiration of Sir John Harrington, and her charms are described in a sonnet from the pen of Sir John when "he firste thoghte her fayre as she stode at the princesses' windowe in goodlye attyre, and talkede to dyvers in the courte yarde." Subsequently the poetical lover addressed her directly in the following lines.

JOHN HARRINGTON TO SWEETE ISABELLA MARKHAM.

> Marvellouse be thy matchless gyftes of mynde,
> And for thy shape, Erithnia rightly growen;
> Recklese of prayse, a prayse rare in thy kinde,
> Great in desert, small in desyre, well knowen;
> A mansion meete where chastitie doth dwell,
> Rype in all goode, of evill the sede unsowen,
> Endewed with thewse that do the rest excell,
> Temp'rance hathe wonne and constancye doth holde,
> Wisdom hath taughte that myldness mastereth might.[2]

The result of the love passages was a marriage between Sir John and Isabella, which took place under the auspices of the Princess Elizabeth in 1554. On her Highness being committed to the Tower in the same year, Lady Harrington was sequestered from her service, and, as already mentioned, was, on account of her so-called heretical opinions, committed to a prison lodging along with her husband, whose offence consisted in having carried a letter to the princess. When, on the death of Mary, Eliza-

---

[1] Hume.   [2] *Nugæ Antiquæ*, vol. iv. p. 256, sonnet xvi.

THE BEQUEST OF PHYLLYPOT.

beth came to the throne, she did not forget the devoted conduct of her attendants nor the indignities they had undergone on her account. She stood godmother to Lady Harrington's son, and gave her many tokens of affectionate regard. Sir John's poetical effusions continued after his marriage, for in 1564 he writes as warmly in her praise as ever he had done. The loving pair lived together near Bath, and brought up a considerable family.[1]

Whilst persecution was cursing the country, Newark received the blessing of a display of generosity worthy to rank with those of Magnus and Brown. In 1556 William Phyllypot, a Newark merchant, made a will by which he gave valuable estates to the borough. The property was reserved to his wife whilst she lived, and on her decease it went to the aldermen and assistants, inhabitants of the town of Newark, and their successors upon certain trusts: first, to maintain and support a certain almshouse, in Coddington Lane, which the testator had built for the reception of five poor men; secondly, for the support of the said five poor men by an allowance of 20s. yearly, to be paid quarterly to each of them; thirdly, to find a certain garment for each of the said poor men, of the value of 6s. 8d.; fourthly, to purchase for the use of the said almshouse coals and firewood of the value of 26s. 8d.; fifthly, to augment the salary of the Grammar Schoolmaster, 40s. a year to be paid quarterly; sixthly, to pay the alderman for the time being 20s. a year as a compensation for his trouble in ordering the said five poor men in the almshouse, overlooking the premises, keeping the same in repair, and passing the accounts. A number of small appropriations were added, and it was directed that the surplus should go towards the paving of the streets, the repair and improvement of the estates, and to "such charges of the town as the most need shall require." The estates are in the parishes of Newark and North Muskham. The ordinary yearly income arising from them, and from dividends on consols, amounts now to about £690. Added to this is the sum of £27 a year received from Dyson's bequest, the late Mr. Dyson having left that sum to go annually to the support of the people in the almshouses. The total income of the charity is thus about £720, and it is expended in accordance with a decree of the Court of Chancery made in the year 1738. The sum of £246:18s. per annum goes in weekly payments to the Bedehouse inmates, who consist of twenty-four old men and women and a matron.[2] From £70 to £80 is expended annually on clothes for them, and for coal and other necessaries £40 to £50 more. The usher of the Grammar School receives £40; the urban Sanitary Authority £120; and the residue, after payment of incidental expenses, is appropriated for the repair and improvement of the estates.

Phyllypot died in 1557, and in the parish church is a brass bearing a portraiture of him in his robes of office as an alderman, and having the following inscription:—
"Here under this stone lyeth buried the body of William Phyllypot, Marchant,

---

[1] *A History of the Markham Family*, by the Rev. D. F. Markham. Printed for private circulation, 1854.
[2] They are also benefited by the charities of Lawrence and Summers, for particulars of which see subsequent pages.

and Elizabeth his wife, which William decessyed the VIII. day of May yn An. Dom. MCCCCCLVII., whose dethe desyryng youe all to have in remembrance, calling to God for mercy." The brass was removed in 1811 from the stone in the south transept to the north wall near the west end, where a marble tablet, to which it was affixed, records the particulars of its removal. The inscription plate, however, still remains in the south transept.

In the first year of the reign of Queen Elizabeth, who succeeded her sister in 1558, there was another gift for charitable purposes which, though on a smaller scale than those already mentioned, is worthy of honourable notice. Mr. Anthony Foster devised all his lands in Meryn Close, Newark, to the Corporation upon trust, to apply the rents for the assistance of those afflicted with the plague. The pestilence had been of frequent occurrence, and its constant presence was a source of great misery and suffering. Its origin has been attributed to the slovenly habits of the people, and to their want of proper comforts.

In 1561 armorial bearings were granted to the borough by her Majesty, at the special request of the Earl of Rutland. A peacock proper between a fleur de lys and a lion passant gardant, form the principal distinctions of the shield. The supporters are a beaver and an otter, the surrounding district having formerly abounded in animals of this description. The crest is a sea mew or gull holding a silver eel in its beak, "the silver eel having long been a distinguished inhabitant of the Trent."[1] For the engraving of the seal which we here present, we are indebted to the courtesy of the Harleian Society (per Mr. Armytage). It should be noted that in Harl. 1400, a lion passant gardant is substituted for the fleur de lys on

sinister side of the chief, and so it is in the original grant, which hangs up in the Town Hall, and a copy of which we have reproduced by photography.

The Queen being favourable to the Reformation, was welcomed on the throne with great joy by the Protestants. She devoted herself actively to the affairs of the State, and to conquering the difficulties which kept springing up around her. Her secretary was Sir William Cecil, the most vigilant, active, and prudent minister ever known in England.[2] Another powerful and influential statesman was the Duke of Norfolk, the splendour of whose family and opulence rendered him without comparison the first subject in England. It was to the ambition of the latter that an event arose which created considerable trouble. His Grace, in 1569, had suggested to him the idea that he was a suitable match for the Queen of Scots, and it was represented that if he

[1] Dickinson, p. 142.   [2] Hume.

could succeed in uniting himself with her, he would compose the dissensions in Scotland, and possess the prospect of a succession to the English throne. The Queen of Scots being induced to take a favourable view of the proposal, the Duke next exerted himself to secure the alliance of the nobility and gentry. Two of Mary's partisans, the Earls of Northumberland and Westmoreland, entered heartily into the conspiracy, and rumours of an approaching rebellion were circulated throughout the north. A force amounting to 4000 foot and 1600 horse was collected, and a manifesto published, declaring that the aim of the insurgents was to re-establish the religion of their ancestors, remove evil counsellors, and restore the Duke of Norfolk and other faithful peers to their liberty and to the Queen's favour.[1]

Secretary Cecil and the Queen, meanwhile, were not inactive. Instructions were issued for the levying of forces, and two armies were soon in the field. The commander of the one was Sussex, attended by Earl Rutland, and Lords Hunsdon, Evers, and Willoughby of Parham; of the other the Earl of Warwick, and Lord Clinton. The two last named received a joint commission, and Newark was selected as a convenient place for the union of the Earl of Warwick and Lord Clinton's troops. Writing to Cecil on the 29th November,[2] Lord Clinton announces his intention of moving to Newark with his whole force, and on December 1 (1569), he suggests that they had better remain there until the arrival of the Earl of Warwick. In a letter to Sir Walter Meeding he states that his horsemen and harquebusiers are in want of training, but there is no lack of arms and armour. On December 3 Lord Clinton writes from Newark stating that he will proceed the next day to Doncaster, taking with him two pieces of ordnance sent from Cecil's house at Burghley. Another batch of troops, under the command of Edward Aylwnby, reached the town on December 28, and remained there until a convoy of horse sent by the Lord Lieutenant joined them. Clinton's and Warwick's forces having united, marched against the rebels on the one side, while Lord Sussex drove them before him on the other. Disheartened and alarmed they fled in all directions. The royal troops had no need to strike a blow, and so soon could the services of some of them be dispensed with, that on January 16 (1570), we find Lord Clinton at Newark writing to Cecil relative to a portion of the treasure sent for paying off the army.[3]

The occupant of the castle during the stay of the troops in Newark was Sir Francis Leeke of Sutton Scarsdale, in Derbyshire. On the 25th June 1560 a lease had been granted to him of the site of the castle, "parcel of the possessions of the Bishop of Lincoln," for twenty-one years at the annual rent of 53s. 4d.[4] During December 1569 Sir Francis was in possession under this lease, for we find him writing various letters to Secretary Cecil, dating them from Newark Castle. In his last, bearing date 28th January 1570, he says, "Now that this tumult is ended, I beg leave to return and visit my sick wife in Derbyshire. The Earl of Sussex and Sir Ralph Sadler will be here to-morrow."

[1] *Cabala*, p. 169.   [2] *State Papers*.   [3] *State Papers*.
[4] *Vide* Rolls of Particulars of Leases, Co. Notts, Augmentation Office, Roll III., No. 55.

Under date 1571, there is in the Augmentation Office a lease to the Mayor and Corporation of Newark of the fines and profits of the fair, perquisites of court, and profits of flesh and fish in the borough, valued at £4 : 13 : 5. Fine £13 : 6 : 8, granted for the benefit and quitting of the town for twenty-one years. This lease is under the seal of the Court of Exchequer.

The Earl of Rutland, who was one of the leading officers of the army of Sussex, petitioned the queen in 1575 relative to the manor of Newark, to which he had taken a fancy. He intimated his desire to purchase of her Majesty the whole of the manor, stating that he had not any house within the county of Nottingham. We do not trace amongst the *State Papers*, from which we glean this information, the reply to the petition, but on reference to the Rolls in the Augmentation Office, from which we have just quoted, we find that a favourable answer must have been sent, subject to the lease held by Sir Francis Leeke; for immediately on the expiration of the tenure of Sir Francis, a lease (bearing date 14th February 1581) was granted to the Earl of Rutland, the countess his wife, and Elizabeth his daughter, for the term of their three lives, of the site of the Castle of Newark. No fine was to be paid in consideration of the decay, as certified by the auditor of the county of Notts, and by commission. The earl was to do all repairs at his own cost, and to pull down the high tower, in default the lease to be void, and the Crown to have any money expended on the castle. Annual rent 53s. 4d.[1] The earl on his death bequeathed the castle and demesne to the countess so long as she continued unmarried. Sir William Cecil (afterwards Lord Burghley) was one of the trustees under the will, and in this way Newark became associated with Queen Elizabeth's distinguished minister. In 1587 Lord Burghley and his co-trustees wrote to John, Earl of Rutland, reminding him of the will of his brother, and requiring that his sister-in-law should be permitted to have the quiet possession of the estate and property. Four years after, namely, on the 4th June 1591, William Lord Roos, son of William Cecil (Lord Burghley), son of Sir Thomas Cecil; and Elizabeth Manners, daughter of Edward, Earl of Rutland, were baptized in Newark Castle. In 1591 a lease of the castle was granted to the Countess of Rutland, William Cecil (Lord Burghley), and William Lord Roos, for their lives, at an annual rent of 53s. 4d.:[2] and in 1593 they had a further lease granted them for their three lives, of all the tithes belonging to the rectory of Newark,[3] for a fine of £13 : 6 : 8, and an annual rent, the lessees covenanting to support the chancel of the church, and to pay a stipend of £10 to the vicar. Gilbert, Earl of Shrewsbury, paid a visit to the place in 1594, and it appears to have inspired his poetic fancies. In a letter to Thomas Phelipps, dated 14th January in that year, he refers to the fact that he had written some verses during his stay. Lord Burghley, notwithstanding his important duties as a statesman, found time to look carefully after the Newark property, for in a memorial of

---

[1] Rolls of Particulars of Leases, Augmentation Office, Roll I.
[2] Augmentation Office, Roll II., No. 47.
[3] Described as possessions of the Monastery of St. Catherine, near Lincoln.

things to be attended to by him, dated 24th April 1594, is mentioned "the decay of the mills at Newark."

The course of the river Trent having been turned, to the detriment of the occupiers of the mills, proceedings arose before the courts, in which the grievance was fully detailed. It appears that formerly the river passed near the town, about 345 yards from the castle. At that time only a small brook ran through Averham, Kelham, and Muskham. This little stream not being sufficient for the wants of the influential family of the Suttons, who resided at Averham, a cut was made to the brook from the Trent, near Farndon. This gave a turn to the whole current, and so much of the water passed that way that a suit was instituted against them by the miller and inhabitants of Newark. The Court directed the owners of Averham to build a weir, and for ever to maintain the same, in order to throw some share of the water into the Newark branch. The Newark mills were a part of the estate of the lord of the manor, and the inhabitants were compellable to grind at the lord's mill.[1] Dr. Stukely states that he saw old proceedings in one or more law-suits, brought in support of this right. The river which now runs under the walls of the castle is the Devon, which takes its rise above Belvoir Castle, the present seat of the Rutland family. The Trent is united with it by means of a navigable cut, but the main portion of the great stream passes over Averham weir, and thence through Kelham. The Devon flows into it below Newark, at a spot known as Crankley Point.

In the 27th year of Elizabeth's reign (1585), an Act of Parliament was passed for the paving of the streets of the borough. It is believed that the work was only proceeded with very slowly, for it was not until the 18th of James I. that the paving of the market-place was begun by Henry Webster, who was Alderman of Newark in 1603 and 1613; and it was then but partially effected, for there was no more than a causeway six feet broad from the house, subsequently Hercules Clay's, at the western corner of the market-place, to the south porch of the church. At this time there was a cross in the centre of the market-place near to which in the pavement were inserted the initials of Webster's name and the date of his work, viz. H. W., 1619.

In the British Museum there is a paper, bearing date during her Majesty's reign (1589), which contains a complaint from the quarter sessions at Newark to Lord Burghley against the conduct of a saltpetre maker. For many years the manufacturers of this useful commodity were a source of great annoyance to the people. Saltpetre was made from the soil of slaughter-houses, stables, and even the floors of dwellings. Being regarded as a national requirement, on account of its use in the manufacture of gunpowder, the "saltpetre men" were armed by the law with full powers to excavate upon private premises in order to obtain the necessary material. The authority they possessed paved the way for extortion. It made them generally regarded as "troublesome fellows," and gave rise to numerous com-

[1] Dickinson.

HOW SALTPETRE WAS OBTAINED.

plaints and disputes. The document in the British Museum to which we refer indicates that the inhabitants of this district felt they had a grievance which needed removal, and they addressed themselves to one associated with the borough to try to obtain a remedy. The petition runs as follows:—

> To the Right Honorable oure verie good Lorde, the Lorde Burghley, Lorde Highe Threasiror of Englande.
>
> Righte honorable, our humble dewties to your good lordshippe premised : may it please the same to be advertised that at the quarter sessions, holden at Newarke, within this countie of Nottingham, there was a generall complaynte made unto us by the whole countrie that one John Ffoxe, saltpeter maker, had charged the whole countrie, by his precepts, for the caryinge of cole from Selsma, in the countie of Nottingham, to the towne of Newarke, within the same countie, being sixteen miles distant, for the making of salpeter, some tounes with five cariages, and some with lesse ; or else to give him four shillings for evrie load, whereof he hath receved a greate parte : uppon which complaynte we called the same John Ffoxe before some of us at Newarke, at the sessions there, to ansuere the premises, and also to make us a propocition what loades of coles would serve to make a thousand weight of salpeter, to the end we might have sette some order for the preparing of the same ; but the saide Ffoxe will not sett doune anie rate what would serve for the makeinge of a thousand. Therefore, we have thoughte good to advise youre good lordshippe of the premises, and have appoynted the clark of the peace of this countie of Nottingham to attend your lordshippe to know your lordshippe's pleasure about the same, who can further inform your good lordshippe of the particularities thereof, if it shall please your lordshippe to give him hearinge : and so most humblie take oure leave.—Newarke, the 8th October 1589.

WILL. SUTTON.	RO. MARKHAM.
NICHS. ROOS.	RAUF BARTON.
JOHN THORNHAGH.	BRIAN LASSELS.

We are not able to ascertain what course his lordship took, but that "saltpetre men" were troublesome for very many years after is amply witnessed by the records that remain. In the year 1626 complaints so loud and general were made that the subject was brought under the notice of Parliament. Amongst the documents at the House of Lords is the draft of an Act "for the preservation of the mine of saltpetre, and increase of the means for making saltpetre, and for the ease of the subject from the grievance they now bear by digging their houses and taking their carriages by petre men. Great grievances (it went on to tell) are now suffered at the hands of the makers of saltpetre, who dig up barns and cellars, and impress carts and horses, to the great loss of farmers and others." The Act, however, does not appear to have come into operation. On the contrary, saltpetre was felt to be a commodity of such increasing service, that in 1627 the king issued a proclamation on the subject. The proclamation stated that the saltpetre makers (notwithstanding the facilities afforded them) were unable to supply the nation with a third part of the saltpetre required, especially in a time of war. It directed, therefore, that John Brooke and Thomas Russell, who had discovered how to make it by a new process, should have power to go from house to house to collect the animal fluids, once in twenty-four hours in summer, and once in forty-eight hours in winter ; and the inhabitants were ordered to save the fluids for their use. It is believed by some historians, that so strict were the laws relating to saltpetre, that corporate bodies were compelled at their own charge to maintain works, so that it might be manufactured from the refuse of their several localities. Whether this was the case or not, it is certain that in the papers of many corporate bodies, bearing date during this period, references to "saltpetre men" occur. Amongst the records of the corporation of Newark we find the following:—24th July 1637. Received of Mr. Thomas Smith for increase of provisions for his Majesty's household, and for the *saltpetre man for this part of the country;* for carriage and other charges concerning the same, and for repairing of the county hall, and for repairing of Laine Bridge for the town of Newark, £3 : 7 : 6, (signed) WILLIAM POCKLINGTON." At length, in 1656, an Act was obtained, forbidding saltpetre makers from digging in houses or enclosed lands without leave of the owners, and the subsequent discovery and importation of rough nitre from the East Indies made "saltpetre men" unnecessary, and rid the country of a long-standing source of serious inconvenience.

The following grants of land during Queen Elizabeth's reign are copied from the Patent Rolls:—

28 Elizabeth, Part 14.

Grant to Jones and Brathwick : pasture in Barber's closes, containing half acre in the tenure of William Waite or his assigns.

29 Elizabeth, Part 2.

Grant to Adams and Butler : one toft in the tenure of Edward Brothering, belonging to Barton St. Lazar.

31 Elizabeth, Part 7.

Grant to Coppinger and Butler : site of the free chapel of St. Leonards', Nr. Newark or hospital, with the advowson of the same.

42 Elizabeth, Part 29.

Grant to Best and Holland, in consideration of money: the rectory of Newark, with all rectorial tithes, the advowson of the vicarage excepted.

On the accession of James the First Newark was honoured with a visit from his Majesty. In his journey from Edinburgh to London to take possession of the throne, he passed through Nottinghamshire. Near to Worksop a band of hunters, dressed in forest uniform, and having with them all the requisites of the chase, advanced to meet him, and gave him a hearty reception. The king was agreeably surprised at the proceeding, and agreed to delay his journey in order to join with them in hunting—a pastime to which he was ardently devoted. The day was accordingly spent in amusement, and his Majesty found plenty to interest him within the confines of "merrie Sherwood." The next day he proceeded through Southwell to Newark. At the former place the chapter, in full canonicals, assembled to greet him, and he was shown through the church, at the size and beauty of which he expressed his surprise. Hearing some of the attendants speak of it in disparaging terms, he exclaimed emphatically, "Vary weel, vary weel, but by my blude this Kirk shall justle with York or Durham, or any Kirk in Christendom."

It was on the 21st of April 1603 that King James arrived in Newark. He was received with great ceremony by the Corporation, and was presented with a large silver gilt cup, for which he expressed his sincere thanks. Mr. John Twentyman, subsequently an alderman of the borough, delivered a congratulatory address in Latin, and it was a composition of so scholarly a character that the king, who is stated to have been a man of cultivated literary tastes, was highly delighted with it. To show his appreciation of Mr. Twentyman's loyalty and ability, he conferred upon him the distinction of "purveyor of wax for the royal household in the counties of Nottingham, York, Lincoln, and Derby." Before leaving, the king desired to hear the address again, and Mr. Twentyman went through it a second time for the gratification of his Majesty. The name of the speaker, however, did not suit the royal ears. James was told that the scholar was a Twentyman, whereupon he ejaculated that he must be a traitor, for the Twentymans pulled down Red-Kirk in Scotland. Subsequently, reflecting that coincidence of name is no criterion for coincidence of thought and feeling, he withdrew his prejudice against Mr. Twentyman, and never visited this district without inquiring after that gentleman's welfare.

Another incident that occurred whilst the king was in Newark does not speak so well for him. It was an act of despotism, if not of cruelty, and set an example of disregard for the law which no king should exhibit before his subjects. A pickpocket was detected attempting to rob one of the spectators at the royal pageant, and he was brought before his Majesty, who immediately ordered him to be hanged. It was urged that the man ought to have a fair and proper trial according to the laws of the country, but James was inexorable. The sentence was carried out, and the man lost his life without the opportunity of making a defence.

In "a true narrative of the entertainment of his royal Majestie from the time of his departure from Edinburgh till his receiving at London," etc.,[1] we have some further details of the proceedings at Newark. We read that "the 21st being Thursday, his Highness tooke his way towardes New-warke-upon-Trent, where that night he lodged in the Castle, being his owne house, where the aldermen of Newark presented his Majestie with a faire gilt cup, manifesting their duties and loving hearts to him, which was very kindly accepted. In this toune and in the court was taken a cut-purse,[2] doing the deed, and being a base pilfering theefe, yet was a gentleman like in the outside. This fellow had good store of coyne found about him, and upon examination confessed that he had from Barwick to that place plaied the cut-purse in the court. His fellow was ill mist, for no doubt he had a walking mate; they drew together like coach-horses, and it is pitie they did not hang together; for his Majestie, hearing of this nimming gallant, directed a warrant presently to the recorder of New-warke to have him hanged, which was accordingly executed. This bearing smal comfort to all the rest of his pilfering facultie, that the first subject that suffered death in England in the rayne of King James was a cut-purse, which fault if they amend not, heaven sodainly send the rest. The king ere he went from New-warke

---

[1] A scarce tract printed in London in 1603, and quoted in Nichol's *Progresses of James I.*
[2] The purses hung from the girdles in those days.

as he had commanded this silken base theefe in justice to be put to death, so in his benyne and gracious mercie, he gives life to all the other poore and wretched prisoners, clearing the castle of them all. This deed of charitie done before he left New-wark, he made these knights,—Sir John Parker of Sussex ; Sir Robert Bret of Devonshire ; Sir Lewes Lewkener of Sussex ; Sir William Mumperson (Richard Momperson) of Bucks ; Sir Francis Ducket of Shropshire ; Sir Richard Warburton of Cheshire ; Sir Richard Wigmore of Herefordshire ; Sir Edmond (Edward) Foxe of Shropshire, and Sir William Davenport of Cheshire. The 22d day being Fryday, his Majestie departed from New-warke toward Bever Castle, hunting all the way as he rode, saving that in the way he made four knights ;" including Sir William Sutton and Sir Roger Askoth, sheriff of Nottinghamshire. Several historians have censured the king for the peremptory way in which he dealt with the cut-purse, condemning the man without trial, and upon his sole warrant. Rapin says : "It cannot be denied that this was beyond the power of a king of England, and directly contrary to the priviledges of the English nation." It is probable his Majesty was warned what the ill effects of such unusual proceedings would be, seeing that he never repeated them ; and endeavoured to leave a reputation behind him, not for severity, but for gentleness and mercy, by setting all the other prisoners in the town at liberty. The warrant for releasing the prisoners at Newark was in the following terms :—

JAMES KINGE.

Sheriffe, Undershcriffe of Nottinghamshier, Alderman of our Towne of Newark, and your deputies, we greet you hartylie well. Whereas we of our Princely power and authoritie doe relese and pardon all prisoners, savinge for wilfull murder, debt, and recusance ; we therefore will and requier you to let at libertie all prisoners detcyned within your jurisdiccion, savinge William Woodroffe, Vincent Brambley, and John Wetherhead, whom you shall deteyne in close prison. It is our will also that fower honest men of good conscience and judgment be chosen as our commissioners, whoe shall conforme to the dett and abilitie of the dettors, giving them dayes of payment, without takinge any forfeitures of their handes, and to take such securitie as the said dettors can give ; and as we pardon the felonie, the fees to be likewise pardoned, that in defect thereof they be not deteyned longer prisoners ; and this out of our Princely and Christian commisseracion we graunt this pardon, willinge you as our officers to effect the same, wherein you doe us good service, keepinge this warrant one of you for the reste, whoe shall exacte the same. Newark, the 22d day of April 1603. The names of the commissioners Ric Hurte, Mayor, Archer Jackson, Humfrie Bouer, Aldermen of Nottingham, Olliver Widdrington, preacher there.

I request and requier you, in his Majestis name, to use noe delaye in the relesinge of the said dettors in forme aforesaid. Will. Hunter.

It is somewhat singular that the commissioners should have been chosen from Nottingham. "The townsmen of Newark were not apparently trusted," adds Mr. Nichols in a footnote ; but why they should not have been, it would puzzle any one to decide. It could not be because they had not found favour with the king, seeing that he kindly accepted their present, and was so far delighted with Mr. Twentyman as to confer upon him the dignity of purveyor of wax, for we presume it was considered a dignity, whatever the duties of the office may have been. Whilst at Newark the king wrote two letters, copies of which we append. The first, it will be seen, is to the Receiver of York for payment of 100 horse on the borders, and the other to the Council at Carlisle for suppressing outrage:—

Mr. Scudamore,

Trustie, etc. Whee for repressing of certain lewd people, who uppon the Confynes of o^r realmes of England and Scotland haue of late comitted fowle disorders, we haue appointed fiftie horsemen of o^r ordinary garrison of Barwick and fīte others newly leuied by the lord of Johnston to attend uppon o^r west march for the prosecution of them, who we order forthe from o^r Prissoners at Carlisle by reason of the late spoyles of the County, are not able to continew in service wthout an augmentation of wages; we haue therefore thought good to require you out of such o^r means as are in yor handes to pt as well unto the lord of Johnston or his assignes for his fiftie he also to the fiftie of o^r garrison of Barwick an increase of pay of eight pence sterls by the d^{te} above the ordinary eight pense accustomed to be allowed unto them, so as the pay of each horse may be for the tyme of this service sixteen pence sterls. The same to take begining from the viijth day of this month of Aprill, and to continew during o^r pleasure. And if you haue not in y^r handes so such of o^r moneys (above that wch is to py o^r ordinary of Barwick and the rest of the borders) then we require you to pay out of y^r own or to borrow so m^{ch} as will suffice for this charge from tyme to tyme. And we will take order you shall be paid it again at London, or allowed it uppon ye accompt according to the acquittances wch for the receipt of the part of this increase you shall haue from the Captains or others who shall receaue the same.

Endorsed 1603, 21 April, To ye Receauor of York for pay of 100 horse on the borders, written at Newarke, Sent from Bever Castle.[1]

Right reverend father in God & o^r right trustie and right welbeloved we haue perused y^r tres sent to us from Carlisle by these two gentlemen, and likewise such instructions as writen you gaue them to be imparted to us, and we haue both heard them o^r selfe and caused them to be heard by our Councell. And forasmuch as to us and to o^r sayd Counsell it seameth upon the most important point of yor tres and instructions we had before giuen direction from Yorke, which when you wrott those tres had not come to you We haile it with saffitie that you for the present be admonished to proceed espetially against those lewd persons as will be in y^r hands as others, accords to those o^r directions sent from Yorke, and so from tyme to tyme you advertise us of yor doings by wch yor advertisements if it shall appeare unto us that the directions already prescribed be not sufficient to remedy the mischief committed, wee will adde thereunto from tyme to tyme what further we shall aduise to be necessary. And you will hauve by reason of the spoyle of the County the horses used there as well as of o^r garrison of Barwick advertized. Lord Johnston's are not able to come to prosecute the service we haue answered their party from eight pence sterls to sixteen pence, and given direction to o^r Receavour of the County of Yorke to pay them after that rate from the [2] dth of this month dui^{rn} o^r pleasures of whom if you cause the Captains to demand an increase of them they shall receaue the same.

Endorsed 22 Aprill, To ye Councillers at Carlisle for repressing outrage, dated at Newarke.[3]

On leaving Newark, after his short but pleasant stay in the borough, King James proceeded by rapid stages to London, to assume the reins of Government. At this time the nation was divided into three great parties. There were the Episcopalians, the Romanists, and the Puritans, and all of them were hoping to secure the favour of the new monarch. In 1604, at a conference at Hampton Court, the king plainly indicated his preference for the Episcopal form of worship. "No bishop, no king,"

---

[1] *State Papers*, Domestic Series, Jas. I., vol. i. No. 45.
[2] Illegible in the original.
[3] *State Papers*, Domestic Series, Addenda, Jas. I., vol. 35.

was his favourite expression, and with this he parried the arguments of the Puritans, who strove to convince him to the contrary. The conference not only elicited the bias of the king's mind; it had a greater and more enduring result. It gave rise to a new translation of the Bible. Forty-seven ministers were appointed to undertake the work. It occupied them three years, and ended in the issue of the noble version which we use at present, and at the commencement of which the address of the translators to his Majesty may be seen.

Though busy with ecclesiastical controversies, the king did not entirely lose sight of the Newark people, by whom he had been entertained with such enthusiastic loyalty. On the Patent Roll for the second year of his reign, there is the record of a new charter granted to the burgesses of the borough.[1] The principal provisions are as follows :—(1) Confirmation of the charter of 15 July, 21 Eliz.; (2) The aldermen of the borough to have power to constitute any of the inhabitants to be their deputies, when absent by illness; (3) The recorder, aldermen, or their deputies, to be Justices of the Peace in the borough; (4) No county or other Justice of the King to have jurisdiction in the borough; (5) The aldermen or their deputies to have power to issue all warrants for any crime, including murder; (6) No alderman or his deputy, or any of the inhabitants of the borough, to be put on any assize or inquisition held out of the borough; (7) Grant to the corporation of a hall called the "King's Hall," in the parish of Newark, with power to them to make therein such by-laws as they think proper for the good of the town; (8) Grant to the corporation of the right to assess the inhabitants, and tax them for such rates as may be necessary for the expenses of the borough; (9) Power given to the corporation to admit any one to exercise any art or trade in the borough; (10) Confirmation to the corporation of all their Property held under any previous charter from the Crown. It is dated by the king at Westminster, 23d July, in the 2d year of his reign.

The Episcopalian tendencies of the king, to which we have referred, were a source of great annoyance to the Romanists. They produced anger and discontent, and it was not long before both these feelings were manifested. In a fit of wild passion, a plot was formed for destroying the two Houses of Parliament (1605). Gunpowder was laid in the cellars underneath, and, as every one knows, Guy Fawkes, a Spanish officer, was entrusted with the task of firing the deadly train. The preparations were diabolical and carefully arranged. Parliament was to receive a terrible blow, and not to know the hand from which it came. Providence, however, ordered it otherwise. The secret was broached, the plot discovered, and the conspirators disbanded. Several were seized at the time; others fled into the country, and were subsequently brought to justice.

Amongst those who escaped for a while and afterwards suffered was Henry Garnett, a superior of the Jesuits, who was by birth a Nottinghamshire man. Mr. Bailey believes him to have been connected with the Whalleys of Screveton, near Newark, and says that he changed his name first to Darcy and then to Garnett, to

[1] Patent Roll, 2 James I. Part 9. The Roll on which it is written is partly injured, and the writing very difficult to make out.

avoid being known as a descendant of that staunch old Protestant family. That he did alter his name seems evident. The judge who tried him said he was "a man of many names, but of no good name." At an early age he went to Rome to be educated, and there his association with the Jesuits commenced. He was acquainted with the object of the plot, and was familiar with its details. On its failure he sought refuge at Hindlip House in Worcestershire, where he was secreted in a chimney. The house was searched by the king's order, and after considerable trouble the hiding-place was discovered. The refugee had marmalade and sweetmeats by his side, but his chief source of maintenance had been by means of a reed passed through a small hole in the chimney. Through this reed, broth and nutritious drinks were conveyed to him, and his life was thereby sustained. After his trial he confessed to a knowledge of the plot, but denied that he participated in it. He was executed on a scaffold erected at the west end of St. Paul's church. He appears to have been a man of considerable acquirements. Sir John Coke made the remark, that "he was endowed by God and nature with many gifts and graces, if the grace of God had been joined with them." Unfortunately his talents were not used as they should have been, and he suffered a sad penalty for a want of that discretion and self-control which are often as absent in the learned as in the illiterate.

In 1609 Newark tolls were ordered to be leased at a rental of eight pounds per annum, and a fine of thirty pounds. The wages of the head master of the Free Grammar School were fixed at £20, and those of the usher at £10.

In 1612 the king paid a visit to Sherwood, attended by a large retinue. He rode from Belvoir to Newark on the 10th August, staying one night at the castle. Here he renewed his acquaintance with alderman Twentyman, and departed, "hunting as he rode."

On the 23d October, in the ninth year of King James's reign, William Bethell, by indenture, gave £10 to the alderman and his assistants of the borough of Newark, to be placed at interest, to be applied for the following principal objects, namely:—6s. 8d. to be paid to the vicar for preaching a sermon once a year, and 13s. 4d. to be distributed yearly amongst the poor. The charity is endowed with 1-96th part of net rents derived from lands at East and West Laughton, Lincolnshire. The ordinary yearly income of the charity amounts to 18s. 1d., and the net income is now applied in payment of 1-3d of the amount of net rents to the vicar, and the remaining 2-3ds are distributed amongst the poor in coal.

In 1613 there died abroad Henry Constable, a son of Sir Robert Constable of the Spittle, Newark. Among the sonneteers who flourished in the reigns of Queen Elizabeth and King James I., Henry Constable deservedly occupies a prominent place. The estimation in which his poems were held by his contemporaries is evidenced by the numerous editions of them which were called for during his lifetime, and the fact that they have been reprinted several times in the present century, shows that they have not yet been wholly forgotten by his fellow-countrymen. Mr. Thompson Cooper, F.S.A., in an able article on Constable and his career,[1] says there

---

[1] *Register and Magazine of Biography*, January 1869.

is no room for doubting that he was Henry Constable of Newark, in Nottinghamshire, even had we not the direct testimony of his contemporary, Roger Dodsworth, the Yorkshire antiquary, who, in enumerating the principal branches of the Constable family, names "Sir Robert Constable, Lieutenant of the Ordnance to Queen Elizabeth, sometime of the Spittle in Newark,[1] father of H. Constable that was banished for religion." Sir Robert Constable served in the wars in Scotland, under the Earl of Surrey, by whom he was knighted in 1570. "He was," continues Mr. Cooper, "like Puttenham, one of the gentlemen pensioners, and like him also, a man of ruined fortunes. Like him also, he was nearly allied to several noble houses, a circumstance which was not forgotten by his son Henry, when he obtained from Sir William Segar a certificate of his descent, as was the custom in those times of persons going abroad. This certificate sets forth that the mother of Sir Robert and grandmother of Henry was Catherine, daughter of Sir George Manners (Lord Roos) sister of Thomas, Earl of Rutland, and niece of King Edward IV., by his sister Anne, Duchess of Exeter. Sir Robert Constable, thus nobly descended, married Christiana, daughter of John Dabridgecourt of Astley or Longdon Hall, in the county of Warwick. This lady was descended from the Lanches Dabridgecourt, who had given protection to Queen Isabella, and who was admitted into the Order of the Garter on its first institution. She was the widow of Anthony Foster. As he is described of Newark, it may be assumed that Sir Robert Constable acquired his estate there in consequence of this marriage, and it seems not unlikely that Foster was the person of that name who was unfortunately concerned in the death of Lady Robert Dudley (Amy Robsart). Sir Robert was a writer as well as a soldier, there being among the MSS. in the British Museum a treatise by him on the ordering of a camp, written in 1576."

Of the birth and early education of Henry Constable comparatively little is known. He is believed to have been born in 1562. On the 11th of June 1578 he matriculated as a fellow-commoner of St. John's College, Cambridge, and proceeded to the degree of B.A. in pursuance of a special grace; January 15, 1579-80. Becoming a convert to the Church of Rome, he went on the Continent; and in the course of his travels visited Italy, Poland, and the Netherlands. In 1591 Sir Robert, his father, died in debt to the Crown, and Henry sold the Newark property to William Cecil, grandson of Lord Burghley, and afterwards Earl of Exeter. In 1592 he issued a small quarto volume entitled "Diana; the praises of his mistres in certaine sweete sonnets by H. C." The lady for whom Constable expresses in his verse an ardent though a hopeless passion, is believed to have been Lady Penelope Devereux, afterwards Lady Rich, and eventually the Countess of Devonshire. The work, with additions and alterations, was republished in 1594, 1597, and 1604. A complete edition of Constable's poems was prepared in 1859, and published under the efficient supervision of Mr. William Carew Hazlitt. In 1595 Constable was at Paris, and whilst there he arranged with the Papal Legate to proceed to the Scottish capital, in company

---

[1] Sir Robert's name will be found mentioned in a lease which we print a few pages farther on.

with the Laird of Bonington, to persuade King James to grant a toleration of the Catholic faith throughout his dominion. "It was thought" (says Mr. Cooper), "that a man of versatile talents like Constable, might be able to practise on the king's mind, and induce him to forsake the Protestant religion for the ancient church to which his ill-fated mother (Mary, Queen of Scots) had been so devotedly attached." The errand, however, was a fruitless one, and Constable retired into Arragon. In 1604 he was confined a prisoner in the Tower, but released towards the end of the year; and constrained to seek refuge abroad. In three years' time he returned to his native land, when he was again arrested and imprisoned. On regaining his freedom, he took up his abode in Paris. In 1613 he was sent to Liege by Cardinal du Perron, to confer with Dr. Benjamin Carier, a new convert to the Romish creed. Whilst at Liege he was seized with illness, and died October 9, 1613. So ended the chequered career of a remarkable Newark man; a man of natural genius and of considerable attainments. In the quaint words of one familiar with him, "he was a great master in English tongue," and had "as pure, quick, and high a delivery of conceit as any gentleman of our nation."

The "visitation" of the borough made in 1569 by Wm. Flower, Norroy King of Arms, was continued by Richard St. George, in 1614, with other enlargements by John Withie, 1631. In the visitation of Notts we have the following :[1]—"The towne and borough of Newark-vppon-Trent, within the county of Nottingham, was incorporated by E6 in the 3 yeare of his rayne, by the names of one alderman and xij. assistants. Queene Elizabeth, in the 21 yeare of her most happy rayne, gaue the authoritye to haue a recorder, making the alderman and the recorder Justices of Peace and quorum, and 4 of the society and ffraternitye to be Justices of the Peace, exempting them 13 from all manner of seruices whatsoever in the county; and lastly, our most gratious souerayne lord King James, in the 2 year of his raigne, did not only confirme all fformer graunts made by his predecessors, the kings and queenes of this land, but also of his most princely disposition towards the town, exempted all the inhabitants thereof from all manner of forayne seruices whatsoever, gieuing them full power to purchase lands and make such orders and laws as should be thought by them more conuenient for the better Gouernment of the towne, hauing both arms and a comon scale belonging thereonto. And at the time of this visitation was Mr. Henery Webster, alderman, and these following recorder and assistants, viz., Mr. Gervas Molineux, recorder, Edmond Metheringham, Peter Key, John Twentiman, Bartholomew Martyn, John Browneley, John Noble, Richard Birketts, Thomas Jennyson, Robert Good, Christopher Haselam, Richard Hering, and John Methringham, John Brownley, coroner."

His Majesty, who had taken a great fancy for visiting among his subjects, was at Newark for one night in 1614. In the Nottingham corporation records, there is this entry: "Mr. Rockett required to go to Newark to-morrow (August 9) to observe the manner of his Majesty's entertainment there." On August 8, 1616, he was at

[1] Published by the Harleian Society.

JAMES I. AGAIN AT NEWARK.

Newark again, and he paid a fourth visit on April 7, 1617, travelling from Lincoln, where he had been enjoying himself to his heart's content. Among the sports which he patronised in the cathedral city was cock-fighting. An old chronicler [1] tells us that he went to the sign of the George by the Stone Bow to see the battles fought. He caused four cocks to be put into the pit, and it "made his Majesty very merrie." From thence he went to the Spread Eagle to see a trial of skill between a fencer of the city and the servant of one of the attendants at Court, who had challenged the city men. "His Majesty called for his porter, who called for his sword and buckler, and gave and received a broken pate and other bad hurts." The other sports and pastimes included horse-racing and hunting, and a race by hunters. On leaving Lincoln the mayor and his brethren attended upon the king, who gave them his hand to kiss, and told them that if God lent him life he would see them oftener. The sheriffs in their gowns, and carrying white staves, and accompanied by a number of men with javelins, went before the king as far as the end of Bracebridge, when they likewise took their leaves. The high sheriff of Nottinghamshire received his Majesty at the farther end of the bridge, and conducted him on his journey to Newark.

Like some of his more noted predecessors, King James was often short of funds. To augment his means he sold the honour of knighthood. It became a kind of stock-in-trade. For a thousand pounds a cavalier could buy the title of "Sir," and about two hundred of them did so. This demoralising barter has been not unfairly attributed more to necessity than to choice. On one occasion James was particularly clear in showing his feeling with regard to it. A person presented himself who had no claim to the honour save from the length of his purse. Approaching the king he held down his head. "Raise it up, man," said his majesty, "I have more need to be ashamed than thee." The extent to which the granting of undeserved dignities had grown, and the frivolous way in which the king permitted his friends to nominate men as barons or knights, is well illustrated in a letter written from Lincoln by Mr. Chamberlain to Sir Dudley Carleton, and dated 5th April 1617.[2] Mr. Chamberlain says, "the king goes this day to Newark. The Lord Hay is yet here plotting where to get his two barons the king has bestowed on him, whereof Sir Edward Carr of Lincolnshire is named as one. Abercrombie, a Scottish dancing courtier, hath gotten likewise the making of two Irish barons, and the dignity of baronet has not yet become so bare but there are lately come in one Egerton of Cheshire and Townshend of Norfolk."

In 1619 a Mr. Chapman bequeathed to the then alderman of Newark and his assistants, and to the vicar of Newark and his successors, certain messuages in Appleton Gate, for the accommodation and maintenance of four poor widows. The charity is endowed with the following properties, viz., £6 : 4s. land tax derived from Laughton estate ; £5 : 16 : 7, land tax derived from Stone and White's estates ; £3 : 6 : 10, land tax derived from Bathley Grange ; 14s. land tax payable by Jonathan Bradley's

---

[1] Quoted by Mr. Nichols in his *Progresses of James I.* [2] *State Papers.*

representatives; and £100 £3 per cent consols invested in the names of the official trustees of charitable funds. The ordinary yearly income of the charity amounts to £19 : 1 : 5, and consists of land taxes and dividends on consols as before stated. The net income is applied for the benefit of four poor widows, each being paid at the rate of 1s. 9d. per week.

A lease of the castle and lordship of Newark was granted in 1620 to Sir Thomas Howard. The castle was described by a contemporary writer as the king's own house (see page 84), and it would appear to have gone from him to Charles, Prince of Wales, his eldest surviving son (afterwards Charles the First), whose feoffees in trust granted the lease.[1] Leases are not as a rule very entertaining reading, but we venture to insert this fully, inasmuch as it gives us a reliable record of the names of many of the occupiers of property within the borough at that period. We extract it from the Parliamentary Survey for the County of Notts.[2]

This indenture made the eleventh day of July, in the eighteenth year of the reign of our Sovereign Lord James, by the grace of God King of England, Scotland, France, and Ireland, Defender of the Faith, that is to say of England, France, and Ireland the eighteenth, and of Scotland the three and thirty, betweene Sir Henry Hobarte, knight and baronet, chief judge of his Majestys Court of Common Pleas, chancellor to the most excellent prince, Charles, Prince of Wales, Duke of Cornwall & of York, & Earl of Chester; Thomas Murray, secretary to the prince his Highness; Sir James Fullerton, master of his Highnesses wardes and liveries; Sir John Walter, knight, his Highnesses attorney general, and Sir Thomas Trevor, kt., his Highnesses controller general of the one part, & Sir Thomas Howard, kt., master of his Highnesses horse of the other part. Whereas the said Sir Henry Robarto, Thomas Murray, Sir James Fullerton, Sir John Walter, & Sir Thomas Trevor do stand and are interested, & possessed for the term of divers years yet ending of and in the castle and lordship of Newark, with the rights, members, and appurts in the county of Nottingham, late parcel of the lands and possessions of the Bishop of Lincoln exchanged whereof the several lands hereafter mentioned are to and for the only use and benefit of the said most excellent Prince Charles. And whereas the late Queen Elizabeth, in and by her three patents under the exchequer date bearing the seven and twentieth day of May, in the three and thirtieth year of her reign, did grant unto William Cecill, then Esqr., and now Lord Burleigh, Elizabeth, Lady Roos, his wife, and William Cecill, their sonn, for terms of their lives and either of them longest living successively, all that close of pasture called the uroo, with the appurts lying and being in Worham Eyrome, in the said county of Nottingham, & all that close with the appurts called Castle close lying and being in Stoke in the said county, late in the tenure of the said William Cecill, now Lord Burleigh, and the said Lady Roos, his wife, or their assigns. And whereas also the said late Queen Elizabeth by three patents under the exchequer seal bearing date the eighteenth day of May, in the said three and thirtieth year of her reign, did grant unto Isabel Countess of Rutland the said William Cecill, Esqr., now Lord Burleigh, and William Lord Roos, for term of their lives and the longest liver of them successively, all the fishing of Boisthorpe lying and being within the lordship of Boisthorpe, in the said county of Notts, with appurts. And whereas also the said late Queen Elizabeth in and by her letters patent under the great seal of England, bearing date the nineteenth day of November in the four and thirtieth year of her reign, did grant unto the said Lady Isabel, Countess of Rutland, the said William Cecill, Esquire, now Lord Burleigh, and William Lord Roos for term of their lives respectively, all those three tenements with appurts situate laying and being in the market-place, Newark, in the said county of Notts, late in the tenure or occupation of Thomas Neucombe

---

[1] We find from the Patent Rolls that it was granted to Charles in 1613.
[2] In the Augmentation Office, No. 20.

under the haull called the Motehall, and also divers other messuages, tenements, tolls, and fishings in the tenure of divers persons hereafter in this present grant mentioned in the said last recited letters patent testified and confirmed since which time the Elizabeth, Lady Roos, Isabel Countess of Rutland, and William Lord Roos are all deceased, and the said William Lord Burleigh is now lawfully interested and possessed for term of life only for all and singular the premises and appurtances in the several fore recited letters patent granted by right of survivorship, as aforesaid.

Now this indenture witnesseth that the said Sir Henry Hobarte, Thomas Murray, Sir James Fullerton, Sir John Walter and Sir Thomas Trevor, by command and warrant of the said most excellent Prince Charles, for and in consideration of the good & acceptable service heretofore done and hereafter to be done unto his Highness by the said Sir Thomas Howard, have granted, and to farm letten, and by these presents do grant, and to farm let unto the said Sir Thomas Howard all that the said close of pasture called the uroo with appurts lying and being in Worham Eyrome aforesaid, in the said county of Notts, and all that close with appurts called the Castle Close lying and being in Stoke, in the said county, now or late in the tenure of the said William Cecill, now Lord Burleigh, and Elizabeth, Lady Roos, his wife, or their assigns, with all and singular appurts, and also all that the castle and site of the castle of Newark aforesaid in the said county with all and singular the rights, members, and appurts whatsoever in the said county of Notts, and all and singular houses, edifices, buildings, barns, stables, dovehouses, yards, orchards, gardens, cellars, halls, chambers, entries, ground and soil, and all other easments, profits, commodities, advantages, emoluments, and heredits whatsoever, with their appurts whatsoever within the walls, site, precinct & circuit of the said castle of Newark, late in the tenure or occupation of Isabel, Countess of Rutland or her assigns ; and also all that piscarie and fishing of Boisthorpe lying and being within the lordship of Boisthorpe, in the said county, with appurts whatsoever, late in the tenure or occupation of the said Lady Isabella, Countess of Rutland, or her assigns, with all and singular appurts, and all those three tenements with appurts sit being and lying in the market-place in Newark in the said county of Notts, late in the tenure or occupation of Thomas Neucombe under the haule called the Motehall, and all that other tenement with appurts late in the tenure of Thomas Hobman ; and another tenement there, late in the tenure of Peter Stowe the younger ; and two tenements or cottages or loft and crofte in Newark aforesaid in a place called the brigg, late in the tenure or occupation of Stephen Johnson ; and four other tenements in Newark aforesaid in a certain street called the Barre gate, that is to say one tenement with a garden, late in the tenure or occupation of John Mercer ; and other tenements with a garden in the street aforesaid, late in the tenure or occupation of Nicholas Gardener ; and other tenement with a garden there in the street aforesaid, late in the tenure or occupation of John Wilkinson ; and one other tenement with a garden in the street aforesaid, late in the tenure or occupation of Richard Erwyn ; and one tenement with a garden in the street aforesaid, in the tenure or occupation of Thomas Wynne without the Barre gate aforesaid ; and one close of pasture there called Great Dyleton ; and one other close of pasture there called Little Dyleton, late in the tenure of Christopher Jenyson ; one close of pasture there over against a certain land called Rutland on the west part, late in the tenure of Richard Standish ; and one other close of pasture there over against the land aforesaid towards the east in the tenure or occupation of Robt. Lubbe ; and one other close of pasture there, late in tenure or occupation of Robert Butcher ; one other close of pasture called the Sandpit close, late in the tenure of William Harrison ; one other close of pasture there called the Great Close late in the tenure of Sir Robert Constable, knt. ; and two closes of pasture there called the pigge lease, lately inclosed out of wast lands, late in the tenure of Bryan Holston ; & two other closes of pasture there out of the said waste lands likewise enclosed in the tenure of William Brockbank & Robt. Bell ; and one other close of pasture there likewise out of the said waste lands inclosed late in the tenure of Thomas Williamson ; and one other close called the Milne close in Newark aforesaid in the tenure of John Goodfield ; and one other close of pasture called the Milne close, late in the tenure of Nicholas Boothe ; and one other close of pasture in Newark aforesaid called the Little Milne close, late in the tenure of

Reynold Hapton; & one other close there in a certain place called Barbar close, late in the tenure of John Mercer; & one other close of pasture called the Well-pitt-head, late in the tenure of Nicholas Gardener; & one other close of pasture there called the lyott in the tenure of John Mercer; & one other close of pasture in a certain street called Milne Gate, late in the tenure or occupation of Hugh Delcine; & one other close of pasture there late in the tenure of Walter Ward; and two other closes of pasture lying & being in the territory of farnedon and within the parish of Stoke, in the county aforesaid, whereof one of them is called Badinge, late in the tenure of Thomas Waite, & the other called Beane lands, late in the tenure of Thom Baffe; & one other close of pasture called the Conygree, together with the warren of Conyes within the parish of Stoke aforesaid, late in the tenure of the Lady Isabel, Countess of Rutland; and one other close of meadows lying and being within the parish of Stoke aforesaid called the Thistle close, late in the tenure of Luke Ottes; & two wanges of meadow lying and being in the territory of farnedon aforesaid, & within the parish of Stoke aforesaid in a certain meadow called the Colney meadow; and one other close of pasture lying and being within the parish of Stoke aforesaide, late in the tenure of William Brockbanke, between the Conygree & the Castle Close; & one other close of meadow there, late in the tenure of the said William Brockbanke; & one other close of meadow there called the barnyards in the tenure of the said William; & one other close of pasture in the parish of Stoke aforesaid, lying and being between the Thistle Close, Conygree, and Colney meadow, late in the tenure of William Marhall; & one wong of meadow, called honeywong, lying & being within the territory of farnedon, in the parish of Stoke aforesaid, late in the tenure of Bryan Houlston; & one piece of pasture called Ellete meare, lying and being in the territory of farnedon & in the parish of Stoke aforesaid, late in the tenure of the said Bryan Houlstone; & one other piece of meadow lying & being in the territory of farnedon aforesaid & in the parish of Stoke aforesaid, called the Grymeholme, near Newark aforesaid, late in the tenure of the said Bryan. Also seventeen wonges of arable land lying & being in the fields & territories of Newark & Northgate; & one piece of meadow lying & being in the meadow of Newark aforesaid, in a certain place called the Norking; & one piece of land, called the forty acres, lying & being in Norking aforesaid; & one other piece of meadow lying & being in the meadow aforesaid, called the five acres piece, late in the tenure of Edward Brotherick; & two other pieces of meadow lying and being in the meadow aforesaid, called the three acre, late in the tenure of Richard Standish; one other piece of meadow in the meadow aforesaid, called pond acre, late in the tenure of the said Richard Standish; & also one other piece of meadow in the meadow aforesaid, called Bounde acre, late in the tenure of the said Richd. Standish; one other piece of meadow lying & being in the meadow aforesaid, called the mantle bound acre, late in the tenure of the said Richard; also fishing in the river of trout under the castle of Newark aforesaid; & in other several fishings late in the tenure of John Goodchild; & also fishing in the water of Devon from the bridge called Marcall Bridge, unto the end of the town of haugton, late in the tenure of the said John Goodchild; & also two pieces of wast ground in Newark aforesaid, late in the tenure of hugh allen; & all that toll called the day toll or passage toll in Newark aforesaid, late in the tenure of Thomas Wynne; also picage & stallage of the marketplace in Newark aforesaid, late in the tenure of John Mercon; & also the market toll of cattle, that is to say of oxen, sheep, and hoggs in Newark aforesaid, late in the tenure of Reginald Hapton; & also the markett toll of horses called the horse market, & the toll of carriages, & carters bringing iron ware to merchandize, & the drift of hoggs once a year in Newark aforesaid, late in the tenure of Andrew Hatrett; & one piece of land called the beast markett hill where the market is kept every Wednesday, & was kept for cattle in Newark; & one other piece of land there called the corn market holden the same day in Newark aforesaid; & two islands in osiers or sallowes in the territories of farnedon, within the parish of Stoke aforesaid, late in the tenure of John Goodchild; & also the site of Mannor or capital messuage of Balderton, near Newark, aforesaid, called the manor of Balderton & twelve exchanges of lands, meadow and pasture to the said late or capital messuage of the manor aforesaid, appertaining or belonging, late in the tenure of Henry

LEASE OF THE CASTLE AND LORDSHIP.

Holcrofte, gentleman; & all & singular houses, edifices, building, barns, stables, pigeon-houses, orchards, gardens, crofts, curtilages, lands, tenements, meadows, pastures, feedings commons, waters, watercouses, poundes, pools, bankes, streams, fishings, fishing places, profitts, comodities advantages emoluments & heredits whatsoever to the same premises any way belonging to or appertaining with all & singular appurts (all great trees, woods, under woods, wards, marriages, mines & quarries, coming, growing, renewing, or being in or upon the premises, or any part or parcell thereof out of his present demise, & grant allways excepted & reserved) To have & to hold the said castle & scite of the castle of Newark aforesaid, & all other the several messuages, lands, tenements, hereditaments & premises with appurts (except before excepted) unto the said Sir Thomas Howard, his executors and assigns from the day of the date of these presents, for & during the term of fourscore & tenne years from thenceforth next & immediately following, fully to be compleated & ended if Thomas Howard & Charles Howard Elgmok sons of the said Sir Thomas Howard or either of them, shall so long live yielding & paying therefore yearly, during the said term the several ancient yearly bank following— viz., for the said castle & scite of the castle of Newark with appurts fifty three shillings & four pence of lawful money of England; for the said fishing of Boisthorpe the yearly rent or sum of sixteen shillings of lawful English money; for the said pasture called the uroo, & Castle close in Worham & Stoke the yearly or sum of forty shillings of lawful English money; & for all other the residue of the premises above mentioned to be demised the yearly rent or sum of three score & four pounds of lawful English money—viz., for the said messuage, lands, tenements, cottages, closes, crofts, gardens, medows, feedings, pastures, closes, rents, fishings in the water of Deven, tolle, pannage, herbage, islandes, osiers, shallows in Newark, Nortegate, farnedon, hawton, Worham, Balderton & Stoke aforesaid, & in the fields of the same the yearly rent or sum of twenty-six pounds thirteen shillings and four pence; for the fishings under the castle of Newark three pounds; for the said pasture called Tolney twelve pounds; for the said warren of conies forty-six shillings and eight pence; for the said scite of the manor or capital messuage of Balderton with appurts four pounds; & for the said toll & farm of the toll sixteen pounds at the feasts of St. Michael the Archangel, & the annunciation of the blessed Virgin Mary for even & equal portions, the first payment thereof to begin at the first of the said feasts which shall next happen after the date of the surrender, forfeiture & other determination of the estate for life of the said William, Lord Burleigh of & in the premises. And also yeilding & paying upon & after the death of either, the said Thomas Howard & Charles Howard, sons of the said Sir Thomas Howard the sum of six pounds of lawful English money, for & in the name of a herriott. Provided always that if the said several yearly rents or any part or parcell thereof be behind & unpaid in part or in all after any of the said feasts in which the same ought to be paid by the space of eight & twenty days, or if the said sum of six pounds referred in the name of heriot be not well & truly satisfied & paid within six weeks next after the death of either of the said Thomas Howard and Charles as is aforesaid, then this present lease & grant to be void & of no effect, anye thing herein contained to the contrary in any wise notwithstanding. And the said Sir Thomas Howard for himself, his heirs, executors, administrators, & assigns doth covenant & grant by these presents to & with the said Sir Henry Hobarte, Thomas Murray, James Fullerton, Sir John Walter, and Sir Thomas Trevor & assigns, that he the said Sir Thomas Howard for himself, his heirs, executors, administrators shall and will from time to time during all the said term at his and their own proper costs, charges, well & sufficiently repair, mend maintain, uphold & keep the said castle & all the other messuages, tenements & cottages in & upon the premises or any part or parcell thereof, & also all the hedges, dithes, fences, mounds, banks, shores & sea walls belonging to the several lands before demised; & all the same so sufficiently repaired & amended, hedges, ditches, fences, walled & inclosed in the end of the said term shall leave & yield up, he the said Sir Thomas Howard, his executors & assigns, having and taking in & upon the premises competent and sufficient house boote if any shall be spent & employed in & upon the premises only, & not elsewhere to be had & taken by the assignment of the Steward of the said manor, or deputy for the time being & not otherwise. And shall & will also within the two years next after the death of the said William, Lord Burleigh, & also after every tenne years during the said terme make & deliver or cause to be made & delivered unto his Highness or his heirs, or the commissioners of his Highness's revenues for the time being, being a true, certain & perfect extent and terrah of the said several premises distinctly & particularly setting forth the true number and quantity of acres of the same, and the butalls & boundaries thereof, and in the whole possessions, they shall then contain; and shall and will also, within one year, next, after the death of the said William, Lord Burleigh, certified by note in writing under his or their hand & seal, unto his Highness, or heirs or the said commissioners of the revenues for the time being, the true number of all such trees, timber, & trees like to be timber as are & at the death of the said William, Lord Burleigh, shall be standing & growing in & upon the premises, & particularly in what grounds the same do grow, & the same trees other then such as shall be allowed for the competent house boote in manner aforesaid, shall maintain & preserve from felling, spoil & destruction during the said term; and in the end or other determination of the said term to leave the same growing upon the premises; and shall & will allow also in every year during the said term, plant & set the number of twenty trees of oak, elm, or ash in or upon some part of the premises, & the same shall likewise preserve and leave growing upon the premises at the end of the present grant & demise. And further, that neither he the said Sir Thomas Howard, his executors, administrators, or assigns shall or will during the said term plow or tear up any of the meadow ground or ancient pasture grounds, parcell of the premises, but the same shall continue as now they are. And lastly, that neither he the said Sir Thomas Howard, his executors, administrators or assigns, or any of them, shall or will at any time during the said terme let, allow, sell or assign the premises or any part thereof for longer time than three years without the speciall license or consent of him or them, which shall have the immediate reversion of the premises first had and obtained in writing, except it be by devise in his last will & testament to his wife or some of his children.—In witness the said Sir Henry Hobarte, Thomas Murray, Sir James Fullerton, Sir John Walter and Sir Thomas Trevor, whereof to the one part of these indentures *By warrant of the said most excellent Prince Charles* have set their hands and seals, and to the other part hereof remaining with the said Sir Henry Hobarte, Thomas Murray, Sir James Fullerton, Sir John Walter, and Sir Thomas Trevor, the said Sir Thomas Howard hath set his hand and seal the day and year first written.

The constant visits of the king to the country districts and the festivities attendant thereon, together with the cost of conveying his Majesty and his retinue, began to be regarded as a somewhat serious burden. The matter seems to have been mentioned to his Majesty, especially with regard to the cost of vehicles, for we find that in 1621 he addressed a letter to the deputy-lieutenants and justices of the peace, setting forth how ready and anxious he was to give ease to his subjects, as to the charge of carts for his removals. He desires them, therefore, to agree amongst themselves as to the best method to be adopted to save expense and trouble, stating, at the same time, that so far as his hunting-parties are concerned, he will pay for the carts himself. The following corporation for "provision for the king's household" in the midland counties, 1622, is from the coucher book of the corporation of Newark.[1]

We weare at Lecester upon the xvii. day of August to treate with the Comissioners, who weare then there, to compound with the counties for all manner of provisions for his Majesty's household, and for cart taking. After long debate concerninge the same, we thought it good and profitable for the

---

[1] Communicated by the late Mr. W. E. Tallents to Mr. Nichols, F.S.A.

countrie to compound in regard that wee shall save some of that which the countrie formerlie paid, and be freed from all the rest. That which the countrie paid yearely to purveyors for beefes, muttons, and porkes amounted to £232 : 13 : 4, beside that which was paid for waxe and for butter yearelie ; and we have compounded to paie but £240 for all theis, and therein to be freed from takinge of carts, single horses, wheate, malt, pullen, and all other things, soe that, if this £240 be duelie paid, the countrie shall be freed from all kinds of takinge. And the rather wee are induced to compound for that Leicestershire then compounded the same daie, and divers other counties have formerlye compounded ; so that wee sawe that those counties that will not compound, wil bee wholy burdened with takers and the rest freed. The articles and condicions agreed upon we haue sent to the Justices of the Peace to be condescended to and subscribed ; and those that like not thereof must signifie in writing their dissent. Wee do conceave that there is true and plaine dealing in the commissioners who did well satisfie us in all doubts. It wilbe expected that everie Justice of the Peace sett downe in writing his likinge or dislikinge of the condicions thereof; and that it be speedilye sent from one to another to the end that the commissioners may have speedye notice of the countries likinge which wee have promised to send to them very shortly and thus we rest, your loving frendes,

Leicester, the 17th daie of August, 1622.   HEN. SACHEVERELL, JOHN WOODE.
I like well these articles, & doe give my consent.—W. BURGHLEY.
I doe agree to these articles.—THO. HUTCHINSON.
I doe agree to theis articles.—JOHN BYRON, W. COOPER, JO. THORNHAGE.
I doe thinke they have done very well, and like very well of it.—JOHN DIGBYE, R. PIERREPONT, RO. SUTTON, FOULKE CARTWRIGHT.
I like well these articles, and consent thereunto.—R. STANHOPE.

By indenture, dated 19th December 1623, John Lilly, enfeoffed Robert Outram and Launcelot Thompson in a messuage called "Bathley Grange," in Bathley, in trust for the alderman and assistants of the borough of Newark, and their successors, to be disposed of among the poor children working in the Jersey school, and in default of such school, to be applied towards the relief of the poor of the said town. The charity is endowed with the following properties, viz., 63a. 1r. 14p. of land situate at Bathley, Notts, let to a yearly tenant at the annual rent of £126. The net income is now applied in stockings purchased from Stone's charity, and in bread, coals, and money (the money being paid to "Chapman and Ellis's" widows) and distributed to the poor of the town.

The king visited Sherwood Forest for the last time in 1624, passing through Newark on the 8th of August. A curious incident is mentioned in reference to the final visit. Sir Thomas Wentworth, afterwards Earl of Strafford, thus writes, in a letter to a friend :—" I will write you news from the Court at Rufford, where the loss of the stag and the hounds hunting the foxes instead of deer put the king, our master, into a marvellous chafe, accompanied with those ordinary symptoms better known to you courtiers, I conceive, than to us country swains. In the height whereof comes a clown galloping in and staring full in his face. 'S'blood,' quoth he, 'am I come forty miles to see a fellow?' and presently in great anger turns about his horse and away he goes faster than he came, the oddness whereof caused his Majesty and all the company to burst out into welcome laughter, and so the fume for a time was happily dispersed." There is no wonder that the countryman was disappointed. James had nothing comely in his personal appearance. He was rather repulsive than attractive.

He was of middle stature, corpulent, his eyes large and ever rolling, his beard thin and his tongue too large for his mouth. His legs, also, says one writer,[1] were very weak, so that at seven years of age he could not walk or stand alone, which weakness made him ever leaning on other men's shoulders, and when he walked it was with a kind of circular motion of his limbs. We can imagine that the appearance of such a figure would somewhat startle the countryman, who had expected to see a Saul amongst the people.

Soon after the departure of his Majesty, a serious fire broke out in the forest, which darkened the air as far as Newark, and caused considerable alarm. A writer who was visiting his friends at Newark at the time, has left on record an account of the disaster,[2] in which he states that it commenced on Monday, the 23d August (1624). It had been a dry season, and the fire was caused by some ill-slaked charcoal that was being carted away, falling among the ling. About noon the bracken, ling, and trees, for a great distance were in flames, and the wind carrying the smoke towards Newark "it made such a greet mist in the aire, that it did darken the sonne withall." The writer goes on to say that many people in Newark came out of their houses, greatly wondering at such a sudden and fearful sight. Most, he says, "did coniecture it to be the sonne in the cliptes, and others said noe, it smelt like fire; the which proufed the most true-ste, for presently vpon came ther commande from the justeses to rayse the cuntery ther aboute, and to bringe pickaxes, spades, and shouelles, to make dikes and trenches to breeke the fire in the forreste: And such a fire as was never knowne in manes memory; beinge 4 mille longe, and a mille and a hallfe ouer all at once: And had it not plesed the Lorde to turne the winde at an instant when it was sesinge vpon a greet and longe wood that was betwene Mancefellde and Nottinggame: which if it had taken houllde, but the Lorde prevented it, which to my knowledge which afterwards I did see, did run up vnder the hy trees above a stone's cast, which if it had got vp into the bowes and branches of the greet trees, it was thought it would have burnt up all the cuntry before it, as far as Nottingegame." The deer in the forest, it seems, escaped the flames, and were seen collected together for mutual protection, for the writer tells us, that "ridinge on his way through the forrest homeward, he saw of the other side of the selfesam hill, a greete herde of faire red deere, and amongst them 2 extreordanary greet stages, the which he never saw the like."

Amongst the miscellaneous references to Newark during the reign of James in the calendars of *State Papers* are the following:—They are not generally of much interest, but it may be useful to give them for the purpose as well of reference as of information. 1605, Nov. 20, grant to Brian Taylor of the office of post-master of Newark for life. 1607, March 13, grant to Gilbert, Earl of Shrewsbury, of the office of constable and steward of Newark and forester of Sherwood for life. 1609, May 29, petition of the alderman, etc., of Newark to Salisbury, for decision on a bill exhibited against

---

[1] Sir Anthony Weldon.
[2] MSS. in the British Museum, quoted in Mr. Robert White's *Worksop, the Dukery and Sherwood Forest*.

them in the exchequer, by the late Countess of Rutland, and now by Lord Burghley concerning rights of tolls and stallage in the market of Newark, with order thereon. 1610, May 16, petition of the alderman and corporation of Newark to Salisbury, and Sir Julius Cæsar, Lord Burghley, and others, commissioners for survey of the bridges and king's hall at Newark; having certified the necessary repairs, they request that order be taken for the same. Annexed is Lord Burghley, and others report to the Court of Exchequer of the survey of the above places and estimate of the cost of repairs. 1620, October 15, Newark, commissioners of Musters of Notts to the council, stating they have completed, trained, and exercised the footbands; but many who were summoned to supply the defects of the horse, do not appear. The names of the defaulters are transmitted. 1622, May 1, letter from Newark of the justices of Notts to the council, stating that they cannot make out the schedule for contributions to the Palatinate by the day appointed. 1623, June 9, Lady Mary Leeke of Newark to Secretary Conway; trusts to his favour and that of the Countess of Exeter, to protect her against her adversaries. In spite of Mr. Leeke's great age, his understanding is perfect, but his self-will threatens to ruin her and her son. She hopes Hawton may be cleared from all incumbrance of debt, etc. On the Patent Roll, dated 11, James the First (part 23), is the record of a grant to William Whitmore of *five water* mills, the tenure of Lord Burghley and *two fulling mills*, parcel of the manor of Newark, late possessions of the Bishop of Lincoln. If there were five water mills, as appears by this entry, we can well understand the outcry that would be raised when an effort was made to divert the course of the stream upon which they were dependent. The beauties of the district were celebrated in verse by Bishop Corbet[1] in his *Iter Borealis*. Writing of a ride between Nottingham and Newark, with special reference to Flintham, which he much admired, the bishop says:—

> We are for Newark after this sad talk,
> And thither 'tis no journey, but a walk;
> Nature is wanton there, and the highway
> Seemed to be private, though it open lay,
> As if some swelling lawyer for his health,
> Or frantic usurer to tame his wealth,
> Had chosen out two miles by Trent to try
> Two great effects of art and industry:
> The ground we tread is meadow fertile land,
> New trimmed and levelled by the mower's hand,
> Above it grows a rock, rude, steep, and high,
> Which claims a kind of reverence from the eye;
> Behind them both there slides a lively stream,
> Not loud but swift: Meander was a theme
> Crooked and rough; but had those poets seen
> Straight, even Trent, it had immortal been:

---

[1] Richard Corbet, D.D., an English divine and poet, raised successively to the bishoprics of Oxford and Norwich; author of a spirited "Narrative of a Journey to France," and of various other poems; born 1582, died 1635.

> This side the open plain admits the sun
> To half the river which did open run;
> The other half ran clouds where the curled wood,
> With his exalted head threatened the flood;
> Here I could wish us ever passing by
> And never past; now Newark is too nigh,
> And as a Christmas seems a day too short,
> Deluding time with revels and good sport;
> So did this beauteous mixture us beguile,
> And the whole twelve being travelled seemed one mile.

The bishop also adverts to the parish church, telling us that "Newark for light and beauty might compare with any."

On the accession of Charles I. an effort was made by the borough to secure additional privileges. On the 22d May 1626 the alderman and assistants presented a petition to the king, praying for a new charter of incorporation, and setting forth the privileges which they desired it should contain.[1] Attorney General Heath reported in favour of the petitioners, recommending that, with one exception, all their desires should be granted; and on the 24th May he received instructions to prepare a bill for the king's signature, in conformity with his report. The new charter having being prepared, received the royal assent, and was forthwith forwarded to the alderman and assistants. It is dated July 1, 1626, and gives to the borough the privilege of appointing a mayor and a recorder. We present a summary of its provisions:—

The charter begins by describing Newark-upon-Trent as an ancient and populous town, and after mentioning the charters and privileges previously granted, continues thus:—"Whereas we are informed that by reason of the situation of the said town upon the river of Trent, the traffic of the said town continually increases, and by reason of the vast plenty of corn and fruits, and other commodities growing in the country thereabouts, which are carried by water for the supply of other parts of this our realm, and by reason also of the great concourse of passengers to the said town travelling from our city of London and other southern parts into our kingdom of Scotland and other parts of the north, the said town is become much more populous now than it has been in times past, and will, therefore, require some more special method of government. . . . Therefore, being minded that from henceforth for ever hereafter there shall be in the said town continually one certain and undoubted method of and for the keeping of our peace, and for the good rule and government of our people therein, and of others coming thereinto; and that the said town shall for ever hereafter be and remain a town of peace and quiet, to the terror and discouragement of evil doers, and a reward to those that do well, and that our peace, and other acts of justice, may be there kept and observed without further delay; and hoping that if they and their successors shall by this our more extensive grant enjoy their franchises, authorities, liberties, and privileges, that then they will hold themselves obliged to do to us, our heirs and successors, the more special and vigorous service; we, out of our special grace and favour, etc., declare and grant that the said town be, and shall for ever hereafter be, a free town of itself." The alderman and assistants are then declared a body corporate by the name of the mayor and aldermen of the town of Newark-upon-Trent. Henry Gill is named the first mayor of the town, and John Brownlow, John Noble, Thomas Jenison, Christopher Haslam, Peter Smith, John Jenison,

---
[1] *State Papers*, Domestic Series.

Thomas Hobman, William Middlebrook, John Stanidge, Henry Clifton, Christopher Wilson, and Robert Outram, the first and original aldermen. The mayor is to be elected on the Day or Feast of St. Michael the Archangel, each year; if he die, or is removed by the aldermen ("for we will," says the charter, "that the said mayor not behaving himself well in his office, or for any other reasonable cause, shall be removable at the pleasure of the aldermen of the said town or parish for the time being, or the major part of them"), another shall be appointed within seven days; on the death or removal, under similar circumstances, of an alderman, another is to be elected within a convenient time after; if the mayor is sick he is to appoint a deputy; a recorder is to be elected; a court of record may be held every Thursday before the mayor, recorder, and aldermen, or three or more of them; no sheriff is to enter except in default of the mayor; the mayor, recorder, and four senior aldermen are appointed Justices of the Peace, and power given to punish offences in the borough; a gaol is to be erected for offenders; the mayor to be clerk of the market, and have the perquisites of the office; a coroner is to be elected; the mayor appointed escheator;[1] a common clerk exercising the duties of clerk of record and clerk of the peace is appointed, Thomas Bullar being nominated as the first; power is given to appoint four officers, called sergeants-at-mace, to attend upon the mayor, and to bear before him maces of gold and silver engraved and adorned with the signs of the arms of England; also to appoint a fit and discreet person as scavenger; and to elect constables. It is directed that all penalties and forfeitures shall be used by the mayor and aldermen, who are exempt from serving at assizes, or on juries and inquisitions; and who have power to call upon all and every inhabitant of the town, of whatever state or condition, and having had them "arrayed, armed, and fortified," to cause them to keep watch and ward day and night for the safer custody, guard, and defence of the town. Any one refusing to obey is liable to imprisonment. The town is to have two seals, one to be kept by the mayor, and the other by the town-clerk; and the last-named is to take recognisances of debtors. All fairs and immunities heretofore granted and enjoyed are confirmed, "albeit the same, or some, or any of them, have or hath heretofore been disused, abused, or discontinued, and albeit the same, or some, or any of them, have or hath been forfeited or lost."

In the following year (1627) Mr. Jno. Wood, of Woodborough, was, under the provisions of the new charter, appointed recorder of Newark. This gentleman was the eldest son of Mr. Robert Wood of Lambley, and grandson by the maternal side of Sir Robert Montague, Lord Chief-Justice of England. He was one of the verderers of the forest of Sherwood, as appears by a petition to King James I. signed by himself and three other persons—Christopher Strelly, Launcelot Rolleston, and Gervase Wylde—to have their rights to certain trees and a few deer restored to them, which had lately been withheld. He married Kathleen, one of the daughters of Richard Hewson of London, merchant, by whom he had issue seventeen children.

Charles, on assuming the reins of power, did not find himself in the happiest of circumstances. His marriage with the Princess Henrietta of France, a Romanist, tended to alienate the Puritans. They looked upon the new queen with suspicion and mistrust. Hence they were not disposed to accord to the throne any great amount of confidence or affection.[2] Whilst his wedding offended the Puritans, his want of means led him to adopt measures that irritated other classes. An expensive Spanish war was in progress, and it needed considerable funds to sustain it. To raise the money Charles summoned a Parliament. He asked them for a liberal sub-

---

[1] The duty of an escheator was to make inquests of trial by escheat. It was an ancient office, and formerly of great use to the Crown.   [2] Confirmed by Hume, vol. vii, p. 65.

sidy, but they made only a very moderate grant, and in his perplexity and chagrin the king dismissed them in three weeks. A second Parliament met in 1626, but it rendered itself equally objectionable to the king, and was dissolved before it had concluded a single Act. To supply his necessities, his Majesty resolved on adopting "new counsels." He and his advisers declared that as the urgency of affairs admitted not the way of Parliament, the most speedy, equal, and convenient method of supply was by a general loan from the subject. Commissioners were appointed to levy the loan, and they were armed with great inquisitorial powers. Among other articles of secret instruction given to them, they were enjoined that "if any shall refuse to lend, and shall make delays or excuses, and persist in his obstinacy, that they shall examine him upon oath whether he has been dealt with to deny or refuse to lend, or make an excuse for not lending? who has dealt with him, and what speeches or persuasions were used to that purpose? and that they also shall charge every such person in his Majesty's name upon his allegiance, not to disclose to any one what his answer was."[1]

Some, notwithstanding the implied danger, endeavoured by reasonable excuses to exonerate themselves from the infliction. Diana, Countess of Oxford, writing to the council from Newark, Oct. 30, 1626, states that the lords have required of her payment of the first entire subsidy of £6 : 13 : 4. The late lord, she says, "set over" his whole estate for the payment of debts, so that she has neither lands nor goods, and only depends on the goodness of her parents. But from the majority of persons in Newark the loans were more easily obtained. The commissioners reported to the council (June 7, 1627) that they had sent up in April, by Mr. William Sturtevant, all money lent by Newark to the king, and that "no person fit to lend refused." The mayor also wrote a similar letter (Sept. 29), stating that "no subsidy man refused to lend."[2] In other parts of England, many persons not only framed legitimate excuses, as the Countess of Oxford had done, but, regarding the proceeding as obnoxious, unwarrantable, and unconstitutional, boldly refused the loans. By warrant of council, they were thrown into prison. Soldiers were billeted upon private houses, the refusers of the loans being specially burdened with the most unwelcome of the guests, and some "of low condition," who had been refractory, were pressed into the service.[3]

For a third time the representatives of the people were gathered together. This was in 1628, and at a period when forced loans, benevolences, taxes without the consent of Parliament, arbitrary imprisonments, the billeting of soldiers, and martial law had produced a strong feeling throughout the country. The commons voted the king a supply, but they determined, before it passed into law, to erect a barrier against further encroachments on their rights and liberties. The celebrated Petition of Right was accordingly framed. To this the king reluctantly assented, and whilst the commons were discussing the subject of tonnage and poundage, declaring it illegal to levy them without the consent of Parliament, he ordered a prorogation.

[1] *Rushworth*, vol. i. p. 419. [2] *State Papers*, 1627-28.
[3] *Rushworth*, vol. i. p. 419; *Hume*, vol vii. p. 101.

On the 20th January 1629 a new Session of Parliament was opened. The principal topic of debate was the old grievance, that of tonnage and poundage. The king was advised to maintain his right to levy these dues, and Parliament, on the other hand, fully intended that no impost of any kind should be laid upon the people without their sanction and consent. A remonstrance was drawn up by Sir John Elliot, to be presented to his Majesty, and handed to the clerk at the table. That officer refused to read it, whereupon Sir John read it himself. The question was coming to a vote, when the Speaker declared he had a command from the king to adjourn. The announcement created an uproar, for the commons were wrathful and resolute. The Speaker was held in his chair by two members, whilst a short remonstrance was framed and passed amidst tumultuous applause. The king in haste despatched the Gentleman Usher of the Lords to the excited Chamber. The members locked the door, and he could not enter until the business was finished. He then removed the mace from the table;[1] Parliament was dissolved; and till 1640 his Majesty did not see fit to require the counsel of the representatives of the people.

Amongst the varied controversies of the period, the religious one concerning fatalism and free will had come prominently to the front. "The first reformers in England, as in other European countries, had," says Mr. Hume, "embraced the most rigid tenets of predestination and absolute decrees, and had composed upon that system all the articles of their religious creed. But these principles having met with opposition from Armenius and his sectaries, the controversy spread to this country. The Armenians finding more encouragement from the superstitious spirit of the Church than from the fanaticism of the Puritans, gradually incorporated themselves with the former; and some of that sect, by the indulgence of James and Charles, had attained the highest preferments in the hierarchy." With the public their success was not so great as with the Church and court, and the commons levelled against them formidable censures. The subject was generally debated throughout the country and the utterance of strong opinions was the result. In a communication from Lord Keeper Coventry to Secretary Dorchester (1630) there is enclosed a letter from the justices of assize for the county of Nottingham, concerning scandalous words, alleged to have been spoken by one Thomas Bullar, town-clerk of Newark. The enclosure states that "Thomas Bullar was charged to have said at Newark, after Christmas last, that my Lord of Holland had got a great office, and he prayed God he had not sold his conscience to get that office; that the king himself was no divine, and that all or most of his Majesty's council were Armenians or Papists." The language was alleged to have been spoken to James Levett; and both Levett and Bullar were cast into prison; the former for omitting to inform the mayor of the words that had been spoken. Levett was afterwards discharged on his bond to appear, and Bullar was ordered for his offensive expressions to give sureties for his good behaviour, and to appear at the next assize.[2] On pretence of pacifying the disputes which prevailed

[1] *Rushworth*, vol. i. p. 660; *Whitlock*, p. 12; *Hume*, vol. vii. p. 161.
[2] *Calendars of State Papers*, 1629-31.

orders were issued from the council forbidding on both sides all preaching and printing with regard to the controverted points. But they were not carried out with impartiality, and therefore were worse than useless.

The utterance on any subject, whether religious or political, of language disrespectful to the great was regarded as a most serious matter, and it involved many unwary persons in difficulties besides the town-clerk of Newark. Clarendon tells us[1] that a waterman belonging to a man of quality, having a squabble with a citizen about his fare, showed his badge, the crest of his master, which happened to be a swan, and thence insisted on better treatment from the citizen. But the latter replied that he did not trouble his head about that goose. For this offence he was summoned before the Marshall's Court, was fined for having opprobriously defamed the nobleman's crest by calling the swan a goose; and was in effect reduced to beggary. Morley was fined £10,000 for challenging and striking in the Court of Whitehall, Sir George Theobald, one of the king's servants.[2] So great a care being taken of the nobility and royal attendants, it was not surprising that words reflecting on the king and savouring of disloyalty should be readily seized upon; and sometimes, on very slight evidence, men were compelled to make elaborate explanations. A gentleman who was subject to much inconvenience through the strict rules that prevailed, was John Beresford of Eagle Hall, near Newark, who, through the unsupported assertions of a servant girl, had to take steps to clear himself, and to satisfy the council that he was truly loyal to the king. In his evidence, taken before two Justices of the Peace,[3] he stated that on the 2d of July (1635), he was at the house of John Monson, Esq., in company with Mr. Monson and Thomas Markham, son of George Markham of Ollerton. Monson asked him "What news at Newark?" where he had been the day before; to whom he replied that he knew no news, but there was mustering and training, and that Mr. Gervase Markham, a kinsman of Thomas Markham, had one of the best horses that were there shown. Thereupon Thomas Markham inquired when they should train in Lincolnshire, and he answered, on the Tuesday following. Markham observed that they had mustered in the south long before, to which he replied that he thought the muster was general. Markham said he had heard there was an order that every earl should be charged with twelve light horse for the king's service; every lord with eight, and so on in proportion. Examinant thereupon fell into commendation of the Earl of Exeter and Lord Newcastle for having in their stables so many able horses for service, but did not name any other lords. In a letter of July 8 Beresford protests to the council that he never had any disloyal thoughts, but should be ever ready and willing to spend his life and fortune in the king's defence against any foreign power or treasonable attempt. On July 13 Thomas Markham of Ollerton was examined on the same subject before Archbishop Neile of York at his manor-house of Southwell. He fully confirmed Beresford's statement as to the conversation that passed, adding that Beresford asked him

---

[1] *Life of Clarendon*, vol. i. p. 72; *Hume*, vol. vii. p. 200.   [2] *Rushworth*, vol. ii. p. 270.
[3] *State Papers*, 1635.

THE LEVYING OF SHIP MONEY.

"What news of Sir William Monson, their countryman?" who was at sea. He said he had heard that Sir William had caused twenty fiddlers to be pressed, six of whom he had taken into his own ship, and further, examinant said he conceived they meant to be merry on board. Being told that a "wench" named Kirby Mossman had reported certain words relative to this conversation, he protested there were no such words spoken, and that, as he hoped to be saved, he was far from such disloyalty. Hearing that the "wench" (Mossman) who stood at the door had made such a report, he went to Mr. Gervase Neville to clear himself. The explanations probably warded off any legal proceedings, but the severities of the Star Chamber in many cases occasioned much comment and discontent. "In order," says Mr. Hume, "to account for the subsequent convulsions, even these incidents (severities) are not to be overlooked as frivolous or contemptible."

A method of taxation to which the king resorted when he had dispensed with the services of Parliament was that known as ship money. The first writs had been issued to seaport towns only, but in 1634 and subsequent years it was levied upon the whole kingdom. In some places the burden, coming at a time of such national perplexity, could with difficulty be borne. At Newark it was not an easy matter to meet the demands that were made. The town was assessed in 1636 at £120, and with all their energy, the authorities were only able to raise £50. On May 28, 1637, the sheriff of the county wrote to the council on the subject,[1] stating that Newark had offered to pay £50, if they might be discharged of all the rest, and suggesting that Retford might very well pay £50 instead of £30, and Newark thus be eased of £20. This was followed, on September 6, by a letter from the under-sheriff, James Webster, stating that Newark had only paid the £50, and the mayor alleged the disability of the town to contribute more than that sum. Mr. Webster added: "There is indeed no trading in the county except in some market towns; but the country people mostly live by husbandry and hard labour."[2] The council, not heeding the plea so graphically put before them, made an effort to obtain the full amount. On September 18 they wrote to the mayor, saying they understood from the sheriff that the town was £70 behind in its contribution. "His Majesty," they added, "has commanded us to require you to finish your collection, and to pay in the same by Michaelmas next, as you will answer your failing herein before this board." In compliance with the peremptory order of the council, the mayor renewed his exertions, and appears to have succeeded in reducing the deficiency to rather less than one-third. On the 29th January 1638 Sir John Lascelles (late sheriff) writes to the council: "I have lately received your letter for £30 unpaid of ship money for 1636. Of this sum £20 is due from Newark, but having called on the mayor for the same, he alleged that the Earl of Berkshire should pay £10 thereof, he having at Newark the castle and mills with the tithes of corn and hay; neither he nor his tenants have paid anything for ship money that year, for I spared assessing the earl and his tenants, conceiving the said premises to be within the precincts of Newark." In the *State Papers*,

[1] *State Papers*, Domestic Series.   [2] *Ibid.*

from which we glean this information, is a letter dated December 3, from Secretary Nicholas to the Earl of Exeter, in which he says the mayor of Newark has signified that having demanded of the earl's servants £3 : 6 : 8 assessed on the earl in that town for ship money, he was answered that the earl would pay the same in London as he did last year. The secretary prays the earl to order the same to be paid to the mayor, who only can give discharge, and it will be an inducement to others of the town to pay their assessments. A similar letter was sent to the Earl of Berkshire for payment of £6 : 13 : 4. Launcelot Thompson, mayor of Newark, writing to Sir Francis Thornhagh, sheriff, March 24, 1638, says:—"I think it will never be my fortune to see you at Fenton. This day I purposed to be there, but the gentle smith has pricked my horse so that he is not able to stir; nevertheless I have sent you by my son £66 : 13 : 4, and for the other £13 : 6 : 8, viz., the Earl of Exeter £3 : 6 : 8, and the Earl of Berkshire £6 : 13 : 4, and Squire Leeke £3 : 6 : 8; I have demanded it in their absence of the servants, and they say that their lords will pay it at London, as they did all the rest. Mr. Leeke is not guilty of much money, neither hath he anything to distrain. You must return him, as the other sheriffs did, and they will make him pay." The Earl of Berkshire subsequently paid all that was due from him for an acquittance in full is filed, dated January 29, 1639. The Earl of Exeter wrote to say that he did not belong to the town, but to the county. The town people assessed him, but they did it for their own case.

We have a more vivid illustration of the difficulties that beset the collection of the tax in a petition presented to the council (June 30, 1637) by John Bradley, constable of North Muskham. Bradley stated that he was charged to levy on Dorothy Caldwell 50s. ship money, and after many denials he required Squire Randall, an inhabitant of the parish, to aid him in making a distress. The Squire was at first willing to do so, but being dissuaded by John Coude, attorney-at-law, refused, whereupon petitioner alone took the distress; Coude, however, interfered, and the rest of the inhabitants, being by him dissuaded, refused to pay. Petitioner reported the matter to the sheriff, and Coude having notice of this, in open market at Newark, endeavoured to assault petitioner, and being prevented, broke out into these words, "Sirrah, you have preferred a petition against me to the council table, but I will make you glad to wait my leisure."[1] Petitioner prayed that the council would call Coude before them. The difficulties that had been encountered in raising the money in Newark would appear to have led the council to reduce the assessment in 1637 and 1638. The reduction, however, considering the impoverished state of the people, was not deemed sufficient; for we find a petition sent to the council towards the end of the last-named year by the poor inhabitants of Newark, "asking for further relief."[2] The petitioners say that the town being incorporated, is taxed at £45 towards the ship money, which sum the sheriff intends to lay upon the town, not having power to mitigate the same. The petitioners set forth their inability to pay the amount, and pray direction to the sheriff or any other

[1] *Calendar of State Papers.*   [2] *Ibid.*

thought fit to examine the truth of the information they give respecting their poverty, and that after such examination the sheriff may lay a moderate and equal tax upon them. In response to this appeal, the council directed the sheriff to ease Newark, and to levy more on the body of the county.

But though there was discontent at the levying of ship money and other grievances, it is probable affairs might have continued without serious disturbance had it not been for Scotland, which Mr. Hume describes as a country that was more turbulent and less disposed to submission and obedience. Charles, attached to the ecclesiastics, raised many of the Scotch prelates to the chief dignities of the State. Canons for establishing ecclesiastical jurisdiction were promulgated, and a liturgy imposed, copied from that of England. These proceedings were regarded as most offensive. A covenant was prepared by the Scotch denouncing Popery, and binding those who subscribed to the document to resist religious innovations. A general assembly was convened, and episcopacy was declared unlawful. Forces were enlisted and disciplined, and arms were imported from other countries. To subdue the insurrection the king, early in 1639, started for the north. The command of his army was entrusted to the Earl of Arundel, and that of the navy to the Marquis of Hamilton. "While the king remained at Newcastle," writes Professor Masson,[1] " and Hamilton's fleet was in the Firth of Forth, the Scots, still anxious to avoid open war, made their last efforts for peace. Letters were addressed to Hamilton, as their countryman, requesting his mediation with the king. Letters of similar import were sent to the Earl of Essex, whose character for liberty and fairness stood as high with the Scots as with the English. Nay, the services of messengers and mediators of humbler rank were gladly used. There was, for example, a certain Dr. Moseley, vicar of Newark,[2] who, taking an interest in the Scottish movement, and wishing to observe matters with his own eyes, had gone into Scotland on a tour of curiosity. He had been going about for some weeks, and had seen a good deal of the Scottish clerical leaders, who found him a good, simple, candid kind of man, and by no means 'Canterburian' in his views. He, on the other hand, found them and their cause by no means so bad as had been represented, and professed that though he had no commission, yet, as an English clergyman, he would consider it his duty, on his return to England, 'to give the king better information about them.' To this good-natured vicar, accordingly, leaving Edinburgh for Newcastle on the 11th May, there was intrusted a supplication to the king, drawn up by Henderson in very 'submiss' terms, together with letters in 'a stouth style,' drawn up by Argyle to the Earls of Pembroke and Holland. And the vicar was as good as his word. He had reached Newcastle and delivered his letters before the 17th of May, on which day we find Mr. Edward Norgate, clerk or secretary to Mr. Secretary Coke, writing from Newcastle to Robert Reade, holding the same office to Secretary Windebank in London :[3]

---

[1] *Life and Times of Milton*.
[2] There are numerous documents bearing Dr. Moseley's signature amongst the Corporation Papers, from one of which we have copied his autograph.   [3] *Calendar of State Papers*, 1639, p. 190.

'I met with Dr. Moseley, vicar of Newark, who seems a grave and well-spoken divine. The doctor tells me, and will make it good with the loss of his vicarage, that during his fortnight's stay in Scotland, he never heard a word from any Scot savouring of disaffection to our king or nation.' As Norgate, like his master, Mr. Secretary Coke, was no friend to the war, he was pleased to hear such a report, but he could not help twitting the doctor a little. 'Seeing the doctor,' he says, 'in a very formal and canonical priest's cloak, I asked him if he durst wear that in Scotland.' The doctor told him that though he had gone a great deal amongst the Presbyterians of all ranks, and though he had been taken in some places for a bishop, yet he had received not the least affront. But the doctor's man, who was by, informed Norgate privately that his master was deaf, or else he would have had a different story to tell. The Scottish women seeing him pass in his priest's cloak, had saluted him with such ejaculations as 'If thou beest a bishop, the deil hold thy head!' 'A cauld cast on thy chaps!' or 'My malison on thee!' the doctor hearing not a word, or taking it all for compliments.'" Though the letters brought by Dr. Moseley were not without some effect, the king resolved that it would be best to try to overawe the Scots by his near personal presence; and with this object he proceeded as far as Berwick. Negotiations were then entered into, and a sudden pacification concluded, in which it was stipulated that he should withdraw his fleet and army, that the Scots should dismiss their forces, that the king's forts should be restored to him, his authority be acknowledged, and a general assembly and Parliament summoned, in order to compose all differences. Good Dr. John Moseley, who had been so energetic in his efforts, had an eye to the main chance in connexion with the settlement of the difficulty. On June 10, 1639, he wrote to Secretary Dorchester,[1] complaining of the hard measure which had been offered him on account of his propositions formerly made touching peace, and soliciting some preferment "out of the good things now in his Majesty's gift, in or near London."

In 1640, when a Parliament was again summoned, instead of proceeding to grant the king supplies, it entered upon a consideration of the grievances that existed. The subjects of complaint were classified under three heads, namely, those with regard to the privileges of Parliament, to the property of the subject, and to religion. Finding so large a field opened for inquiry, and fearing that supply might be indefinitely postponed, Charles solicited the House by new messages. To allay the alarm and mitigate the disgust which ship money had created, he informed the House that he never intended to make a constant revenue of it, that all money levied had been expended in equipping the navy, but that he would totally abolish the obnoxious impost by any law which the commons should think proper to present to him. In return, he asked for his necessities a supply of twelve subsidies (about £600,000) and that payable in three years. A warm debate ensued on the king's proposal, but it did not come to a vote; for seeing that his adherents were out-

[1] *Calendar of State Papers.*

numbered, his Majesty dissolved Parliament, and thereby fanned still further the flame of popular discontent.

Disappointed of Parliamentary subsidies, the king resorted to other expedients, borrowing from his friends, and enforcing a loan wherever it was possible to do so. Urged to once more try the effect of an appeal to the representatives of the people, his Majesty summoned a great council of peers at York. When the council met, the king, who had been assured they would insist upon a properly constituted Parliament being convened, told them he had resolved to take that course. On the 3d of November 1640 the celebrated Long Parliament met, and commenced active business. The Earl of Strafford and Archbishop Laud were impeached, and two other advisers of the king saved themselves from a similar fate by flight. On the 22d of November 1641 it was resolved in the commons, by a majority of eleven, to draw up a remonstrance, complaining of the king's previous government. Charles, believing that much of the boldness thus displayed was exhibited through his own inactivity and pliability, was advised to assume a firmer and more determined attitude. Accordingly he took the unwise step, early in 1642, of accusing Lord Kimbolton and five active members of the House of Commons of high treason. A sergeant-at-arms in the king's name demanded of the House the five members, but was sent back without any positive answer. Next day the king went in person to the house, accompanied by his usual armed retinue of two hundred men. He declared that he should proceed against the accused in the legal way, but that he must have them. The five members were not in the house at the time, and the king departed amidst cries of "Privilege." Apprehensive of danger from the temper of the multitude, who had been greatly aroused by the incident, the king retired to Hampton Court, and subsequently went to York. It was evident to all parties that a great crisis was at hand.

Soon after the king's arrival at York he heard that it was intended to remove a large quantity of arms and ammunition from Hull to London. He resolved, therefore, to visit Hull, which was under the control of Sir John Hotham, and to prevent such a proceeding. He started with several hundred attendants, and on his arrival found the gates closed against him, the bridge drawn, and the walls manned (April 1642). Sir John, speaking from the walls, told his Majesty that he durst not open the gates being trusted by Parliament. The king replied that it was not possible for him to sit down by such an indignity, and ordered Sir John to be proclaimed a traitor. Sir John, nevertheless, refused to yield; and with much indignation his Majesty returned to York, resolving to reduce the refractory town by force. That the people might fully understand his intentions, he summoned several of the trained bands to attend him at Beverley, and sent a proclamation to Parliament, intimating that if they wished the use of force to be avoided they must deliver Hull into his hands. If they conformed themselves, he would endeavour to settle the distractions that prevailed, but if they declined, "God and all good men must judge between them;" and he appointed a day on which he would expect their answer at Beverley. In the meantime preparations were in progress. The trained bands who had been drawn from Nottinghamshire were reviewed at Newark in the middle of July. An address was delivered to them by Lord Newark, of which the following is a copy.[1]

Gentlemen, and my good countrymen all.

These noble gentlemen and myself have called you together by virtue of his Majestie's commission of array directed to us. I shall acquaint you with the grounds and reasons of it, which are these, the defence of his most sacred person, of your liberties, laws, religion, and the just privileges of both Houses of Parliament. These are the ends of this commission, and of all his Majestie's actions and endeavours, they tend hither as to their proper centre and place of rest: I know herein you easily beleeve me; the least doubt cannot remain with them that have so often had his royall word, his solemne and frequent protestations to this purpose, and the word of a king is sacred as his person; what then are his solemne protestations?

I hope this is the farthest journey you shall take, and that your countrey shall be the onely spheare wherein you are to move, I am sure his Majesty heartily desires it should be so: but if there be urgent and necessary occasions that you must goe further, I will accompany you, and not any shall be exposed to that hazzard I will not be myselfe; your trouble shall be mine, your danger mine, all fortunes I will participate with you, and my care of every one of you shall be equall to that I shall have of my selfe. I should have been glad to have found anywhere such zeale and readinesse to serve the king; but rejoyce much more to find them here amongst you, my countreymen, in this place, the place of my birth and my affections. It should argue some diffidence I had of you to perswade you to obedience and loyalty to your prince, and, indeed, I should lose time in so doing, when I already see your hearts full of them; and well may they be so to him that is so carefull and tender of the good of you, so gracious a prince, as unexampled in vertues as in royalty: besides, I should but lay open my owne folly in thinking any arguments could be more prevalent and of greater efficacy with you then those I have already named, your religion, the safety and preservation of your prince, of your lawes, and liberties, and of all that is dear and near unto you; to these I may adde the faithfull keeping of those religious oaths and protestations you have taken; with whom these would not be powerfull I am sure nothing under Heaven could, no not Heaven itselfe.

I have acquainted the king, and fully, with your forwardnesse to serve him, and told him that this countrey hath beene onely remoter from his person, but as neere to him in heart as Yorkshire, and that in our dutifull affections to him we will not be second to any subjects he hath. I have no more to trouble you with: you may all now depart every one to his own home, where I pray God you may happily live and enjoy the benefit of those good lawes the care of former times hath transfered to you, and the goodnesse of his Maiesty hath bestowed, and is still ready to bestow more upon you.

To encourage the good affections of Nottinghamshire which seemed almost entirely to be devoted to his service, and to stimulate his friends in Lincolnshire, his Majesty made a journey to Newark, in July, and delivered a speech to a meeting of the knights, gentlemen, and freeholders of the county, who had assembled to greet him. The address delivered in Newark was as follows:[2]—"Your honest resolutions and affections to me and your country, for the defence of my person and

---

[1] My Lord Newark's speech to the trained bands of Nottinghamshire, at Newark, 13th July 1642, concerning His Majestie's Commission of Array. London, printed by Edward Griffin, 1642.

[2] *Vide* a pamphlet entitled "His Majesty's Two Speeches: one to the knights, gentlemen, and freeholders of the county of Nottingham, at Newark; the other to the knights, gentlemen, and freeholders of the county of Lincoln, at Lincoln. London, printed by Robert Barker, printer to the King's most excellent Majesty, and by the assignees of John Bull. MDCXLII."

the laws of the land, have been, and are so notable, that they have drawn me hither only to thank you: I go to other places to confirm and undeceive my subjects, but am come thither only to thank and encourage you: you have made the best judgement of happiness by relying on that foundation which the experience of so many hundred years hath given such proof of—the assurance and security of the law: and assure yourselves when laws shall be altered by any other authority than that by which they were made, your foundations are destroyed, and though it seems at first but to take away my power, it will quickly swallow all your interest; I ask nothing of you (though your demeanour gives me good evidence that you are not willing to deny), but to preserve your own affections to the religion and the laws established; I will justify and protect those affections, and will live and die with you in that quarrel."

After a day's stay at Newark, his Majesty proceeded to Lincoln, and thence returned to Beverley. The Earl of Holland, on behalf of the two Houses of Parliament, presented a petition to him, requesting him to forbear all preparations and actions of war, and promising that if this were done, they should be ready to "lay down all those preparations which they had been forced to make for their defence." His Majesty, in reply, requested that Hull should be delivered up to him, and that the navy should be entrusted to such as he should direct; contending that he ardently desired peace, and had taken no measures except such as were necessary for his own safety. He added that he should expect a full and positive answer by the 27th of July, till when he should make no attempt to force Hull, "hoping in the affection, duty, and loyalty of the petitioners." Having obliged himself not to proceed against Hull until the 27th of July, the king resolved to make another progress into the neighbouring counties. Doncaster, Nottingham, and Leicester were visited, the king being at Nottingham on the 21st. Returning towards Hull, he received a message from the Parliament that they could not for the present, with the discharge of the trust reposed in them for the safety of the king and kingdom, yield to the demands of his Majesty. War seeming inevitable, further preparations were made on both sides. From York the king issued a declaration, recapitulating what he described as the insolent and rebellious actions of both Houses, and forbidding his subjects to yield obedience to them. At the same time he published his proclamation requiring all men who could bear arms, to repair to him at Nottingham by the 22d of August, on which day he would set up his royal standard there, "which all good subjects were required to attend." On his journey to Nottingham, the king passed through Newark and Southwell. He was at Newark on the 17th, Southwell on the 18th, and Nottingham on the 20th.

At Nottingham he held a review of his cavalry, which then numbered eight hundred. At the close of the inspection, news was conveyed to him that under orders from the Earl of Essex two regiments of foot were marching to Coventry to take possession of that town. Charles felt it desirable either to intercept or to precede them, and without delay hastened forward with the troops under his control. He reached Coventry before the Parliamentarians, but the inhabitants closed the gates of their town against him. The king demanded admission, and sent men to enforce his demand. The Mayor refused to comply, and the burgesses fired on the soldiers. The king was much chagrined at the indignity, but not having the means to force the barricades, he retired somewhat dispirited. As one writer puts it [1]—"The unhappy retreat which looked like a defeat and the rebellious behaviour of Coventry made his Majesty return to Nottingham very melancholy."

When the king reached Nottingham, his affairs were not in a very encouraging condition. In a brief narrative of the civil wars in the midland counties, written many years ago by a Mr. Savage of Southwell,[2] we are told there was hardly an army sufficient to form a guard for the royal person. Nor were the people readily aroused. The writer says: "The countrie came in very slow, and everything wore a melancholy aspect; while daylie accounts came off the success off the Parliament levies." On the 22d of August (1642) the king, surrounded by about eight hundred horse and a small body of militia, proceeded to a part of Nottingham known to this day as Standard Hill, where the proclamation was read. It was about six o'clock in the evening when this remarkable ceremonial took place. First, the herald commenced to read the proclamation, but he had not gone through many sentences when he was interrupted. The king had some scruples as to the wording, which caused him to take the paper from the herald and examine it. Having slowly corrected several passages on his knee, he returned it to the herald, and the reading of it aloud proceeded slowly, for the man had a difficulty in understanding his Majesty's interlineations. Then the trumpets sounded and the standard was brought forward bearing the motto "Render unto Cæsar the things which are Cæsar's." But no one knew where to erect it. The sky was cloudy and the wind blew with violence. At last the standard was planted in the castle on the top of a tower after the example of Richard III., the latest known precedent.[3] The next day it was not visible. The wind had blown it down, and the occurrence was regarded by the populace as an evil omen. Mr. Savage says: "Many evil presages were said to be observed att the time off setting up the standard, but what affected the people's minds more than anything off this sort was, that the royal standard had not been raised many hours before it was blown down. It is surprising what a general damp of sorrow satt on every face after this accident, as if they understood it for a warning that the cause should never prosper. The tempest continued so great that it was the 25th [4] before it could be sett up again, and even then not in the same place, for att first it was erected on the high tower off the castle, and now in a field hard bye."[5]

At this juncture the king was prevailed upon to send suggestions for peace to

---

[1] *History of the Rebellion.* By Jacob Hooper, Esq. The work (2 vols.), to which we shall have occasion to refer hereafter, is evidently an old one, though there is no date attached. It bears the following curious imprint:—"Printed by R. Walker and T. James, and delivered *gratis* to the customers to the Cambridge Journal."
[2] Entitled *Coritani Lachrymantes*, and quoted by Mr. Dickinson.   [3] Guizot.
[4] Clarendon says it could not be fixed again for a day or two until the tempest was allayed.
[5] This account is also corroborated in the *History of the Rebellion.* By Jacob Hooper, Esq.

the Parliament. He was not very willing to resort to such an expedient, and for some time stoutly objected to do so; but the counsel of his friends prevailed. They argued it was most probable that out of their pride and contempt of the king's weakness the Parliament would refuse to treat; which would be so unpopular a thing, that as his Majesty would highly oblige the people by making the offer, so they would lose the hearts of them by rejecting it; which alone would raise an army for his Majesty: That if they should embrace it, the king could not but be the gainer, for by the propositions which they should make to him, he would be able to state the quarrel so clearly, that it should be more demonstrable to the kingdom than it yet was that the war was on his Majesty's part purely defensive, since he never had, and now would not, deny anything, which they could in reason or in justice ask: That this very overture would necessarily produce some pause and delay in their preparations, or motions of their armies, for some debate it must needs have, and during that time men's minds would be in suspense, whereas his Majesty should be so far from slackening his preparations, that he might be more vigorous in them, by hastening those levies for which his commissions were out.[1] Accordingly, a message was despatched to the House desiring that some fit persons might be appointed by his Majesty and the Parliament to accommodate matters between them. The reply sent by the Parliament concluded thus:—"Until your Majesty shall recall the proclamations and declarations whereby the Earl of Essex and both Houses of Parliament, and their adherents and assistants, and such as have obeyed and executed their commands and directions, according to their duties, are declared traitors or otherwise delinquents; and until the standard set up in pursuance of the said proclamation be taken down, your Majesty hath put us into such a condition that whilst we so remain, we cannot, by the fundamental privileges of the Parliament, the public trust reposed in us, or with the general good and safety of the kingdom, give your Majesty any other answer to this message."

The Earl of Warwick, one of those who had been proclaimed a traitor, had previously written to the king on the subject.[2] He informed his Majesty that he had received his letter of dismission from the navy, and with it an ordinance of Parliament for his continuance in the employment. He besought the king to consider the great strait he was in between these two commands. He hoped his Majesty had always been assured of his fidelity, and begged that he might not be divided between two authorities. The reply was written by Sir Edward Nicholas, and is dated at Newark (13th July 1642). Sir Edward says he has presented his lordship's letter to the king, who was nothing satisfied with it, and commands him to signify that his Majesty conceived that nothing could have induced his lordship to commit treason. Sir Edward adds he is sorry to be the messenger of such an answer.[3]

As some of the king's friends had prophesied, the delay to which the negotiations

---

[1] Hooper's *History of the Rebellion*.
[2] *Vide* Fifth Report of the Historical Manuscripts Commission, Appendix, p. 38.
[3] *Calendar of State Papers*.

gave rise was not without advantage to the Royal cause. Recruits arrived in Nottingham from various adjoining counties, and "an extraordinary number for a single town from Newark." Yorkshire contributed a large contingent, and the king found himself at the head of a substantial army. Seeing the good effect of his overtures on the people, he once more sent propositions to the Parliament, and then on the 13th of September set out for Wales amidst the "acclamations of the countrie." He halted first at Derby, and proceeded thence to Shrewsbury, gathering additional forces on the way. An engagement in which Prince Rupert beat a body of Parliament horse was succeeded by the battle of Edge Hill (Oct. 23), an undecisive conflict, which wasted about five thousand lives.

Newark, occupying an important position, possessing a strong fortress, and commanding the passage of the Trent for a considerable distance, was anxiously regarded. Both sides recognised its importance and appreciated its advantages. Mr. Savage states that the rebels proposed to make Newark their principal station in this part of the world. Mrs. Hutchinson, however, in the memoirs of her husband, Colonel Hutchinson, the eminent Parliamentary soldier, makes it appear that the design was mutual, and that the sheriff who wished to secure Newark for the king was somewhat wily in his course of procedure. She says:—"After the battle at Edge Hill, Sir John Digby, the high sheriff of Nottinghamshire, returned from the king, and had a design of securing the county against the Parliament; whereupon he sent out summonses to all the gentlemen resident in the county to meet him at Newark. Mr. Hutchinson was at the house of Mr. Francis Pierrepont, the Earl of Kingston's third son, when the letter was delivered to him, and another of the same to Mr. Pierrepont; and while they were reading them, and considering what might be the meaning of this summons, an honest man of the sheriff's neighbourhood came and gave them notice that the sheriff had some design in agitation, for he had assembled and armed about fourscore of his neighbours to go out with him to Newark, and, as they heard, from thence to Southwell, and from thence to Nottingham, through which town many armed men marched day and night, to their great terror. Mr. Hutchinson, upon this intimation, went home, and, instead of going to meet the sheriff, sent an excuse by an intelligent person well acquainted with all the country, who had orders to find out their design; which he did so well that he assured Mr. Hutchinson if he and some others had gone in they would have been made prisoners; for the sheriff came into Newark with a troop of eighty men with whom he was gone to Southwell, and was to go the next day to Nottingham to secure those places for the king. Mr. Hutchinson immediately went with his brother, and acquainted them at Nottingham with this intelligence, which they had likewise received from other hands. . . . The high sheriff and the malignant gentry, finding an opposition they expected not, wrote a letter to Mr. Francis Pierrepont and Mr. John Hutchinson, excusing the sheriff's force that he brought with him, and desiring a meeting with them to consult for the peace of the country, security of their estates, and such like fair pretences; which letter was civilly answered them again, and the treaty kept on foot some fourteen days, by letters signed by the Lord Chaworth, Sir Thomas Williamson, Mr. Sutton, Sir Gervas Eyre, Sir John Digby, Sir Roger Cooper, Mr. Palmer, and Mr. John Millington. At length a meeting was appointed at a village in the country on the forest side, where Mr. Sutton should have met Mr. John Hutchinson. Mr. Hutchinson came to the place, but found not Mr. Sutton there, only the Lord Chaworth came in and called for sack, and treated Mr. Hutchinson very kindly; when Mr. Hutchinson, telling my lord he was come according to appointment to conclude the treaty which had been between Nottingham and Newark, my lord told him he knew nothing of it. Whereupon, Mr. Hutchinson being informed that some of my Lord Newcastle's were to be in that town that night, and that Mr. Sutton was gone to meet them and conduct them into the country, returned to Nottingham, where he received a kind of lame excuse from Mr. Sutton for his disappointing of him, and for their bringing strange soldiers into Newark, which they pretended was to save the town from the plunder of some Lincolnshire forces. But Mr. Hutchinson, seeing all their treaties were but a snare for him, would no longer amuse himself about them; but being certainly informed that Henderson, who commanded the soldiers at Newark, if he were not himself a papist, had many Irish papists in his troops, he, with the rest of the gentlemen, sent notice to all the towns about Nottingham, desiring the well-affected to come in to their assistance; which the ministers pressing them to do upon Christmas day 1642, many came to them and stayed with them till they had put themselves into some posture of defence. As soon as these strange soldiers were come into Newark, they presently began to block up and fortify the town, as on the other side they at Nottingham began works about that town; but neither of them being yet strong enough to assault each other, they contented themselves to stand upon their own defence."[1]

From this period Newark and Nottingham stood in marked antagonism. The former clung to the last to the fortunes of the king, whilst Nottingham held to the Parliament, and willingly fought for it. During the winter (1642), the Marquis of Newcastle brought to Newark a stout garrison, intended for its defence. The object of this was twofold. The Parliamentary leaders in Lincolnshire were scheming to take the town by surprise, and the strengthening of the force in Newark defeated their design. It acted also as a barrier to the junction of the forces in South Lincolnshire with those in Yorkshire under Lord Fairfax. An effort, slight and unsuccessful, appears to have been made to sweep away the obstructive garrison. Two troops of cavalry were sent stealthily from Lincolnshire to capture the town, but their whereabouts was made known to Mr. Twentyman, a descendant of the worthy alderman of whom we have already spoken. This gentleman directed a youth named Foster to beat an alarm upon a drum, which he did so vigorously that the bulk of the inhabitants were speedily got together. The weapons with which they armed themselves were those that came first to hand. Some brought sticks and spits, and others rushed to the defence with pitch-forks. The trained bands were called in, the Lincolnshire side of the town garrisoned, and a message despatched to the Marquis of Newcastle

---

[1] *Memoirs of Colonel Hutchinson*, pp. 131-2, 140-1.

for reinforcements.[1] The Parliamentarians made an attack, but were vigorously repulsed, and compelled to retire. They subsequently re-assembled at Grantham, where they established their head-quarters.

After the defeat of the attacking forces, the town was left unreservedly in the hands of the Royalists, and became one of their best and most serviceable strongholds. From it assistance was rendered to the cavaliers of the neighbouring counties. On January 5, 1643, Sir John Henderson, the governor, writes to Mr. Guildford Slingsby, secretary to her Majesty at Pomfret:[2]—"Last night the Lincolnshire gentry desired my assistance in advancing their affairs, and although I had not my Lord General's express orders, yet considering the necessity of the service, I granted them thirty dragoons and twenty horsemen for three days, as they expect this day to have four or five hundred men. This will make a great diversion of the enemy's forces. I beseech you move the Lord General for the sending of more men. The intention is to seize upon Grantham and Bever (Belvoir) Castle. There are two pieces of ordnance, and abundance of ammunition, and some arms in Bever Castle. There is no force at all in Nottingham except Captain Quhyt's [White's], who has retired to the castle, and victualled it. They have cast the pieces of ordnance in Nottingham, which lie as yet in the town. If, for my regiment of a thousand musquets, which I am not able to raise, being thus employed, his Lordship would be content that I might levy five companies of Scots lancers, amounting to three hundred, I would undertake to get them quickly, and do very good service with them."

Early in 1643, when the political atmosphere all around had become thicker and more threatening, the works at Nottingham were pushed hastily forward. Fortifications were made, the workmen engaged in the breastwork receiving eightpence per day, which was raised by weekly collections. Gates were made at Chapel-bar and Cow-lane bar, two of the principal entrances, and a drawbridge was constructed over the Leen. Having completed these necessary works of defence, the Nottingham men turned their eyes towards Newark, and resolved upon a determined effort to win it. Messengers were sent to Lincoln and Derby by the Parliamentary committee at Nottingham, propounding a scheme for attacking the borough. An arrangement was made that at Candlemas troops should advance from the three counties, and should surround Newark for the purpose of making a simultaneous onslaught. News of the plot reached Newark, and caused instant activity. The town presented an animated scene. Entrenchments were made, strong chains were placed across the principal entrances, the garrison was reinforced under the command of Sir John Henderson, several troops of horse were obtained from the Marquis of Newcastle, and the trained bands were again called in.

At the appointed time the Parliamentarians advanced in strong bodies. The men from Nottingham and Derby met about a mile from Newark on the western side, and the Lincolnshire men, who were commanded by an officer named Ballard, approached from the opposite direction. An ambuscade had been laid by the

---

[1] *Vide* MSS. of Mr. Twentyman, quoted by Dickinson.   [2] House of Lords' Calendar.

FIRST SIEGE OF THE BOROUGH.

Newarkers to intercept the Lincoln troops, and to sweep down upon them on a given day. The weather proving very stormy, the Lincoln soldiers delayed their march, and thus escaped the plot that had been laid for their destruction. The combined forces of the besiegers numbered about a thousand men; but the brave garrison in Newark were in no way dismayed. To show the enemy how little they cared for such antagonists, the cavalry, led by gentlemen from the county who had taken refuge in the borough, rode boldly up Beacon Hill, and dared the Lincolnshire horse to an encounter. The latter, however, declined the challenge, and the only reply was the firing of cannon, though the bombardment was carried on at too great a distance to do any damage. On the following day a determined attack commenced. The Nottingham and Derby men, under Colonel Hutchinson and Sir John Gell, advanced to the works, and driving back the few troops within them, entrenched themselves on their opponent's ground. At the same time Captain King, on the Lincolnshire side, took possession of one of the streets, removed the chain at the end, and got a small cannon in working position inside a house. For some reason or other, Ballard at this juncture ordered Captain King to retire, and the garrison, relieved of the necessity of watching his movements, rushed with all their energy upon the Nottingham and Derby contingents. A smart struggle was fought in the trenches, and its result was doubtful until an alarm was spread by a Lincolnshire trooper which caused two hundred of his comrades to retreat. The Derbyshire men joined in the panic and decamped, leaving the Nottingham men to themselves. These, under Colonel Hutchinson and Captain White, fought as long as their ammunition lasted, and then went away. The garrison prepared to follow them, but the firing of cannon covered the retreat, and prevented any further combat. In recognition of their valour, General Ballard presented the Nottingham men with two pieces of ordnance; "but still," says Bailey, "great dissatisfaction prevailed among the troops at the result of the enterprise and the conduct of the commander-in-chief during the operations of the assault."[1]

In some quarters the conduct of Ballard was severely commented upon. He was described as a person of respectable and decayed family,[2] who had seen much service abroad, and had received many favours in his earlier days from the gentlemen who were located within the walls of Newark Castle. It was only after repeated entreaty that he could be induced to march against the town, and when the troops came in front of it, he placed the ordnance at such a distance that it was non-effective. Ballard, according to the assertions of his detractors, was determined at any hazard to save his old patrons. He would not suffer his men to stir when the garrison sent out a foraging party, and he even sent a trooper with the alarm to the attacking force to flee for themselves! Such were the statements of the defeated army, but they can scarcely be regarded otherwise than as excuses for non-success. On the departure of the discomfited assailants, the governor of Newark determined to provide against such unpleasant and dangerous surprises for the future. As a matter of prudence

---

[1] *Annals of Nottingham*, p. 680.   [2] *Memoirs of Colonel Hutchinson*, p. 143.

he caused the houses in North Gate to be burned, including a stately mansion belonging to the Earl of Exeter, erected on the ancient site of St. Leonard's Hospital. The fortifications were improved; Wiverton House and Shelford Manor were garrisoned, as were also the residences of the Earl of Newcastle and Sir Roger Cooper of Thurgarton Priory.[1] In June the queen visited Newark, from which place she addressed a letter to the king, dated June 27 (1643), informing him of her movements, and criticising his proclamation, which she describes as showing "too much fear." The original is in French, partly in cipher, which is deciphered in the king's handwriting.[2] It is as follows:—

My dear Heart—I received just now your letter by my Lord Saville, who found me ready to go away, staying but for one thing, for which you will pardon two days' stop, it is to have Hull and Lincoln. Young Hotham, having been put in prison by order of the Parliament, is escaped, and hath sent to 260[3] that he would cast himself into his arms, and that Hull and Lincoln should be rendered. He hath gone to his father, and 260 waits for your answer, so that I think I shall go hence Friday or Saturday. I shall sleep at Werton, and from thence to Ashby, where we will resolve what way to take, and I will stay there a day, because the march of the day before will have been somewhat great, and also to know how the enemy march; all their forces of Nottingham at present being gone towards Leicester and Derby, which makes us believe that it is to intercept our passage. As soon as we have resolved I will send you word; at this present I think it right to let you know the state in which we march, and what I leave behind for the safety of Lincolnshire and Nottinghamshire. I leave 2000 foot, and wherewithall to arm 500 more; twenty companies of horse; all this to be under Charles Cavendish, whom the gentlemen of the country have desired me not to carry with me against his will, for he desired extremely not to go. The enemy have left within Nottingham 1000. I carry with me 3000 foot, thirty companies of horse and dragoons, six pieces of cannon, and two mortars. Harry Germyn commands the forces that go with me, as colonel of my guard, and Sir Alexander Lesley the foot under him, and Gerard the horse, and Robert Legge the artillery, and her she majesty generalissimo over all, and extreimley dilligent am I with 150 waggons of baggage to govern in case of battle; have a care that no troop of Essex's army incommode us, for I hope that for the rest I shall be strong enough, for at Nottingham we have had the experience, one of our troops having beaten six of theirs, and made them fly. I have received your proclamation or declaration, which I wish had not been made, being extremely disadvantageous for you, for you show too much fear, and do not what you had resolved upon. Farewell, my dear Heart.—From Newark, 27th June 1643.

During her short stay in Newark her Majesty ingratiated herself into the good graces of the people. Mr. Savage says, the courtesy of her behaviour brought so great an increase to her forces that she had not arms sufficient for the men. When she was about to leave, the ladies pressed her to remain longer. They urged her to stay until her forces had taken Nottingham. Her Majesty replied that she was under the command of the king, and was going to march elsewhere by his orders, adding, moreover, that whilst she lamented not being able to comply with their request, she rejoiced in being able to set them an example of obedience to their husbands.[4]

[1] Amongst Prince Rupert's papers (quoted in Warburton's *Life of the Prince*, vol. ii. p. 218) is a lengthy document on "the benefit of putting a balancing force into Lincolnshire." The writer, whose name does not appear, says the foundation of such a force might be drawn from the garrisons of Newark, Wiverton, and Belvoir, and that a thousand spare muskets and three hundred cases of pistols at Newark might be assigned to the service.
[2] *Harl. Mis.* (King's Cabinet Opened).   [3] The Earl of Newcastle.   [4] *Vide* Echard's *Hist. Eng.*

From Newark her Majesty, accompanied by Charles Cavendish, proceeded to Southwell, and remained there two days, in doubt whether to attack Nottingham or to pass by it and join the king. A communication from his Majesty decided the question, and they proceeded by stages to Burton-on-Trent. This place was taken by storm, and, with the exception of Nottingham, the leading passes of the river thus fell into the hands of the Royal troops.[1] Nottingham, surrounded on all sides by hostile stations, remained true to the Parliamentary cause, though fears were entertained that it would have to yield to the force of superior numbers. To guard as much as possible against attack, the Corporation ordered the bulwarks of the town to be repaired, and at the suggestion, it is believed, of Cromwell the command of the forces in the district was entrusted to Sir John Meldrum, an old and experienced officer, who had seen active service abroad. A large body of the king's troops, under Charles Cavendish, menacing Gainsborough, Sir John massed his forces, and marched to the relief of that town, being joined on the way by Cromwell, who, though only holding the rank of colonel, was rapidly coming into notice for his bravery and sagacity. The united forces encountered the Royal army, and a hand to hand engagement ensued. Cromwell, at the head of his famous regiment of heavy armed horse, the "Ironsides," did serious execution, and so vigorous and well-sustained were the attacks that the king's forces gave way. The "General," Charles Cavendish,[2] and other officers of note were killed on the spot, and about 500 rank and file lost their lives in the battle (July 1643).

Prior to his death, Cavendish had expressed a wish to be buried at Newark, and he was accordingly conveyed thither. His body lay in state for several days, and was then consigned to the tomb amidst a regret that was prevalent throughout the borough. The General possessed many good qualities which endeared him to the troops, and, as it has been well observed, "his premature death was a real loss to the country" and to the cause of the king. During the engagement the Marquis of Newcastle advanced to support Cavendish, but having to construct a bridge of boats in order to cross the river, he was unable to get over in time to render that assistance which would have been invaluable at such a juncture. He had the mortification of witnessing the discomfiture of his friends without the ability to render aid. The Marquis avenged the annoyance and defeat, for he laid siege to Gainsborough on the return of Sir John Meldrum to Nottingham, and after an assault of eight days, during which time many smart encounters were fought, the place surrendered to his forces. In the meantime, Sir John Meldrum, with his men, joined the main body of the

[1] Charles Cavendish left her Majesty at Burton, and returned to his command near Newark. Her Majesty continued her journey to meet the king, and suffered some privations on the way for want of food. In a letter dated Walsall, July 9, written in French, and given in the Royal Reports on Historical MSS., she says: "Am so much harrassed that this day I give myself all the rest I can. We have been two days without eating any meat, except the last day, and it was cold and from Newark. I dare say I have not slept three hours a night, but all that pleases me since it is to show you by all my actions that I have no pleasure but that of serving you."

[2] Cromwell relates that his officer "slew him (the General) with a thrust under the short ribs," and Mr. Carlyle relates how "he dared to kill this honourable person."—*Cromwell's Letters*, vol. i. p. 186.

Parliamentary army, and the command of the garrison at Nottingham was entrusted to Lieutenant-Colonel Hutchinson. In order to place the town in as good a state as possible for defence, munitions of war were stored in the castle, and a meeting was called with a view of uniting the inhabitants and arranging for active service. At this meeting Colonel Pierrepont informed them there were three alternatives for the burgesses, either to leave the town and secure themselves in other garrisons, or stay in the castle, or stand in the works and have their throats cut. On this intimation, some went into the country, some took shelter with other garrisons, and some stayed in the town. The entire garrison only amounted to 300 men, but these were determined fellows, and were so confident of their prowess, that on the visit of Major Cartwright with a summons from the Marquis of Newcastle for the surrender of the castle, the governor boldly said he scorned to yield, a bystander (Mr. Geo. Hutchinson) adding that, "If my lord would have that poor castle, he must wade to it in blood."[1]

Colonel Hutchinson's integrity would appear to have been put to a severe test immediately after this occurrence. Sir Richard Byron, who had gone to assist at Newark, urged him to save his estates from the ruin which awaited him by joining the Royal forces, and promised to interest himself in his behalf. To this the Colonel replied in indignant terms, saying that he had resolved to persist in the place which it had pleased God to call him to defend. Up to this period Nottingham had escaped any attack from the Marquis of Newcastle; but it was not without its dangers and its difficulties. The loyal garrison at Newark, who were as brave as they were enterprising, did not remain inactive. They determined, if there was nothing to be done at home, they would seek something to do. Accordingly, they turned their attentions to Nottingham, and amply retaliated for the attack that was organised by the Nottingham men in the preceding February. Time after time they advanced upon the borough, now openly, now stealthily, and were several times on the verge of subduing the garrison.

The first expedition from Newark against Nottingham (in September 1643) was commanded by Sir R. Byron. The object in view was to obtain possession both of the town and castle, and to do this required a combination as well of boldness as of stealth. Well-armed and equipped, with daring spirits and under a brave leader, the Newark troops advanced speedily but cautiously to the town. The governor of Nottingham, fearful of attack, had directed several precautionary measures to be taken. The lanes adjacent to the castle were ordered to be blockaded and the horse to be quartered in them. The orders, however, were but tardily and carelessly obeyed, for before the blockade had been erected, 600 of the Newark cavaliers had entered the town. Mrs. Hutchinson says they were admitted by the treachery of one Alderman Toplady,[2] "a great malignant;" but whether they found admittance by treachery or ingenuity, they were fortunate enough to enter in the dead of the night before any alarm was given. The sentries

---

[1] *Memoirs of Colonel Hutchinson*, p. 165. [2] *Ibid.* p. 176.

were captured, two-thirds of the Nottingham soldiers quartered in the town were seized in their beds, and the rest escaped, some to the adjacent villages, and others to the castle. So quietly was the work effected that the governor of Nottingham knew nothing about it until the following morning, when the Newark troops foolishly fired upon some of the soldiers from the castle as they were coming into the town. Directly these men found themselves assailed, they hastened back to the castle and gave an alarm. The Royalists pressed close upon them, but they were too late to enter the castle grounds before the gates were closed. On discovering the startling position of affairs, the governor called out the garrison, and on doing so, found to his dismay that not more than a third of them had remained in their quarters through the night. The total did not exceed 100, and there were no officers in point of rank save the governor and his brother.

In this emergency messengers were hastily despatched to Leicester and Derby for assistance, and by way of intimidating the besiegers, cannon balls were fired into those quarters of the town where they were principally congregated. Nothing dismayed at the vigorous firing from the castle walls, but rather encouraged by their successes, the Newarkers courageously returned the fire, and seeing that the tower of St. Nicholas's church was on a level with the platform of the castle, they cheerfully mounted it, and poured such a hail-storm of bullets on to the castle grounds, that the men could not stand to the guns without wool packs being placed before them, and even then they were not able to pass from one gate to another, nor relieve the guards, but at the extreme hazard of being shot. Being completely masters of the town, the Newark troops made free with the provisions in the houses, and are said to have "plundered and ransacked at pleasure."[1] For want of a better place to put them in, the prisoners were for a time confined in sheep pens in the market-place, and guarded by soldiers. Subsequently they were removed to a fort that the besiegers had constructed at the Trent Bridges, and from thence both they and the booty were conveyed by boats to Newark.

After the Newark cavaliers had been in undisturbed possession three days, Sir Richard Byron sent a letter to the governor desiring a meeting at St. Nicholas's Church. Sir Richard, as we have said, wished to bring about an arrangement and to win over the governor to the Royalist side. The letter was conveyed by Major Cartwright, but it did not meet with a favourable reception. The governor regarded it as a trap set by his skilful and daring antagonist. He therefore sent no written answer, but commanded the bloody flag to be raised, and discharged three shots at the church steeple, as an indication both of his refusal and his defiance. On the fifth day, seeing no chance of subduing the castle, Sir Richard and his forces began to retire, to the no small relief of the garrison, who had been kept in a constant state of uneasiness and alarm. As the Royalists were retiring (September 23d), Major Hutchinson and his troops attempted to harass them in the rear, and an affray took place in which a few were badly wounded, and twenty-

---

[1] This is Mrs. Hutchinson's assertion; the only one on the subject.

five taken prisoners. Sir Richard Byron's horse was so injured that it fell dead in the next street, and Sir Richard, after a struggle, escaped with the loss of his hat.[1] A detachment under Captain Hacker was left in charge of the new fort at the Trent Bridge, and the remainder of the Newark forces returned in safety to their homes.

Immediately on the retirement of the Cavaliers, 400 Parliamentary soldiers from Leicester and Derby arrived in the town. These men are said to have been as "dexterous at plunder as at fight,"[2] and the unfortunate Nottingham people were robbed as much by their friends as they had been by their enemies. The governor did his best to induce restraint, and to utilise the men who had been sent to aid and not to embarrass. Two cannon were brought into the market-place, and the governor requested that an attack might be made on the new Trent Bridge fort. The major from Derby, who was "an old dull-headed Dutchman,"[3] assured the governor that 10,000 men could not take it, and the idea was, therefore, temporarily abandoned. The cannon were taken back to the castle, and the governor entertained his visitors and friends at a banquet. The men who could not fight with swords did their duty manfully with knives and forks, vanquishing all before them; for peace hath her victories no less renowned than war.

Though the old Dutch major had affirmed that 10,000 men could not capture the fort at the bridges with the eighty Newarkers within it, the governor of Nottingham, when the timid lethargic Dutchman had returned to Derby, resolved to take advantage of the first favourable opportunity that arose, and to make an effort to rid the town of the proximity of dangerous foes. Learning that the main body of the garrison of Newark had made an expedition into Lincolnshire, leaving their friends at the bridges isolated, the troops, horse and foot, lying in the district adjacent to Nottingham were called together, and about eleven o'clock one Monday morning, during a storm of wind and rain, they advanced through the meadows and planted their colours within gunshot of the fort. The pioneers flung up a breastwork, and the governor went back to the castle for the cannon. In his absence the troops from the fort made a desperate sally. The pioneers were put to flight, but the soldiers remained firm, and the Cavaliers had to return to their quarters. In the meantime, a message having been sent to Derby, the old major and his men returned to the assistance of their Nottingham friends. The major still retained his opinion that the fort was impregnable, but the governor was not to be moved again by discouraging argument. Under his direction a trench was cut, and the cannon were placed within range of the fort. Seeing but little chance of withstanding a combined attack, the Cavaliers deemed it prudent to retire. On the fifth night of the siege they abandoned the fort, and broke down two of the arches of the bridge to prevent the besiegers coming in pursuit. The victors found in the fort fourscore sheep, a hundred loads of coal, twenty quarters of oats, a quantity

---

[1] Mrs. Hutchinson's *Memoirs*, p. 179. [2] Bailey's *Annals*, p. 698.
[3] *Memoirs of Colonel Hutchinson*, p. 182.

of hay, and a considerable weight of lead, but "this spoil having previously been gathered from the burgesses of the town or the inhabitants of the vicinity, was no real loss to the retreating company."[1]

The Nottingham soldiers were naturally elated at the departure of the enemy, and to increase their joy news was brought to them the same week, that the forces which went from Newark, joined with Henderson's, had received a great overthrow by Cromwell, and that Lord Newcastle had been forced to raise the siege of Hull (October 12, 1643). The favourable intelligence put the garrison of Nottingham in good spirits, and when they came to reflect on the narrow escape they had had, they could not but feel cause for great rejoicing. As Mr. Bailey says, the condition of their affairs had been such, that, had the Newarkers possessed a great gun or a mortar of any calibre during the five days they were in possession of the town, they could scarcely have failed to have captured the fortress, seeing that the garrison consisted of but fourscore men.

Unable thus far to complete their object, the spirits of the Newarkers were not daunted or dismayed. A plan for a renewal of the attack upon Nottingham, was decided upon in January 1644, and a little strategy was interwoven with valour. To throw the Nottingham people off their guard, they caused intelligence to be conveyed to the governor of Nottingham Castle, that "all the forces in Newark were marched out upon a design against Sleaford." Fortunately for Nottingham, Colonel Hutchinson disbelieved the news, and, regarding it as a trap, commanded all the soldiers and townsmen to sit up that night, and watch lest the enemy should enter in. As to what followed, we must refer to Mrs. Hutchinson, whose account is the only available record of the transaction. She says:—"The next morning, being Tuesday, two of his intelligencers came and brought word very early that the design was against Nottingham. After them the horse scouts came in with the news of their approach, the enemy's scouts and they having fired upon each other. Hereupon a strong alarm was given throughout the garrison, and a foot company sent down from the castle to the works, and the horse were there set with them, to dispute the enemy's entrance into the town; but the horse, perceiving the enemy's body to be a great one, retreated to the castle, and the foot seeing them gone, and none of the townsmen come forth to their assistance, made also an orderly retreat back to the castle, in which there was not a man lost or wounded. The works being imperfect and quitted, were easily entered, though the cannon that played upon them from the castle took off wholly the second file of musketeers that entered the gates. The first was led up by Lieutenant-Colonel Cartwright, who two days before had sent to the governor for a protection to come in and lay down his arms. The enemy being entered, possessed themselves of St. Peter's church and certain houses near the castle, from whence they shot into the castle-yard and wounded one man and killed another, which was all the hurt that was done our men that day. The governor was very angry with the horse for coming up so suddenly, and stirred them up to such a

[1] *Annals of Nottingham*, p. 702.

generous shame, that they dismounted, and all took muskets to serve as foot, with which they did such very good service, that they exceedingly well regained their reputations. Having taken foot arms, the governor sent one of his own companies with part of them, and they beat the Cavaliers out of the nearest lanes and houses, which they had possessed, and so made a safe way for the rest to sally out and retreat as there should be occasion. When this was done, which was about noon, the governor sent out all the rest of the horse and foot to beat the enemy out of the town. Sir Charles Lucas, who was the chief commander of all the forces there, had prepared a letter to send up to the governor to demand of him the castle; or if he would not deliver it, that then he should send down the mayor and aldermen, threatening that if they came not immediately he would sack and burn the town. There were at that time above a thousand Cavaliers in the town, and as many in a body without the town to have beaten off the Derby and Leicester forces, if they should have made any attempt to come in to the assistance of their friends in Nottingham. On the other side the Trent were all the forces Mr. Hastings could bring out from his own garrison and Belvoir and Wiverton to force the bridges. All the Cavaliers that were about the town were about three thousand. When Sir Charles Lucas had written his letter, he could find none that would undertake to carry it to the castle, whereupon they took the mayor's wife, and with threats compelled her to undertake it; but just as she went out of the house from them, she heard an outcry, that "the Roundheads were sallying forth," whereupon she flung down their letter and ran away; and they ran as fast from four hundred soldiers who came furiously upon them out of the castle, and surprised them; while they were secure the castle would not have made so bold an attempt. But the governor's men chased them from street to street, till they had cleared the town of them, who ran away confusedly; the first that went out shot their pistols into the thatched houses to have fired them, but by the mercy of God neither that, nor other endeavours they showed to have fired the town, as they were commanded, took effect. Between thirty and forty of them were killed in the street, fourscore were taken prisoners, and abundance of arms were gathered up, which the men flung away in haste as they ran; but they put some fire into a hay barn and hay mows, and all other combustible things they could discern in their haste, but by God's mercy the town, notwithstanding, was preserved from burning. While their foot marched away, their horse faced the town in a valley where their reserve stood till towards evening, and then they all drew off. Many of them died on their return, and were found dead in the woods and in the towns they passed through. Many of them, discouraged by this service, ran away, and many of their horses were quite spoiled: for two miles they left a great track of blood, which froze as it fell upon the snow, for it was such bitter weather, that the foot had waded almost to the middle in snow as they came, and were so numbed with cold when they came into the town, that they were fain to be rubbed to get life into them, and in that condition were more eager for fires and warm meat than for plunder; which, together with their feeling of security, saved many men's goods; as they did not believe that an enemy, who had unhandsomely, to speak truth, suffered them to enter the town without any dispute, would have dared, at such great odds, to have set upon driving them out. Indeed, no one can believe, but those that saw that day, what a strange ebb and flow of courage and cowardice there was in both parties on that day."[1]

This ebb and flow of courage, as Mrs. Hutchinson describes it, was continuous, for the Newark men no sooner recovered their strength after one affray than they were ready for another. Their valour kept up an ebb and flow of troops between the two towns to an extent unequalled elsewhere in the country at this eventful period. A month had not elapsed from the date of the last attack to the arrangement of another, in which still more ingenious devices were resorted to to gain the mastery. A plan was devised for introducing soldiers on a Saturday in the guise of market-people and capturing the Trent Bridge. Details of the plot were conveyed to Nottingham by Cornet Palmer, who had been a prisoner at Newark, and arrangements were forthwith made to apprehend the daring Cavaliers on their arrival. It was about eleven o'clock on Saturday, the 17th of February (1644), that the disguised soldiers began to put in an appearance. They were dressed as market men and women, but had concealed pistols, long knives, hatchets, daggers, and great pieces of iron. When about a dozen had passed the bridge, they were set upon and captured. The others, seeing the ill success of the ruse, decamped; nine were overtaken, and with their captain leaped into the Trent. Of these four were plucked out of the water, and five drowned, while the captain swam safely to the opposite shore and escaped. There were several skirmishes after this, including one at Shelford, which was held by Cavaliers. They were, however, between small bodies of troops, and possess no features of special interest.

While these casual conflicts were occurring, a movement was on foot of great importance. The Parliamentarians were planning the overthrow of Newark by an organised attack on an extensive scale. By the latter end of February (1644) arrangements had been made for a vigorous effort to deliver the country from what Mrs. Hutchinson describes as "the pernicious enemy." Sir John Meldrum, commander of the Roundheads in the midland counties, proceeded steadily towards Newark with as many troops as he could possibly collect. They numbered 7000, and the force, powerful though it was, was materially augmented by the arrival of 1000 cavalry from Leicester and Derby, commanded by Sir Edward Hartup, and 500 from Nottingham, under the control of Colonel Hutchinson. Newark had thus arrayed against it 8500 men, well armed and possessing a powerful train of battering artillery and mortars. The disposition of the besieging forces was as follows:—Sir Michael Hubbard had his quarters at Balderton, two miles to the south, Sir John Meldrum took his stand at the Spittal, to the north-west, and Lord Willoughby of Parham had his forces at the hill about a mile from the town to the east. What, in the face of these alarming preparations,

---

[1] *Memoirs of Colonel Hutchinson*, pp. 204-7.

was the condition of the besieged? For a satisfactory answer we must turn to Mr. Savage's little history. He says: "The inhabitants were all loyal, the fortifications strong, and the garrison well supplied. The numbers in the place were always from 4000 to 5000 foot, better than 500 horse, and all the inhabitants able to bear arms did so. The walls were in good condition; its four famous gates well guarded, and plenty of cannon on its walls." They were thus well prepared for a powerful and determined defence.

As soon as the besieging forces had settled themselves in their quarters, they bombarded the town. From a manuscript of Mr. Twentyman, we learn that thirteen pieces of ordnance and two bombs were fired in the course of every night against the town by the besiegers. Nor were the loyal garrison at all inactive. Whilst the artillery returned the fire, a portion of the cavalry escaped over Muskham Bridge into the surrounding country to collect a force from the different garrisons in the district that were in favour of the king. So successful were they in their levies that, according to Mrs. Hutchinson, they collected 2000 men, and with these they quartered near Nottingham, putting that town in a state of great alarm. Mrs. Hutchinson says: "There was a fast kept at this time in Nottingham to seek God for His presence with the armies, and before the first sermon was ended the Newark horse came to the town side and gave a strong alarm, and continued facing the town till night, at which time they returned to their quarters." On their retirement the governor conveyed information of the matter to Newark, and on his arrival there he found Sir John Meldrum had made preparations for a general assault on the town. But Sir John's impetuosity was not shared by his comrades. They could not be prevailed upon to agree on the advisability of prompt action. They preferred a policy of delay, and at a council of war a resolution was come to not to commence the attack for the present. What Sir John's feelings must have been on finding that all his preparations had been to no purpose may be readily imagined. He did not openly quarrel with his brother officers, but that he was uncomfortable in his command is evident from Mrs. Hutchinson's narration. For when the governor of Nottingham, in readiness to return to his garrison, called on Sir John to take his leave, "Sir John entreated him that he would return again and be among them as much as he could," at the same time making a sad complaint of the "envyings, heartburnings, and dissensions that were among the several commanders, so that he had much ado to hold them together."[1]

Information of the danger in which Newark stood from the presence of so formidable a force had meanwhile been conveyed to his Majesty, and to Prince Rupert who was then at Chester. Writing to the latter on February 10, Sir Richard Byron had informed his Highness that "the rebels take the boldness for want of force, to repel them to quarter in divers towns within three or four miles of this garrison; they are twelve columns of foot and twenty troop of horse; if they should do no more than continue where they are, they shall hinder

[1] *Memoirs of Colonel Hutchinson.*

the money and provisions that should maintain themselves; great bodies of the enemy threaten to unite to the hazard of this plan;" and he leaves it to his Royal Highness's care for timely assistance.[1] On the 18th of the same month the king forwarded to the prince, by the hand of E. Nicholas, his private secretary, copy of a remonstrance from commissioners of Lincoln and Nottingham, representing the state of those counties and of Newark, whence (as they believed) Cromwell and Manchester were levying forces to fall upon Newark. The king recommended the matter to Prince Rupert's "prudent decision and despatch making a proportionable diversion of those their designs and the succouring of Newark."[2] Other letters reached the prince, including one from Lord Digby, recommending the especial care of defending Newark, and His Royal Highness lost no time in starting to the relief of the town. Marching to Shrewsbury, and thence to Wolverhampton, his forces being augmented as he proceeded by the addition of recruits, he arrived presently at Ashby de la Zouch, where he was informed that 2200 men, under Sir Edward Hartup, who had been despatched by Sir John Meldrum, were stationed near the bridge over the Soar about a mile from Loughborough. Their purpose was either to interrupt Major-General Porter, or to prevent his journey with Lord Loughborough, for thither, with four regiments of horse and one thousand musketeers of Lord Newcastle's men, was Porter now come from about Newark, to hinder the further inroads of the Parliament troops into Leicestershire. Daily slight skirmishes had passed among the troops; but Meldrum's men (commanded by Sir E. Hartup) not being able to force the passage, and hearing of Lord Loughborough's drawing out his force, stole away. The retirement of Sir Edward's forces enabled Prince Rupert to continue his march unimpeded, and to receive additional strength by the junction with his troops of those commanded by Major-General Porter and Lord Loughborough. The united forces passed rapidly on and quartered in a close near Bingham, eight miles from Newark.[3] Colonel Hutchinson had heard of them as they passed by Nottingham, and despatching two troopers in the dead of the night, informed Sir John Meldrum that Prince Rupert had gone by with an army, estimated at about 6000 men, and would in all probability be with them on the following morning.

Colonel Hutchinson was not wrong in his despatch. The prince lost no time in advancing to Newark, where his presence had become greatly needed. Not only had the inhabitants been isolated from the neighbouring country, but they had been exposed to a constant fire from thirteen pieces of ordnance. Ever since Sir John Meldrum's forces surrounded them their lives had been those of privation and constant danger. The food had been consumed sparingly, and day by day the cannon balls were knocking down the houses over their heads. It must have been with intense anxiety that they awaited the arrival of help; and when it did

---

[1] "Prince Rupert's Correspondence;" Appendix to Warburton's *Life of the Prince*, vol. i. p. 495.
[2] *Ibid.* p. 497.
[3] Clarendon's *Rebellion*, iv. 592; Baker's *Chronicle*, 551. These authorities say the besiegers were so dubious of the prince's close and rapid approach that they disbelieved their own scouts.

arrive they were for a time unaware of its proximity. Sir John's forces had so blocked up all entrance to the town that it was with the greatest difficulty the prince could devise a means of informing the Newark garrison of his immediate presence. His Highness had taken a somewhat circuitous route in order to reach the town. With the view probably of avoiding Hubbard's forces at Balderton he had passed at the back of that village, and from thence fallen into the line of the Coddington road. His first business was to endeavour to secure the co-operation of the garrison, so that when the attack came, it might be made jointly. An account of the manner in which he succeeded in his design, and of the ingenious way in which the governor replied, is preserved in Mr. Savage's narration. He says : "The prince had provided him with a character under which they were to correspond, but haveing sent two messengers with this and the news off his arrivall, and only one off them haveing got into the town, the governour was afraid lest the enemie should be in possession off the other, and therebye become acquainted with his intelligence if it should be intercepted. He sent att length the following message, which he thought would not be understood, if the character in which it was wrote should be, by anybody but those it was directed to, nor dared he to trust the messenger with any knowledge of the intelligence he carryed, for so many deserted every daye when they had opportunity that he did not know how to trust any one. The words off the letter were these: 'Let the OLD DRUM on the north side be beaten early on the morrow morning.' By the 'old drum' was meant Sir John Meldrum," and so the arrangement for a joint action was made.

It was on the morning of the 21st of March (1644) that the successful effort to rid Newark of the investing forces was commenced. Sir John Meldrum had drawn up his army in battle array near the Spittal. Here all the infantry were concentrated, with a bridge of boats over the river. The horse had been despatched to the bottom of Beacon Hill to receive the prince as he descended, and they were drawn up into one main body and two wings. The prince's forces were divided into five divisions, having two troops to each. In the first, to the right, were Captains Gardner and Richardson, then the Lord Grandison and Sir Thomas Dallison, and next the troops of Lord Dillon and Sir Lewis Dives. The prince commanded his own Life Guards, and close to them were the troops of Major Legge, Lieutenant-Colonel O'Neil, and Major-General Porter. The field word of the Cavaliers was "King and Queen,"[1] that of the Parliamentarians, "Religion." An eye-witness of the proceedings writes :[2]—"His Highnesse, having intelligence of their amassing themselves into one body, which he supposed a preparation to march off suddenly, advanced his van of horse upon the spurre, to overtake them ; the rest of our horse had order to keep along with the fort cannon and ammunition : coming neare the Beacon Hill, a mile shorte of Newarke, we perceived some horse of the enemie's, who, upon our

---

[1] It was also "For God and for the King," *vide* old ballad.
[2] "An account of the raising of the siege of Newark, written by an eye-witness to a person of honour"—a pamphlet of the period.

approach, drew doune the other side to their oun grosse ; ours thus easie gaining the Hill increased his Highnesse naturall courage, upon his apprehension besides of having many advantages upon a retreating enemy, whereupon, 'Courage,' says he ; 'let's charge, in God's name, with the horse we have, and ingage them till our reare and foot be marcht up to us ;' trooping thus to the edge of the Hill, he perceived the most of the enemies in battalia (horse and foot) neare the Spittle, all the meane, except foure great bodies of horse, who expected us at the descent of the Hill ; the prince thus ordered his oune few forces ; first himselfe and his oun troope of Life-guard undertook to attaque that body on the left hand, appointing my Lord Loughborough's troop to second him, and Colonell Charles Gerard's troop to be as a reserve."

The prince led the attack, charging the enemy with great impetuosity. Immediately, on the first shock, the Parliamentarians doubled, then fell from two to six deep, and returned the charge with such effect that some of the prince's troops would have been dispersed had not Captain Martin rushed to their assistance. Reinforced, the Cavaliers hurled back their opponents, and the prince himself pierced deeply into the enemy's lines. His boldness and dashing bravery nearly cost him his life ; for being easily recognised, he became the object of attack. Three sturdy men rushed vigorously at him ; one he killed with his own sword, the second was pistoled by Master Montaign, the third, as he took hold of the prince's collar, had his hand nearly chopped off by Sir William Neal. Immediately he was released from this peril, having received no other inconvenience than a shot in his gauntlet, the prince heading Sir Richard Crane's troop, charged through the enemy, and pursued them to their works at the Spittal. The other Parliamentary troops, who had been engaged against Lord Loughborough, were also repulsed, not, however, without a great effort, requiring all his lordship's strength, courage, and ingenuity. In the engagement Colonel Gerard was shot in the arm, and being much bruised by the fall of his horse, was taken prisoner. As soon as the rebel troops had been thrust back to the Spittal, where the foot were encamped, a pause ensued, during which each side prepared for renewing the encounter.

When the forces had had breathing time, and were somewhat refreshed, the prince again led the attack, and a desperate conflict ensued. Sir John Meldrum's troops fought courageously, but were driven away by main force. Some retreated over the bridge of boats on to the island ; four troops, with several companies of foot, hurried away to Muskham Bridge, where they remained until the evening, when, breaking the bridge behind them, and throwing a cannon into the Trent, they hastened to Nottingham. The main body stood some little distance from the Spittal, having lost, in addition to the slain, about 100 prisoners, three of whom were captains and five cornets. As if by general consent, a second period of quiet succeeded, lasting for about half an hour. During the self-imposed armistice the Parliamentarians drew all their horse and foot within the Spittal works, whilst the prince waited the arrival of the foot under Colonel Tillier, and the rear of the horse, which had been left about two miles behind. On obtaining these reinforcements, the prince put his troops in order, and both sides saluted each other with a volley of shot. Colonel Tillier received orders to march up the riverside and capture the bridge of boats. This he essayed to do, but finding it strongly guarded, he returned out of reach of the cannon. Loughborough's men were placed on the hillside as a reserve, and whilst they stood in readiness for action other bodies of troops charged the enemy's works.

During the heavy fighting outside the town, Sir Richard Byron, with a portion of the garrison, made a diversion on the south-east side. At this juncture news reached the prince that the enemy were greatly distressed for want of food. A deserter assured him that they were not able to live for more than two days, so short was their supply. On hearing this, the prince resolved to reduce them by famine rather than by sword. Being concentrated at the Spittal, they were easily surrounded. On the south side was the town, on the east the prince, on the north Colonel Tillier, and into the island on the west his Highness sent 500 horse, with 200 of the Newark troopers. Sir Richard Byron cut off all traffic between the Spittal and Muskham Bridges, by advancing so high into the island as to intersect them, and thus the besiegers found themselves completely besieged. The prince was about to make the investment more secure by casting up a redoubt between the two bridges, when the enemy sent to desire a parley.[1] After the hard work that had been undergone, the prince was not loth to come to terms, especially as he found from an intercepted letter that Fairfax was advancing. Accordingly, he despatched Sir Richard Crane and Sir William Neale as his representatives, whilst the Parliamentarians chose Sir Miles Hobard and Sir John Palgrave. The deputies discussed terms, and those which were finally approved of were these:—

1. That all match, bullet, powder, cannon, and all other firearms be delivered.

2. That all soldiers march away, with their swords by their sides, and colours and drums.

3. That all officers march without molestation, with their arms and horses, for themselves and servants, and all bag, baggage, money, and whatever doth truly belong to themselves.

4. That all troopers and dragoons march with their swords, horses, and colours.

5. That his Highness send a convoy to protect us from any injury, two miles from the utmost of his Highness's quarters.

RICHARD CRANE, MILES HOBARD,
WILLIAM NEALE, J. PALGRAVE.

Dated March 22, 1644.

---

[1] An old account says they sent a trumpeter. Warburton, in his *Life of Prince Rupert*, vol. ii. p. 396, states: "A short time before dusk Gerard (who had been taken prisoner) was seen limping out of the enemy's entrenchments," bringing proposals for a surrender.

An eye-witness of the siege, on whose graphic account,[1] sent to a "person of honour," we have relied for many of the details we have given, says: "Besides these conditions, his Highnesse gave instructions to his commissioners to insist upon a demand of some prisoners before taken, which was also granted. Hereupon next morning the rebells marched out; but for the horsemen's carrying away their arms, and others their pikes, with more than was conditioned, our unruly soldiers (especially those that had been so before used at Lincolne by the Parliamentiers) taking this occasion to quarrel with the rebells, took more from them than by the articles they should have done. But for this were divers of them slashed by the Prince, and the rebells' colours sent back unto them. The rebells thus gone, we had leasure to carry off their arms and ammunition, consisting of betwixt three and four thousand musquets, and a great quantity of pikes and pistolls, with the cannons they left behind them; of these we found eleven fair brasse pieces, one a basiliske of Hull, foure yards long, shooting 32 ball; one of their ordnance was found at Muskham Bridge, and the carriage of the other. Two goodly mortar pieces were also left us,—the least shooting 80 pounds Granado, and the other twelve stone and eight pounds,—and all their ammunition. The number of the slaine we know not, but we think they lost towards ninescore or two hundred, and we about halfe as many slaine and wounded. Thus, after just three weeks' siege, was Newarke happily relieved. His Highnesse hath appointed a thanksgiving for this on Sunday, by which the world may see him to be as devout as valiant." Mr. Savage says the powder that was taken was "a mightie seasonable relieffe." He adds: "It is strange that all through the war there was always a complaint off the scarcitie of powder on the king's side. . . . The prince left the arms behind him which had been taken from the enemie, for they were much wanted, many loyal gentlemen off the town and countie being desirous to bear arms and assist in defending that important pass Newark, if they could be had."

The following poetical description of the siege is supposed to have been "written by Sir William Davenant, or some one, about the Marquis of Newcastle, he being a gentleman of grandeur, generosity, and loyalty." The writer of *Ladye Shakerley*, who quotes the lines, says, "We came possessed of these rhymes by a fellow hawking of tracts and verses."[2]

> Old Newark's walls lay compassed by three armies in the field,
> And Meldrum, Hubbard, Willoughby, vow'd to God they'd make them yield;
> But the loyal hearts within swore they never would give in,
> For as long as they had life, they would keep it for the King.
>
> They were three to one against them; they surrounded all the town,
> And the four old gates they yearned to break them down;
> And Hubbard, Meldrum, Willoughby, said, "Ye'd better now give in,
> And we'll grant you easy terms, though you're fighting for the King."

---

[1] "His Highnesse, Prince Rupert, raising of the siege of Newark-upon-Trent, March 21, 1643-4, written by an eye-witness to a person of honour."

[2] Also quoted by Mr. Briscoe in his *Nottinghamshire Facts and Fictions*.

And the one-to-three looked out from the grand old wall in scorn,
And they made a deep, dead silence while the Herald blew his horn,
For gallant Sir John Henderson was governor within,[1]
And he'd sworn upon the Cross to keep it for the King.

So the Herald answered proudly, in the name of all the rest,
"We know what the mercies of the wicked are, at best ;
If you storm the town we'll blow it up ; we never will give in ; .
And our gates will keep you long enough—false rebels to your King.

"We've guns enough, we've men enough, our hearts are strong and true ;
We will burn the city down, but we'll never yield to you ;
We can starve and we can die, but we cannot live to fling
Our brave old gates wide open to you—traitors to the King.

"So tell your rebel leaders we are loyal to the last,
And when our bread is eaten, we then must keep our fast ;
We can do and we can dare, but old Newark's walls shall ring
With no battle-cry but ours—for God and for the King !"

Oh, the Roundheads snuffled Psalms, and swore below their breath,
When the rebel leaders heard this challenge to the death ;
And they vow'd they'd sack the town, for it was a shameful thing
To make the godly wait so long by this fighting for the King.

For many weeks and many months they bravely held their own,
Till famine, with her hungry eyes, went up and down the town ;
And men then never left the walls— they could not face within
The faces of the children that were starving for the King.

And the women brought the food to the men that kept the wall,
And they tried to watch them smiling as they ate it, crumbs and all ;
For they knew that but for them, and the little ones within,
They would die in one brave sally for God and for the King !"

Then one gallant fellow said, "We can do, and we can dare,
Aught but watching tender women, so patient, take their share ;
I will advertise Prince Rupert, and our homes once more shall ring
With merry children shouting for God and for the King !"

They dressed the brave young Cavalier, ready to do and dare,
They dressed him like a Roundhead, they cut close his waving hair ;
Then the maiden he had wooed and won stept in amid the ring,
And before them all she blest him, for God and for the King.

---

[1] Mrs. Hutchinson says that Sir Richard Byron had come to be governor some time before the siege, and the constant references to the actions of Sir Richard in other old accounts, together with his letter to Prince Rupert seeking relief for the garrison, would seem to bear out the assertion. On the other hand, Mr. Savage speaks of Sir John Henderson as being governor until shortly before the third siege, when he was called away to other duties. The letter of his Majesty (p. 134) directed to Sir Richard Byron "Governor," shows clearly that he was governor of Newark immediately after the siege, if not during its progress.

He looked into her deep-set eyes, he gave her one long kiss,
Then he turned him to his comrades, "I pray you grant me this ;
If the foe,"—he could not say it, but he touched his pistol spring,
And they swore to do his bidding, by God and by the King.

And the rebels knew the garrison and death were face to face,
And they hoped a few days more now would make them sue for grace ;
They knew the Prince was on his way, their scouts did daily bring
Fresh tidings of his marching on for God and for the King.

But they knew how small his force, and they deemed their scouts did lie
When, with terror in their faces, they swore the Prince was nigh ;
For they never dreamt that he dared the battle to begin
With a handful of wild troopers, for God and for the King.

But Essex sent nine hundred horse to watch his little band,
And Ashburnham had wrote the Prince "he hoped they'd all be —— ;"
The Prince left *them* to watch his foot, and five hundred horse did bring,
To charge three rebel armies, for God and for the King.

So cheerily at midnight blew Prince Rupert's bugle-horn,
And old Newark rose before them, as rose the early morn ;
Then he looked upon his troopers, and his troopers looked on him,
And he knew to death they'd follow, for God and for the King.

They gained the Beacon Hill, and the town beneath them lay,
The rebel army round the walls gathered in dense array.
The grand old castle still from her battlements did fling
The Royal Standard proudly, for God and for the King.

And the river by the castle still murmuring did run,
For ever, ever murmuring and glittering in the sun,
Unheeding of the tumult, of the strife and tears within,
Of those who still fought bravely, but were starving for the King.

All around, and on the foe, Rupert's eagle eye did fall ;
Then he turned him to his troopers, five hundred in them all ;
And then his voice rose loud and clear above the shouts and din —
Rose clear and high his battle-cry, "For God and for the King."

They are seen upon the hill-top, all dark against the sky,
They are sweeping down the hill-side to death or victory ;
They have burst upon the rebels, and Newark heard the hymn
(None ever sounded sweeter), "For God and for the King !"

They are round him, all those Roundheads, they surround his little band,
They are fighting against hundreds, they are fighting hand to hand ;
And ever in the thickest fight, where shot like hail poured in,
Rose loud and high that dauntless cry, "For God and for the King !"

The garrison have sallied out, the foes fall back a space,
For Rupert presses onward : neither give nor ask for grace ;

And ever in the hottest fight, above the battle din,
His battle-word is clearly heard, "For God and for the King!"

They have won the bridge, those troopers! They will keep it to the death,
And the foes are drinking hard in the crimsoned stream beneath;
And down the grey hill-side Rupert's Foot is marching in,
And echo high the battle-cry, "For God and for the King!"

They have sheathed their bloody blades at his word, those troopers wild,
For he swore he'd shoot the first that harmed a woman or a child;
And the foe have begged for quarter, they are ready to give in,
And leave Newark and her standard to God and to the King.

As he entered the old gates one cry of triumph rose
To bless and welcome him who had saved them from their foes;
The women kiss his charger, and the little children sing,
"Prince Rupert's brought us bread to eat from God and from the King."

And that brave young Cavalier, ready to do and dare!
She will find him near the bridge—she is gone to seek him there,
Close beside old Newark's walls, but he never heard them ring
With many children shouting "For God and for the King!"

News of the success of Prince Rupert's expedition, and of the gallant behaviour of the garrison and people of Newark, was conveyed to his Majesty, who was then at Oxford, and elicited from him a letter, which we extract from the old minute-book of the Corporation.

KING CHARLES Y^e FIRST of Blessed and Glorious Memory, His Gracious Letter to Y^e Corporaĉon.

CHARLES R.

Trustie and well beloved wee greet you. As wee must acknowledge the great blessing of God in the reliefe and preservation of that our Toune of Newark from the Rebells by the seasonable arrival of our forces, and the Prosperous command of our deare nephewe Prince Rupert, so wee are very sensible of y^r singular care and courage in the defence of ye place, till ye succour came: wee assure you wee shall always remember it to y^r advantage. And wee require you to let all those officers and gentlemen who with industry and courage have assisted you in this great service, know that wee shall take very particular notice of their severall affeccons, and hope in due time in some degree to reward them. And for that Corporacion itselfe wh. did so darly, and hath so constantly given such eminent testimony of their affeccon and loyalty to us in this so generall a defeccon, you shall let our Maior, Aldermen, and inhabitants of that our good toun know that wee will give them some such signall of our extraordinary acceptance and value of their duty, as may be an evidence to the whole kingdom thereof. In the meane time, wee would have them send us a copie of their charter, that wee may upon view thereof make such additions of grace, favour, and advantage to them as may be most convenient for them. And in the preamble of the same leave a monum^t to posterity of their faithfull and loyall demeanour, wee having a greater sense of their meritt toward us than we can express. And so wee bid you farewell.—Given at our Court at Oxford, the 26th day of March 1644.

By his Majesty's Command,

GEORGE DIGBY.

To our trustie and well beloved Sir Richard Byron, Knight, Governor of our toun of Newark.

Numerous letters of congratulation, on the raising of the siege,[1] were sent to Prince Rupert. The king writes from Oxford (March 25, 1644): "I assure you that this (as all your victories), gives me as much contentment in that I owe you the thanks as for the importance of it, which, in this particular, believe me, is no less than the saving of all the north." His majesty adds: "How to follow up this (indeed beyond imaginable) success, I will not prescribe you; yet I cannot choose but send you, by my Lord Digby, the thoughts of that countrie which I call yours; earnestly desiring you to consider, and judge well, the contents of his letter; remembering to eschew Hannibal's error in not right using, as well as you imitate him in getting of victories."[2] Lord Digby on the following day (March 26) despatched an inflated letter. He says: "I shall not use congratulation to your Highness for your late incomparable success at Newark; our sense of it here is as much beyond expression as the action itself beyond; for as it had a concurrence of all parts in it to make it glorious to your Highness, so had it a conjecture of all circumstances, of time, place, and relation, to improve and heighten the advantage of it to his Majesty's service; and therefore all my congratulations upon this subject shall be to his Majesty, not so much for his present victory as for you," and much more to the same purport.[3] The next was a droll one, from Trevor, who wrote: "Give me leave humbly to join myself with the courtier, the scholar, indeed people of all ages, all sexes, all faculties, bells and bonfires, in congratulating your happy success in the aid of Newark, by attributing to you so eminent courage and conduct, all on this side of idolatry."[4] The prince also received letters of congratulation from Lord Newcastle, then at Durham, and many others. His Royal Highness was so high in favour that he was to have whatever arms, men, and money he required. Even the queen thought of placing herself under the protection of her victorious nephew.[5]

It is understood to have been during the earlier part of this siege that Hercules Clay (afterwards mayor of the borough) and his family had a remarkable escape. Mr. Clay occupied a house at a corner of the market-place, now the site of Messrs. Godfrey and Riddell's bank. For three nights in succession he dreamt that the besiegers had set his place on fire, and he became so impressed with the circumstance that he and his family quitted their abode. They had no sooner done so than a bomb fired from Beacon Hill, and believed to have been aimed at the governor's house, which was opposite Mr. Clay's, fell on the roof of Clay's dwelling, and passing through every floor set the whole building in flames.[6] The tradition is, that a spy, blindfolded and bearing a flag of truce, came from the Parliament army on the hill to the governor's

---

[1] Clarendon calls it "a prodigious and unexpected victory."
[2] *Life of Prince Rupert*, vol. ii. p. 398.   [3] *Ibid.* vol. ii. p. 399.   [4] *Ibid.* p. 400.
[5] Letter from Trevor to Prince Rupert, March 28, 1644:—"Her Highness may desire to move into your quarters and be within your charge."   [6] Dickinson.

house, and was able on his return so accurately to describe its situation as to make the shot all but successful.[1] To commemorate his fortunate deliverance, Mr. Clay inserted a clause in his will, giving to the mayor and aldermen the sum of £100 to be placed at interest by the vicar's consent for the vicar's benefit, to preach a sermon on the 11th day of March annually, and another sum of £100 to be secured and applied in a like manner for the benefit of the poor. The charity is now endowed with 20-96th parts of the net rents derived from lands at East and West Laughton, Lincolnshire. The ordinary yearly income amounts to £18, one half of which is given to the vicar for a sermon, and the remaining half to the poor of the town in penny loaves. A tablet to the memory of Hercules Clay is in the parish church. The inscription, partly in Latin and partly in English, the Latin with two Greek words, may be rendered thus:—

> "Sacred to the memory of
> HERCULES CLAY, Alderman of Newark,
> Who died in the year of his Mayoralty,
> Jan. 1, 1644.
> On the 5th of March, 1643,
> He and his family were preserved
> By the Divine Providence
> From the thunderbolt of a terrible cannon
> Which had been levelled against his house
> By the Besiegers,
> And entirely destroyed the same.
> Out of gratitude for this deliverance,
> He has taken care
> To perpetuate the remembrance thereof
> By an alms to the poor and a sermon;
> By this means
> Raising to himself a monument
> More durable than Brass."

> "The thund'ring Cannon sent forth from its mouth the devouring Flames
> Against my Household Gods, and yours, O Newark.
> The Ball, thus thrown, Involved the House in Ruin;
> But by a Divine Admonition from Heaven I was saved,
> Being thus delivered by a strength Greater than that of Hercules,
> And having been drawn out of the deep Clay,
> I now inhabit the stars on high.
> Now, Rebel, direct thy unavailing Fires at Heaven.
> Art thou afraid to fight against God—thou
> Who hast been a Murderer of His people?
> Thou durst not, Coward, scatter thy Flames
> Whilst Charles is lord of earth and skies.
>
> Also of his beloved wife
> Mary (by the gift of God)
> Partaker of the same felicity.[2]

---

[1] "Notes on Newark;" a lecture by Mr. Sketchley. [2] The Latin portion of the epitaph ends here.

> Wee two made one by his decree
> That is but one in Trinity,
> Did live as one till death came in
> And made us two of one agen ;
> Death was much blamed for our divorce,
> But striving how he might doe worse
> By killing th' one as well as th' other,
> He fairely brought us both togeather,
> Our soules together where death dare not come,
> Our bodyes lye interred beneath this tomb,
> Wayting the resurrection of the just,
> O knowe thyself (O man), thou art but dust."

The writer of the epitaph, whoever he may have been,[1] has followed the old legal method of calculation in regard to the dates, thus creating an apparent diversity, to which reference ought to be made. The year in which Mr. Clay died was 1645, the year of his mayoralty, and the entry in the parish register, is as follows :—"January 1, Hercules Clay, maior." So, too, with respect to the siege, which is stated on the epitaph to have been in March 1643. It occurred in 1644, as we have already shown. The difference arises, as many of our readers will, doubtless, be aware, from the fact that, at the time the epitaph was written, New Year's Day would be on the 25th of March. It was not until 1752 that the first of January became the initial day of the legal, as it had long been of the popular year. Before that time it was customary to set down dates between the 1st of January and the 24th of March inclusive, thus :— January 30, 1643-4, meaning that popularly the year was 1644, but legally 1643.[2] In accordance with this system the parish registers of the period are made up from March to March; thus we have the register from March 24, 1644, to March 24, 1645, headed throughout 1644, the date 1645 not being introduced until we reach March 25 of that year. The autograph which we have copied is from a document[3] bearing date November 23, 1644; and was thus signed by Mr. Clay about a month before his death. The epitaph describes the bomb as falling on the 5th of March; yet Mr. Clay directed that in commemoration of his deliverance the sermon and distribution should be on March 11. Lastly Mr. Dickinson states (p. 233) that the will of Mr. Clay is dated December 11, 1694, and we find it has been so printed in other publications in which reference to the charity has been made. It is obviously a misprint for 1644, and we feel constrained to mention that such is the case to prevent further perpetuation of the error. We have not been able to ascertain when the tablet to the memory of Mr. Clay was erected, but it is not referred to in Thoroton, who gave a tolerably long list of the monuments

---

[1] The initials on the tablet are G. H.

[2] We may here mention that the dates we have given are, in all cases, those of the popular, and not of the legal year.

[3] A formal order on the treasurer for payment of money. The order we found amongst the Corporation Papers.

in the church in 1677, nor in Throsby's additions to Thoroton, published in 1790. It is, however, mentioned by Samuel Buck, who published in 1726 a copy of the chief engineer's plan of the redoubts, forts, and fortifications around Newark on the occasion of the final siege in 1646. This plan shows, amongst other things, "the supposed course of the bomb, which (to quote Buck's words), being pointed at the governor's house, fell on Alderman Hercules Clay's, from which his personal and memorable deliverance by a dream is piously perpetuated by an annual sermon and alms of his own donation, as a Latin inscription upon his marble tomb in the southeast angle of the church amply testifies." The descendants of Mr. Clay are occupying highly respectable and responsible positions in various parts of the country, and in the list of subscribers to this volume, the names of some of them are, we understand, included.

Mr. Clay's house was only one of many that suffered during the severe bombardment to which the town was subject. A shot fell on the house of Alderman Baker, subsequently mayor of the borough; a second shot fell on the residence of Mr. Christopher Wilson; and a third passed through the steeple of the church, but did no material damage.[1] All these shots are stated to have come from the cannon on Beacon Hill, which continued to play unceasingly until Prince Rupert came to the rescue, and gallantly forced the besiegers to retire.

It will be readily understood that a defeat like that which Sir John Meldrum's forces had sustained would not be without its effect in daunting the spirits of the vanquished Parliamentarians and their colleagues. Not only in Nottinghamshire, but in adjoining counties, the depressing influences of the calamity were plainly noticeable. Several garrisons in the northern part of Lincolnshire fled, as in a panic. "Indeed," says Mrs. Hutchinson, "such a blow was given to the Parliament interest in all these parts, that it might well discourage the ill-affected, when even the most zealous were cast down and gave up all for lost." At Nottingham precautionary measures were actively taken. It was not unnaturally supposed that the Prince's troops would retaliate by attacking the borough, and the governor took all the measures of defence that lay in his power, flooding the meadows and strengthening the fortifications at the Trent Bridges. That the Royalists were debating the desirability of advancing on Nottingham soon became apparent. Three days after the engagement at Newark a letter was sent from the Royal commissioners, telling the governor "that the Parliament forces had quitted Gainsborough, Lincoln, and Sleaford, and that the prince intended to advance against Nottingham, and to fire the town if he (Colonel Hutchinson) did not immediately throw down the works, which, if he should not do, the world would then take notice of him as the only ruin of his native country." To this stern message the governor returned reply that, "as he never

[1] There is at the present time, in the possession of Mr. Edward Marshall of Leicester, a cannon-ball which was taken out of a beam in the roof of the north aisle, during the churchwardenship of the late Mr. James Lang, plumber, Stodman Street. This ball is believed to have been fired from Beacon Hill, the hole in the N.E. cant of the spire being in a line with the spot in the roof where the ball was found.

engaged himself in this service, with respect to the success or actions of other places, so, though the whole kingdom were quitted except this town, he would yet maintain it as long as he was able, and he trusted that God would preserve it in his hands; but if it perished, he was resolved to bury himself in the ruins of it; being confident that God would afterwards vindicate him to have been a defender, and not a destroyer, of his country." A copy of the letter which the Newark commissioners sent to the governor, was supplied to one Francis Cooke, a "malignant" inhabitant of Nottingham, with a request that he would communicate it to the whole town. In the difficult dilemma in which he was placed, the governor of Nottingham despatched a messenger to the Earl of Essex earnestly soliciting assistance, and the earl returned a civil and encouraging reply. Meanwhile the prince bade farewell to Newark, and proceeded not towards Nottingham, as had been anticipated, but to Shrewsbury, thence to Lathom House, and next to the relief of York, which had become hard pressed by the besiegers.

For a short time comparative quietude prevailed in the town. But the calm was not of long duration. As Mr. Savage justly observes, Newark was "destined to feel the weight off the enemies exertions during the whole of the warre." At the latter end of the year (1644), the committee of both kingdoms sent down an order for all the horse of Nottingham and Derbyshire to join with three regiments of Yorkshire, and quarter about Newark to straiten the enemy there. An expedition was forthwith started, but did not succeed in straitening the enemy so much as in exposing its own weakness and incompetence. Mrs. Hutchinson says:[1] They met at Mansfield, and thence marched to Thurgarton, where Sir Roger Cooper had fortified his house, and lined the hedges with musketeers, who, as the troops passed by, shot and killed one Captain Heywood. Hereupon Colonel Thornhagh sent to the governor, and desired to borrow some foot to take the house. The governor accordingly lent him three companies, who took the house with Sir Roger Cooper and his brother, and forty men in it, who were sent prisoners to Nottingham, where, although Sir Roger Cooper was in great dread of being put into the governor's hands, whom he had provoked before upon a private occasion, yet he received such a civil treatment from him, that he seemed to be much moved and melted with it. The foot had done all the service, and run all the hazard, in taking the house, yet the booty was all given to the horse; this they had very just reason to resent; but, notwithstanding, they marched along with them to Southwell, and there were most sadly neglected and put upon, keeping outguards for the horse, and had no provisions, so that the governor was forced to send them some out of his garrison, or else they had been left to horrible distress. Hereupon they sent to the governor to desire they might come home; but upon Colonel Thornhagh's entreaty and engagement that they should be better used, the governor was content to let them stay a little longer, till more horse came up, which were sent for out of Yorkshire. In the meantime, those who were there already did nothing but harass the poor country;

[1] *Memoirs of Colonel Hutchinson*, p. 268.

and the horse-officers were so negligent of their own duty, and so remiss in the government of their soldiers, that the service was infinitely prejudiced, and the poor country miserably distressed. The Nottingham horse, being in their own country, and having their families in and about Nottingham, were more guilty of straggling than any of the rest; and Captain White's whole troop having presumed to be away one night when they should have been upon the guard, the Newarkers beat up our quarters, and took almost two whole troops of that regiment. White's lieutenant, without any leave from the colonel, thereupon posted up to London, and contrived a complaint against the governor, to make him appear guilty of this disorder; but soon after the Newarkers gave them another alarm, and the Parliament horse made so slender an appearance that the officers, thereupon consulting in a council of war, concluded that the design should not be prosecuted without more force, and for the present broke up their quarters."

Several skirmishes took place during the winter, which, though they did not involve much loss of life, indicated the determined activity of the opposing forces. On one occasion a party had been from Newark into the adjacent villages to trouble the Parliament's friends by levying contributions upon them. The Nottingham committee, hearing of the proceedings, sent a detachment of horse to drive away the tax-gatherers. On their approach the Newark men retired, leaving their booty and five or six of their comrades behind them. The Nottingham soldiers were not content with this, but pursued the enemy. As the old proverb puts it, "Much wanted more, and so lost all;" for, a stronger body of Newarkers arriving, the Nottingham forces were completely routed, Major Meldrum, Lieutenant Smith, and about thirty others being taken prisoners. On the 27th of November Sir Richard Byron, governor of Newark, and Sir Gervas Lucas, made a dash at Melton Mowbray, and took "six or seven hundred men, arms, etc., together with the committee of Leicester— viz., Staveley Hazelrigg and Captain Hacker." Sir Edward Hartopp's cornet alone escaped. "The committee had come to gather up the rents of all such as were not so perfect rebels as themselves." They were all taken to Belvoir Castle, and having seen them securely lodged there, Sir Richard Byron returned with his men to Newark.[1]

The year 1645 opened dismally for Newark. The enemy, constantly suffering from the daring valour of the Newark troops, had begun to assemble in considerable numbers to compel their surrender. The dangers and privations of a third siege were imminent, and to add to the difficulty there were traitors within as well as foes without. From a letter written at the time by one Joseph Rhodes, we learn that a dastardly plot was formed for betraying the garrison, and letting the rebels gain by stealth what they were unable to effect by force. Fortunately the design was discovered early enough to prevent mischief, and the leader of the gang of cowardly schemers was thrown into prison. The letter of Rhodes, which is directed to Prince Rupert, reveals other important particulars. Differences had arisen respecting the governorship, and it was proposed to associate with Sir

[1] *Mercurius Aulicus*, p. 690.

A PLOT TO BETRAY THE GARRISON.

Richard Byron in the direction of affairs a minister named Rhodes (perhaps the writer of the letter), and this was an indignity which the loyal and courageous Byron was not disposed to submit to. Rhodes writes as follows:—

May it please your Highness.

Upon my coming to Newark I found the enemy gone from Southwell and all parts beyond the river where they had invested us, having only removed their quarters a little farther off; and, no doubt, if there was that care requisite taken within us, we should not fear so much without. There was very lately a damnable plot for the betraying of this garrison. Captain Clay, the chief, apprehended, and divers others fled upon it; and I dare justify it with my life there is no other way to prevent that, or such-like miscarriages, but by continuing your Highness's resolution to settle these parts by some person of gallantry, knowledge, and integrity. I humbly beseech your Highness to give me leave to acquaint you with that which indeed ought not to be concealed, that Lieutenant-Colonel Whichcote, who came down with me bringing a letter to Sir Richard Byron from his mother, the Lady Byron, who lyeth in Merton College (Oxford), which letter opened of itself, being slightly made fast by a cover of paper, wherein these words, amongst others, were, that she was told that Prince Rupert had joined in commission with him, for the government of Newark, Rhodes, the minister; and if it be so, she advised him either not to suffer him to govern there, or to give up his commission; besides, she added, "There are governors in these parts who will not give up their government but keep it against Prince Rupert's will. I shall use all means to cross Rhodes's desire, and I would advise you to get Sir Jervase Clifton, and the rest of your friends, to write to the king or Prince Rupert that they will not have Rhodes to govern there." This letter, and these very words, being copied out by us, came to the governor's hands, which I shall be ready to justify by Lieutenant-Colonel Whichcote and myself with our lives and salvation, all which your Highness, in your wisdom, will make use of.

I beseech your Highness to give me leave to come home nearer to the preservation of this place once more, that unless there be some speedy course taken, this garrison will never be sufficiently victualled by our government here, the enemy taking just occasion of advantage by our nakedness, as well of the understanding part for government as victual. There either hath or will wait on your Highness, a gentleman, one Major Wheeler, from Newark; I beseech your Highness to examine him strictly upon his reputation, of the condition of these parts, and particularly of the carriages of our forces, drawn out when the enemy went from Southwell, from Friday, the 3d of January, to the Wednesday after; and I am confident, however some here may attempt the biassing of him to represent things their own way, yet he hath so much known gallantry, that he will give your Highness full satisfaction therein, he being personally engaged in all that action. As for that commission your Highness was pleased to give me, and which I left with you, I do, with all readiness and humility, submit it and myself to your Highness's wisdom, and if my appearing in it may in the least manner prejudice his Majesty's service, I desire it may never be thought upon more; only be pleased to give me leave to add, that whoever they are that may blast it or me, are they who never served his Majesty with that zeal and fervour as I have ever done, without the least ends of mine own; and, if your Highness be pleased to give credit so far to me, you may safely believe no man more able and faithful to give a just account of all the carriages here unto whomsoever your Highness shall command hither. This being all I have at present to trouble your Highness, with humble desire of your Highness's pardon for this honest presumption, I shall remain ever your Highness's most obedient faithful servant,

JOSEPH RHODES.

May it please your Highness to give me leave to take such notice, that just upon the despatch of these, Major Wheeler being employed to this end, that Sir Richard Byron should write and be desirous of some other to command abroad, but himself continue his command within the walls; herein also give me leave to speak with all clearness, and that from the mouths of the best and chiefest officers,

that his Majesty's service cannot be done, but we necessarily destroyed if both one and other be not.
. . . hands of some able to manage it; but this is the device of our commissioners, who do nothing wherein their own in.[1] . . .

For Prince Rupert's Highness.

Newark, Jan. 10, 1645.

What the complaints were which dissatisfied parties made against Sir Richard Byron we are unable to ascertain. Mrs. Hutchinson tells us that the officials with whom Sir Richard had disagreed were the king's commissioners, and she further says that so many factions prevailed on all hands that "it was as if discord had infected the whole English air with an epidemic heartburning and dissension." The disputes in regard to Newark resulted in the removal of the brave Byron from the governorship, Sir Richard Willis being entrusted with the command in his stead.

By February Newark, in the centre of a circle of foes, had become reduced to a condition of much distress. Famine and disease had both made their appearance, and had begun to create deadly havoc. Desperate sallies had to be made to obtain supplies. The soldiers became weakened for want of food, and in addition to the pangs of hunger, they had to submit to the alarm and danger of occasional cannonading. In the midst, however, of their difficulty and distress, no thought of surrender appears to have been entertained. On the contrary, the garrison defended the town with praiseworthy vigour, and waited with anxiety, but with confidence, the arrival of assistance. Communication had been opened with Prince Rupert, and his Highness determined to make another effort for the relief of the town. Accordingly he despatched Sir Marmaduke Langdale, an officer of considerable experience and courage. How Sir Marmaduke fulfilled his mission is well narrated by an officer in his service, whose manuscript was printed in 1782.[2] The writer states that the order delivered to Sir Marmaduke, who was then at Leicester, was to get what force he could together, and a certain number of carriages with ammunition, which the Governor of Leicester would deliver to him, together with a quantity of provisions, especially corn and salt, in order to relieve Newark. He then goes on to say:—"This town had long been besieged; the fortifications of the place, together with its situation, rendered it one of the strongest in England; and as it was the greatest pass in the kingdom, so it was of vast importance to the king's affairs. There was in it a garrison of brave old rugged boys, fellows that, like Count Tilley's Germans, had iron faces, and they had defended themselves with extraordinary bravery a great while, but were now reduced to exceeding strait for want of provisions. Accordingly we received the ammunition and stores, and went away for Newark. About Melton Mowbray, however, Colonel Rositer (25th Feb.) set upon us with above 3000 men; we were about the same number, having 2500 horse and 800 dragoons. Rositer, like a brave officer as he was, charged us with great fury, while we defended ourselves with all the eagerness

---

[1] Quoted in Bailey's *Annals of Nottinghamshire*, vol. ii. p. 732.
[2] *Memoirs of Prince Rupert*, vol. iii. pp. 48-50.

we could, and withal gave him to understand we were not to be beaten as soon as he expected. While the fight continued doubtful on our side, our people, who had charge of the carriages and prisoners, began to enclose our flanks with them, as if we had been marching; which, though it was done without orders, had two very good effects, and did us extraordinary service. First, it secured us from being charged in the flank, which the enemy had twice attempted, and secondly, it secured the carriages from being plundered, which had spoiled our expedition. Being thus enclosed, we fought with great security; and though Rositer made three desperate charges upon us, he could never break our line. Our men received him with so much courage, and kept their order so well, that the enemy, finding it impossible to force us, gave over the attack, and drawing off, left us to pursue our orders. We did not offer to chase them, but were contented enough to have repulsed and beaten them off; and our business being to relieve Newark, we proceeded. If we are to reckon by the enemy's usual method, we gained the victory, because we kept the field, and had the pillage of their dead; but otherwise neither side had any very great cause to boast. We lost about 150 men and as many hurt; they left 170 on the field, and carried off some. How many they had wounded we could not tell. We got 70 or 80 horses, which served to remount some of our men, who had lost theirs in the fight. We had, however, this disadvantage, that we were compelled to march on immediately after the service, the enemy having only to retire to their quarters, which were hard by. This was an injury to our wounded men, who were afterwards obliged to be conveyed to Belvoir Castle; and from thence we advanced to Newark.

"Our business at Newark was to relieve the place, and this, whatever it might cost, we resolved to do; although, at the same time, to avoid fighting unless we were compelled to it. The town, at this time, was rather blocked up than besieged; the garrison was strong, but ill provided; we had sent them word of our coming and our orders to relieve them, and they proposed some measures for our doing so. The chief strength of the enemy lay on the other side of the river; but they, also having some notice of our design, had sent over forces to strengthen their leagues on the opposite side. The garrison had often surprised them by sallies, and indeed, had chiefly subsisted for some time by what they had brought in by this means.

"Sir Marmaduke was at first for a general attempt to raise the siege, but was dissuaded from this by the consideration that if he should be beaten, which by possibility might be the case, the town would then be certainly lost. Having arrived at their destination about two hours before night-fall, the horse drew up before the enemy's works, they at the time making preparation for an assault, and seeing no foot soldiers expected our dragoons would dismount, and attack them. They were in the right to let us attack, if such had been our design, because of the advantage of their batteries and works; but as we intended only to amuse them at this point, their caution only effected our intent; for while we thus faced with our horse, two regiments of foot, which came up to us but the night before, and which were all the infantry we had, with the waggons of provisions and 300 dragoons, taking a compass clear round the town, on the east side, and so on by the south, till they came opposite the castle, and near to the river. Upon a signal agreed upon before, the garrison sallied out at this very juncture with all the men they could spare; and dividing themselves into two parties, whilst one party moved to the left to meet our relief, the other fell upon that body which faced us. We kept in motion, and, upon this signal, marched to their works. Our dragoons fired upon them, and the light horse wheeling and counter-marching often, kept them in continual expectation of an attack. By these means the enemy were kept employed and their attention distracted, whilst our foot, with the waggons appearing on that quarter where they were least expected, easily defeated the advance guards, and forced their post; where, entering the leaguer the other part of the garrison, who had sallied that way, came up to them, received the waggons and entered with the dragoons safely into the town. That party which we faced on the other side of the works knew nothing of what was done till it was over. The garrison then retreated to the town in good order; and we drew off, having finished what we came for with little fighting. Thus we plentifully stored the town with all things wanting, and with the addition of 500 dragoons, after which we marched away."[1] Effectual relief having thus been provided, making it impossible for the town to be reduced through famine for some time to come, the besiegers early in March thought fit to retire, leaving the town again open and free.

On the withdrawal of the besieging forces, troops from Newark advanced to Southwell and cut off a regiment of Parliamentarians who were stationed there. In Lincolnshire they successfully attacked Grantham, and penetrated as far as Barton-on-Humber, returning with a load of money, plate, and arms. Another expeditionary force went as far as Wirksworth, in Derbyshire, and adroitly succeeded in capturing a Parliamentary committee stationed there for the governance of that district. Hearing that the governor of Nottingham was in London, a scheme was devised for seizing the fort at the Trent Bridge. On a Sunday morning at the latter end of April (1645) a Newark party stormed the fort, captured it, and put to death nearly the whole of the troops on garrison at the time. The event threw Nottingham into an uproar, and had it been followed by a vigorous assault on the town and castle, both might have been taken. Colonel Hutchinson, hearing of the matter whilst in London, went to the Parliament and told the House how the Newark men had taken the fort and, for aught he knew, the garrison also. He then hastily returned home and erected a small fort near to the Trent Bridge, in which he placed a lieutenant and thirty men. Detecting the design, which was, if possible, to enclose them, the Newark troops sallied forth and drove the lieutenant and his party away. After this, finding that they were not supported by a larger party, they abandoned

---

[1] This account is confirmed in some of its more important details by Mr. Savage in his brief narration of the wars. He has, however, fallen into error as to the date, for he states the raising of the siege to have been in the summer. Neither Mr. Savage nor the officer above quoted mention who was in command of the besieging army.

the fort and rejoined their friends on the south side of the Trent, having gallantly, and in the face of superior numbers, held the place for nearly a month.

In May (1645) the king entertained the idea of proceeding to Newark, where he had so many loyal and active adherents. He thus writes to the queen from Stone:—

> Stone, Fryday, 23d May. Deare Hart—This is more to tell thee where I am, then for any great newes I can send thee at this tyme, for since the Rebelles ar gone from Chester, I haue not fixt any certaine desyne, as not yet being surly informed, what the Scots, on the one syde, or Fairfax (with his new-moulded army) on the other, ar doing; it is possible wee may meet with some of them to-morrow, if it be trew (according to some probable intelligence) that a strong party of Rebelles ar coming to Strafford, w[ch] if so we shall goe asyde to salute them: otherwaise we shall goe straight to Vxater & so towards Newarke to joyne with some of my forces thereabouts, & expect the coming of Charles Garrat & newes from Goring; whom I have commanded to aduance that way with all speed, because I fynde (most asseuredly) that all the Rebelles' armys ar gathering together Northeward, to distresse this, or (as themselues usually call it) a King caching, of w[ch] (according to comparative probability of former yeares) they ar lykely to haue smalle comfort: I will not send thee westerne newes, but leave those to my sone, lykewaise I hope Adrian May (whom I could not send safely away till now) will picke some good freshe newes out of the west to present thee with, though what he carryes from hence will be but stale: So praying as hartely for thy healthe as successe to myselfe, I rest eternally thyne. [Endorsed] 1645. To my Wyfe, 23d May.[1]

The king did not come to Newark, but sat down before Leicester.

In response to an application from headquarters, the Newark cavalry, which had rendered itself justly celebrated for its valour, was despatched to the assistance of the king at Leicester. His Majesty possessed a formidable force, and had determined to wrest the town from the hands of the few Parliamentarians by whom it had been held since the retirement of Sir Marmaduke Langdale. On the 30th of May a summons to surrender was sent by Prince Rupert to the committee, and not being acceded to, the attack commenced. The Newark cavalry arrived during the progress of the action, and coming up fresh when the king's troops were nearly worn out with fatigue, they rendered conspicuous service. Armed only with swords and pistols they faced the musketry and great guns of the garrison, mounted the breach, and, as Clarendon states, led on by a brave commander, Colonel Page, were the first among the Royalists who forced their way into the town, and planted the black flag of Rupert amidst the ruined fortifications of the desolated place.[2] The capture of Leicester seems to have aroused the Parliamentarians to extra efforts. Fairfax, whose army had been greatly recruited, hastened from Oxford to retrieve the loss. He met the Royal forces near Naseby, and the celebrated battle which shattered the king's prospects was fought on Saturday the 14th of June. The Royalists were completely routed, and Fairfax, with his triumphant army, marched to Leicester.

---

[1] *Vide* Reports of Royal Commission on Historical MSS.
[2] That part of Leicester where the attack was made is still named "the Newarke." One hundred and forty waggon loads of plunder obtained in the town, were sent off by the Royalists to Newark.

In the Naseby battle the Newark horse, to the number of 1200, took a prominent part. They were under the command of Sir Richard Willis, and when the plan of battle[1] was arranged, they were placed as a reserve to the left wing along with the king's regiment of foot, the king's Life Guards (horse) and Prince Rupert's regiment of foot. During the conflict they were attacked by the right wing, commanded by Cromwell and led by Colonel Whalley. They were beaten, though they fought stoutly, and maintained a retreating fight among the gorse bushes.

The best and strongest garrison which now remained to the king was that of Newark. Thither many of the Royalists repaired, riding direct from the fatal field at Naseby, and never drawing the rein until safe within the shelter of the Newark walls. Three months later they were joined by the king, who had determined to proceed northwards in order to unite with the Scotch force which Montrose had successfully collected in his favour. It was at the beginning of October[2] when his Majesty arrived in Newark, where he was cordially and affectionately welcomed. He stayed in the town above a week, rectifying errors which had arisen in the management of the garrison through the extravagant habits of Sir Richard Willis, the governor. Sir Richard had levied contributions almost at will from the surrounding country, and dwelt in the castle in great state, assisted by a staff of twenty-four general officers. The king employed himself in reducing their great expenses, regarding them as injurious to his cause. The luxurious Cavaliers resented this reformation, and complained that they alone had been blamed and visited, while Goring and Granville acted as they pleased without rebuke. A report now arrived that Montrose had obtained another victory, and the king once more set forth in search of a conquering army that he could call his own.[4]

On leaving Newark his Majesty marched northwards with the limited forces that remained at his disposal. The first day he reached Tuxford, and on the next he arrived at Welbeck, where he remained two days. Writing from Nottingham, October 15, 1645, to Mr. Gilbert Millington, Colonel Hutchinson says: "The king's quarters at present are about Welbeck, and Worsop Manors, where he has not above 1500 horse, and those so tired and ill-armed that he is able to do little service with them. During their quartering on the south side of the Trent near us we continually alarmed them, and found them of so daunted and dejected spirits that twenty of our men charged fifty of theirs in a town where the queen's regiment quartered, and killed and took thirty of them, and if ours had had more strength they must have brought away many more; they took thirty horse with some good luggage. At another time forty of ours charged a hundred and twenty of theirs at Langar, routed them, killed near twenty, and took fourteen, one of whom is a major, who is sore wounded. Cannot say what the king intends, but reports are some for

---

[1] Plan of battle, by De Gomez, engineer to Prince Rupert, copied in Warburton's *Life of Prince Rupert*.

[2] The king was in Newark about the middle of August, but passed hurriedly through on his way to Oxford, where news reached him of Montrose's success.

[3] Walkers' *Historical Discourses*, p. 145.   [4] *Prince Rupert's Life*, vol. iii. p. 198.

the relief of Skipton, others Chester, and some say that Colonel Rositer so visited their quarters that they make trial of others for more security."[1]

During the king's stay at Welbeck, the governor of Newark visited him, and he was also waited upon by the commissioners of Nottinghamshire and Lincolnshire, who proposed to assemble in his behalf a body of infantry at Doncaster. Whatever hopes were raised by the loyalty of Newark and the promises of the commissioners were destined, however, to be ruthlessly dispelled. While at Welbeck the news reached his Majesty that the Scotch army that was advancing towards him was not in his interest, but in the interest of the Parliamentarians. Montrose had met with little success, and the Parliamentarians had raised a strong force, which had marched beyond Newcastle. In this dilemma Lord Digby urged the king to retire for shelter to Newark, and this he resolved to do. He proceeded as far as Southwell, when he was informed that a body of Nottingham men were marching to arrest him. On receiving this news, he hurried forward to Newark, and it was fortunate that he did so, for he had hardly left Southwell an hour before two hundred of the enemy's horse entered the town.

The dates and particulars of the king's wanderings in the early part of October may be gathered from the subjoined extract from the *Carolinum* :—

October 1645.

	Nights.	Miles.
Thursday, the 2nd, dinner at Ridgheath, the rendezvous ; supper at Lichfield, the Close	1	22
Friday, the 3d, no dinner at Tongue ; supper, Mr. Sutton's	1	15
Saturday, the 4th, no dinner at Newark : supper, Lord Danecourt's[2]	9	26
Sunday, the 12th, to Tuxford, the White Hart	1	12
Monday, the 13th, dinner in the field at Welbeck ; supper, Marquis of Newcastle's	1	12
Tuesday, the 14th, no dinner at Newark ; supper, Lord Danecourt's	18	12

From Newark the king directed the following letter to Belvoir :—[3]

Charles R.

Trusty & wellbeloved, Wee greete you well. Whereas Wee have for the present thought fitt to dispose our horse in this & all other garrisons in these parts, whereby they may bee ready for any service, our pleasure & comand to you, therefore, is, that you imediately provide in that our garrison fit accomodation for Generall Gerrard's horse, beeing about 300 besides your owne, and that you assist them in levying & bringing in provisions for the supply both of horse & men out of the severall towneshipps allotted for their provisions during their stay with you. Herein Wee expect you shall employ your best care & diligence. And so Wee bid you farewell. From our court at Newarke, this 6th of October 1645.

By his Matie's Comand, EDW. WALKER.

[Addressed] To our trusty & wellbeloved Sr Gervase Lucas, Knight, Governor of Belvoir Castle.

Complaints having reached the king relative to Colonel Legge, one of the most active of his adherents, his Majesty wrote expressing his unwillingness to believe the rumours :—

[1] *Vide* Reports on Historical MSS. [2] *The Friary* ; see page 64.
[3] *State Papers, Domestic*, October 1645.

FROM THE KING TO SECRETARY NICOLAS.

For what concerns Will Legge I have no suspicion of but what Lord Digby [cipher] informed me, which satisfies me as to what I have done, but will not believe him guilty of [cipher] trickery before I see more particular proofs.[1]

Newark, Oct. 10.

The king appears, however, to have altered his mind and to have dismissed Legge. He had previously written to Prince Rupert relative to the loss of Bristol, stating that the manner in which it had been surrendered by the prince was the greatest trial of his constancy that had yet befallen him.[2] Accompanying the letter his Majesty sent a passport to the prince to leave the kingdom—"to pass from these dominions into the parts beyond the sea."

The prince, as may readily be imagined, was greatly grieved and mortified at these letters from his uncle, whom he had served with such earnestness and fidelity. He wrote, however, a temperate reply to the king, intimating that he should deem it his duty to make a full explanation, and expressing his belief that if the king had heard his account of the transaction he would not have censured him. Prince Maurice warmly espoused his brother's cause, and though letters arrived from the king forbidding Prince Rupert to approach, he determined to visit his Majesty at Newark, whatever the consequences might be. The prince's proceedings will be best gathered from the following notes to his diary.[3] "Then the prince had a letter from the king to discharge him of the generalship, and Legge of the government of Oxford; Bristol having made a suggestion that he held correspondence with the Prince Elector, though he never wrote one letter to him. The king was then at Newark, and the prince resolved to break through the enemy, and go to the king, and he accordingly took his troop, about eighty in number, and went to Banbury, where Prince Maurice came to him, and accompanied the prince, and there laid his design to get through Northampton, and came to Burghley, to the Duke of Buckingham's house, which was a Parliament garrison; and as he marched by it the garrison came out, and one that was governor there had been formerly in his Highness's troop. The prince drew his troops into two divisions in a broad highway there, and the governor had but a small forlorn hope, which they beat in. The governor came with the gross of his body, and knowing the prince, he came up with his pistol and missed fire, and then cried for quarter; but the prince shot him dead, and then in a short time the rest fled. Now that the prince's design of breaking through was known at London, they laid fifteen hundred horse for him at several places. After this the prince marched and came to a bridge not far from Belvoir Castle, where there were three hundred horse more. The prince stood first towards the horse as if he would charge them, and then upon a sudden turned, and the enemy followed him; the prince turned and fought them, and beat them twice, by which the other

---

[1] Evelyn's *Correspondence*, vol. v. [2] Clarendon's *Rebellion*, v. 252.
[3] Notes to Prince Rupert's diary, not in his handwriting, but compiled from his words and from the anecdotes of those who served with him. *Vid. Memoirs of Prince Rupert*, vol. iii. p. 193.

COUNCIL OF WAR AT NEWARK.

forces of the enemy being alarmed, they came up to the prince. Says the prince to his people, 'We have beaten them twice, we must beat them once more, and then over the pass and away,' which accordingly they did. Then the prince sent away his papers and baggage to Belvoir Castle." The prince was again attacked before he reached the shelter of the castle, but he drove his assailants away, and so "fair and softly" came to Belvoir.

When the king heard of the prince being so near, he wrote a letter to him, by which he required him to stay at Belvoir until further orders, and reprehended him for not having given obedience to his former commands. Notwithstanding this, he came next day to Newark, and was met by the Lord Gerard and Sir Richard Willis, governor of the town, with one hundred horse, two miles on his way. About an hour after, with his train, he came to court, and found the king in the presence-chamber, and without ceremony told his Majesty that he was come to render an account of the loss of Bristol, and to clear himself from those imputations which had been cast upon him. The king said very little to him; but meat being brought up, went to supper, and, during the time, asked some questions of Prince Maurice, without saying anything to the other. After he had supped, he retired to his chamber, without admitting any further discourse; and the prince returned to the governor's house (of which we give an illustration),[1] where he was well treated and lodged.  The king, how displeased soever, thought it necessary to hear what Prince Rupert would say, that he might with more ease provide for his own escape from thence, which it was high time to make; so he appointed the next day to hear his defence, which the prince made with many protestations of innocence, and how impossible it was long to defend that fort after the line was entered. His Majesty did not suspect his nephew to have any malicious design against his service, and had no mind to aggravate any circumstances which had accompanied that action, and therefore, after a day or two's debates, caused a short declaration to be drawn up, by which Prince Rupert was absolved from any disloyalty or treason in the rendering of Bristol, but not of indiscretion.[2] The document was as follows:—

CHARLES R.

Whereas, our right dear and entirely beloved nephew, Prince Rupert, did, at a Council of war, held by us, at Newark, the eighteenth of this instant, October, there being then present our right

---

[1] The governor's house was the ancient house in Stodman Street, represented in the engraving. It has recently been repaired and renovated, but the upper storeys have been carefully preserved in their original form. The house is occupied by Messrs. Jenkinson and Son, jewellers, of Newark and Retford.

[2] *History of the Rebellion*, by Jacob Hooper, Esq., vol. ii. p. 805.

trusty and well-beloved cousin and councillor, Montague, Earl of Lindsey, Lord Great Chamberlain of England; our right trusty and right well-beloved cousin, Richard, Earl of Cork; our right trusty and well-beloved Jacob, Lord Astley, Field Marshal-General of our army; John, Lord Bellasis, Captain-General of our horse-guards; and Charles, Lord Gerard, Lieutenant-General of all our horse forces; our trusty and well-beloved Sir Richard Willis, knight and baronet, governor of Newark; and John Ashburnham, Esquire, our treasurer at war; desire to clear himself for the rendering the city and garrison of Bristol, with the castle and forts thereof; and thereupon produced a narrative of the matter of fact during the siege, with the articles for the rendering of those places; which being accordingly read and considered, we were then pleased to say that we did not believe our said nephew to be guilty of any the least want of courage and fidelity to us, in the doing thereof; but withal, we believed that he might have kept the castle and fort a longer time; we having absolutely resolved speedily to have drawn together all the forces we possibly could, and to have hazarded our own person for his relief; our design being so laid, as that in probability it would have succeeded. To which our said right dear nephew answered, that whatever he did therein was by the advice of the Council of war of that garrison; and that he could not, in his judgment, possibly expect such relief. Besides, he alleged that he had not received from us any intimation thereof; but said that if he had, he would have maintained those places to the last man, though the tender regard he had to the preservation of so many officers and soldiers was the chief reason that induced him to capitulate for the whole; they having so long and faithfully served us. All which our said right dear nephew humbly submitted to our judgment; who, upon which, at a second hearing, before ourself, this twenty-first day of October, the lords and others above named being then likewise present, and, upon a serious consideration of the whole matter, we were then pleased to declare that we were fully satisfied that our said right dear nephew, Prince Rupert, is not guilty of any the least want of courage or fidelity to us, or our service, in that action; and we then gave leave to the lords and others, above specified, to declare their opinions on that point; who, upon our leave, and a full consideration of the narrative formerly delivered, did unanimously concur with us; declaring likewise, that our said right dear nephew is not guilty of any the least want of courage or fidelity to us, or our service, in that action.

Given under our sign manual, at our Court, at Newark, this twenty-first of October 1645.[1]

The matter having thus been settled the king resolved to take means for his own escape. The change of the posture of the enemy and Poyntz's coming to the north side of the Trent, made his Majesty resolve to begin his march on the Sunday night, being the 26th of October; which resolution he imparted to none but two or three of the most trusty. But the differences were grown so high between the governor and the commissioners, and had been so much increased by the mutual contest which had been between them in the presence of the king, that there was no possibility of reconciling them, and very little of preserving the garrison, but by the removal of the governor, which was so evident to the king, that he resolved on that expedient, and on the Sunday morning, sent for Sir Richard Willis into his bedchamber, and after many gracious expressions of the satisfaction he had received in his service, and of the great abilities he had to serve him, he told him his own design to be gone that night, and that he resolved to take him with him, and to make him captain of his horse-guards in the place of the Earl of Lichfield, who had been lately killed before Chester (which was a command fit for any subject), and that

[1] *Memoirs of Prince Rupert*, vol. iii. p. 201.

he would leave the Lord Bellasis governor of Newark, who, being allied to most of the gentlemen of the adjacent counties and having a good estate there, would be more acceptable to them. Sir Richard Willis appeared very much troubled, and excused the not taking the other command as a place of too great honour, and that his fortune could not maintain him in that employment. He said that his enemies would triumph at his removal, and he should be looked upon as cast out and disgraced. The king replied that he would take care and provide for his support, and that a man could not be looked upon as disgraced who was placed so near his person; which he told him he would find to be true, when he had thought a little of it. So his Majesty went out of the chamber and presently to the church.

When he returned from church, he sat down to dinner; the lords and others of his servants retiring likewise to their lodgings. Before the king had dined, Sir Richard Willis, with both the princes, the Lord Gerard and about twenty officers of the garrison, entered into the presence-chamber. Willis addressed himself to the king, and told him that what his Majesty had said to him in private was now the talk of the town, and very much to his dishonour. Prince Rupert said that Sir Richard Willis was to be removed from his government for no fault that he had committed, but for being his friend. The Lord Gerard added that it was the plot of the Lord Digby, who was a traitor, and he would prove him to be so.[1] The king was so surprised with this manner of behaviour, that he rose in some disorder from the table, and would have gone into his bed-chamber, calling Sir Richard Willis to follow him, who answered aloud that he had received a public injury, and therefore that he expected a public satisfaction. This, with what had passed before, so provoked his Majesty that, with greater indignation than he was ever seen possessed with, he commanded them to depart his presence, and to come no more into it; and this with "such circumstance" in his looks and gesture, as well as words, that they appeared no less confounded; and departed the room, ashamed of what they had done; yet, as soon as they came to the governor's house, they sounded to horse, intending to be presently gone. The noise of this unheard of insolence quickly brought the lords who were absent and all the gentlemen in the town to the king, with expressions full of duty, and a very tender sense of the usage he had endured. There is no doubt he could have proceeded in what manner he would against the offenders. But his Majesty thought it best, on many considerations, to leave them to themselves, and to be punished by their own reflections; and presently declared the Lord Bellasis to be governor; who immediately betook himself to his charge, and placed the guards in such a manner as he thought reasonable.[2] In the afternoon a petition and remonstrance was brought to the king signed by the two princes and about four and twenty officers, in which they desired, that they and Sir Richard Willis might receive a trial by a court of war.

---

[1] See *Edward Walker*, p. 149. [2] Hooper's *History of the Rebellion*, vol. ii. p. 808.

The document was as follows:—

COPY OF PRINCE RUPERT'S PETITION, ETC., DELIVERED AT NEWARK.

May it please your most excellent Majesty,

Whereas, in all humility, we came to present ourselves this day unto your Majesty, to make our several grievances known; we find we have drawn upon us some misconstruction by the manner of that, by reason your Majesty thought it appeared as a mutiny. We, therefore, the persons subscribed, with all humbleness and carefulness present unto your Majesty that we, who from the beginning of this unhappy war have given testimony to your Majesty and the world of our fidelity and zeal, do think ourselves unhappy to lie under your Majesty's censure. We do, in all humility, present these reasons unto your sacred Majesty, rather in writing than personally, lest we should hazard a second misrepresentation. That many of us trusted in high commands in your Majesty's service, have not only our commissions taken away without any reason or cause expressed, whereby our honours are blemished to the world, our fortunes ruined, and we rendered incapable of trust or command from any foreign prince; but many others, as we have cause to fear, are designed to suffer in the same manner.

Our intention in addressing ourselves to your Majesty, and our submission now are, that your Majesty will be graciously pleased that such of us as now labour under the opinion of unworthiness or incapacity to serve your Majesty, may at a council of war receive knowledge of the cause of your Majesty's displeasure, and have the justice of defence after what can be alleged against us, and, in particular, concerning this government (of Newark), and if, upon the severest examination our integrity and loyalty to your Majesty shall appear, that then your Majesty be graciously pleased to grant us either reparation in honour against our enemies, or liberty to pass into other parts, which are the humblest desires of your Majesty's most obedient and loyal subjects and servants.[1]

In conversation, the petitioners said they hoped his Majesty would not look upon this action of theirs as mutiny.[2] The king said he would not now christen it, but it looked very like one; as for the court of war, he could not make that a judge of his actions; but for the passes, they should be immediately prepared for as many as desired to have them. The next morning passes were sent them, and in the excitement of the occasion, swords are said to have been drawn in the king's presence. Thus Pepys, in his *Diary* states:—"My Lord Bellasis told us how the king, having newly put out Prince Rupert of his generalship, upon some miscarriage at Bristol, and Sir Richard Willis from his governorship of Newark, at the entreaties of the gentry of the county, and put in my Lord Bellasis, the great officers of the king's army mutinied, and came in that manner with drawn swords into the market-place of the town, where the king was, whereupon the king said, 'I must horse,' and there himself personally, when everybody expected they should be opposed, the king came, and cried to the head of the mutineers, which was Prince Rupert, 'Nephew, I command you be gone.' So the prince, in all his fury and discontent, withdrew, his company scattered."[3]

The account, however, appears to be somewhat exaggerated. Sir Edward Walker, who was present in Newark, does not allude to such a riotous scene as that said to have taken place in the market, and he would doubtless have done so had it occurred. That swords were drawn, seems evident, but they were unsheathed in the heat of quarrel, and not by way of mutiny, or as an insult to the king. A Parliamentary Journal says:—"At length the king was enforced to rouse himself, and

---

[1] Evelyn's *Memoirs*, v. 150. [2] Hooper's *History of the Rebellion*. [3] Pepys' *Diary*, vol. i. p. 329.

to interpose between their angry swords, and commanded peace to be observed; the malady being treated without, but not within. The king, not many hours after, sent for the two princes—who, being come unto him, he assured them that, in this present condition wherein he was, it brought some comfort to him to see them with him, which comfort he desired might be continued, having of late been so exercised with afflictions upon afflictions, that he needed no addition to them. For his own part, he made no doubt of their fidelity, but he said that, after having so many obligations to him, if they should now nourish any secret design to turn into his adversaries, either through fear or hope, that, he was afraid, would bring but little credit to them. To this Prince Rupert answered, that he honoured his Majesty too much to take offence at anything he pleased to have done, that he was well pleased if his Majesty would acknowledge his innocency; to which we hear that his Majesty made reply, he did. The princes, being departed from the presence of his Majesty, repaired presently to Gerard, with whom they took new counsel, and disclaiming to remain at a court wherein the Spanish and Irish factions did mingle, they called together their friends, about four hundred, and marched to Worton (Wiverton) House, fourteen miles from Newark; the king looking out of a window, and weeping to see them as they went."[1]

On the night of the 3d of November (1645), accompanied by about five hundred horse, his Majesty left Newark, and marching by the Trent for some miles, escaped the notice of his enemies and turned across to Belvoir. Here he was provided with guides to conduct him to Oxford, and with as little delay as possible he proceeded to that city. On the day that he left Newark, he wrote a letter to the Marquis of Montrose, expressing affliction at his inability to send him assistance, and his sense of the eminent fidelity and generosity the Marquis had shown in his service. His Majesty assured him that his less prosperous fortune, so far from lessening his estimation of him, would rather cause his affection to "kythe the cleerlier" to him.[2]

Newark had by this time become closely invested. In addition to the extensive forces under the control of the Scotch commander, the troops from Nottingham, Derby, and Leicester, had arrived under General Poyntz, and a strong detachment had marched from Grantham under General Rosseter. The Scots established their headquarters between Newark and Kelham; General Poyntz was between Newark and Farndon; Colonel Rosseter at Balderton, which the English made their headquarters; Colonel Theo. Gray at Coddington; Colonel Henry Gray at Winthorpe. There were two lines of circumvallation drawn, one inner and one outer, and these were strongly protected by means of a profusion of redoubts and bulwarks. The construction of the redoubts was not carried on without considerable loss and difficulty. The garrison seized every opportunity of disconcerting the besiegers. Furious sallies were made, and a heavy cannonading maintained. Colonel Hutchinson had several narrow escapes; whilst going to view the works a cannon ball killed a brother officer

---

[1] *Mercurius Britannica*, King's Pamphlets, vol. ccxxxii., No. 5.
[2] Preserved amongst the papers of the Marquis of Montrose.—*Vide* Reports on Historical MSS.

who was riding abreast of him. On another occasion he had not left his tent above a minute before it was torn to pieces by a shot, and the sentry killed. The works of Newark consisted of bastions about twenty in number, each connected by a curtain; they commenced at the river Devon, three furlongs and one perch north and south from the castle, and completely surrounded the town from these points. The whole line of defence was seventeen furlongs and a half, or nearly two miles and a quarter; its distance from the queen's sconce was 330 yards, from the centre of the marketplace to the extent towards Balderton 500 yards. A deep ditch ran parallel to these works, which the besieged had generally the opportunity of having filled with water. The bridge over the Devon was defended by what was called an iron turnpike, or kind of chevaux de frize, besides which there was a strong redoubt at the distance of a furlong, in front, on the road leading to Kelham. This, together with the king's and queen's sconces, formed the whole of their outworks. There had been a fort at the Crankley's, but that was now within the enemy's line of circumvallation. Muskham Bridge was broken down at Prince Rupert's relief, and that at Kelham was in the same state, the passage being occupied by a bridge of boats.[1]

The Scots, to maintain their forces, applied to Parliament, who voted them £1500 monthly. The money not being promptly forthcoming, the Scots petitioned for the grant to be made effectual.[2] In order to raise the funds which the English as well as the Scotch commanders required to supply so large an army as that quartered before Newark, the Lords and Commons in Parliament assembled issued an ordinance directing a levy to be made upon "the eastern association," and the counties adjacent. The ordinance, which was printed pursuant to the direction of the Parliament,[3] states that "for the better reducing of Newarke, and securing the several counties hereafter named, there shall be forthwith raised the several sums of money in the several and respective counties and cities hereafter named." The amounts to be levied from the "several and respective" places were as follows:—County of Norfolk £2187:5s., city of Norwich £113:4s., county of Suffolk £2187:5s., county of Essex £2088:5s., county of Cambridge £572, Isle of Ely £225:8s., county of Huntingdon £315:11s., county of Hertford £752:10s., county of Bedford £309:7s., county of Northampton £139:4s., county of Leicester £77:15s., county of Derby £159:12s., county of Lincoln £640:7s., and county of Rutland £55:18s. These sums were to be reimbursed to the counties and cities out of the estates of delinquents.

The opening of another year (1646) saw Newark still in the midst of enemies. Now and then there was a bold sally by the garrison, and on one occasion more than two hundred of the troops under General Poyntz were killed and taken prisoners. On both sides, the utmost determination to conquer prevailed. During March an attempt was made to induce the garrison to yield without further bloodshed. From a pamphlet printed in April of the same year we have an account of these negotiations. The

---

[1] Shilton's *Hist. Newark*; also shown on a plan of the fortifications made at the time by the chief engineer. Copied by Buck, and published 1726. [2] *Lords' Journals*, vol. viii. p. 197.
[3] Imprinted at London for John Wright, at the King's Head, in the Old Bayley, 13th August 1645.

pamphlet commences with a letter from the Commissioners at Newark to the Speaker of the House of Commons, and encloses the summons made to the garrison to surrender, and the governor's reply.[1]

To the Hon. WILLIAM LENTHALL, Esq., Speaker of the Honourable House of Commons.

SIR—On Saturday we met with the Earls of Lothian and Dunferlyn, the Lord Belcarris, Sir David Hume, Sir Thomas Carre, Sir Thomas Ruthen, Mr. Glandonnon, and Mr. Johnston, committee of the Parl^t. of Scotland, and did that day agree upon, and send summons into Newark; we have here enclosed sent you copies of our summons and the answer; and since the mercy of the Parl^t. is neglected, we hope by such other means as God and you have put into our hands, ere long to reduce that place. The Yorkshire committee have written unto us to be disengaged of the promise of repayment what the counties of Lincoln, Leicester, and Nottingham, should for the present lay out for the quarters of their horse (in regard their ordinance was expired, and that they sensibly find by experience they are like to expect no more moneys considerable, so long as the Scotch Horse continue those heavy burdens upon the county): we, therefore (and for that without present payment these countreys cannot long provide for their horse) shall be necessitated to send them into Yorkshire, and the line being now finished, we hope they may be spared, without much prejudice to the service. Colonel Poyntz doubts not but suddenly to turn the course of the river Trent, which ran close under Newark, and will in a little time turn the river Smite into a new channel, that their mills may not be helpful to them, or the water hinder the approaches on the north side Trent. The field-officers have viewed the most convenient place for forts, to shoot either into the town or sconces, which are in preparation, and will speedily be finished. We shall lose no time to make a good end of this service; and we beseech the House that their promised and often-ordered payments to the three companies of the Isle of Ely and the other forces may be duly observed. We have received a letter from the committee of the eastern association, which declares their great care and pains for payment of their garrison soldiers, and we hope the execution of their orders will not be neglected.

Your humble servants,
W. PIERREPONT.   W. ARMYNE.
THO. HATCHER.   EDW. ASCOUGHE.

THE SUMMONS TO NEWARK.

We, the committee of both kingdoms, being sent and authorised to use our best endeavours for the reducing the town and garrison of Newark, do hereby (in the name of both Houses in the Parl^t. of England, and for the use of the king and Parl^t.) demand of you, that you forthwith surrender the same into their hands; it is the pious care of the Parl^t., to prevent the effusion of Christian blood, the wasting of the country, and the destruction of towns. We shall esteem ourselves happy in being instruments to averte those miseries; and shall therefore grant to you, the gentlemen with you, and the town, honourable and fair conditions; which, if you shall now neglect, and will let nothing but experimental sufferings declare unto you your unavoidable ruine; you are to give an accompt to God, to this present age, and to posterity, for all the blood that shall from henceforth be shed, for the wasting of your native and neighbouring counties, and destruction of so considerable a place; you may not, nor can any in reason expect (and most assuredly on the faith of honest men, you shall not hereafter obtain from us) such terms as we are now willing to

---

[1] A letter to the Hon. William Lenthall, Esq., Speaker to the House of Commons, from the Commissioners employed by the Parliament for the reducing of Newark, together with the summons of the Commissioners of both kingdoms to the governor for the delivering up of the said town for the use of the king and Parliament, and the governor's answer thereto, appointed by the Hon. William Lenthall to be forthwith printed and published. London, printed by Edward Husband, printer to the Hon. House of Commons, April 6, 1646.

afford you. We sent no summons until you and all with you might see we were able by force to attain what we much rather desire by treaty ; the Parl^t. have 16,000 horse and foot at present before your town, souldiers of experience, united, and in health and courage. This is no way mentioned as if we trusted in the arm of flesh (God the Lord of Hosts hath manifested that we fight His battles), but to shew you the vast expenses which will be occasioned by the continuance of this siege (for which your estates must answer), and that your holding out may not further tempt the Almighty ; And thoughe you should not regard your own ruine, though some others should be of that your opinion, shall yet that wealthy town be sacked, and others perish with you that see their own misery and would avoide it? A prudent man, a souldier, cannot live or die in reputation of peace of spirit, to maintain a place not so long tenable, as till it can be relieved, of which you cannot have the least hope ; flatter not yourselves, relief is not to be had ; Chester was nearer succours and considerable armies for them in the West and in Wales ; now scarce can be seen what remains of either. Was not that strong city of most great importance? were they not very often promised? did not all assurances to be relieved come to them? They had none ; that place is surrendered. Your health, if you rightly consider in what state you are, promises you certain and sudden destruction. You are prepared in some things for defence ; you know and we know you are not for some others. Consider these things seriously, and you cannot but through them see your ruine to be inevitable, if you do not avoide it by accepting what is now offered. We will expect your answer on Monday next by eleven of the clock in the forenoon at Balderton.

Signed in the name and by the warrant of the committee of both kingdoms, by Rutland Lothain.
Balderton, March 28, 1646.

To the Governor of the town and garrison of Newark, the gentlemen there, and the mayor, aldermen, and burgesses of the town.

THE GOVERNOR OF NEWARK'S ANSWER TO THE SUMMONS.

March 31, 1646.

Having received a paper subscribed by the committee of both kingdoms, directed as to a committee governour, by putting the gentlemen and corporation in equal commission with me (though the joining us together was with the intention to divide us), I shall in answer thereto desire you to reflect upon the king's letter of the 23d of March, sent to the two Houses of Parl^t. (which I received from your own quarters), where, in a full compliance with all their desires, upon the most gracious conditions that ever prince propounded, he offers to disband his forces and to dismantle his garrisons. To what end, then, do you demand that of the steward, whereof the lord and master makes a voluntary tender? I conceive it my duty to trace his commands, not to outstrip them ; so that, though honour and conscience would permit the delivery, yet civility would retard it. Least his Majestie's act of grace be frustrated by my over hasty speed, I shall waive the arguments wherewith you endeavour to evince my consent ; I am neither to be struck into apostasy by the mention of fair conditions in a misty notion, nor to be frightened into dishonour by your running division upon the force of Chester. For as I do not measure my allegiance by my interest to the former, so I do disdain that poverty of spirit, as by resemblance of Chester to suffer by example ; I can be loyal without copy, and I hope this garrison shall never be the transcript of their calamity. You may do well to use your fortune modestly, and think not that God Almighty doth applaud your cause by reason of your victories, or that He hath not a blessing in store for ours. Whereas you urge the expense of the siege and the pressure on the country in supporting your charge there, since occasioned by yourselves, I am not concerned ; yet in order to their ease, if you will grant a pass to some gentlemen to go to the king and return, I may then know his Majestie's pleasure, whether, according to his letter, he will winde up the business in general, or leave me to

steer my own course. Then I shall know what to determine; otherwise I desire you to take notice that when I received my commission for the government of this place, I annexed my life as a label to my trust.
F. BELLASYSE.

Newark, March 31.
To the Commissioners of both kingdoms.

A few days after the reply had been sent, the garrison manifested their determination to resist if need be to the uttermost. A vigorous onslaught was made on the quarters of General Poyntz, and the works were carried by storm. Many were put to the sword, and others being driven back into the Trent, were drowned. When the impetuous Cavaliers returned, they carried back with them scores of prisoners, which was not perhaps a wise proceeding, seeing that they needed to be maintained, and that their presence added much to the suffering of those confined within the walls of the town.

Whilst Newark was thus holding out with its accustomed gallantry, the king's position at Oxford had become extremely critical. Three proposals were being considered by his advisers—first, whether it were not better he should attempt to obtain conditions from the Parliamentary army than be exposed to certain ruin in the garrison; secondly, whether an effort should be made for him to break through the army, and tender himself to the two Houses at Westminster; and lastly, whether he should try to get privately beyond the seas. The king and his council were debating which of these schemes would be for the best, when there arrived Mons. Montreville, an agent from France, who had instructions to treat with the commissioners of Scotland, then in London, and to endeavour by all the means he could devise, to induce them to moderate their desires with regard to the covenant and other particulars, which they had hitherto rigidly insisted upon. To aid him in his mission, he was told he might assure them that if they would come to terms, the king should go into their army as it lay before Newark. The commissioners embraced the proposal made by the agent, and shortened the work by giving him authority to repair to Oxford and to comply in all things with the king's desires, so that he might dispose his Majesty to go speedily to their army. The king appears to have approved of the negotiation, but scrupled what security he should have for the due performance of the conditions agreed upon.

The agent tendered him the engagement of the Crown of France, which, in favour to the Scots (he affirmed), was obtained by them, and that that security was part of the commands he stood charged with. He proffered that his Majesty should peruse his instructions on the point, or have with all expedition any other satisfaction he should require. When that part was examined, the king declared that he fully rested upon that engagement, and finding all things ready for a conclusion, sent the agent to the Scots army to acquaint them with what had passed, and to desire (if they adhered to the treaty) they would send a strong party of horse to Gainsborough to meet him, providing that he would not be bound to anything till he received an account how the agreement relished in the army; resolving, that if by any means, he could have reasonable terms (in the interim) from either the English Parliament or the army, he would not go to the Scots. Negotiation with the Parliament failed, and Montreville sent word from Southwell that he found the commissioners of Scotland residing with the army not fully resolved to concur in the articles of agreement which the commissioners at London had submitted for his Majesty's satisfaction.[1] The next day, however, more letters came from him, in which he intimated that all difficulties were reconciled, and that David Lesley, their lieutenant-general, had orders to meet his Majesty with 2000 horse at Gainsborough. This news was so welcome to the king, who despaired of any other reception, that he resolved to attempt a passage through the English army (April 26), and proceed to the Scots.

For a detailed account of what took place on the arrival of the king near Newark, after a somewhat perilous journey, we must turn to the narrative of Mr. Ashburnham, who accompanied his Majesty the whole of the distance, and from whose account we have gathered some of the preceding particulars. He writes:[2]—"After nine dayes travell upon the way, and in that time haveing passed through fourteene guards and garrisons of the enemies, wee arriv'd safe at the Scotts army before Newarke; where being come, his Majestie thought the most proper place for his reception by the generall and Scotts commissioners would be the house of the French agent (at Southwell), that all circumstances belonging to the treatie betweene his Majestie, the Crowne of France, and the kingdome of Scotland, might be adjusted. Manie lords came instantly to waite on his Majestie with professions of joy to finde that hee had so farr honour'd their armie as to thinke it worthy his presence after so long an opposition; some of them desireing to knowe wherein they might best express their gratitude for the greate confidence hee had in them; his Majestie reply'd that hee should be well satisfied for the hazards he had runn to get to them if they would cheerefullie apply themselves to perform the conditions upon which hee came unto them; the Lord Lowthian (as his Majestie was pleas'd to informe mee) seemed to be surpriz'd with the word 'conditions,' and affirm'd that hee had never been privie to anie thing of that nature, nor did hee beleeve that anie of the commissioners resideing in the armie had anie more knowledge of that treaty than himself. Whereupon his Majesty desired the French agent to summe up his instructions from the Crowne of France, and to make a narrative of his negotiations thereupon with the Scotts commissioners resideing in London, which when hee had done, some of the lords did assure his Majestie that they were altogether ignorant of those particulars, and that, therefore, the treaty being with their commissioners at London, and they being a distinct bodie of themselves could not be responsible, or anie way concern'd therein."

We must here interrupt the course of Mr. Ashburnham's interesting narrative in

---

[1] Montreville, when at Southwell, lodged at the King's Arms Inn, now the Saracen's Head. He conferred with the Scots commissioners in the Archbishop's Palace, a noble structure, which was afterwards demolished by the rebels. *Vid.* Letter of Dr. Stukeley quoted by Dickinson, p. 86.

[2] "A narrative by John Ashburnham of his attendance on King Charles the First from Oxford to the Scotch army, and from Hampton Court to the Isle of Wight."

order to mention that the Scots commissioners with the army not only repudiated any participation in the treaty, but from first to last denied that they were cognisant of the king's intention to throw himself into their midst. Their letter from Kelham to the Parliament was as follows:—

"Right Honorable—The earnest desire which we have to keep a right understanding between the two kingdoms moves us to acquaint you with that strange Providence with which we are now surprised, together with our carriage and desires thereupon. The king came to our army yesterday in so private a way that after we had made search for him, upon the surmises of some persons who pretended to know his face, yet we could not find him in sundry houses. And we believe your Lordships will think it was matter of great astonishment to us, seeing we did not expect he would have come in any place under our power. We conceived it not fit to inquire into the causes that persuaded him to come hither, but to endeavour that his being here might be improved to the best advantage for promoting the work of uniformity, for settling of religion and righteousness, and attaining of peace according to the league, and covenant, and treaty, by the advice of the Parliament of both kingdoms, or their commissioners authorised for that effect. Trusting to our integrity, we do persuade ourselves that none will so far misconstrue us as that we intended to make use of this seeming advantage for promoting any other ends than are expressed in the covenant, and have been hitherto pursued by us with no less conscience than care. And yet for further satisfaction, we do ingenuously declare that there hath been no treaty nor capitulation betwixt his Majesty and us, nor any in our names, and that we leave the ways and means of peace unto the power and wisdom of the Parliaments of both kingdoms. And so far as concerns us, as we have a witness in Heaven, we are confident to make it appear to the world that there is nothing more in our desires, than in all our resolutions and proceedings, to adhere to the covenants and treaty. Our gravest thoughts shall be taken up in studying, and our utmost abilities employed in acting, those things that may best advance the public good and common happiness of both kingdoms, wherein, by the help of the Most High, we shall labour to use so much tenderness and care, that we hope it shall soon appear that our actions have been the issue and result of honest and single intentions. And further, we cannot (in a matter of so deep consequence and common interest) but seek your Lordships' advice; for which effect we have also written to the committee of estates of Scotland, with intention to move, by your joint councils and resolutions that we at last, after a seed-time of many afflictions, may reap the fruits of truth and peace. In this confidence we remain, your Lordships' humble servants,

LEVEN.	HUME.
BELCARRIS.	GLENDOWYN.
R. OF FREELAND.	LOTHIAN.
DUMFERLING.	T. CARRE.
	JOHN JOHNSTONE."

The secretary of the Scots army, in his relation to the commissioners,[1] confirmed the letter. He said, "On Tuesday morning his Majesty came to Southwell to the Scots army, and General Leven having intelligence that his Majesty was come unto their garrison, for some officers that were upon the guard that saw him had some suspicion of him that it was the king, who, making it known, a search was made three hours before they could hear where he was; and about noon his Majesty sent to General Leven, letting him know where he was, and that he was then with the French agent, and that he would cast himself upon them; whereupon there was advertisement

---

[1] Printed pursuant to order of Parliament by Elizabeth Purstow, London, May 11, 1646.

given to the Scots commissioners of his Majesty being there, who with General Leven went to his Majesty and caused him to remove his quarters to Kelham, where there was much amazement to see unto how low a condition his Majesty was brought."

The king was naturally astonished at finding the commissioners repudiate any expectation of receiving him. "His Majestie," continues Mr. Ashburnham, "demanded how hee came to be invited hither, and what reason they had to send him word that all differences were reconcil'd, and that David Lesley was to have met him with a partie of horse. They answered that it was verie true, for they approved well of his Majestie's confidence in them, beleeveing that the end of his honouring their armie with his residence was onlie to have made that the place where hee intended to settle a peace with his two kingdomes; in short, such was the indisposition of the Earle of Lowthian towards his Majesty as hee (being president of that councill, and of good credit amongst them) would never suffer anie discourse to be made to his Majestie other than the takeing of the covenant, and subscribeing all the nineteene propositions for the satisfaction of both kingdomes; things, that as they were most distant from his Majestie's resolution, being most averse to his conscience and honour, so they were most unexpected from persons so highly favour'd by the greate adventures hee had undergone for them. To this usage they presently added restraint to his person, setting strict guards upon him, and grew in all things so rigid and severe, as to mee there seemed little distinction (either in discourse or anie part of the entertainment) betweene his Majestie and his subjects, so that from these proceedings the king did plainly discover that they intended to evade all performances of conditions upon the treaty, by their not being privie to what those commissioners at London had done.

"It was clear the Scots were absolutely resolved to make the best market they could of the prize in their hands, but whilst they were thus exercising their unnatural dominion over their soveraigne, a messenger was sent them for a conference with the commissioners from the Parliament, resideing in the English army, which blocked up Newarke on the other side. At which meeting, the English commissioners (as I was informed by one who was present at the debate) desired that the persons of his Majestie and myselfe (who only came with him) might be delivered into their hands, which if they should refuse to doe, a charge would justly lye against them, that wee were come thither by some privat invitation, and pressed hard the separation that the action would necessitate betweene the two nations, if anie such practize should bee discovered; but certainly the Scotts wanted not confidence to deny their knowledge thereof to them who had done the same to his Majestie before. As to their delivery of his Majestie, they told them that, though they could not in honour consent to the giveing up of anie man who came to them upon trust and confidence, as his Majestie had done, yet desired them to beleeve that his comeing thither should in no wise bee prejudiciall to the interest of either nation, but rather an advantage to all, they could promise to themselves; hopeing they should be better understood by the Parliament of England, than to conceave they had any hand in that action, other than by such opportunities to worke the wished-for designs for both kingdomes in relation to Church and State.

"Yet, notwithstanding all the protestations they made of their ignorance of his Majesty comeing to them, and their resolution to continue faithfull to the Parliament during his abode there, the English Commissioners parted with them altogether unsatisfied, which strooke no little terror into the Scotts; insomuch that, at their returne to the king, their discourse seemed to be of a more temperate complexion, and their applications to carrie with them more reverence than before; intimating that probably, when the nobility of Scotland should meete with all their Commissioners, those things insisted on by his Majestie to be the subject-matter of the past agreement would then be thought fit to be consented to, and therefore propos'd to march speedily to Newcastle, whither they were all to come; and that they might rise from the siege with more honour and securitie to themselves, they desir'd that his Majesty would send to the Lord Bellasis (then governour of Newarke) to surrender that place to the English, upon as honourable termes as they could obtaine, that whilst they were busied in receiving the towne, the Scotts might have more leisure and less interruption in their march to Newcastle; concluding that if his Majestie would so doe, they would not be wanting in their services to him, when there should be occasion. Howbeit, his Majestie well knew that the true ground of that proposition was their fears that the English would rise from the seige of Newarke, and follow them in the reare; yet, upon the whole matter, this offer qualified somewhat the rigidness of their former entertainments, though his Majesty continued still deeply sensible of the greate misfortune hee had drawne upon himself in comeing hither; in the sad apprehension whereof hee began to turne his thoughts another way, and to designe his remoove out of their hands, commanding mee, that if I had aquaintance with anie of the Commissioners from Parliament, to take the opportunity of his sending to the Lord Bellasis, to desire him that hee would procure mee a meeting with some of them, his Majesty resolveing, if that were granted, to give mee authority to treate of his comeing to them upon termes of honour and safety; which accordingly I did, nominating to the Lord Bellasis Mr. William Pierrepont, but the Lord Bellassis told me (for I got leave to speake with him when hee had obeyed his Majestie's commands of surrendring the towne) that Mr. Pierrepont would by no means admit of anie discourse with me in the condition I then stood, the action of waiting on the king to the Scotts armie rendring mee more obnoxious to the Parliament than any man living; and so those thoughts of his Majesty going over to the English vanished."

Some of the details thus given by Mr. Ashburnham rest on his testimony alone, but others are fully confirmed, and especially his references to the treatment of the king at Kelham. The secretary to the Scots affirms that "care was taken for fresh clothes and other refreshments for his Majesty." This may have been the case, but that the king was rigidly guarded and somewhat unceremoniously treated is affirmed by several authorities. Mr. Savage avers that "nothing could be worse off than the condition off the king. From this time his Majesty found himself entered upon a state

Y

of thorough captivitie, in which he experienced afterwards no other variety than that of frequently changing his jail and his jailers, till the time of his unhappy execution." On the evening that the king arrived at Kelham, the Scots, as briefly mentioned by Mr. Ashburnham, procured an order from him to Lord Bellasis for the surrender of Newark. The message was received by the garrison with the greatest grief. It was believed that the place was strong enough to hold out for several months, and after resisting so much, the brave defenders did not relish the idea of suddenly yielding. The governor, Lord Bellasis, is stated to have shed tears, and the soldiers united with him in his sorrowful feelings. Nor were the townsmen wanting in valour. William Baker[1] is said to have headed three deputations of the townspeople to his lordship, assuring him of their strength both in provisions and ammunition, and begging him to disobey his Majesty's orders. In this difficulty, the governor decided to send to the king, and to acquaint him with the loyalty of the town. His Majesty's reply was conclusive. He wrote as follows :—

BELLASYSE.—Such is the condition of affairs at the present, that I can give no hope at all of relief, nor of better conditions than those I sent you last night ; wherefore, the best for my service will be that you conclude upon them with all expedition ; the chief reason being that, according to my design, I am necessitated to march with the Scotts army this day northward, but cannot move till this agreement be consented to by you. CHARLES REX.

There was no alternative but to yield, and Lord Bellasis accordingly proceeded to treat with the besiegers for that purpose. The conditions upon which he consented to give up the town were of a most favourable character. They were as follows :—

ARTICLES Agreed and Concluded the sixth day of May 1646, between the Commissioners hereunder named, authorised by the Committee of the Parliament of both kingdoms of England and Scotland, on the one part, and the Commissioners hereunder named, authorised by the Right Honorable John, Lord Bellasyse, Lieut.-General to his Majesty, of the Counties of Nottingham, Lincoln, and Rutland, and Governour of the Town and Castle of Newark, of the other part ; touching the Surrendering of that Garrison, and the Castle, Forts, and Sconces thereunto belonging, to the Committees of both kingdoms, for the use of the Parliament of England.[2]

1. That the town and garrison of Newark with the castle, forts, sconces, ordnance, mortar-pieces, arms, ammunition, provisions, and necessaries of war (not hereafter expressed), be surrendred on Saturday next, by ten of the clock, into the hands of the committee of both kingdoms, or whom they shall appoint for the use of the Parliament of England, without imbezelling any of them.

---

[1] Dickinson says it was William Baker who headed the deputations, and that he was mayor at the time. A reference to the list of mayors, however, shows that Mr. Baker was not elected to the office until November. Mr. Thos. Smith was therefore mayor when the town was surrendered. Thoroton says (vol. i. p. 391) : "Mr. Smith, the valiant maior, upon his lordship communicating to him the king's order, urged the said governor with tears, to trust God and sally."

[2] Ordered by the House of Commons to be printed, May 11, 1646.

2. That the Governour of the said garrison, the Lord Bellasyse, shall march away with his servants, horses, arms, and their proper goods, to any garrison he shall name, not besieged or blockt up, or to his own house, there to remain unmolested (submitting to all ordinances of Parliament), and also, that the said Lord Bellasyse shall have liberty upon desire, any time within three moneths, to passe beyond seas, and to have passes granted for himself and his servants accordingly.

3. That all officers in commissions, or that have formerly been in commission, shall march away with their horses, arms, and their proper goods, the common souldiers, horse and foot, with their money, clothes, and swords, to any garrison not besieged or blockt up, or to their houses, as they shall make choyce of. And those that have not money, to have free quarter in their march, and not to march above ten miles in one day unless they please, and to have a convoy and carriages provided for carrying away their goods; hostages being given for the return of the convoy and carriages: And such goods as cannot be removed, the owners shall have three moneths' liberty to dispose of them.

4. That all such officers and gentlemen now in the garrison, who shall desire to depart this kingdom, shall, upon signifying thereof to the commissioners of both kingdoms, any time in three moneths, have passes for that purpose for themselves and servants, ingaging themselves during their stay to do no disservice to the Parliament.

5. That all such officers and souldiers, as by reason of sicknesse, wounds, or otherwise, are not able to march out at the time appointed, shall have liberty to stay in the town, or some other convenient place, till they be recovered; and such as are not able to provide maintenance for themselves shall have care taken of them.

6. That all noblemen and gentlemen in the said garrison shall have liberty to march forth the same, with their horses and arms, and their known menial servants, with their horses and swords, to their own houses, there to remain unmolested, submitting to all ordinances of Parliament: and to have liberty to carry away their own proper goods then, or at any time within three moneths, or to have passes for themselves and servants to go beyond sea upon desire, within three moneths; and in the meantime to engage themselves to do nothing to the disservice of the Parliament.

7. That all clergymen in the said garrison shall have liberty, with their horses, servants, and their own proper goods, to march to any garrison unblockt up, or not besieged, or to their own houses, there to remain unmolested (submitting to all ordinances of Parliament).

8. That the mayor, aldermen, and inhabitants of the said garrison, shall not be molested in their persons, priviledges, goods, or estates (submitting to all ordinances of Parliament), but to enjoy the same liberties, and to have the same protection as all other towns have which are under the power of the Parliament.

9. That the ladies, gentlewomen, wives, widows, children, and servants belonging to any of the persons mentioned in the former article, or any others, shall have liberty to march forth of the said garrison with their coaches, horses, and proper goods, as in the sixth Article. And if any of them, by reason of sickness, or any other just reason, cannot march forth, then they shall have liberty to stay there till their recovery, and then to depart unmolested.

10. That all prisoners now in the said garrison, castle, or forts, or any other prisoners of war taken by either party since the siege began, shall forthwith, upon signing these Articles, be set at liberty, unlesse they be detained for criminal offences, charged upon them not as souldiers.

11. That all persons comprised within these Articles, grounded upon the summons of the 27th of April, which began this present treaty, be recommended to compound with the Parliament for their estates, as coming in before the 1st of May; so as they do effectually prosecute such compositions within two moneths next ensuing the date hereof.

12. If any of the persons above mentioned shall violate any of these Articles, or any part of them, they shall lose the benefit of all the said Articles.

13. Lastly, That for the performance of these Articles, hostages be mutually given, and that a

cessation of arms be continued by both sides, till the time of surrender, according to these Articles. And that guards and convoys be appointed to protect the gentlemen and souldiers in their march from violence.[1]

Signed by us, authorised by the commissioners for both kingdoms.

ALEXANDER POPHAM.   RICH. THORNTON.
FRAN. THORNHAUGH.   GILBERT CARRE.
JOHN HUTCHINSON.   PHILIP TWISTLETON.
WALTER SCOT.   A. DOUGLAS.
HENRY GRAY.   JOHN ARCHER.

Signed by us, Commissioners for the Lord Bellasyse,

MARM. DARCY.   J. ATKINS.
GER. NEVIL.   ANTH. GILBY.
THO. INGRAM.   SIMON FANSHAW.
BRY. PALMS.   HUGH CARTWRIGHT.
A. EYRE.   EDW. STANDISH.

The deplorable condition of the town at the period of the surrender is graphically described in a manuscript preserved in the library at Tatton Park, and communicated to Mr. Dickinson by Mr. A. H. Eyre. The writer, a Parliamentarian, whose initials only (S. R.) are appended, says:—"Truly it is become a miserable, stinking, infected town; I pray God they do not infect the counties and towns adjacent, which is the care of the Commissioners, that way to be taken to prevent. Yesterday the Commissioners came up to see them march out of Newarke: they carried not much out of the town, for they had very few carriages. We have gathered together 4000 armes already, and there are many more; which, by reason of the sickness in divers places, the officers dare not yet venture to fetch out, nor make that diligent search, which will afterwards be made, so soone as with safetie may * * Those of Newarke garrison, from the greatest to the least, doe all of them generally seeme to be much discontented at hearing that the king had delivered himself up to the Scots, and are much troubled at the hearing thereof, which makes many of them repent that ever they were engaged in the service, being like men in amaze at the hearing of it. And when 800 of them had marched out with the Lord Bellasis, the Governor, and it was expected that they should name to what garrison they should march, they would not nominate any garrison to march to, for the further service of the king in the design against the Parliament.

"But as all the rest that came out of Newarke, who were above 1000 more, so they went away every one to their owne homes; so that as I confesse, I know not where they could have easily found out any garrison unbesieged to march to, according to the Articles; so they did not care to put themselves into any other prison in that service in which they have received so little satisfaction. The Governor hath been very punctual and the conditions very exactly observed. They labour much to compound with the Parliament.

[1] The articles are similarly given in the pamphlet containing the relation of the Secretary to the Scots army referred to on page 159. There are, however, one or two differences in the copies, which are worthy of notice. In the names of the commissioners of Lord Bellasis, Robert Sutton appears in the place of Hugh Cartwright, and Balmes is substituted for Palms.

"The countrie thereabouts are all summoned to come in with spades, shovels, pickaxes, and other necessaries, on Monday next, to assist in the demolishing of the workes of Newarke, which are very many, strong, and formidable. I believe they will come in very joyfully to that worke, which tends to so much and great an ease to all those parts, as they have found by wofull experience, since they felt the oppression of that garrison and others, of all which they are now clear, and all will be buried in the ruins of this, which they are forthwith to level. Doctor Deane, Doctor Hurst, Doctor March, and divers other malignant clergymen in Newarke, who, with the gentrie, as Alderman Atkinson, and the rest of the malignant townsmen and others are very sad in the towne, so as they walk away in a mournful posture, the troubles of those parts being now most troubled in their own thoughts.

"The Scots are marched northward with all their body of horse and foot; the horse march before the king, and with them Lieut.-General David Lesley. They march along with great rejoicing that they have the king with them. I believe that a party of horse will goe before with the king towards Newcastle. They say that they have dealt plainly with the king since he came into their army. We have taken great care to prevent the souldiers from plundering, though some of them did very well remember how they were stripped at Spittle. The governor hath had very great care of all things in Newarke to see that nothing should be imbezzled, and hath showed himself very noble. There is a great change by which God hath given us experience of His great power in bringing downe the hearts of the proud and haughty. Our commissioners have endeavoured to continue all amity and loving accord with the Scots, who, I believe, will grant to have his Majesty disposed of as both Kingdoms shall agree, and in the meanwhile to remain with General Leven's army, where he shall dispose of him; and General Leven hath carried on things since he came to the army with great wisdom and moderation, and it is said that he is much troubled what to do to please both kingdoms in the matter of giving account about the king. Newarke is now open and free again, and the tradesmen are preparing to furnish their shops. Our soldiers have already bought divers things of them, and the country have a free market, but it cannot be expected to be much whilst the sickness is in the town; but to God be the praise, who hath done this great worke for us, to deliver this stronghold of the enemies into our hands. I pray God that others (so oppress'd) may have the like mercy, and peace and truth be settled amongst us."

The sickness to which allusion is made in the foregoing account was probably a malignant fever of unusual violence. In Thoroton it is described as "the plague," and such was the definition frequently given in his day to serious outbreaks of epidemic disease. On reference to the parish registers at Newark, we do not find any mention of the calamity, but in the register of the parish of Stoke,[1] in which parish the Castle and a large portion of Newark would be included, there is a fearful list of the deaths that occurred, each entry being marked with a large cross. Preceding the list are the

[1] We desire to acknowledge the courtesy of the Vicar of Stoke, the Rev. A. W. Bailey, in bringing the register for our inspection.

words, "All those names that have ye crosse before them, did dye of ye plague; from which plague, good Lord, deliver us." The first deaths were those of "Richard, son of Thomas Walker, *alias* Custance and Ellen his wife," who were buried the 28th of May. It is evident from this that the disease made its appearance in May, and it continued during July, August, and September, with appalling severity. Families were rapidly thinned, several of the same household being buried in one day, and so fast did the people die when the pestilence was at its height, that some were buried on their own land, instead of being conveyed to the parish graveyard. Thus, after one death is the entry, "buried in ye field," and after another (that of Edward Shenton, son of Thomas), "buryed in his croft." Amongst the other entries are the following:— " Peter and John Hasolam, that came from Newark and boarded at William Simpson's, died of ye plague and were buryed 30th July," and on the 3d of August William Simpson and his daughter-in-law were also buried. "A youth from Newark, that lodged at Ruth Bagguley's, dyed of ye plague and was buryed 2d September," and there is a list of Bagguleys, Parnhams, Brocktons, and others, who were swept away. Before the pestilence subsided, the parish clerk, who was one of the Bagguleys, caught the infection, for we read "Robert Bagguley, the parish clerk, dyed of ye plague and was buryed ye 7th of September." Against this entry there is a cross of extra size, and at the end of the fearful list is this sad statement: "There dyed in the towne of Stoke, 1646, eight score and one, whereof of the plague seven score and nineteen. William Lloyde, vicar, 1646." The year before the plague there were only nine deaths in the parish, and the year after six.

A list of the noblemen and gentlemen slain in the king's service, in or near Newark, contains the names of the following:—Earl of Kingston, and Colonels Beton and Herne, slain between Newark and Gainsborough; Lieutenant Colonel Markham of Ollerton and Colonel Cavendish, slain between Newark and Gainsborough; Colonel Leeke, son of Lord Deincourt, slain near Newark; Lieutenant-Colonel Pavier, slain between Newark and Lincoln; Colonel Stanhope, Major Clifton, and Captain John Clifton, slain at the capture of Shelford House; Colonel Ferdinand Stanhope killed at Bridgford; Sir Troilus Turberville, Captain of the King's Life Guards; Sir Ingram Hopton and Sir Charles Bowles; Major Thomas Whitmore, Sir John Ramsey, and Captain Smith, belonging to the garrison of Newark, slain in different engagements in the neighbourhood; Captains Anthony Orde, Thomas Cole, and Pelham, killed at the last siege. Mr. Carey, Mr. Jennings, and Mr. Lathom, persons of note, were slain near Newark. On the side of the Parliament the loss was also great, including a great number of officers and men of rank. In the parish registers we find the following entries of burials at Newark:—In 1645, April 7, Captaine John Rogers; May 4, Captaine Robert Sandersonne; July 16, Thomas Bishoppe, a Leifetenant; August 12, Captaine Robert Bencoinne; August 15, Collonell Lowther, governor of Pontefract; October 6, Captaine Parsons; December 21, Collonell Charles Leake; and in 1646, January 14, Liefetenant Thomas Cole; 19, Liefetenant Thomas Cartwright; 28, Captaine Dercy Washington; February 6, Captaine William Wharton; February 12,

A MINT AT NEWARK CASTLE.

Captaine Henery Hutton; February 27, Major Newtonn; March 2, Captaine Edwarde Twentyman; March 20, Captaine Anthony Orde; 26, Mr. Samuel Reniger, Liefetenant of horse; 27, Captaine William Pelham; May 1, Captaine Mirhill; May 3, Captaine William Witchrote. At an earlier period is the following, "Lord Barinet Douer, generall ouer quene ffoursis." He was interred in the altar vault, June 27, 1643.

The orthography of the register at this period is very remarkable, *e.g.* Sessiles = Cecil, and Curinal Senione = Colonel St. John. Dugdale's *Diary*, under date of June 21, 1643, has the following: "The queene's forces ... advanced from Newark towards Nottingham ... Baron Done slayne on y^e K p'te." And under date of June 24 (the register distinctly says the 27th), the following: "The Barron Done buried in y^e Quire of Newarke Church, in ye vaut at ye east end, wth great solempnity." The baron is mentioned as having been a kinsman of the Prince of Orange, and, in order to ascertain the correctness of this statement, Mr. Edward Peacock, F.S.A. communicated with a Dutch friend of his, learned in historical and genealogical matters, who thus replied:[1] "Your baron Done or Douer, a kinsman of the Prince of Orange, can be only a younger son of the well-known German family of Dhona, sometimes written Dona. In the extensive genealogy of the Dhona or Dohna family, given by Hubner in his genealogical tablets, I see many of them registered, but without a date of their death; and, as your baron has not given his Christian name before dying, it will be most difficult to ascertain whether he was any of those mentioned in the said book. I have not the least doubt, that the one who fought and died in England, anno 1643, was a younger son of that family, who were to be found wherever any war was going on."

Amongst matters incidental to the siege may be mentioned the fact that, with the sanction of the king, a mint was established at the castle. Quantities of plate, brought in by the nobility and clergy, were converted into half-crowns, shillings, ninepences, and sixpences, with which to pay the troops. They were shaped as shown in the accompanying engraving; the crown between C.R., and the value in Roman numerals on the obverse; the year in which they were struck, and O B.S. (*obsidium* siege) on the reverse. An account of what was taken in Newark on the surrender, given by the Parliamentary writer, whose description of the town after the last siege we have already quoted, includes the following items:—One great piece of ordnance, called Sweet-lips; eleven other great pieces of ordnance; two mortar-pieces; divers drakes and small pieces; four thousand arms gathered; divers arms not taken in; forty barrels of gunpowder; many thousand (pounds) weight of bullets and lead; match and other ammunition, proportionable and plentiful; little fresh meat, only

[1] *Notes and Queries*, September 8, 1877.

poultry, and that very scarce; salt meat, some plenty, but much of it tainted and not fit to be eaten; butter and cheese, some store; beer and wine, many barrels; corn, good store; fuel for fire, very little." The following marched out of Newark to their own homes, at the termination of the siege:—Lord Bellasyse, governor; Lord Davencourt; Lord Lexington; Dr. Farmer, chancellor of Lincoln; Dr. Dean of York; Dr. Hurst, and other clergy; Sir John Burrell; Sir Guy Palms; Sir Charles Dallison; Sir George Hennings; Sir Robert Fedway; Sir Jarvis Skroop; Sir Philip Constable; Sir Thomas Ingram; Sir Bryan Balmes; Sir Jarvis Neville; Sir Simon Fanshaw, and other knights; Major General Eyre; Colonel Gilby; Colonel Trollope; Colonel Herne; Colonel Darcy, and Colonel Atkins. The most "malignant" aldermen, that is the most persistently and daringly loyal, were, according to the same authority, the Mayor of Newark, Alderman Atkinson, and Alderman Standish.

The judge-advocate of the garrison was John Cleveland. He was a scholar and a poet of considerable popularity. He wrote various works, which went through numerous editions. When besieged in Newark, he was not idle. He composed a volume entitled *The Muses' Mistress, a storehouse of rich fancies, written at succedaneous hours, during the action at Newark*. A correspondence between him and a Parliament officer at Grantham has been preserved. It relates to the fact of the officer's servant having stolen £133 of his master's money, and then absconded to the other side, entering what Cromwell's Captain facetiously terms "the Ark at Newark." The letters are very witty, but it is doubtful whether the judge-advocate ever took much trouble in searching out and punishing the offender. The following song is said to have been written by him, in order to cheer the garrison :—

NEWARKE.[1]

OUR braines are asleepe, then fyll[2] vs a cupp
   of capporing sacke & clarett;
here is a health to King Charles! then drinke it all op,
   his cause will fare better for itt.
did not an ould arke saue Noyo[3] in a fflood?
   why may not a new arke to vs be vs[4] good?
wee dread not their forces, they are all made of wood,
   then wheele & turne about againe.

Though all beyond Trent be sold to the Scott,
   to men of a new protestation,
if Sandye come there, 'twill fall to their Lott
   to haue a new signed possession;
but if once Lesly gett [them] in his power,
   gods Leard! heele play the devill & all.
but let him take heed how hee comes there,
   lest Sweetclipps ring him a peale in his ears.

---

[1] "Very probably writ by Jack Cleveland during the siege of Newark-upon-Trent, to cheer the garrison, when he was Judge-Advocate.—P[ercy]."   [2] MS. vis *or* vus.—F.   [3] Old Ark—Noë.—P   [4] As.—F.

> Then tosse itt vp merrilye, fill to the brim!
>   wee haue a new health to remember;
> heere's a health to our garrisons! drinke it to them,
>   theyle keepe vs all warme in December.
> I care not a figg what enemy comes,
>   for wee doe account them but hop-of-my-thumbes;
> for Morrise,[1] our prince, is coming amaine,
>   to rowte & make them run againe.
>   ffins.[2]

The story goes that when Cleveland was at last taken, he presented himself to his captors with all the conscious dignity of a prisoner of importance; and the contemptuous indifference with which they suffered him to go his ways, the collapse at once of his loved cause and fancied celebrity, broke the poor poet's heart. His poems and remains were (in 1659) collected together by E. Williamson, who dates an address "to the discerning reader," from "Newark, November 21, 1658," which begins, "It was my fortune to be in Newark when it was besieged:" Cleveland was buried in 1659 in the Church of St. Michael, Paternoster, City of London. His portrait, by Dobson, is in Bridgwater House, London.

Another production may be mentioned as forming part of the somewhat prolific literature of the last siege. It is from the pen of Colonel Dymock, and is entitled "England's Dust and Ashes raked up, or The King and People beguiled, being an Historical Narrative, or a Generall Treatise upon the present Warre, whose unlawfulnesse and authors are so plainly set out as to present his Majestie's sufferings and the malice of his adversaries to a more near and convincing discovery. Being likewise a truculent object which this generation must behold with feare, the next with thanks, and to the world's end with detestation and wonder. And lastly a true Glasse, wherein every subject that hath a conscience may view it, that if he finds anything stand wrong in the dresse of his allegiance to his Prince, by this he may right it, *nulla salus uniquo bello*. Penned at the last siege and surrendry of Newark-upon-Trent, by Colonel Thomas Dymock, his Majestie's true servant." (Printed in the yeare 1648.) The work commences with an address to the King, in which the writer unfolds his objects as follows:—"When I observed the fainting language of unprevailing armes to draw short breath, speak but seldome, and with a feeble utterance, almost all swords being put to silence in your just quarrell; I found it then high time to flourish my pen against your conspiring Catilenes, as David did his sling at the brow of the Philistine; unlikely weapons to cope with Gyants, yet I wish, sir, to this of mine a successe like his, to lay the proud monster groveling, which, glorying in his own strength, presumes to defie you, that so (without hurting his head, which I am confident he hath not), I may kill or wound him at the heart with his own usurped sword, the Scripture."

---

[1] Maurice.—P.

[2] Bishop Percy's *Folio MS. Ballads and Romances*, Hale's and Furnevall's edition, vol. ii., part i. p. 33, 1867.

In a catalogue of topographical works issued by Mr. Hotten in 1873, there is mention of another publication entitled "Newark: Orders from the Lord of Hostes for regulating the Hostes of the Lord, set down in a sermon preached at the Leaguer before Newark, on Friday, 27th March 1646, upon occasion of a publick Fast kept by English and Scotch armies before Newark, to seek a blessing from Heaven in the present siege of that garrison" (4to, 1646). A note in the catalogue says, "The discourse came from the mouth of Edward Reyner of the City of Lincoln."

In the possession of His Grace, the Duke of Northumberland, is a volume of letters, entitled *Royal Letters*. Reference is made to it in the recently issued *Reports of the Royal Commission on Historical Manuscripts*. We are told, "this collection appears to have belonged to Prince Rupert, and to have passed through his natural daughter, Ruperta, to her great grandson, the late Sir George Bromley, of East Stoke, near Newark. On the fly-leaf of the volume occurs *Cha aug oulk*, 1808. It was probably purchased by the Duke of Northumberland." The letters are not fully calendered, but a few extracts have been made to show the nature of the collection. Amongst the letters is one from Charles, Count Palatine, to the Queen of Bohemia, dated 8th May 1646, wherein he says:—"I doubt not but y^r Mat^y knoweth afore this of the King's arrival wth the Scottish army afore Newarke. Havinge been some days privat in the French resident's Montreuil, his house near it; it was ten days afore they knewe heere what was become of his Mat^y. I pray God that this way he hath taken may produce his and his kingdom's welfare and security." We may also notice two letters in French from Charles I., supposed to be to Prince Rupert. They have no signatures attached, nor is the year mentioned in which they were written. They are printed in an interesting book[1] issued by the late Sir George Bromley, and, as they contain local allusions, we give translations of them:—

YORK, *April the 7th.*

I have received your letter in which you inform me of your coming. I will make all the possible speed to start; but our army has gone to pursue the enemy, which fly so before them, that, until I have heard from them, I cannot exactly tell you on what day we shall start, but it will be in three or four days. In the meantime, I should be glad to know what forces you bring with you, and what cannon, in order that I may regulate myself on that; also what distance you can walk in a day, and the places where you will pass between where you are and Newark. I leave you to choose where you like to stay between where you are now and Newark, from this time until I inform you that I start; and if you wish to advance as far as Newark, let not your troops go beyond that place; and as for yourself, if you like to come as far as here let me know and I shall send you a convoy. I am not in the habit of taking with me only my regiment of infantry and cavalry (as I wish to take nothing from that army), which will accompany me to Newark. But I hope it will soon be able to follow, if necessary; for I believe their work will soon be done in this country. I will say nothing more, except that I am very much obliged to you for having come to take me, and that I am truly yours.

---

[1] A Collection of Original Royal Letters, written by Kings Charles the First and Second, King James the Second, and the King and Queen of Bohemia; together with Original Letters written by Prince Rupert, Charles Louis, Count Palatine, the Duchess of Hanover, and several other distinguished persons, from the year 1619 to 1665, dedicated with permission to his Majesty, by Sir George Bromley, Bart. London, printed for John Stockdale, opposite Burlington House, Piccadilly. MDCCLXXXVII.

I have already sent you over to inform you of what I think right for you to do. This bearer has promised me to remit you this note, which is to tell the same thing as the other. If you like to advance as far as Newark, or near it, do which you like best, but let not your forces pass beyond Newark. And as for yourself, if you like to come, let me know, and I will send you a convoy. This country is so ruined by the armies that I should be afraid lest your troops could not subsist. I hope in a day or two to inform you when I shall start, for our army having found nothing at Pontefract, the enemies having left on their arrival, they have followed them to Leeds, where they have commenced to fight to-day. I hope to hear something about it by to-morrow, which I shall let you know immediately. In the meantime inform me what forces come with you, in order that I may regulate myself accordingly, and if you have any cannon or not. As for forces, I will take with me only my two regiments of horse and foot. The army, or a great part of it, will come with me as far as Newark. But if we defeat the rebels, as I expect, all will be right here. There will only be Hull left to reduce, which I believe will be very easy, and Yorkshire will be free. I hope you will know my short writing (little hand).

April 9th.

It is needless to add that the design of his Majesty to take the greater part of the army with him to Newark was never carried into effect.

Sir Richard Byron, who was knighted by the king, and who distinguished himself as the Governor of Newark, held a command at the battle of Edge Hill. He succeeded to the peerage on the death of his brother, in 1652, and died in 1679, aged 74. It is recorded on his tomb at Hucknall Torkard, the burying-place of the Byrons, that he and his brother suffered much for their loyalty, and lost all their fortunes, "yet it pleased God so to bless the honest endeavours of the said Richard, Lord Byron, that he repurchased part of the ancient inheritance, which he left to his posterity, with a laudable memory for great piety and charity." Sir Richard Willis, another of Newark's governors, was at one time Colonel-General of the counties of Lincoln, Nottingham, and Rutland. He was the son of Richard Willis of Horningsey and Fen Ditton, Co. Cambridge, and was created a baronet by King Charles in 1646. Sir Richard married Alice, daughter of Dr. Thomas Foxe, of Waltham Abbey, grandson of the martyrologist. He had an only son, Thomas Foxe Willis, on whose death, in 1701, at the age of 89, the baronetcy conferred on his father became extinct. Sir Richard died in 1690, and was buried at Fen Ditton, in the county of Cambridge. The gallant Lord Bellasis is stated to have been killed in a drunken quarrel in France,[1] and the peerage subsequently became extinct.

In the diary of Abraham de la Pryme,[2] published by the Surtees' Society, under date 1696, are two curious entries descriptive of incidents that occurred in connection with the sieges of Newark. The first is as follows :—"*August* 13. This day Mr. Rawson, an old, learned, and ingenious gentleman, that was at the siege of Newark in Cromwell's days (told me) in one sally that the besieged made, a blackamore took

---

[1] *Memoirs of Prince Rupert*, vol. iii., footnote to page 203.
[2] Abraham de la Pryme was curate of Broughton Linc in 1695, and was removed in 1697. See Hunter's *South Yorkshire*, vol. i. p. 181.

a Scotch soldier prisoner, upon which the poor Scot, being almost frightened out of his wits, prayed heartily, saying, 'O God! O God! have mercy upon me sawl, have mercy upon me sawl, de deel's got my body, the deel's got my body;' and the fellow was so frightened he would not follow the black, so that he was forc'd to kill him. He says he was in this sally, and saw this thing." Under date 21st Dec. is this entry, which we copy as written :—" The Anderson's is a worthy and honourable family, great lovers of the church, and of unity and peace. Stephen Anderson was a great loyalist in K. C. the First's days, and was almost ruined thereby, altho' that he had a vast estate. All Appelby then was his, and he sould it to aid the King. He gave at one time 800 pounds to compound for his estate. He maintained for several years a troop of horsemen at his own charges, and had his house at Manby thrice sacked, and everything that he had taken away from him—not only household goods, but also all his beasts and horses. He was in the siege of Newark. He had four sons, which were then but young, which four are now alive, viz., Sr Stephen Anderson, Edmund Anderson, Francis, and Edwin. When a party of the enemy sacked his house the last time, they inquired hard for Francis, his little son, who was then at nurse in the town of Manby, to have got him, and to have made his father redeem him, which so frightened the nurse, that she takes the child, dresses it and herself all in raggs, and ly's it on her back, and away she ran with it to Newark, and got safe into the town. Mr. Edmund and a sister that he had were carry'd about almost a whole year, from place to place, the one in one panyer, the other in another, but God be thank'd, never got any harm. These four brothers are yet alive. This I had yesterday from one of them."

In the *Lords' Journals*[1] there are various items of more or less interest; one is an order for £20 to the messenger who brought the good news of the taking of Shelford House. Another entry is a draft order for payment of £100 to Colonel Carleton, who brought the first news of the surrender of Newark (May 15, 1646). Captain Bedford, who also brought news of the surrender, was paid £20. The other entries relating to Newark include the following, which are of sufficient interest to merit reproduction :—

Dec. 21, 1644.—Petition of Isaac Demergue, chirurgeon (to the Parliament). Has been in the service of the State, as steward to the Lord Willoughby of Parham's regiment, and there is due to him £233 for arrears of pay; but he has been arrested by one Smyth, at the White Hart in the Strand, and imprisoned in the Marshalsea. Petitioner, who has three times lost his estate, been three months imprisoned in Newark by the king's forces, and has many maimed soldiers under his hand, prays either that his arrears may be paid, or he himself released. L. J. vii. 109.

Petition of the inhabitants of that part of the county of Nottingham lying on the north side of Trent to the committee of the Lords and Commons, complaining of the hardships they suffer at the hands of the Scots army.

Dec. 23, 1645.—Petition of Lady Brudenell on the behalf of Thomas, Lord Brudenell, her husband. Lord Brudenell was, by the violence of the ruder sort of people, driven from his usual habitation into

---

[1] *Vide* Reports of Royal Commission on Historical MSS.

the king's quarters, which is the only delinquency that can be proved against him. He is now taken prisoner at Hereford, and committed to a common gaol; and being very aged, and deprived of all means of subsistence except petitioner's fifth part, is utterly disabled to endure a strict restraint without certain ruin. Prays that he may be brought before their lordships, and such a course be taken that a person of his age and quality may not perish in his confinement. L. J., viii. 61.

Annexed :—

Answer of Lord Brudenell to the charges of recusancy made against him. Was never in Beever (Belvoir) Castle after the death of George, Earl of Rutland, nor acquainted with the governor, and did not contribute to the support of the garrison. Was not acquainted with the raising of horse about Lincoln, but at that time was living quietly at Northampton; never raised any regiment or marched at the head of any regiment, but, being forced out of his own house, was driven for safety into Newark, and went thither upon his bailiff's horse; was forced from all his dwellings, and wandered to eight or nine places for safety only. He was pursued, and his lady and servants pillaged upon their way to London (he having escaped out of the coach), notwithstanding the commanders saw the pass from the house. (Undated.)

Jan. 6, 1646.—Paper from the Scots Commissioners respecting the maintenance of their forces before Newark, &c. L. J., viii. 89.

Jan. 12, 1646.—Letter from the committee with the Scots at Newark, and the commissioners of the Scots army. Seventeen papers, presented to the house this day by Lord Montague. L. J., viii. 344-350.

June 6, 1646.—Draft order for the payment of £10 to John Taylor, the messenger who brought the letter from Major-General Poyntz from the leaguer before Newark. L. J., viii. 362.

June 8, 1646. Letter from the Scots Commissioners to the Speaker of the House of Lords, stating that the letter published in the king's name, mentioning that offers have been made to his Majesty by the Scots, is false, and that those against whom complaints were made are discharged from their army. L. J., viii. 364.

June 27, 1646.—Petition of Richard Woolph of Stamford, in the county of Lincoln, grocer. In April 1644, information having been given to the Earl of Manchester that petitioner had been in the king's quarters at Newark, though not aiding the enemy, he was fined £200, but this sequestration was afterwards taken off; he has since contributed to all Parliament taxes, and afforded free quarters to their soldiers, and has, besides, been plundered by the enemy, so that he is ruined in estate and credit; notwithstanding, the committee at Lincoln have again sequestered him for the old offence, and taken an inventory of his goods, amounting to £270, and forced him to give bond for the same. Prays the house to interfere in his behalf. L. J., viii. 398.

Aug. 6, 1646.—Draft order appointing commissioners to take the account of all free billets, and assessments imposed upon the county of Nottingham for maintenance of the Scots army whilst before Newark. L. J., viii. 456. In extenso.

Jan. 13, 1646-7. Petition of Elizabeth, Countess Dowager, to William, late Earl of Exeter. By constantly adhering to Parliament she has incurred great losses by the burning, plundering, and spoiling of her houses and goods about Newark and elsewhere; but she has chosen to bear those losses in silence till she can no longer forbear, on account of her many wants and debts. She prays for relief out of the compositions of delinquents' estates. L. J., vii. 670.

Amongst some hundreds of old papers belonging to the Corporation, stored in several large old oaken chests in an anteroom of the Town Hall, we find a bill, dated 21st June 1647, as follows:—" Demanded by Corporal Maude, for arrears due to ye soldiers, ffor 20 soldiers' pay for three weeks at 10s. a man, £30 : 00 : 00 ; for 9 weekes' pay of 10 soldiers at 10s. a man, beginning 8th of March 1646, £45 : 00 : 00." By a receipt attached, it appears that the money was duly paid. A more extended particular of money given to soldiers for arrears of pay shows a total disbursement of £60 : 11 : 10. Under date 2d of August 1647, there is a warrant to the chamberlains, signed William Baker, Mayor, ordering payment to a person of 20s., being half-year's allowance for carrying "crippldc." It must not, however, be supposed that this had any special reference to the wars, and to persons crippled or wounded thereby, seeing that the payment was in vogue in 1641, before the war broke out, as appears by another warrant which we noticed, bearing date 4th August in that year. We had hoped to find amongst the Corporation Papers many of an interesting nature, relating to expenses incurred both in connection with the wars and the various visits of his Majesty to the borough. We have only, however, been able to find the following, bearing date during the wars, in addition to those above mentioned :—" Ffor the Corporation, January 5, 1643. A banquet for my Lord Withrington £2 : 7 : 8. Layd out for ye work in Appleton £10 : 0 : 0." In the same account are these other items :—" November 20. Sug^d nutts and tobacco for Coll. Thornhagh, at Mr. Maior's, 2s., 6d. 26th. More for Col. Thornhagh, at Mr. Maior's, 2s. 4d." The following is a receipt for a gratuity :—" Received, the 22d August 1645, of Mr. Edw. Standish, Maior of Newarke, the sum of £5, for a gratuity, given to his Maties servants from the saide Corporation. I say rec^d by me,

"W^m. PAMAN."

The king's sconce, to which reference has been frequently made, stood beyond St. Leonard's, in the two fields of hillocky ground between Northgate and the river. The queen's sconce was on the left of the Farndon Road, now known as the Sconce Hills. The site of the Scotch camp is still visible in two fields near to Kelham. The destruction of the earthworks of Newark and the dismantling of the castle commenced on the 11th of May 1646, pursuant to an order of the Parliament, and in a short time, by the vigorous use of picks and crow-bars, the gang of men who had been summoned to the work converted the castle from a powerful military stronghold into a shattered ruin. A paper,[1] containing interesting historical and descriptive particulars of the venerable and once formidable building, has been courteously placed at our disposal by the Right Rev. the Bishop Suffragan of Nottingham (Dr. Trollope, F.S.A.) After brief references to its erection by Bishop Alexander, and to events thereat which we have fully described in preceding pages, and the expression of an earnest hope that what still exists of the interesting old structure may long be preserved as a visible record of the past, his lordship writes :—

"Castles of the time of Henry I. and Stephen still retained the characteristics of the earlier Norman period, but were greatly enlarged. Those built soon after the Conquest had square or oblong keeps, with a square tower at each angle projecting slightly beyond the main walls, and one or more shallow buttresses between them, of which the White Tower, London, and the Castles of Rochester and Newcastle, are familiar examples. These were usually surrounded by an inner and outer court, or

---

[1] Read at a meeting of the Lincoln Diocesan Architectural Society. Jan. 23, 1871.

baily, protected by walls and moats, or ditches, according to the character of their sites. The next change was the addition of a tower in the centre of each face of the keep, similar to those at the angles, as in the instance of Dover Castle, erected at the commencement of the reign of Henry III., and sometimes were greatly expanded, so as to enclose a large central court, although still retaining the external characteristics of the smaller and loftier keeps of earlier examples. At Sleaford, the castle built on the edge of the little river Slea, protecting it on one side, was on the other three sides defended by an outer and inner moat, fed by that stream; and most probably the same arrangement existed at Newark Castle, where the Devon could be so readily forced to serve in its defence, both having been built by the same person, at the same time, and on similar sites, in which water constituted an important feature.

"Perhaps I need hardly say that no trace of any Roman work is to be found on the site of Newark Castle, nor have any materials provided by Roman hands been incorporated in any part of its structure. I have been most anxious to discover what portions of Bishop Alexander's have survived the lapse of time, and I am very glad to say not only that fragments of his work still undoubtedly exist, but that these are easily separable from all after-work, so that no mistake, or even doubt, can exist as to what remains of the original Norman stronghold of Newark.

"After the Bishop had wisely selected the site for his proposed Castle on the edge of the Devon, and close to the old Roman Fosseway, he found that there was not sufficient room for his stronghold between them; hence his first step was to apply for a licence from Henry I., empowering him to divert the course of that road so as to enable him to secure the requisite space for the Castle, and a large pond[1] near it; and the diverted road and a still existing charter prove that his request was granted. This last is entitled, 'Carta R. II. 1., de stratâ et calceto de Newarc,' and runs thus—'H. R. Angl., Ric Bassett et A. de Vere & S. Concedo quod Epis. Lincolniæ divertat regiam viam stratam quæ transibat per villam suam de Newercâ per eandem villam suam quacunque voluerit, et concedo ipsi ut faciat calcetum vivarii sui. T. G. Cancellario. *Mon. Angl.*, vol. 8, p. 1272.' Then the following more precise licence respecting the desired fish-pond was subsequently accorded to Bishop Alexander, entitled, 'Carta ejusdem regis facta Alexandro Episcopo Lincolniæ de Vivario suo apud Newarcam,' and running thus—'H. Rex Angl., omnibus baronibus & S. Sciatis me concensisse Alexandro Ep. Lincolniæ quod faciat fossatum et calcetum vivarii sui de Newarcâ supra chiminum Fosse et chiminum ipsum per eandem villam, sicut voluerit, divertat.'

T. W. Albini Britoni,
apud W. ster,
'Ibid. p. 1274.'

[1] This fish-pond was doubtless so formed as to serve in part for the better defence of the Castle, whilst it was a most useful adjunct of such strongholds, as well as of monasteries, for breeding and preserving fish and water-fowls, such as swans, geese, and ducks; and it is a curious fact that one of the oldest inns of Newark, close to the Castle, although now modernised, has for its sign "The Swan and Salmon."

"And, lastly, the Bishop obtained a third Royal licence, allowing him to build a bridge over the Trent, as a means of approach to his Castle. It is entitled, 'Carta præfati R. H. de ponte super aquam de Trentâ,' and thus worded—'H. Rex., Angl., Justiciariis & S. Sciatis quod concessi Alexandro Epis. Linc. ut faciat fieri unam pontem super aquam Trente ad castellum suum de Newareâ, ita quod non noceat civitati mea Lincolniensi, neque burgi meo de Nottingham, et si nocuerit talem eum faciat quod non noceat. T. Epis. Sarum, N. Cancellario, et Eustachio filio Johannis apud Fomas.' 'Ibid.' This last charter, it will be observed with interest, is addressed to Thomas, Bishop of Salisbury, uncle to Bishop Alexander. And now we must endeavour to gather up the Architectural character of the Castle of Newark.

"We cannot ascertain with precision the size of its area, because all trace of its eastern limit has disappeared; but from existing remains we find it was 294 feet long on the western side, and 84 feet from its north-western angle, to the centre of the gatehouse in the northern elevation, so that, if this feature stood in the centre of that elevation, it was 168 feet long; and of this there was evidence before the Castle precincts were freed from the numerous buildings encumbering them, the form of the lower part of an hexagonal or octangular tower at the same distance eastward of the gatehouse, as the existing one on its western side. It was always protected by the Devon on the west, and most probably defended by a double moat on the other three sides, as has been before stated; but of these there is now no trace. It was built of oolite, and had thick and lofty walls, defended at the angles by square towers, probably repeated at intervals; its entrance was most carefully protected, first by a barbican on the northern edge of the moat, and then by the strong gatehouse on the opposite edge, that still remains, between which was a drawbridge. Of this Castle we have three fragments left, viz. the above-named gatehouse, and part of an adjoining wall west of it, a square tower at its south-western angle, and a small adjunct left in the lower part of the western wall by the subsequent rebuilders of that portion of the Castle. We will first describe the largest and most interesting fragments of Alexander's Castle, viz. the gatehouse: this stands on the northern side, and consists of a massive tower, oblong in plan, and three stories high, having walls 9 ft. thick. It is 44 ft. 6 in. long from north to south, and 30 ft. wide from east to west. Attached to this on the east is a staircase-turret, square in plan, but containing a circular newel staircase 10 ft. by 10 in. wide, including the newel, giving access to the upper stages of this building. The outer doorway to this was on the east side originally, but is now on the south side. The steps are almost worn away, and the building above is of the simplest character, in the formation of which very coarse gravel is a component part of the mortar employed. Above, this turret assumes an octagonal form, and the newel is of much smaller diameter. In the external face of the basement stage is a fine arched entrance, now inaccessible from the loss of the barbican opposite, to which access was no doubt formerly supplied by a causeway. This outer face of the gatehouse is shored up by a massive buttress on either side, finished above with a stepped coping and a massive roll-mould, whence springs a flat pier or buttress reaching to the top of the

wall, the eastern one being still quite perfect. Between these piers is the entrance, having plain massive piers surmounted by a semicircular arch composed of two plain unchamfered members and a hood-mould, enriched with the double fillet and scallop ornament, but was never provided with a portcullis or doors. The string above this is ornamented with the saw-tooth device. In the second stage were three semicircular-headed windows, now filled in with masonry, but the outlines of which are distinctly visible, although partly interfered with by two subsequently inserted Tudor windows. The ornamentation of the string above the stage may be termed the folded ribbon. In the upper stage above this were two small semicircular-headed windows with pillared jambs, also now filled in, but these appear to have had square heads internally, from an examination of their construction. Passing under the outer archway, another is reached of similar character, in which were doors, intended to be secured against intruders by the insertion of a massive beam laid across them, large and deep square holes for the reception of which still remain on either side. Behind this archway, on the west, is a small recess for the use of the warder, supplied with a little aperture under an arch, looking like a peephole; on each side of this portion of the entrance is a low plinth, perhaps intended for seats, and above remain the holes of the timber of the flooring of a chamber. A third similar archway, but without doors, constitutes the southern entrance to the gatehouse. Above this are the remains of a circular window in the upper stage, applied to one of the usual Norman character within, having only a semicircular head and vertical jambs. In the east and west walls of the second stage are similar windows having pillared jambs and a massive roll moulding which, together with one last mentioned, although placed at a much higher level, light one large room, which may have been used as a chapel, and if so, was that of St. Philip and St. James, provided by Bishop Alexander. On the west side of the gatehouse is a portion of the contemporary wall, which is at first slightly recessed, and then again brought forward; in this last is a large semicircular-headed window, now filled in. At the point where this Norman walling joins the later work, the difference of their character and materials is admirably exemplified; for the first is built of an oolite stone never subsequently used, with irregular courses of unshapely character and wide jointing, and also has this uncommon feature—viz., that the inner, as well as the outer angles of the work, are invariably built with the same ashlar bonding, serving as an index to Alexander's work wherever it is detected, whilst the after-work is built of larger and more carefully-worked courses of red sandstone, with narrower joints. In the angle between the gatehouse and the adjoining wall on the west is a little arch supporting a small projection giving access from one wall to the other; and in the west wall of the former, just below this, is a semicircular-headed doorway, now filled in.

"The second fragment of Alexander's Castle stands at the south-west angle of its area, and probably represents all its lost compeers. It is a lofty rectangular tower, twenty-four feet from north to south, and fifteen feet from east to west above its massive basement, which is, at least in part, a subsequent addition, as may be seen from the examination of its southern face. It consists of four stages, each of which is stepped, and its western face batters considerably. It is only relieved by its ashler quoins, and a roll mould above its lowest stage. The original parts of several of its windows remain, but their heads have been replaced, and other windows inserted. Adjoining its southern face is a small piece of the contemporary south wall of the Castle. Here the peculiar quoining before mentioned will be observed. In this tower King John is said to have died; but there is no foundation whatever for the tradition.

"The third Norman fragment is in the lower part of the west front of the Castle, and, from the character of its stone-work, is easily detected, both within and without. It projects by means of a splay from the face of the more modern wall around it, and in this is a small semicircular-headed doorway. This is now stopped up with masonry, but it clearly communicated with the two arched outlets on the external side of the wall, and both are constructed of the same oolite used by Bishop Alexander's builders. This constituted a Garde-robe, according to mediæval phraseology.

"Having thus picked out and described the earlier portions of this ancient stronghold, we will now examine the rest. It is quite clear that Newark Castle was almost entirely rebuilt in the first quarter of the thirteenth century of red sandstone externally, and grey lias within, when a different style of architecture prevailed, and a different mode of building was adopted. Of this period are the whole western façade, and that portion of the northern one between the north-west angle tower and the remnant of the older Norman work adjoining the gatehouse, excepting the south-west tower, and a little fragment of the older work near to it. Then the present large sexagonal tower arose in the place of one that probably corresponded with that still remaining at the south-west angle of the Castle; a similar smaller tower was built in the middle, and the old Norman south-western wall was allowed to remain, next to which what may be regarded as a wide buttress, was added to the new work, for the purpose of supplementing its strength. The whole of this rises from an inclined base, only broken by a segmental-headed doorway, serving as a water-gate in its northern half. A little above this is a range of five slits, the only admissible lights at so low a level. In the storey above are three rather spacious arched-headed windows, the sills of which are thirty-one feet above the ground-line; but now there are no traces whatever of their having had mullions, although tracery, apparently of a later date, formerly existed in their heads, from the evidence of an old engraving of the Castle, if that evidence is trustworthy. Two of these windows are on the north side of the central tower, and the third on the south side, beyond which is a small, contemporary, two-light window, deeply splayed within, through the great thickness of the Castle wall. No doubt there were other minor windows, or slits, of this period, but most of these were subsequently replaced by larger ones. The whole was surmounted by an embattled parapet, pierced by archers' slits, one alone of which now remains, adjoining the south-western tower. On the lower part of this front three blackened circles serving as targets may be detected, as well as the marks of many shots fired at them. These were probably used by the militia at the beginning of the present century. During the Perpendicular period, and apparently in the reign of Henry V. or VI., a large oriel window was erected towards the north end of the west front, the details of which are weak, but it must have proved a very enjoyable addition to the room in which it was placed. Above it, externally, is a shield bearing three leopards, and within, on its north side, this shield of arms is repeated. Several other windows were also inserted at the same time, more at a later Perpendicular period, and more again during the Tudor dynasty, which it would be tedious to describe. The particular use of the several rooms in the Castle cannot be even suggested with safety, except that of the one called the crypt, in the northern part of the west front. This is a large vaulted apartment, 45ft. long and 22ft. wide, having a vaulted roof supported by a central arcade of four semicircular arches, rising from slender octagonal pillars, and wall brackets. From the simple character of its pier caps, etc, and the form of its vaulting arches, it has been pronounced to be Norman, but it is clearly a part of the early thirteenth century work of the Castle, as indicated by the distinctive Early English character of the base moulding of some of its pillars. Its wall facing the Devon is 7 ft. 6 in. thick, and is lighted by four of the five little slits before spoken of, the fifth lighting a little slip adjoining the northern end of it, supplied with a doorway, perhaps intended for the use of the guard on duty. A fresh staircase was supplied to this very interesting room a few years ago at its southern end; but the original one is at the opposite end, and consists partly of steps, partly of inclines, leading first to the doorway of the slip, then to that of the room itself, and thence to the Castle court above; but part of this is now walled up, and the remainder is thought to have been a dungeon, but in reality only consisted of a portion of this means of access from the area of the Castle to its water-gate. From its position half-way between the western entrance of the Castle and its court above, almost beyond doubt it served as the guard-room of the garrison. The large apartment above, lighted by an oriel and other windows, probably constituted the hall, next to which would be the withdrawing room, and other state apartments. Here, as in the case of most old castles and monasteries, there are the reports of the existence of dungeons, and of course of a subterranean passage of prodigious length, founded in some measure on fact; but as a rule such sub-structures, when fully investigated, are more commonly found to be cellars rather than dungeons, and the mysterious passages have to assume the extremely unromantic term of sewers."

Whilst the castle and earthworks, which had sheltered so many devoted subjects of the king, were being rendered useless, the captive monarch was in safe custody. On the 3d of February 1647 he was delivered up by the Scots to the English commissioners at Newcastle for the sum of £400,000, one half to be paid instantly, and another in two subsequent payments.[1] When intelligence of the final resolution of the Scottish nation to surrender him was brought to the king, he

[1] Rushworth, vol. vii. p. 326.

happened at that very time to be playing at chess.[1] Of this event Dryden has written in one of his songs :—

> "So have I seen a king on chess—
> His rooks and knights withdrawn,
> His queen and bishops in distress—
> Shifting about, grown less and less,
> With here and there a pawn."

On the 3d of June he was seized by Cornet Joyce and escorted by 500 horse to the army, who subsequently made Reading their headquarters. From Reading the king was conveyed to Hampton Court, and contriving to escape from his captors, he proceeded to the Isle of Wight, where, though received with great demonstrations of respect, he was in reality a close prisoner,[2] more carefully guarded than he had been before. In the meantime ill feeling had developed between the English and the Scotch, and with a large army the latter invaded this country. Cromwell, who had been quelling an insurrection in Wales, started to meet them. On his way he passed through Southwell, occupying the same apartments as those which had been used by the king and Montreville. The soldiers were quartered in the town and villages, and there being a scarcity of stable room, some of the horses were placed in the antechoir of the church. The two great armies met in Lancashire, and the battle of Preston was fought (August 17, 1648). The Scots were completely routed, and the Duke of Hamilton, their leader, made prisoner. Some of the scattered and dispirited Royalists, who, in their fierce enmity to the Parliament, had assisted the Scots, to the best of their ability, fled, after the defeat, to various parts of the country, seeking shelter wherever they could escape recognition. Thus the gallant Sir Marmaduke Langdale, who had once relieved Newark in its extremity, made his way to this county, and in company with two or three brother officers took up a lodging at a little alehouse on Colonel Hutchinson's land, at Owthorpe. For a few days they enjoyed their seclusion, but unluckily for them a country fellow, suspecting that they were no ordinary travellers, communicated with Mr. Widermpoole, who had served as Major under Colonel Hutchinson. This gentleman forwarded the information to the Colonel, and the result was the surrender of the whole party, who were forthwith marched off to Nottingham Castle. Sir Marmaduke was a prisoner for some months, and he then contrived, by bribing one of the guards, to make his escape.[3]

Whilst the Cavaliers who continued in the profession of arms were hunted down and dispersed (many joining the naval force which Prince Rupert had organised),[4] those who returned to their homes to resume their occupations or to look after their pro-

---

[1] Burnet's *Memoirs of the Hamiltons*.   [3] Hume, vol. viii. p. 88.
[2] *Memoirs of Colonel Hutchinson*, p. 324.
[4] The whole Cavalier system was transferred at once from military into naval details; generals became admirals, colonels captains, soldiers marines, and garrisons ships' crews.—*Memoirs of Prince Rupert*, vol. iii., p. 259.

perties were punished with equal rigour. The estates of the "delinquents," as they were termed, were forfeited, or had to be compounded for by heavy money payments. How to avoid the severe losses that stared them in the face was the business that for a time absorbed and superseded all other. At Newark money matters were in the forefront, for disputes had arisen amongst the gentlemen who advanced loans for the king as to the way in which the burden of financial responsibility should be borne. According to Mrs. Hutchinson, a resident of Newark named Atkinson, along with several other rich men, lent money to the commissioners when the town was first fortified to enable the construction of defensive works, and the commissioners had entered into bonds for the repayment of the loans. The bondsmen were Mr. Sutton[1] (Lord Lexington), Sir Thomas Williamson, Sir John Digby, Sir Gervas Eyre, Lord Chaworth, Sir Thomas Blackwell, Sir Roger Cooper, Sir Richard Byron, and others, and the sum for which they were responsible was between £8000 and £10,000. Of this £1500 was due to Atkinson, and that gentleman, fearful of losing his money, pressed for payment. The commissioners offered him the amount without interest, but he would not accept the principal unless the interest was added, and commenced legal proceedings. Sir Thomas Williamson was openly arrested for the debt in Westminster Hall, "upon which Mr. Sutton and he being maddened, put in a bill in Chancery against Atkinson and others, praying that they might set forth to what ends and uses this money was lent to the said gentlemen."[2] They knew very well that if Atkinson confessed that he had lent his money to be used for the defence of Newark against the Parliament, he would not get much sympathy. All he seems to have recovered was £600, and the evidence that he received that sum will be found a few pages farther on in the copy which we give of a petition presented by the unfortunate commissioners to Charles II. at the Restoration. It will be seen that amongst the debts paid by some of the commissioners is the entry, "Mr. Atkinson £600;" amongst the debts given as "contracted but not paid" is "Mr. Nicholas Atkinson £200," but whether this was the same individual is doubtful, as the Christian name appears to have been inserted by way of distinction. Thomas Atkinson was mayor in 1641, and he would probably be the rich man who lent the larger sum.

[1] Robert Sutton, afterwards first Lord Lexington of the second creation, was born in 1594. There is a curious entry in the parish register of Averham, which marks the untimely death of one of Mr. Sutton's retainers: "A.D. 1618, Richard Linley, clerk to Mr. Robert Sutton, Esq., and Matthew Bromley, servant to Sir George Manners of Haddon, knight, each of other in single combat slaine, were buried the twentieth day of June." The feud between the servants did not extend to the masters, or was speedily adjusted; for Mr. Sutton shortly afterwards married Elizabeth, daughter of this Sir George Manners, whose son, on the failure of male heirs to the elder branch, succeeded his cousin as eighth Earl of Rutland. Early in 1643-4 Mr. Sutton joined the king at Oxford; his estates were in consequence sequestered by the Parliament, and his house at Averham burnt by the troops. In reward for his services, and as some compensation for his losses, Mr. Sutton was, in 1645, created Lord Lexington by Charles I. At the surrender of Newark in the following year he fell into the hands of General Fairfax, and, to avert the wrath of his captors, subscribed the covenant. He succeeded in recovering his estates on the payment of a heavy fine (£5000), but the Parliament refused to acknowledge the validity of his patent of peerage, and he was compelled to relinquish the title until the Restoration, when he resumed it. He died in 1668. Vide Lexington Papers, pp. 2, 3.   [2] Memoirs of Colonel Hutchinson, p. 326.

How Atkinson and others who had lent money to the commissioners succeeded in recovering any portion of it, does not appear. Instead of the Parliament assisting them, it laid claim to the money itself, declaring the various sums to have been forfeited by the lenders, and directing the debtors to pay in the money to the Parliamentary committee, who were to hand it over to Colonel Hutchinson as a recompense for the pecuniary losses he had suffered through his devotion to the triumphant cause. "Hereupon," says Mrs. Hutchinson, "Sir Thomas Williamson and Lord Lexington, who, being men of the best estates, were principally looked upon for the debt, applied themselves to Colonel Hutchinson, begging as a favour, that he would undertake the management of the order of sequestration given out upon their estates; and would also oblige them by bringing in several other gentlemen that were bound to bear proportionable shares. The Colonel, to gratify them, got the order of sequestration and brought them to an accommodation, wherein every man according to his ability agreed upon an equal proportion;[1] and the gentlemen, especially Mr. Sutton, acknowledged a very great obligation to the Colonel, who had brought it to so equal a composition among them; and then, upon their own desires, the order of sequestration was laid upon their estates, but managed by one of their own bailiffs, in order to free them from inconveniences that otherwise would have come upon them. Some of them made use of it to get in arrears of rent which they knew no other way of getting, and for which at that time they pretended the greatest sense of gratitude and obligation imaginable. The Colonel also procured them days of payment, so that whereas it should have been paid at Michaelmas 1648, it was not paid till a year after; and for these and many other favours on this occasion he was then courted as their patron, though afterwards this civility was like to have been his ruin."[2] The sequestration thus made to meet Colonel Hutchinson's claims did not deprive the commissioners of their subsequent responsibility for the borrowed money, for according to their petition they paid many of the debts (including Atkinson's £600), and suffered imprisonment for others which they were unable to discharge by reason of the sequestration.

The king, meanwhile, was still a prisoner, and preparations for his trial were in progress. On January 20, 1649, a tribunal, self-created and styled the High Court of Justice, met in Westminster Hall. The king objected to submit himself to its jurisdiction, for the peers alone, according to an ancient maxim of the constitution, could sit in judgment on a peer. Objection and defence were alike in vain. After a so-called trial of seven days' duration, sentence of death was pronounced, and on the 30th of January the unfortunate monarch was beheaded in front of the banqueting-hall of Whitehall Palace. Amongst those who gave evidence against the king was Robert Loads of Cotham, near Newark. He deposed that about October 1642 he saw the king in rear of his army in Reynton field upon a Sunday,

---

[1] At the Restoration Lord Lexington (Mr. Sutton) and others introduced a Bill in Parliament for a return of the money out of the Colonel's estates, with the accumulated interest, and managed to get it "huddled through."—*Memoirs of Colonel Hutchinson*, p. 414.   [2] *Ibid.* p. 327.

where he saw many slain on both sides. He further said that he saw the king in Cornwall, near the house of my Lord Mohun about Lestwithill, in corn harvest, 1644. In the register of Cotham, after the baptism in 1608 of one Robert Loads, is the following note, "This Robert Loads, tyler, was one of the witnesses examined against his sovereign lord, Charles I., of ever blessed memory."

The wars so largely monopolised notice during the reign, that there are few local references apart from them to be met with. There are, however, the following entries in the *Calendars of State Papers* :—1626, January 22. Letter from Newark of William, Earl of Exeter to Conway. Begs a license to be absent, both from the coronation and the Parliament, having a grievous fit of gout. This, he says, is not written to save charges. Before he attended the king into Kent, both he and his wife had all things ready, both for the entry and the coronation. 1633, April 15. Letter from Justices of the Peace for Nottinghamshire to the Council. They hope to have the highways all repaired before the 18th of May. They state what has been done to the great bridge over the Trent at Newark. The bridge cannot be suddenly completed, but there is a good ford near to it which has been passable the greater part of the winter for horsemen and coaches. 1635, December 18. Charges laid against Thomas Atkinson, postmaster of Newark, addressed to some one styled "your honour," who was the proprietor of the mills at Newark. Atkinson's servants were charged with taking horses for posting from persons who came to the mills with corn to be ground. The corn was removed from the horses backs and left in the street, and occasionally even mares with foal were thus taken. People were fain to bring their corn to be ground by night.

The dealings with the estates of "delinquents," which had been actively begun before the execution of the king, were not settled for some time after. In cases where the properties were subject to mortgage, the interests of the mortgagees had to be considered, and the applications for composition sometimes came through them. The castle of Newark and lands in Newark, Stoke, and Averham, held by the Earl of Berkshire, had been mortgaged (in 1642) to the Speaker of Parliament (Mr. William Lenthall), the Lady Katherine Gargrave, and Mr. Hugh Woodward, for £2060, and when the Earl compounded to save his estates, he craved a saving on the Newark property in respect of the mortgage. The castle and lands were of the yearly value of £240, but the demolition of the castle had reduced the value materially, and this was another point submitted to consideration. The matter came on for hearing in February 1650, and we find the following entries relating thereto in the *Royal Composition Papers* :—

ROYAL COMPOSITION PAPERS, 1st Series, vol. 40, p. 39.

A true particular of the estate of Thomas, Earl of Berks, held by Grant from the late king, wherein there are two lives yet, being called the Castle of Newark, and lands in Newark, Stoke, & Averham, in the County of Nottingham, which are now in the possession of William Lenthall, Esq., Speaker of Parliament, the Lady Katherine Gargrave, and Hugh Woodward, Esq., the same being mortgaged to them for payment of £2060, 3d November 1642, with interest for the same, which, with the charges expended in recovery hereof, over & above what hath been received, amounts to £2520 & more, & are of the value hereafter mentioned.

The said castle & lands were before the late troubles besides repreises of the yearly value of £240. Out of which is desired consideration for the demolishing of the said castle by order of Parliament, which, whilst it stood, was great advantage to the letting of the said estate.

HUGH WOODWARD.

FIRST SERIES, 7mo. Maii 1650, vol. 28, page 561.

GENT.—We think fit to give you notice that the case of the Honble the Speaker of the House of Com, & the Lady Gargrave concerning the Castle of Newark & the lands there, belonging to the Earle of Barkshire, is now in examinacon before us. And that we shall very shortly give you further direccons therein till when you may respit any pceedings therein.

ROYAL COMPOSITION PAPERS, 1st Series, vol. 40, p. 45.

According to an order of the 29th Aug. 1650, upon the desire of the Honble William Lenthall, Esq., Speaker of the Parliament, to be admitted to compound for a mortgage of part of the estate of Thomas, Earl of Berkshire, upon the Act of 1st Aug. instant, we find;

That the said Earl of Berkshire, being possessed for the term of 90 years, if Thomas Howard & Charles Howard his sons, or either of them so long live, of & in the site & castle of Newark & lands in Newark, Stoke, & Averham in the county of Nottingham, being of the yearly value by the particular now delivered of £240, by his indenture bearing date the 16th of May 1642, whilst the said Earl sat at Westminster a member of the late king's House of Lords, as is certified by Mr. Speaker, did mortgage the said castle and lands unto Mr. Speaker, the Lady Catherine Gargrave, & Hugh Woodward, Esq., & others, under this proviso, to be void upon payment of £2060 with interest thereof, the 3d of November 1642, with a further proviso that the said Earl should enjoy the same till default of payment thereof, as by the said deed of mortgage aforesaid, under the hand & seal of the said Earl, & proved by Henry Steghous, one of the witnesses, endorsed to be sealed and delivered at or very near the day of the date for non-payment, whereof the said mortgagees entered for same as the garrison of Newark was surrendered to Parliament.

And they alledge that they will make it good upon their account with the auditor, that on & above all the money which they have received out of the profits of the said lands or otherwise there is still due to them of that debt, £2450 at least, which is also dispossessed by the said Hugh Woodward, & I find that the said Earl of Berkshire compounded there, the 12th day of June 1649, upon articles, at a tenth, & did insert in his particular the said castle & land, being of the yearly value of £240, but did crave a saving for the same in consideration of the mortgage before mentioned.

So it is submitted to judgment whether the mortgagees shall not be admitted to compound for the said castle & lands, deducting their debt aforesaid, according to the said act of the 1st of August instant.

18th Feby. 1650.
JOHN LEECH.
JOHN ROADINGS.

We have not been able to trace the matter farther, but, as one of the mortgagees was no other than the Speaker of Parliament, there can be no doubt every consideration would be shown him in the settlement of the question.

In 1655, during the precarious continuance of the Commonwealth, John Johnson, by his will, dated 22d October in that year, gave £50, the interest whereof was yearly to be employed towards the most necessary repairs of the church windows. The charity is now endowed with 5-96th parts of net rents, derived from lands in

East and West Laughton, Lincolnshire. The ordinary yearly income amounts to £4 : 19 : 2, and the net income is handed over to the churchwardens, for repairs to the church windows, in accordance with the will of the benefactor. Mr. Johnson also gave, by the same will, a rent charge of £5 per annum for the following principal objects, namely: for the use of fifty of the "poorest and ancient" widowers and widows of Newark, to be paid yearly to the mayor or churchwardens on the 20th of December, and distributed the day after; and he gave four cottages in Parish Lane, in Newark, to be for ever enjoyed by four old widows to be therein placed in succession by the appointment of the mayor and aldermen, and he willed that John Johnson, his heirs and assigns, should for ever after out of certain lands devised to him by the said will, uphold and repair the said four cottages. The charity is now endowed with an annual rent charge of £5 payable by His Grace the Duke of Newcastle, and the net income is applied in paying to 48 poor widows and widowers, 2s. each, on the 21st of December annually.

On the 3d of September 1658 Cromwell died of ague. His son succeeded to his station, but did not hold it above five months. On his resignation he retired to his farm at Cheshunt, and lived in peace to an extreme old age. Whilst affairs were in a state of the greatest disorder, and a return to a monarchy became every day more anxiously desired, General Monk, who had formerly held a commission in the Royalist army, marched from Scotland to London with 7000 troops. He was everywhere well received, and at no place more so than at Southwell. The Rev. Mr. Mompesson presented him with a copy of complimentary verses in which much was said of the blessings of kingly government, and how ardently it was now desired by the people of the country. As he passed with his troops through the town the inhabitants assembled in the churchyard at the side of the wall, and followed him down the street shouting, "God bless you, General, may heaven prosper you with success in your good designs." A new Parliament was summoned, and when Monk told it that the exiled Charles had sent a messenger who was waiting for admission, the news was received with shouts of delight. A warm invitation was sent to Charles, who gladly returned to his native land. On May 29, 1660, he made a public entry into London, and was received with the greatest enthusiasm. Newark, ever loyal, sent up to his Majesty addresses of laudation and congratulation. The soldiers of Cromwell settled down to their former occupations. Several who had been concerned in the execution of Charles I. were tried and condemned.

Colonel Hutchinson, the ex-governor of Nottingham, was arrested and conducted to Newark. Mrs. Hutchinson relates how, on Sunday the 11th of October (1663), soldiers entered the house, conducted by Atkinson, a Newark man, and told the Colonel he must go with them. The Colonel inquired for their commission, and they showed him an order from Mr. Francis Leeke, one of the deputy-lieutenants, directing them to seize Colonel Hutchinson and to bring away from his house what arms they could find. It being night-time, "a stormy, pitchy dark, black, rainy night," the Colonel desired they would stay until morning, but they persisted in going at once, and took him with them to Newark. Arriving there about four o'clock in the morning, the Colonel was lodged at the Talbot, with two soldiers to keep guard over him. The name of the landlord was Thomson, and when Mrs. Hutchinson sent her husband some clean linen, Thomson seized the messenger and kept him prisoner two days. Subsequently, he misbehaved himself in the Colonel's chamber, whereupon the Colonel snatched up a candlestick and, says Mrs. Hutchinson, "laid him over the chaps with it." Mr. Leeke and others, hearing the disturbance, came into the room, and, on being informed of what had transpired, and that the Colonel had resolved to eat no more in that house, caused him to be taken to the next inn (Mr. Twentyman's), where he was civilly treated. On the 19th October Mr. Leeke, with a party of horse, took the Colonel to the Marquis of Newcastle's, where he was dismissed, and returned to his home. On the 22d, however, he was again arrested and carried back to Newark. Mr. Leeke, having occasion to go to London, left the Colonel in charge of the mayor, (Mr. Herring), who sent a gaoler to remove him to prison. Colonel Hutchinson refused to leave the Inn without a warrant from a magistrate, but the mayor sent five constables and two soldiers, and forcibly conveyed him to gaol. Though very unwell, he was kept in gaol from the 23d to the 28th, when he was taken by Beck, the gaoler, to Twentyman's inn, preparatory to being sent with a guard to London. "Thus," says Mrs. Hutchinson, "the Colonel took his last leave of Newark, which being a place he had formerly subdued, and replete with so many malicious enemies to the whole party, and more particularly to him, upon no other account but that he had been the most formidable protector of the other party in this county, he expected far worse treatment from the generality of the town, who were so far from joining in joy at his captivity that, when he was forced through their streets, they gave him very civil respect, and when he came away civil farewells." Subsequently the Colonel was taken to Sandown Castle, in Kent, where he died, September 11, 1664, in the 49th year of his age. His body was embalmed and removed to Owthorpe, where it was buried.

Those who had suffered losses in defence of the late king were hopeful of recompense, now that the second Charles was seated securely on the throne. The commissioners for the county of Nottingham who had contracted debts in erecting the fortifications at Newark applied for a reimbursement of the ruinous outlay to which they had been subject. Their first petition was shelved, whereupon they sent a second, the principal portions of which have been preserved. It ran as follows:—

> The Second Petition of ROBERT, LORD LEXINGTON, THOMAS WILLIAMS, Bart., Sir JOHN DIGBY, Sir HUGH CARTWRIGHT, —— KNIGHTLEY, JOHN COOPER, ROBT. MELLISH, and THOS. HOLDERS, Esquires,
>
> Most humbly sheweth that your petitioners did, with great humility present to your Majesty a former petition, in which they did ——— garrisoning the town of Newark upon Trent.
>
> Your royal father of ever glorious memory—as well by his commands as by his royal letters—commanding us not only to expend what we had of our own, but as much more as our credits would extend unto, for the use of the garrison, which we readily obeyed in regard of the great——his Majesty

was pleased to give us by his letters, and especially one of the 13th of Jan. directed to the Lord Byron, then governour of the said garrison, and to be communicated to us, which said letter, with the former petition, was presented to your Majesty, which you was most graciously pleased to read, and then thereupon promised your petitioners to consider of some way to disengage and to reimburse the therein expressed debts of £15,000, and did accordingly recommend your petitioners to Mr. Secretary Nicholas to take care of their petition, that some way might be found for their relief and satisfaction ; now so it is, that nothing having been done in the same, may it please your sacred Majesty, nothing having been granted towards the relief of your said petitioners, some of them still being in prison for these engagements and others of them being in like danger, they humbly pray your Majesty would be pleased to grant unto them a lease for 99 years of lands and grounds disparked, together with all your right & interest in the forest & chase of Needwood, disparked and in common in the counties of Derby & Stafford, and part of your Dutchy of Lancaster, as the same stand and were divided by survey in the year 1648, betwixt the commons & the late rebel and usurper, Oliver Cromwell, under yearly rent of £100, which is as much improvement to your Majesty's revenue, and your petitioners hope in some time that it may——towards the £15,000 they disbursed and stand indebted, &c., &c.

And your petitioners will ever pray, &c.

A schedule of several sums of money borrowed upon bonds and otherwise by his late Majesty's commissioners of the county of Nottingham, and expended in the defence and preservation of the garrison of Newark, according to his Majesty's command, whereupon they became liable for the same, and are paid by some of the commissioners :—

DEBTS UPON BOND WHICH ARE PAID.

To Mr. Barrett	£530 0 0	Brought forward	£7564 0 0
„ Mr. Chambers	1500 0 0	To Mr. Bolles	150 0 0
„ Mr. Clay	636 0 0	„ Mr. Trass	100 0 0
„ Mr. Trueman	320 0 0	„ Mr. Camm	100 0 0
„ Mr. William Cook	100 0 0	„ Earl of Scarsdale	1500 0 0
„ Mr. Newton	1000 0 0	„ Mr. Stanhope	400 0 0
„ Mr. Alderman Johnson	840 0 0	„ Mr. Zouch Wild	1.0 0 0
„ Mr. Christopher Wilson	200 0 0	„ Mr. Rawsons	40 0 0
„ Mr. Rooksby	200 0 0	„ Mr. Alderman Wilson	100 0 0
„ Messrs. Stones and Fisher	200 0 0	„ Mr. Robert Martin	31 0 0
„ Mr. Alderman Baker	156 0 0	„ Mr. Alderman Standish	100 0 0
„ Captain Hawley	132 0 0	„ Mr. Peter Dickinson	136 0 0
„ Mr. Shipman	100 0 0	„ Mr. Alderman Standish	51 0 0
„ Mr. Marshall	100 0 0	„ Mr. Draper	650 0 0
„ Mr. Pasey	800 0 0	„ Mr. Thomas Goodson	40 0 0
„ Mr. John Martin	100 0 0	„ Colonel Errington	100 0 0
„ Mr. Atkinson	600 0 0	„ Mr. William Reason	53 0 0
„ Mr. Wilkinson	50 0 0	„ Mr. Mason	50 0 0
Carry forward	£7564 0 0		£11,285 0 0

DEBTS UPON BOND WHICH ARE NOT YET PAID, viz., in 1661, Feb. 14th.

To Sir Guy Palmes	£200 0 0	Brought forward	£588 0 0
„ Sir Gervas Clifton	168 0 0	To Mr. Alderman Smith more	70 0 0
„ Sir Hugh Cartwright	200 0 0	„ Mr. Alderman Hanks	75 0 0
„ Mr. Alderman Smith	30 0 0		
Carry forward	£588 0 0		£733 0 0

The total of the debts upon bond as they were affixed to the petition presented to his Majesty Feb. 14, 1661 . . . } £12,018 8 1

Debts contracted and acknowledged by the said commissioners which are yet unpaid and demanded by several persons, as follows:—

	£	s	d		£	s	d
Mr. Langholm demands	150	0	0	Brought forward	270	0	0
Hays the baker	40	0	0	Mr. Brown	300	0	0
John Hoyes	20	0	0	Mr. Geo. Cartwright	131	0	0
Mr. Palmer	60	0	0	Mr. Nich. Atkinson	200	0	0
Carry forward	£270	0	0		£901	0	0
The Lord Byron for several sums disbursed for the garrison					500	0	0
Sir John Digby for money disbursed by him about the powder mill					320	5	9
Sir Hugh Cartwright for arms delivered by him into the garrison					458	9	4
Sir Hugh Cartwright for corn delivered by him for the garrison					300	0	0
The total of the debts without bonds but acknowledged and subscribed by all the commissioners to be due and unpaid					£2479	15	1
The total demanded by our petition					£14,498	3	2

Besides the great charges, not only in law suits, about the said debts, but also by long imprisonment of some of the said commissioners who were sued for most of the said debts, both in Chancery and at common law, they having been disabled to pay the same by reason of the sequestration upon their estates and their heavy compositions for them.

And besides that interest has been paid ever since and is yet paid for most of the greatest debts above said, but neither charges nor interest is accounted in any of these particulars, but only the principal debts. This is a true copy of all the particulars delivered, together with a petition, February 14, 1661, as signed by H. C.

The document, it will be seen, mentions that some of the commissioners were consigned to prison. This statement is verified by a petition presented to the Lord Chancellor and others, March 3, 1661-2,[1] by Sir John Digby, prisoner in the fleet. Sir John states that he had joined with Lord Lexington, Sir Thomas Williamson, and others, by command of the late king, in borrowing £11,000 for the garrison of Newark; that he had offered to pay his share, but the others having compounded, left him alone; and he had been in prison five years. He therefore prayed that Lord Lexington, Sir Thomas Williamson, and others, might be enjoined to have him discharged. On March 20, 1661-2, a warrant was issued to relieve Sir Thomas Williamson of £500, ship money levied on the county during his shrievalty, and by him paid in 1648 for the use of the garrison of Newark. And two years later (1663) £10,000, due to Lord Byron, Lord Lexington, Sir Thomas Williamson, and others, the late king's commissioners for Newark garrison, was paid in full.[2]

Whilst the commissioners were in doubt whether they should ever obtain any portion of the money due to them, the inhabitants of Newark, wisely determining to have some recompense for their sufferings, endeavoured to secure the additional privileges

---

[1] Calendar of State Papers.   [2] State Papers.

which had been promised by Charles I. On July 27, 1661, they forwarded a petition to the king for a renewal of their charter with additions, mentioning the promise made by the late king, but obstructed by the wars, and stating that they had lost £40,000 by the burning of a sixth part of the town when it was made a garrison, by erection of works, moneys lent and never repaid, quartering of soldiers, etc. The subject was referred to the attorney-general for his consideration, and he reported as to the several additions which it might be fitting to permit, on account of the eminent loyalty of the town during the rebellion. The carrying out of the suggestions was delayed several years, but a new charter came in 1667. The old rights and privileges were by it ratified and confirmed, the town was declared a free borough, and power was given to elect two burgesses for the borough to serve in Parliament, the burgesses to be chosen by the mayor and aldermen for the time being and their successors, and by all the inhabitants of the borough for the time being, "who pay and contribute, shall pay and contribute, or ought to pay and contribute, Scot and Lot in the said borough." Freemen of the town were declared exempt from paying toll throughout England, and the extent of the liberties and jurisdiction of the mayor and aldermen were thus defined "unto and through the parish of Newark aforesaid and the whole castle of Newark and the scite thereof, and all those water-mills commonly called Newark mills." The mayor and aldermen were to have and enjoy all and singular the goods and chattels of felons and fugitives, "extents, outlawries, waifs, estrays, treasure-trove, and deed, happening, chancing, or arising within the borough;" and a *Custos Rotulorum* was appointed, Henry, Duke of Newcastle, being nominated the first. The office of coroner was ratified and confirmed, as was also the power of creating four justices. Authority was given to commit offenders to the county gaol, as well as to the gaol at Newark; and to purchase and possess manors not exceeding the yearly value of £300. The Court of Record might hear plaints up to £300, but not beyond. The mayor was to have the return of all writs, and two fairs were appointed to be held, one on the 21st and 22d of October, and the other on the Friday and Saturday before Lord's Day, called Careing Sunday. The right and patronage of the rectory of Winthorpe was given to the mayor and corporation, and lastly, it was directed that the clauses and grants of these letters patent should be "good, firm, valid, and effectual."

By deed or will, dated 14th March 1663, John Martin gave the use of £50, to be paid to the mayor and alderman, to be laid out in coals, and distributed by them yearly at Christmas. The charity is endowed with 5-96th parts of net rents derived from lands at East and West Laughton. The ordinary yearly income amounts to £4 : 10 : 5, and the net income is applied in the purchase of coals for distribution.

In the summer of 1665 the plague, raging with fearful virulence in London, spread to various parts of the country, and Newark is one of the towns which it is stated to have visited. Tradition says that the infection was conveyed direct from London in some patterns of woollen cloths sent to a draper in the market-place. "Be this, however, as it may," remarks Mr. Dickinson, "the disease is said to have carried off more than a third of the inhabitants; and it continued to rage so great a length of time that the streets were entirely grown over with grass. The inhumation of bodies was prohibited within the precincts of the town, and a large pit was opened at the southern extremity of Millgate, not far from the bridge over the Devon, into which it has been rumoured the dead and dying were promiscuously conveyed by a cart every morning before sunrise." We give the statement in the form Mr. Dickinson puts it, qualified in its details by the expressions "it is said" and "it has been rumoured." For our own part, though we have searched carefully, we cannot find any record to verify the account. The parish registers contain no more entries of deaths than in previous years, and there is no marginal reference indicating the existence of a plague or any other serious infection, though such references are frequently met with in the registers of places that suffered from similar calamities.[1] In the account book which contains a record of the collections at church, we find the following items:—August 2, 1665, collected towards the relief of the towns infected with the plague, to be transmitted to the Archbishop of York, £2:3:8; for the same use, September 6, £2:10:8; for the same, October 4, £1:5s.; for the same, November 8, £1:3s. It appears, therefore, that the charity of Newark was successfully enlisted on behalf of the towns that did suffer, but whether Newark had so fearful a share in the calamity as that indicated in the traditional account above referred to, is more than we should care to affirm on the evidence before us.

For a considerable period there appears, from the parish registers, to have been collections at the parish church of Newark in aid of places that had suffered, not only through plague, but from serious outbreaks of fire or other calamities. In some years there are records of six or seven collections for the repair of damage done by fires or inundations, and the towns and districts assisted are not those in the Midlands alone, but in all quarters of England, and even in Wales. The collections were made in many cases "by virtue of letters patent from the High Court of Parliament," and the objects for which contributions were solicited ranged over a wide field, extending from the restoration of a church to the redemption of captives. On September 28, 1662, there was collected for rebuilding the church at Scarborough £1:9:9½. On June 6, 1669, there was "collected for the relief of captives under the dominion of the Turks" £1:4:3, the figures being thus put in the parish register, £01:04:03. On May the 15th in the same year there was "collected for the redemption of the English slaves in the Turkish dominions £06:11:03. On February 1, 1672, collected for the great fire in London, near Russell Street, in St. Martin's in the Field, £1:15:4. July 14, 1672, for the University of Oxon. £1:7:6. On February 10, 1674, collected for "y⁰ redemption of y⁰ slaves in Algiers" £5:12:8; January 28, 1681, collected for the Protestants in Poland £1:16:8½; February 12, 1681, collected for the French Protestants £5:2:4¼. In 1686, July 18, the large sum of £23:1:5 was con-

---

[1] The register of Stoke for instance, quoted on pages 165-6.

tributed for the same object. There were also collections for the Irish Protestants; for a steeple fallen at Chalfont, St. Peter's, Buckinghamshire; for repairing the pier at Hartlepool; for the fishery at Folkestone; for the University of Oxford; and for St. Andrew's harbour, Scotland. In 1692 there was a collection for poor sufferers, by casualties at sea, several for the relief of captives, and seven for fires, in various parts of England. On July 14, 1700, there was collected for the redemption of the captives in Fez and Morocco the sum of £3 : 8 : 6½, and lastly, in 1715, the sum of £2 : 15 : 8 was raised for the cow-keepers of Middlesex, Surrey, and Essex. Whilst speaking of what the parish registers of this and subsequent periods reveal, we may mention numerous entries of marriages performed by the mayors and aldermen for the time being, and also by justices of the peace. As a specimen we give the following, under date 1654:—"Richard White, miller, and Frances Easte, widow, both of this parish, after the publication of the banns of matrimony three several Lord's Days, and no objection made, were *contracted* by Mr. Wightman, one of the justices of the peace for Nottinghamshire." Another expression used instead of "contracted" is "did put the consummation in the presence of many witnesses." The services of Mr. Benjamin Wilson, who was mayor in 1653, were in special request. There are numerous entries of weddings at which he officiated, and when the love fever reached him, as it seems to have done in due course, a Mr. Christopher Wilson performed the marriage ceremony.

On receipt of the new charter in 1667 the town proceeded to elect two burgesses to serve in Parliament, and a further election took place in 1677, when difficulties which had arisen had been finally settled. Some curious particulars of the proceedings at the last-named contest, and of other matters relating to the town, may be gleaned from a perusal of the following letters from the Savile correspondence in a volume (LXXI. 1858) of the Camden Society's publications. We are indebted to Mr. R. F. Sketchley, B.A., for copies of the letters; the interesting explanatory footnotes are those of the editor of the volume (Mr. W. D. Cooper):—

[1] HENRY SAVILE TO HIS BROTHER, GEORGE VISCOUNT [AFTER MARQUIS OF] HALIFAX.

Paris, September 30, N. S. [16]76.

". . . If y^u can possibly send time enough to Rufford that a buck may be sent to Mr. Robert Atkinson at Newark for the election of their new mayor on Michaelmas day, you will oblige me extreamly, and I think he does very well deserve it, and must have a very great mind to it that could write hither to me for it." . . .

SAME TO SAME.

Sedgebroke, April 11, [16]77.

"I am just now arrived here, and am mett by some of my Newarkers, who tell me of the cruellest accident that could possibly befal my present pretensions, viz.,

---

[1] Born at Rufford 1641 or 1642; Envoy Extraordinary at Paris; Vice-Chamberlain and Commissioner of the Admiralty between 1680 and 1687; date of death uncertain, some time between 1689 and 1700.

that vote of parliament about expences at elections, which has put Newark in such a rage that the common people say it was I that procured the vote, and that an uncle of mine did it for my sake;[1] so that they filled a frock with straw and carry'd it about the town and set it up in the market place, and called it the ten pounds burgess, and had burnt it but for the mayor, who came in his pontificalibus to prevent any further riot. You must needs think, if I do recover this unlucky accident, it must cost me both pains and money, and if it were any uncle of mine who proposed this vote, next under God and my cousin Thynne, I may very well owe a disappointment to him, which would be very shamefull to me; in a word, what may not I expect that is unlucky? I hope to pacify this rabble with the help of some friends, and having time till to-morrow sevennight, which is the day of election; sooner it cannot be, because of the fair at Gainsborough and the market-day. In the mean time it were worth giving a year of life that this insupportable week were past; but what must not younger brothers do in some cases! *Gaudeant bene nati.* . . .

"H. S."

SAME TO SAME.

Newarke, April 16, [16] 77.

"Sir Rob. [Markham][2] and I came hither on Thursday morning last; since which time I have been so continually drunk that I could never have time either to write to London or ride to Rufford. Sr Richard Rothwell had been at so great an expense before we came, that we found it impossible to hope for a voice in this town if we stuck to the new order of the House of Commons, and not to the old custom of England; nay we were fain to double our reckonings to them. We were not the contrivers of that damn'd vote, as was particularly laid to my charge; but I hope I have pretty well convinced them of the contrary, but at so dear a rate that I doubt, whether I succeed or not, I have quite broken my back, and shall do my heart if I return unsuccessfull to London, after pains and trouble taken that I would not undergoe again to be an emperor instead of a burgess. But I find whatever is undertaken out of the pride of a man's heart brings great anxiety's at long run; and, though I should succeed, which is far from a certainty, I have reason to wish I had never seen nor heard of this town; but our measures now at court are so taken that it is esentiall to a man's succeeding there to be of the Parl^{mt} which if I am destin'd not to be, I must be content with my poverty. . . . Because of the mart at

---

[1] Although Newark was the last borough enfranchised by a royal charter, granted so late as 4th April 1667, the electors fell at once into the "good old ways" of other and more ancient towns. The Commons Journals show that the committee appointed on 12th November 1675, on the exorbitant drinking and expenses at elections, were directed to prepare a bill: they were on 20th November ordered to report, and on 15th February 1676-7 a bill was introduced and read a second time to regulate these expenses; and on the 19th, on its being ordered to be committed, a clause was presented to prevent bribery and excessive treating at elections. No further notice appears on the Journals of a bill, but the resolution against corrupt practices was passed, which gave such offence to the worthy electors of Newark. Treating had become a very common practice at elections.

[2] Sir Robert Markham stood on the same interest with H. Savile, and Penistoun Whalley stood with Sir Richard Rothwell. The numbers polled do not appear on the records of the corporation.

Gainsborough, the day of election could not be till Thursday, which is the day I wish for more than a lover ever did for a wedding night to be at an end of more noise and tumult than ever poor mortal was troubled with; I have been all this day sick to agonyes with four day's swallowing more good ale and ill sack than one would have thought a country town could have held; and this worthy employment must be begun again to-morrow, though I burst for it; therefore pray for me and pity me, for I would gladly change my next three days with any slave at Algiers."

SAME TO SAME.

Barraby, April 21, [16] 77.

"I need say no more to you but that I am y^r first burgess of Newarke, and Sr Rich^d. Rothwell the second,[1] by what steps I will tell you on Thursday next; but I have been most handsomly obliged by Sr Robt. Markham in very serious earnest, and my burgessship, as I told you before, suits better with my pride than with my purse; but, if I were to have lost this place at which I now am, it must have been sacrificed for the honour of y^r family, when I had once appear'd; and I can only say as Francis ye 1st, when he was taken prisoner, *Tout est perdue hors l'honneur*, for the same[2] will stun y^u as much as it will trouble me; but I repent it not, though the payment will be heavy."

---

[1] Mr. Savile and Sir Paul Neale had been returned in 1673 under the new charter, but, as the parliament was sitting and the writ had not been issued by the House of Commons, they were not allowed to take their seats. On 31st January 167$\frac{2}{3}$, therefore they petitioned the Commons claiming their seats as being duly elected, and the petition was referred to the committee of privileges: on which nothing was done till 10th May 1675, when other parties petitioned the House complaining of undue means and practices resorted to for obtaining the charter for sending two members. This petition was also referred to the committee without effect: the matter still lingered, and at length Sir W. Coventry and Mr. Guy, Secretary of the Treasury, were tellers, on 26th February 1677, in a majority of 147 to 98 noes, determining to hear the petitioners at the bar; they were heard on 21st March, when a resolution that Mr. Savile and Sir Paul Neale were duly elected was negatived by a majority of one (102, 103). Ultimately a writ was issued to the corporation on 7th April. That the exertions of Henry Savile in procuring the adjustment of the difficulties about the charter might be suitably acknowledged, the corporation passed an address, which, with all its defective Latinity, I am enabled to give through the kindness of Mr. T. F. A. Burnaby, Clerk of the Peace, who also informs me that the corporation books contain no record of the election of 1673, or of that of 1677. The address was as follows:—

"M. Æ. Henrici Savilij, Armigeri, Hoc. D. D.D. Sen. Nevarcæ. Nos Praetor et Senatores Municipij Nevarcæ super Trentam in agro Nottingamiensi insigniora Henrici Savilij Armig' merita atq' beneficentias inestimabiles illo in nos collatas, penitus penitusq' sentientes, quippe nihilo minus propriarum animi dotium prosapiaeq' nobilitatis quam qua cluit apud Principem suum, gratiae ergo haud indigno quem ambiant omnes et in delicijs habeant quorum aures illius beaverit nomen, qui indulto sibi soli favore ac proclivi ad evehendam hujus Burgi Rempublicam ardore praesenti nostro postprius abdicatum, diplomate Clementissimum Regem Carolum secundum, supremum Dominum nostrum, exorato, multis in locis non abs re hujusce corporis mutato, ministris aulicis ne quidem mimino à nobis honorario vel eo nomine praemio pro more et ex debito auctis quibus scilicet à Regiâ Majestate factum est satis nos ornavit, volentesq' cum tanti Benefactoris et beneficij memoria Corinthio aere sit perennior, tum posteris cui Chartam referimus acceptam innotescat, quinetiam ab hoc Burgo de gratiâ illi nepotibusve reponendâ parum laboretur praecaventes; Hisce praecipimus Instrumentum hoc in tabulas publicas perscribi ibidemq' gratitudinis erga illum nostræ testimonium et suorum erga nos quibus solvendis non sumus officiorum in monumentum ut ponatur conservari. Anno Æræ Christianæ Milessimo sesquicentesimo septuagesimo septimo, Annoq' Regni dicti Domini Regis etc. Vicesimo nono.

Savile Correspondence. *Camden Society*, 1858, vol. lxxi., pp. 46-7.   [2] ? Sum. R. F. S.

Same to Same.

Whitehall, May 8, [16] 77.

"... I find ... that the heavens being on my side, you were forced to call at my famous borough of Newarke instead of Filkerton [*sic*] Ferry, which I threatned the town I should have been your passage had I lost my election. You must needs believe every letter that gives me an account of my expences makes my heart bleed as much as my purse; but the bill of £100 when it comes shall be paid. ... In the mean time, I am glad you saw Mr. Atkinson and Mr. Morris, who I hope, when they take the air to pay their duty's to you at Rufford, will be welcome as well as the rest of the aldermen of the towne. I could be glad also that you would, according to y^r promise to me, use Frank Chesham for your cooper, if a man of that profession be of use to you, and let him have a good bargain in a little wood for his trade; as also Andrew Keppis for your pewterer; in a word, all Newarke men who voted for me being employ'd by you in their several vocations may turn some day to account to y'self, besides being a present obligation to me."

Earl of Halifax to H. Savile.

Windsor, August $\frac{1}{2}$1, [16] 79.

". Your friend my Ld Daincourt will try at Newark, but sayeth he will not be at any charge, which maketh me doubt his success; for I doubt your noble friends there will not much approve a dry election, as a thing of ill example, and tending to introduce presbytery, by the way of small beer, besides the detriment it may bring to his Mat^y revenue of excise."

No other letters of local interest appear in the volume.

On the 8th March 1678 Anthony Collingwood, by his will, gave to his wife all his houses and lands for life, and after her death he gave his lands in reversion that were purchased by him of Henry Girton, lying in Farndon, in the county of Nottingham, and in Allington, in the county of Lincoln, to the mayor and aldermen of Newark, in trust, for the better enabling the vicar of Newark "to maintain prayers, commonly called Divine Service, to be performed twice every day in the week, in the parish church of Newark." He also gave his house, in Stodman Street, to the said mayor and aldermen, to be held by them, after the death of his wife, for ever, to the use of the poor of the said town. He also gave his house, in Carter-Gate, for the repairs and better support of the fabric of the parish church.

The charity (having reference only to that part which was included in the testator's devise of his house in Stodman Street), is endowed with the following properties, namely: £819:13:5 invested in 3 per cent consols in the names of the official Trustees of Charitable Funds; £147:12:8 invested in 3 per cent consols in the names of the official Trustees of Charitable Funds. The ordinary yearly income of the charity amounts to £29 : 0 : 2, and consists of dividends on consols as above mentioned. The net income is now applied in the purchase of coals, and distribution of the same amongst the poor of the town on the 2d February and 21st December annually; also in the purchase of clothing to the value of £5, and distribution of the same amongst Chapman and Ellis's widows.

At a meeting of the Town Council on Saturday, 17th April 1679, it was announced that Emma Watson had, by her will, dated 8th December, 1675, left the sum of £50 to be paid to the corporation for them to let out the same to yearly interest, to be used in buying coals or corn for the poor people at the discretion of the mayor and aldermen. The charity is endowed with 5-96th parts of net rents derived from lands at East and West Laughton, Lincolnshire. The ordinary yearly income amounts to £4 : 10 : 5, and is applied in purchase of coals and distribution of the same amongst the poor of the town.

In 1683 a disastrous flood occurred along the Trent valley, and the fields on the river-side in the neighbourhood of Newark were deeply inundated. The breaking up of a frost, accompanied by much snow, caused the river to overflow its banks, and the force of the stream was such as to sweep down the Trent Bridge at Nottingham, and do other serious damage. In the Reports of the Commissioners on Historical MSS. there is a mention of a small book of poetry, 12mo. temp. Charles II. "upon the late inundation of the river Trent," by Thomas Winnard, A.B., St. John's, in the possession of E. P. Shirley, Esq. The scene is described as " Muscham and Holme, two opposite villages on the river-side near Newark," and the poem begins—

> " When heirs and widows hoarding fresh supplies
> Bottle up teares wrung from St. Swithin's eyes."

In 1685, after an illness of a week, King Charles II. breathed his last. Amongst the miscellaneous references to local matters of interest during his reign in the *Calendars of State Papers*, we find the following:—1660, June 7. Petition of Joseph Thompson of Newark for the place of postmaster there, in consideration of service during the late wars, annexing a certificate by John, Lord Bellasyse, and ten others, of the faithful service of the above, and that Thos. Atkinson, a pretender to the place deserted the service of the late king. 1660, July 6. Petition of Thomas White to the king for presentation to the vicarage of Newark, void by the death of Hen. Truman, and now possessed by Sam. Hawkes, an intruder, with reference therein to Drs. Sheldon and Earles, and their report, July 7, in favour of the petitioner. 1660, July. Petition of Anne, widow of Colonel William Staunton, stating her husband fought for the late king through the wars, raising troops at his own charge. On the surrender of Newark, his family were exposed to the cruelty of the enemy, and by composition he lost most of his paternal estate and her jointure. 1660, August 11. Account by Captain Luke Whittington of his services and sufferings. He raised troops for the siege of Hull, Newark, etc. 1663, November 11. Warrant for creating Francis Leeke, of Newark, a baronet. 1664, October

18. John Russell to the Navy Commissioners, stating that the justices of Newark have given warrants for 300 loads of timber. 1665, July 11. Dr. Thomas Fuller to Williamson. Begs aid in detecting a fraud, also delay in the business of Newark; the incumbent is his friend, will resign as may best serve his end, and thinks he (Fuller) will be acceptable to the town. 1666. Petition of Thomas Fuller, D.D., for presentation to the vicarage of Newark-upon-Trent. 1666, April. Petition of John Wright, *John Cromwell*, and two others, prisoners in Newark, to the king for release; were committed $2\frac{1}{2}$ years ago by the Duke of Newcastle, Lord Lieutenant of Nottingham, though they never broke the peace, and have remained there ever since, without being called before any magistrate. 1667, April 25. Reference to the Lord Treasurer on the petition of Colonel Thomas Howard, for the stones and materials of Newark Castle and a lease of the site of the same.

A quarter of an hour after the death of Charles II. his brother, the Duke of York, took his seat at the council as King James II. (1685). He declared his resolve to govern according to the laws, and to uphold the Church of England. Loyal addresses poured in from every side, the horizon cleared, and all around seemed bright and promising. He had not, however, been on the throne many months before there was a rising under Monmouth, who came over from Holland, and issued an address wherein he denominated the king a traitor, a tyrant, an assassin, and a popish usurper. At Sedgemoor, near Bridgwater, the royal army overthrew the rebels, and Monmouth took to flight. He was captured near the New Forest, and suffered death on Tower Hill. Scores of the rebels were hanged at Taunton, and Chief-Justice Jeffreys passed through the whole of the Western Circuit sentencing criminals by the dozen, and leaving in his wake a wide track of blood. James, who was a staunch Romanist, believing that he was now securely seated on the throne, began to unfold his designs. What he aimed at was the complete restoration of the Romish worship in Great Britain, but the people were too firm and too closely welded to Protestant principles to submit. In two years James found that instead of shaking the Protestant Church, he had shaken the foundations of his own throne. One of his devices was very ingenious. He published a declaration of indulgences, permitting all to worship in their own way. This looked like a step in advance on the road to liberty. But whilst he professed to give freedom with one hand, he tried to suppress the power of the people with the other. Writs were issued, *quo warranto*, to take away the last new charters granted by Charles II., in order to make such alterations as would cause them to be conformable to the Royal will.

Amongst other places on which James forced the acceptance of a new charter was the borough of Newark (1686). The charter appointed William Martin to be mayor till the feast of St. Michael following; Henry Savile, Esq., John Marris, William Basseldine, George Berkett, Robert Marris, Isaac Sherwin, William Twentiman, William Hobman, John Girton, Richard Read, William Rastall, and

Alexander Clark, aldermen for life, "unless removed for ill behaviour or any other reasonable cause." Robert, Lord Lexington, was appointed Recorder for life, and John Hobman, town-clerk during good behaviour. The power of choosing the two representatives in Parliament was vested in the mayor, aldermen, freemen, and freeholders of forty shillings value. The most important reservation, however, was that "any or all of these corporations or their successors should be at all times removable at the king's pleasure under privy seal." Acting upon the power which he had thus reserved to himself, the king directed (1687) who were to be appointed to the various offices. In the Corporation Minute-Book are the following entries:—

The order of council for regulating the corporation at the Court at Whitehall, the 24th of February 1687. By the king's most excellent Majesty, and by the Lords of his Majesty's most Hon. Privy Council. Whereas, by the Charter lately granted to the town of Newark-upon-Trent, in the county of Nottingham, a power is reserved to his Majesty by his order in council to remove from their employments any officers in the said town, his Majesty in council is pleased to order, and it is hereby ordered that Robert Marris, Mayor, and Ald. William Martin, George Berkett William Twentiman, William Hobman, and John Girton, be and are hereby removed and displaced from their aforesaid offices and places in the said town of Newark-upon-Trent. JOHN NICHOLAS.

THE KING'S LETTER—JAMES R.

Trusty and well-beloved, we greet you well; whereas we have by order in council thought fit to remove Robert Marris from being Mayor of Newark, William Martin, George Berkett, William Twentiman, William Hobman, and John Girton from being aldermen of our said borough, we have thought fit hereby to will and require you forthwith to elect and admit our trusty and well-beloved Samuel Ellis to be Mayor, and one of the Aldermen: Robert Heron, Gilbert Standish, William Welby, Timothy Ellis, and William Haslam to be aldermen of our said borough in the room of the persons above mentioned, without administering to them any oath or oaths (but the usual oath for the execution of their respective places), with which we are pleased to dispense in their behalf, and for so doing this shall be your warrant, and so we bid you farewell. Given at our Court at Whitehall, this 25th day of February 1687, in the fourth year of our reign.

The proceeding upon this regulation took place on the 3d day of March, when his Majesty's order was complied with. To Nottingham the king sent two men with authority to displace such members of the corporation as would not answer the king's gracious design in favour of the "dissenters." The secret intentions of the monarch, clumsily hidden beneath plausible pretext, were still more clearly revealed in a letter written by the Deputy-Recorder of Nottingham, who went to London to solicit for a new charter. When he had been in the city a short time, he wrote that his Majesty had referred the petition to the Attorney-General, and that all the corporation's desires were granted, "only in the business of the election of officers of the town Mr. Attorney-General will not be persuaded to let the populace have any vote, as being a matter contrary to his Majesty's design, and tending to disturbance among themselves (the corporation), and he will limit all elections of mayor, aldermen, councillors, coroners, sheriffs, chamberlains, etc., to be chosen by the mayor, aldermen and common council, and no others. This," continues the deputy-recorder, "will be a new thing to you." He adds further:—" His Majesty reserves to himself a power of displacing any members of the corporation, and also to nominate and appoint others to succeed such as shall be removed. These are the terms upon which all charters are granted at this day, and none are to pass without them." That the Nottingham people did not approve of such terms is evident from a letter written by the mayor, and signed by five of the aldermen, stating that they had called a Hall, and were troubled at nothing but the exclusion of the popularity or common burgesses in the election of the town officers which they had always voted for. "They will, without doubt," says the letter, "look upon it as a great infringement of their privileges, and have a very ill eye upon us, supposing it to be done by our means; and cause them to apprehend ill of the Government, which we would by no means have them to do."

In all quarters the king's ill-concealed pro-Romanist designs aroused opposition. When he ordered his declaration of indulgence, permitting all to worship in their own way, to be read from the pulpits on two successive Sundays, the London clergy disobeyed, and the Primate Sancroft, with six bishops,[1] drew up a petition against the declaration. James was not one to bear opposition with a good grace, and the Crown lawyers received directions to institute a prosecution. The prelates were committed to the Tower, where they lay for a week, and were then set free on bail. Their trial took place before the Court of King's Bench. They were charged with having published a false and malicious libel. The jury said "not guilty," and London was ablaze with illuminations in honour of such a verdict. On the day that the bishops were acquitted a letter had been sent to William, Prince of Orange Nassau. It was signed by many of the leading noblemen and clergy of England, and invited him to come with an army to aid them in defending their liberty and their faith. William accepted the invitation, and landed at Torbay, in Devonshire, Nov. 5, 1688. In four days he reached Exeter, with a force of 15,000 men, and was received everywhere as the champion of the Protestant faith. James started to meet him, but every day his army diminished. People flocked to William's standard, whilst the adherents of James grew less and less.

In the month of November the Princess Anne privately withdrew from Court, and sought refuge at the house of the Bishop of London (Compton). From there, with the Bishop, Lady Churchill, Lady Berkeley, and other persons of distinction, she travelled by coach to Nottingham. The Earl of Dorset, with 40 horsemen, accompanied her thither, and a few days after her arrival the Earl of Devonshire gave her a guard of 200 men. From the entries in the mayor's book, it appears that a request was presented to the Corporation to take upon themselves the charge of maintaining a guard of honour for the princess. At first they declined, remarking that they were already considerably in debt; but some insinuations being made against their loyalty, they eventually subscribed £100 towards the expenses of the guard.

[1] One of the bishops was Bishop White of Peterborough, who had been for a short time Vicar of Newark.

ENDOWMENT OF THE JERSEY SCHOOL.

From Nottingham she retired to Oxford, where Prince George of Denmark, to whom she had been previously married, met her with a detachment of the Prince of Orange's forces. Seeing his ranks grow thinner and thinner, the courage of James began to "ooze out." His warlike proclivities vanished. At first he determined to hazard all on a great battle. Now he was resolved upon flight. His wife and son were sent over to France, and he started in a small vessel from Sheerness. Being seized by some Kentish fishermen, he was brought back and kept a prisoner, until released by an order from the Lords, and he then passed to London and Rochester. Subsequently he effected his escape, and landed in France, where he was welcomed by the French monarch. A convention declared the throne vacant, and William and Mary became king and queen, being crowned at Westminster (April 11, 1689). The Declaration of Rights settled the Crown first on the children of Mary, and then on those of Anne, and failing these, upon the children of William by any other wife. The son of James II. and his posterity were thus shut entirely from the succession.

In 1688, the last of the reign of James II., Henry Stones of Newark, by his will, dated 6th July, gave the sum of £1400 to be paid to certain trustees therein named, whom he empowered to purchase lands therewith, and to settle the same in trust for the Corporations of Lincoln and Newark, for the following principal objects, namely, for the employment of poor people in work, living and inhabiting within the precincts and limits of the said Corporations of Lincoln and Newark, the moiety of the said £1400 to be settled for the use of the Jersey School in Lincoln, and the remainder to the like use in Newark. The charity is endowed with the following properties, viz.:—a Jersey School and five small houses adjoining, occupied by the Mistress of the Jersey School, and Chapman and Ellis's four widows; 70-95th parts of net rents derived from lands at Besthorpe and Girton, Nottinghamshire; and £3167 : 14 : 1 invested in the 3 per cent consols in the names of the official trustees of charitable funds. The ordinary yearly income of the charity amounts to £311, and consists of 70-95th parts of net rents derived from lands at Besthorpe and Girton, Nottinghamshire, and dividends on the above mentioned 3 per cent consols. The net income is applied in the maintenance of the Jersey School, in payment of the Mistress's salary, and wages to poor women in knitting worsted (spun in the Jersey School) into stockings.

During the following year (1689) a handsome silver bowl and thirteen cups were added to the Corporation plate through the generosity of the Hon. Nicholas Saunderson. The bowl has a movable rim, with rests like the top of a chess castle, intended, it might be thought, for punch ladles, but the inscription shows that the vessel was designed as a munteth cup for cooling or washing wine-glasses, which would be hung round the rim. It runs thus:—"This munteth, and thirteen cups, were given by the Honourable Nicholas Saunderson to the Corporation of Newark-upon-Trent, A.D. 1689." Monteth is taken from the name of the inventor. As Dr. King says:—

> "New things produce new words, and thus Monteth
> Has, by one vessel, saved his name from death."

Of the other Corporation plate, the largest silver tankard was presented by Daniel Crayle, a retired London banker, whose bust and monument are in the south transept. The smaller one was presented by John Johnson. The Loving Cup was given by the Hon. Henry Savile in 1687. The maces were the gift of King Charles the First.[1]

In the diary of Abraham de la Pryme[2] (as published by the Surtees' Society in their 54th vol. p. 44) are the following items:—"Not being well pleased with the country, tho' I was mighty much made on there, and had everything that I could desire, I, however, began my journey for Cambridge again on the 1st of July 1694. The first day I ridd by Newark (which is a very handsome town, well situated, and of great trade; there are the reliques of a mighty large and strong old castle, built, after the old manner, like forts, which castle held out mightily in Cromwell's time for the king) to Grantam, which place is famous for a delicate high steeple." Under the year 1695, November 9, after giving some account of King William the Third's journey to Lincoln and Nottinghamshire, he says (p. 73):—"I am credibly told that the town of Newark presented him with a silver sceptre, curiously cut and ingraved, but he would not accept thereoff. Then they presented him with a bagg of gold, but he refused that also, he telling them that the taxes were great, etc. But at Lincoln he received one of fifty broads and fifty guinneys."

By will, dated 23d December 1690, Lady Frances Leeke[3] gave £100 for the use of the poor of the parish of Newark, and £200 to be laid out in communion plate for the service of the church. As a result of the first-named bequest a charity is in existence endowed with 5-96th parts of the net rents derived from lands in East and West Laughton, Lincolnshire. The ordinary yearly income amounts to £9:0:9, and is applied in the purchase of coals, and the distribution of the same amongst the poor. Out of the second bequest there were purchased one large paten or dish for the bread, 22 in. in diameter; two large flagons, each 15½ in. in height, and 5½ in. in diameter; four less ones; two large cups, each 12 in. in height, and 5½ in. in diameter; two bread plates, and two candlesticks, each 20 in. in height, and 9 in. on the bottom square. We may add that Robert Palmer, clerk, and Susanna Anfield, subsequently gave two pieces of plate, in the form of ladles, for the purpose of collecting alms. Richard Jackson and Robert Beck presented a small salver. The whole of the articles are of massive silver.

In the same year that Lady Frances Leeke founded her charity (1690), Dr. Thomas White, Bishop of Peterborough, gave to the poor of the parish of Newark £240 to be laid out in lands, and £10 yearly to be paid out of the rents thereof to the said poor for ever, and the remainder to the vicar for his pains in

---

[1] "Notes on Newark." A lecture, by R. F. Sketchley, B.A.
[2] De la Pryme was descended from one of the foreign families who settled in the Levels in the days of the drainage. He was now returning from Hatfield, his native parish, to Cambridge, where he had taken his B.A. degree the preceding January.
[3] For particulars of the Leeke family see preceding pages.

distributing the same; which he directed should be done yearly, on the 14th day of December by the said vicar in the church porch, in the presence of the churchwardens or overseers of the poor, among twenty poor families or persons of forty years of age equally (husband and wife reckoned as one person), who should, before receiving the same, distinctly repeat the Lord's Prayer, the Apostles' Creed, and the Ten Commandments without missing or changing one word; and no one should receive the charity twice till all the poor of the parish had received it once. The donor in his will states: "I do desire that it may be observed that I design this gift, not only as a corporal but as a spiritual alms, for the good of the souls as well as of the bodies of the poor; having with sorrow of heart noticed the inconceivable ignorance which prevails amongst the poorer sort of people, that they are (at least very many of them) Christians only in name, but know not why they are so, nor what it is they are to believe, or practise, or pray for, to answer the ends of the Christian profession; to encourage them therefore to learn the fundamentals of the Christian religion, I have bequeathed this charity, which I do desire the vicar to distribute with a good conscience according to these directions, that the ends which I purpose by these resolutions may be obtained."[1] The charity is now endowed with 25-95th parts of net rents derived from lands at Besthorpe and Girton. The ordinary yearly income amounts to £77. The net income is applied in £10 being distributed amongst poor persons on the 14th of December annually by the vicar, and the rest is given to him for his pains in distributing.

The church was enriched by the munificence of Dr. White with an excellent library. It appears that when a boy he had resided in Newark, and had received the rudiments of his education at the Grammar School. From the school he proceeded to St. John's College, Cambridge, and having entered holy orders, returned to Newark as its vicar. He resigned the vicarage in 1666, and passed rapidly through a succession of preferments. He was Archdeacon of Nottingham in 1683, and two years later became Bishop of Peterborough. In that capacity he signed the petition to James II. against the reading in the churches of his declaration of indulgence, and was one of the seven bishops who were sent to the Tower of London for libel. Notwithstanding his objections to the proceedings of James, he did not relinquish his loyalty to that monarch. He refused to take the oath of allegiance to William and Mary, and was suspended from his functions. He died in London in 1698, and was buried in St. Paul's Cathedral. A proof of the literary taste of the learned prelate is afforded in the selection of the books for the library, the value of some of which time has greatly enhanced. Among the twelve hundred volumes which he bequeathed are the Polyglot Bible, the best edition of Camden, several important topographical works, and a peculiarly rare work by Sir Francis Willoughby, on Ornithology. The library occupies an upper room on the south side of the church, and a catalogue of it was published a few years ago.

A contest for the representation of the borough, which aroused more than

[1] *Vide Corporation Minute-Book.*

ordinary interest, occurred in 1699. The candidates were Sir Francis Molyneux, Mr. John Raynor, and Mr. Saunderson. Sir Francis Molyneux and Mr. Saunderson were returned by the mayor. Mr. Raynor petitioned the House of Commons on the 12th of December. The petition set forth that Mr. Raynor was duly chosen a burgess to serve in Parliament for the borough of Newark; but that many illegal practices were used by Edward Hobson, then mayor of the town, and others, in favour of Sir Francis Molyneux, "who polled several for him who were not qualified, and refused several who were qualified, who would have voted for the petitioner." Snow, one of the petitioners, said " the mayor, at the election, took him by the hand, and told him he was glad to see him, he having promised to vote for Sir Francis Molyneux; but after he declared he voted for Mr. Raynor, the mayor said he had no vote, and bade the officers turn him down." The House referred the case to their committee of privileges and elections; and upon the 11th day of January 1700 Sir Rowland Gwynn, the chairman, made his report. The resolution of the committee, with which the House agreed, declared that Mr. Raynor was the sitting member, and that Sir Francis Molyneux had not been duly elected. The House further resolved " that the mayor, aldermen, and all inhabitants within the said borough who pay *or ought to pay* Scot and Lot, have a right to vote in the election of burgesses to Parliament for the same." They then committed Edward Hobson, the returning officer of the borough, to the custody of the sergeant-at-arms for his irregular practices, in which custody he soon after died.[1]

In 1702 Queen Anne, second daughter of James II., ascended the throne, to the exclusion of her brother, James Francis Edward, a Roman Catholic. Amongst the addresses of congratulation that were offered to her Majesty, was one presented by Mr. Matthew Jenison, the owner of the Friary at Newark, who received on the occasion the honour of knighthood. The Jenisons were an old Newark family, as will be seen from the following interesting notice of them, for which we are indebted to Captain A. E. Lawson Lowe, F.S.A. Christopher Jenison, the first of his family who appears to have been connected with the town of Newark, seems to have been a wealthy tanner residing in what was then called " the market stead." He filled the office of alderman in 1580 and 1593 and again in 1605, and dying, January 13, 1606, was buried in the parish church, where there was formerly a monument to his memory. He married Elizabeth, daughter of Edward Kelsterne, of Newark, draper (alderman in 1559, 1568, and 1578), and left several children. Leverett Jenison, one of his younger sons, married Isabella, daughter of Henry Webster, alderman of Newark, in 1613, whilst Thomas Jenison, the eldest son, was himself alderman of Newark in 1616, and being appointed, together with his eldest son John, amongst the first and original aldermen of Newark, under the new charter, he became mayor of Newark in 1628. This Thomas Jenison married Mary, daughter of Sir John Savile, Bart., of Lupsett Hall, in Yorkshire, by whom he had several children. His daughter, Barbara, married her cousin, the Reverend

[1] *Journals of the House of Commons.*

John Savile, Rector of Thornhill, near Wakefield, and had a son, George, who succeeded to the baronetcy on the death of his kinsman, Sir John Savile, Bart., in 1704. Edward Jenison, who appears to have been the leading physician in Nottingham of his day, was one of the younger sons of Thomas Jenison. John Jenison, the eldest son of Thomas, was an apothecary, and was alderman of Newark under the old charter in 1622, and mayor in 1635. He left two sons: Matthew, who purchased the Friary estate from the Earl of Scarsdale, and was mayor of Newark in 1654, and Leverett, who followed his father's profession and was mayor of Newark in 1664, and who inherited the Friary upon the decease of his elder brother. Mr. Leverett Jenison died in 1689, and was succeeded by his elder surviving son, Matthew, who thereupon inherited a very considerable estate.

The circumstances to which the Jenison family owed a very considerable portion of their wealth are (if we may credit the tradition related by Dickinson) remarkable indeed. "In Mr. Jenison's house," says Dickinson, "were many subterraneous vaults, of great depth and intricacy, which had belonged to the religious of former times. During the siege of Newark these were considered as the most secure depositories for money, plate, title-deeds to estates, and, in short, for whatever was valuable, and might become an object of plunder to the Republicans in the event of their becoming successful. Thither, then, the wealthiest of the inhabitants repaired, from time to time, as the danger became imminent, or as they were called out on sorties, or on expeditions, with all their treasures, as to a secure asylum. Many of these were cut off in the field of battle; some were every day dropping off by the common incidents of life; not a few departed never to return, owing to various disasters, as imprisonment, sickness, age, and casual mortality: it is not unreasonable to suppose that even some few from indolence, from the distracted state of affairs, nay, even from an over-weening confidence in their friend, might omit to reclaim these valuable deposits till times should become more peaceable, and the acknowledged possession of wealth less dangerous. In the meantime old Mr. Jenison dropped into the grave, and his son came unconsciously into the possession of unclaimed property to an immense amount. It has been already observed that the son was brought up to the same profession as his father, and it was not long before an event occurred which was followed, as far as concerned his interest, by circumstances and advantages nearly similar to those which the civil wars of the former reign had produced to his ancestor. This was the great plague in the reign of King Charles II. It has been noticed in a former page that few places suffered so severely, in proportion to the number of their inhabitants, by this dreadful visitation as the town of Newark. The tradition of the place is, that the infection was conveyed directly from London by some patterns of woollen cloths which were sent to a draper in the market-place. Be this, however, as it may, the disease is said to have carried off more than one-third of all the inhabitants, and it continued to rage so great a length of time that the streets were entirely grown over with grass. The inhumation of dead bodies was prohibited within the precincts of the town, and a large pit was opened at the southern extremity of Mill Gate, not far from the bridge over the Devon, into which, it has been rumoured, the dead and dying were promiscuously conveyed by a cart every morning before sunrise. This melancholy mortality is said not only to have taken off the small remnants of old families that had been spared by the previous troubles and their concomitant scourges, pestilence and famine, but to have swept off whole generations of new inhabitants, who had been encouraged, by the return of peace, to settle in the place. These circumstances, however, not only secured Mr. Jenison in the undisturbed possession of those deposits which had descended to him from his father, for which there were no longer any claimants, but is confidently said to have brought a great accession of similar fiduciary wealth into his coffers, of which few inheritors survived to disturb his enjoyment."[1]

Matthew Jenison, the fortunate inheritor of this strangely-acquired wealth, was brought up to the profession of the law, but it would not appear that he ever practised as a lawyer. In 1702 he received the honour of knighthood from Queen Anne, on presenting an address on her accession to the throne. Sir Matthew seems to have been a strenuous advocate for the enclosure of the open lands in the parish of Newark, a proceeding from which he would, doubtless, have derived large pecuniary benefit, but his attempts met with very general opposition. An undated document relative to this is quoted by Dickinson, and is of sufficient interest to warrant its reproduction in these pages:—

Wee, the severall persons whose hands and seales are hereunto subscribed and set, doe by these presents for our respective heires, executors, and administrators, covenant, promise, and agree, to and with the mayor, aldermen, or body incorporate of the burrough of Newark-upon-Trent, in the county of Nottingham, their successors and assignees, to bear and pay our severall shares and proportions of all such charges, expences, and ffees, as have been or shall be expended incident or necessary in carrying on, defending, managing, and prosecuteing all such suites at law and in equity as have been already brought, or shall happen to arise or to be advised to be commenced, for the opposing or throwing open the severall parcells of ground lying in the fields of Newark aforesaid, lately inclosed by Sr Matthew Jenison, knight, and John Jenison, clerke, or either of them, or by any other person or persons in what name or names soever such suite and suites now are or at any time shall be commenced. And the said mayor and aldermen, for themselves, their successors, and assignes, doe covenant, promise, and agree, to and with the said severall persons, their executors, and administrators, by these presents, to bear and pay their joynt share and proportion of the charges, expences, and fees, now and at all times hereafter, according to the true intent and meaning of these presents.

Signed and sealed for and on behalf of the right honourable Robert, Lord Lexington, by George Cartwright, Esq., in the presence of William Snell, Matthew Heron, Mordicai Hilton.   GEORGE CARTWRIGHT.

Signed and sealed by T. Howard, Esq., in the presence of Timothy Ellis; and alsoe in the presence of a servant of the said Mr. Howard, which waited of him in his chamber and held the inkhorn whilst the said Mr. Howard signed and sealed, he then having the gout upon him.   THOMAS HOWARD.

---

[1] We have adverted on a preceding page to the tradition regarding the Plague, and explained the absence of any corroborative evidence.

Signed and sealed by Mr. S. Ellis, in the presence of R. Hacker, Richard Reade, Jun.

SAMUEL ELLIS.

Signed and sealed by the Mayor and aldermen, under their comon seal, in the presence of John Hobman, Samuel Baily.

WILLIAM POCKLINGTON, Maior.
ROBERT MARRIS.
RICHARD READE.
MATTHEW ALVEY.
RICHARD RAWSON.
SOLOMON BETTISON.
EDWARD HOBSON.
WILLIAM HASLAM.

Sir Matthew Jenison was considered, in his day, to be the most influential Whig in Newark, and repeated struggles for the honour of representing the borough in Parliament, combined with the extravagant, dissolute life which he led, involved him in difficulties, and he first mortgaged the Friary to Sir Francis Willoughby, Bart., of Wollaton, and ultimately sold it to Thomas, first Lord Middleton. During the latter part of his life he became entangled in a Chancery suit, and the chancellor not only decreed against him, but condemned him in costs. These he determined not to pay, and for his contempt of court was committed to the Fleet prison, where he died. Sir Matthew Jenison was never married. His younger brother, the Reverend John Jenison, had died in his lifetime, and his sister, Anne, who had married Mr. Francis Bradford, had left an only surviving daughter, Elizabeth, who married Sir Samuel Gordon, Bart., and carried the remnant of the Jenison estate into that family. The arms borne by the Jenisons were—*Azure, a bend (wavy) or between two swans argent*, which were duly allowed to the family at the visitation of 1662.

By will, bearing date 12th May 1704, Timothy Ellis vested his three chambers by the churchyard over part of the then butchers' shambles, in trust, with Timothy Ellis and his heirs and Samuel Rastall and his heirs "for the support, relief, and maintenance of three poor widows of Newark town of sixty years of age, such as never had any collection from the said town ; and for the support of that disposition he ordered the profits of the said shops under them and widow Burnett's house at the churchgate, Rushton's house in North Gate, and Primrose and Chantry's house in Castle Gate, to be applied for the repairs of the said chambers, shops, and houses, and maintenance of the said poor widows ; and he willed withal that out of the revenues of the same the said poor people should have yearly bought, and should wear constantly, purple gowns of baize signated with these three letters, viz. S. T. E., upon every one of their right sleeves in open view and sight."[1] On the removal about the year 1775 of the property in the shambles, in order to open and enlarge the avenues and approaches leading to the church and churchyard, the widows were taken to the houses in Guildhall Street. The charity is now endowed with the following properties, viz.—£2 : 5s. annual rent charge payable by Mr. W. F. Handley's executors out of a house in Northgate, and £1 : 7s. annual rent charge payable by

[1] Report of the Commissioners for inquiring as to Newark charities, 1829.

Mr. J. P. Lacy's executors out of a house in Castle Gate. The net income is applied in payment of weekly allowances to the three poor widows.

On a brass plate in the north aisle of the parish church is the following inscription:—"Here lies the body of Mr. Thomas Summers, who died August 7, 1708, in the 57th year of his age, leaving to the poor of the corporation £500 to be paid after the decease of his mother, according to his will, out of his land at Carlton-on-Trent to five beadsmen 5s. a week, and the other part remaining to be given to the use of the other poor of the said Corporation upon Candlemas Day in every year for ever." The charity which Mr. Summers founded is endowed with the following properties, viz.:—50-96th part of net rents derived from lands at East and West Laughton, Lincolnshire. The ordinary yearly income amounts to £45 : 3 : 9. It is applied in payment of a shilling each per week to five beadsmen, and the remainder is utilised in the purchase of coal and distribution of the same to the poor on the 2d of February annually.

In 1710 an election took place, when Sir Thomas Willoughby, of Wollaton, and Mr. Richard Newdigate were chosen for the borough of Newark. A petition was lodged against their return by Mr. Richard Sutton, but it was without success. In the year following Sir Thomas was raised to the peerage by the style of Baron Middleton, and was succeeded in the representation of Newark by Brigadier-General Sutton. In 1713 eight bells were cast for the steeple of the church by the direction of the new member. An inscription placed at the time in the belfry stated that "Richard Sutton, Esq., the Honourable Brigadier-General of Her Majesty's forces, gave £200 for the new casting of six bells and metal for two new bells in this steeple; as also the branch candlesticks in the church and chancel." There were inscriptions on the bells, which have been justly described as more creditable to the owner's liberality than to the poet's talents. They were as follows:—

		cwts.	qrs.	lbs.	ozs.
1st. Ex dono Hon. Brigadier Sutton, A. R. 1713	.	7	0	1	0
2d. Do. do. .	.	7	0	26	0
3d. Pack and Chapman, London, fecit 1775 .	.	"	"		
4th. Brave Sutton rais'd us to declare					
The joys of peace; the end of war		10	1	0	0
5th. If Sutton's praises we could speak,					
Much sweeter echoes we should make		13	3	1	10
6th. Whilst here we're loud in Sutton's fame,					
What place rings not of his bright name?					
Ely Stansfield, Vicar, 1713		15	1	11	10
7th. Arma virumq. Cano., Richard Read, Richard Hawding, churchwardens; Abraham					
Rudball of Gloucester cast us all, anno domini 1713 . . .		20	1	7	7
8th. Multi cum fuimus nos resonare fecit,					
Honor Iis Brigadier Sutton 1713,					
Solomon Pettinson mayor, Joseph Marris, churchwarden		28	1	7	7

About the year 1842 the bells were recast by Messrs. Taylor of Loughborough, and two new ones added.

There is in the library of local literature in connection with the Nottingham Free Public Libraries a curious broadside, giving "An account of the Phænomenon which appear'd at Elston, near Newark, March the 7th 1716," which we transcribe. It is written in the first person, but the writer, who was probably the vicar of the parish, has omitted to furnish his name. It is as follows:—"I observ'd in the North-West a long and broad stream of light, issuing out of a darkish cloud (betwixt twenty and twenty-five degrees of the horizon North-East as near as I can guess), like to the beams of the sun setting in a drizling evening, the stream pointing directly towards the zenith. I was somewhat amaz'd at it, considering the sun had been more than an hour set, and the moon's rising not being till the morning. Presently, after some other streams issued out of another cloud, near to the former, with a very unusual light, and with variety of colours, black, blue, flame-colour, yellow, etc., and so more and more till all that part of the heavens was overspread. During this whole time, never was seen such contentions (as it were) as betwixt these meteors: being all in confusion, and darting one against another, with an incredible force and swiftness, for about an hour and a half. Thro' all that region of the air where this confusion and strife (for I can term it nothing else), was, the stars appear'd clear as thro' a thin bright smoke, or as the sun sometime thro' a thin bright cloud. The other part of the heaven toward the North-East was very clear, the stars bright and twinkling, as in Winter's cold night when there is no moon; about nine at night, these meteors (as I may so call them) in great measure disappear'd, but not quite; some faint sort of contentions (as it were) were still perceiv'd; and about ten o'clock they broke out again with a fresh violence in the same manner as before, and so continued till about half an hour past eleven. About twelve, a bright globular body appear'd as big as, and like the sun at its rising, but not quite so clear. Indeed, it was the most astonishing sight I ever yet beheld: during this time, the light was such, that I myself (tho' now almost sixty years of age) and another clergyman did read several titles of the books in the Bible, without any use of art. The night was calm, not so much as a breath of wind was perceiv'd. It began, according to my opinion, in the North-West and so drew round to the South-East."

At a meeting of the town council in 1720 it was provided that every member of Parliament elected for the borough should become a freeman. The resolution stated "that every person or persons not already made free, or a free inhabitant of the borough that shall hereafter stand as a candidate or candidates for the borough in Parliament, shall, at the first court of record to be held for the borough, after he or they shall first ask or desire any vote or votes of the electors of the said borough by themselves or their friends now in open court, then and there desire to be made a freeman of the said borough, and that the said person or persons so desiring the same shall, upon the payment of £40 to the chamberlain for the use of the corporation, etc., immediately be made and declared a freeman of the said borough and not otherwise, which said sums so raised shall be lent to freed men of the said borough without any interest upon security to be given for the repayment thereof at the end of one year." In the same year an ordinance was passed to this effect: "Whereas of late several persons have resorted with certificates from places distant to this borough of Newark with intent to keep public-houses by selling ale and beer, though perhaps they have been refused licenses for so doing at the last place of their abode, or are persons of idle lives; we, therefore, the mayor and aldermen of the said borough, do agree and declare that no license for selling ale and beer, or for the keeping of a victualling house in the said borough, shall be granted by us or any of our successors to any person or persons whatsoever resorting or coming to this borough from any place of Great Britain without paying, or causing to be paid, to us or our successors the sum of £10." At a subsequent meeting, it was ordered "that whereas of late several persons have resorted to this our borough under the titles of hawkers and pedlars by license, and these have hawked and carried about, and exposed for sale divers goods and merchandise under pretence and under colour of their licenses, etc., all which being very much to the prejudice and damage of the tradesmen or persons who are freed men in our borough, and who for many years have sold such goods, etc., we do order and declare that henceforth no hawker or pedlar shall expose for sale any goods or merchandise except those in the Acts of Parliament described: the penalty for any offence shall be 10s. for the first, 20s. for the second, and 40s. for the third."

We copy the following advertisement from an old Nottingham paper:—" A subscription of cocks to be fought at the house of Mr. James Thomlinson at the White Hart, Newark, for two guineas a battle; to be shown and weighed on Monday, 29th of this instant (May 1738), and to fight the three following days, and any gentleman who pleases to send any cocks may have them carefully fed by James Peters senior, and William Garnon, feeders. *N.B.*—There will be an ordinary every day at the aforesaid house."[1] Not only did the brutal sport of cock-fighting find numerous patrons, but the prize ring was occasionally occupied by competitors in human form. In a paper of some years later, viz. October 1767, we came across an account of a battle in Appleton Close between a Claypole farmer and a noted London gambler for £10. The disgusting combat lasted twenty minutes, during which time the farmer knocked down the gambler twenty times, and was hailed the winner by a great crowd who had assembled to enjoy the spectacle!

In 1745 the exiled Stuarts, encouraged by France and Spain, made a bold rush for the throne of England. Charles Edward Stuart landed near Moidart, on the coast of Inverness-shire, and at the head of seven hundred clansmen marched southward, gathering numerous reinforcements on the way. To quell the rebellion a subscription was entered into by the inhabitants and corporation of Nottingham. The mayor was authorised by the king to levy forces, grant commissions, and discharge other necessary duties of a military as well as a civil character for the defence of the town against the Scotch rebels. The Duke of Kingston, with the assistance of the noblemen and gentlemen of the county, raised a regiment of light cavalry.

[1] *Weekly Courant*, published at Nottingham.

The total subscriptions received amounted to £8525 : 10 : 6. On the 13th October came into Nottingham 72 carriages belonging to the artillery, 18 baggage waggons, 16 cannons, 2 mortars, 200 mattresses, 500 Dutch and 200 English foot, with Wade's regiment of horse complete. The artillery lay all night in the marketplace, where thousands flocked to see it. The next morning they set forward for the north, with their swords newly ground, and everything in order, as if they were to have engaged the enemy directly. During the summer a body of English and Hessian troops, to the number of about 6000, encamped for a while on Wheatley Hills, near Retford, and whilst halting at Retford they made a stable of the church for their horses.[1]

In the meantime Charles, who had become the idol of many of the Scottish people, entered England by the western border, and took Carlisle in three days. The English Jacobites came very slowly around him, though he moved through districts where, during the civil war, devotionate loyalty to his ancestor had been manifested. One of the towns he marched into was Newark, and Mr. Sketchley informs us he has heard it stated that the troops were regaled with ale in Guildhall Street. The statement, however, must, he says, be taken as a tradition wanting confirmation from other sources. On the 4th December Charles reached Derby, and this was the end of his onward journey. His troops were far from being united, and though success had held them together thus far, bickerings and jealousies succeeded. At their instigation he retreated, and his forces were routed by the Duke of Cumberland at Culloden Moor, nine miles from Inverness. The Duke of Kingston's cavalry took part in the engagement, and three Nottingham butchers are said to have slain fourteen of the enemy. Charles fled to the mountains, and eventually made his escape to France. His latter days he spent in Rome, and though the Jacobites long drank to the king over the water, the rebellion of 1745 was the last effort of the exiled family to regain the throne.

In 1751, a contested election, which had become an event of very rare occurrence, took place at Newark. The Dukes of Rutland and Newcastle, who had considerable influence in the town, had been in the habit of nominating the representatives, and there had been no contest for about forty years. On this occasion, however, Dr. Bernard Wilson, the vicar, started an opposition, the candidates being Mr. Cracroft, one of the Doctor's relatives, and Lord William Manners, who again offered himself in conjunction with Mr. Job Staunton Charlton. The Doctor and his nominee were unsuccessful in their effort, and in 1754, when, on another election occurring, the Doctor started a third candidate in the person of Mr. Dalaval, he was again unable to make headway against the two powerful houses of Belvoir and Clumber.

From 1739 until 1757 there is no record in the corporation book, but the following, written and signed J. Sykes, mayor, will explain the omission:—" It may appear very bad to our successors that there is so long a space of time passed over

[1] *Piercy's History of Retford.*

without any minutes of the proceedings of the corporation being inserted in this book ; for the more clearly explaining this matter, and for the satisfaction of persons who may succeed, we choose to declare the reason. Mr. Lund, a late alderman, by some means got this book into his possession, and it was never restored to this chamber until his death, and was thought to have been lost."

There seems to have been an uncomfortable scene in the church about this period, for we find that at a meeting of the mayor and aldermen, on the 3d January 1757, it was agreed that an application be forthwith made to the Court of King's Bench for an information against Mr. Edward Graves and Mr. John Marshall, for the insults offered to Mr. Mayor and the rest of the corporation in the church on Saturday last, and that the same be paid in an equal proportion "by us whose names are hereunto set." Eleven signatures are appended. At another meeting, on the 20th of February, it was agreed that Mr. Henry Foster and Mr. William Poyntell be added to the persons against whom an information is to be lodged. At a meeting on the 9th of June it was resolved that the corporation do proceed against the persons who insulted the mayor and corporation in the church on the 1st and 7th of January last, by a petition to the Court of Chancery, provided Mr. Mayor and the town-clerk shall, on consulting counsel, and laying before them the depositions of witnesses, find that the said court will give them relief on that account. What eventually became the result of the proceedings does not appear from the minutes.

In 1757 there died a gentleman well known in Newark, and whose abilities had earned for him considerable reputation—we mean Dr. David Hartley. He was born at Illingworth in 1705, was the son of a Yorkshire clergyman, and was the eldest of eight children. In 1720, when only fifteen years of age, he was admitted to Jesus' College, Cambridge, and from there he went to London to study medicine. Having obtained his diploma, he settled in Newark, but did not succeed in obtaining a very lucrative practice. The income he derived was so limited that he was compelled to adopt other means of gaining a livelihood, and obtained the mastership of the Grammar School. Whilst holding this appointment he wrote, anonymously, several treatises on medical subjects, which attracted the notice of an eminent physician in London. The writer was traced, and, through the interposition of friends, induced to relinquish his tutorship at Newark, and settle at Bury St. Edmunds. This was a step in advance, but he was not destined to remain in the comparative seclusion of a small provincial town. His influential friends turned his thoughts towards London, and held out to him an inviting prospect of success, which so large a sphere as the metropolis afforded. The glitter of the picture drew him within the great city, but he did not stay there long. What induced him to relinquish London life we know not. All we know is that he went from London to Bath, where he practised until 1757, when he died of a painful disease—that of stone. His writings were numerous, and full of deep thought. The earliest publication to which he attached his name related to lithiasis, and to this subject, on account of his own malady, he devoted a vast amount of attention and study.

A Mrs. Stephens had prepared a remedy for stone, consisting especially of a mixture of calcined egg-shells and Castile soap.[1] Dr. Hartley warmly approved of the recipe, and published (in 1738) ten cases of persons who had taken Mrs. Stephens' medicines, one of them being that of "the Right Reverend the Lord Bishop of Bath and Wells." Of his own case he says:—"It is now more than a year that I have had the usual symptoms of the stone in the bladder, with some suspicions of that in the kidneys. This made me listen to the accounts of Mrs. Stephens' medicines, and upon inquiring particularly into some cases, I was encouraged to try them. I have since been more particular in my inquiries, and here offer ten cases to the public, with an abstract of some experiments taken from a journal which I kept of them. The first nine cases are signed by the gentlemen themselves, the last rests upon the authority of the person therein named.... My design in printing these cases and experiments is to engage the public to purchase the discovery of the medicines from Mrs. Stephens. She offers this at £5000, and is ready to submit the effects of the medicines which she discovers to any examination which gentlemen of worth and skill shall propose." He subsequently published "*De Lithontriptico*, a Joanna Stephens, nuper invento. Dissertatio Epistolaris Auctore Davide Hartley, A.M. et R.S.S.," to which he added "*Conjecturæ quædam de Sensu, Motu, et Idearum Generatione*. Editio secunda, Bathoniæ, 1746."

In 1739 Parliament awarded to Mrs. Stephens for her discovery the sum of £5000, a vote which was doubtless due in a great measure to Hartley's powerful advocacy and influence. Experience has not been favourable to the continued use of this specific, but that the doctor firmly believed in it is shown by the recorded fact that he himself took upwards of two hundred pounds' weight of soap. Warburton, in one of his letters, says,[2] speaking of Hartley's death, which occurred in August 1757, "We have just lost too, a more philosophic visionary, Hartley, a martyr to Mrs. Stephens' medicine," insolvent!

The principal work on which the doctor's literary reputation rests was issued in 1748. It is entitled, *Observations on Man, his frame, his duties, and his expectations*. In this work, which consists of two volumes, he developed the hints and inquiries of Locke on purely materialist principles. "The association of ideas he made the foundation of all intellectual energy, and derived it from certain vibrations of the nerves."[3] The following reference to him is in *Whistlecraft*, by J. Hookham Frere,—

"Not from Locke's associations,
Nor David Hartley's doctrine of vibrations."

Hartley Coleridge was named after him, and in his *Religious Musings* Coleridge says of him,—

[1] *British and Foreign Medical Review*, vol. xii. p. 391.   [2] *Warburton Letters*, 4to, p. 187.
[3] *Biographical Treasury* (Maunders), p. 442.

> "And he of mortal kind
> Wisest, he first who marked the ideal tubes
> Up the fine fibres through the sentient brain."

The doctor had a son, David, who rose to some eminence. He became M.P. for Hull, and was a warm supporter of Lord Rockingham. He took an active part in vindicating the rights of America, and as Minister Plenipotentiary, signed at Paris the definitive treaty of 1783. He died in 1814, at the age of eighty-three, Senior Fellow of Merton College, and Father of the University. One of his inventions was a plan for rendering houses fire-proof; which consisted chiefly in forming the floors of double boards, placing a thin sheet of metal between the two; the idea being that if the lower layer of boards was consumed by fire, the sheet of metal would prevent the fire from spreading to the boards above. Parliament voted £2500 towards building a house on this plan, which was erected on Putney Heath in 1774, and visited by the king and queen, who breakfasted, it is said, in an upper room of it, whilst a large fire was kindled on the floor of the room below. The experiment at first seemed to promise a great success, and an obelisk was built near the house in honour of Mr. Hartley. Subsequent trials, however, showed that the plan was of but little practical value, and it was wholly forgotten in a few years. The house at Putney was converted into a private residence.[1]

At a meeting of the town council on the 16th November 1758, the mayor read the following letter from Mr. Job Staunton Charlton, one of the representatives in Parliament for the borough:—"I hear with pleasure that there is a proposal of applying to Parliament this session for an Act to enclose Everton lordship, that you may be enabled more effectually to carry on the great purposes for which those estates were given; I beg the favour of you to make my compliments to the corporation and the trustees, and acquaint them, I shall be much obliged if they will honour me with the care of the bill in the House of Commons, and give me leave to pay their share of the expense there. The uncommon zeal and spirit which has lately exerted itself for the promotion of the common weal of your town shall always have my warmest assistance, let who will oppose it." The town-clerk was ordered by the mayor and aldermen to express their thanks, and to state that they would accept the offer. The enclosure took place in 1762.

In 1760 George II. died suddenly of heart-disease, and George III. ascended to what has been aptly and accurately described as a glorious throne. In Newark, as elsewhere, the occasion of the accession of the new monarch was one of general rejoicing. We have no details of the proceedings at Newark, but in Nottingham there were great festivities. The principal inhabitants paraded the streets with music and streamers, preceded by the mayor and aldermen in their scarlet robes, the sheriffs, chamberlains, and common council in their official dress, and the clergy in full canonicals. Several sheep were roasted whole in the market-place, and there were grand illuminations and fireworks at night.

---

[1] Sir Richard Philip's *Morning Walk from London to Kew*, 8vo, 1817. See also *Notes and Queries*, August 26, 1876.

PERSECUTION OF A PREACHER.

At a meeting of the corporation of Newark on the 25th November it was ordered that an action be brought by the searchers and sealers of leather appointed for the borough against Thomas Wright, tanner, for refusing to allow them to search and seal his leather. At the same meeting it was ordered that the following plate be sold:—a tankard, the gift of Mr. Thomas Hobman; a cup, the gift of Mr. Camm; a beaker, the gift of the same gentleman; four salts, the gift of Mr. Birket; a thick-eared cup, the gift of Mr. Johnson; two large salts and seventeen spoons, also the gift of Mr. Johnson; one salt, the gift of Mr. W. Wombwell, and two odd seals. The total weight of these articles, which formed part of the old corporation plate, was 152 oz. 9 dwt., and they were sold at the rate of 5s. 6d. an oz., realising £41 : 18 : 6. The purchaser was Henry Bagerley.

About the year 1760 an attempt was made to steal the communion plate from the parish church. The rascals arranged that one of their number should secrete himself in the church at a funeral. In the night he let his companions into the church, who together (three in number), by the help of instruments, forced open a strong iron chest in which the silver was deposited. They also broke open the outside case of another iron chest, which contained the deeds and writings belonging to the estates of the town, and in which the trustees kept the money arising therefrom, but they could not force the inside one. This appeared to be their principal object, for the communion plate they left as they found it; all the booty they procured was the money in the poor's box, a small sum. One of the offenders, who, it appeared, had broken out of Newgate only the night before the robbery, was transported the assizes following for robbing a house in Nottingham.[1]

Mr. Thos. Lee, an earnest Wesleyan preacher, visited Newark in 1761, and he has left on record an account of the persecution he met with in the town. He says: "Towards the end of my sermon the mob threw a large quantity of eggs filled with blood and sealed with pitch, which made strange work wherever they alighted. Some thousands were gathered in the streets. I requested the mayor to send an officer to guard me through them. He said he would go himself, and he did go to the gate, but when I was gone out, he immediately went back. I was presently surrounded, and they soon began to throw mire and clods of earth and stones in abundance. This they continued to do all down the street, till we came to the preaching-house. Our friends, finding there would be no safety there, brought my greatcoat into the stable, and advised me to mount and gallop through the mob, which I purposed to do. Accordingly I mounted, but some of them held the gate and others beat both me and my mare in so violent a manner that I thought it would be the best to dismount, and go the back way, but here also the mob met me, beat both me and the mare, and when I endeavoured to mount, pulled me back, and the mare got from me. They then dragged me along, sometimes on my feet and sometimes on the ground, to the side of the Trent, swearing they would throw me in, but they were not agreed in this, so they brought water and poured it upon me from head to foot. A painter then

---

[1] Throsby's additions to Thoroton.

came with his pot and brush, and laid it on plentifully. They still surrounded me, throwing dirt and beating me till I could hardly stir. Then they offered to let me go if I would promise never to come again, but this I could not do. Just then a man came cursing and swearing and threatening, offended, it seemed, at their proceedings, on which most of them left me and dispersed."

A native of Newark, who died in 1762, Dr. Robert Taylor, had a singularly changeful career, that is neither uninteresting nor uninstructive. He was born in April 1710, his father being the landlord of the Turk's Head public-house. He received his early education at the Grammar School, and passed from thence to Trinity College, Cambridge. Desiring to become a physician, he devoted himself to the study of medicine, and gained a high reputation for his attainments. On receiving his diploma he settled in Newark, and was plodding quietly along when a circumstance arose which brought him face to face with fame and fortune. Lord and Lady Burlington were on a visit to the Duke of Rutland, at Belvoir, when his lordship was seized with a serious illness. A messenger was despatched to Newark for medical aid, and Dr. Taylor was taken over to wait upon the noble patient. For a time his lordship's life was despaired of; but, after a while, the malady yielded to the skill and unremitting attention of the medical man; his lordship was restored to health, and Dr. Taylor returned to Newark loaded with praises and with gratitude. Nor did the matter end here. The illustrious guests who were staying at the castle had been so impressed with a sense of the doctor's abilities that they determined to do something for him. Yielding to their solicitations, he removed to London, where he was introduced to the highest society. Lady Burlington took him in her carriage—introducing him to the nobility as a prodigy of skill, and she and her friends procured for him the appointment of physician to the king. With such influence at his back, combined with unquestionable abilities, the doctor advanced with rapid strides.[1] But he no sooner reached the top of the ladder than he began to come down again, and his fall was even more rapid and extraordinary than his ascent had been. Giddy with the applause and the honours which were showered upon him, he became extravagant and haughty; he wasted his substance, and alienated his friends; his practice dwindled down to minute dimensions, and he sank, suddenly, into the very midst of debt and difficulty. Illness succeeded upon adversity, and he died in 1762 without a penny to leave behind. A grand mansion which he had been erecting at Winthorpe was sold, and it is even said that the body could not be brought to Winthorpe to be buried, because an offended creditor threatened that he would seize upon it for debt in case any attempts to remove it were made.[2] However this may be, there is no doubt the interment took place in the burial-place of Audley chapel, but a few years after the remains, together with those of his infant son, were conveyed to Winthorpe and placed in a small vault which his widow had prepared for their reception. Mrs. Taylor survived fifty years,

---

[1] He delivered the anniversary oration before the College of Physicians in 1757. This, and the Latin epitaph on his father in Newark church, are the only specimens of his literary talent extant.

[2] Bailey's *Annals*, p. 1262; *Dickinson*, p. 282.

dying at the advanced age of 86. A neat tablet in the church at Winthorpe bears the following inscription :—

To the Memory of
ROBERT TAYLOR, M.D.,
Physician in Ordinary to his Majesty,
Who died the 15th May 1762, Aged 53.
Also
Of ELIZABETH TAYLOR, his wife,
Who died 10th May 1812, Aged 86 ;
And of ROBERT TAYLOR, their infant son.
This Monument is erected
By their only Daughter,
ELIZABETH CHAPLIN.

The races at Newark in 1763 lasted three days, and three prizes of £50 each were offered. There was a numerous attendance of noblemen and gentlemen, who were so pleased with the sport that they opened a subscription for next year's races with eighty guineas. On the first race evening, Tuesday, October 11, by order of Lord George Sutton, the play of "the Jealous Wife" was performed, at which the Marquis of Granby and several others of the nobility, the two borough members, the members for the county, and all the neighbouring gentry were present, and were highly entertained.

In 1765 there died, at his residence in London, Dr. William Stukely, the learned antiquary, to whom reference has been made in the earlier pages of these Annals. Mr. Stukely was born at Holbeach, in Lincolnshire, in 1687, and received a portion of his early education at the Free School at Newark. In 1703, though only sixteen years of age, he was admitted to Bennet College, Cambridge, where he devoted his time principally to medical studies. In 1709 he took the degree of Bachelor of Medicine, soon after which he settled as a physician at Boston, in his native county. In 1717 he removed to London, where honours fell thickly upon him. He became F.S.A. in 1717, F.R.S. in 1718, M.D. in 1719, and was admitted a Fellow of the College of Physicians in 1720. Maunders (*Biographical Treasury*) says of his subsequent career: "In 1726 he went to reside at Grantham, where he acquired great reputation as a medical practitioner, but repeated attacks of the gout induced him to relinquish his profession, and enter into holy orders, and he was presented to the living of All Saints, Stamford. In 1747 the Duke of Montague gave him the rectory of St. George the Martyr, Queen Square, London, where he died in 1765. Dr. Stukely pursued his antiquarian researches with an unusual degree of spirit and enthusiasm, and he made important accessions to our knowledge of the early monuments of human art and industry belonging to our native country. His principal works are :— *Itinerarum Curiosum, or an Account of the Antiquities and Curiosities of Great Britain*, 2 vols. folio ; *Palæographia Sacra, or Discourses on the Monuments of Antiquity that relate to Sacred History*, 4to ; *An Account of Stonehenge*, folio ; *Palæographia Britannica*, 4to ; *The History of Carausius*, 2 vols. 4to." It was after he became an inhabitant of Stamford that he used to spend a considerable portion of every year in

Newark, where, by the ties of relationship, he was much connected and universally esteemed. During his visits here he made his observations on the antiquity of the town and neighbourhood, enriching the margins of Thoroton and other histories with his valuable and interesting notes. He was buried in a private manner at East Ham, in Essex, in a spot which he had selected when on a visit to the rector of the parish.

In the same year that Dr. Stukely expired (1765) there died also Lady Mary Wortley Montague, a lady of great accomplishments, who has left a lasting literary reputation behind her. She was the eldest daughter of the Earl of Kingston, and was born at Thoresby, in the year 1690. In her youth she was remarkable for the readiness with which she made herself familiar with the classical and several of the modern languages. In 1712 she married Edward Wortley Montague, eldest son of the Hon. Sydney Montague, a gentleman who sat as a Member of Parliament, and was, on the accession of George I., an active supporter of the administration. From letters written by her ladyship it would seem that Mr. Montague had at one time an idea of contesting Newark, but was dissuaded from so doing. Writing to him in 1713, her ladyship says, "I cannot be sorry for your declining Newark, being uncertain of your success. Lord Lexington has considerable interest there. If you have any thought of standing there, you must know how he is affected, though I am afraid he will assist Brigadier-General Sutton, or some other Tory. Newdigate will certainly be chosen again. Upon the whole, it is the most expensive and uncertain place you could stand for." Her ladyship was no bad prophetess, for her predictions became verified in every particular. Lord Lexington supported General Sutton, and Mr. Newdigate was chosen again. In 1716 Mr. Montague was appointed Ambassador to the Sublime Porte, and it was whilst they were living in Turkey that her ladyship wrote her well-known letters. It was in Turkey also that she learnt the practice of inoculation, with the introduction of which into England her name has become indelibly associated. Her ladyship tried the experiment on her infant daughter, and finding it successful, recommended it amongst the nobility and gentry, whose adoption of it caused it to become general amongst all classes, and to remain so until it was superseded by the more approved method of vaccination.

On October 17, 1767, the Right Honourable the Earl of Lincoln and Lord George Sutton were sworn as aldermen of Newark, on which occasion their lordships gave an "elegant entertainment" to the gentlemen of the town and neighbourhood. In 1768 Mary Sturtevant, by her will, dated October 29th, devised £200 to the churchwardens and inhabitants of Newark, the interest of which was to be disposed of on Christmas Day among poor widows. In pursuance of the decree of the Court of Chancery, the legacy was laid out in the purchase of £230 : 4 : 3 three per cent consols. The dividends are now received half-yearly, and are distributed in half-crown doles to poor widows, at the discretion of the churchwardens. At a meeting of the council on the 15th March the Right Hon. John Shelley was admitted a freeman of the borough of the company of fellmongers. The Duke of Newcastle having been elected mayor, desired leave to resign his office on account of his avocations rendering it impossible for him to reside in the town. The resignation was accepted.

The rivalry existing between the supporters of the dominant party and the friends of Dr. Barnard Wilson extended to other contests than those in which Parliamentary honours were concerned. Prior to the election of churchwardens on Monday and Tuesday, April 4 and 5, 1768, active preparations were made for a great trial of strength, and the polling took place amidst a scene of considerable excitement. The corporation side, as it is termed in the newspapers, polled 359 votes, and the Doctor's interest 315 votes, but on a scrutiny it was affirmed that the Doctor's party had a majority of 18. A mandamus for the swearing in of the Doctor's friends arrived in the course of a day or two, and thus the reverend gentleman came off with flying colours.

On Michaelmas day, in the same year, the Right Hon. the Earl of Lincoln was sworn in mayor of Newark. After the council meeting his lordship invited the members of the corporation to a "genteel" entertainment.

In the annals of crime within the borough a case of murder, which occurred in February 1769, occupies a prominent place from the peculiarity of the circumstances under which it was perpetrated, and the strange conduct of the principal actor in the tragedy. The victim was a man 79 years of age, a pawnbroker named Thomas Burril, and the persons accused of the murder were three Claypole men—William Hebbe, Daniel Hebbe (his brother) and Thomas Moore. Burril had received from one of the Hebbes a watch in pawn for 30s., and an unsuccessful attempt had been made to regain possession of the watch without refunding the money advanced upon it. On the 17th February, about four o'clock in the afternoon, the Hebbes were seen to go to Burril's house, and heard to say, on their return, that they had "done for the old rogue." No notice, however, was taken of the matter until next day, when Mr. Burril was found lying dead on the house floor. There were no external marks of violence; but a surgeon testifying that the deceased had met with his death by unfair means, the coroner's jury brought in a verdict of wilful murder against some persons unknown. Suspicion naturally attached to the Hebbes, and one of them, in order to clear himself, produced a witness to testify that he was at home at six o'clock on the evening of the murder. The other two absconded, but a "hue and cry" being raised, they were pursued and apprehended at Welbourne, in Lincolnshire. At the magisterial examination, which lasted from ten to twelve hours, a considerable amount of circumstantial evidence was forthcoming, but the principal testimony was given by the prisoner, William Hebbe, who confessed that he had participated in the affair, having received part of the cash stolen from Burril, but alleging that his brother and the man Moore were the actual murderers. In his confession he stated that, under the pretence of treating the old man, they purchased some ale, into which they put 2 oz. of "laudanum drops." The liquor threw him into a profound sleep, and then they strangled him. The evidence of the surgeons proved that death had resulted from strangulation, and the three men were committed for trial. They were removed to Nottingham gaol, each man being chained under a horse, and, on arriving at Nottingham, William Hebbe addressed himself to the spectators, bidding them take warning by his position.

At the assizes in March more than twenty witnesses were examined. There being no positive evidence against Daniel Hebbe and Moore beyond the assertions of their fellow prisoner, they were acquitted; but William Hebbe having made a voluntary confession, the jury found him guilty, and he was condemned to death. He requested that Moore might be permitted to fix the rope, and the request was complied with. On the day appointed for the execution at Nottingham, he and Moore were put into a cart, and when within sight of the gallows, he requested some singers, who were accompanying him, to sing a penitential psalm, in which he joined with great earnestness, his voice being heard above all the rest. At the gallows he made a speech, and fixed the cord himself, instead of permitting Moore to do so. Then taking a paper from his pocket, he kissed it, pressed it in his right hand, and recommending his soul to God, was launched into the other world. While hanging on the tree, the paper was taken from his hand, and proved to be a tender letter from his wife. His body was taken to St. Ann's Well, and dissected by two eminent surgeons, who, says the *Nottingham Journal*, "pronounced him to be the finest subject they ever saw for dissection." The same paper concludes its account of the execution in a somewhat curious fashion :—" Thus died William Hebbe, much admired and much lamented, his many failings seeming to be buried in his expressions of true penitence, and in the uncommon manner in which he made his exit!"

When the time for again appointing churchwardens came round (1769) the old spirit of rivalry revived, and there were preparations for a renewal of the contest. Three and four guineas are stated to have been given for a vote[1] to secure the election of some of the candidates. Lord George Sutton, the Marquis of Granby, and many of the gentry of the district, came into the town to render assistance, and were received with great acclamation by an immense crowd. Riotous proceedings being feared, the high sheriff, Mr. Robert Foster, a resident in Newark, suggested that all the electors should poll by tallies, and that each side should take all possible means to preserve the public peace. The proposition was not accepted, nor was the poll proceeded with, for one of two reasons. On the one side, the reason given was that some friends of the corporation candidates objected to polling by tallies, and declared they would give a guinea per vote more than their opponents. It was also stated that as large sums had been given away, and as there was a prospect of dangerous riots, which would preclude a fair and free election, it would be wise to abandon it altogether. On the other hand, it was maintained that the corporation candidates had such a majority of electors in their favour, that the opposing party had no alternative but to yield. Whatever may be the true version, the fact remains, that about nine o'clock on the election morning (28th March) the contest was discontinued, and at eleven o'clock Mr. Lacy, Mr. Ridgill, Mr. Stevenson, and

[1] *Nottingham Journal.*

Mr. Sketchley who were supported by the Duke of Newcastle, Lord George Sutton, the corporation, and most of the principal inhabitants, were declared duly elected.

During a heavy storm on Friday, September 15, about two o'clock in the afternoon, the lightning pierced through the steeple of the parish church, damaged the wheel of the sixth bell, and threw out several stones. Fortunately no other mischief was done.

Until the year 1770 the access to Newark from the north was, by reason of the overflowing of the river, often impracticable. At these times a boat was used at an exorbitant rate from Newark to Muskham, five guineas having (according to Mr. Shilton) been frequently paid for conveying a carriage and the passengers. At that period the idea was suggested by the landlord of the King's Head, Mr. Joseph Wright, that an elevated road might be formed, interspersed with arches. This was accomplished under the auspices of a Mr. Simpson, at a cost of £1200, and it now bids defiance to all ordinary floods.

At a council meeting on the 26th January 1771 it was resolved "to request the Right Hon. Lord George Sutton to reside in the town." The same year the corporation gave their assent to the bill for the North Muskham enclosure. In the following year Lord George was elected mayor, but declined taking upon himself the office.

Dr. Wilson died on the 30th April 1772. Mr. Dickinson gives a lengthy biography of him, containing particulars of a very curious character. He, says the Doctor, was the son of a mercer of Newark, and being a lad of promise, some of the principal inhabitants procured him admission to Westminster School, and on his proceeding to Trinity College, supported him liberally by their joint contributions. He distinguished himself as a youth of "lively parts and some erudition," and managed to ingratiate himself into the good graces of several youths of superior rank and fortune, amongst them being Thomas, afterwards Duke of Newcastle. Meanwhile his father had taken the Friary, where he subsisted on his little property, the kindness of his friends, and the income derived from the payments of several lady boarders. Amongst the latter was a Miss Bradford, a young woman having, in addition to a good appearance, a fortune of £1200. When Wilson left Cambridge and returned to his father's house, he made love to Miss Bradford, and succeeded in securing her affections. On the vicarage of Newark becoming vacant, the influence of the Duke of Newcastle procured it for him, and Wilson being an effective preacher, the parishioners were well satisfied with the appointment. In 1717 Mr. Wilson published a translation of discourses by eminent members of the French Academy, and this he dedicated in fulsome language to Sir George Markham, the member for the borough. Sir George rewarded him for his flattery by giving him the management of large estates in Lincolnshire, and recommending him as a husband to Miss Ogle, the daughter of an Irish gentleman. Though residing in a splendid mansion which he had erected for himself, and accompanied in his magnificence by Miss Bradford, he paid his addresses to Miss Ogle, and also to Lady Elizabeth Finch, and a Miss Davis. Miss Ogle persuaded her uncle to leave him a fortune. Lady Elizabeth disdainfully rejected his advances, whilst Miss Davis sued him for breach of promise, and recovered £7000 damages. Miss Ogle subsequently became a lunatic, and found an asylum with her friends at Dublin. Wilson, though liberated on this ground from his promise to marry, became involved in lawsuits with the Ogle family. These were compromised by the payment of £30,000, of which £20,000 went to the elder Ogle, and the remainder was divided between the younger children.

After the settlement of these broils the Doctor privately married his first love, Miss Bradford, at the church of Claypole, near Newark. But one cause of difference and difficulty was hardly ended ere another arose. The vicar quarrelled with his patron, the Duke of Newcastle, and endeavoured to subvert his influence in Newark by lending money to the inhabitants, establishing charity schools, distributing gifts, and the like. At several elections his efforts were, as we have already shown, actively used in opposition to the duke, and the antagonism does not appear to have ever been annihilated. In 1772, at the advanced age of eighty-three, Dr. Wilson caught a severe cold, which terminated in a fever, and produced his death. It is said that nearly £5000 were found in different parts of his house, consisting principally of guineas of Queen Anne's reign, and half-crowns of the time of William III.

By a codicil to his will, bearing date 31st May 1769, after reciting that he had bequeathed the residuum of his personal estate to Robert Cracroft, Esq., Dr. Wilson directed that the said Robert Cracroft should, out of the said residuum, pay the sum of £40, to be distributed yearly for ever to such poor and necessitous families of the town of Newark as the vicar of the town should direct; £20 of the money to be distributed on every 21st day of August, being his birthday; and the other £20 to be distributed on every 11th day of January, being the birthday of his late most valuable friend, Sir George Markham, deceased. On each day of distribution a sermon was to be preached by the vicar on the subject of loving God and our neighbour, or upon the duty of charity, or the misapplication of public charities. For these sermons the vicar was to receive £10. By a subsequent codicil, dated 7th June 1770, Dr. Wilson gave to his nephew, Robert Cracroft, and his heirs, £100 a year, from premises in the market-place, to be distributed by him amongst fifty necessitous Newark families of sober and religious life and conversation; also £10 to be distributed amongst twenty poor widows; and £10 to the vicar, "so long as he should behave himself with decency and respect to the said Robert Cracroft, his heirs and assigns." The bequests in the last codicil were void, under the statute of 9 George II., c. 36. Those of the first codicil are received by the vicar in half-yearly sums of £25, of which he distributes, on 11th January, £20 to eighty poor persons, in sums of 5s. each, and on 21st August he makes another distribution of a like sum to the same number of recipients. A list of the persons receiving the charity is entered in a book which is deposited in the church. The remaining

£10 the vicar retains to his own use, in accordance with the provisions of the will. A tablet in the church, to the memory of Dr. Wilson, bears the following inscription :—

> Sacred to the memory of BARNARD WILSON, D.D.
> Upwards of forty years vicar of this place ;
> A man of sense, politeness, and learning,
> without pride, reserve, or pedantry.
> Possessed of an affluent fortune,
> His hand was ever open to relieve the necessitous.
> His extensive charities when living,
> and ample benefactions at his decease,
> have raised him a living monument in the hearts
> of the poor.
> He departed this life on the 30th of April 1772,
> Aged 83 years.
> Robert Wilson Cracroft, Esq., his nephew,
> has, with gratitude and affection, inscribed this to his
> memory.

In 1772 an Act of Parliament was obtained "for improving and completing the navigation of that branch of the river Trent which runs by the town of Newark from a place called the Upper Weir in the parish of Averham to a place called the Crankleys in the parish of South Muskham." The preamble of the Act states that "whereas the town of Newark is possessed of a considerable trade in corn, wool, coals, and other merchandise, and the said branch of the river Trent, which runs by the side of the town, may, by improving the channel thereof and by making proper cuts and other works, be rendered navigable at all seasons of the year, and a more regular intercourse of trade would thereby be opened ;" commissioners were therefore appointed with power to construct dams of stone or brick and to do other works necessary for improving the means of navigation.[1] In making the cut many cannon balls, which had been used during the sieges, were taken out of the soil.

At a meeting of the town-council on the 26th January 1773 the mayor and aldermen affixed the common seal to a petition to Parliament for selling portions of Brown and Phillipot's estates at and near Newark, and building a town-hall and shambles with the money arising therefrom, and ground and houses for enlarging the churchyard. An Act was accordingly passed, the title of which ran as follows:—"An Act for the sale of certain charity estates therein mentioned, and to apply the money arising therefrom to the building of a town-hall and shambles in the town of Newark-upon-Trent, and in the purchase of lands and hereditaments for enlarging the churchyard of the said town, and for opening the avenues thereto, and for laying out the residue of the money in purchasing other lands to be settled to the charitable uses therein mentioned." The first stone of the new Town Hall, which is one of a very substantial character, was laid during the year. The front is composed of Mans-

---

[1] Acts of Parliament for Newark in the Stock Library.

field stone. The basement storey exhibits a beautiful specimen of rusticated masonry. "A perfect Doric entablature," as Mr. Shilton describes it, forms the completion of the two other storeys, the centre of which is supported by columns of that order, whose symmetry will bear the most critical inspection ; behind these columns is a commodious recess, technically termed a Loggia, with a balustrade in front. The sub-Loggia, originally proposed to be used as a corn-market, as also the sub-hall, used as a butter-market, are well paved ; the latter is divided into colonnades by columns of the compound Tuscan order ; the ceiling is divided into rather small square compartments, which increases the firmness of the superincumbent floor. A handsome geometrical staircase of stone leads to the large hall, which is 80 feet long, 30 feet wide, and 30 feet in height. In the centre of each side is a handsome chimney-piece of Italian marble. The room is extremely well lighted by six lofty circular-headed windows in the sides, and one at the upper end. It is used for public meetings, soirees, balls, concerts, etc., and the quarter sessions for the borough are held in it. In the piers between the windows, and likewise at intervals in the bow ends, are double pilasters corresponding with the columns before described. Fronting the market-place is a commodious room known as the council-chamber. Its length is 35 feet, breadth 20 feet 8 inches, and height 16 feet. It is well lighted by large windows looking towards the market, and at night by means of elegant lustres depending from the ceiling. In this chamber the council hold their meetings, and the borough petty sessions take place here twice a week. Adjoining the chamber are two smaller rooms, used either as retiring rooms or for committee meetings.

The following were employed in erecting and finishing the Town Hall and its adjacent wings :—Architect, Mr. J. Carr, York ; superintendent, Mr. W. Matthews, Newark ; mason, Mr. Mew, Mansfield ; bricklayer, Mr. Palmer Sheppard, Newark ; carpenter and joiner, Mr. Baker, Retford ; slater, Mr. W. Lewis, Nottingham ; plasterer, Mr. Moses Kilmister, Derby ; carvers, Messrs. G. Barrett, Newark, and Thickstone, Doncaster ; plumber and glazier (hall), Mr. J. Smalley, Newark ; plumber and glazier (wings), Mr. S. Watson, Newark, Mr. J. Holmes, Newark ; painter, Mr. J. Smith, Newark. Upwards of £17,000 are said to have been expended in the erection and completion of these edifices.[1]

The frost was so intense during the early part of January 1774 as totally to impede the navigation of the Trent through nearly its whole course from Nottingham to Newark.

A theatre at Newark was built this year in Middle Gate. It stood on the site of the grocer's shop now occupied by Mr. Welch.

From the termination of the civil wars until 1775 there had been a wooden bridge very meanly constructed over the Devon, a little below the castle. The keeping of this bridge in repair was an expense annexed to the lease of the Crown lands lying in the borough, which had for many years been in the possession of the Duke of

[1] Shilton's *Hist. Newark*, p. 372.

Newcastle. In the year 1775 his Grace was advised to take down the dilapidated old structure, and to erect one of more durable materials. Accordingly, one was built of brick faced with stone.

The celebrated Bishop Warburton, who was born at Newark, died at his palace in the city of Gloucester, in January 1779. Of the family to which the learned prelate belonged, and of their first association with this town and district, Captain A. E. Lawson Lowe thus writes us :—" The Warburtons of Warburton and Arley in Cheshire were amongst the most ancient families in that county, their descent being derived from one Hudard or Odard, who is said to have come into England at the time of the Norman invasion. William Warburton, a younger son of Peter Warburton, Esq. (the third son of Sir Piers Warburton of Arley, by Elizabeth his wife, sole daughter and heiress of Sir Richard Winnington of Winnington), distinguished himself as a Royalist in the civil wars of the seventeenth century, and especially under Sir George Booth at Chester. He subsequently came into this county and settled at Shelton, where he practised as a lawyer and became coroner for the county, an office which he held until his death. His first wife, Margaret Brooke, was a member of an ancient Cheshire family still seated at Norton in that county; but, according to Ormerod,[1] she left no issue. He afterwards married Frances, daughter of Robert Awfield, of Elston, in Nottinghamshire, and widow of George Armstrong Esq., of Scarrington (who, as Thoroton[2] tells us, 'reproved a vile Parliament soldier for swearing and cursing, and was by him stabbed to death'), by whom he had three sons.[3] At the herald's visitation of 1662 this William Warburton was summoned amongst the other gentry of the county, and established his right to armorial bearings, namely,—*Argent, a chevron between three cormorants, sable. Crest, a Saracen's head affrontée, couped at the shoulders proper, wreathed about the temples, argent and gules, issuing therefrom three ostrich feathers, or.* These arms, boldly carved in stone, with the name 'William Warburton' beneath, still remain affixed to one of the pillars in Shelton church; and there is also a large slab, bearing an inscription to his memory.

"His second son, George, was likewise a member of the legal profession, and established himself at Newark, of which place he eventually became town-clerk, and is said to have been much esteemed for his integrity. He was married about the year 1696 to Elizabeth, daughter of William Hobman, alderman of Newark, by whom he had several children, whose baptisms are recorded in the parish registers between the years 1697 and 1704. He died in November 1706, and was buried on the 19th of that month within the parish church. William Warburton, his eldest son, was born December 24, 1698, and was baptized January 5, 1698-9. He was first educated at the Free School under Mr. John Twells, whose son, an attorney in Newark, subsequently married one of Warburton's sisters. From thence he was sent to the Grammar School at Oakham, where he continued until 1714,

---

[1] Ormerod's *History of Cheshire*, vol. ii. p. 3. [2] Thoroton's *Antiquities of Nottinghamshire*, p. 119.
[3] Watson's *Life of Bishop Warburton*, p. 2.

when his cousin, the Rev. William Warburton, being elected to the mastership of the Newark Free School, he was taken home and placed for a short time under his tuition. That same year he was articled for five years to Mr. John Kirke, an attorney practising at East Markham, in this county. He was subsequently duly admitted into one of the law-courts, and is said to have practised for several years as an attorney in his native town, and seems to have been an unsuccessful candidate for the office of town-clerk. It has been stated that Warburton was for some little time a wine merchant in the borough,[1] but nothing in confirmation of this has been seen. He was ordained as a deacon December 22, 1723, and took full orders March 1, 1727, and shortly afterwards he was presented to the vicarage of Greasley, near Nottingham, which benefice he only held for about a year, when he resigned it, having been presented by Sir Robert Sutton to the rectory of Brant Broughton. He married, September 5, 1745, Miss Gertrude Tucker, niece and heiress to Ralph Allen, Esq., of Prior Park, near Bath (the 'Squire Allworthy' of 'Tom Jones'), by whom he had an only son, Ralph, born in 1756. In 1766 he obtained royal license for his son and his posterity to assume the surname of Warburton Allen."

Having thus quoted a sketch of the Warburton family, compiled with Captain Lowe's usual accuracy and care, it will be interesting to trace in fuller detail the bishop's active and successful career. It is a noticeable fact that, like others who could be named, who have risen to eminence, he gave no indication in his schoolboy days of the possession of any unusual talent. One of the masters at Oakham when *The Divine Legation* appeared, expressed the greatest surprise, declaring that, when at school, he had always considered Warburton as the dullest of all dull scholars. On his return from Oakham to Newark he worked with unusual assiduity, and had the advantage of constant assistance from his competent relative, who was at the head of the school.[2] The kind-hearted master, we are told, employed all the time he could spare in instructing Warburton, and used to sit up very late at night with him, to assist him in his studies.[3] The effect of the careful training which he underwent, and the studious habits to which he became accustomed, was very beneficial. He passed successfully as a solicitor when he came of age, and on leaving the law for more congenial employment in the Church, he continued to work with great zeal and earnestness. A year after he had been admitted a deacon, namely in 1724, he issued a volume of translations in prose and verse, and in 1726 he contributed notes to Theobald's edition of Shakspeare. In 1727 he published his *Inquiry into the Causes of Prodigies and Miracles*, and then, having previously been admitted to full orders, he settled at Brant Broughton, pursuing his studies with diligence in the quietude of his country residence. It was from Brant Broughton that he gained the title of the Lincolnshire parson, of which he was apparently fond, for we find him adverting to it with noticeable pride in several of his contro-

[1] *Gentleman's Magazine*, vol. lii. p. 288.
[2] Dr. Zachary Gray says that Warburton "was a schoolmaster at Newark." It is possible he assisted his cousin, which may have given rise to the supposition.
[3] Letter from Archdeacon Warburton in Hurd's edition of Warburton's works, vol. i. p. 5.

versial writings. During the time that he lived in comparative seclusion he added greatly to his stores of learning, and planned, and partially executed some of his most notable publications. He usually spent a great part of the night in study, and as an instance of his intenseness of thinking, and perhaps, too, of his absence of mind, it may be mentioned that he rode past Fulbeck Hall, whilst it was on fire, without noticing it. Said he, "I saw no fire or bustle." It was rumoured that he spent so much time in contemplation and study, that he could spare little to attend to the requirements of his parish—a rumour which is embodied in Churchill's satirical lines:—

> "A curate first, he read and read
> And laid in—while he should have fed
> The souls of his neglected flock—
> Of reading such a mighty stock,
> That he o'ercharged the weary brain
> With more than she could well contain."

In 1736, after a nine years' interval, Warburton issued an elaborate treatise on the *Alliance between Church and State* which excited considerable attention in many quarters. Bishop Hare, to whom he had sent a present of his book, wrote:—"I had formerly been very agreeably entertained with some emendations of yours on Shakspeare, and was extremely pleased to find this work was by the same hand. Good learning, great acuteness, an ingenious working head, and depth of thought, will always please in an author, though we are not entirely in the same ways of thinking." Dr. Horsley writes[1]:—"Warburton, in his *Alliance between Church and State*, hath shown the general good policy of an Establishment, and the necessity of a test for its security, upon principles which Republicans themselves cannot easily deny. His work is one of the first specimens that are to be found, perhaps, in any language, of scientific reasoning, applied to a political subject." In 1737 he justified his reputation as a learned and indefatigable author by giving to the world the first volume of his great work on *The Divine Legation of Moses*. A more generous tribute to the ability exercised in its composition cannot be found than that contained in an article in the *Quarterly Review*, on Hurd's edition of Warburton's works. The writer says:—"To the composition of this prodigious performance Hooker and Stillingfleet could have contributed the erudition, Chillingworth and Locke the acuteness, Taylor an imagination even more wild and copious, Swift and perhaps Eachard the sarcastic vein of wit; but what power of understanding except that of Warburton could first have amassed all these materials and then compacted them into a bulky and elaborate work so consistent and harmonious? The principles of the work, as well as its execution, are alike bold and original." The writings of Warburton had not unnaturally caused him to be talked about at Court, and when the queen expressed her desire to have a person of learning in attendance, the Bishop of Chichester had no hesitation in recommending Warburton to her notice.

[1] *Review of the Case of the Protestant Dissenters*, Pref., London, 1787.

Her Majesty, however, was seized with a sudden illness, and died on the 20th November 1737.

In 1739 Warburton drew up and published a short defence of Pope's "Essay on Man."[1] The Essay had been attacked by M. de Crousaz, who had attempted to show that it was constructed on the principles of Spinoza,[2] and contained a dangerous system of irreligion. Pope was extremely pleased with Warburton's defence, and an intimate acquaintance arose between the poet and the commentator. In the spring of 1740 he visited Pope for the first time, and in an account of his visit which he gave to Dr. Middleton, he says:—"I passed a week at Twickenham in the most agreeable manner; Mr. Pope is as good a companion as a poet, and, what is more, appears to be as good a man." One of the results of the intimacy that had arisen was the introduction of Warburton to Mr. Allen of Prior Park, Bath,[3] and whilst staying at the residence of that gentleman the fourth book of Pope's *Dunciad* was read and approved, the rest being finished in the course of 1742. In the following year Warburton edited the four books complete, and so much to the author's satisfaction, that he engaged him to sustain the like office with regard to the rest of his works. In May 1744 Pope died, leaving to Warburton half his library and the whole of his unsold copyrights, valued by Johnson at £4000. Soon after Mr. Pope's death Warburton received a letter from Mrs. Cockburne, a lady of great abilities, lamenting that event, and soliciting some explanation of his system of moral obligation. He sent a courteous reply, dated from Newark, January 26, 1645, wherein he says:—"I am just now returned home," after staying at Bath and London.[4] In September 1745 Warburton married Miss Gertrude Tucker, a favourite niece of Mr. Allen, and shortly afterwards he was unanimously appointed to the preachership at Lincoln's Inn. In 1747 he issued an edition of Shakspeare's works, which he had undertaken at the instance of Pope. When it appeared, it aroused a spirit of hostile criticism, for Warburton not only made free with the text but was severe on previous editors. In a letter to Bishop Hurd, he says:—"I have, as you say, raised a spirit without designing it. And while I thought I was only conjecturing, it seems I was conjuring. So that I had no sooner evoked the name of Shakspeare from the rotten monument of his former editions, than a crew of strange devils, and more grotesque than any he laughs at in the old farces, came chattering, mewing, and grinning round about me."

Disregarding his critics, Warburton continued his literary labours with ever increasing energy. In 1750 he published *Julian*, a discourse concerning the earthquake which defeated the Emperor Julian's attempt to rebuild the Temple of Jerusalem. Speaking of this work some years afterwards, he said it had had a great

---

[1] The late Dr. —— informed Dr. Warton that when Warburton resided at Newark he and several others held a club, where Warburton used to produce and read weekly essays in refutation of Pope's "Essay on Man," This poem he afterwards found it convenient to defend.—*Malone.*

[2] The system of Spinoza is that matter is eternal, and that the universe is God.

[3] Fielding's "Squire Allworthy;" the owner of extensive property.

[4] See Appendix to Hurd's *Life of Warburton.*

effect in France, where freethinking held its head as high as in England. "This," he says, "is a consolation to me, as my sole aim is to repress that infernal spirit." In 1751 he issued a noble edition of Pope's works, and "from henceforth," says Bishop Hurd, "we see him only in his proper office of Dean." Promotions followed with great rapidity. Step by step he mounted the ladder. In 1753 he was made prebend of Gloucester; in 1754 he was appointed chaplain to the king; in 1755 he was made a prebend of Durham, and had conferred upon him, by the archbishop, the degree of D.D.; in 1757 he became Dean of Bristol; and in 1760 was made Bishop of Gloucester. He continued his literary labours until 1770,  when his faculties began to decay. His reasoning powers gradually left him, his bodily strength wasted away, and he died in January 1779 almost without a struggle.[1]

Warburton, in the midst of his literary popularity and glittering success, never forgot his early association with Newark. Writing to a friend of his, Charles Yorke, who had been on an excursion in Nottinghamshire, he says:—"It would have been the greatest pleasure to have dropped upon you at Newark. I could have led you through delicious walks, and picked off for your amusement, in our rambles, a thousand notions which I hung upon every thorn as I passed thirty years ago." When beyond seventy, his rambles in Newark were still fresh in his memory; writing to the Bishop of Worcester, he states:—"I think you have heard me say that my delicious season is the autumn, the season which gives most life and vigour to my mental faculties. The light mists, or, as Milton calls them, 'the steams' that rise from the fields on one of these mornings, give the same relief to the view that the blue of the plum (to take my idea from the season) gives to the appetite. But I now enjoy little of this pleasure compared to what I formerly had on an autumn morning, when I used, with a book in my hand, to traverse the delightful lanes and hedgerows round about the town of Newark, the unthinking place of my nativity." Of the literary abilities of Warburton there can be no two opinions. Dr. Johnson, alluding to his abundant and well-applied reading, aptly observes that "his table is always full. He brings things from the north and the south, and from every quarter. He carries you round and round without carrying you forward to the point, but then you have no wish to be carried forward." Of the social and personal characteristics of Warburton some interesting particulars are given in a letter, dated Feb. 12, 1785, of Dr. William Cuming, of Dorchester, to Dr. Lettsom. Cuming had, it appears, formed a most unfavourable opinion of the Bishop. From a perusal of his polemical and critical works he was disposed to regard him as "stiff and conceited in his opinion; dictatorial in his sentiments, and treating everyone who thought differently from himself with the most sovereign contempt." The conclusions that he arrived

[1] The engraving of Warburton, which we have introduced on this page, is from the painting at Gloucester Palace, copied in Bishop Hurd's edition of Warburton's works and elsewhere.

at after an acquaintance with Warburton may be gathered from the account he gives of his introduction to the Bishop, and the conversation that passed between them. He writes:—

"It is above 30 years ago that Ralph Allen of Prior Park first came to pass about three months in the summer annually at Weymouth; his niece, Mrs. Warburton, was always of the party.... I had been introduced to Mr. Allen's acquaintance soon after his first arrival, and was always professionally employed by the family. After a few years, the Bishop, whom I had never seen, came to pass a month of the summer with Mr. Allen at Weymouth. I was soon after sent for, to attend some one in the family. After having visited my patient, Mrs. Warburton took me by the hand, and led me into the dining-room, where we found the Bishop alone. She presented me to him with 'Give me leave, my lord, to introduce to you a friend of mine, to whom you and I have great obligations, for the care he has repeatedly taken of our son.' He received me courteously enough, but I own to you I felt an awe and awkward uneasiness. I determined to say but little, and to weigh well what I said. We were left alone; it was an hour to dinner; he soon engaged me on some literary subject, in the course of which he gave me the etymology of some word or phrase in the French language, with a 'Do not you think so?' I ventured to dissent, and said I had always conceived its origin to be so and so. To this he immediately replied, 'Upon my word, I believe you are in the right; nay, 'tis past a doubt; I wonder it never struck me before.' Well, to dinner we went: his lordship was easy, facetious, and entertaining. My awe of him was pretty well dissipated, and I conversed with ease. Some time after dinner, when he was walking about the room, he came behind me, tapped me on the shoulder, and beckoned me into an adjoining room. As soon as we entered, he shut the door, seated himself in an armed chair on one side of the fireplace, while he directed me by his hand to one on the opposite side. My fit immediately returned; I expected to be catechised and examined, but it was of short duration. He said, he was happy in this opportunity of asking the opinion and advice of a gentleman of my character respecting some complaints he had felt for some time past, and which he found increasing. On this my spirits expanded; I did not fear being a match for his lordship on a medical subject. He then began to detail to me the complaints and feelings of those persons addicted to constant study and a sedentary life. As I mentioned several circumstances which he had omitted in his catalogue, and which he immediately acknowledged, I gained his confidence. He was sensible I was master of my subject.... I explained to him the rationale of his complaints, and showed him the propriety of the diet, exercise, and regimen, which I recommended to him. In short, we parted, to join the company, very well satisfied with each other. I found my disgust and prejudice gradually abate. During several subsequent years I had repeated opportunities of being in company with him, and never saw a single instance of that fastidiousness and arrogance, so conspicuous in his writings. He always received me with great good-humour; I conversed with him easily and familiarly. On all subjects he showed an attention and deference to the opinion of others. He had a great fund of anecdote, and told his stories with much humour and facetiousness."[1]

Mr. Malone records that Burke, the first time he saw Warburton in company, sat next to him at dinner without knowing who he was, and that being much struck with his talk, he at last observed, "Sir, I think it is impossible I can mistake; you must be the celebrated Dr. Warburton; *aut Erasmus aut Diabolus.*" Warburton, adds Malone, "though so furious a controversialist in print, was very easy and good-humoured in company, and sometimes entertaining."[2] Mr. Dickinson says that in the social intercourse of private life he was often easy, even to a degree of playful-

[1] Nichol's *Literary Illustrations of the 18th Century*, vol. ii., p. 838.
[2] Prior's *Life of Malone*, p. 370.

ness, and relates the following anecdote, which was told him by the late Dr. Lynford Cary, master of Jesus College, Cambridge:—"Mrs. Warburton, a complete woman of the world, unable or unwilling to appreciate the value of her husband's talents, was never so happy as when she could promote the mirth of the moment by holding him up to derision, and had more influence with him than such a woman ought to have possessed. She had a near relation, a general in the army, whose uniform she obtained for the occasion, and persuaded the bishop to dress himself in it, in order, as she assured him, to be convinced that his martial air would have been much better suited to the army than to the Church. Teased with her importunities, he complied, but had scarcely finished the labour of his toilette when a door opened, and a numerous party of guests, who had been invited for the occasion, were admitted and introduced, by the facetious lady, to 'Brigadier General Moses,' in allusion to the great work on which he founded his principal pretension to literary reputation."[1]

In conversation and in his letters he produced many clever expressions, some of which have become famous. He has the credit of the noted distinction between orthodoxy and heterodoxy—"Orthodoxy is my doxy and heterodoxy is another man's doxy." To him also is attributed the saying that "there are two things for which every man thinks himself competent—managing a small farm and driving a whisky." When Lord Lyttleton, who had held the office of Chancellor of the Exchequer for a short time, was obliged to retire from incapacity and was succeeded by Mr. Dowdeswell, Warburton observed to Hawkins Browne that there was a curious contrast between the two ministers, for "the one could never in his life learn that two and two made four, while the other knew nothing else."[2] Instructing Hurd how to make his way in the world, he says:—"In your commerce with the great, if you would have it turn to your advantage, you should endeavour, when the person is of great abilities, to make him satisfied with you, when he is of none, to make him satisfied with *himself.*" Johnson and Warburton were contemporaries, but they only once met, as Boswell records, namely, at the house of Mrs. French, at London, well known for her elegant assemblies. The interview proved mutually agreeable. On one occasion it was told the Doctor that Warburton had said, "I admire Johnson, but cannot bear his style," to which he replied, "That is exactly my case as to him."

Warburton destined his only son for the law, but, to the great grief of his parents, he died in his nineteenth year. For several years before his demise the bishop was almost imbecile, and took little interest in anything. Cradock relates (but only as a report) that just before he died a momentary revival of intellect took place, and he asked his attendant in a quiet, rational tone, "Is my son really dead or not?" The servant hesitated how to reply, when the bishop repeated the question in a firmer voice. The attendant then answered, "As your lordship presses the question, I must say he is dead." "I thought so," said Warburton, and soon after expired.[3] In the

---

[1] Dickinson's *Newark*, footnote to p. 201.   [2] Timb's *Century of Anecdote*, p. 435.
[3] Watson's *Life of Warburton.*

cathedral of Gloucester, where the bishop was buried, is a neat marble monument bearing the following inscription :—

To the memory of
WILLIAM WARBURTON, D.D.
For more than XIX years Bishop of this See,
A Prelate
Of the most sublime genius and exquisite
Learning,
Both of which talents
He employed, thro' a long life,
In the support
Of what he firmly believed
THE CHRISTIAN RELIGION,
And of what he esteemed the best establishment of it,
THE CHURCH OF ENGLAND.
He was born at Newark-upon-Trent
Dec. 24, 1698,
Was consecrated Bishop of Gloucester
Jan. 20, 1760,
Died at his palace in this city
June 7, 1779,
And was buried near this place.

At an election at Newark in July 1780, on the occasion of a dissolution of Parliament, Lord George Sutton and General Sir Henry Clinton were returned by a considerable majority. Sir Henry was at the time of the contest serving in America in connection with the war whereby the United States secured their independence. About a month before his election, namely, on the 23d June, news had arrived of the capture of Charlestown, South Carolina, by the forces under his command, and had elicited great enthusiasm in Newark, Nottingham, and other towns. On the 27th of November the House of Commons passed a vote of thanks to General Clinton and Earl Cornwallis for the services they had rendered. The victory was, however, but the precursor of a defeat. In 1781 Lord Cornwallis was, by the skilful movements of Washington, shut up in Yorktown and compelled to surrender with 7000 men. The war lingered until 1783, when the independence of the thirteen United States was formally acknowledged by treaty.

Another subject of interest, contemporaneously with the American War, was the efforts of Mr. Pitt to bring about a reform in the representation of the country. In 1781 Lord George Sutton presided at a meeting at Mansfield, in support of Mr. Pitt, when a petition was adopted in favour of the abolition of at least fifty of the "rotten boroughs," as they had begun to be styled, the enfranchisement of the proprietors of copyhold inheritances, and the shortening of the duration of Parliaments. Mr. Pitt introduced a scheme, but was unsuccessful.

The severity of the laws of the period, which made serious theft a capital offence, resulted in the execution of a man named Cooper Hall, who had committed a robbery near Newark. Hall was arraigned at the county assizes on March 9, 1782, before Mr. Justice Buller, charged with stealing a bill of exchange for £120, on the 18th of the previous November, from the mail-cart running between Tuxford and Newark. The jury brought him in guilty. Hall's behaviour after condemnation was penitent, and consistent with his position. On Wednesday, the 27th March, the procession to Gallows Hill set out, the malefactor being "indulged" with a chaise. His suffering at the fatal spot was greatly aggravated by the circumstance of his hanging upon the rope as the cart was moving from under him, which caused the knot to slip to the back of his neck. He died in the 31st year of his age, and his remains were removed to Newark for interment.

Lord George Sutton died at Kelham on the 9th of January 1783, aged fifty-nine years, and was succeeded in the representation of Newark by his second son, Mr. John Manners Sutton. His lordship was the third son of the Duke of Rutland, by Bridget, daughter and heir of Robert Sutton of Lexington. By his death the Colonelcy of the Militia became vacant, and the Hon. Mr. Willoughby, son of Lord Middleton, was appointed to the command. Shortly afterwards the force, which had been on severe duty for five years, was disbanded.

On the 29th of May 1783 it was ordered by the town council that the expenses attending the keeping of the Dutch prisoner here be paid out of the corporation stock. France, Spain, and Holland were in arms against Britain during the latter years of the American War, and it is probable that the Dutch prisoner was a person who had been captured in one of the engagements.

Employment being scarce and provisions dear, an effect of the stagnation consequent upon the wars, the number of vagrants was considerably augmented. To meet the pressing demands for relief, the corporation voted £9 to be distributed by the mayor. News of the signing of the treaty of peace between his Majesty and the United States of America reached Newark early in September, and intelligence was also brought that at the same time peace had been concluded with France and Spain. The satisfactory tidings were received with public demonstrations of joy.

One of the most curious entries on the minutes of the corporation occurs under date of 1784. A gentleman who had been elected to the honourable office of alderman, desired to be excused from accepting it, and he pleaded not only that his business would not permit him to attend to the duties, but that he had a certificate for a conviction for housebreaking assigned to him, by which he had a legal exemption!

Parliament was dissolved on the 25th of March 1784, and an election took place at the beginning of April, when Mr. John Manners Sutton and the Right Hon. Constantine Lord Mulgrave were returned for Newark. His lordship had previously been appointed a burgess of the borough of the company of cordwainers. At the meeting of the corporation, which took place on his lordship's admission as a burgess, it was resolved to present an address to his Majesty upon "the late change of ministers, and the present situation of public affairs." The address was approved at a general meeting of the inhabitants, but a copy of it has not been preserved upon the minutes of the corporation.

The butchers hesitating to accept the accommodation provided at the back of the town-hall, by the erection of shambles, the town-council resolved upon an effort to clear them out of the market-place and to force them into the new quarters. On the 22d of May it was resolved that the town-clerk apply to the Duke of Newcastle to let the corporation have a copy of his grant of the manor of Newark, "that the same may, together with the corporation charter, be laid before counsel to consider how far a regulation of the stalls in the market may be made, so as to oblige the butchers to go into the shambles and make use of the shops there." On the 5th August, it was ordered that a pinfold, to detain the goods impounded by the mayor and aldermen, be built at the end of Barnby Gate, upon the place where the pinfold heretofore stood.

For the third time Mr. Pitt, undaunted by his previous reverses, and encouraged by his ever-growing popularity, resolved to introduce a bill for reform in Parliament. This was in the session of 1785. His specific plan was to disfranchise thirty-six rotten boroughs, giving compensation to those who regarded them as property; to transfer the right of election to counties and unrepresented large towns; and to extend the franchise in counties to copyholders. On the 9th of March a meeting of the freeholders of Nottinghamshire, convened by the High Sheriff, and numerously attended, was held at the Old Assembly Rooms, Newark, to express approval of the measure. Mr. Joseph Sykes, Major Cartwright, and Mr. Dickinson Rastall, were amongst the speakers, and a petition to Parliament in favour of the bill was unanimously agreed to. Mr. Pitt introduced the measure in April, and it was again rejected by a large majority.

We have spoken of the rigour of the laws of the period, and a further illustration is afforded in the case of Thomas Cobb, who was executed at Nottingham, on the 27th July 1785, for housebreaking at Normanton-on-Trent, near Newark. Cobb, described as a poor man with a large family, had been to his parish for relief, and returning through Normanton at night, he asked for shelter at a public-house. His request was refused, and he thereupon retired into an outhouse; whilst there, he observed the landlady place her pocket on a chair under the parlour window, and when she had gone to bed, he took out a pane of glass and stole the pocket. There was little in it of any value, but he was condemned to death, and suffered at Nottingham.

A parish workhouse, near the Beaumond Cross, was erected in 1786, out of some of the charity estates. It contained within its walls the borough gaol and numerous apartments for the accommodation of the poor. Over the entrance door was the following inscription:—"This workhouse built from the estates of Magnus Brown and Phillipot, 1786."

In the Rev. John Wesley's Journal, under date 24th June 1786, is the following brief but complimentary entry:—"I preached at Newark, one of the most elegant towns in England." About a year afterwards a Wesleyan chapel was built.

A noticeable event in the history of the borough is the introduction of the first printing-press. Dr. Cotton states[1] that the art of printing was first introduced into Newark in 1788, but Mr. Briscoe informs us that there are two works in the collection of local literature in the Nottingham Free Public Reference Library printed before that year. The earliest is the *Book of Common Prayer*, "so transposed and methodised as that all the prayers may be found in the same order they are publickly read." The editor was the Rev. W. Lewis, A.M., Rector of Barnsdale, who was assisted by "other divines." This work contains several quaint woodcuts of Scripture subjects, and portraits of kings James and Charles. It was "printed and sold by J. Tomlinson and S. Creswell," in 1778, or ten years earlier than the date fixed by Dr. Cotton as the year of the introduction of the typographic art in Newark. In 1782 there issued from the press of James Tomlinson of Newark *The History of the Civil Wars in Germany, from the year 1630 to 1635*, which was "written by a Shropshire gentleman," and edited by E. Stavelay of Newark. This work was printed from manuscript which had been in the editor's possession many years. In 1792 was issued by Cartwright *Journals of Transactions and Events during a Residence of Sixteen Years on the Coast of Labrador* (3 vols. quarto), and in 1793 was published *The Cocker* (on cock-fighting), quarto, printed at Newark. During the present century numerous books have issued from the Newark press, and will, we hope, long continue to be produced with ability and credit.

The king, who had been out of health for some time, had so far become affected mentally that towards the close of 1788 he was decidedly insane. "I am afraid," wrote Mr. Grenville[2] on the 7th of October, "that it would be very sanguine indeed to say that there is even any hope that the king will recover both his health and his understanding." When Parliament met in November, and the serious condition of his Majesty was made publicly known, a diversity of opinion arose as to the proper course to be pursued in such an unprecedented emergency. Mr. Fox maintained that the Prince of Wales was entitled to assume the reins of government during the continuance of the sovereign's illness and incapacity; but Mr. Pitt urged that, unless with the express consent of both Houses of Parliament, the prince had no more right to assume the government than any other individual in the country. In case of the interruption of the personal exercise of the royal authority without any previous lawful provision for carrying on the government, it belonged, he said, to the other branches of the Legislature on the part of the nation at large "to provide according to their discretion for the temporary exercise of the royal authority in the name and on the behalf of the sovereign, in such manner as they should thing requisite." Mr. Pitt's view of the question commanded the approval of 265 members of the Lower House, and it so far gratified the corporation of Newark that at a meeting on the 23d January 1789 it was unanimously resolved that an address be presented by the

---

[1] In his *Typographical Gazetteer*. [2] W. W. Grenville, *Court of George III.*, vol. i. p. 431.

corporation to the Right Hon. W. Pitt, setting forth their thanks to the said William Pitt for his conduct; also to the two members for the borough, and to the 265 members of the House of Commons who maintained the constitutional right of the Lords and Commons of this realm, to supply the defect arising from the present unhappy incapacity of the sovereign. That Mr. Guthrie, mayor, Mr. Sketchley, Mr. Jesson, Dr. Buck, and the town-clerk, do immediately prepare an address for that purpose. The address which they prepared was as follows:—

To the Right Hon. WILLIAM PITT, Chancellor of his Majesty's Exchequer.

We, the mayor and aldermen of the borough of Newark-upon-Trent, in the county of Nottingham, in common council assembled, and the recorder, gentlemen, clergy, and inhabitants of the said borough whose names are hereunto subscribed, desire to express our sincere thanks to you for your general Parliamentary conduct since you have been the minister of this country, for your great attention to the political and commercial interests of this kingdom, and the dominions thereunto belonging, particularly for your very able and manly conduct in supporting the rights of the people in Parliament, and for your zealous and faithful attachment to our most gracious sovereign; and we further beg leave to express our thanks to the Right Honourable Lord Mulgrave and Col. John Manners Sutton, our worthy representatives in Parliament, and to the other 265 patriotic members of the House of Commons who supported you in maintaining the constitutional right of the Lords and Commons of this realm to supply the defect of the personal exercise of the royal authority arising from the present unhappy incapacity of our beloved sovereign.

Whilst the Regency Bill, which it was thought advisable to introduce, was under discussion, a great amendment took place in the king's condition. On the 25th February the issue of bulletins by the royal physicians was discontinued, and on the 10th of March it was announced to Parliament that his Majesty had, by the blessing of Providence, recovered from his indisposition, and was able to attend to public affairs. The gratifying intelligence produced great rejoicings throughout the kingdom. At Newark the town-hall was beautifully adorned with lights and transparencies, as were likewise all the large inns and principal houses. At a meeting of the corporation on the 21st of March an address was prepared, congratulating the king and royal family on the restoration of domestic comfort, and uniting in a fervent hope that his Majesty might "long enjoy every felicity, and continue to reign as the king and father of a free, loyal, and grateful people."

Parliament, having nearly completed its full term of seven years, was dissolved soon after the prorogation in June 1790, and at the election of members for Newark, to serve in the new Parliament, the spectacle of a well-fought contest was witnessed. Mr. John Manners Sutton, who sought re-election, and Lieutenant Colonel William Crosbie, were energetically opposed by Mr. William Paxton, a gentleman of large fortune in Wales. Mr. Paxton had issued his address as early as April 24, soliciting the support of the "worthy and independent electors," who, he understood, desired a change in the representation, and declaring that as his situation in life rendered him perfectly independent, his sole motive for offering himself was "the honour of representing so respectable a body of men." The printing-press being in full operation, there was no lack of circulars, "squibs," and placards; but the chief warfare of words that arose was as to whether or not Mr. Dickinson Rastall had offered his interest in the borough to Colonel Manners Sutton for £3000. Mr. Rastall indignantly repudiated the assertion, and made an affidavit on the 7th of May, declaring his innocence of the charge. He stated that "it had always been his opinion that if great property united with great rank had a claim to the compliment of one member for Newark, it was the duty of every man who had property or influence within it to prevent any further encroachment on the liberty of the inhabitants; that for this reason it had long been his determination to oppose the election of more than one member connected with any of those great families who had of late years represented the town, and that therefore he had never made any offer or proposition, nor had he wished to make any offer or proposition, which could in any degree militate against this general view." On the 15th of May Mr. John Manners Sutton issued his address, wherein he regretted that severe illness had prevented him paying his personal respects to them on a recent occasion, and added, "If an independent discharge of the duties of a British senator, if an hereditary attachment to the principles of our constitution, and if an interested concern for the welfare of the town of Newark be circumstances which may entitle me to a renewal of your confidence, I can entertain no doubt of meeting with the same honourable support I have previously experienced whenever the day of election shall arrive."

The election took place on the 18th, 19th, and 21st days of June, and for Mr. Paxton 57 more votes were tendered than for either of the other candidates. According to the old construction of the charter and the received interpretation of the resolution of the House of Commons, in 1703 "all persons who paid or *ought to pay* Scot and Lot were entitled to vote for members of Parliament." The mayor (Mr. Milnes), however, as the returning officer, put a different construction on the words, and rejected all voters whose names did not appear in the parochial books as ratepayers. From a circular issued on the evening of the 19th June we learn that his worship had rejected 128 votes of Paxton's friends, and 40 votes offered on the other side. As a consequence of the rejection of votes, Mr. Sutton and Colonel Crosbie were declared elected. Mr. Paxton petitioned the House of Commons against the return on the ground that he had a clear majority of votes according to the recognised principle of the original charter. On the 22d March 1791 the committee appointed to try the merits of the petition confirmed the interpretation which the mayor had put upon the charter, and upon the previous resolution of the House of Commons.[1]

During the session of 1790 an Act was obtained for the better paving, lighting, and cleansing of the streets, lanes, and other public passages, and places of the town of Newark-upon-Trent, in the county of Nottingham, and for removing the market

---

[1] The addresses, "squibs," etc., together with a list of voters who polled, were issued by D. Holt, printer, Stodman Street. From these we have gathered most of the details given of the contest.

for butcher's-meat, in the said town, for regulating the said market, and for repealing an Act made in the 27th of Queen Elizabeth, entitled "An Acte for the pavinge of Newarke-upon-Trent, in the countie of Nottingham."

The first number of a Newark newspaper, printed by D. Holt, in Stodman Street, on the site of the present *Advertiser* offices, was issued on October 5, 1791. In the number for October 12 we find an advertisement, announcing that post waggons set out from the Bull and Mouth, in Bull and Mouth Street, London, every morning at 11 o'clock, and arrived in Newark in about 48 hours, whence goods were conveyed immediately to Southwell, Ollerton, Worksop, Lincoln, Sleaford, and other places. In the paper of December 7 there is the following curious paragraph:—"Last week, in digging a grave in our churchyard, the sexton found a skull, in the orifice of the mouth of which a glass bottle was inserted, containing a small quantity of liquor. From this circumstance we may conjecture the remains of some old toper had been deposited there, whose friends were desirous that he should not be deprived, when dead, of that favourite beverage which, when living, he so much admired." A singular accident is reported to have happened on the 8th December; the paragraph runs thus:—"On Saturday as Mr. Edward Driver, son of Mr. Robert Driver of Kelham, near this town, was shooting sparrows near his father's barn; having shot once and killed but two, he charged the piece still higher; in firing a second time the barrel flew from the stock, and stuck in his forehead so fast as to support itself horizontally, requiring the united efforts of two persons to draw it out. Twelve pieces of bone have been extracted, and he yesterday saw a glimmering of daylight for the first time since the accident happened." The weather, during the winter, is reported to have been very severe, so much so that several persons in the neighbourhood of Newark were frozen to death.

The last of the famous election contest had not as yet been heard. At the March assizes in 1792 several persons were charged with committing acts of bribery at the election in 1790. Why the trial had been deferred so long does not appear, but Mr. Holt's Newark paper gives a brief account of the assize proceedings, from which we learn that one of the defendants was Mr. Dickinson Rastall. The jury gave an unanimous verdict of acquittal, to the great joy of the Newark people. The populace went to Muskham, the residence of Mr. Rastall, and insisted on drawing him in his carriage to Newark, with drums and fifes and flags. An immense concourse from the neighbouring village joined the throng, adorned with blue ribbons. They proceeded through the market-place to the bank, where Mr. Rastall alighted, after having addressed the multitude in the following words:—"I most sincerely thank you for this testimony of your regard to me. However little concern I might feel for my own personal safety, as the father of a family I must receive great satisfaction from that event you are now celebrating; but permit me to assure you that the strongest impression which it makes on my mind arises from the consideration that the verdict of those honourable men, which gave security to my property, conferred it in an equal degree on your liberties and the privileges of my native place." In the evening an enormous bonfire was made in the market-place, and three sheep were roasted whole.

The progress of the French Revolution was now the all-absorbing topic of conversation. It was excited chiefly by three causes—the infidel writings of Voltaire and Rousseau, the oppression of the lower orders by insolent nobles, and the want of money consequent on the reckless extravagance of the French Court.[1] The state of opinion in England may be partially ascertained from the proceedings of "associations in support of the constitution," at the meetings of which the danger was set forth to which the public peace and order were exposed "by the circulation of mischievous opinions founded upon plausible but false reasoning." The circulation of dangerous doctrines was alleged to be mainly carried on by the industry of clubs and societies; and the pernicious opinions were embodied in the terms "the Rights of Man—Liberty and Equality—no King no Parliament." Paine, who was prosecuted for libel in issuing *The Rights of Man*, was, at the time of his trial, a member of the National Convention of France, and he took occasion to write an insolent letter to the Attorney-General, wherein he said that "the terrible examples" that had taken place in France ought to have some weight with men in his situation.[2] The nation was greatly agitated by the revolutionary tendencies that were manifested, and when a proclamation was issued for preventing tumultuous meetings and seditious writings, both Houses of Parliament voted loyal addresses, and many cities and towns followed their example. The corporation of Newark at a meeting on the 4th of June (1792), unanimously adopted an address to his Majesty, wherein they said, "it was much to be lamented that in different parts of the kingdom there were many factious and disorderly persons who, by their seditious publications and criminal conversation, were endeavouring to subvert the constitution of this country, and thereby to promote anarchy and confusion." The corporation considered all associations that were formed for the purpose of introducing wild theories and speculations, and interfering with the constitutional rights of Parliament, had a dangerous tendency, and ought to be suppressed by his Majesty's loving and faithful subjects.

A measure, entitled the Alien Bill, passed the House of Lords, and came before the Commons for its second reading, in December. On that occasion Burke "mentioned the circumstance of 3000 daggers having been bespoke at Birmingham by an Englishman, of which 70 had been delivered. It was not ascertained how many of these were to be exported, and how many were intended for home consumption." The Parliamentary history then adds:—"Here Mr. Burke drew out a dagger, which he had kept concealed, and with much vehemence of action threw it on the floor." The orator, pointing to the dagger, said:—"This is what you are to gain by an alliance with France; wherever their principles are introduced, their practice must follow." The bill passed on the 4th January 1793, and when M. Chauvelin for the French Republic, protested against it as a violation of the treaty of commerce,

---

[1] Dr. Collier's *History*.   [2] Charles Knight's *History*, vol. vii. p. 248.

by which the subjects of the two nations had liberty to come and go freely, he was informed that his Majesty did not see fit to receive his letters of credence. On the 21st the French Republicans executed their king, and on the 24th M. Chauvelin was ordered to retire from this country within eight days. Active preparations had been made for the war which soon followed, and sums of money for distribution were collected in most towns and villages. On the 29th of June (1793) the society that had been formed in Newark for raising a fund for the relief of the widows and children of such soldiers as might die or be killed in the service of their country, transmitted to Sir E. Pellew ten guineas, to be disposed of as he should think proper, amongst the widows and children of the brave men who gloriously fell on board the "Nymphe," in the late signal action with the French ship "La Cleopatra," and also expressed to him the admiration felt in Newark at his and his brother's gallant conduct on a day ever to be recorded in the annals of the country.

The anxiety that had been manifested to suppress sedition, and to preclude the possibility of the revolutionary flame spreading from France to England, was fully shared by the Government, and so active and sensitive were they that numerous prosecutions were directed against the printers of publications, some of which were bad enough, while others could not, in calmer moments, be classed in the same category as the exciting and pernicious literature of the French revolutionary period. At the assizes for Nottinghamshire, on Friday, the 19th of July, before Mr. Justice Wilson, Daniel Holt of Newark, the printer of the Newark paper to which allusion has been made in preceding pages, was convicted, by a special jury, on two informations filed, *ex officio*, by the attorney-general, one for republishing a letter by Paine, entitled, "An Address to the Addressers on a Parliamentary Reform," and the other for reprinting and publishing a paper entitled, "An Address to the Tradesmen, Artificers, Labourers, and other Inhabitants of the Town of Newark, on a Parliamentary Reform." The writer of the last-named Address, whose name did not transpire, had ventured to air his views on Parliamentary corruption in the following terms :—" If the present inequality of representation and length of Parliaments be the causes of Parliamentary corruption, as they undoubtedly are, we must remove the causes before the effect will cease. By a corrupt Parliament is meant that which, instead of being a shield against unnecessary taxation, is the hired instrument whereby the nation is pillaged ; that which, instead of proving a check upon the Crown when disposed to engage in unnecessary and ruinous wars, is the bribed tool by which the nation is first gulled into an approbation of war, and afterwards drained of its blood and treasures to carry it on. . . . A moment's reflection will convince any candid man that in such elections, annually repeated, there could be no such thing as bribery, and if a ballot were added, all undue influence of wealth or authority would be guarded against. Bribery and threats out of the question, who could have an interest or temptation to promote any licentiousness ? It has already been shown, also, that in parliaments so elected, and so dependent on the esteem, and confidence, and power of the people, it would be as impossible for a minister to obtain support by corruption as now it is impossible to find support without corruption." And much more to the same purport.

This was undoubtedly plain speaking, but what would now be passed over as an uninfluential expression of individual opinion, was, at a time when wild revolutionary principles were rampant in a neighbouring country, regarded as dangerous, and in conjunction with Paine's more virulent and abusive pamphlet "calculated to excite and stir up discontent and sedition." An association had been formed in Newark, as in many other towns, for "the support of the constitution," and had passed a resolution declaring that they would take every measure which the law empowered them, to punish the authors, publishers, and distributors of all seditious writings. Soon after Mr. Holt's publications made their appearance, he was served with a notice that informations had been filed against him, and his trial took place at the assizes in July. The information for selling "The Address to the Addressers" was first heard, and after a trial of five hours' duration, the special jury withdrew. In half-an-hour they returned with a verdict of "guilty." The trial for reprinting and publishing the second Address next came on before a special jury, with a similar result. Sentence was deferred until a later period. In the *London Gazette* of the 26th of August there appeared a notice to the effect that, as it had been represented to the king that on Tuesday night, July 23, several inflammatory sentences were written upon the walls and doors of houses, etc., over the greater part of the town of Newark, supposed to be on account of the trial of Mr. Holt, and threatening one of the witnesses at such trial, his Majesty would offer a free pardon to any one, except the actual writer, who would discover his or her accomplice, together with a reward of £100 to be paid by the Right Hon. the Lords Commissioners of his Majesty's treasury, upon the conviction of one or more of the offenders. To this amount the Newark association for the support of the king and constitution added £20. On the 20th of November Mr. Holt appeared before the Court of King's Bench to receive judgment, when his counsel (Mr. Erskine) submitted that it was competent for him to suggest that his client had been illegally convicted and ought to have a new trial. The attorney-general intimated that he did not desire to shut out the application, but he had doubts as to whether it was now in time or not. After some discussion on the point Mr. Erskine waived the claim for a new trial, and proceeded to address the Court on the decision which had been arrived at, contending that the publication of the address to the people of Newark was not with a seditious intention, and that sufficient evidence had not been adduced to warrant the conclusion that the defendant had any evil motives. The attorney-general in his reply alleged that Mr. Justice Wilson at the assizes had submitted to the jury the question of seditious intent, and the jury had, by their verdict, given a complete answer. Lord Kenyon thereupon overruled Mr. Erskine's objections, and Justices Ashurst, Buller, and Grose expressed their concurrence in his lordship's ruling. Defendant was then remanded, and on the Wednesday following was brought up to receive sentence. Mr. Justice Ashurst delivered the judgment of the court in the following terms:—

Daniel Holt, you have been tried and found guilty, on two several indictments, for printing and publishing two very atrocious libels, the one entitled an "Address to the Addressers," and the other entitled "An Address to the Tradesmen, Mechanics, Labourers, and other Inhabitants of the Town of Newark on the Subject of a Parliamentary Reform." The first of these libels alludes to his Majesty's most gracious proclamation, which is in everybody's memory, and to the addresses of loyalty sent from all parts of the kingdom in consequence of it. These loyal addresses very much counteracted the designs of men of such a description as the author of this publication. The general tendency of this libel is to bring his Majesty's proclamation into contempt, and to insinuate that these addresses did not contain the genuine sentiment of the loyalty of his Majesty's subjects, but that they had been set on foot by corrupt and interested men; that the system of our Government was a system of tyranny and oppression; and that the formation of it was radically bad, and wanting reformation; and that a Parliamentary reform was to be brought about by the people only, and not by the Parliament, of Great Britain. And it daringly recommends a national convention to be held as the proper means of reform. This publication also tends to traduce and vilify all kingly governments in this and all the countries of Europe, and boldly calls on the subjects of this kingdom to insurrection and revolt; and insinuates that the example of a neighbouring nation was proper to be followed in this. This paper falls very little short of high treason, and certainly stands in the very first rank of sedition. The second of these libels most grossly and impudently asperses the Parliament of this kingdom, and brands them with the imputation of venality and corruption, and calls for a Parliamentary reform. As to the mode by which that reform was to be conducted, this paper does not so largely enter into it; that had been sufficiently pointed out by the former publication, entitled "An Address to the Addressers," which recommends it to be done by a national convention. The bloody advisers of such a measure have been acting a scene in a neighbouring country, which, when we look upon it, we have the strongest reason to congratulate ourselves on our own condition when compared with the tyranny, rapine, murder, and desolation which have ravaged that unfortunate country. It has been alleged, in extenuation of your crime, that you were not the author or the first publisher of this pamphlet. But how does that apply in your favour? Was it not enough that such a horrid production had been once stifled in the birth, and must you foster and nourish the unnatural and diabolical offspring, and give it fresh life and existence? Though the nation in general had shown their abhorrence and detestation of the doctrines contained in this publication, yet you were determined to cram it down the throats of his Majesty's subjects. What has been said in extenuation for the second publication can stand you in little stead. With respect to the subject of the publication, that it was published ten years ago, and that you only republished it, and therefore are innocent, and that it could only mean the Parliament which then existed, and not the present Parliament of Great Britain, let any man of common sense take that paper in his hand, and say whether the utmost extent of charity can consider it a simple, innocent republication. If you had meant it in that view, why not publish it with the ancient title, and why not state that it was published in such a year? Though even if you had done that, it ought not inevitably to retain that sense; but you yourself give it a present application. You address it to the "Tradesmen, Mechanics, and Labourers, and other Inhabitants of the Town of Newark on the Subject of a Parliamentary Reform." How are they to know that ever it was published before? how can they apply it but to the present existing Parliament of Great Britain? The learned judge who tried this information left the case to the jury in a fair and candid way. He put this question to them, "Are you satisfied that the defendant published this paper with a malicious intent or not?" There could not be two opinions on the subject among honest men, and the jury found you guilty. The malignity of this paper having been established by the jury, it only remains for this Court to do its office. This Court will always know how to temper mercy with justice where there is room for it, but here there is no palliation as to the first of these libels, at least your own counsel owned that nothing could be said for you. It behoves, then, this Court to try what can be done by the severity of punishment. And though there are but small hopes of your reformation, it may at least operate to deter others from being guilty of the same enormities. This Court has taken the magnitude of your offence into their consideration, and this Court doth order and adjudge that for the first libel you pay a fine to the king of £50, and that you be imprisoned in his Majesty's jail of Newgate for the term of two years; and that for the second offence you pay a further fine of £50, and be imprisoned in his Majesty's jail of Newgate for the further term of two years; and that after the expiration of your imprisonment, you find security for your good behaviour for the term of five years, yourself in £200 and two sureties in £50 each, and that you be imprisoned till such fines be paid, and till such sureties are found, as aforesaid.

During the first year of his imprisonment at Newgate Mr. Holt issued to the townspeople of Newark a lengthy vindication of his conduct and principles. He stated that reformation, and not revolution, had ever been his object, and that he should not be diverted from attempting by legal and peaceable means to secure reform. "I have," he wrote, "embraced it (the cause) from choice, from conviction, and from a principle of duty; and persecution, imprisonment, or compulsion, shall never oblige me to abandon it. The mere act of selling the pamphlets no more proves the improper intention of my mind, than my selling the *Alcoran* proves me to be a believer in the doctrines of Mahomet; or vending the writings of Pythagoras convicts me of being a believer in the transmigration of souls."

But the anxiety and excitement which had been manifested about reform became, through the war with France, abundantly neutralised by the spirit of patriotism. At the beginning of 1794 the French Government threatened invasion, and the people forgot all about home legislation in their eagerness to defend themselves and their beloved country against the evil designs of the enemy. The regular forces were speedily increased, and the Government, in their desire to arm the public, advocated the formation of bodies of volunteers, and especially of yeomanry cavalry.[1] On the 17th of April an Act was passed "for encouraging and disciplining such corps or companies of men as shall voluntarily enroll themselves for the defence of their counties, towns, or coasts, or for the general defence of the kingdom during the present war." In June (1794) a county meeting was held at Mansfield to consider the several plans recommended by Government for the internal defence of the kingdom, when it was resolved to raise a corps of cavalry. A subscription was started to defray the cost, towards which numerous gentlemen in Newark contributed, the corporation sending a donation of £100. In all quarters the talk was of the defence of king and country against the French, and many illustrations of the exuberant and impetuous loyalty that prevailed are to be found amongst the papers of this exciting and anxious period. In South Hants, a private belonging to the militia is reported to have met an Italian selling images. One representing a monarch on horseback was declared by the Italian to be the King of France, and a pedestrian figure was said to be the King of England. The soldier, on hearing the explanation, broke all the images to pieces. For the offence he was brought before a magistrate and fined

---

[1] Knight's *History of England*, vol. vii. p. 304.

15s., to raise which amount he had to pawn his watch. The officers of the regiment subsequently had the man brought before them, and asked him for an explanation of his conduct. His reply was that "his blood boiled to see the King of France on horseback, and the good King of England tramping it on foot." The officers were so amused at the answer, and so pleased with the spirit it manifested, that they subscribed the money, and the watch was redeemed.

While the volunteers were forming and training, the army and navy were in successful motion. The earliest in the series of great naval victories was that of Admiral Earl Howe, on the 1st of June (1794), an event which aroused special interest in this county from the fact that the hero of the fight was of a Nottinghamshire stock, and the owner of Langar, in the vale of Belvoir. His lordship was in command of the Channel Fleet, waiting at Portsmouth for intelligence that the Brest Fleet had put to sea. This fleet was declared by French journalists to be the most formidable that had ever anchored in Brest harbour; and they proclaimed that "all burn with desire to fight the enemies of their country to the very banks of the Thames, and under the walls of London."[1] On the 2nd of May Lord Howe sailed into the Channel, and after cruising about many days in foggy weather, he sighted the enemy on the 28th of May. The English fleet consisted of twenty-six sail of the line, and five frigates; the French Admiral had an equal number of vessels under his control, though many of them were of larger size, were better armed, and more numerously manned. A preliminary engagement took place on the evening of the 28th, but it was on the 1st of June that the memorable action took place. After a desperate fight, the French Admiral beat a hasty retreat, leaving half his dismasted ships behind him.[2] The English captured seven vessels, but one sank before the adequate assistance could be rendered to her crew. The news of the great victory caused the greatest gratification, and everywhere inspired feelings of determination and confidence. With a due regard to the interests of those who had lost friends in the action, the Newark Society for the Relief of the Widows and Children of Soldiers and Sailors transmitted to Lord Howe fifty guineas, as a small token of their gratitude to the memory of their gallant countrymen who so nobly fell on the glorious 1st of June. In sending the money, the Society, in a letter signed on their behalf by Mr. Roger Pocklington, said:—"As Britons, we sincerely share with our countrymen in those honest effusions of joy which have pervaded this island, and as inhabitants of the county of Nottingham, we feel a degree of local pride on the present occasion, in its having given birth to the commander in an action wherein gallantry and conduct were never more highly distinguished, ample as is the page which records the naval merit of this country." Lord Howe, in reply, said he was very thankful for the money, and by no means insensible to the flattering compliment paid to him.

A corps of volunteer infantry which had been raised in Newark held a meeting in September, when Mr. William Handley was elected captain, Mr. R. Marshall,

[1] Knight's *History of England*, vol. vii. p. 306.   [2] *Ibid.* p. 307.

lieutenant, and Mr. E. S. Godfrey, ensign. The sum of £150 was promptly subscribed towards defraying the expenses of the corps, and the following declaration was adopted :—" We, the undersigned, convinced that it is our duty to assist the Executive Government in protecting our laws and constitution, declare that we enter the Corps of Newark Volunteer Infantry to defend our town and its precincts, and by a prompt assistance to the Magistrates, and submission to our Officers, ensure due obedience to the laws, and preserve the peace of the same. Further, we declare our determination to provoke no one by insult, but in every situation to demean ourselves as peaceable inhabitants and good subjects, and, to prove to all the world the purity of our intentions, have severally taken the following oath :—I, A. B. do sincerely promise and swear that I will be faithful, and bear true allegiance to his Majesty King George, and that I will support the constitution of my country as established by law. So help me God."

The ceremony of consecrating the standards of the corps took place in the following year (1795), on the 4th of June—the anniversary of his Majesty's birthday. About half-past ten o'clock in the morning the whole corps, consisting of upwards of 100 men, met in the market-place. On their right hand a troop of Windsor Foresters, commanded by Captain Cobourg, and quartered in the town, was drawn up, and on their left a troop of the Nottingham Yeomanry Cavalry, headed by Cornet Brough. A procession took place soon after eleven o'clock, when an escort from the infantry conducted the standards furled from the town-hall, attended by the mayor and aldermen in their robes, and accompanied by the officers of the corporation and a large number of country gentlemen. The members of each corps then marched to the church, where, after depositing the colours upon the communion table, divine service was performed. A discourse was preached by the Rev. Mr. Brooke, chaplain to the corps, from the 13th and 14th verses of the 2d chapter of the first Epistle of Peter—" Submit yourselves to every ordinance of man for the Lord's sake : whether it be to the king, as supreme ; or unto governors, as unto them that are sent by him for the punishment of evil-doers, and for the praise of them that do well." At the conclusion of the service the ensigns proceeded to the altar to receive the standards ; the " Union Jack " being presented by Mr. William Handley, captain commandant, whilst the local flag, with the town arms upon it, was presented by the mayor (Mr. David Stephenson). The officers of the corps marched to the altar and saluted the standards, and the whole of those present then returned to the market-place, where the colours were saluted by the corps, and several volleys fired. In the afternoon a sumptuous entertainment for the corporation and the whole corps was provided at the Swan and Salmon Hotel. After dinner the town-clerk, in a suitable address, returned the thanks of the corporation to the officers and men of the Newark Volunteer Infantry, for their loyal and spirited conduct in stepping forth at this critical period to preserve the peace of the town, and to protect the constitution from its foreign and domestic enemies.

The prevalence of war and the stagnation consequent upon so much national excitement and anxiety, had had a serious effect upon the home markets, and wheat advanced by rapid stages to over 100s. per quarter. Much distress prevailed through the scarcity of food, and want of the common necessaries of life led the starving masses in some places to adopt lawless measures. In Newark, riotous feelings became prevalent, and a large mob, consisting mostly of women, after clamouring for bread, made a rush at a cargo of flour lying at the wharf, and seized fifteen sacks. With the booty thus obtained, they made their way to the market-place, when the volunteers appeared upon the scene, and dispersed them. Twenty-seven constables were sworn in to preserve the peace, and the town then resumed its tranquil state. The entry made in the orderly book of the volunteers was as follows:— "The infantry assembled by order of the deputy-mayor to suppress a riot, and to take possession of some wheat taken forcibly out of a boat, the property of Mr. T. W. Winter. It was guarded all night by the infantry, who were divided into four divisions on the occasion." An eye-witness has left on record the following memorandum[1]:—"The wheat was taken out of the boat principally by women and exultingly brought into the market-place. The infantry took possession of it and guarded it opposite the head inn, the Kingston Arms, kept by Mr. Midgeley. The town-clerk then read the Riot Act opposite the White Hind in Stodman Street, etc. The wheat was then removed to the town-hall, guarded all night, and from thence restored to the owner."

The same privations that had caused the people of Newark to raise a clamour for food induced the people of London to assail the king, on his way to Parliament (October 29), with cries of "Bread! bread! Peace! peace!" One of the windows of the state carriage was broken by a stone, or by a shot from an air gun. "The king," says Mr. Knight, "manifested his wonted courage amidst the groans and hisses of an excited mob. An address to his Majesty was voted in both Houses, and a bill was passed for the safety and preservation of his Majesty's person and government against treasonable and seditious practices and attempts." At a meeting of the corporation of Newark on the 19th November, an address was framed congratulating his Majesty on his escape. It ran thus:—"We beg leave, with the most unfeigned regard and affection, to show our extreme detestation and abhorrence of the atrocious attempt that has been made against your Majesty's sacred person at a time when your Majesty was about to exercise one of the functions of our most invaluable constitution. We lament exceedingly that there should be in your Majesty's dominions a set of people so depraved and infatuated by the diffusion of such disorderly principles, but when we reflect what are the sentiments of a few men in the most elevated situations, our wonder ceases that the weak and profligate should be so misguided by the mischievous influence of example."

In March 1796 the price of corn at the Newark market was as follows:—wheat, 107s. to 110s. per qr.; oats, 27s. to 34s.; beans, 44s. to 47s.; barley, 42s. to 45s. In May there died Mr. William Simpson, landlord of the Robin Hood public-house.

[1] MS. notes of the late Mr. Frederic Eggleston.

He was a man of great corpulency, and was seized with an apoplectic fit at the very moment of exerting his vocal powers in favour of one of the conservative candidates who had come forward to represent the town in the new Parliament. The election took place about the end of May, when Mr. Thomas Manners Sutton, Colonel Mark Wood, of Carmarthen, and Mr. Paxton, went to the poll. "At twelve o'clock at night (says the *Nottingham Journal*) Mr. Paxton, finding a very great majority of the unpolled voters in the interest of Mr. Sutton and Colonel Wood, sent a deputation to inform them that he declined any further contest. At one o'clock on Saturday the newly-elected members were chaired in the market place, and subsequently a plentiful dinner was provided in the town-hall."

On November 15, 1796, the following address was sent to Mr. Sutton for presentation :—

TO THE KING'S MOST EXCELLENT MAJESTY—THE ADDRESS OF THE NEWARK VOLUNTEER INFANTRY.

We, your Majesty's most dutiful and loyal subjects, the Newark Volunteer Infantry, beg leave to assure your Majesty of our inviolable attachment to your Majesty's sacred person and the constitution of these kingdoms. As a means of securing a continuance of the blessings we enjoy, and to protect the same from the attacks of any foreign or domestic enemy, we humbly tender our services in case of invasion, wherever your Majesty shall please to direct. SAMUEL OLIVER, *Captain.*

The renewed prospect of invasion which had arisen towards the end of 1796, and which probably called forth the spirited offer of the Newark volunteers, caused serious alarm throughout the country, and as the unsettled and critical condition of affairs produced commercial distrust, there appeared an immediate probability of a general panic and a wide-spread ruin. The pressure upon the Bank of England became greater week by week, until, on the 25th of February, the Directors informed the Chancellor of the Exchequer that they could pay in specie no longer. A Cabinet Council was summoned, and the result was the issuing of an order stopping payment in coin, but with a notification that the general concerns of the bank were in the most affluent condition, and that the bank would continue their usual discounts, paying in bank notes. At a great meeting of merchants, in London, it was unanimously resolved to accept notes, and in the provincial towns meetings were held, at which similar decisions were arrived at. In Newark a large assemblage of gentry, clergy, merchants, and other inhabitants took place in the town-hall "to consider the propriety of giving every possible support to the public credit and commercial engagements of the town and neighbourhood at this juncture." The mayor (Mr. Thomas Spragging) presided. Resolutions were passed to the effect that the alarm that so unnecessarily agitated the minds of the public had been caused intentionally by the enemies of the country, and that it was incumbent upon every man who had the welfare of the nation at heart to endeavour, as far as possible, to defeat the intention, in full confidence that there was no real cause for the alarm if the people themselves did not give reality to the supposed distress of the country by withdrawing that mutual confidence which alone could support credit. The meeting believed that the same circumstances which had operated with the Government to restrain the payments in cash at the Bank of England, presented an adequate reason for the other banks declining to make such payments at this crisis. A vote of confidence in the local banks was passed, and those present promised to take as usual, in all payments, the notes issued by them.

On his Majesty's birthday (June 4) the Newark volunteers assembled in the market-place at eleven o'clock and fired three volleys; in the afternoon the mayor and corporation, and others, to the number of 200, dined together at the old assembly rooms. Amongst the toasts given were, the Duke of York and the army, Lord Bridport and the navy, and a speedy return of the disaffected to loyalty. The non-commissioned officers dwelling with the supplementary militia were treated to dinner at the Pack Horse, and every private had a shilling given him to drink his Majesty's health. The yeomanry dined at the Rutland Arms.

On the 6th of November a public meeting was convened, at which an address was voted to his Majesty on the late decisive naval victory gained by Admiral Duncan and his gallant companions in arms.[1] The subscribers to the Fund for the Relief of the Widows and Orphans of Soldiers and Sailors remitted 50 guineas to the admiral to be distributed by him.

By his will, dated December 1, 1797, Mr. George Lawrence, formerly of Newark, merchant, gave to the mayor and aldermen of the borough the sum of £1000 upon trust, to invest the same; and the interest thereof he directed to be applied towards the allowances to the alms men and women who should be elected into the almshouses founded by William Phillypot in Newark, or in providing clothes or other necessaries for them. The charity is now endowed with £1839 : 1 : 7, invested in 3 per cent consols in the names of the official trustees of charitable funds. The ordinary yearly income amounts to £55 : 3 : 6, and the net income is applied in payment to twenty Beads people of 1s. per week each, with 24s. extra at Christmas.

During the winter the threats of invasion were continued. Buonaparte, who had gained the confidence of the republic, had accepted the command of an army, which was to endeavour to hoist the tricoloured flag on the Tower of London. In view of such an effort, considerable sums of money were raised for the defence of the kingdom. The members for Newark gave £100 each, and at a council meeting on the 9th February (1798) it was resolved that the sum of £100 be immediately subscribed and paid into the Bank of England to be applied out of the corporation stock as a voluntary contribution towards the exigencies of the State; that the further sum of £50 be annually paid as a voluntary contribution, during the war, out of the corporation purse; and that for the purpose of defraying such sum, the annual allowance to the mayor for the feasts be suspended during that period. On the 13th April it was ordered that the sum of £100 be subscribed out of the corporation stock, for defraying the expenses of the Newark Volunteer Infantry, and that the shares in the Trent Navigation be sold to pay the subscription and defray

[1] The ships of Holland were scattered by Admiral Duncan off the Dutch village of Camperdown.

the corporation debts. In consequence of a letter from the Lord-Lieutenant, a meeting of Newark volunteers was held, when it was resolved to march to any part of the southern district comprehending the coasts of Lincoln, Norfolk, Suffolk, and Essex, in case of invasion or imminent danger. It was also thought proper to augment the corps, and as soon as it became known that men were needed for active home service, thirty recruits enlisted. Meanwhile Buonaparte had made a few rapid visits to the ports bordering the English Channel, and had seen the arsenals and the gun boats. On his return, he persuaded the French Government to postpone the scheme and to permit him to embark an army for Egypt, in order to pave the way for the conquest of India. On the 19th of May he left Toulon, and landed at Alexandria on the 28th. Nelson, who had been on the look-out, saw the French flag on the walls on the 1st of August, and the fleet of Admiral Brueys at anchor in the Bay of Aboukir. The great naval battle of the Nile followed, and when the news of Nelson's success reached England, it occasioned great rejoicings. The festivities were renewed when intelligence arrived that Sir John B. Warren had defeated the Brest squadron. Newark was splendidly illuminated, there being, we are told, "some charming transparencies that had a most beautiful effect."

During 1800 the country was in a condition of great distress. The price of wheat had reached the enormous sum of 134s. per quarter, and was still on the increase. In February the sale of bread which had not been baked twenty-four hours was prohibited. Brown bread was to be eaten instead of white, and the people were officially exhorted to economy. In consequence of the distress riots arose, and the assistance of the volunteers was required in restraining the violence of the half-starved populations. On March 12 Major Marshall announced to the Newark volunteers the contents of a letter he had received from the Duke of Portland, referring to the disturbances, and requiring the assistance of the corps in aid of the civil power, which was readily granted. Towards the end of the year the riots had become still more serious, and appeared likely to extend to this neighbourhood. On September 2 the infantry assembled in Newark in consequence of a letter from the magistrates at Southwell, intimating that a mob intended to liberate some rioters confined in the House of Correction, and requesting assistance. The mayor, however, declined to permit the men to go, on account of threats as to what would transpire at Newark in their absence. In the spring of 1801 the price of the quartern loaf had advanced to 1s. 10½d. A good harvest was fortunately reaped, and in October the price fell to 11½d. The volunteers who had been of such service in the emergency had discussed amongst themselves the question of receiving pay. At a meeting of the Newark corps, on October 1 (1801), a letter was read from the Duke of Portland, intimating that pay would be allowed if required, whereupon a vote was taken, when there appeared a majority of seventy against, and twenty in favour of, receiving pay. Two days later information arrived in the town that preliminary articles of peace between England and France had been signed in London by Lord Hawkesbury and M. Otto. The volunteers accordingly assembled in the afternoon and fired nine volleys, and the following toast was enthusiastically drunk by the whole corps, "Peace with all Europe ; and God bless the King."[1]

Though the preliminaries of peace had been arranged the Newark troop of Yeomanry Cavalry, with a patriotic view to possibilities, intimated to his Majesty that they were perfectly ready to continue their services. Their spirited offer was graciously received by the king, the following letter being sent by Lord Hobart to Lieut.-Col. Eyre :—

Downing Street, December 31, 1801.

Sir— I have taken the earliest opportunity of laying before the king your letter of the 27th inst., communicating the handsome and public-spirited offer of the Newark troop of Yeomanry Cavalry, to continue their services during his Majesty's pleasure, and I have it in command from his Majesty to express the cordial satisfaction with which he has received so strong a testimony of attachment to his person and Government as that which you have conveyed on the part of the troop under the command of Captain Chaplin. The continued service of the Yeomanry Corps, under present circumstances, has already been recommended in my circular letter of the 10th of October last, to the Lords Lieutenants of counties, and his Majesty's ultimate determination with respect to the immediate object of your communication will be signified as soon as I shall have received the king's commands for that purpose. I am directed by his Majesty, in the meantime, to say, that his experience of the extensive benefits derived from the invaluable institution of the Yeomanry Corps, has led him to consider its continuance, as far as can be rendered consistent with the necessary occupations and convenience of those of whom such corps may be composed, as highly important to the public interest ; and under the impression, his Majesty will at all times reflect on the offer now made by the Newark Troop of Yeomanry with every sentiment of the warmest approbation.—I am, sir, your most obedient, humble servant, HOBART.

On March 25, 1802, the peace of Amiens between Great Britain, France, Spain, and Holland put an end to hostilities, though only for a brief period.

A young man named George Thompson, twenty-one years of age, was executed March 23, 1803, for stealing a portmanteau, the property of Mr. Edward Smith Godfrey, attorney of Newark, from the coach-office in that town, and his crime was aggravated by an attempt to stab the person who seized him as he was getting off the coach, in the yard of the White Lion Inn, Nottingham.

One year and six weeks after the peace of Amiens the war with France was renewed, "and now," writes Mr. Knight,[2] "the land bristled. The spirit that was raised in France by the Duke of Brunswick was raised in England by Buonaparte. The pressure of taxation, the desire for a reformed House of Commons, the remembrances of despotic acts of Government, the sympathy with Republican France—all was forgotten in the one absorbing impulse for the defence of the soil." In July (1803) it was proposed by the Secretary for War that an enrolment should be made of men in every parish between the ages of seventeen and fifty-five. Fox objected to the compulsory provisions of the bill. "Go round," he said, "from house to house, and ask those who would be willing to serve their country in the hour of danger ; there would not be five refusals in 500." The words were perfectly true, for in less than a month the volunteer movement had spread with such rapidity that the

[1] MSS. of the late Mr. Frederic Eggleston, an eye-witness. [2] Knight's *History*, vol. viii. p. 425.

PRESENTATION OF COLOURS.

number enrolled had increased from 60,000 to 300,000. Newark, we may be sure, had not been behindhand in such a crisis. The first corps had been disbanded at the general peace, and their colours deposited in the church. But the patriotic spirit burst forth again, and at a meeting in the town-hall to form a new corps 906 enrolled their names. An offer to raise eight companies was transmitted to his Majesty, and accepted. On Thursday, November 17 (1803), the men were inspected by Lieutenant-Colonel Kane, the reviewing officer of the district; their appearance attracted the Colonel's particular notice, and he was pleased to express his perfect approbation of them. On the same day, also, he reviewed the Newark troop of Nottingham Yeomanry Cavalry, who were complimented by him on their high state of discipline.

In the following year, namely on April 27, 1804, the Newark volunteers, to the number of 538, marched to Retford on permanent duty. They returned home on May 8, and were met at Muskham Bridge by the Newark Yeomanry, consisting of 100, the Southwell Volunteers 300, and those of the Trent Vale 160. The total who proceeded to the market-place was thus 1098. The Lieutenant-Colonel Commandant was Thomas Thoroton, Esq., of Flintham, and the Lieutenant-Colonel, Thomas Bradshaw, Esq., Newark. On the 30th of August a very interesting ceremony took place:—the consecration of colours presented to the Volunteers by Mrs. Thoroton. The corps assembled in the market-place about twelve o'clock, when, after a very animated address and appropriate prayer of consecration from the Rev. J. Brooke, their chaplain, Mrs. Thoroton presented the colours. Addressing the Colonel Commandant, she said:—

It is impossible for me to express how much I feel interested in the welfare of the Loyal Newark Volunteers. Permit me, sir, as a token of my sincere regard and attachment, to present to your corps these colours. May they ever lead you to victory! May they be an encouragement to you in the day of battle, and prove a terror to our enemies, and convince them of the valour and invincibility of Britons, when fighting for their God, their country, and their king!

Colonel Thoroton, on receiving the colours, returned the following answer:—

In the name of the Loyal Newark Volunteers, I return you our thanks for the honour you have conferred on the corps in presenting to us our colours. Be assured, madam, these colours shall be defended with all the courage and zeal that British soldiers are capable of exerting. We well know that the loyalty and public spirit which have ever distinguished the town of Newark and its neighbourhood, so often and so well tried on many former occasions, affords the strongest pledge that when this corps, which I have the honour to command, is called out into active service, it will do its duty, not only to the satisfaction and credit of the place in which it was raised, but in such a manner as to entitle it to the general thanks and praise of the country. Called upon as we are, by the most powerful of all motives that can influence the human mind—the protection of our wives and children, and of everything dearest to us in private life, and also of everything that is held most valuable in public opinion, our religion, our laws, our country, and our king—I will venture to affirm there is but one sentiment that glows in the breast of every individual in this corps, and, I believe, of every one here present,—"To conquer or to die in their defence." How soon this corps may be called upon to join our brother soldiers in the field is yet uncertain; but from the state of the enemy's preparations to invade our shores, the time is probably not far distant; but let the time come when it may, it is an animating

2 K

reflection to be assured that the country is sufficiently prepared for its defence; and from the loyalty, spirit, and unanimity that pervades every part of these kingdoms, let the unprincipled invader come when he will, he shall repent severely of his presumptuous temerity. May we, with the assistance of Divine Providence, maintain safe and unsullied the colours which have this day been presented to us!

Then turning to the ensigns, the Colonel added :—"Gentlemen, I commit these colours into your hands, satisfied they will be defended as becomes the name and character of British soldiers." The Colonel afterwards addressed the corps in the following terms :—"Before I dismiss you, I take this opportunity of assuring you how much satisfaction and pleasure I feel at the high state of discipline this corps has now attained. I beg to return my sincerest thanks to every officer, and to every individual in it, for their unremitting attention to their military duty; for their exemplary conduct during the time they were on permanent duty at Retford, and which so very deservedly gained much honour and credit to their regiment. My acknowledgments are particularly due to Lieut.-Colonel Bradshaw, to whose indefatigable pains and exertions this regiment owes, in a very essential degree, its high character and state of discipline, which I hope it will be the pride and ambition of the Loyal Newark Volunteers ever to support and maintain."

Colonel Thoroton, in his address, alluded to the active preparations made for the invasion of England, and the subject was naturally uppermost in the minds of the whole country. "To cross the Channel with an army, and to terminate in London the rivalry of the two nations, was the prodigious enterprise to which Buonaparte applied his faculties during three successive years." But the ambitious project was never carried out. The combined fleets of France and Spain were shattered by Nelson, and though Napoleon continued for years his daring military schemes, the proposed descent on England was abandoned as altogether impracticable. The volunteers of Newark were not called upon to fight, but the readiness with which they sprang to their feet at the call of duty, is a testimony to their gallantry and to the loyalty of the town.

On Sunday, November 11, 1804, the new organ at Newark, built by the celebrated maker, England, was played upon for the first time, to a very crowded congregation. Cathedral service was rendered by the Southwell Choir, and a very excellent discourse on the occasion was delivered by the Rev. Joshua Brooke.

We find the following advertisement in the Newark paper, published at this period :—

COCK PIT, NEWARK.

A main of cocks will be fought there on Tuesday and Wednesday, the 29th and 30th January, 1805, between the gentlemen of Lincolnshire and the gentlemen of Nottinghamshire, for five guineas a battle, and a hundred guineas the main. To show twenty-one battles on the main, and ten bye battles; a pair of cocks to be on the pit each morning at nine o'clock.

Newark, *January* 17, 1805.

A more healthful and innocent recreation was provided for the public in 1809. On Monday, May 8th, in that year, a bowling-green was opened in the presence of about eighty subscribers. The green is delightfully situate, and continues to be a favourite resort for townspeople on summer evenings.

A case of forgery in Newark resulted in the execution of the offender—Thomas Lampin, thirty-four years of age, a native of Crediton, in Devonshire. Lampin was tried at the County Hall on July 22 (1809), before Sir Simon Le Blanc. He was found guilty of forging a bill of exchange for £100, with intent to defraud Mr. Peter Selby, of Newark, and received sentence of death. He was hanged at Nottingham on the 2d of August, leaving behind him a wife and two children.

The king having reached the fiftieth year of his reign, on October 26, 1809, a national jubilee was held. The event was celebrated in Newark with all that energy and affectionate attachment to the throne which had ever distinguished the town. A liberal subscription was raised, and food plentifully distributed to the poorer inhabitants. The mayor and corporation, and the Newark troop of volunteer cavalry, attended divine service in the morning, when an appropriate sermon was preached by the Rev. J. Brooke, to a crowded and attentive congregation. A very numerous party of gentlemen of the town and neighbourhood dined at the town-hall, among those present being Lord Manners and Mr. John Manners Sutton, his brother, Mr. Henry Willoughby, M.P., Mr. Henry Fynes, M.P., and many others. At Kelham an ox and two sheep were roasted and distributed.

The desirability of forming a dispensary, for the relief of the sick poor, was discussed in 1812, and at a large meeting held on the 24th of October, a liberal subscription was started for the purpose of founding such an institution. The mayor was requested to confer with the medical gentlemen in the town, and to prepare regulations for the guidance of the establishment, to be submitted to a future meeting.

In the midst of local movements, all eyes continued to be watching with eagerness the progress of the great war. Early in July 1813, the welcome news arrived, that a great victory had been won, on the 21st of the previous month, at Vittoria. "The allied army under my command," wrote Wellington, in his despatch, "gained a complete victory, having driven the enemy from all their positions, having taken from them 151 pieces of cannon, 415 waggons of ammunition, all their baggage, provisions, cattle, treasure, etc., and a considerable number of prisoners." To celebrate the event a great fête was held in London, on the 20th of July, and there were rejoicings in most provincial towns. At Newark a public meeting was held at the bowling-green. Sir David Rae, Bart., Lieutenant-Colonel of the Royal West Middlesex Militia, was quartered with his regiment in the town, and he ordered the regimental band to accompany a dance, and to perform appropriate festive and martial music. The officers of the regiment and upwards of 300 persons assembled, and we read in the newspapers that "the serenity of the evening, the charming effect of the music from the balcony of the building (the colonnade of which was decorated with laurel), and the general joy that beamed on every countenance, all combined to render the scene most agreeably enchanting."

The continuance of the war had brought up the price of wheat to 120s. per quarter, and the winter of 1813 proving severe, the distress was considerable. At the commencement of 1814 a liberal subscription was entered into by the inhabitants of Newark, for the purpose of distributing soup and bread to the poor during the continuance of the storm. The depth of snow on the roads was such as to greatly impede traffic.

At Nottingham, the transit of all kinds of goods to and from the town was suspended for some days. The frost, which had commenced on the 27th September 1813, began to break up on Sunday, February 6 (1814), and on the following Tuesday the ice on the surface of the Trent having also melted, there was a great inundation.

The end of the war was fortunately approaching. The ambition of Napoleon had received many checks, and after the battle of Leipzig, his prospects were very gloomy. Rapidly the allies marched to Paris, and the French Senate declared that Napoleon had forfeited the throne. On the 4th of April he abdicated, and retired to Elba. On the 23d of the same month a convention was signed in Paris, by which it was stipulated that all hostilities should cease, that the foreign armies should evacuate the French territory, and that the boundaries of France should be the same as on the 1st of January 1792. When the intelligence reached England, the nation became almost frantic with joy. In every town and village the two-fold event was gladly celebrated. On Thursday evening, 9th June, there was a general illumination throughout Newark, which drew together the largest concourse of people that had been seen in the town for years. On Friday a ball was held, which was attended by upwards of 300 persons. On Saturday there was a dinner at the town-hall, and ordinaries at several public-houses. Two bullocks and 28 sheep were roasted in different parts of the town, four hogsheads of ale given away in the market-place, and £200 distributed amongst the labouring classes, to enable them to regale themselves at their homes. In the illuminations on Thursday evening, the town-hall stood foremost. The two outer columns in front were decorated with spiral wreaths, and the centre ones with clusters. There were festoons above, and the intercolumniations were richly decorated with G. R., and a star and crown; the figures of the lion, unicorn, and justice, at the top, each having a collar of variegated lamps, gave to the whole a magnificent appearance. The wings (then inhabited by Mr. Moore and Mr. Wallis) exhibited two beautiful transparencies, the one an emblem of peace with the inscription :—

> "War (thanks to Providence) at length is o'er,
> And peace revisits Britain's happy shore,
> Long may the olive flourish in her hand,
> Europe rejoice, and plenty bless the land;
> The laurel Wellington entwine, and bloom
> Unfading over Pitt and Nelson's tomb."

Over the other wing was Britannia with her hand resting on a pedestal, on which was printed :—"My sons have done their duty."

A special meeting of the town-council was held on the 30th of June, when an address was agreed to, congratulating his Royal Highness the Prince Regent, on the recent happy change in the political state of Europe. The address stated :—"We desire to offer to your Royal Highness our congratulations upon the recent happy change in the political state of Europe, a change for which the world is not less indebted (under Divine Providence) to the wisdom and firmness of his Majesty's counsels, and the brilliant and unexampled exertions of this country in the common cause, than to those illustrious allies, whose magnanimity and moderation in the hour of victory were only equalled by the perseverance and valour which achieved it." The address regretted that the indisposition of the king prevented him participating in the general joy felt at the downfall "of the common desolater of Europe," and went on to refer with satisfaction to the well-merited honours conferred by his Highness on the gallant officers who had taken part in the struggle. The address concluded :—" It must be a source of the greatest satisfaction to your Royal Highness that, in the steady pursuit of the counsels and enlightened policy of your father, the objects of the protracted warfare have at length been attained, and the glory of our country carried to the highest pitch of renown."

But the sky, now bright and promising, speedily became overclouded. The radiant sunshine of peace gave place once more to the war cloud. Eleven months passed in comparative quietude, and then news came that Napoleon, still restless and daring, had left Elba, had landed on the coast of Provence (March 1, 1815), and was marching to Paris. The French soldiers flocked in thousands to his banner, and in twenty days he once more held the capital and the throne of France. Europe, enraged at this utter disregard of oaths and treaties, again took up arms. At Waterloo the strength of Napoleon was scattered to the winds. Defeated and disheartened, he was sent, a prisoner, to end his days on the island of St. Helena. In the ever-memorable battle several Newark men were engaged, one of whom, Robert Jackson, a private in the Royal Horse Artillery, died as recently as October 14, 1878.

Amongst the local casualties of the year 1815 may be mentioned two serious coach accidents. On Saturday, August 12, the "Accommodation" coach, very heavily laden, going from Nottingham to Newark by way of Southwell, was overturned near Averham, by which accident Mr. Ringrose of Langford was so severely hurt that he died on the following Monday. A John Smith of Newark was injured, a man named Ridley had his shoulders dislocated, Serjeant Brogden of the Militia his leg broken and the cap of his knee removed, Mr. Clark of Skegby his arm broken, and several others were very much bruised. At the inquest on Mr. Ringrose, a verdict was given that he was killed by the overturning of the Nottingham coach, which was occasioned by the carelessness of the driver. Another coach accident took place in September. The Wellington post coach, travelling from Boston, was overturned in Newark, the horses taking fright at some rubbish which had been left on the road. The outside passengers were much hurt, one of them (Mr. Martin Bower, of Retford) surviving the fall only about four hours. A Mr. Rice, of London, also died from the effects of injuries received to his leg. Subsequently, at the Nottingham assizes, Will Bradley, the driver of the "Accommodation" coach, was charged with the manslaughter of Mr. Ringrose, but the evidence not substantiating the allegation of negligence, he was acquitted.

Many noble acts of heroism were exhibited during the wars, but none were more conspicuous for their gallantry than the 42d Highland regiment, whose numbers, after the battle of Waterloo, were reduced from 1000 to 400. A division of this small remnant, under the command of Lieutenant-Colonel Dick, marched through Newark on Tuesday, the 23d January 1816, on their way to the North, when they were received by the mayor and corporation, and all the principal inhabitants. The bells were rung and flags were hoisted. The men were regaled and a ball was given in honour of the officers at the town-hall.

A smart shock of earthquake was felt in Newark and throughout most parts of the county, on Sunday, March 17th. It came on with a rumbling noise, accompanied by a quick, convulsive tremor, which lasted about two seconds. Persons who were in the streets at the time described the sound as resembling that of the rattling of a carriage on the pavement. Speaking of its effects at Nottingham, Mr. Bailey, in his annals of that town, says:—"It was felt at half-past twelve P.M.; and as divine service was not over at the churches, nor some of the chapels, great alarm was experienced by the congregations. At St. Peter's and St. Nicholas's the consternation was so great that service had to be suspended for a few seconds, and one lady was borne out in a state of insensibility. The pillars supporting St. Mary's tower were visibly shaken; but fortunately the attention of the crowded congregation was so engrossed by the eloquent discourse of the sheriff's chaplain, and the presence of the judge and his retinue, that the vibration was comparatively little regarded, and consequently the alarm was but slight. In various parts of the town and neighbourhood glasses and other things were shaken off shelves, window casements were thrown open, and other striking indications manifested of the extent and force of the subterranean movement."

The winter of 1816 was equal in severity to some of its immediate predecessors. A meeting was held in the town-hall, early in December, to consider the best means of relieving the poor, when it was resolved to provide soup and other food for distribution. The sum of £300 was immediately subscribed, and it was subsequently greatly increased. During the ten weeks preceding March 1 (1817), the poor were supplied weekly with upwards of 3000 lbs. of beef and 1900 pints of soup, which were distributed to more than 800 families consisting of 2000 persons; 664 families were relieved with coal, and the committee purchased a large quantity of potatoes, which they sold at twopence per peck to those who had soup tickets. The price of the quartern loaf at the commencement of March was one shilling and three pence farthing.

The condition of the country at this time was of a very serious description; agitation, distress, and a feeling of insecurity prevailed. Lord Sidmouth in the House of Lords, and Viscount Castlereagh in the Commons, brought forward measures for the temporary suspension of the Habeas Corpus Act; the extension of the Act of 1795, for the security of his Majesty's person, to his Royal Highness the Prince Regent; and for embodying into one Act the provisions of certain Acts relative to tumultous meetings, debating societies bound together by secret oaths, or by fraternised branches over the kingdom. In the midland districts the Luddites had instituted a Reign of Terror, and some who had been captured, had been tried in Nottingham in the previous August, and acquitted amidst a scene of intense excitement. In February (1817) an official order was issued directing that the assizes for the county of Nottingham should be held at Newark instead of at Nottingham, "in consequence of insults offered to the judge, and the menacing conduct of the rabble at the previous assizes." The Prince Regent, however, countermanded the order, and the business of the assizes was transacted at Nottingham as usual. One man was arraigned and condemned, but the majority of the Luddites were tried at Leicester, and six of them were executed.

On the lamented death of her Royal Highness the Princess Charlotte Augusta, November 6, 1817, a meeting of the inhabitants was held to consider the most proper mode of observing with due solemnity the day appointed for the funeral. It was resolved to close the shops on Wednesday, November 19, the date of the interment, and evening service was held at the church, attended by one of the largest congregations ever assembled within the edifice. The sermon was preached by the Rev. J. Bartlett, from Job ii. 10. Addresses were forwarded by the town to the Prince Regent and the Prince Leopold of Saxe-Coburgh, condoling with them on their severe bereavement. Replies were duly received, that from Prince Leopold being as follows:—

CLAREMONT, *December* 20, 1817.

SIR—I have this day had the honour of presenting to the Prince Leopold the address of the mayor, recorder, aldermen, and inhabitants of the borough of Newark-upon-Trent, on the recent deplored event at Claremont. The Prince Leopold receives these assurances of true affection and interest in his welfare with full and earnest confidence in all the sympathy and participation in his grief that the inhabitants of Newark have so feelingly manifested in their address, and he looks with fervent and assured consolation to that high and sacred source of mercy, to which, in their affectionate condolence, they lead his thoughts and hopes of restored happiness.—I have the honour to be, sir, your most obedient and humble servant, ROBERT GARDINER.

Thos. Bland, Esq., mayor, Newark-upon-Trent.

A similar service at the church to the one above mentioned was held on the interment of the Queen on Wednesday, 2d December, and on the 5th an address of condolence was forwarded to the Prince Regent by the town-council.

In the summer of 1818 the vicarage house, situated about 50 yards north from the choir door, was taken down, and its site, together with the appurtenances extending to Parsons Mount, attached to the churchyard. This was considered at the time a very great improvement, as the burial-ground had become extremely crowded. The present residence allotted to the vicar is in Appleton Gate, nearly opposite the east window of the church. This property was many years in the family of Martin, when it devolved to the late Richard Forster, Esq., of whose executors it was purchased for the present purpose. At the same period the upper part of the spire, to the extent of 15 feet, being deemed in a ruinous condition, and consequently dangerous, the course of stones constituting the dilapidated portion was carefully lowered to the ground, a firm basis acquired, and the elegant pyramid reconstructed under the direction of Messrs. Willis and Marshall, masons, in a manner which seemed to bid defiance to further concussions. The top stone was put on August 4, 1818, and on Saturday evening, the 8th inst., at twenty minutes past six, the weathercock was placed on the spindle : the bells were rung in honour of the event, and there was also a band of music playing on a platform erected from the top window of the spire. Before refixing the weathercock, as above stated, it was made considerably lighter by cutting off a pair of outstretched wings with which it was previously ornamented.

Another severe winter, that of 1819, having added to the distress, a meeting of the inhabitants of Newark, convened by the mayor, was held in the town-hall on January 18, 1820, to take into consideration the expediency and best means of providing some relief for the poor during the inclement season, when the sum of £378 was subscribed for that purpose, and the paper ordered to be left for additional signatures. It was the unanimous opinion of the meeting that the most effectual and proper relief to the poor on all occasions was by employment, as far as the same could be effected; and a committee, chosen from the gentlemen present, were requested to find as much employment as possible for such as were out of work, and to pay a proportion of the wages for extra labour out of the subscriptions. It was also resolved that soup, and such articles of food and necessaries as might be thought useful by the committee, should be immediately provided for temporary relief.

The long reign of George III. closed on the 29th January 1820. His Majesty died at the age of eighty-two, having been king for sixty years. The corporation of Newark being desirous of showing every mark of respect to the memory of the deceased monarch, it was resolved at a meeting on the 4th of February "that the maces and the corporation seat in the church be put in mourning, and that the beadle be also put in mourning, and that if his late Majesty's funeral shall remain fixed for Wednesday the 16th inst., or any other Wednesday, the mayor be requested to give notice of holding the market of that week on the preceding day, that the day of interment may be observed with the solemnity suitable to that mournful occasion." It was also resolved "that the mayor do request the officiating minister of the parish to perform divine service on that day, that the corporation do attend in procession from the town-hall, and that the sermon be preached by the Rev. J. B. Wittenoom." It was further agreed "that the mayor publish a handbill requesting that the shops in the town be closed during the whole of the day of interment;" a request that was duly complied with.

On the 10th February it was resolved "that the mayor and aldermen do meet in their gowns, attended by all the mayor's officers and constables, on the following day, to proclaim his Majesty King George IV." It was decided "that four dozen of wine be ordered for the purpose of drinking the king's health out of the gold cup, that six half-hogsheads of ale be distributed to the populace, and one shilling each allowed to the constables who attend, and a guinea to the mayor's officers, to drink his Majesty's health." Subsequently a public meeting was held, when an address to his Majesty was passed, expressing attachment to the throne, and a firm determination to support the laws and constitution of the country.

It was during this year that Mr. Shilton published his account of Newark, and

he describes the celerity with which the mail from London to York was conveyed as being admirable, as its limited time allowed not more than twenty-seven hours. Seven coaches passed through Newark daily; they were as follows:—the Union (Kingston Arms), the Rockingham (Castle and Falcon), Nelson (Mr. Gilstrap's, Kirkgate), Highflyer (Mr. Gilstrap's), Wellington (Royal Mail Tavern, Beaumond Street), Edinburgh Mail (Mr. Gilstrap's), Glasgow Mail (Kingston Arms). The coaches for the cross roads were—Nottingham Coach (Mr. Gilstrap's), Lincoln Coach (Mr. Gilstrap's), Nottingham Accommodation (Robin Hood), Lincoln Accommodation (Castle and Falcon), and the Tallyho to Manchester (Castle and Falcon).

At the annual meeting of the Newark troop of Yeomanry Cavalry, a number of gentlemen of the town and neighbourhood having expressed a wish to dine with them, "for the purpose of testifying at this particular crisis their attachment to the king and constitution," on Monday, December 18 (1820), two hundred and seventy gentlemen sat down to dinner in the town-hall, and many were refused tickets from fear of inability to accommodate more than that number. The company were delighted with the truly loyal, manly, and patriotic sentiments that were expressed by the gentlemen who addressed them. The speakers were the recorder (Mr. Balguy), Mr. Godfrey, Mr. Manners Sutton, Mr. Tallents, and others.

The rejoicings and festivities on the day of the coronation of George IV. (July 19, 1821) were generally participated in by all classes. In the morning the corporation, preceded by the children of the National Schools, went in procession to church, where prayers were read and an excellent discourse delivered by the Rev. William Bartlett, the vicar, to a crowded congregation. After divine service, the different committees of management repaired to their respective streets to superintend the preparation of the repast, which had been provided by public subscription, for the poor inhabitants, and at one o'clock upwards of 5000 men, women, and children sat down to a plentiful dinner of plum-pudding, beef, mutton, and ale. At three o'clock an excellent dinner was served at the town-hall for the gentlemen of the town and neighbourhood, and the Newark troop of Yeomanry Cavalry, who had been invited to join on this loyal occasion. Upwards of 250 gentlemen sat down to dinner. The utmost conviviality prevailed during the whole of the evening, and some of the party did not separate until three o'clock in the morning. On the following evening there was a ball at the town-hall, which was largely attended, and other public demonstrations of joy took place in various parts of the borough.

The first stone of a new chapel for the Independents, was laid at Newark on Wednesday, October 23, 1822.

The career of a poet of extraordinary abilities, who, amidst the exciting events of the anxious period to which we have been referring, had monopolised a vast amount of attention, came now to an abrupt close. On the 19th of April 1824 Lord Byron died at Missolonghi, in Greece, where he had gone to fight the battle of liberty, and his remains were brought for interment to Hucknall Torkard in this county, the burying-place of the noble family to which he belonged. Of the remarkable literary career of the noted bard who thus succumbed at the early age of 36 years, we need say nothing in these pages. Nor is it within our province to dwell upon the details of his private life, replete as they are with items of spicy romance, and with stories of lamentable excesses. It may not, however, be uninteresting or inappropriate if we advert briefly to the connection of the noble poet with Newark, and to the circumstances out of which his association with the borough arose. It is well known to those who have made themselves familiar with the biography of Byron, that, in his early youth, when staying with his mother at Southwell, he made many intimate friends in that pleasant little town. At a somewhat later period, he occasionally stayed at Newark, lodging at the Kingston Arms, now the Clinton Arms Hotel, and invariably calling to inspect the stock of books on sale at Ridge's shop. Writing to Miss Pigot at Southwell, he says :—" I shall pass very near you on my journey to Newark, but I cannot approach. If you have a letter, order it to be left at Ridge's shop, where I shall call, or the post-office. If your brother would ride over, I should be very glad to see him ; he can return the same night, or go home the next morning. The Kingston Arms is my inn."

It was the Ridges of Newark, to whom his lordship refers—the late firm of Messrs. S. and J. Ridge—who had the honour of first introducing Lord Byron to the public as a poet, and not this alone, but who were the means of making the place "classic ground," by causing it to be habitually frequented by the then youthful bard, at the most critical and interesting period of his life, when his genius was being gradually developed, and his poetical capacity progressively matured. A son of the elder partner in the firm aforesaid, who was a boy at the time, tells us with what pride they received the visits of the then embryo poet at their house; though it could scarcely be for his poetic fame, for he had none at that time; his new-fledged wings had not yet begun to soar. Proud they had indeed great reason to be, as time rolled on, and at no distant day either; for it was the very volume which first saw the light, through their agency, at Newark, his *Hours of Idleness*—the slashing criticism of which in the *Edinburgh Review* called forth that clever retort of his— *English Bards and Scotch Reviewers*—which gave its youthful author such occasion to exclaim, "I awoke one morning and found myself famous." No, it could not be the juvenile bard, as such, whom they were proud to harbour, but only as the "sprig of nobility" that he was ; though soon it came to pass that the glare and glitter of the lordly rank was totally eclipsed by the brightness of his glory as a poet.

Lord Byron's connection in early life with Newark arose from his mother, after leaving Newstead Abbey, having taken up her residence at Southwell. His youthful lordship himself, having left Harrow, was then at Trinity College, Cambridge ; and it would seem to have been whilst spending the long vacation at Southwell, in 1807, being then in but his nineteenth year, that he first thought of printing (though only for private circulation) a selection from a miscellaneous mass of his poetical effusions, written when scarcely past his boyhood. Moore, in his *Life of Byron*, thus briefly relates the story of what may be called his poetical nativity, and that which has conferred on Newark the honour of being its birthplace:—" The idea of printing his juvenile poems first occurred to him in the parlour of that cottage which, during his visits to Southwell, had become his adopted home. Miss Pigot, who was not before aware of his turn for versifying, had been reading aloud the poems of Burns, when young Byron said 'that he too was a poet sometimes, and would write down for her some verses of his own which he remembered.' He then, with a pencil, wrote those lines beginning, 'In thee I fondly hoped to clasp,' which were printed in his first unpublished volume. He also repeated to her the verses, 'When in the hall my father's voice,' so remarkable for the anticipations of his future fame. From this moment," continues his biographer, "the desire of appearing in print took entire possession of him; though, for the present, his ambition did not extend its views beyond a small volume for private circulation. The person to whom fell the honour of receiving his first manuscripts was Ridge, the bookseller at Newark; and while the work was printing, the young author continued to pour fresh materials into his hands, with the same eagerness and rapidity that marked the progress of his maturer works."

This volume, whilst going through the press, was the cause of incessant visits by the impatient young poet to Mr. Ridge's house, and at his *house* in preference to his *shop*. The house-door was in a line with that of the shop. There were two steps up to it, as there are still; for the premises, though modernised and improved a little, are yet substantially, it appears, in much the same "outward form" they at that time presented. Byron, we are told, used to skip up the two steps to the house-door as best he could with his lame foot, give with the brass knocker his hurried *rap-a-tap*, which, from its peculiarity, always foretold his awaiting presence without; so that after scarce a moment's delay the door was opened, and my lord was forthwith shown upstairs into the drawing-room, where, in due course, he was respectfully waited upon by Mr. Ridge, generally with his hands full of "proof slips," and mentally prepared to undergo the perplexity and trouble to which the "second thoughts" of the apprentice author would too often subject him, involving, as they did, alterations extending frequently to the remodelling of couplets, and even to the substitution of one poem for another.

The printing of these poems was completed in November 1806; it is a thin quarto volume of sixty-six pages, with the simple title *Fugitive Pieces*, and is inscribed "To those friends at whose request they were printed, for whose amusement and approbation they are solely intended, these trifles are respectfully dedicated by the author." There is also a short preface or notice:—" As these poems are never intended to meet the public eye, no apology is necessary for the form in which they now appear. They are printed merely for the perusal of a few friends to whom they are dedicated; and as most of them were composed between the ages of fifteen and seventeen, their defects will be pardoned or forgotten in the youth and inexperience of the author." There is no table of contents: the dates appended to the poems range from 1802 to October 9, 1806. The first complete copy was sent to the Rev. John Thomas Becher of Southwell, who, objecting to a certain poem for its too warm colouring, forthwith expressed his well-meant censure to the young author in some verses. Byron replied both in verse[1] and in prose, and called in immediately the copies which had been distributed, and in Mr. Becher's presence burnt the impression; Mr. Becher's own copy and a second which had been sent to Edinburgh, probably to Pigot, alone escaped the *auto-da-fé*. Surely no poet ever showed greater docility or modesty. These two copies still survive; the former copy, with "J. M. Pigot" inscribed by Byron's hand, came into the possession of Miss Pigot, who bequeathed it, with other relics of the poet, to Mrs. Webb of Newstead Abbey, where it is preserved with watchful care. The second copy has ever since remained in the Becher family; and the present possessor, Mrs. Becher, widow of the son of Byron's wise monitor, keeps it among her choicest treasures. The Newstead copy is imperfect, wanting pp. 17-20 inclusive, and eight pages at the end.[2]

Immediately after the sacrifice of the quarto edition, Byron commenced the preparation of another to replace it; in six weeks it was printed and ready for distribution. It is a small 8vo. of 144 pages, contains considerable additions, and bears the title "Poems on various Occasions, Virginibus Puerisque canto. Newark: printed by S. and J. Ridge, MDCCCVII."[3] The dedication remains as in the earlier edition, but the short notice differs, and is as follows:—"The only apology necessary to be adduced, in extenuation of any errors in the following collection, is, that the author has not yet completed his nineteenth year. December 23, 1806."

Aroused by the flattering encomiums of some of the Scotch literati to whom presentation copies had been sent, Byron decided to give to the public that which had hitherto been restricted to private circulation, and published an amended and enlarged edition (187 pp.), "Hours of Idleness, a series of poems, original and translated, by George Gordon, Lord Byron, a minor. Newark: printed and sold by S. and J. Ridge, 1807." In lieu of the short notice prefixed to the two previous editions, is a preface of nearly six pages, and the book is without a dedication. This edition sold well. Byron eagerly watched for public opinion. "Does my publication go off well?" he asks of Miss Pigot. "Has Ridge sold well, or do the ancients demur? What ladies have bought? What the devil would Ridge have? is not fifty in a fortnight, before the advertisements, sufficient sale? Ridge does not proceed rapidly in Notts,—very possible. In town things wear a more promising aspect, and a man whose works are praised by *reviewers*, admired by *duchesses*, and sold by every bookseller in the metropolis, does not dedicate much consideration to *rustic readers*." This edition called forth the violent attack from the *Edinburgh Review*, but before the article appeared, a new edition was called for. It, nevertheless, bore traces of the punishment he had received. The title is altered to "Poems, original and translated, by George Gordon, Lord Byron." The minor of the

---

[1] *Hours of Idleness* (1st edition), p. 118.   [2] Elze's *Byron*.
[3] In September 1876 a presentation copy from the author to H. E. Pigot was sold by auction for £25 at a bazaar on behalf of the volunteers at East Retford.

first disappears in the second edition, also the long preface; it is dedicated to the Earl of Carlisle.[1] The publishing of *English Bards and Scotch Reviewers* was offered to the same firm at Newark, but they, guided by their London agent, declined to have anything to do with a production so dangerously suggestive of libels.

The business intercourse between the noble bard and his Newark printers seems to have been throughout of a mutually satisfactory character. It is true there are several unfavourable expressions to be found in Byron's published letters. He uses a harsh epithet on one occasion because the printer had mistaken a word of "a handwriting which no devil could read;" and he introduces in another epistle a charge of piracy, because he had heard that Ridge had reprinted the *Hours of Idleness* in spite of his lordship's inhibition. The first-named cause of complaint is comparatively trivial, and the second was capable of a complete and honourable explanation. It appears that, as the book sold, Ridge informed Lord Byron that the edition was "just out," meaning, as any publisher under similar circumstances would mean, not that there were no copies on hand, but that it was time to commence reprinting. Byron resolved to close the issue with the current edition, but meanwhile Ridge not only sold all that were "made-up," but, as he frankly told his lordship, "reprinted some sheets to make up the few remaining copies." "How trivial in its origin, and baseless in reality, was the grave charge of piracy in this case," says a recent writer,[2] "and how little Lord Byron, even at the time, meant to reflect upon his respectable neighbour and printer, is illustrated by the fact that, as long as he remained in England, when visiting Newstead, he used to testify his respect by calling and purchasing a few books at the shop at Newark. And so little, on the other hand, did Ridge or his family suspect the existence of any feelings or expressions like those alluded to that one of them, who happened to be in London in 1819, was, I believe, the first person to give Murray the information of surreptitious editions of the *Hours of Idleness* and *Bards and Reviewers* being in the press; and the publication of which was, in consequence, immediately restrained by an injunction from the Lord Chancellor." As illustrative of the confidential and friendly intercourse that passed between the noble poet and his first printers, we may refer to three letters which were received by Ridge 1807-8, and which were recently laid before the public.[3] In the first letter, which bears date January 12, 1807, his lordship informs Mr. Ridge that several of the papers are in the habit of publishing extracts from his volume, and that, as publisher, he ought to put a stop to it. "You will," he says, "act upon this as you think proper, and proceed with the second edition as you please. I am in no hurry, and I still think *you* were *premature* in *undertaking* it."

[1] There is still retained upon the premises in the market-place, Newark, the printing-press at which the different editions referred to were printed, and also the small woodcuts and metal casts which were introduced into the edition of *Hours of Idleness*, 1807; also copies of the *Poems*, 1807, for private circulation; *Hours of Idleness*, 1807, the first public edition; and *Poems*, 1808, the second public edition.
[2] "D," in *Notes and Queries*, vol. vi. 2d series, p. 303.
[3] *Notes and Queries*, 2d series, X, p. 362-3.

In the second, dated November 20, he says he is happy to hear everything goes on well, though he is of opinion the first edition had better be entirely sold before the printing of a second is risked. Directions are given as to certain poems which are to be omitted, and others substituted, and various matters incidental to the printing are referred to. Still anxious that no loss should accrue, his lordship adds :—" Remember, I have advised you not to risk it a second time, and it is not too late to retract. However, you must abide by your own discretion." The third letter is dated from Dorant's Hotel, February 11, 1808, and runs thus :—" Something has occurred which will make considerable alteration in my new volume. You must *go back* and *cut out* the whole *poem* of '*Childish Recollections.*' Of course you will be surprised at this, and perhaps displeased, but it must be *done*. I cannot help its detaining you a *month* longer, but there will be enough in the volume without it; and as I am now reconciled to Dr. Butler, I cannot allow my satire to appear against him, nor can I alter that part relating to him without spoiling the whole. Will, therefore, omit the whole poem. Send me an *immediate* answer to this letter, but *obey* the directions. It is better that my reputation should suffer as a poet by the omission, than as a man of honour by the insertion." And the kindly intercourse between author and printer, of which these letters are an evidence, was never marred by unfriendliness or dispute.

Such were Lord Byron's beginnings as a poet; and Southwell must share with Newark in the interest they possess as the opening of one of the most rapidly brilliant poetic careers that any English poet has ever had the greatness of genius to accomplish. Moore was of opinion that his residence at Southwell had a soothing and humanising effect on his too turbulent and impetuous nature. "With the exception of the brief bewildering interval with Miss Chaworth," he remarks, "it was at Southwell alone that an opportunity was ever afforded him of profiting by the bland influence of female society, and of seeing what woman is in the true sphere of her virtues—home. The amiable and intelligent family of the Pigots received him within their circle, and in the Rev. John Becher the youthful poet found not only an acute and judicious critic, but a sincere friend." These are reminiscences that well deserve to be mentioned in the annals of Newark, to which the noted subject of them may almost be said to have more or less belonged.

But another of Byron's biographers looks less favourably than the poet Moore has done on those doings of the noble bard which so closely connect him with Newark. In a volume entitled *The Life and Writings of Lord Byron*, published anonymously, with special allusion apparently to the first public edition, it is remarked :—" At the age of nineteen Lord Byron, at the importunity of friends, made a small collection of those poems which, having been circulated privately, had excited considerable interest. The volume, accordingly, appeared the same year from the neighbouring printing-press at Newark, to which, however, the execution did little honour in point of correctness or elegance." But this is not only an unnecessary, but an unjust remark. This volume is still extant, and can testify for itself. And we repeat that it did great credit to the town, in fact, it was in fit accord with that distinction which the interesting incidents here referred to combine to confer upon Newark—at a period, too, when but few provincial towns of similar size were capable of such an achievement.

Turning from the literary world, in which Byron was so prominent, to the commercial, we find the royal speech, at the commencement of 1825, exulting in the public prosperity which prevailed. "There never was a period in the history of this country, when all the great interests of the nation were at the same time in so thriving a condition." So, at least, said the monarch; but unfortunately, the happy state of things did not long continue. Money being plentiful, large amounts were ventured in extensive speculations. The gambling propensities of human nature were brought into action, and the banks were drained of money, that it might be invested in wild schemes for accumulating wealth. As the fascinating bubbles burst, distrust and confusion succeeded. Bank after bank, unable to withstand the sudden drain which excited customers put upon them, had to succumb. The effects of the panic would have been still more serious, but for the prompt action taken in many places. Meetings were held to express confidence in the local banks, and promising not to press them in the hour of difficulty. At Newark, a meeting convened by the mayor, was held at the town-hall, on the 19th of December. The following resolution was unanimously agreed upon:—"We, the undersigned, feeling convinced that the present difficulty attending all money transactions arises from a groundless panic, and being desirous to avert the incalculable inconvenience and evil that must arise from a want of public confidence, do hereby declare our entire conviction of the stability of the banks at Newark, and our determination to accept their notes in all payments." To this the principal townspeople and gentry appended their names.

At the close of the session on the 31st May 1826, the royal intention was announced, to dissolve without delay the present Parliament. The principal question before the public was that of Catholic emancipation, but the dissolution "had no reference to the state of political parties, but simply had regard to the convenience of the time for a general election." At Newark, the candidates were Mr. H. Willoughby and General Sir William Henry Clinton, who sought re-election, and Mr. S. E. Bristowe, of Beesthorpe Hall. The two first named issued brief addresses, announcing themselves as staunch defenders of "our excellent constitution in Church and State." Mr. Bristowe published a longer statement, wherein he said, that having read and thought a great deal about the unfortunate condition of the country, he felt quite convinced that nothing but a fair and equitable representation of the people, joined to an unalterable determination to retrench the lavish expenditure of the public wealth, could ever replace England in that glorious situation which she had hitherto held among the nations of the globe. Mr. Bristowe went on to say that he considered the state of the Corn Laws unjust and unreasonable; the Game Laws were productive of endless misery and abuse, and the condition of the poor in

Ireland called for alleviation. The final abolition of slavery would also have his support, though, in the interests of all parties, he should feel bound to act with caution. The contest was a vigorous one, and some disturbances occurred when the excitement was at its height. The polling took place on the 9th and 10th of June, and ended in the re-election of Messrs. Willoughby and Clinton, by considerable majorities, the numbers being as follows:—Willoughby 647; Clinton 595; Bristowe 296. In consequence of the excited state of the town, the ceremony of chairing the successful candidates was deferred. In their address, the re-elected members said they had foregone the ceremony and the celebration of the day of election by the usual festivities in deference to the opinion of their friends, founded upon circumstances to which they alluded with reluctance, and which they hoped had their origin principally among those who were not electors of the borough. They renewed their pledge of undiminished attachment to Church and State, and expressed their readiness to promote the local and individual interests of the electors. Mr. Bristowe attributed his disappointment to the lateness of his canvass, and expressed a hope that another time the borough would return at least one member of independent principles. On the 25th July Mr. Bristowe's friends invited him to a dinner at the Castle and Falcon, and made preparations for his reception. At half-past two o'clock they set out from the Beaumont Cross, headed by a band of music, and marched to Kelham, to meet him there. Blue streamers were carried, bearing the words "Bristowe and liberty," and other similar inscriptions, a long procession paraded the principal streets, the church-bells rang merrily at intervals, and an address was delivered by Mr. Bristowe in the market-place, opposite the Clinton Arms Inn.

A meeting of persons interested in the question of the proposed repeal of the Corn Laws, was held at Newark on the 17th January 1827. The Rev. W. Clay of Westhorpe presided, and it was unanimously resolved "that it was the duty of every man whose welfare depended upon the prosperity of the farming interest to stand forward and oppose any alteration in the present system that should not fully recognise and provide for the protection of the home grower." A petition to Parliament was adopted.

The strenuous efforts which the Roman Catholics were putting forth to obtain their share of political power and influence gave rise to meetings in various parts of the country. Amongst the petitions presented to Parliament was one from the mayor, aldermen, and upwards of 1100 of the inhabitants of Newark, expressing an opinion that such power could not be conceded without a violation of those securities which were absolutely necessary to the preservation of the Protestant Establishment. The petitions were forwarded in March to the Duke of Newcastle and Mr. Henry Willoughby for presentation to both Houses. A marked difference of opinion on the subject, however, prevailed in the town, for, in the *Nottingham Review*, we find the following given as the concluding portion of an address from Newark in favour of concession. "We humbly beseech your Majesty, that their emancipation be unaccompanied with mortifying restrictions, which, under the name of securities, would only serve to depreciate the gift in the estimation of the receiver. The love of your subjects for the best of monarchs, and their invincible attachment to the happiest of constitutions, are the strongest securities; our everlasting gratitude will erect around your sacred person such bulwarks as no enemy whatever shall be able to overthrow."

The remains of his Grace the Duke of Gordon lay in state at Newark on Friday, June 20, 1827, on their way to Gordon Castle in Banffshire. The family titles take date from 1736, when the first Earl of Huntly was created; the title of Marquis of Huntly was conferred by James VI. in 1599, and that of Duke of Gordon in the county of Banff in 1684, by Charles II.

A tremendous storm of thunder and lightning accompanied with heavy rain passed over the town and district early on the morning of Monday, 30th July 1827. A traveller on the road from Newark to Lincoln described the trees, hedges, and fields as appearing to be enveloped in one vast sheet of fire. At Claypole the church was struck by the electric fluid and damaged. Several trees were split near the town, and a woman at Collingham lost her life. At Gotham four sheep were killed.

Another meeting in reference to the proposed repeal of the restrictions affecting Roman Catholics was held at the town-hall on Monday, the 5th May 1828, when a petition was adopted praying Parliament not to remove those barriers which the wisdom of their ancestors erected around the Protestant constitution. The petition received 775 signatures.

Lieutenant-General Sir W. H. Clinton, Bart., having accepted the stewardship of the Chiltern Hundreds, a new writ for Newark was moved for in the House of Commons on Monday, Feb. 23, 1829. On the Wednesday morning following the intelligence reached Newark, and in the course of the day Mr. Michael Thomas Sadler (see engraving), of the firm of Messrs. Fenton, Sadler, and Sadler, linen merchants of Leeds, issued an address offering himself as a candidate to represent the town.

The causes which led to the resignation of the gallant general and to the appearance of Mr. Sadler in the field are thus stated:—"The Cabinet had determined to concede to the fullest extent the Catholic claims. Sir William H. Clinton, who held the appointment of Lieutenant-General of the Ordnance, was thereupon informed that the 'open question' system was at an end, and that all persons holding office would be required to support the line of policy now adopted by the Government. But Sir William had been returned by the borough on a positive declaration of his hostility to the Romish demands. He had repeatedly voted against those claims, and had already in the present session been entrusted with a petition signed by nearly the whole of his supporters in the borough deprecating the proposed concession. It was therefore clearly impossible that he should obey the word of command in this instance. The alternative of course was taken.

He applied for the Chiltern Hundreds, and gave back his trust with a clear conscience into the hands of his constituents. There was probably no individual in the kingdom who felt more acutely on the subject than Sir William's noble relative, the Duke of Newcastle. Being the largest proprietor in the borough of Newark, the inhabitants had always been accustomed to seek for one of their representatives among the members of his Grace's family; and it was in this way that Sir William Clinton's connection with the borough originated. On learning his relative's intention, his Grace, feeling the most lively interest in the discussions which were just opening in the House of Commons, and remembering Mr. Sadler's speech at the Pitt Club Anniversary of the preceding May, wrote to him for the purpose of recommending him to proceed to Newark without delay, and there to announce himself a candidate for the vacant seat. After much hesitation, he decided on responding to this call, and at once set out for Newark, where he found that letters had already been received by the persons most in his Grace's confidence desiring their best exertions in his favour."[1]

In the address which Mr. Sadler issued on his arrival at Newark, he stated that his political principles were strictly those of the Revolution of 1688—in short, he was an humble but determined advocate of that sacred cause, Protestant ascendency. His views regarding the true policy of the country were thus expressed:—"It is the duty of the legislature carefully to watch the public expenditure, in order to enforce economy so far as is consistent with the efficiency of our necessary establishments; to encourage with foreign nations a liberal interchange of the products of industry, where it would be mutually beneficial, to the exclusion of a competition where it would be ruinous; to proceed with all real and practical reforms, which do not impair the character and destroy the integrity of the constitution; and finally, to preserve that tranquillity and peace, domestic and foreign, at every sacrifice save that of national honour, which is so necessary to reinforce the energies and heighten the prosperity of the country." As soon as the address was issued, Mr. Sadler proceeded actively with his canvass, and had every prospect of an unopposed return.

On Saturday morning, however, a letter was received from Mr. Thomas Wilde, "one of his Majesty's counsel learned in the law" (see engraving), intimating his intention of contesting the borough, and at three o'clock in the afternoon he arrived, accompanied by his nephew. A large concourse of people lined the road from Newark to Balderton, to which place Mr. Wilde's friends drove to meet him. At Balderton the horses were taken out of the learned serjeant's carriage, and the populace drew it down Balderton Gate, through the Newark market, and round by Castle Gate and Lombard Street, to the Castle and Falcon Inn, from the windows of which

house he addressed the electors. He dwelt upon the "unconstitutional conduct"

[1] *Life of Mr. M. T. Sadler*, pp. 111-112.

of the Duke of Newcastle in endeavouring to impose upon the borough a nominal representative with whom they were utterly unacquainted," and said that he relied on "the independent spirit of the people, and not the patronage of a peer." The Hon. Mr. Law also spoke. The nomination on Monday, March 2, was a scene of great excitement. Mr. Sadler's friends displayed pink flags, on one of which was printed, "Sadler and no Popery." Serjeant Wilde's party were attended by a band of music, and blue flags were exhibited inscribed with "Now or Never," "Wilde and Independence," "Freedom to Newark," and similar mottoes. The vicar, the Rev. W. Bartlett, proposed Mr. Sadler, stating that the writings of that gentleman and his speeches had met with his entire approbation: Mr. Sadler would maintain the Protestant principles—the principles of freedom—and he felt it his duty as a minister, to stand forward and support him. Mr. John Orme Norton seconded the nomination. Mr. Kelk proposed Serjeant Wilde, and the nomination was seconded by Mr. J. L. Simnitt, who stated that he had received a discharge from the duke for having voted for Mr. Bristowe in a previous contest. In his speech, Mr. Sadler emphatically denied that he was a nominee, and said he offered his best services, unshackled in his opinions, without remuneration or reward. Serjeant Wilde commented at length on Mr. Simnitt's discharge, which he read to the meeting, and urged the electors to "rescue Newark from thraldom." In regard to Catholic emancipation, though strongly opposed to Popery, he could not see the danger of admitting Catholics into the House of Commons, as the few were more likely to be converted by superior numbers, than superior numbers by the few.

During his speech the back part of the hustings gave way, having been broken by men climbing up from behind. Several persons were thrown down, and those in the rear being compelled to press forward, the mayor was slightly hurt. The show of hands was in favour of Serjeant Wilde, and a poll was demanded by Mr. Robert Caparn, legal adviser for Mr. Sadler. The polling forthwith commenced, and at the close of the day, Serjeant Wilde had received 138 votes, and Mr. Sadler only 47. The learned serjeant jubilantly told his supporters that the sky was indisputably blue, to which Mr. Sadler wittily retorted he would take the liberty of prognosticating that the setting of to-morrow's sun would change its colour to red. The prediction was fulfilled; for at the close of the second day, Mr. Sadler had a majority of 73. On the third day the polling continued with unabated vigour. There were occasional interruptions on account of disputed votes, and one in particular occupied a considerable time. It was occasioned by a man named Mason coming up to poll, and on being asked the usual question, "Whom do you poll for?" replied "Serjeant," and then made a long pause. While he was thus wavering, the poll-clerk repeated the names of the candidates; and as soon as the word "Sadler" was mentioned, the man said "Ay, Sadler," and the poll-clerk immediately recorded the vote for Mr. Sadler. The man, however, said, "He did not mean that! he meant Serjeant Wilde;" but this was objected to by Mr. Sadler's party. Much confusion and disputation ensued, Mr. Sadler's party claiming the vote, and the serjeant's party insisting the vote was theirs. The mayor was ultimately requested to attend in the hall to decide the matter, and a long discussion took place. The mayor insisted that no person should speak while he examined the poll-clerk respecting the vote in dispute—he then put several questions to him, and upon receiving the clerk's answers, was going to decide upon it, when Mr. Serjeant Wilde interfered. He told the mayor he would never allow a returning officer to do that which he had not allowed a judge, viz. to decide a matter before he had heard both sides, and requested the mayor would hear the statement of the man himself. The man was appealed to again, who said, "He wished to vote for Serjeant Wilde." Mr. Sadler came forward, and said he would agree to the proposition made by the Hon. Mr. Law, viz. for the vote to be entered Serjeant Sadler, making a special memorandum of it. (Laughter.) Mr. Serjeant Wilde would not agree to the proposal, as there was no such candidate. Mr. Sadler then, by the advice of his friends, withdrew his opposition to the vote, and it was recorded for Mr. Serjeant Wilde.

In the warmth of his zeal and the confusion of the moment, a gentleman (brought into the hall in a sedan) voted for the candidate to whom he was opposed. On the usual question being put, "Whom do you vote for?" he hesitated to answer; but, on the name of Serjeant Wilde being mentioned, he signified his assent, and the vote was registered accordingly. Immediately after, he found he had voted for the Blue Candidate, and was not a little affected. About four o'clock a circumstance occurred which gave rise to great mirth. An elderly female, dressed in a "Newark blue frock" and man's hat, presented herself with great confidence to the poll-clerks to tender her vote, to the infinite amusement of the gentlemen on both sides. The following dialogue ensued :—

Mr. W. Wilde. What is your name?
Woman. John Bettinson.—(Peals of laughter.)
Mr. W. Wilde. Where do you live?
Woman. Water Lane.
Mr. W. Wilde. What are you?
Woman. Waterman.
Mr. W. Wilde. Whom do you poll for?
Woman. Blue.—(Considerable laughter.)
Mr. — Sadler. I object to this vote.
Mr. Wilde. Upon what grounds?
Mr. — Sadler. Because he is not a man.—(Great laughter.)

The incident naturally caused much merriment, and the advocate for "Universal Suffrage" walked off, without a muscle of her countenance having been affected during this ludicrous scene.

The poll closed on Friday March 6, having lasted five days, when the numbers were for Mr. Sadler 801, for Serjeant Wilde 587. The number of electors polled was thus 1388; the number unpolled 288. At the declaration which took place from the hustings, in the presence of an immense crowd, Mr. Sadler affirmed that he went to Parliament as free and unembarrassed as any man that ever entered the House.

Serjeant Wilde maintained, however, that they had only sent his friend's body to Parliament, his mind and his understanding being at Clumber. On Saturday Serjeant Wilde sent presents of tea to many poor families and widows, and had a procession through the town; subsequently there was a tea and dance, the ladies being adorned with blue ribbons, and the men wearing blue frocks. Mr. Sadler had gone at once to London, to attend to his Parliamentary duties, but his friends distributed tickets for tea, during the ensuing week. In less than a fortnight after his election, Mr. Sadler made a speech in the House of Commons, on the subject of removing the disabilities affecting Roman Catholics, contending that neither the established constitution of the country, nor the oaths they had taken, permitted them to throw open the doors of the House to the admission of Popery. The speech, for a maiden effort, was unusually clever, and created somewhat of a sensation. The *Morning Post* described it as "one of the most able, luminous, and comprehensive speeches heard within the walls of Parliament since the ever-memorable days of the immortal Pitt." The *Standard* made a similar assertion, and the *Morning Journal* said it made a powerful and favourable impression on the House.[1] On the 24th July a dinner was given to celebrate Mr. Sadler's return.

On Good Friday 1829 the town was visited with a fearful thunderstorm. To many who were assembled at the time in the parish church, to commemorate the crucifixion of their Lord, it brought to remembrance the awful period, when He was suspended on the cross, and the veil of the temple rent in twain. Just as the Rev. J. Wild, the curate, was finishing the reading of the second lesson for the day, a vivid flash of lightning darted through the church, and for a moment seemed to envelope the place in one complete blaze. At the same instant the rev. gentleman was deprived of his eyesight. He was conducted out of the desk, and medical aid immediately procured, but although a glimmer of light returned for a short interval, total darkness succeeded.

In September a memorial signed by one hundred and eleven persons was presented to the mayor, stating that discharges had been given in the name of the duke to upwards of 200 electors who had declined voting for Mr. Sadler, and requesting his worship to call a public meeting of the inhabitants to consider the subject. The mayor declined to accede to the request, whereupon the requisitionists issued notices themselves. The meeting took place on Monday morning the 5th of October (1829) in a large booth erected in an open space adjoining the Independent Chapel. A report was presented entering at great length into the subject, and stating that notices of the meeting had been sent both to the duke and to Mr. Sadler. His Grace in reply wrote a letter dated Clumber, September 28, wherein he said, "If I rightly understand the object of the requisitionists it is to assert the cause of freedom and independence. No man on earth values both more than I do, but as I respect the liberty of others, so must I demand that others shall not attempt to interfere with the freedom and independence which are my right as well

---

[1] The bill subsequently passed the House by a majority of 178.

as theirs. According to my interpretation of the advertisement, you meet to deliberate upon an interference between my tenants and me. Is it presumed, then, that I am not to do what I will with my own? or that I am to surrender my property and the inherent rights belonging to it into the hands of those who desire to deprive me of it? This is the simple question to which I answer, Whilst the laws of England exist and are respected, I shall permit no clamour nor threats, nor even force itself, to deter me from doing as I may think fit with my own property." His Grace then went on to advise them not to enter into an unjust crusade. He asserted that he and his ancestors had always been ready and prominent benefactors of Newark, and that, whilst they were the constant and best friends of the town, they naturally looked for entire confidence and grateful co-operation—not an assumed distrust and faithless disunion. The letter of his Grace was much commented upon at the meeting, and subsequently in the public press. The resolutions carried included the adoption of a petition to Parliament against a renewal to the duke of the lease of the Crown lands.

During the severe winter of 1829-30 above £800 were subscribed in Newark for the distressed poor, the list being headed by £100 from the Duke of Newcastle, and a similar sum from Lord Middleton. The borough members gave £50 each, and Serjeant Wilde £50. Meat was sold at 1½ per lb.; and flour at 8d. per stone. 120 blankets were purchased, and after being marked, were lent to the very aged, the bedridden, and the sick, to be returned on the 1st of July following, at the townhall. The number of families relieved with meat and flour was 975; of individuals averaging 3½ persons to each ticket issued, 3412. The scale of distribution was as follows:—Meat: to a man and his wife, 3 lbs.; to a single person 2 lbs.; to each child in a family, ½ lb. Flour: to each person entitled to purchase 2 lbs. of meat, ¼ stone; to ditto 3 or 4 lbs. of meat ½ stone; to ditto 5 or 6 lbs. of meat, ¾ stone; and to ditto 7 or 8 lbs. of meat, one stone of flour.

On the 1st of March 1830 Mr. P. B. Thompson, the member for Dover, presented to the House of Commons the petition from Newark, praying that the leases of Crown lands in the borough, granted to the Duke of Newcastle, might not be renewed. He stated that the borough contained about 2000 houses, and about 10,000 inhabitants. The duke held about 200 houses in his own right, and exercised an influence over individuals owning an equal number. If a gentleman wanted a field, or a tradesman a garden, he might obtain it from the Crown lessee, but he must, as the duke put it, give him "his entire confidence and grateful co-operation." The lease, besides houses, consisted of 960 acres of valuable land about Newark, besides chief rents, tolls of markets and bridges, and influence over certain charities. It was first granted in 1760 to the Earl of Lincoln, by the Duke of Newcastle, then Prime Minister, for £36 per annum; it was renewed in 1815, and was then raised to £2060 per annum. After commenting upon these statements, and affirming that, with one exception, every tenant of the Crown lessee who voted for the unsuccessful candidate received notice to quit, Mr. Thompson moved for a select committee, to make further inquiries. Viscount Lowther argued against it, contending that the petitioners had made many inaccuracies in their allegations. Twelve houses and 26 cottages were all the Crown owned in Newark, and when the lease was renewed, in addition to the increased rent, a fine of £2500 was paid. Mr. Fynes Clinton said the electors of Newark were in number 1388; the tenants on the Crown lands having votes were 74, seven of whom voted for Serjeant Wilde; yet it was stated that the 74 Crown tenants decided the election in favour of Mr. Sadler! After some remarks from Sir F. Burdett, Mr. D. W. Harvey, Lord Howick, and Mr. Hobhouse, Mr. Sadler said he admitted that in cultivating a connection with the town of Newark he had sought the aid of persons possessing local property and influence, but he had likewise canvassed the inhabitants, and had borne with him a commanding majority of unbiassed votes, which no efforts of power could have withheld. He denied that he was exposed to the operation of sinister influences, and could most conscientiously say that the noble duke, who had acted in a humane and considerate manner in all his transactions with the town, had left him to pursue his own line of conduct. Mr. Secretary Peel said it had been assumed that seven persons out of seventy had been deprived of their houses, but no one had proved the allegation that menaces had been applied. It was only fair that property should have its just influence, whether it belonged to a peer or a commoner. The lease would expire in 1836, and there was no cause for interference. There voted for a select committee 61 against 194, majority against, 133.

Whilst the excitement consequent on the election and petition was still rife, another contest arose. The demise of King George the Fourth having caused a dissolution, a writ for the election of two members for Newark was received on Sunday night, 25th July (1830), and on the following Monday the mayor and the town-clerk, attended by the officers, proclaimed the same from the balcony of the town-hall, and appointed the Monday following, at nine o'clock, for the election to take place. The candidates were Messrs. Willoughby and Sadler, who sought re-election, and Mr. Serjeant Wilde. Some weeks prior to the reception of the writ, the two first-named gentlemen had issued their addresses, and they appear to have commenced a personal canvass on the 28th of June. The friends of Serjeant Wilde announced that as soon as the last honours had been paid to the remains of the late king, the serjeant would solicit the suffrages of the people. Accordingly, on July 17, he made a public entry. He was met by a procession at the clump of trees on the Balderton Road, and escorted to the borough by a large number of persons. The procession was on an elaborate scale, the principal features being the following:—Mr. Hitchins, as the preserver of public tranquillity, mounted on a charger, richly caparisoned, wearing the sword of justice, three parts sheathed, and in his right hand an olive branch, emblem of peace; a band of drummers and fifers; discharged tenants bearing their discharges upon escutcheons dressed with crape; a deputation from the serjeant's committee, walking in rows of four, with blue silk sashes; Mr. Bristowe jun., Mr. Charles Pearson, agent, and Mr. Kelk; a "Dove" bearing an olive branch, borne before eighty daughters of voters, dressed in white with caps decorated with blue ribbons, and each carrying a basket of flowers; Serjeant Wilde on horseback; Captain Turner's band from Grantham; two freemen bearing the Bible, "Crown and Constitution," two freemen bearing a large gilt key, on a blue cushion; the sisters of the Female Friendly Society, dressed in white, preceded by the mother; the children of the discharged tenants; a golden eagle with wings extended; sons of voters, with cockades and sashes, numerous banners with mottoes, and some of the voters' wives dressed in white, walking arm and arm between the rows of the voters.

The procession passed through the principal streets of the town. From the window of the Blue Bell the crowd was addressed by Serjeant Wilde, and he subsequently spoke from the Castle and Falcon. The serjeant's address was issued two days after, and from this time the contest proceeded with the greatest vigour. The serjeant's friends determined to honour him with another public entry on the 30th July, and made arrangements accordingly.

The friends of the "united interest," not to be outdone, prepared for Messrs. Willoughby and Sadler a public reception on the 31st. They stated that "they had not thought it requisite hitherto to have recourse to pomp and pageantry, but an enthusiastic feeling having sprung up, surmounting all objections, there would be a triumphant entry—no laboured programme, no studied arrangement of banners, no theatrical effect, no wooden Bibles, no gilt keys, no golden eagles, in short, no artificial aids to excitement; but all in the good old English style." The candidates were therefore met on the Muskham Road between the Newark and Muskham bridges, an immense concourse escorting them in the following order:—The senior elector of the borough (Mr. George Brown, aged eighty-eight) led the procession on horseback, followed by twenty other equestrians; then a band of music playing lively marches; next several pink flags; then several hundred voters on foot six abreast, decorated with pink ribbons; followed by a great crowd of the fair sex; the band occasionally relieved by a party of drummers and fifers; after which about three hundred horsemen wearing pink favours at their breasts, and velvet rosettes of the same colour on the bridles of their horses, flanked by a large and excellent band, and more flags; the candidates (supported by their agents, Mr. George Hodgkinson, and Mr. Robert Caparn) followed in an open chariot drawn by six grey horses, the postillions wearing pink velvet jackets; the carriage of John Handley, Esq., filled with the ladies of his family, and upwards of twenty other carriages, most of them drawn by four horses, the postillions all wearing pink jackets alike, brought up the rear of a procession nearly a mile in extent. The candidates addressed the crowd from the windows of the Clinton Arms Hotel.

The nomination took place on Monday, August 2. Mr. Willoughby was proposed by Mr. W. F. Handley and seconded by Mr. James Thorpe; Mr. Sadler was proposed by Mr. Alderman Fillingham and seconded by Mr. John Orme Norton.

Serjeant Wilde was proposed by Mr. S. Bristowe and seconded by Mr. T. H. Massey. The show of hands was declared to be in favour of Mr. Willoughby and Serjeant Wilde, whereupon a poll was demanded for Mr. Sadler. The polling lasted from the 2d to the 6th of August inclusive. The numbers were for Mr. Willoughby 775 ; Mr. Sadler 746 ; Serjeant Wilde 652. The successful candidates issued a brief address of thanks. The serjeant maintained that the power of the duke had again triumphed over the wishes of the people.

The all-absorbing topic of Parliamentary Reform continued meanwhile to be anxiously debated. Under the pressure from without, Sir R. Peel and the Duke of Wellington made way, in December 1830, for the administration of Earl Grey. When Parliament re-opened in February (1831), the declaration of the new Ministry, pledged to retrenchment and reform, was eagerly awaited. Lord John Russell introduced the scheme of the Government in a plain, calm speech. It was proposed to disfranchise 60 boroughs, having each less than 2000 inhabitants ; to take one member from each of 47 boroughs with less than 4000 inhabitants ; and to reduce the representatives of one borough from four to two. Seven unrepresented towns were to return two members each ; and twenty smaller towns were to return one each. The total number of members in the House was to be reduced from 658 to 596. Instead of the old rights of election in boroughs, a household franchise of £10 was substituted. When Lord John Russell read the names of the boroughs to be disfranchised, wholly or in part, there was great excitement in the House. Lord Eldon wrote :—" There is no describing the amazement this plan of reform has occasioned." The debate which ensued lasted for seven nights. On the 21st the bill came on for a second reading, and after two nights' discussion, was carried by a majority of one. On the 18th of April the House went into committee, when General Gascoyne moved that " it was not expedient to diminish the number of representatives for England and Wales." Mr. Sadler seconded the resolution in an eloquent speech. The vote was taken at a late hour on the 19th, and the resolution was carried by a majority of eight. The Ministry resigned, and there was an appeal to the country.

The election for Newark took place at the commencement of May. The candidates were Mr. W. F. Handley, Serjeant Wilde, and Sir Roger Griesley. Mr. Sadler, though he had greatly increased his reputation as an orator, did not present himself for re-election. His biographer says :—"The excitement prevailing, rendering the result of an election at Newark extremely doubtful, and Mr. Sadler's parliamentary friends being desirous of placing his return to the next Parliament beyond a doubt, he was advised by the same noble friend who had originally been the means of introducing him to the legislature, to become a candidate for Aldborough in Yorkshire ; a borough in which his Grace possessed the natural influence of large property, and for which Mr. Sadler continued to sit during the remainder of his parliamentary career."[1] In the absence of Mr. Sadler, who had proved so success-

---

[1] *Life of Mr. M. T. Sadler*, p. 263. In August 1831 Mr. Sadler brought under the notice of Parliament the question of Poor Laws for Ireland ; in October he pleaded the cause of the English agricultural labourers ;

ful an antagonist, Serjeant Wilde secured a substantial majority. The voting took place from April 28 to May 3, and the numbers at the close of the poll were Wilde, 849; Handley, 746; Griesley, 678. The serjeant received no less than 599 plumpers, and on the 20th of May he was presented, by his friends, with a piece of plate, in acknowledgment (as the inscription testified) of "the splendid ability, unwearied perseverance, and disinterested public spirit" he had displayed in maintaining the two previous contests of 1829 and 1830.

Parliament opened on the 14th of June (1831), and the reformers being now in a majority, a Bill passed the Commons in September by 345 votes against 236. In October, after five nights' debate, the measure was rejected by the Lords. Great excitement ensued; there were riots at Derby, and at Nottingham a frantic mob set fire to the castle. At Newark, it is creditable to record, strict order prevailed, and the re-introduction of the Reform Bill was quietly awaited. In December Lord John Russell brought in the new measure, and it passed its second reading on the 18th. It reached the Lords in March (1832), and in committee of that House the first principle of the measure—the disfranchising of boroughs—was rejected. The Ministry resigned, but were induced to resume office on obtaining the king's permission to create such a number of peers as would ensure the passing of the Act. On the 4th of June the Bill passed by a majority of 84, and three days later, having received the royal assent, became the law of the land. On the 16th of August Parliament was prorogued, and politicians were everywhere active in view of the inevitable dissolution.

At Newark three gentlemen presented themselves before the electors. Mr. Handley and Serjeant Wilde, who had both supported the Reform Bill, sought re-election, and a third candidate appeared in the field, a stripling who, having passed through a successful university career, had bidden farewell to his college, and turned his thoughts from scholastic to parliamentary distinctions. The young politician who made his *début* at Newark on this memorable occasion was Mr. W. E. Gladstone. On the invitation of the Duke of Newcastle, whose influence was still powerful within the borough, he had consented to undertake a contest, and to see if one of the seats, at the disposal of the electors, could not be secured in the Conservative interest. As might naturally be expected, the undertaking at such a conjuncture was very arduous. The reformers, having just emerged from a successful struggle, were on the popular side, and not only were they supporting a winning cause, but their favourite candidate, Serjeant Wilde, was an eloquent and experienced politician, who knew how to turn every favourable point to good account. To make headway against such a formidable opponent required a combination of influence and ability, and involved

in March 1832 he introduced his bill for regulating the labour of children and young persons in the mills and factories, and became a champion of the ten hours' movement; in December 1832 he was an unsuccessful candidate for Leeds, and his parliamentary career closed. Mr. Sadler was a Fellow of the Royal Society, and the author of several works. He died at Belfast, July 29, 1835, aged fifty-five, and his remains rest in Ballylesson churchyard. There is a statue in memory of him in Leeds Parish Church, and another in the Museum of the Leeds Philosophical Society, Park Row.

a contest of far more than ordinary severity. "It was," says Mr. Gladstone, "altogether a peculiar period. Wilde, who had to fight for Parliamentary existence, was a powerful antagonist, with a squad of lawyers from London to support him. It happened, on the other hand, that it was my first introduction to the world, from which I had been unusually severed. The excitement of my first canvass was such as I have never undergone before or since." The remarkable position which Mr. Gladstone has attained has contributed still further to render the election in question a very notable one, and we make no apology, therefore, for entering into the details at some length.

The circumstances under which Mr. Gladstone came to Newark to enter the arena of party warfare, and the first experiences he met with as a politician, we have the privilege of stating in his own words. The right honourable gentleman thus writes us:—"I had been well known to Lord Lincoln at Eton and Oxford. I received the duke's invitation, sent through my father, at Milan, in July 1832, and came home in consequence. The duke was invited by the Red Club to act. I arrived at Newark, after a journey of forty hours, from Torquay, at midnight, on Monday, 24th September 1832, an absolute personal stranger, aged twenty-two. Next morning I set forth on my canvass, with band, flags, and badges of every kind, and perhaps a thousand people. The constituency was, I think, 1570 in number, and the duke's tenants rather under one-fourth. But his influence was my sole recommendation. It was, however, an arduous contest, extending, with intermissions, over three months. The canvass was old-fashioned and thorough. We went into every house, be it what it might. Even paupers were asked for their 'influence.' 'Oh, sir!' replied one old woman, 'my influence is but very shallow.' A clergyman recently come entered another old woman's house with a memorandum book, which happened to be red. 'God bless you, sir,' she cried ; 'I wish you success.'"

On the 8th of October a large meeting of the Red Club was held for the purpose of presenting to the president (Mr. E. S. Godfrey) a silver ticket, in acknowledgment of the services he had rendered to the Conservative cause. The presentation was made on behalf of the Club by Mr. Robert Caparn, the secretary, and Mr. Gladstone, who was present, delivered an address. The favourable impression which Mr. Gladstone had produced during his brief sojourn may be gathered from the statement of one of the papers, that his election had already become regarded as beyond a doubt. In a publication, called *Old England*, it was asserted that there were 650 voters connected with the Red Club, every one of whom had promised to support Mr. Gladstone. Other electors, to the number of 240, had also promised, and there were 100 who had made no promise at all. The matter was, therefore, settled. "And who," asks the paper, "is Mr. Gladstone? He is the son of a friend of Mr. Canning, a Liverpool merchant. He is not more than twenty-four years of age (22), but he has won golden opinions from all sorts of people, and promises to be an ornament to the House of Commons."

The political subjects discussed with the candidates in the course of the vigorous and complete canvass that took place, were principally those of reform and the abolition of slavery. A large number of the electors were ardent supporters of the anti-slavery agitation, and a Society had been formed in the town to assist the noble philanthropists who desired to sweep the abominable system of slavery from British territory. Each of the candidates was promptly and rigidly questioned by the Society as to the views he entertained, and had either to give decisive and satisfactory replies, or to submit to a stern opposition. Mr. Gladstone was appealed to while his candidature was in progress; but for a full explanation of his opinions the Society and the electors had to await the issue of his election address. This was published, not at the commencement, but at the completion of his canvass. It was dated October 9, and ran as follows :—

To the Worthy and Independent Electors of the Borough of Newark.

Gentlemen—Having now completed my canvass, I think it my duty as well to remind you of the principles on which I have solicited your votes as freely to assure my friends that its result has placed my success beyond a doubt. I have not requested your favour on the ground of adherence to the opinions of any man or party, further than such adherence can be fairly understood from the conviction that I have not hesitated to avow that we must watch and resist that uninquiring and undiscriminating desire for change amongst us, which threatens to produce, along with partial good, a melancholy preponderance of mischief, which I am persuaded would aggravate beyond computation the deep-seated evils of our social state, and the heavy burthens of our industrious classes; which, by disturbing our peace, destroys confidence and strikes at the root of prosperity. This it has done already, and this we must, therefore, believe it will do.

For a mitigation of those evils we must, I think, look not only to particular measures, but to the restoration of sounder general principles—I mean especially that principle on which alone the incorporation of Religion with the State in our constitution can be defended; that the duties of governors are strictly and peculiarly religious, and that legislatures, like individuals, are bound to carry throughout their acts the spirit of the high truths they have acknowledged. Principles are now arrayed against our institutions, and not by truckling nor by temporising, not by oppression nor corruption, but by principles they must be met. Among their first results should be sedulous and especial attention to the interests of the poor founded upon the rule that those who are the least able to take care of themselves ought to be most regarded by others. Particularly it is a duty to endeavour by every means *that labour may receive adequate remuneration*, which unhappily, among several classes of our fellow-countrymen, is not now the case. Whatever measures, therefore, whether by the correction of the Poor Laws, allotment of cottage grounds, or otherwise, tend to promote this object, I deem entitled to the warmest support, with all such as are calculated to secure sound moral conduct in any class of society.

I proceed to the momentous question of slavery, which I have found entertained among you in that candid and temperate spirit which alone befits its nature, or promises to remove its difficulties. If I have not recognised the right of an irresponsible Society to interpose between me and the electors, it has not been from any disrespect to its members, nor from any unwillingness to answer their or any other questions on which the electors may desire to know my views. To the esteemed secretary of the Society I submitted my reasons for silence, and I made a point of stating those views to him in his character of a voter.

As regards the abstract lawfulness of slavery, I acknowledge it simply as importing the right of one man to the labour of another; and I rest it upon the fact that Scripture—paramount authority on such a point—gives directions to persons standing in the relation of master to slave, for their conduct in that relation; whereas, were the matter absolutely and necessarily *sinful*, it would not regulate the manner. Assuming sin is the cause of degradation, it strives, and strives most effectually, to cure the latter by extirpating the former. We are agreed that both the physical and moral bondage of the slave are to be abolished. The question is as to the *order* and the order only; now Scripture attacks the moral evil *before* the temporal one, and the temporal *through* the moral one, and I am content with the order which Scripture has established.

To this end I desire to see immediately set on foot, by impartial and sovereign authority, an universal and efficient system of Christian instruction, not intended to resist designs of individual piety and wisdom for the religious improvement of the Negroes, but to do thoroughly what they can only do partially. As regards immediate emancipation, whether with or without compensation, there are several minor reasons against it, but that which weighs with me is, that it would, I much fear, exchange the evils now affecting the Negro for others which are weightier—for a relapse into deeper debasement, if not for bloodshed and internal war. Let *fitness* be made the condition of emancipation, and let us strive to bring him to that fitness by the shortest possible course. Let him enjoy the means of earning his freedom through honest and industrious habits, thus the same instruments which attain his liberty shall likewise render him competent to use it; and thus, I earnestly trust, without risk of blood, without violation of property, with unimpaired benefit to the negro, and with the utmost speed which prudence will admit, we shall arrive at the exceedingly desirable consummation, the utter extinction of slavery.

And now, gentlemen, as regards the enthusiasm with which you have rallied round your ancient flag, and welcomed the humble representative of those principles whose emblem it is, I trust that neither the lapse of time nor the seductions of prosperity can ever efface it from my memory. To my opponents my acknowledgments are due for the good humour and kindness with which they have received me, and while I would thank my friends for their zealous and unwearied exertions in my favour, I briefly but emphatically assure them that if promises be an adequate foundation of confidence, or experience a reasonable ground of calculation, our victory *is sure*.—I have the honor to be, gentlemen, your obliged and obedient servant, W. E. GLADSTONE.

Clinton Arms, Newark, Tuesday, Oct. 9, 1832.

"This address," writes Mr. Gladstone, "certainly justified criticism. It was that of a warm and loyal Tory, who was quite unaware that it contained in it the seeds of change to come. I remember that the duke, a singularly kind, honourable, and high-minded man, questioned me a little about the passage on the wages of labour, which seemed somewhat to startle him. But he was far too delicately considerate to interfere."

After the address had been issued and discussed, Mr. Gladstone and his friends continued to be busy amongst the voters. The right hon. gentleman tells us the activity was great, and the speaking incessant. "I never," he once declared, "worked harder or slept so badly, that is to say, so little."[1] Early in December there was a meeting of more than ordinary consequence. We transcribe the following from the *Nottingham Journal*:—"On Tuesday morning, December 4, 1832, a special general meeting of the Newark Red Club was held at the Old Assembly Rooms (now the Drill Hall, Carter Gate), at half-past eleven o'clock, for the purpose of affording an opportunity to the ladies of Newark of presenting a most elegant and appropriate flag to the members of that Society. The large room was crowded to excess with the ladies of Newark and neighbourhood, and the Red band attended and played appropriate tunes. The flag, composed of rich silk and adorned with a device similar to that borne upon the Red

[1] *Vide* letter to Mr. Godley of Newark, in *Daily News*, 16th November 1876.

Club ticket, was most beautiful. After the secretary (Mr. Robert Caparn) had opened the meeting by stating the object for which it was called, one of the ladies stepped forward, and handed to the president (Mr. E. S. Godfrey) and members of the club an address, speaking of the pleasure which it afforded them to witness the growth of the Red Club, as the good old Red cause was 'the only means by which the welfare and lasting prosperity of an ancient borough, which has so often been distinguished for its loyalty, can be safely secured.' The address proceeded :—' We beg sincerely to congratulate you on the circumstance of your energies being first called into action to secure the return to Parliament of so estimable a character as Mr. Gladstone, a gentleman whose high mental endowments and excellency of heart fully qualify him, in our estimation, for filling the important and responsible situation in which you are desirous—and we feel the greatest confidence in your being able—to place him.' After some cordial words of thanks from the president, Mr. Gladstone said his worthy friend Mr. Godfrey had rightly attributed to him a desire to express his gratitude for the complimentary notice of him, which had been read in a manner adequate to the occasion. He only wished that Mr. Godfrey could likewise have endowed him with the power. But often as he had had to lament his inability to meet their kindness, he never felt it so strongly as he did at that moment. He agreed with his worthy friend as to the exclusion of all wearying and irritating topics, and would confine himself to the immediate subjects of their meeting—the flag and the ladies—he would rather say, the ladies and the flag. He heartily rejoiced in the extraordinary countenance given to their cause by the gentler sex, not only because they reaped honour and encouragement from their smiles, not only because they graced by their presence those ruder assemblages, but for one yet weightier reason. The Red party were stigmatised as the friends of tyranny, and as men determined to grind the faces of the poor, to trample on the necks of the oppressed, and, in particular, to perpetuate the thraldom of the negro. Now, he was willing to allow their opponents all possible latitude of thought and expression, but he really did think it was a little presumptuous that they should arrogate to themselves a monopoly of the feelings of justice and humanity, when they, the supposed oppressors, numbered among their friends so preponderating a portion of that sex which was pre-eminent for acuteness of conscience and gentleness of feeling. He therefore maintained that such an assumption was but little credible, and appealed to the presence of the ladies as a positive argument in their favour. Now he was proud, not only of their principles, not only of his supporters, but of the very emblem chosen for their cause. He could not forget that they were marshalled under England's favourite ensign, and it would lead them to victory. They all knew how the red flag of England had ever been the symbol both of national moderation and of national power; how it had waved during the awful period of revolutionary war 'as a signal of rallying to the combatant, and of shelter to the fallen.'[1] When every throne of the Continent had crumbled into dust beneath the tyrannous strength of France, England

---

[1] These words are quoted from a speech of Mr. Canning.—W. E. G.

remained the last refuge of civilisation, and the last hope of mankind. Our countrymen did not dally, or compromise, or concede, but they stood boldly in the breach, firm in their reliance in Almighty Power, and so that refuge became sure, and that hope proved triumphant. The blast which tore every other ensign to tatters served only to unfold their own, and display its beauty and its glory. Nor would that meeting, comparatively trivial though it might seem to some, be void of its purpose and its use if it served to combine more strongly in their minds the cause in which they were at present engaged with those indelible recollections associated with the red flag of England. No man could say whether the civil struggles into which the country was entering might not prove even more arduous than those in which she had been heretofore engaged. They knew that they stood on the brink of an awful war—a war of principles; and he lamented the insanity of ministers in tempting Providence, as it were, to its commencement. But when it had once commenced, who could tell what shore would not re-echo its thunders, what distant land it would not clasp in its desolating embrace? Dishonour now threatened their ancient flag. It had been unfurled for bloodshed in a cause where no necessity urged, where no insult ever had been offered, nay, admitting even the false and frivolous cause of glory as a motive for war, what glory was to be gained in a war of sixty millions against two?'[1] They would all join him in the humble, and earnest, and anxious prayer that this unhappy enterprise might speedily be terminated. In the meantime they would look forward with confidence to their own struggle, and, conscious of the justice of the end, would be scrupulous, also, in their choice of the means. When that struggle had been closed, when they could congratulate themselves on having attained an object they had made their own, and when he, for his own part, hoped to have the high honour of being himself chosen the representative of an independent and upright constituency; in that day of exhilaration no man who was present, and, certainly, least of all the humble individual who had then the honour of addressing them, would forget who had cheered them through the contest, and were ready to crown them at its close, or would undervalue his obligations to the ladies of Newark. Mr. Tallents followed, stating that Mr. Gladstone's return was beyond the possibility of doubt. After some remarks from Mr. Thomas Godfrey, the band struck up 'God save the King,' which was sung by the whole company with a simultaneous burst of loyalty and harmony, and the meeting separated, highly gratified at the events of the morning."

It wanted now but a week to the election. On either side every nerve was being strained. The Whigs were anxious to break through the ducal influence, as well as to further their principles. The Conservatives, who had been somewhat alarmed at the success of the reform movement, wished to give a check to the "indiscriminate spirit of change," by the return of Mr. Gladstone. But though the excitement grew great, the interest of this memorable election was chiefly local. In the

[1] In answer to a question as to what these observations refer to, Mr. Gladstone says:—"I think they refer to the measures of war adopted, without a declared state of war, against Holland by France and England. But I do not think the report (of this speech) was corrected by me."

country generally no unusual importance attached to the issue of the contest. The franchise in Newark had not been enlarged by the Reform Bill, and the only change that had been made in the electoral lists had been done in the new process of registration.[1] There was, therefore, nothing of an experimental nature involved, and those fiery orbits, commonly known as "the eyes of the country," did not glare upon the borough. The nomination was fixed for Tuesday, December 11, and of the proceedings we have the full details preserved in the Nottingham papers. It will be seen that the slavery question was in the fore-front throughout, and that Mr. Gladstone, who was represented by the Whigs as the friend of the planters, had to run the gauntlet of hostile questioning.

At ten o'clock the gates of the area under the town-hall were thrown open, and the space was speedily crowded. A platform rising step above step was fixed at one end of the place, but there were no seats of any kind, nor the least accommodation for writing. For seven hours was every one obliged to stand, closely crowded together in this dark place, without the possibility of getting away. The usual preliminary proceedings being gone through, the mayor, Mr. James Thorpe, took the oath as returning officer, and entreated a patient hearing for all. Mr. James Prior Lacey, in a neat speech, proposed their late representative and fellow-townsman, William Farnworth Handley, Esq., as a proper person to be elected their member, who had been indefatigable in the discharge of his parliamentary duties. Mr. Thomas Withers seconded the nomination. Mr. Mills proposed the re-election of their excellent friend, Mr. Serjeant Wilde, as the advocate of civil and religious liberty, of every practicable reform in the Church, State, and Law, and above all as a friend to the unconditional emancipation of the negro. Mr. Thomas Gillson, in seconding this proposition, entered upon a long eulogium of Mr. Serjeant Wilde's parliamentary conduct, and of his qualifications to represent them. (Cheers, and cries of "Now for the slave-driver.")

Mr. Edward Smith Godfrey said that he differed most essentially from the opinions formed of the two gentlemen already proposed, and he should therefore propose a third candidate. He admitted that we were now arrived at a most important crisis, and though he himself had not been favourable to the Reform Bill, it behoved him and all others to be obedient to it, as the law of the land. He rejoiced that they were arrived at a new era in the elections for Newark: the united interest was at an end.[2] (Cheers.) He had long disapproved of that union, and he was consoled for the last defeat by its having put an end to the coalition. He should not enter upon the comparison of the merits of his candidate with those of the late members (cries of "He's a lad"), but as it was necessary to bring to the great council, talent, information, honesty, and good moral conduct, he could, on these grounds, recommend Mr. William Ewart Gladstone, who had, at no distant period, received the highest honours of one of our great seminaries of learning. Mr. Godfrey then entered upon the subject of colonial slavery to some extent.

Mr. Dyson, in a short panegyric, seconded the nomination. Before the candidates addressed the electors, it was intimated that several persons wished to ask questions of the candidates; several of the latter querists, however, made speeches to introduce their questions, which prolonged this part of the business more than two hours.

Mr. Gillson asked Mr. Gladstone why he had not made his appearance at a meeting, which had been called by the electors in the market-place, to hear the opinions of the candidates?

Mr. Gladstone said, Because it was refused to be held by the constituted authorities, who had the only legal right of convening it.

---

[1] *N.B.*—The franchise was progressively contracted by the extinction of the Scot and Lot voters.—W. E. G.
[2] The united interest was, I *think*, Mr. Manners Sutton's interest, and that at this time it went with Mr. Handley, who had not a great deal to give to the Reds in return.—W. E. G.

Mr. Gillson asked, What was the reason of his finding his way to Newark, and by what means he had been invited?

Mr. Gladstone said he was aware that the name of the Duke of Newcastle would be flung in his teeth, but he would reserve that for his address; he came by the invitation of the Red Club, to whom he was not personally known, nor was it likely, as he had not courted publicity; but the Red Club had applied to the Duke of Newcastle to know if he could recommend a fit and proper person to represent Newark in Parliament; application was in consequence made to him (Mr. Gladstone.) That was a short and intelligible history of the affair.

Mr. Gillson asked if he was not to be considered as the nominee of the Duke of Newcastle; and being asked by Mr. G. to define the word "nominee," said he meant one sent by the Duke of Newcastle to be pushed down the throats of the electors.

Mr. Gladstone said that, according to such a definition of the word, he was no nominee, because he was not forced upon the electors against the will of any one.

Mr. Kelk having expressed his disgust at hearing the family of the Gladstones were traffickers in human *flesh*,[1] and his disapprobation of quoting Scripture for political purposes, as Mr. Gladstone had done in his addresses—a practice which had done more injury to religion than all the infidels and atheists that ever lived—asked if he knew of such a passage in the Bible as that of Exodus xxi. 16, "He that stealeth a man and selleth him," etc., and whether his father was not a dealer in human flesh?

Mr. Gladstone said he was perfectly aware the crime of man-stealing was condemned in Scripture.

Mr. Kelk then proceeded to ask a series of questions as to recent alterations of the laws, and whether Mr. Gladstone wished to re-enact the former statutes, when he alluded to a return to "sounder general principles," in his address of the 9th of October. Ought a man be put to death for forging a one pound note the same as for killing a fellow-creature?

Mr. Gladstone said that he did not allude to the principles of late years, but he had in his mind the manly and God-fearing principles of our forefathers, two hundred years ago. [Mr. Kelk; What! when they burnt witches?] As to the recent subject alluded to by Mr. Kelk, he was friendly to the repeal of the Test and Corporation Acts, and to Catholic emancipation, of which his father had been a uniform supporter; he was extremely glad to see the difference made between forging a £1 note, and taking the life of a fellow-creature in punishment, and was not for taking human life, except in cases of extreme necessity. As to the subject of the Reform Bill, he thought very few men would wish to retrace their steps, without making a trial of the measure, but he should simply say, that had he been in Parliament, he should have opposed it.

Mr. Andrews said, that as Mr. Gladstone had not thought proper to answer the questions proposed by the Newark Anti-Slavery Association, he would now put them. This part of the subject occupied a very considerable period, and turned almost into a debate on the slavery question, which would occupy some pages to detail. The following may be considered as the most important parts of it :—

Mr. Gladstone conceived that man could have a property in the labour of his fellow-man, but could have none in his soul, nor a right to interfere between it and revelation; he considered the state of things in the West Indies most desirable to be got rid of, but the people of this country were culpable for the former inactivity on this subject; he thought it vain to grant the slaves political rights till they were changed in their nature by the influence of Christianity, but he regretted the hostility of many planters to this being done. On the subject of the missionaries, he would answer in precisely the same words as the learned serjeant, by affording every facility to Christian instruction being diffused ; nor was he opposed to any denomination nor to any individual missionaries, except such as deviated into political questions. The sum of his argument against immediate emancipation was, that the plantations would cease to be cultivated, and the supply of sugar would be then from the Brazils,

---

[1] We inquired on what rumour this assertion could be founded? Mr. Gladstone replied :—"My father was a West Indian proprietor; and it may have been supposed that he had been concerned in the slave trade (only abolished twenty-five years before), which he had not.

where slavery reigned, with the slave-trade in all its horrors. He would not entertain the question of compensation, to the prejudice of the rights of the slave, though he considered that the question of remuneration should be inquired into.

A long discussion ensued upon this subject, to prove, on the one hand, that in San Domingo and Antigua, where slaves had been emancipated, that good order and prosperity had followed, and on the other, to show that the reverse had taken place.

Mr. Kingdom, after an eulogy on the diffusion of information, inquired whether Mr. Gladstone would support the repeal of the taxes on knowledge?

Mr. Gladstone said, before he consented to the reducing of any tax, he must be aware whether it could be spared; he understood by "taxes on knowledge" the newspaper duties; the press was an engine of immense power for good or evil, over which it was necessary for the law to exercise some control; the offences of newspaper editors were not capable of reparation in the same manner that other offences were; he considered the bail required from newspapers to be useful,[1] and he confessed that the appetite for political controversy should be restricted; he was therefore friendly to the principles of the present laws.

Mr. Bonifant said, that no town had done more to forward the cause of the ballot than Newark, which had called forth the sympathies of every constituency in the kingdom; he wished to know Mr. Gladstone's opinions on that matter?

Mr. Gladstone said he did not mean to pledge himself, but his conviction certainly was most decidedly opposed to the vote by ballot.

Mr. Kelk asked whether Mr. Gladstone would wish to have a repetition of this amusement annually, triennially, or septennially, and whether he could give any reason why the page of a newspaper should be stamped, and that of the Bible be exempt?

Mr. Gladstone said he preferred septennial parliaments; and he would not subject the Bible to a stamp duty, because it was exclusively the object of good, while the newspaper required restriction, not being of divine origin, and being of doubtful good.

Mr. Handley and Serjeant Wilde having spoken, Mr. W. E. Gladstone commenced his address by adverting to the arguments which had been adduced on the subject of slavery, and proceeded with much energy and animation, but the patience of the people was exhausted, and they would hear no more, drowning his voice with hooting and clamour. The *Journal* says:—"The lateness of the hour (half-past four o'clock in the afternoon), the weariness of standing for nearly seven hours in a dense crowd, without the possibility of change of position, were circumstances, both to Mr. Gladstone and to those around him, sufficient to render it anything but desirable to be detained with another three hours' speech, which, from Mr. Gladstone's talents, we were far from thinking was not possible, though we, at the same time, thought it highly improbable. How far a man possessing the discernment of Serjeant Wilde could feel justified in occupying the attention of the meeting to the entire prevention of his competitor to reply [for had not the hour been so late he would have been heard], we cannot easily conceive; but according to our view, we think there was a manifest injustice, whether it was an error of head or heart." The mayor then put the question to a show of hands; for Mr. Serjeant Wilde an immense majority appeared, for Mr. Handley about one-fourth of those present, and for Mr. Gladstone very few except his friends on the hustings. The mayor declared the show of hands to have fallen on the two former, and a poll was demanded for the latter.

In the course of the afternoon, an attack took place upon the banners of the Reds, three out of four being thrown down and torn in pieces. The polling commenced at nine o'clock on the Wednesday morning in the five districts, and from the first the friends of Mr. Gladstone pressed forward, and placed him at the head of the poll. His majority was greatest about noon, when he was 100 ahead of

[1] We may mention that until recent years no newspaper could be published unless the proprietors were registered and could find sureties.

Mr. Handley, and more than 200 before Mr. Serjeant Wilde; in the course of the day, this was gradually reduced. The great strength of the Reds lay in the Market-place district, No. 1, and the Lombard Street, No. 3; that of the Blues in Carter Gate, No. 4, and a small majority in Castle Gate, No. 5. At the time that the poll was closing, a great number had assembled in the market-place, and the bands and banners of the three separate parties were all near the town-hall. A warm discussion began relative to the alleged coalition and renewal of the "united interest," and a tumult ensued; the Reds speedily retreated, and escaped with the loss of one flag, but the yellow and orange banners of Mr. Handley were surrounded, and after a long struggle, were one after another thrown down and torn to pieces. The numbers at the close of the day were, Gladstone 690; Handley 618; Wilde 564. In reference to other incidents, Mr. Gladstone writes:—"After the close of the poll, and in pitch dark, I spoke to a friendly crowd out of the window of my sitting-room in the Clinton Arms. A man on the outer line of the crowd flung at me a stone nearly the size of an egg, which entered the window within a foot of my head. He was seen and laid hold on. I understood at the time that he arranged the matter by voting for me on the next day."

On Thursday it was evident that the division of the borough into districts had enabled the great majority of the available electors to poll the first day, and the voting proceeded very slowly. In the morning the friends of Mr. Serjeant Wilde made a push, and approached nearer to Mr. Handley, but in the after part of the day fell back to their former situation, and, at the close, the majority against the Serjeant was still further increased. The numbers, when the polling ended, were, Gladstone 882; Handley 793; Wilde 719. "Thus," says a Whig journal, "Newark is again returned under the nomination of the Duke of Newcastle, or, to use the language of the Red Club, the recommendation of his Grace."

The results of the elections throughout the country were, however, greatly in favour of the Reform party. Only 147 Conservatives found seats in the House. The first work which the Government undertook was the passing of a Coercion Bill for Ireland. Next came the Irish Church Temporalities' Bill. It dealt with the revenues and position of the Church in Ireland, and was opposed by Mr. Gladstone. Then followed the abolition of slavery in the British Colonies. In the debate upon this great scheme Mr. Gladstone made a maiden speech on the opposition side, not condemning the measure, but urging a due regard for the interests of the planters. In the course of his address the honourable member dealt with the personal question which had been alluded to in an exaggerated form at the nomination at Newark, and which had been adverted to in a milder fashion by one of the speakers during the debate. He said:—"About six years ago the estate of Vreedon Hoop came into my father's possession. Out of 550 slaves, 140 were aged and infirm persons. In the year 1826 the crops were exceedingly small, amounting to only 257 hogsheads of sugar for 370 persons, which gives an average of 1100 to 1200 lbs. for each slave. In anticipation of the decrease which, from the state of affairs, it was foreseen would take place, about 200 additional persons were placed upon the estate, raising the entire number to 570. I find that the slaves on the estate ordinarily finish their work by 3 P.M., and, as regards punishment, I have a letter in my pocket, dated 20th of April, which shows that, since the month of January—a period of nearly four months—the punishments on that property of 450 negroes amounted to—just one." The honourable gentleman then went on to refer to the great question of slavery, pointing out how delightful it would be to all involved, if a system, "begun in atrocious crime and grevious sin," could be brought to a satisfactory termination. He trusted, however, that the opinions of those who denied the claims of West Indian planters would not be adopted by the House. "I should bewail such an event, not most for the sake of the West Indian, but for the sake of the slave, for the sake of this House, and of this mighty empire, which stands erected, not upon the basis of physical force, but on the foundation of superior intelligence, superior honour, and superior virtues. I should deplore such a catastrophe as the signal of downfall, and as the harbinger of an universal desolation."

Of the personal appearance of Mr. Gladstone at this period, and of the favourable impression he had created by his oratory and his earnestness, we have an account given us by Lord Albermarle. His lordship writes:—"One evening, on taking my place (in the House of Commons), I found, on his legs, a beardless youth, with whose appearance and manner I was greatly struck. He had an earnest intelligent countenance, and large, expressive, black eyes. Young as he was, he had evidently what is called the ear of the House, and yet the cause he advocated was not one likely to interest a popular assembly—that of the planter *versus* the slave. I had placed myself behind the Treasury bench. 'Who is he?' I asked one of the ministers. I was answered, 'He is the member for Newark! a young fellow who will some day make a great figure in Parliament.' My informant was Geoffrey Stanley, then Whig Secretary of the Colonies, and in charge of the Negro Emancipation Bill, afterwards Earl of Derby; and the young Conservative orator was William Ewart Gladstone —two statesmen who each subsequently became Prime Minister and leader of the party to which he was at the time (1833) diametrically opposed."[1]

From this period Mr. Gladstone took an active part in the business of Parliament. In December 1834 Sir Robert Peel was called upon to form a Ministry, and in 1835 there was an appeal to the country. The date of the election for Newark was Monday, January 5th, on which day two bands paraded the streets, and the bells rang merry peals. Mr. W. F. Handley having withdrawn, there was no contest. At ten o'clock Mr. Gladstone and Serjeant Wilde, with their friends, mounted the hustings in front of the town-hall, and about 4000 persons were in the market-place.. Mr. Gladstone was proposed by Mr. T. S. Godfrey, and seconded by Mr. Branston; Serjeant Wilde was proposed by Mr. Massey, and seconded by Mr. Dobbs. The election over, mutual congratulations ensued, and the mayor, after expressing his gratification at the good feeling which prevailed, requested that the shops

[1] Lord Albermarle's *Fifty Years of my Life*, ii. 309.

might be closed after twelve o'clock, and the day observed as a general holiday. Mr. Gladstone, in his address, denied that the Government were opposed to all change, and contended that they were the only true Reformers. Serjeant Wilde affirmed that the return of his amiable and talented friend, without hostility, was a satisfaction to the Blues, and that the duke, if he came to the town, would be met with a smile of kindness from all parties. At two o'clock the "chairing" of the newly-elected members took place. Bands were playing, flags flying, and bells ringing, and the scene was of the most animated description. Mr. Gladstone's procession set out from the Clinton Arms Inn, and Serjeant Wilde's from the Castle and Falcon. The gay red chair which Mr. Gladstone occupied was fixed over the springs of a four-wheeled carriage, drawn by six beautiful grey horses, with riders dressed in red silk jackets. Serjeant Wilde's chair was imposing, but, says a Conservative paper, with an amusing tinge of prejudice, "it had nothing like the appearance of the Red chair." The Serjeant was also drawn by six fine greys. The principal streets were paraded by both members, and the processions meeting in Kirk Gate, mutual congratulations took place. The bands struck up "God save the King," and the multitudes cheered enthusiastically.

The times generally were exciting, and parties were balanced with tolerable evenness. When the House met on the 9th February (1835), 618 members, besides 4 tellers, divided on the question whether Sir Charles Manners Sutton should be re-elected Speaker, or the Right Honourable James Abercromby be chosen to fill the chair. The votes for Abercromby were 316, for Sutton 306. Towards the close of March, the subject of the temporalities of the Church of Ireland was reintroduced by Lord John Russell. In April his lordship carried his motion, that any surplus revenue of the Church, not required for the spiritual use of its members, should be applied to the general education of all classes of the people without religious distinction. The division was fatal to the Ministry, and Lord Melbourne assumed office.

On Thursday, 11th June 1835, a dinner, in honour of Mr. Gladstone, was given in the town-hall. Nearly 200 gentlemen attended, including many of the clergy and influential gentry of the neighbourhood. The hall was profusely decorated, among the inscriptions on the banners being "Gladstone and the Conservative cause," "The king beloved by all his people," and "Unity is strength." A conspicuous feature in the decorations was the red flag which had been presented by the ladies. The chair was taken by Mr. T. S. Godfrey, supported by Mr. Gladstone on his right, and Sir R. Howe Bromley, Bart., on his left. Mr. W. E. Tallents presided at the left hand table, supported by Mr. John Gladstone, father of the honourable member, and the Mayor of Newark presided at the right hand table, supported by Mr. Robertson Gladstone. In response to the toast of his health, which was drunk with great enthusiasm, Mr. Gladstone spoke on the subjects of municipal and Church reform, urging that the duty of the Conservatives was to maintain the union of Church and State. There were, he said, two classes, called

Conservatives and Reformers. The latter cried aloud against institutions, and the Conservatives contended for the existence of them, and in no small degree they were more the foes of abuse than those who arrogated to themselves the name of Reformers. True Conservatives hated abuse, as it gave strength to their enemies, but the false Reformers loved abuse, because it supplied them with a weapon against the institution itself. The honourable gentleman spoke strongly in favour of maintaining the Irish Church, contending that they could not disturb its property without breaking public faith and affecting private honour. The speech throughout is described in the report as having been delivered in a style of most impressive and graceful oratory. Mr. Gladstone senior also spoke. After alluding to the pleasure which that day's proceedings afforded him, the venerable old gentleman, in a tone of deep feeling, expressed his gratitude to God for having imbued the mind of his son with those principles which, he might be allowed to say, had always governed his conduct, and would, he hoped, abide with him through life, for he might truly state that they had grown with his growth, and ripened with his maturer years. He had no doubt that those principles would always animate his son in the discharge of his duties, and that he would esteem it a sufficient reward if he could secure their approbation.

On the 20th of June 1837 William IV. died at Windsor Castle, and at the general election, consequent on the accession of Queen Victoria, Mr. Gladstone and Serjeant Wilde were again elected for Newark, without opposition. The proposed alienation of the revenues of the Irish Church had naturally drawn much attention to the question of Church establishment, and had aroused considerable controversy. Various publications dealt with the subject, and one of the most widely read and valuable contributions to the debate was a work written by Mr. Gladstone, published at the close of 1838. It was entitled, "The State in its relation with the Church, by W. E. Gladstone, Esq., Student of Christ Church, and M.P. for Newark," and it dwelt upon the advantages of maintaining a close union between Church and State. Amongst those who opposed the teaching of the book, whilst admiring its author, was Lord Macaulay. In the *Edinburgh Review* for April 1839 his lordship contributed a lengthy criticism, going fully, and with his usual ability, through many of the points raised. In his opening sentences he thus adverts to the member for Newark :—" The author of this volume is a young man of unblemished character and of distinguished parliamentary talents, the rising hope of those stern and unbending Tories, who follow, reluctantly and mutinously, a leader whose experience and eloquence are indispensable to them, but whose cautious temper and moderate opinions they abhor. It would not be at all strange if Mr. Gladstone were one of the most unpopular men in England. But we believe that we do him no more than justice when we say that his abilities and his demeanour have obtained for him the respect and good-will of all parties. His first appearance in the character of an author is, therefore, an interesting event ; and it is natural that the gentle wishes of the public should go with him to his trial." His lordship then proceeds to rebut Mr. Gladstone's views. Mr. Gladstone did not, we believe, reply to his lordship's criticism, but addressed to his critic a kindly note, cordially acknowledging the candour and single-mindedness which had been exhibited. "How much this letter pleased Macaulay is indicated by the fact of his having kept it unburned, a compliment which, except in a single instance, he never paid to any of his correspondents."[1] Mr. Gladstone's views upon the whole question were more publicly stated in the autumn of 1868 in *A Chapter of Autobiography*, published at that time.

Towards the close of 1839 Serjeant Wilde, Mr. Gladstone's colleague in the representation of Newark, accepted office as Solicitor-General. He issued his address seeking re-election on the 23d of November, and two days later a Conservative candidate entered the field in the person of Mr. Frederick Thesiger. On hearing that opposition to his candidature was contemplated, the learned serjeant published a longer manifesto, in which he pointed to his parliamentary efforts, and remarked that there were few members of any party who did not at that moment deem his return important to the maintenance of the constitutional efficiency of Parliament itself. "Whatever credit," he said, "may be claimed for the representatives of larger boroughs than Newark the high talents of my amiable coadjutor, so justly estimated by all parties, secure you from any disparaging comparison, so far as he is concerned; and I humbly venture to hope that I also have not given occasion for such comparison." The learned serjeant stated that his political tenets had undergone no change, and expressed his conviction that the electors would return him again to his sovereign, "carrying to the foot of the throne the confirmation of her gracious choice." Mr. Thesiger, in his address, which is dated from the Clinton Arms, November 26, stated that the contest was one of principle, not of personal feeling against the Solicitor-General, and the question at issue was, Did the learned Serjeant represent the sentiments of the constituency of Newark or not? He (Mr. Thesiger) believed that he did not, and the electors would now have an opportunity of determining the question, and of showing whether they approved or disapproved of the policy of the Government. The canvass was thereupon vigorously prosecuted on both sides, and a large number of addresses and squibs was issued. It was not until January 16, 1840, that a writ was moved for in the House of Commons, and by this time the excitement had been worked up to a high pitch. The nomination took place on Thursday, January 23, and by nine o'clock in the morning the whole borough was astir. The Red bands and banners might be seen proceeding one way, and the Blue band and banners accompanied the Solicitor-General another. On the hustings Serjeant Wilde was supported by Sir Robert Heron, Bart., of Shelton, M.P. for Peterborough, Mr. John Handley, Mr. T. H. Massey, and many others, wearing blue ribbons. Mr. Thesiger, with his pink ribbons, was supported by the Earl of Lincoln, M.P. for South Notts., Mr. T. S. Godfrey, Mr. William Waldegrave, Mr. Pelham Clay, and a large number of gentlemen. The Solicitor-General was proposed by Mr. John Handley, and seconded by Mr. Thomas Hackett Massey; Mr. Thesiger was pro-

[1] *Life and Letters of Lord Macaulay.*

posed by Mr. T. S. Godfrey, and seconded by Mr. Thorpe. The Solicitor-General spoke from half-past nine until a quarter to twelve o'clock. Mr. Thesiger made a brief speech amid considerable interruption. During the address several red herrings and penny loaves were thrown at him, but he bore it all, says the report, "with great good humour, declaring that the loaves and fishes, as of yore, fed a multitude." A struggle for the Red banners followed, but they were hoisted, amid cheers, into the windows of the Clinton Arms, and so preserved. The show of hands was in favour of Serjeant Wilde. The polling took place on the 24th and 25th, amid the greatest excitement. A better illustration of the severity of the contest cannot be afforded than that which the numbers present, the official declaration of the poll being as follows:—Wilde 541; Thesiger 532. The small majority of nine by which Serjeant Wilde was returned gained for the contest the title of the "number nine" election, a definition which it still retains.

Of the subsequent careers of the two talented lawyers who were thus pitted against each other, a few particulars will not be out of place. Sir Thomas Wilde shortly afterwards terminated his connection with Newark, and sat for Worcester from July 1841 (in which year he was made Attorney-General) until July 1846, when he was raised to the bench as Chief Justice of Common Pleas. In July 1850 he obtained the highest legal honours, being appointed Lord Chancellor, and raised to the peerage by the title of Lord Truro. He resigned office in February 1852. His death took place at his town residence in Eaton Square, in November 1855, at the age of seventy-three years. Mr. Thesiger was the son of Charles Thesiger, Collector of Customs in the Island of St. Vincent, West Indies. He was born in London 1794. He was called to the bar of the Honourable Society of Gray's Inn in Michaelmas Term 1818, and went the home circuit, in which he took a leading position, and was made a King's Counsel in 1834. A month after his rejection at Newark he was elected M.P. for Woodstock, which borough he represented in the House of Commons until 1844. In that year he was elected M.P. for Abingdon, and sat for that borough until 1852, when he was returned for Stamford, retaining his seat as its member until he was made Lord Chancellor in 1858. Sir Robert Peel had in 1844 chosen Mr. Thesiger for the vacant solicitor-generalship, and in the ensuing year he succeeded Sir W. Follett as Attorney-General, retiring in the following year on the downfall of Sir Robert Peel's ministry. He was recalled to the same office by Lord Derby in 1852, and when his lordship succeeded to power again in 1858, Sir Frederick became Lord Chancellor with the title of Lord Chelmsford. In Lord Derby's third administration he again sat on the woolsack, but when Mr. Disraeli became premier in 1868 he gave place to Lord Cairns. He died on the 5th of October 1878. That both the candidates in the celebrated election of 1840 should have reached the high dignity of Lord Chancellor is at least a remarkable if not an unprecedented occurrence.

A short time after the close of the contest the Conservative Society, which held its meetings in the front room of the Saracen's Head Hotel, decided to have portraits painted of Mr. Gladstone and also of Mr. Thesiger. The work was entrusted to Mr. W. H. Cubley, artist, of Newark, and that gentleman proceeded to London, where he had sittings from Mr. Gladstone at Carlton House Terrace, and from Mr. Thesiger at Bryanstone Square. The portraits were finished in due course, and on being hung upon the walls of the Club-room a special meeting of the Society was held, at which speeches appropriate to the occasion were delivered. Mr. Gladstone, to whom the portrait had been shown, expressed his satisfaction at the way in which the work had been executed, and Mr. Cubley was also complimented at the meeting on the efficient result of his efforts. At the dissolution of the Society, which took place some years later, the portraits were offered for sale, and were purchased by Mr. Alderman Branston, in whose possession they now remain. By the courteous permission of that gentleman we have obtained an engraving of the portrait of Mr. Gladstone, which we here present. Those who remember the right honourable gentleman during his early career at Newark describe him as being a fine, healthful-looking man. His figure was somewhat slim; his face was plump, with scarce a line upon it; his cheeks possessed the ruddy glow of health; his hair was dark and plentiful; his eyes were large and expressive; and his countenance was animated with an ever-varying expression. There is little in the portrait which we copy to remind one of Mr. Gladstone  as he now is. The massive forehead and earnest eyes are the same, but in almost every other respect the face has undergone those marked changes which are brought about by the irresistible instrumentality of time and care.

In May 1841 Lord John Russell announced the intention of the Government to propose a fixed duty on corn, instead of the sliding scale which was then in operation. In the budget it was proposed to keep the existing duty on colonial sugar, and lower it on foreign sugar. The debate upon the proposition developed into a discussion of the great subject of free trade, which had been warmly agitated for two or three years. Lord John Russell argued for free trade in corn, and Lord Palmerston contended that it was impossible a great country like England could go on protecting without other countries following its example. The game was one which two could play at. The trade which was free was the trade that was carried on with intelligence, enterprise, and success. The majority, however, was averse to an alteration. On a vote being taken in reference to sugar duties, the Government were defeated by thirty-six. On the 27th May Sir Robert Peel moved a resolution expressing want of confidence in the Ministry, and after one of the most extensive debates on record, it was carried by a majority of one. The Ministry resigned, and the dissolution of Parliament was announced on June 23. At the general election which succeeded, the candidates for Newark were Mr. Gladstone, who sought re-election, and Lord John Manners on the Conservative side, and Mr. Thos. Benjamin Hobhouse, a free trader. The Conservatives had the ducal influence again in their favour, and the Manners Sutton interest also came in with Lord John Manners. Mr. Hobhouse's chances were still further lessened by the fact that he did not arrive in Newark until the day before the nomination. This event took place on Monday, June 28. Mr. Gladstone was proposed by Mr. T. S. Godfrey, and seconded by Mr. Branston. Lord John Manners was proposed by Mr. G. Hodgkinson, attorney, and seconded by Mr. Harvey Readitt. Mr. Hobhouse was proposed by Mr. T. H. Massey, and seconded by Dr. Dobbs. After the nomination Mr. Gladstone addressed the assemblage in a long speech, in which he attempted to prove "that a large loaf was a great evil, and free trade a new curse." So states the *Nottingham Review*. Mr. Gladstone states, "It is evidently an exaggerated description, but I took my stand with Sir. R. Peel and my leaders in favour of protection." Mr. Hobhouse defended what Mr. Gladstone had termed the "shuffling administration," and argued in favour of a repeal of the Corn Laws. At daybreak on Tuesday the town was in that state of excitement which usually exists at an election. A volunteer band arrived from Claypole, and several fights took place, particularly in the market, where a waterman named Lilley was badly injured. At the close of the poll the numbers were, Gladstone 633; Manners 630; Hobhouse 394.

The result of the elections generally was antagonistic to the free trade principle, and Sir Robert Peel became Prime Minister, with Mr. Gladstone as Vice-President of the Board of Trade and Master of the Mint. The right honourable gentleman arrived in Newark on 9th September 1841 to seek re-election after accepting office. He was heartily welcomed, merry peals being rung on the church bells, and his supporters cheering lustily. Attended by a band and with flags flying, Mr. Gladstone proceeded with his canvass. The nomination took place on September 14. Mr. Gladstone, accompanied by the Earl of Lincoln, was escorted to the hustings, and there being no opposition, was declared duly elected. He and his friends subsequently paraded the town, and in the evening dined together at the Clinton Arms Hotel. We pass on to the 3d of April 1845, when Sir Robert Peel brought forward the plans of the Government respecting the improvement of the Roman Catholic College of Maynooth, and proposed a grant of £30,000 a year to be secured by Parliament. "It was," says Mr. Gladstone, "supported by me as an independent member," but by many it was stoutly resisted. Churchmen and Dissenters held meetings denouncing the measure as a renunciation of the Protestantism under which the empire had flourished. The Bill, however, was carried by considerable majorities. Meanwhile the anti-protectionists had continued their efforts, and Sir Robert Peel had been coming over to their side. At a Cabinet Council in December, Sir Robert laid before his colleagues a scheme having for its ultimate object the extinction of protective duties. Lord Stanley and the Duke of Buccleuch signified their inability to support such a measure, and in consequence of the Cabinet dissensions Sir Robert tendered his resignation. Lord John Russell was sent for, but failed to form an administration, and Sir Robert was requested to continue in office. The announcement of Sir Robert's free trade proclivities created some excitement. On December 31 a meeting of the members of the Nottinghamshire Agricultural Protection Association was held at Newark to consider the subject. About 500 agriculturists attended. Resolutions were passed pledging the meeting to support the amount of protection which the law afforded. A memorial was adopted expressing the utmost pain and astonishment that Sir Robert Peel and a Conservative Ministry had resolved to lower protection. "We are convinced," said the memorialists, "that we cannot exist as farmers without protection, and we are determined to uphold it by every means in our power." The Duke of Newcastle, who had been appealed to for an opinion, had previously written expressing his hearty desire to co-operate with the Society in so important a cause in such a perilous emergency.

In the meantime Lord Stanley resigned, and Mr. Gladstone, who had retired from office some time previously, succeeded him as Secretary of State for the Colonies. The Duke of Buccleuch would not at once decide upon resigning. The other members of the Cabinet declared their determination to support Sir Robert in the course he intended to pursue. When Parliament assembled in January 1846, the Prime Minister announced his policy. He confessed that his views on the subject of protection had undergone a change. He did not consider that there was any reason to feel humiliated and abashed in avowing this change, but he should feel humiliated if, his opinions having undergone a change, he had shrunk from the avowal of it by the fear of a charge of inconsistency. He then went on to state that he could no longer defend the Corn Laws, and to announce the various duties he proposed to repeal. In the usual course of things, Mr. Gladstone, having accepted office, had to be re-elected either by his old constituents or by others. Being at direct variance with the Duke on so important a subject as that of free trade, he determined not to appeal to Newark again. On Wednesday the 7th of January an address from him was distributed in the borough. He stated that he should on several accounts have been desirous of giving the borough an opportunity of pronouncing judgment on his public conduct by soliciting a renewal of the trust which he had already received on five successive occasions, and held during a period of thirteen years. But as he had good reason to believe that a candidate recommended by local connection to the favour of the electors might ask their suffrages, it became his painful duty to announce his retirement on that ground alone from a position which had afforded him so much honour and satisfaction. His vindication, whenever and wherever it might be offered, would be raised upon no merely apologetic plea, but upon the assertion that he had acted in obedience to the clear and imperious calls of public obligation, and with the same purpose which he had ever sought to follow of promoting the interests of the community, and of all classes of which it was composed. The *Journal* having expressed an opinion that Mr. Gladstone's Maynooth vote had something to do with his retirement, the right honourable gentleman wrote to the editor of that paper as follows:—" Allow me respectfully but positively to assure you that neither the Maynooth College Bill, nor any commercial policy of the Cabinet, past or prospective, nor any other public question, has had the smallest effect in determining my conduct. The motives by which I have been influenced have been exclusively of a personal character." That the Duke of Newcastle felt strongly on the subject of protection is evidenced by his conduct in the case of South Nottinghamshire. His son the Earl of Lincoln espoused Sir Robert Peel's principles, whereupon the Duke opposed him, and he was ousted from his seat, Mr. T. B. T. Hildyard being returned in his place. The candidate who was nominated for Mr. Gladstone's seat at Newark was a Mr. Stuart. An effort was made by the free traders to induce Mr. Gladstone to contest the borough, but it was not open to him in honour to comply with the request. He had to seek return elsewhere, and his political connection with Newark was at an end.

In order to preserve as far as possible the continuity of the foregoing account, we have not interposed any references to other local events occurring between 1832 and 1846. There were, however, several of a noteworthy character that ought not to pass entirely unnoticed in these Annals. We find that on the evening of Friday, December 21, 1832, the town was lighted with gas for the first time, when crowds of people paraded the streets, admiring the lights and the improved appearance which they gave to the shops.

On the 25th March 1836 there was a terrible storm of thunder and hail. The steeple of the parish church was struck and some pieces of stone dislodged.

The Crown estates in and near Newark were offered for sale on Tuesday, October 11, 1836, and the three following days. The proceeds of each day's sale were as follows:—Tuesday, £18,040; Wednesday, £25,800; Thursday, £23,500; Friday, £22,945; total, £90,285. The greater portion of the lots was purchased by Mr. Tallents for the Duke of Newcastle.

In 1837 the erection was completed of a Roman Catholic church in Parliament Street, dedicated to the Holy Trinity. It is a neat Gothic edifice, and owed its origin to the profuse liberality of the Rev. Dr. Waterworth, a learned and indefatigable writer of great repute amongst the Catholics. Dr. Waterworth, whose principal work was *The Faith of Catholics*, died at the Old Hall, in Mill Gate, adjoining the church, March 28, 1876.

In 1837 Christ Church, Lombard Street, was opened. It is a neat edifice in the Early English style, and the cost, £3000, was raised by subscription. In 1839 an organ was presented to it by Mr. Gladstone, the member for the borough.

The proclamation of Queen Victoria took place on June 26, 1837. A procession passed through the streets, and the health of her Majesty was drunk enthusiastically. On the coronation of the Queen, June 28, 1838, there were great rejoicings. The corporation and magistrates having breakfasted together at the town-hall, went to church, where the national and Sunday school children of all denominations assembled after service. The children paraded the streets, and then returned to the market-place to sing the National Anthem. They were subsequently regaled with roast beef and plum pudding. Dinners were given in various places; the town was beautifully decorated, and at night there was a grand display of fireworks at the bowling-green.

On Monday, May 20, 1839, as some workmen were lowering a mound of earth on a site near the old castle, intended for a beast market, they discovered three human skeletons; on Tuesday another was dug out, and the following week four more were found. They were all about three feet below the surface, and from the position in which the bodies lay, it was conjectured that the spot had been used as a burying-place for the garrison.

On the 5th of August 1839 there was a high flood, and thousands of acres of hay and corn were laid under water.

At the close of 1839 died Mr. William Hilton, R.A., the son of a native of Newark, and the painter of the beautiful picture, "The Raising of Lazarus," which hangs over the western door of the parish church. Alluding to his death, the *Spectator* said that British art had lost one of its brightest ornaments, and the Academy a distinguished and valuable member. Mr. Hilton, always delicate in constitution, and of uncertain health, sustained a severe shock by the sudden death of his wife under unusually distressing circumstances, and this blow was thought to have given a fatal impetus to the internal disease that ultimately terminated in dropsy. He was entirely devoted to his art, and having no children, his whole aim and energies were shared between his profession and the active duties of his office as Professor of Drawing in the Antique School at the Academy. His manners were mild and unassuming. In all the relations of life he was amiable and honourable, and he was high in the estimation of all who knew him. He was only in his fifty-third year, and under ordinary circumstances might have added many to the list of fine pictures on which his high reputation as a painter of historical and poetical subjects is based. The picture of the Raising of Lazarus was presented by Mr. Hilton to Newark Church as an altar-piece. The following inscription on a brass plate was placed on the centre of the bottom part of the frame in 1838:—"To the Church of St. Mary Magdalene, Newark, this picture is presented by William Hilton, Esq., R.A., in affectionate remembrance of the native town of his father, A.D. 1821."

Owing to the severe weather in January 1841 a committee was formed to relieve the necessitous poor. Mr. Gladstone subscribed £20, and the Solicitor-General (Serjeant Wilde) £50.

In 1842 the old peal of bells at the parish church was recast, and converted (with additional metal) into a peal of ten. The great bell of the old eight was taken down on Saturday, February 19, 1842. The remainder of the peal and frames were taken down during eight days—viz. from March the 7th to the 15th, six men being employed. The last passing bell rung on the old tenor was for Elizabeth, wife of Mr. William Hall, on Christmas Eve, 1841. Mr. Hall was, at the time, head churchwarden. The new bells arrived by boat on Monday, April 25, 1842, and were met by the ringers at the top Roving. Having got on board, they rang a peal on the hand-bells until they came to "Huddlestone Top Wharf," Mill Gate,

THE NEW PEAL OF BELLS.

where many people came to see the bells. The Notts Society of Change Ringers were appointed by the churchwardens of Newark to open the new peal, and on Wednesday week, May 25, they assembled at Newark for that purpose. The bells were raised at eight o'clock in the morning, and 600 changes were rung. The Sheffield Change Ringers then raised the bells, and after accomplishing nearly the same number of changes, they desisted. The bells were then oiled, and short peals were rung at intervals during the day. The Nottinghamshire ringers pronounced the bells at Averham to be the finest peal of six in the county, having rung a peal of 720 "Kent or Treble Bob" on their return home. At Newark, on the evening of Wednesday, their performances on the hand-bells gained them very great repute. On the hoisting of the bells into their places in the tower they were each of them named by parties who were present.

The following were the inscriptions on the bells:—

1. This peal was recast and hung by Taylor and Son, Loughborough. Glory to God on high.
2. Peace on earth, good will toward men. John Corby, sexton, 1842.
3. A voice from the temple a voice from the Lord.
4. John Taylor and Son, founders, Loughborough.
5. John Taylor and Son, founders, Loughborough.
6. Holiness to the Lord. John T., founder, Loughborough.
7. J. G. Bussell, vicar, J. Branston, W. Hall, G. Ingledew, J. Bentley, churchwardens. The year of our Lord's Salvation, 1842. To the glory of God.
8. Fear God, honour the king. J. Taylor, founder, Loughborough.
9. Deo et Excelsior. J. Taylor, founder, Loughborough.
10. Call a solemn assembly. John Taylor, Oxford and Loughborough, bell-founder, 1842, late of St. Neots and Bridge Devon.

The weights of the bells are as follows:—

	FROM THE SEXTON'S LIST.			FROM *Stamford Mercury*.		
	Cwt.	qr.	lb.	Cwt.	qr.	lb.
1.	7	1	11	7	1	8
2.	7	0	8	7	0	8
3.	7	3	24	7	3	14
4.	8	3	4	8	3	4
5.	8	0	3	8	3	0
6.	10	1	13	10	1	12
7.	13	1	13	13	1	12
8.	15	3	17	15	3	17
9.	20	3	6	20	3	6
10.	32	3	27	32	3	27

The third bell of the old peal was recast by Pach and Chapman, London, in 1775, and the tenth, in 1821, by Taylor and Son of St. Neots, the predecessors of the firm who cast the present peal. On the tenth, cast in 1821, was inscribed, "I to church the living call, and to the grave do summon all. Taylor and Son, St. Neots, *fecit* 1821." In 1846 two of the bells, the treble and second, were taken down, and two others hung in their stead. The change was made on account of one being cracked and the other out of tone. In the *Leicester Mercury* for March

PUBLIC BUILDINGS ERECTED.

19, 1842, is the following paragraph:—"Six large trees were felled a short time ago in Bosworth Field for the purpose of making the framework of a set of bells about to be put up in Newark church, and whilst the workmen were employed in sawing the beams and cutting into the heart of the tree, they met with some obstruction, which was found to proceed from a bullet supposed to have been lodged there in the battle of Bosworth Field in 1485."

Previous to the restoration of the church, which we shall describe presently, there was a board in the ringers' chamber stating that Holts' peal of 5040 changes or grandsire triples was rung in three hours and fifteen minutes on the 16th May 1816, and not a single error occurred in the 40,320 oscillations of which this difficult peal is composed. On the south wall of the chamber, a great height from the floor, was the following list of sextons, with the dates of their appointments, viz. Wm. Palfreyman, 1721; Thomas Hinchley, 1725; J. Chapman, 1761; John Corby, 1775; John Corby, January 1, 1796. Below this was . . .

Yᵉ RINGERS' ORDERS.

If you a hindrance to yᵉ ringers be, Twopence for it must be yᵉ sexton's fee;
With hat or spurs on don't begin to ring;
Twopence you forfeit if you touch a string;
Don't swear nor curse; shun these stumbling-blocks.

The law gives twelvepence, or else go to the stocks.
Who brawls or wrangles whom yᵉ major part Finds to be guilty shall pay his quart;
Who rings an hour-bell, be it night or day, If he o'erthrows, he shall his sixpence pay.

The Wesleyan chapel in Barnby Gate was opened on July 2, 1846. The entire cost, including the site, was £5261 : 18 : 4, and accommodation is provided for upwards of 1400 persons. The opening services were very largely attended, and the proceeds amounted to £493 : 15 : 6. A new organ was placed in the chapel in 1858. The Methodist New Connection Chapel was opened on Sunday, October 29, 1848.

The Corn Exchange in Castle Gate was opened for business in September 1848. The building was erected from the design, and under the superintendence, of Mr. Duesbury of London. The cost was £4300.

On the evening of the 1st September 1853 the town was visited by a frightful storm. At the end of Lombard Street the water was eighteen inches deep. Several buildings were struck by lightning. The electric fluid entered the steeple of the church, and did some damage.

The year 1855 witnessed the re-opening of the magnificent parish church of Newark after a restoration of a most extensive character. Naturally enough we have had occasion to refer in preceding pages to matters connected with the church, and it now becomes our duty to present an account, not only of the work of the restoration, but of the main features of the sacred edifice, its architecture, and its monuments. In inquiring into the date of various portions of the grand old building, our labours have been materially lightened by the courteous permission of the Right Rev. the Bishop Suffragan of Nottingham (Dr. Trollope), to include a paper which he prepared on the subject in 1871. As this paper describes the construction of the church, giving the probable dates of the principal portions of it, we cannot do better than present it to the reader first of all; adding such further information as we have been able to obtain, and thus leading down to the period when the restoration gave to the interior of the building the splendid appearance which it now presents. His lordship writes:—

"To many, an attempt to describe so grand a church as this may seem to be an unusually difficult task from its great size and importance, but, in reality, churches of much more modest dimensions are often fully as difficult to elucidate as their proudest compeers; and in this case I have the great advantage of profiting by the past labours of two of the most distinguished Members of our Society,[1] Mr. George Gilbert Scott and Prebendary Dimock, instead of having to trust wholly to my own resources, which I acknowledge with most grateful thanks.

"Through their investigations and the great advance made in the knowledge of Mediæval Ecclesiastical Architecture, now for so many years fostered by this and kindred Societies, we have no difficulty in ascertaining the dates of the several portions of this grand old Parish Church. The first sight of it from the Railway Station, or any other point on the outskirts of Newark, is very striking, rising as it does far above the town, as though to attract a blessing upon the secular labours of the numerous inhabitants below, whilst its tower and spire dominate above the rest of the fabric in unrivalled grandeur. The appearance of this last feature varies from different points of view, and from some of these its squinches may be considered to be too much pronounced, so as to interfere injuriously with the general run of the spire lines; whilst the comparatively large open passages through the tower pinnacles are defects that could be easily remedied by supplying them with doors. The very long horizontal line of the body of the church, relieved only by a sancte bell-cot at the east end of the nave and a similar feature containing a figure of St. Mary Magdalene at the east end of the chancel, is not pleasing, but yet serves to indicate its grandeur. On a nearer view, it will be seen that its general character very much resembles that of St. Mary, Nottingham, and constitutes a framework for the numerous expansive windows intended for the display of painted glass in superabundant profusion. Another characteristic is the embattled parapets surmounting the clerestory, aisle, and transept walls. The details partake of the insipidity of the later Gothic period, but, from the great beauty of the tower, the commanding height of the spire, as well as the vast size of the fabric, it constitutes a most noble place of Christian worship.

"The better to understand the character of this church, it will be well to shut out from view, as far as possible, all its several features, until each portion is required for particular inspection and imaginary reconstruction.

"There are now no traces whatever of the church that once stood on this spot

[1] The Lincoln Diocesan Architectural Society, for whose meeting in June 1871 the paper was prepared.

in which King Edward, the saintly Confessor, once worshipped, and upon the high altar of which Leofric, the great Earl of Mercia, and his celebrated wife, Godiva, sister and heir of Thorold of Bucknal, reverently deposited a deed-gift of its profits, which they presented to the then Collegiate Church of Stow; but we will now describe the several features of the existing fabric *seriatim*.

"First we have the four central piers of a lost cruciform church, of which they are the sole remnants, excepting a contemporary crypt beneath. These are clearly of a Transitional character, when the Norman style had for the most part yielded to the incoming influence of the succeeding style, or of the close of the twelfth century, and probably formed part of a church built by the monks of the Gilbertine Priory of St. Catherine, Lincoln, after its profits had been given to them by Robert de Chesney, Bishop of Lincoln. It was smaller than the present church, but from the position of its crypt beneath the reredos of the present chancel, we gather that it was not much shorter, although narrower than it.

"From the slenderness of these piers, it is clear that they never served to support a central tower; and after a minute examination of this church, Mr. Scott thinks it probable that its former nave had aisles, a clerestory, and aisle chapels attached to the chancel, and opening into the transepts.

"So much for the earliest features of this church; and now we will advert to the next portion, and the most beautiful of all—viz. the lower part of the tower.

"This was built about 1230, when the Early English style reigned supreme in all its perfection and structural excellence. It stands upon three arches beautifully moulded and enriched with the dog-tooth ornament, opening severally into the nave and aisles, but not according to the first design of the architect employed, although he, no doubt, was the author of all. This has been demonstrated very clearly by Mr. Scott, whence we gather that this tower at first stood out clear of aisles, but that whilst the building was going on, it was determined to pierce the side walls with arches, and to prolong the nave aisles so as to overlap them, as evidenced by the inserted jambs of the side arches, and the waste of the niches and ornamental work on the northern and southern faces of the N.W. and S.W. tower buttresses, imbedded in the western walls of the aisles; and also by the character of the arches above these jambs, which are built in the usual structural manner, demonstrating that they are not after-insertions, and of the roof weatherings above these, which are clearly contemporaneous with the walls in which they appear, while the whole work is of precisely the same date and character. It will also be observed that the pitch of the roofs of the tower aisles was considerably higher than that of the nave aisles.

"This lower and earlier portion of the tower rises only one stage above the nave roof, and is a noble feature, grand in design and excellent in detail. Unfortunately a Perpendicular window has been inserted in its western face, which is as incongruous as it is unneeded. Above, it is enriched with a fine arcade, and the bold, effective, diagonal diaper, used so freely in Bishop Grossetête's work at Lincoln

Cathedral. We have now got the central piers of a very late Norman church, and part of a grand Early English tower far westward of it. Next we have to deal with the spacious nave of this church, required for the use of the always church-loving and church-using people of Newark.

"Perhaps until the first quarter of the fourteenth century this consisted partly of the old Transitional church, and partly of newer work, corresponding with the date and character of the tower; but about 1313 a general rebuilding of the whole, except the tower, was contemplated, and in part set on foot by the parishioners, of which there are evidences on all sides. First we have the whole of the present south aisle, and part of the east elevation of the chancel as evidenced by its buttresses and base mouldings, by a richly sculptured and decorated reredos at the east end of the south aisle, as well as by the foundation of the north aisle, and a niche within it at the west end, adjoining the transept. But man can only propose; for, after the altar of the chapel of St. Mary in the south aisle had been consecrated, August 3, 1315, by the Archbishop of Armagh, through the authority of the Archbishop of York, indicating that some progress had been then made with this design, the work came to an end for a considerable period; and when it was recommenced, fashion had led architects and their employers to change their designs, as they no doubt thought, for the better. Before this took place, however, most happily the upper stage of the tower, and grand spire above it, had been completed, apparently *circa* 1350. In each face are coupled belfry lights below a crocketed pedimented hood-mould. On each side of these is a canopied niche containing a figure of an apostle or saint, and above a smaller niche, also containing a corresponding figure. This stage is surmounted by a parapet enriched with quatrefoils and crocketed pinnacles at the angles.

"From the tower the spire rises grandly. Its angles are softened by a roll mould, and it is perforated by four tiers of lights. Unfortunately the upper portion has been tampered with, perhaps when the finial was renewed in 1793. In the last quarter of the fourteenth century the nave was built, and the more precise date of its construction is indicated by some heraldic bearings carved upon the cap of one of the south aisle pillars, viz.—a shield bearing England impaling quarterly *or*, an eagle displayed *sa.*, *g.*, a lion double queued rampant, *arg.*, for Richard II. and his queen Anne, daughter of Charles of Luxembourg or Charles IV., Emperor of Germany, son of Jean l'Aveugle, king of Bohemia, who was slain at Cressy, and Elizabeth of Pomerania, his fourth wife. As King Richard married Anne of Bohemia in 1383, and she died in 1394, the building of this portion of the church must have taken place within those limits.

"Next followed the chancel, when the Norman piers of the old chancel arch were heightened and surmounted by a new arch. This was built in 1489, at the joint cost of the Prior and Convent of St. Catherine, Lincoln, and certain benefactors of Newark. Next followed the little chapel on the north side of the altar; between the two easternmost pillars of the north aisle arcade is a chantry chapel, founded by

Thomas Merying, of Newark, who, according to his will, dated August 17, 1500 desired to be buried on the spot where the sepulchre of our Lord was wont to be set up at Easter, and that a chapel should be built there, for which he left means, and also for the maintenance of a priest to say masses for his soul. The patronage of the chantry he left in the hands of his kinsman, Sir William Merying. Subsequently his brother, Alexander Merying, also of Newark, was buried beside him, in accordance with his will, dated August 25, 1506. The base of this little chapel facing the north aisle, and on the east, is enriched with panels containing shields of arms belonging to the Merying family and its connections, among which are the Nevile, Leke, and Beckering bearings.

"In a corresponding position opposite is the mortuary chapel of Robert Markham, in which, according to his will, dated May 16, 1505, he was buried. Within was his tomb bearing this legend, *Orate pro animabus Roberti Markham, armigeris et Elizabethe uxoris ejus;* but this has long since been removed, to serve as a burial-place for a family of the name of Herring. The base of the outer side of this chapel is panelled, and within each panel is a shield of arms illustrating the armorial bearing of the Markham family and their connections. Above is an open panelled screen surmounted by a cornice and a trefoiled ridge. Probably all of these now open panels were once filled with paintings, like two still remaining at the east end of the lower range, which evidently form one of a series of subjects illustrating the Dance of Death. On one of these appears the figure of a man in his prime, richly dressed, with his hand in his gypciere, or purse, suspended from his girdle, and on the other a figure of Death with a flower in his hand, said to be a red rose, but in reality a carnation, as an emblem of the shortness of life, which he holds up towards his gaily-dressed neighbour.[1]

"Behind the reredos is the Lady Chapel, once flanked by two other chapels having canopied niches for statues. The transepts are the latest features of this church; but the southern one must have been completed before the year 1539, and almost beyond a doubt both were finished before that date. This last constituted the Chapel of the Holy Trinity. Here were buried Alan Fleming and William Phyllypot, who, with Joan, his wife, filled the south window of this transept with painted glass.

"The date of the Chancel Screen, called 'the Reredose,' and the maker of it, are mentioned in one of the corporation records, as contained in an agreement, dated December 21, 1508, between the churchwardens of Newark and Thomas Drawswerd, kerver, of York, releasing him from all further liability with respect to the making of 'le Reredose' of Newark Church. The side screens, as well as that in the chancel arch, are superb. The last half of the choir stalls was erected by John Smythe, Rector of Newark, in accordance with his will, made in 1521, who therein directed his executor, Sir Roger Walished, to cause to be made the whole

[1] For fuller details see pages 37-39.

half part of the stalls, to be situated on the right side of the choir, in honour of St. Mary Magdalene, of Newark, viz.—at the cost of £25, on condition that the said executor be without suit or trouble concerning his (the testator's) benefices, and the residue of his goods.

"The original font, when perfect, can hardly have been worthy of this grand church, and now has an insignificant and incongruous appearance. Its octangular mediæval stem is placed upon a poor square base. In each of its faces is a niche containing figures of two Apostles, and round its plinth is this inscription, formed of letters delicately and most fancifully carved, in which birds, animals, and foliage are curiously intermingled—*Carne rei nati sunt hoc Deo fonte renati*, or, Those born accused by the flesh, are reborn in God in this Font. The original bowl was destroyed during the time of the Civil War, and the present one was given by a loyalist of Newark at the Restoration, as recorded on a brass plate inserted in the shaft of an adjacent pillar—'This font was demolished by the Rebels, May 9, 1646, and rebuilt by the charity of Nicholas Ridley, 1660.'"

In supplementing the information about the church, given thus far in so interesting a form by the Bishop Suffragan, we have to notice other monuments in addition to those to which reference has already been made. On a brass plate affixed to a column towards the south door is a long Latin epitaph to the memory of John Taylor, who died on the 27th of October 1739. Mr. Taylor was a publican in Newark, and kept an inn known by the sign of the Turk's Head, in Kirkgate. He was the father of the celebrated Dr. Taylor who wrote the epitaph. A monument near to the south door commemorates the virtues of the Rev. Gustavus Broughton, M.A., who died November 17, 1760. Mr. Broughton was a native of Newark, was educated at St. John's College, Cambridge, and was for some time vicar of St. Martin's, Leicester. The monument was erected by his widow, who died in 1763, and was buried near him. There are inscriptions on contiguous stones to the memory of other members of the same family. A brass plate in the north aisle has a Latin inscription in memory of Mr. John Twells, who died in 1713; and there is a gravestone over the remains of Mr. William Snell, attorney, once mayor of Newark, and Mary, his wife. The former died in 1710, and the latter in 1724. The family of Snell is said to have derived its descent from Sir Andrew Snell, in the time of Henry VII. Sir Andrew, according to Mr. Dickinson, distinguished himself at Bosworth Field, and assisted in placing the diadem on Henry's head. A Captain Richard Snell served in the civil wars, and was in garrison at Newark. Another brass plate is to the memory of Mr. John Milnes, thrice mayor of Newark, who died January 1, 1739, aged 77. Mr. Milnes was a member of another old Newark family. In very remote times the corn mills at Newark were celebrated, and, so far as can be ascertained, the road to them always bore the name of Milne Gate. An inscription on the pavement is to the memory of Mary, the wife of the Rev. Davis Pennell, who died January 8, 1803. Mr. Pennell was vicar of Newark, and his wife belonged to the family of Drury of Nottingham. In the north aisle, in Thoroton's time, were two portraits with the draper's arms over them, and the following inscriptions:—

> Orate pro animabus JOHANNIS BOSTONE Merceri
> Et WILLIELMI BOLI filii dicti Johannis
> Qui Willielmus ob. 4 Die Aprilis Anno dom. 1551
> Quorum Animabus, &c. &c.

And on a brass plate affixed to one of the pillars:—

> Pray for the soule of THOMAS GRIFFETH, gentleman,
> which decessed the V day of March, Anno Dom MV XIX
> on whose soul I H U have mercy. Amen.

There is also the following:—

> To the memory of Mr. JOHN JOHNSON, alderman, and twice mayor of this loyal and unanimous corporation of Newarke, who deceased the 24th day of January anno dom' 1659, and lies interred near this place, with hopes of a ioyfull resurrection.
> Hoc grati animi ergo triste monumentum posuit
> Johannes Johnsonus cognatus ejus

By the north-east corner upon marble, in the wall, was a long Latin inscription, with several Greek words interspersed, to the memory of Henry Trewmann. Another monument is to the memory of John Joyce, of Belvoir, Esq., deceased in Lent 1608. Mr. Joyce served the Earl of Rutland first as secretary and then as steward of the household. In the south aisle is an inscription to Mr. William Hobman, who died in 1659, and who belonged to an old and respected Newark family. Members of another noted family are buried here. A monument commemorates Mr. John Heron and Jane, his wife, the former of whom died on the 8th of December 1727, aged sixty-three, and the latter on the 14th of November, aged seventy-one. The inscription gives the following details:—He was the son of Robert Heron, who died on the 16th of May 1709. Robert was the son of Thomas Heron, fifth son of John Heron, Esq., of Bockenfield, in the county of Northumberland, a younger branch of the ancient barony of Heron in that county, whose sons and family were eminently loyal to King Charles I., in whose service the above-named Thomas was major of the regiment of horse commanded by Colonel Robert Dalyson, and also captain of a troop therein. Mrs. John Heron was youngest sister and executrix of Mr. Daniel Crayle, whose monument she erected in the south aisle of the church. Another monument is to Mrs. Anne Taylor, youngest daughter of Mr. John Heron, and first wife of the celebrated Dr. Taylor, by whom a very eulogistic inscription was put up. In the cross aisle is an altar tomb to the memory of Robert Brown, the benefactor of Newark. In the south transept is a monument to Mr. Daniel Crayle, who died in 1727. He was the son of Mr. Richard and Mrs. Jane Crayle of Newark, and amassed a large fortune as a banker in Lombard Street, London. A fine brass in the north aisle bears a portrait of Mr. William Phyllypot, alderman, and Elizabeth, his wife, "which Wylliam," says the inscription, "decessyed the viii day of May, Anno Dmi. MCCCCCLVII., whose dethe desyryng youe all to have in remembrance, calling to God for mercy." In the choir are buried the Atkinson family. A monument with effigies records the virtues of Thomas Atkinson, who died in 1561. Another commemorates a follower of Charles I.:—

> Here lyeth the body of ROBERT RAMSEY, Esquire,
> Servant to His Majesty,
> Who died the 9th day of April 1639.

Amongst the inscriptions referred to by Thoroton, is one to the memory of John Smith, vicar, who died 14th August 1521. There is also one on a stone to Robert Whitcombe, merchant, of Calais, who died in 1447; one to Robert Kirkebye, first master of the Song School, who died in 1573; and Elizabeth his wife; one to Mr. William Leverett, physician, and thrice alderman, who died 15th March 1579; one to Dr. John Burton, vicar, who died 3d February 1475; and others. There are also buried there members of the following families:—Linthwaite, Hill, Spragging, Clough, Ridghill, Martin, Cheetham, Swift, Dranfield, Broadhurst, Hawden, Handley, Snell, Tomlinson, Twelch, Twentyman, Crampern, Derry, Sketchley, Cumberland, Rastall, Haslam, Herring, Pocklington, and others.

In olden times there was much beautiful painted glass in the windows of the church, for the display of which they were particularly well adapted. Captain A. E. Lawson Lowe states:—"In the time of Charles II., when Thoroton wrote the *Antiquities of Nottinghamshire*, a very considerable amount of old stained glass appears to have remained in the windows of the parish church. The glass in the great east window of the chancel seems to have been given towards the close of the fifteenth century by Thomas Mering, the founder of the chantry chapel on the north side of the high altar, who was the younger son of an ancient family which had possessed the neighbouring manor of Mering since the time of the Norman invasion; and along the bottom of the window there was formerly an inscription recording his name, with that of Elizabeth, his wife. Thoroton likewise mentions another window 'which Thomas Mering and Mary, his wife, caused to be made,' and which was adorned with three shields displaying the arms of Mering impaling Nevile of Rolleston, and Mering impaling Leeke, together with the arms of Babington. If this Thomas Mering is identical with the one previously named, as seems probable, it must be inferred that he was twice married. Another window was given by Thomas, first Lord Burgh of Gainsborough, and likewise dated from the latter part of the fifteenth century, for that nobleman was raised to the peerage by King Henry VII. in 1487, and died about nine years later. His lordship had married a daughter of Thomas, Lord Roos, and in the centre of the window was a shield bearing the arms of Burgh quartering Percy and Strabolgi, and impaling Roos quartering Badlesmere. There were also two other shields in this window, the one with the arms and quarterings of Burgh impaling Cobham, and the other with the arms of Fitz-Hugh impaling Burgh, denoting the marriages of the son and daughter of the donor—Sir Edward Burgh, his son and heir, having married Anne, daughter and heiress of Sir Thomas Cobham, of Sterborough, in Kent, whilst Elizabeth, his daughter, married Richard, sixth Lord Fitz-Hugh. In another window there were the arms of Pierrepont impaling Manvers and Heriz, together with the arms of the baronial house of Fitz-Williams, and some other coats. In one of the windows of the north transept there were likewise the arms of Cardinal John Kemp, Archbishop of York and afterwards of Canterbury, who was presumably a benefactor to this church previous to his translation from the former province. In the same part of the church were the arms of Cromwell quartering Tateshall, Chaworth quartering Caltoft, Plumpton quartering Foljambe, Harthill impaling Leeke, and Markham quartering Leeke, together with the heraldic insignia of the families of Rempston, Bozon, Martell of Chilwell, Barry of Tollerton, and Leeke of Kirkton. The glass in the principal window of the south transept, which displayed the old royal arms of England, with the arms of the noble family of Deincourt, was given, in 1539, by William Phelypot, and bore an inscription desiring the prayers of the faithful for the good estate of the donor, and of Joane, his wife. This William Phelypot was possibly identical with, but was more probably the father of, William Phyllypot, alderman of Newark in 1550, and founder of the Bede houses in Barnby Gate, who died in 1557, and whose brass effigy was originally placed in this transept, but was removed to the north aisle in 1811. The old royal arms—France and England borne quarterly—together with numerous smaller shields, bearing the arms of the Lords Deincourt, viz.—*Azure, a fesse dancettée between ten billets or*, and the arms of the Deincourts of Knapthorp, a junior branch of the baronial house, viz.—*Argent, a fesse dancettée between ten billets sable*, yet remain in the east window of the south aisle, having been removed to their present position from the great window of the south transept at the restoration of the church. The remainder of the armorial bearings have all disappeared.

We come now to advert to the restoration of the church. The first step taken towards it was at a meeting held at the town-hall on Friday, the 25th of August 1848, to receive the report of Mr. T. C. Hine, the architect, of Nottingham, when it was decided to commence by restoring the roofs of the whole of the south aisle, including both nave and chancel. This was followed by the exposure of the whole of the beautiful west window, by raising the floor of the ringing chamber (which was formerly on a level with the transom of the window), the ceiling under the present ringing floor being panelled to correspond with the roofs of the church. In the year 1849 Mr. Spreckley, painter, voluntarily cleaned about four of the pillars at the east end of the church by chemical process from the extraordinary number of coats of paint with which they were covered, thus bringing out the carving of the capitals with all the freshness and sharpness of their original state, which good example was followed by several gentlemen of the town, each taking a pillar, and restoring it in the same manner at his own expense. These gradual though slight developments of the beauties of the fabric seemed to prepare the minds of the people for a continuation of the work, and on March 2,

1852, a public meeting was held for the purpose of taking into consideration the re-arrangement and restoration of the interior of the church, at which the Duke of Newcastle proposed, and the mayor (Mr. W. N. Nicholson) seconded, the following resolution :—" That it is the opinion of this meeting that, by a judicious re-arrangement of the sittings in the parish church, the accommodation to the parishioners would be very considerably increased, whilst at the same time the magnificent beauty of the interior would be no longer obscured and disfigured by inappropriate galleries and unsightly pews." Other resolutions were proposed for entering into a subscription, and a committee was appointed, on which the Duke of Newcastle consented to act. Before the close of the meeting the Duke offered to give £250. Mr. J. H. Manners Sutton (one of the borough members) had previously promised £200. The amount promised before the close of the day was £2700, five of the principal inhabitants having put down their names for £100 each, and a great number for £50 and £25 each. A meeting of the committee was held on the 13th April Easter Tuesday) following, when the vicar, in opening the business of the meeting, stated, "that the subscriptions already promised amounted to £3866, which, with nearly £1000 (from the accumulated fabric fund) in his own hands, was sufficient to authorise the committee to take the necessary preliminary step of appointing an architect." The Duke of Newcastle proposed the appointment of Mr. Gilbert Scott, believing him to be fully competent to carry out a work which was almost of national importance. Mr. Scott was finally elected by the committee, and after his plans had been approved by them, they were placed in the town-hall in the month of August, following, for the inspection of experienced parties selected by Mr. Scott to compete for the works. The highest tender was above £6000, and the lowest, Mr. W. M. Cooper of Derby, £4000. The contractor commenced in the early part of January 1853. Divine service was held in the nave until Sunday the 3d of July 1853, after which it was held in the town-hall during the remainder of the period of restoration.

Previous to the alterations, the nave was cumbered by lofty galleries and unsightly pews; the west end, extending to and including the north and south doors, was divided from the nave, forming what was called the ante-church, from which there were entrances through a ponderous mass of wood-work to the aisles and galleries. Of these galleries, that on the south side appeared to be much the oldest, and was in the most dilapidated condition. The deep front gallery and north gallery were of more modern date, and still more recently, within the memory of some of the inhabitants of Newark, the north and south transept galleries, extending up to the screen, were constructed at the expense of persons who required accommodation in the church. The pews that filled the nave were six feet high, and divided in an irregular and unsightly manner, those in the transepts especially being literally packing boxes of the most inconvenient description (the projection of the galleries rendering them nearly useless). The few free seats or sittings for the poor were in the aisles, and consisted of uncomfortable benches standing on the stone floors, the pews forming a high wall on the right hand and on the left. To the credit of the poorer part of the congregation, let it here be testified, that seldom was one of these miserable seats left unoccupied. The general effect of the nave was wretched and gloomy, smothered with the intrusive galleries which cut in half the beautiful windows, nearly obliterating the lower parts, and preventing the fine proportions of the pillars and arches being seen; in fact, there was no point from which any complete idea of the beauty of the interior of the edifice could be obtained. The walls of the church were whitewashed, and the arches and mullions of the windows either painted or colour-washed. The ceilings of the chancel, the north aisles and north transept, had as the old wood-work decayed, from time to time been restored with plaster, the bosses and other ornamental wood-work being replaced, and painted stone colour. A restoration of the fine oak screen, creditable for the time at which it was executed, inasmuch as the details of the original designs appeared to have been adhered to, had been made about forty years before, since which the whole had been painted the all-prevailing stone-colour. The fine picture, the painting of the "Raising of Lazarus," occupied the position of altar-piece, and had superseded pictures of Moses and Aaron of more ancient date, which in their turn had been preceded by a white plastered background, on which were found in bold black letters with red initials the Ten Commandments, of a date supposed to be shortly subsequent to the Reformation.[1]

The improvements that were made on this state of things may be briefly enumerated. The work commenced by removing the whole of the plastered ceilings which extended through the entire length of the north aisle and the centre roof of the chancel, and replacing them with oak; the old carved bosses and ornaments, some of which in the north chancel aisle were very old and curious, being carefully replaced, and new ones of similar design substituted where necessary. The ceilings of the nave and north transept, which were found to be in a very good state, were carefully repaired, and made to correspond in colour with the restored portion of the work; the whole of the galleries and pewing in the church were removed, the stone-work of the pillars, arches, and windows, and ashlar-work of the walls cleaned and carefully repaired, and the plastering of that part of the walls that required such a covering, entirely removed. The flooring throughout the church was taken up, and the ground levelled, and covered with a thick layer of concrete. The momumental slabs were relaid in as nearly as possible their original positions, the rest of the flooring that proved in good condition being used in the chancel aisles. The floor of the nave was laid with Minton tiles, in plain red and black, and in the chancel with encaustic tiles, in a very effective manner. In the chancel, a new reredos in Ancaster stone of beautiful design, replaced Hilton's picture, which found a resting-place in the north transept, and subsequently, over the western door. The first stone of this beautiful piece of workmanship (the reredos) was laid on the 16th of March 1854 by the curate of the parish, the rev. gentleman

---

[1] See the illustration facing p. 210 of the church before restoration.

RESTORATION OF THE CHURCH.

having previously deposited underneath, in a receptacle prepared for it, a leather case delivered into his hands by the vicar, containing a record of the event written upon parchment. The ceremony was performed in the presence of the vicar and churchwardens, the mayor and restoration committee, and a large number of ladies and gentlemen. The celebrated monumental brass of Alan Fleming, which was at the back of the old reredos, was removed and fixed on the south transept wall, near the place where it was first discovered. The screen had the paint removed, and was restored with an almost incredible amount of labour, the greatest portion of the upper part of the carved work being new. The old stalls, miserere seats and desks, throughout the chancel were repaired and restored. The organ was removed from the rood loft, and placed in the south chancel aisle, the entry to the vestry being through the centre of it.

As the work progressed the windows of the nave and transepts (with the exception of the central west window, and the west window of the south aisle, which had been previously restored) were found in very bad condition, and were consequently relaid throughout with Hartley's rough plate glass in quarries, the stonework repaired, and proper iron stanchion bars put in. The walls of the nave were lined to the height of 6 ft. with substantial oak panelling, having a battlement top, and the nave was reseated throughout with open oak seats, having beautifully moulded and carved ends with poppy heads, the variety and beauty of which, and of the exquisite carved tracery in the cross aisles, and of the stalls in the corporation seat, are a perfect study for those interested in the work of church restoration. The pulpit and prayer desk, the designs and workmanship of which are worthy of examination, together with a lectern of oak, were placed immediately in front of the screen. A heating apparatus, capable of raising the temperature of the church to 55 Fahrenheit in the coldest weather, was fixed under the vestry; and the lighting has been effectively carried out by brass gas standards of admirable design and workmanship, and of correct character, the chancel having, in addition to two standards more elaborate than those in the nave, a fine gasalier to correspond with the standards. The gasalier is a very splendid ornament suspended from the roof in the centre of the choir, and containing 88 lights. The two gas standards are placed one at each extremity of the lower steps of the sacrarium, and contain 26 lights each, the effect of which, when illuminated and viewed through the ancient screen, is magnificent. There are also nobly designed standards of a large circular form surmounted by a coronet containing lights, each placed down the centre of the nave, and of smaller design, containing lights on the aisles and transepts. Every hand of these standards is ornamented with leaves in imitation of clusters of flowers. The pulpit is not lighted with gas. The west doors are protected by curtain lobbies, having heavy crimson curtains supported from ornamental ironwork.

The works were under the exclusive direction of Mr. Geo. Gilbert Scott, architect, London. Mr. James M. Johnston was clerk of the works. Contractors

—Mr. W. M. Cooper of Derby for the general restoration; Messrs. Foster and Andrewes of Hull for the organ and case; Mr. Haden of Troubridge for the heating apparatus; Messrs. Skidmore of Coventry for the gas standards and ornamental part of gasfittings; Mr. W. N. Nicholson, Newark, for the mechanical part of the gasfittings and ironwork for windows; Mr. E. Bousfield, of Newark, for the windows; Mr. John Cooper, Newark, for new wood ceiling and other works in the vestry.[1]

The age of the old organ taken down in 1804 (which was said to have been one of the oldest in England) is not known, but it was supposed to have been brought from the castle. Throsby, writing in 1790,[2] speaking of the interior of the parish church, says:—"The organ is a disgrace to everything around it, the case is painted with ruddle, and the pipes in front are as foul as time and neglect could make them." It contained ten stops in a painted deal case, and was placed on the rood loft. In 1804 a new organ, containing a variety of stops, was erected by England. It was opened on the 11th of November 1804, by the organist and choir of Southwell Minster. In 1836, shortly after the appointment of Dr. Dearle as organist, several improvements were made in the organ by Mr. Bishop of London. Among these may be mentioned the addition of pedals, and one octave of large pedal pipes; of a cremona stop in the choir organ, and a claribel in the great organ. The swell was also extended in the compass, and a horn introduced. The organ was re-opened on Friday, December 9, 1836, by two full cathedral services, with a choir of sixty voices, including part of the choirs of Lincoln and Southwell, with several members of the Lincoln and Newark Choral Societies, for whose accommodation a temporary gallery was erected in front of the organ. The sermon in the morning was preached by Archdeacon Wilkins, from the words, "Let everything that hath breath praise the Lord." The sermon in the evening was preached by the Rev. H. R. Harrison, Rector of Elston and Rural Dean, from 98th Psalm, 5th, 6th, and 7th verses. On the restoration of the church the instrument was, on the recommendation of Mr. Scott, removed to its present position in the south chancel aisle, and a new case provided for it from the designs of that eminent architect. In August 1865 Mr. Reay, the present organist, submitted a scheme for additions and alterations, which was adopted, and subscriptions being readily forthcoming, the work was placed in the hands of Mr. Henry Willis of London. The organ was by him entirely rebuilt, and the number of stops nearly doubled, the amount expended being about £650. It now has four complete rows of keys, a separate pedal organ, and contains about 2600 pipes. The stops are thus distributed:—great organ 12, choir organ 7, swell organ 11, solo organ 8, pedal organ 9,—all of which, with two exceptions, are through. The quality of tone is exceedingly fine, and many of the single stops — notably the *tuba mirabilis* — are of unusual excellence. The re-opening

---

[1] *Vide* the "Book of Services at the Re-opening." To the description of the restoration, printed at the end of this book, we are indebted for many of the particulars here given.

[2] Throsby's *Additions to Thoroton*, vol i. p. 401.

services took place on Thursday, June 21, 1866, the sermon in the morning being preached by the Ven. Archdeacon Mackenzie, and that in the evening by the Rev. Thomas Todd, M.A., rector of Newton. In the afternoon there was an organ performance by Mr. Reay, which was largely attended.

The church was re-opened, after the restoration, on Thursday, the 12th of April 1855, the following choir being engaged, under the direction of Dr. Dearle, to take part in the services for the day:—Mr. Miller from Cambridge; Messrs. Ashton and Hemingway from Durham Cathedral; Messrs. Thacker, Strickland, and Harley, from Peterborough Cathedral; Messrs. Mason, Brooke, and Turton, and four choristers, from Lincoln Cathedral; Messrs. Spencer, Holt, Charlesworth, and Thomas, and four choristers, from Southwell Minster; four of the choir of St. Philip's Church, Sheffield; the twelve choristers of Newark church choir; ten members of the Grantham singing classes; and ten members of the Newark Choral Society. The morning was ushered in by merry peals from the fine-toned bells of the church, rung by the Sheffield Society of Ringers, who had been engaged for the occasion. At the morning service every part of the church was filled with a highly respectable congregation. Among the nobility and gentry present were:—The Duke of Newcastle; Earl Scarborough (Lord-Lieutenant of the county); Lord H. Clinton; Mr. J. H. M. Sutton, M.P., and Mrs. Sutton; Mr. G. F. H. Vernon, M.P., and Lady S. Vernon; Mr. W. H. Barrow, M.P.; Sir Thos. White, Bart., and Lady White, etc. Shortly after eleven o'clock the Worshipful the Mayor (Mr. W. Ragsdale), accompanied by Mr. T. F. A. Burnaby, the town-clerk, and preceded by the officers of the corporation bearing the golden maces, entered the church and took their seats in front of the lectern. The organ prelude was then played, and the long procession of about 200 of the surpliced clergy took place down the centre of the nave, and they continued slowly to advance until their numbers had nearly filled up the space within the screen, which they entered. Immediately the service commenced, the Rev. J. H. Henderson intoning, and the full choir responding.

The *Venite Exultemus* and Psalms for the day were sung by the choir. The first lesson (1 Kings viii. 22-61) was read by the Rev. H. Plater. It will be seen on turning to the passage it was exceedingly appropriate to the occasion, being the prayer and supplication of Solomon at the dedication of the Temple. The singing of Dr. Dearle's *Te Deum*, which followed, developed alike the novelty and excellence of the doctor's composition, the capabilities of the organ, and the abilities of the choir. After the *Te Deum* the Rev. J. G. Bussell, the vicar of the parish, read the second lesson. The Rev. J. H. Henderson (precentor of Ely Cathedral) having resumed his place, intoned the Creed, the Lord's Prayer, etc. The beautiful anthem of Mendelssohn, "O rest in the Lord," after the third collect, was executed as a solo alto by Mr. Miller of Cambridge. Before the communion service the solo tenor of Mendelssohn's anthem, "Then shall the righteous shine forth as the sun," was sung by Mr. Ashton of Durham, and followed by Handel's "Hallelujah Chorus" by the full choir.

The prayer and decalogue in the Communion Service were read by the Lord

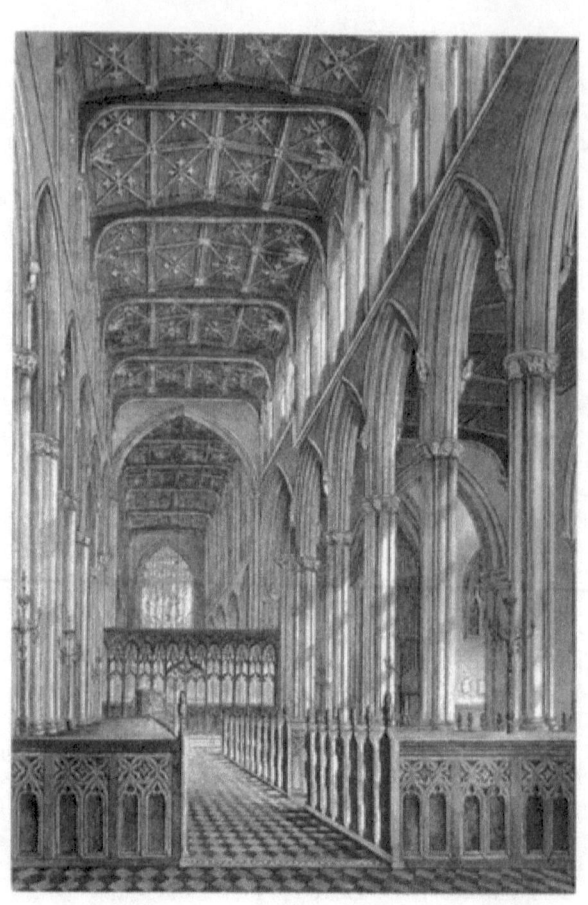

RESTORATION OF THE CHURCH.

Bishop of Lincoln, with Tallis's responses to the Commandments by the choir. The Epistle was read by the Rev. Dr. Hook, and the Gospel by the Rev. Archdeacon Wilkins. The Nicene Creed was chanted after Tallis, and the congregation joined in singing the 100th Psalm. The sermon was preached by the Bishop of Lincoln, and, on its conclusion, a collection was made towards the restoration fund, amounting to £438 : 8 : 3.

At half-past three a luncheon took place at the town-hall under the presidency of the Duke of Newcastle, when above 300 sat down to a very excellent repast. The usual toasts on such occasions were given, and heartily responded to.

At the evening service the bishop and clergy entered at the north door of the chancel, and the choir by the west door. The first lesson, 2 Chronicles 7th chapter, was read by the vicar; the second, James 1st chapter, by the bishop. In addition to the recitative and air "Comfort ye" and "Every valley," the chorus "And the glory of the Lord" was effectively performed by the whole choir. The sermon was preached by the Rev. Dr. Hook, vicar of Leeds, who chose as his text the 2d verse of the 87th Psalm. After the final anthem the bishop left his stall, and advanced to the doors of the choir, where he gave his benediction to the people. The collection at this service amounted to £101 : 14 : 10, making the total amount for the day £540 : 3 : 1.

During the winter of 1855 the weather was very severe. A sheep was roasted on the Trent, at Fiskerton, on Saturday, February 24; and a cricket match was played at the same time and place.

In October the Queen passed through the town. The train stayed five minutes at the Great Northern station, which had been elegantly decorated for the occasion. There was a large attendance to give her Majesty a loyal greeting. The guard of honour was supplied by the Royal Sherwood Foresters.

An official notice from the Secretary of State directed that no interment should take place in the churchyard at Newark after the 1st March 1856. A new cemetery was opened on the London Road, where burials have since taken place.

On the 29th of May of the same year there were great rejoicings on the conclusion of the Crimean War. The Sherwood Foresters assembled in the market-place and fired a *feu de joie*.

An election occurring in 1857, Mr. Charles Dickens, the celebrated novelist, was requested to become a candidate. The circumstances under which the invitation was given were these:—Mr. W. H. Cubley was conversing with a gentleman, a personal friend of Mr. Dickens, as to who would be an eligible and desirable man to contest the borough in the Liberal interest. The names of local personages were canvassed, and then Mr. Cubley suggested that Dickens, being a popular writer, would be a useful, and probably a successful, candidate. The suggestion was heartily approved, and a letter was forthwith despatched. It elicited the following reply, which is still in Mr. Cubley's possession :—

Tavistock House, 11th March 1857.

DEAR SIR—I beg to assure you that I satisfied myself long ago that I am much better and much more usefully employed in my own calling than I could hope to be in the House of Commons. I believe no consideration on earth would induce me to become a member of that incoherent assembly.

Faithfully yours,

CHARLES DICKENS.

A celebrated physician, who had been associated with Newark in his earlier years, died in 1857—we refer to Marshall Hall, M.D., F.R.S. From the very interesting biography published by his widow, we learn that at fifteen years of age he was sent to Mr. Moore, a chemist of Newark, whose place of business was near the town-hall, but, disliking his position there, he prevailed upon his father to remove him. "At Newark," writes Mrs. Hall, "he formed a close friendship with Mr. Robert Cook, then studying for the medical profession, and the two friends together pursued anatomy and other subjects connected with medicine. Feeling the deficiency of his early education, the energy of his character soon developed itself in vigorous and unaided efforts to repair it. He imposed upon himself the task of writing Latin exercises, which he regularly sent once a week by a carrier to be corrected by his friend the Rev. Robert Almond, then curate of Basford. In a letter written to a sister, from Newark, he says, 'I already feel that I can be unremitting in my studies. I rise very early; so much so, that Mr. Cook says he thinks I intend to live without sleep.' It appears that whilst at Newark he taught himself to play the flute, though he certainly never devoted much time to it. In another letter to his sister, he says, 'Bring me all the music you can, as I intend, if I can find time, to practise a little on the flute.' He insisted on trying to improve his sisters in French by correcting their exercises, which, for that purpose, were sent to him regularly. He also gave amateur instruction to the sisters of a friend at Newark in Latin, chemistry, and short-hand writing. . . . Mr. Cook relates that, being called up to visit a patient very early one morning before daybreak, on coming downstairs he found his young friend Hall hard at work studying medicine and chemistry. When Mr. Cook expressed his surprise, Hall said, 'I am determined to be a great man.'" On leaving Newark, it was decided that Hall should adopt the medical profession, and in October 1809 he repaired to Edinburgh. In after years his ambition to become a great man was fully realised. His writings were replete with valuable information, the result of patient labour, and his reputation as a physiologist extended not only through this country, but in medical circles in Europe and America. Famous as a physician, accomplished as a writer, exemplary as a Christian, there are few who have left so good a name behind them.

On November 27, 1857, Kelham Hall, the residence of Mr. Manners Sutton, which had just been restored at a great cost, was destroyed by fire. A local writer thus describes the disaster:—"The interior of the building, as seen from the bay window at the end, presents a scene of desolation seldom witnessed, for all the splendid contents of the many rooms have become ashes, and lie scattered along the ground floor, intermingled with broken marble, elaborate carvings, molten bell metal, calcined illuminations and manuscripts; while looking upwards, broken segments, dislocated masonry, overhanging brickwork, and tottering chimneys, all testify of the power of the element, and the completeness of the destruction." In clearing away the débris, the workmen found numerous relics of fancy and ornamental goods, among the number being a skeleton of a splendid golden workbox which was presented to a lady of the family by Queen Charlotte. About five years after the fire a new hall was erected of elegant design and commodious proportions.

Of the Sutton family, to whom Kelham belongs, so distinguished has it been, and so intimate its association with Newark, as these Annals testify, that the following details, for which we are indebted to Captain A. E. Lawson Lowe, will be perused with interest:—"The grandiloquent inscription upon the monument in the mortuary chapel in Kelham Church to Robert, second and last Lord Lexington, states that 'the house of Sutton,' of which he was a member, 'had given Earls to Warwick and Leicester, and Lords to the Barony of Dudley.' According to the pedigree in Thoroton's *Antiquities of Nottinghamshire*, the Suttons of Averham derived their descent from one Hervey, who held a moiety of the manor of Sutton-upon-Trent, under Alan, Earl of Richmond, at the time of the Domesday survey; but though we may assume this to be correct, it must be obvious that at so early a period little evidence can be adduced in support of this portion of the pedigree. The descent of the family from Hervey de Sutton, who lived in the time of King Henry the Second, seems, however, fully borne out by contemporary documents. Hervey de Sutton and Robert, his son, were benefactors to the Priory of Worksop. Robert died beyond the seas in his father's lifetime, but he had two younger brothers, Richard (who confirmed his father's gift to the Prior and canons of Worksop in 1236) and Roland. Richard de Sutton had no male issue, and his lands were divided at his death amongst his five daughters and coheiresses, all of whom were married and left issue. Roland de Sutton, the youngest brother, married Alice de Lexington, in whose right he acquired the manor of Averham, which continued for more than 400 years to be the seat of this ancient house. Richard de Lexington, feudal lord of Lexington, now called Laxton, the father of Alice, had another daughter, Cecilia, wife of William de Markham (ancestor of the Markhams of Cotham and Sedgebrook), and five sons, four of whom were in holy orders. John de Lexington, the eldest, was keeper of the Great Seal to Henry the Third. Robert was an eminent lawyer, and one of the King's Justices of Assize, and likewise an ecclesiastic, being a canon of Southwell, and for some years Prior of Lenton; Henry was Dean, and afterwards Bishop of Lincoln; whilst Peter and Stephen were both priests, the former holding the Rectory of Gedling, near Nottingham. All five brothers dying without issue, their lands were divided amongst their two sisters and coheiresses. By Alice, his wife, the elder of these ladies, Roland de Sutton had two sons, Sir William and Sir Robert, the elder of whom (according to Thoroton's pedigree) was ancestor of the noble house of Dudley. Sir Robert de Sutton, the younger son, had the manor of Averham, which continued with his posterity. His lineal descendant, Sir Thomas Sutton of Averham, married Catherine, daughter of Sir Thomas Bassett of Fledborough, and there is a curious piece of carving on the south porch of the church at Averham, introducing the arms of Sutton—*Argent, a canton sable*, impaling those of Bassett, with the initials T. S., and other devices. This Sir Thomas Sutton died in 1526, and was the great-grandfather of Sir William Sutton of Averham, a courtier of Queen Elizabeth, who, by Dame Susanna, his wife, daughter of Thomas Cony, Esq., of Basingthorpe, in Lincolnshire, had a numerous issue, and dying in 1611, in his fifty-third year, was buried on the north side of the altar at Averham, where a quaintly inscribed monument, bearing the recumbent effigies of the knight and his lady, yet remains. Robert Sutton, his eldest son, was born in 1594, and was raised to the peerage as Baron Lexington in 1645, for his faithful services to the king during the civil wars, and as some compensation for the losses he had sustained. Lord Lexington died in 1668, in his seventy-fourth year, and was buried at Averham. The inscription upon his monument states that "He was a loyal subject and lover of his country, a good husband, father, friend, landlord, master, and neighbour." His only son Robert, who succeeded him in his title and estates, was a distinguished diplomatist, and fulfilled the duties of various responsible offices during the reigns of William and Mary, and Anne. He married Margaret, daughter and sole heiress of Sir Giles Hungerford, of Colston, in Wiltshire, who died in 1703. His only son died in 1713 at Madrid (where his father was at that time residing as Ambassador to the Court of Spain), and his body, concealed in a bale of cloth, was conveyed to England and interred at Kelham.[1] Lord Lexington died at Averham in 1723, and in him the title expired, and the elder branch of the Suttons of Averham became extinct in the male line. In the mortuary chapel on the south side of the chancel at Kelham there is a ponderous marble monument, already referred to, upon which are the effigies of the second Lord Lexington and his wife, classically treated and somewhat peculiarly placed, *dos à dos*. Having no surviving male issue, Lord Lexington devised his estates to his only daughter, Bridget, Duchess of Rutland, wife of John, third Duke of Rutland, K. G., for her life, and afterwards to her second son, Lord Robert Manners, on condition of his assuming the name and arms of Sutton. Lord Robert died without issue in 1772, when the estates devolved upon his next brother, Lord George Manners, who also assumed the name and arms of Sutton, and was for some years Colonel of the Nottinghamshire Militia. His lordship represented Newark in Parliament from 1780 until his decease in 1783, and was the great-grandfather of the present possessor of the Kelham estates. Henry Sutton, Esq., a younger brother of the first Lord Lexington, was the father of Robert Sutton, Esq., whose younger son, Brigadier-General Richard Sutton, purchased the Scofton estate near Worksop, and became ancestor of the Suttons of that place. In 1713 the six old

[1] The *Lexington Papers*, edited by the Hon. H. Manners Sutton, p. 7.

bells belonging to Newark parish church were recast and two new bells added to the peal at the expense of Brigadier-General Sutton, who represented the borough from 1711 until 1737, when he died. His elder brother, the Right Honourable Sir Richard Sutton, K.B., married Judith, Countess Dowager of Sunderland, by whom he had two sons. John Sutton, Esq., the elder son, died without issue, and his younger brother, Richard, sometime Under Secretary of State, was created a baronet on his retirement from office in 1772. Sir Richard Francis Sutton, Bart., is the present representative of this branch of the family."

A magnificent stained glass east window, placed in the parish church to the memory of the late Prince Consort, at a cost of about £1000, was opened for the inspection of the public on Easter Sunday 1864. The stonework of the window is of the fifteenth century, and consists of fourteen transome lights with the tracery of the period above. The subjects chosen have been, for the upper tier of lights, the Ascension of our Lord into heaven. In the centre light is seen the figure of the Saviour robed in white garments, surrounded by an immediate circle of flaming seraphim, beyond which extends, through the side lights, a rejoicing choir of angels, who are represented on a ruby ground, each angel playing some musical instrument and singing the glories of God. This portion of the subject is enclosed by a semicircular band of clouds, which marks the distinction between heaven, into which our Lord is ascending, and earth, from which the apostles anxiously watch their Master's ascent. In the centre light is St. Peter with his keys, and next to him St. John, the other apostles being represented in the side lights. In the lower tier of lights, the subjects are chosen from the principal events in our Lord's life. In the centre lights is represented our Saviour on the cross, with adoring angels on either side. At the foot of the cross kneels Mary Magdalene and the city of Jerusalem is seen in the distance. On one side of the cross stand the devout women, the blessed Virgin Mary, Salome, and Mary Cleophas; and on the other side, St. John, the beloved apostle, and the centurion. In the outer dexter lights are, in the upper part, the Adoration of the Magi, and in the lower, the Annunciation. In the outer sinister lights are, in the lower part, the visit of the holy women to the sepulchre, where they find only an angel in a white garment, and in the upper part is the incident "Noli me tangere," the appearance of our Lord after His resurrection to Mary Magdalene. The whole of this window is executed in the style of the fifteenth century; a period peculiarly rich in its ornamentation, as exhibited by the profusion of diaper, and the elaborateness of the framework of the medallions. The work was executed by the Messrs. Hardman and Co., of London and Birmingham, who employed, in carrying it out, the best materials that could be procured.[1]

The events of the last few years, which will be fresh in the memory of most local readers, may be briefly summarised. On the 18th October 1864 the Duke of Newcastle died at Clumber, and his funeral was attended by many from this town and neighbourhood.

[1] See the illustration of the east end of the church facing p. 256.

In January 1867, owing to a sudden thaw, there was an immense flood; Kelham Road was a considerable depth under water, and several narrow escapes occurred.

On Wednesday and Thursday, February 27 and 28, 1867, the extensive estates of Lord Middleton, in Newark and the neighbouring parishes, were sold by auction in the town-hall. There were in all three estates. The Caunton estate, which realised £26,000; the Winthorpe estate, which realised £43,100; and the Newark estate, which was disposed of in an hour and a half, realised £23,120, making a total of £92,000 for the whole estates. Mr. Pott was the auctioneer.

A feeling of deep regret was created in the borough early in 1870, when intelligence arrived of the death at Melbourne of Mr. Edward Denison, one of the members for Newark; a young gentleman of great abilities, whose earnestness as a philanthropist had won for him a large amount of respect and admiration. Mr. Denison was the son of the Bishop of Salisbury, and was born in 1840. He was educated at Eton and at Christ Church, Oxford, where, notwithstanding interruptions in his reading, caused by the state of his health, he took a second class in law and history. In the autumn of 1867, the second year of the distress in the East End of London, he took up his quarters in Stepney, and spent eight months amongst the London poor as a voluntary agent of the Society for the Relief of Distress. During that time he built and endowed a school, and gave lectures to workmen. In January 1868 he visited Ossington, the residence of his uncle, the Speaker of the House of Commons (the Right Hon. J. E. Denison, created Viscount Ossington), and from a letter which he wrote under date Jan. 17, it appears the Speaker suggested that he should offer himself as member for Newark.[1] Adopting the suggestion, he contested the borough, and in November (1868), after a somewhat protracted canvass, he was returned. With unvarying earnestness he continued the study of his favourite subject—the best method of dealing with pauperism, and relieving the poor; but his health becoming worse, he was advised either to spend the winter at Cannes, or to go to Australia. He chose the latter alternative, and arrived in Melbourne early in January 1870. Within a fortnight after he had landed (January 26), he breathed his last, and thus terminated a career that had given abundant promise of real usefulness, and of ardent devotion to the public service.

On the morning of Tuesday, June 21, 1870, there occurred one of the most terrible railway accidents that has ever happened in the kingdom. A goods train from Manchester and Sheffield passed Newark station at 1.24 A.M. and, when near the Clay Lane bridge, leading from Barnby Road, the axle of one of the waggons broke, causing some trucks to run off the down line and extend over the other. A heavily-laden excursion train from London returning to Leeds, Bradford, and elsewhere, came up at the same moment, and a fearful crash ensued, resulting in the death of eighteen persons, and in serious injury to many others. At the inquest, under the presidency of Mr. Coroner Griffin, a verdict was returned to the effect that the deaths had resulted from the accidental breaking of the axle of a

[1] *Letters and other Writings of the late Edward Denison*, p. 61.

waggon, and recommending that some means should be devised for the periodical testing of axles in the future.

In 1873 the district of St. Leonards was formed; and the commodious new church in Northgate was opened on January 28, in that year. The church is built of stone, is in the early decorated style of architecture, and consists of a nave 72 feet by 25 feet, chancel 30 feet by 25 feet, with chancel aisles, and north and south aisles 72 feet by 11 feet. It will accommodate 600 people, and the total cost, including site, was about £4000.

In October 1875 the district through which the Trent passes suffered from extensive floods. The water began to rise on Wednesday the 20th, and on Thursday the Trent overflowed its banks, sending a deluge over thousands of acres, and doing considerable damage. The scene from Newark Castle was remarkable. The water rushed past the walls of the ruin in a huge torrent, and almost as far as the eye could reach the fields presented the appearance of a vast lake, the tops of the hedges and hovels, the railway and the great north road, being visible above the water line.

The present century has, fortunately, been prolific in useful public buildings and institutions. In addition to those which we have already mentioned, we may name the following:—Newark Stock Library and Middleton Newsroom, which occupy a building in the market-place given to the members by Lord Middleton in 1828; the Savings Bank in Lombard Street, commenced in 1817, and removed to its present quarters in 1832; the Mechanics' Institution, started in 1836; the Mount National Schools,—those for girls erected in 1826, and for boys in 1838; Christ Church Schools,—the boys' schools erected in 1850, and the girls' in 1856; a new Wesleyan Chapel and Schools at the North End, erected in 1868; a new Baptist Chapel on the Hawton Road, opened in 1876; and a new Chapel for the Primitive Methodists, opened in 1878. It has also been determined to erect a new Hospital and Dispensary, and a site for the purpose has been selected on the London Road.

With this we close our record of the past. As we do so, glancing back over the history of by-gone times, feelings of thankfulness and hopefulness predominate— thankfulness, because, compared with previous centuries, we live in a bright age full of golden opportunities and invaluable privileges—hopefulness, because all around us there are cheering signs that the future of the "good old town" of which we have written may be prosperous and happy. Newark may never more be distinguished by the appellation of "the Key of the North;" it may never be a military stronghold to attract the envious gaze of rival armies; it may never be "a centre of strength for the combatant and a place of refuge for the fallen." But it may be the abode of commercial activity and intellectual culture, may take a worthy part in the social history of a privileged country, and find an honoured place in those peaceful annals which tell of bloodless victories and enduring conquests—the glorious achievements of the cultured brain and the Christian heart.

APPENDIX.

PAULINUS BAPTIZING IN THE TRENT (PAGE 7).

The tradition that Paulinus, the missionary bishop who received episcopal ordination July 21, 625, baptized in the Trent near Newark, rests in a great measure on the supposed identity of Newark with the ancient Tiovulfingacester. The Venerable Bede writes:—" Now, as touching the faithe and beliefe of this province, a certaine prieste and abbot, a man of good credit and to be believed, whose name is Deda, of the monastery of Partney, told me that one of the elders of that convent, as he reported himself, was baptized with many other of the people there at noneday by Byshope Pauline, in the presence of King Edwine, and in the fludde of Trente near the city of Tiovulfingacester."[1] Partney, according to Giles, was a cell to Bardney, a celebrated monastery near Lincoln, of which Deda was made the first Abbot. But where was Tiovulfingacester? Stark, in his excellent *History of the Bishopric of Lincoln*, thus defines it :—" About five miles south of Agelocum (probably the modern Littleborough) on the eastern bank of the Trent, stood an ancient Roman city, called Tiovulfingacester. It seems to have been a place of much importance, and is presumed by some to have derived its name from the situation on which it was built, at the point where the river Till of the moderns (the Tiovul of the Romans) emptied itself into the river Trent, and where, at a subsequent period, Henry II. cut a canal or dyke, the Fossdyke, connecting the river Witham with the Trent." But the site thus indicated is not that which other writers have chosen. Southwell, some forty miles south-west from the place described by Mr. Stark (Torksey), has, by the editor of the *Hist. Mon. Brit.* (Fol. London, 1844), as well as by Leland, been regarded as the Tiovulfingacester referred to by Bede; whilst others have claimed the distinction for Newark. The province in which Paulinus preached was that of Lindsey, which was "the first on the south side of the river Humber, stretching out as far as the sea" (Bede). The seat of the bishopric was at Sidnacester, which Mr. Dickinson claims to have been Newark, but the evidence is undoubtedly very much stronger in favour of Stowe. Newark was, however, included in the province, and whether it can justly claim to be Tiovulfingacester or not, it seems to have been visited by the bishop. In the *Memoriale Fratri Walteri de Coventreia*, edited by Stubbs—a work of the thirteenth century, but no doubt derived from some good authority, it is stated that Thomas the Elder, the twenty-fifth Archbishop of York, claimed Lincoln and Lindsey, and besides Stow *and Newark*, because Paulinus, the first Archbishop, converted them to the faith and founded the church at Lincoln (25tus archiepiscopus fuit Thomas senior. "Iste juste columniavit Lindecolinam, et Lindeseyam, et præcipue Stouwe et Neuwerk eo quod Paulinus primus archiepiscopus convertit eos ad fidem et ecclesiam Lindecolnensem fundavit."—vol. i. 23).

[1] Stapleton's *Bede*, p. 70.

NEWARK GIVEN TO STOWE (PAGE 8).

The See of Lindsey was successively filled by Eathericus and Eadnothus II. The latter died in 1049, and was buried at Dorchester. He was succeeded by Ulfus or Wlfwi, who procured from the liberality of Leofric and his wife Godiva a grant of Newark and other possessions in the district. The charter in Latin is given in Kemble's *Codex Diplomaticus Ævi Saxonici*. It is No. 818, but is marked with an asterisk, as being of doubtful authenticity. It may be thus translated :—Godgifu [Godiva], the wife of Leofric [Leuric], an English earl, to the most renowned and reverent Victor, our apostolic [father], by whatsoever in Christ appears most dear. As the universal Catholic people, with the whole Christian religion, and with all holiness, have united to elect thee glorious, it beseems thee to receive the prayers of thy handmaiden for a short time with unprejudiced ears. I pray thee, therefore, most especially, oh pastor, that you will confirm with your authority, the gifts which I, for the redemption of the soul of my husband, and of mine, have given to the blessed mother of God, Mary at Stowe, even as the countrymen, bishops, and abbots as well as earls, the names of whom have been subscribed, have corroborated. These are the names of the possessions—Newarke, to wit, and Fledborough, with their appurtenances; and Branthon and Martin Well, with appurtenances. These, therefore, I have given to the Mother of the Lord, by my collar and my gold vermiculated pendant (?)
✠ I Eadward, king of the English, have granted the liberty of this donation, holding freely the chief dignity of the whole realm. ✠ I Ealdred, Priest, elected to the archiepiscopal seat of the Church of Canterbury, have given my consent to this royal gift. ✠ I Wlfwi, bishop. ✠ I Leofric, earl. ✠ I Harold, earl. ✠ I Tostig, earl. ✠ I Siword, "duke," and many others.
The apostolic ✠ sign.
For I consent to this gift with all my heart, and confirm by the Roman authority, and return the charter signed with my seal. But if any one shall be so bold as to cancel this, he shall be doomed eternally with Pilate, Judas Iscariot, and Caiaphas as well, and with their companions to Acherontic fire.
The grant of Leofric and Godiva to Wlfwi appears to have been executed in 1054. It was further confirmed by William the Conqueror :—"Me confirmasse donationem quæ Leofricum comes, et Godiva, sua conjux ecclesia sanctæ Mariæ Stowensis dederunt." Lincoln having become the bishop's see, Bloet, who had been chaplain to the Conqueror, proposed to proceed with the consecration of the cathedral, A.D. 1092. But Thomas, Archbishop of York, objected. He claimed that Newark, Stowe, Louth, Lincoln, and the whole district of Lindsey, were unjustly and forcibly detained from his jurisdiction. The controversy was settled by a payment to the king, and an agreement was entered into, under the sanction of William Rufus, whereby, in consideration of the gift of an abbey and church, Thomas relinquished his claim for ever.

THE BUILDER OF NEWARK CASTLE (PAGE 9).

Hollinshead gives the following particulars of Bishop Alexander, the builder of Newark Castle, and his uncle, the Bishop of Salisbury :—"Stephen began to repent himself, although too late, for that he had granted license to so many of his subjects to build castles within their own grounds, and amongst others he vehemently suspected Rodger, Bishop of Salisbury (who had done very much for him), and Alexander, Bishop of Lincoln, nephew to the said Bishop of Salisbury, or (as some thought) more near to him in kindred. For the said Rodger had builded divers castles; and the said Alexander likewise, following his uncle's example, bestowed his money that way very freely, having builded one castle at Newarke, and another at Sleeford. The king, therefore, having committed both these bishops to prison, he threatened to keep them without either meat or drink, if they would not cause these castles to be delivered into his hands; whereby he obtained them; and moreover found, in the Bishop of Salisbury's coffers, forty thousand marks, which he took to his own use by way of confiscation. This ingratitude of the king so wounded the bishop's heart, that, taking thought for the loss of his houses and money, he pined away, and died within a little while after.

"This Rodger, Bishop of Salisbury, was in the days of William Rufus a poor priest, serving once in a village near the city of Caen in Normandy. Now it chanced that the Lord Henry, the king's brother, came thither on a time, and called for a priest to say mass before him; whereupon this Rodger coming to the altar, was by and by ready, and quick at it; and therewithal had so speedily made an end thereof, that the men of war then attendant on the said Lord Henry affirmed that this priest above all other was a chaplain meet to say mass before men of war; because he had made an end when many thought he had but newly begun. Hereupon the king's brother commanded the priest to follow him, insomuch that, when opportunity served, for his diligent service and ready despatch of matters, when Henry had attained the crown, he was by him advanced to great promotions; as first, to be Chancellor of England; after Bishop of Salisbury; growing still into such estimation that he might do more with the king than any other of the council."

KING JOHN AT NEWARK (PAGE 13).

The *Close Rolls* show that the king had been at Newark some time before his death, and was therefore acquainted with the castle and the accommodation it afforded. The entries on the Rolls prove that he was at Newark on the 29th and 30th of May 1207. There is an order to the Sheriff of Norfolk and Suffolk dated at Newark on the 29th, and there are several mandates to the Barons of Exchequer directing payment for wines, etc., purchased for the king's use, bearing date May 30th. (Teste me ipso apud Newere xxx^{ti} die Maii.) There are other letters of the king from Newark of similar date. One acknowledges receipt of money "in our chamber at Newark," from the bailewick of Knaresboro'; another orders the giving up of certain land; and a third is a notice of the receipt of sixty pounds of the revenues of the bishopric of Exeter. The following are translations of the most interesting of the entries relating to Newark:—

"The king to the Barons of the Exchequer. Pay ye to William, Archdeacon of Huntingdon, for 48 doles of wine, two marks for each dole, and six doles at three marks, bought at Boston, for our use. Pay also the same for fifteen doles of wine bought for our use, and of which we have caused four doles to be sent to Hareston, and three to Clipstone, and three to Melbourne, and three to Lexington, and one to Cliff (or Clive), and one to Southwell. Pay also to the same for fifteen doles which we have expended (consumed) at Newark and Southwell, Gringley, Woodstock, Witney (?) at the Ascension and Pentecost. Pay also to the same the carriage of the same thirty doles. Witness, myself at Marlborough the 12th of October, by William de Cantelope senior, and Daniel, the butler, in the ninth year of our reign."

The following appears to relate to a bribe given to the king to obtain an award:—

"The king to the barons, etc. Know ye that William, the son of Wakelin, has paid us one palfrey which he promised us for acting in respect of the cause which was between him and the Earl of the Island in the matter of the land in Pochley on the night of the Ascension of the Lord, in the 8th year of our reign, at Newark, and hereon we charge you that in this matter you shall cause him to be quit. Witness myself, at Woodstock, 11th of June (1207)."

In Henry the Sixth's reign it was not considered incompatible with the usages of the period for the king to exercise an all-powerful influence in securing a verdict. When John Paston brought an action against Lord Molynes for waste and damage, and indicted him and his abettors for felony, the sheriff, who was well disposed towards him, gave notice that he had received a distinct injunction from the king to make up a panel to acquit Lord Molynes.[1] " To show the cheapness of justice in these times (equalled apparently in previous times), when court favour went for everything and right for nothing, John Paston himself tells us that the document on which the sheriff acted was one that could be procured for 6s. 8d."[2]

Another entry on the *Close Rolls* is as follows:—"The king to Reginald de Cornhill, etc. We command you that you shall cause (us) to have by the bearer, in the presence of Brien de L'Isle, two hauberks and four haubergeons and six 'capellos ferreos' (iron hats), good ones, so that he shall be acquitted of you, and charge, etc. Witness myself, at Newark, 30th day of May, in the 8th year of our reign." We append other entries:—[3]

P. 166. A.D. 1214.

"The king to his Barons of the Exchequer, etc. Pay ye to Brian de L'Isle £9 : 15 : 3, which he paid according to the witness and testimony of lawful men for the passage of our . . . from Ireland through England by our order, and 30s. 10½d. in maintenance (feeding) of our dogs at Beverley, and 60 shillings for . . . which we received at Pembroke by the hands of Robert de Percy, and ten shillings and fourpence for eight quarters and one bushel . . . of our venison to be salted at Southwell, and 10 marks for making brattishes at Newark, and £10 for guarding the Castle of Banbury (?), and £12 for making the dovecot at Lexington by our order. Witness myself, the 25th day of May, in the 9th year of our reign." The brattishes were wooden hoardings which were erected on castle walls. They projected over the wall, and were covered. The front was high enough for a man to shoot out of when standing. Stones were dropped through the flooring upon the heads of the assailants, whilst the roof protected the men engaged in defensive operations. The next following items are equally interesting.

P. 291. A.D. 1216.

"The king to the steward of the Lord Bishop of Lincoln, greeting. We command you that you shall receive from our esteemed and faithful Philip Mark, your castle of the Bishop of Lincoln of Newark, giving security that thereby no injury shall arise to us or our realm, because we have commanded the same Philip that he shall deliver it up by the oath and witness of lawful men. But if you shall be unwilling to receive it, and damage shall thereby accrue to your lord, it shall not be imputed to us when the same Philip shall be ready to deliver the same to you, nor by us to him when it stands, so that you can have the same, and know that we have commanded the Lord Bishop of Bath and Glastonbury, who is the chief guardian of the bishopric of Lincoln, that he shall cause it to be received. Witness myself, at Corfe, 17th day of July."

P. 291. A.D. 1216.

"The king to J. of Bath and Glastonbury greeting. Know ye that we have commanded

---

[1] *Paston Letters*, Mr. Gardner's edition.   [2] *Edinburgh Review* (Notice of Paston Letters), No. 297, p. 144.
[3] We are indebted to Mr. W. H. Stevenson of Hull for his serviceable assistance in preparing these transcripts of the *Close Rolls*.

APPENDIX.

Philip Mark that, by the oath and witnessing of lawful men, he shall cause to be delivered to the steward of the Lord Bishop of Lincoln, your brother, his castle of Newark, which, by our order, he has custody of, and when the chief and superior guardians of the bishopric of Lincoln shall appear, we command you that you shall give orders so that the castle shall be received from our bailiff; and if by chance, while he is absent, damage shall arise to your brother, because you will not have received his castle, or had not received it from our bailiff, such shall not be imputed to us or to him. Witness myself, at Corfe, the 17th day of July."

THE DEATH OF KING JOHN (PAGE 14).

Though we have discarded in the body of the work the various statements attributing the death of King John to poison, it may not be uninteresting to advert here to some of the curious assertions which have been made by old authorities upon the subject. Thus Walter Hemingford (or rather Hemingburgh), who died in 1347, tells us that the king hearing the Abbot of Swineshead had a fair sister, a prioress in the neighbourhood, sent for her; that the abbot was uneasy about it, and the hospitaller of the monastery said to him, "Do but absolve me, father, and pray for me, and I will rid the earth of this monster;" that the abbot was scrupulous, because he was a king; that the hospitaller proceeded, nevertheless, and as he knew the king loved new pears, brought some that were all poisoned, except three that he had marked, and offered them to him; upon which the precious stones (in the king's rings) began to sweat! The king said to his host, "What is this you have brought me? poison?" "Not poison," said he, "but excellent fruit." The king, by way of precaution, bade him eat one, which he did, taking one he had marked; then he bade him eat another, and he did so; then a third; after which the king ate one himself, and died the same night. A second account is that of Caxton, which varies in every respect from Hemingburgh's curious tale. Caxton says: —The king hearing it said, when he was at the abbey, how cheap corn was, answered, "He would make it so dear that a penny loaf should be sold for a shilling." Upon this an indignant monk put the poison of a toad into a cup of wine, and drank to the king, which made his Majesty pledge him in return the more readily. After the king had taken the draught, finding himself ill, he asked for the monk, and when it was told him he was dead, "God have mercy upon me," said he, "I doubted as much;" and so he died in two days. A third account, given by John Fox from the *Fructus temporum* agrees as to the manner of poisoning the king, but says it was on account of the language he had used in reference to Lewis the Dauphin, who was popular at Swineshead Abbey. As against these contradictory tales may be set the accounts of several other writers, some of whom lived in King John's time. Matthew Paris intimates that grief and anxiety were thought to have been the source of the king's malady, and to have thrown him into a fever. The disease was increased by the patient's own imprudence, "auxit autem aegritudinis molestiam perniciosa ejus ingluvies, qui nocte illâ de fructu persicorum, et novi ciceris (cider, since M. Westminster calls it pomarium : according to Dr. Fuller, this part of the country was celebrated for its pippins called Kirton pippins), potatione nimis repletus febrilem in se calorem acuit fortiter et accendit." Richard de Morins, author of the *Annals of Dunstable*, who died 1242, says, without intimating anything about poison, that the king died in the castle of Newark, on crastino Sancti Lucæ. The *Annals of Margan*, which terminate 1232, and the *Annals of Waverley*, written about the same time, only say that the king died after three or four days' illness at Newark. We may conclude, therefore, that the king began to be ill at Swineshead from sorrow, anxiety, and other kindred causes; that he, nevertheless, started the next day on horseback for Sleaford, but was obliged to betake himself to a litter; that at Sleaford he was seized with dysentery, and next day was carried to Newark Castle, where he died. The Abbot of Croxton was his physician at Newark (*vide* Matthew Paris), but he did not arrive until the malady was past cure. After his death he was embowelled by the abbot, either at Newark Castle or Croxton, the bowels being buried at Croxton, and the body at Worcester. To those who would care to go still farther into the subject, we heartily commend an elaborate and scholarly article, written by the Rev. Samuel Pegge, in 1772. It may be found in the *Archæologia*, vol. iv. p. 29.

HENRY III. AND THE CASTLE (PAGE 15).

The following entries are translated from the *Close Rolls*:—

"The king to the Constable of Newark, etc. We command you that you shall receive 50 marks, which the Dean of Lincoln will cause to be delivered to you, and you shall send the same to Philip Mark (Sheriff of Notts.) Witnessed at Lexington, the 30th day of December 1216."

P. 284.   A.D. 1216.

"The king to Philip Mark greeting. We command you, as we have commanded others, that you shall deliver to Robert de Gaugy[1] the Castle of Newark; and whatever we may have commanded you before for destroying (throwing down) the same castle, you shall in no wise destroy or allow it to be destroyed, but you shall either retain it in your hands or deliver it to the said Robert. Witness, etc."

It is clear from this that the castle had a narrow escape. The king had so far made up his mind to destroy it, that he issued orders to that effect. He immediately after recanted, countermanded the orders, and appointed Robert de Gaugy keeper of the fortress. What a different history that of Newark would have been if the town had been deprived of that centre of strength which made it a conspicuous stronghold in troublous times!

P. 378.   A.D. 1218.

"The king to Philip Mark, greeting. We command you that, in the allegiance you hold to us, and as you love us, you shall, with an armed band and with as many armed men as you can, meet our venerable father, the Lord H. Bishop of Lincoln, with others of our faithful subjects, at a day and place which the same Lord Bishop of Lincoln will signify to you, to compel Robert de Gaugy to render up his castle of Newark, if he shall have refused to deliver it to him and you.

"These are the names of the knights who have letters of warrant, because they were with the army of our lord the king at Newark:—Reginald de Braose, William de Cuapewell, Roger de Beauchamp, Simon de Kimberley, Geoffrey de Caxton, Phillip de Strelley, Wm. de Beauchamp, Richard de Claudun, John Marr, John de Balun, Geoffrey de Lucy, John de Fresnay, Guy de Walterville, Henry de St. Valery, Elias de Beauchamp, Richard de Percy, William de Colvill, John de Welhagh, William de Luddington, Guy de Waterville, Thomas de Pirho, William de Ros, Roger de Cauz, Hugh de Nevill."

[1] Misspelt Gangi on p. 16. We desire here to point out and rectify the mistake.

APPENDIX.

PARCHMENT MAKING AT NEWARK.

The Issue Roll of 44 Edward III. records a payment to Richard, the parchment-maker of Newark, on the 16th May, by John Capan, for 50 dozens parchment, at 2s. 10d. per dozen, for the king's use, as well as for that of the Privy Seal £7 : 1 : 8 (*Issue Roll*, 44 Edward III. p. 132). There is another entry on the 5th October of money paid to the same for 84 dozen parchment at 3s. for the king's use, etc., £12 : 12s. (p. 283).

THE BEAUMONT CROSS (PAGE 19).

Captain Lowe calls our attention to the fact that amongst the charters preserved in the Bodleian Library at Oxford, is one dated at Neuwerk, the Saturday next before the feast of St. Luke the Evangelist, 3 Edw. II. (1310), whereby Ralph, son of Peter de Neuwerk, grants to William de Asseballock and his heirs a toft in *Beumond* in Newark, for an annual rent of one penny. In the same collection there are four other undated charters, probably contemporary with the one just mentioned. By the first of these, William, son of William Crag', of Neuwerk, the younger, grants to William Asseballock, of Neuwerk, his heirs and assigns, one plot of land in Newerk lying in *Beumnd*. By another, Peter Waleys of Honedleyn, quit claims to William Asseballock of Newerk all his right in a plot of land in Newerk, lying in *Beumond*, between the plot of Ralph, son of Peter, and a plot of the said William's. By another, Robert de Cotum grants to William Asseballock one plot of land without Newerk, lying in *Beumond*. And by the fourth, Robert Salter of Newerk grants to William Asseballock and Beatrice his wife, and John their son, a messuage in *Beumond* in Newerk, they paying an annual rent of sixpence to the Bishop of Lincoln for all secular services. It may be noted that there are four other early charters in the same collection relating to Newark; two of these, dated respectively in 1393 and 1394, refer to "le Apiltongate" in Newark, and the two others, one of which is dated in 1404, whilst the other is probably *circa* 1380, both relate to lands in Newerk and in Northgate near Newerk. *Vide Calendar of Charters and Rolls, preserved in the Bodleian Library*, pp. 275, 276.

Rimmer, in his *Ancient Stone Crosses of England*, pp. 70, 71, 72, states that the cross was built by the Duchess of Norfolk, who married John, Viscount Beaumont, who fell at the battle of Towton Moor, and adds : " Newark by the old road would be about 73 miles from Towton, and here the body of Beaumont was brought for interment, and the cross of which we are writing was erected by his widow to his memory." He further speaks of it as a valuable example of a memorial cross, as the date is so completely fixed.

No authorities are quoted, and if the statement that the cross is a memorial of John, Lord Beaumont, is based merely upon the name, the charters that have been quoted supply abundant evidence that what was then a suburb of Newark was known as *Beumnd* or *Beumond* at a far earlier date than the cross (to judge by the style of its architecture) was erected.

PLACES OF REFUGE (PAGE 43).

The following are exact copies of the entries in the *Sanctuarium Beverlacense* (Surtees Society), to one of which we have referred on page 43 :—

(29th day of July in the 2d year of the reign of King Richard the Third). Richard Cox of

Newark, in the county of Nottingham, the same year and date [as above] likewise came for the death of a certain William at Newark aforesaid, slain by him with a staff (baculum) on Monday before . . . of the blessed Mary Magdalene last, and was sworn and admitted."—P. 152.

"The 30th day of December in the (8th) year of the reign of King Henry VIII., John Bristow, late of Newark, in the county of Nottingham, tailor, came to the perpetual peace of St. John of Beverley, for the homicide [murder] committed upon James Jackson [Jakson] late of Newark aforesaid, and for all other causes, etc., and was admitted to the foresaid liberty, and sworn, as is the custom, etc."—P. 172.

"Christopher Thomlynson, late of Newark, in the County of Notyngham, glover, on the 10th day of December, in the year of the reign of King Henry VIII. . . . came to the liberty and sanctuary of St. John of Beverley because he was attached for the buying of an unknown man, three yards of woollen cloth suspected. And afterwards the same Cristofer [sic] was taken to the prison of our lord the king at Nottingham. And then and there Thomas Clerk, of Newark aforesaid, mercer, became pledge and bond ['fidejussor'] of the said Cristofer [sic], but afterwards the aforesaid Christofer feloniously fled from the custody of the said Thomas, etc., and for other causes touching the safety of his body, and was admitted and sworn, etc." —P. 204.

MAGNUS AND QUEEN MARGARET (PAGE 47).

The following is a letter written to Magnus by Queen Margaret of Scotland. The idea of the reverend doctor being requested to seek out and purchase small hounds and bloodhounds of the best kind is somewhat droll, to say the least of it.

"RIGHT TRUSTY AND WELL-BELOVED FRIEND—We commend us unto you, in our most hearty manner, praying you right effectuously that you will get and send to us three or four brace of the best *ratches* (small hounds) in the country, less or more, for hares, foxes, and other greater beasts, with a brace of blood hounds of the best kind, that are good, and will ride behind men on horseback: and this we exhort you to do as you will do us singular empleasure, and report special thanks of us therefor. And the Trinity preserve you.

Your friend,

MARGARET R.

Written at Edinburgh, the 8th day of January 1526.

To the Right Honourable, our trusty friend, Master Thomas Magnus, Archdeacon of East Riding, etc.

In *Miscellaneous Antiquities*, No. II., printed by Horace Walpole at the Strawberry Hill press in 1772, speaking of Sir Thomas Wyat the elder, it is said:—"That he had the post of Master of the Jewel Office under Henry VIII. appears by a book which was shown to the Antiquarian Society by Mr. Will, one of their members, June 22, 1734. It was the original account of the king's jewels, every leaf being signed with Henry's own hand, and was intituled, 'A Vewe and Accomptis of all and singular the Kinges Jewellis, stone, perle, plate of golde and of silver, in the custodye and kepynge of Sir Henry Wyat, Maister of the Kinges Jewellis . . . and the true poyz and waight of every parcel of the same, taken by the Rt. Revd. Father in God, John, Archbp. of Armachan [Armagh, we presume], Maister Thomas Magnus, Archdeacon of Estriding, and Sir Wm. Kingston, Kt., deputed Commissioners by the Kinges Highness for the same purpose the 14 daye of February the XII. year of our soveraine Lorde Kinge Henry the VIII.'"

APPENDIX.

CROMWELL NEAR NEWARK.

In the combined attack in spring 1643 Cromwell was an element,[1] though he did not take part in the engagement; nor does he ever appear to have been actually at Newark. In May he was at Grantham, from which town he directs a letter (May 13) describing a victory which he had gained over the enemy. They faced, he says, within two miles of the town, numbering "one and twenty colours" of horse troops, and three or four of dragoons. Cromwell's forces consisted of about twelve troops; "some of them so poor and broken, that you shall seldom see worse." After the dragooners had fired on both sides for the space of half an hour or more, Cromwell charged, and put the Cavaliers to flight, taking forty-five prisoners and four or five colours. Mr. Carlyle says there is no tradition at Grantham as to the scene of the skirmish, which must have been some two miles out on the Newark road. May states that Cromwell had two notable skirmishes near Grantham, in one of which he defeated a strong party of the Newarkers, "where the odds of numbers on their side were so great, that it seemed almost a miraculous victory." The opinion of Mr. Carlyle that the Cromwells came from Cromwell, near Newark, is highly interesting. He says:—"The small Hamlet and Parish Church of Cromwell, or Crumwell (the Well of Crum, whatever that may be), still stands on the eastern edge of Nottinghamshire, not far from the left bank of the Trent. From this, without any ghost to teach us, we can understand that the Cromwell kindred all got their name in very old times indeed. From torpedo rubbish-records, we learn also, without great difficulty, that the Barons Cromwell were summoned to Parliament from Edward the Second's time and downward; that they had their chief seat at Tattershall, in Lincolnshire; that there were Cromwells of distinction, and of no distinction, scattered in reasonable abundance over that fen country —Cromwells, sheriffs of their counties there, in Richard's own time."

CHARLES I. AND SIR RICHARD WILLIS (PAGE 151).

In the "Diary of the Marches of the Royal Army during the great Civil War," kept by Richard Symonds (from the original MSS. in the British Museum, edited by C. E. Long, M.A., for the Camden Society 1859), some further details are given of the scene at Newark, between Prince Rupert, Sir Richard Willis, Lord Gerrard, and Charles I. The writer, under date Sunday, Oct. 26, 1645, says, that when the prince and his friends entered the presence, the king had almost dined. Prince Rupert came in discontentedly with his hands at his side, and approached very near the king, whereat his Majesty presently commanded all to be taken away, and rising from the table, walked to a corner of the room. Willis spoke first, and portions of the conversation are given in the Diary. The prince observed that it was Lord Digby who had caused all the distractions which prevailed among them, to which the king replied, that they were all "rogues and rascals" who said so. At this, Lord Gerrard bowed and went out. The prince showed no reverence, but went out with his hands at his side. All the train followed them, and the king was left in private with Sir Richard Willis. Sir Richard informed his Majesty that a corporal and ten boys were able to do as much service as all his commissioners in Newark; and recommended that all the soldiers in the garrison should be collected in a body to march after Fairfax, who was then about Taunton. Newark river was fordable, and in the town were about 4000 foot. The king approved the proposition, but Digby and Ashburnham being jealous, prevailed on his Majesty to relinquish the idea. The result of it all was that Sir Richard was removed from the governorship, and left the town with

[1] Carlyle's *Cromwell's Letters*, vol. i. p. 174.

his officers and 800 men. "Had it not been," adds the chronicler, "for Sir Richard himself, when his men heard that he was turned out of the Government, they had quitted all the guards and left the king's service, for at the first noise of it, many of them toare their colours in the market-place; which was not done by his instigation or insinuation, but out of love to him, and showing their discontent."

THE FINAL SIEGE OF NEWARK (PAGE 154).

Some particulars, which we have not heretofore given of the Final Siege of Newark, may be gleaned from the correspondence printed in the *Parliamentary and Constitutional History of England*, vol. xiv. The Earl of Leven writes, that on the 26th of November (1645), having approached within a mile of the town, he caused the troops to "draw a live dike" to Muskham Bridge, whereupon he placed musqueteers, and sought all means to cross the river, and storm the sconce on the other side; but the garrison, apprehending the design, sallied out before the break of day, and attempted to destroy the bridge. They were beaten off, and on setting fire to the draw-bridge, the besiegers drove them back, and extinguished the fire, which made them forsake their works, so that Lord Leven became master both of the bridge and the sconce. Under date of March 1646 we have the information given us that "the siege went but slowly on. Every inch of ground was disputed by the besieged." The Earl of Rutland, in a letter dated from Lincoln, March 3, wrote word that their whole army on the south side the Trent were drawn together; the farthermost foot quarters were about a mile from the town; others were at Farringdon (Farndon), Houghton (Hawton), and Balderton, and so to the Trent again at Winthorpe." In a letter of March 18, the Earl and Lord Montague state that Colonel Legard's regiment has arrived from York, healthful and full of courage. One of the bridges across the Trent, against Winthorpe, is ready, and the other will be finished in a day or two. The whole cannon from York has come to Winthorpe. One strong fort is made to secure the bridge, and another is preparing near the enemies' great sconce. The culverins (long slender pieces of ordnance) and the mortar pieces were at Balderton and Farndon, and the great mortar piece was to be at Nottingham on Wednesday. In a letter of March 31, their lordships say:—"Colonel Poyntz doubts not but presently to turn the river quite into a new channel, that their mills may not be helpful to them, or the water hinder the approaches on the north side Trent. The field officers have viewed the most convenient places for forts, either to shoot into the town or sconces, which are in preparation and will speedily be finished." Early in May Lord Montague writes that the king and three others have arrived at Southwell, and then follows a letter from Lord Lothian to the Parliamentary Commissioners announcing the surrender of the king to the Scotch army, an event which, the writer says, "has overtaken us unexpectedly, filled us with amazement, and made us like men that dream." Then Lord Montague and others wrote to the Committee of Both Kingdoms a letter, dated Balderton, May 6, stating that on the previous evening, about six o'clock, they met with the Scots' Commissioners in the meadows, between Kelham and Farndon, and were told that the king was come to Kelham, to Lieutenant-General David Lesley's quarters. Strict guard was kept about the house where the king was, and none suffered to have access to him without permission, except M. Montreville, the French agent. Particulars of the surrender of Newark, with copies of the articles agreed upon, were shortly afterwards reported.

SUFFERERS FOR LOYALTY.

From a small octavo volume, entitled "A Catalogue of the Lords, Knights, and Gentlemen who have Compounded for their Estates" (London, printed for Thomas Dring at the signe of the George in Fleet Street, neare Clifford's Inne, 1655), a copy of which has been obligingly lent us by Mr. W. D. Warwick of Newark, we learn the names of those in Newark and the neighbourhood who had to suffer severely for their loyalty to Charles I. The following names, with the amounts paid by way of composition, will be interesting:—Gilbert Atkinson and John, his son (set £50 per annum, 2 lives), paid £42 : 10s. ; Thomas Aitkinson, Newark, £268; John Barker, Southwell, gent., £234; Redman Burrell, Fulbeck, Lincoln, Esq., £770; Christopher Berresford, Fulbeck, Esq., £365; William Baker, Newark, £80; Robert Butler, Southwell, Esq., £679 : 10s.; Hugh Cartwright, Edingley, Esq., £320; Sir Roger Cooper and Cecil, his son, Thurgarton, £1943; Sir Gervase Clifton, Clifton, £7625; Cecil Cooper, Thurgarton, gent., £3 : 6 : 4; Richard Draper, Flintham, gent., £248; Henry Gill, Newark, £63 : 13 : 4; Christopher Haslam, Newark, £141; William Hobman, Newark, £31 : 13 : 4; Gervase Lee, Norwell, £560; Francis Leek, Newark, £2352; Sir Robert Markham, Sedgebrooke, £1000; Richard Marshall, Newark, £550; Robert Martin, Newark, gent., £100; John Martin, Newark, £37 : 6 : 8; William Martin, Newark, £855 : 14 : 4; John Quiningborough, Newark, £40; Elizabeth Rogers, Everton, £250; William Staunton, Staunton, £828 : 3 : 6; Thomas Somminers, Newark, £45 : 5s ; Robert Sutton, Averham, £4861; Joseph Thompson, Newark, £1; Sir Thomas Williamson, East Markham, Kt. and Bart., £3400; Dove Williamson, Fulbeck, £60; George Wells, Newark, £40; William Wilson, Newark, £35 : 4 : 4. The total number of those who compounded appears to have been 3157, and the amount paid £1,296,762 : 8 : 1.

THE WARBURTON FAMILY.

Reference to the parish registers of Shelton shows that some slight correction is necessary in the brief account of the descent of the Warburton family (pp. 223, 224), which was based upon that given by Watson in his *Life of Bishop Warburton*, as there mentioned. The first of the family who settled in Nottinghamshire was William Warburton, younger son of Peter Warburton, Esq. (the third son of Sir Piers Warburton of Arley, in Cheshire), who was living at Shelton in 1605, as the registers record the interment of his son John on the 13th of September in that year. William Warburton died at an advanced age, and was buried at Shelton on the 23d of May 1653, leaving by Anne, his second wife (who was buried at Shelton on the 28th of December 1661), a son, William, and it was he, and not his father, who served in the Royalist army in the civil wars, and became the husband of Frances Awfield, and the father, by her, of George Warburton, town-clerk of Newark, whose elder son was the Bishop of Gloucester. This second William Warburton was buried at Shelton on the 5th of November 1669. George Warburton was his third son, and was born at Shelton on the 29th November 1659, and baptized there on the following day.

MISCELLANEOUS ITEMS.

A fair at Newark appears to have been held as far back as the reign of Edward III. Under date the first year of that king's reign is the following entry in the *Rotuli Parliamentarium* (vol. ii. p. 439 *a*) "Henry Bishop of Lincolne prayeth a longer time for the continuance of his fair of Banbury and Newark? Answer, let him have a writt of the king's grace." The celebrated Boy Bishop had a Newark gentleman as guardian of his property. In an introduction to "Two Sermons preached by the Boy Bishop, temp. Henry VIII., and at Gloucester, temp., Mary," by E. F. Rembault, Ll.D. (*Camden Miscellany*, vol. viii., 1875), is the following:—"A York computer, A.D. 1596, gives a very circumstantial account of the visitation made by the Boy Bishop in that year. This curious roll . . . purports to be the account of Nicholas of Newark, guardian of the property of John de Cave, boy bishop, in the year of our Lord [15]96." Then follows a full epitome of the account, which is also given entire in the appendix. In the register of the parish of Stoke is an entry of the marriage, on the 30th of January 1588, of "William Sisill (Cecil), Esq., son and heir-apparent of the Right Worshipful Thomas Sisill, Knight, and Elizabeth, daughter of the Right Honourable Edward, late Earl of Rutland." The marriage took place in the chapel of the Castle of Newark, and the register is signed by Mary Manners, and fifteen other witnesses. In the *Calendar of State Papers*, 13 Henry VIII. A.D. 1521, is the following entry:—"[Thomas Lord Darcy] Payments in the 11th and 12th years . . . to the four Friars Observant at Greenwich, Hampton, Richmond, and Newark, a half-year at Mich., £6 : 13 : 4." The poem on the inundation of the Trent, alluded to on page 195, and said to be by Thomas Winnard, is given in Cleveland's Works. At p. 291 of *The Works of Mr John Cleveland*, 1687, is the poem commencing as we have described, and occupying four and a quarter pages in length. It does not, however, appear in an edition of Cleveland's Works printed ten years earlier, namely, in 1677.

PARLIAMENTARY REPRESENTATIVES.

We have naturally been anxious to ascertain when Newark first sent representatives to Parliament, and, with that object in view, have made various inquiries, the result of which we here present. It appears that though the town had occasionally the privilege of sending a member to the great council of the nation, it was not regularly represented until the reign of Charles II. One of the first publications to which we turned was "The Parliamentary writs and Writs of Military Summons, together with the Records and Muniments relating to the Suit and Service due and performed to the King's High Court of Parliament and the Councils of the Realm, or affording Evidence of Attendance given at Parliaments and Councils." The volumes are edited by Mr. Francis Palgrave, F.R.S., and were printed by command of his Majesty George IV., in pursuance of an address of the House of Commons (1827). The work includes all the records which show the constituent parts of the ancient legislative and remedial assemblies of England, beginning with the reign of Edward I.; the period when they first assumed a definite organisation. It contains (1) the writs of summons addressed to the prelates and earls, and to the individuals generally, but not invariably designated barons, proceres, or magnates, "and also to the justices, clerks, and others of the council; (2) proxies of the prelates, earls, and proceres; (3) precepts and mandates issued by the metropolitan and diocesan prelates requiring the attendance of the inferior clergy; (4) writs for the election of members to the Commons House of Parliament and returns." The first reference we find of a local nature does not indicate any return by the town, but relates to an influential individual, who was doubtless a native of Newark. It is as follows:—"1283. Rhuddlan (place of meeting), 1st Feb., Commission empowering Henricus de Newerk and Thomas de Normanville to order and dispose of the service which had been granted at York by the knights, 'hiberi Hommes communitates,' and all others of the counties beyond the Trent, assembled before

APPENDIX.

the Archbishop of York and Anthony Bek, Archdeacon of Durham." Next, of uncertain date, "Letters patent addressed to the clergy of the counties beyond Trent, about the Assembly at York, in the quinzaine of the Purification of the Virgin Mary, 16th Feb." enjoining them to give full faith to Henricus de Newerk, Archdeacon of Richmond, substituted as the king's commissioner, in the place of Antonius Bek, employed in other affairs. Also of uncertain date, a Commission empowering Henricus de Newerk to act accordingly. 1283. Aberconway, 18th Mar., Commission for assessment and collection of the thirtieth in the counties of Cumberland, Lancaster, Northumberland, Westmoreland, and York. The assessors and collectors to be assigned by Henricus de Newerk[1] and Thomas de Normanville. In 1297 Henricus de Newerk, Archbishop of York, was summoned to the council or Parliament, held before Edward, the king's son, at London, on the morrow of St. Michael, Sept. 30 (25 Edward I). We also find the archbishop returned as possessing lands in Nottinghamshire and Derbyshire. But though an influential native of Newark was taking, at this early period, an active part in the government of the country, we do not find any representatives elected by the town. There are returns for Nottingham, and also for the county during the reign of Edward II., with the amounts paid to the representatives for their services; but we meet with no mention of Newark. The town was, however, represented in a Great Council, called to consider the interests of trade, held at Westminster, Sept. 26, 1337 (2 Edward III.), as appears by the Parliamentary writs and returns, the necessary authority for the election having been addressed to the bailiffs of Newark on Sept. 2. In 1340 Robert Stuffyn de Newerk was summoned to Parliament (*Vide* Rymer's *Fœdera*, vol. ii. p. 111, 4 edit. 1816). Robert Stuffyn was apparently a wool merchant of Newark, for in 1338, Godekyn de Revele, "Marchaunt de Almayne" (Germany) prays Parliament for remedy that he had bought eight sacks of wool in the county of Nottm., "pur eut faire son profitt," and had sent these sacks to the house of Ralph Sausemer, when "Esteveur le Heyr," who was assigned to seize the possessions of those who were of the alliance of the King of France, in the said county, took these eight sacks into the king's hands, and (we quote as in the original) "les bailla en garde à Robert Stuffyn de Newerk, tant q'il avoit autre maundement. Et puis avoit le dit Robert en maundement d'estre a l'Eschekier a certeyn jour & la feust le dit Robert charge par Tresorer & barons, de sauver le dit leyne [wool] a l'oeps nostre Seigneur le Roi, en supposaunt qe le dit Godekyn est de l'alliance le Roi de Fraunce, come il ne est pas. Par quoi le dit Godekyn prie deliveraunce de la dite leyne, & qe le dit Robert soit descharge." To which the king and his council replied that they did not want to harm the German merchants, who were "de l'amitié le Roy," and that the wool should be given up to Godekyn. In the same year prayed "Reynere de Evelane and Godefr Kirkhere, Marchaunts de Braban" (Brabant), that they had bought twelve sacks similarly, and had "mistrent en la meson William Durant de Newerk, & lui baillerent la clef de mesine la meson," and similarly, "Esteveur le Heir" seized them, and "les bailla en garde à Robert Stuffyn de Newerk," and a similar answer was returned (*Vide Rotuli Parliamentarium*, vol. ii. pp. 101 *b* and 102 *a*). That Stuffyn was a merchant appears from the writ of summons in Rymer to him and other merchants, and the warehousing wool appears to prove he was a wool-merchant. The wool of Notts was probably taken to Newark for exportation to Germany and Flanders. We pass now over a long period. We do not meet with any further reference to Newark as returning representatives until 1592, when one Holles opposed Sir Gervase Markham. Mr. Dickinson gives this as his earliest reference, and does so on the authority of *Talbot Papers* (vol. i. *Herald's Coll.*) It appears therefrom that the contest was of a violent character, and that the Earl of Shrewsbury wrote

[1] We have referred to Henry de Newark on p. 20. He died in 1299.

APPENDIX.

to Lord Burleigh apprising him of the probability of a battle between the friends of the respective candidates. No other contests are mentioned in any records we have met with, and we must fall back on the apparently correct assertion of Willis in his *History of Parliamentary Boroughs*, that though Newark first sent members in the 2d Edward III., it was not regularly represented until the time of Charles II. (*Vide* 2 vol., p. 24 preface). Since that period the representatives of the borough have been the following :—

1661. (The first Parliament of Charles the Second.) Sir Richard Rothwell, and Sir George Markham were elected.
1673. Mr. H. Savile and Sir Paul Neale returned under the new charter, but unseated on petition in 1677.
1677. Mr. H. Savile and Sir Richard Rothwell.
1689. (The first Parliament of William and Mary). George Savile, of Rufford, and the Honourable Conyers Darcy.
1700. John Raynor and James Sanderson were declared by a vote of the House of Commons to be the sitting Members; and Sir Francis Molineux, who had been returned by the Mayor, not to have been duly elected.
1707. James Sanderson and John Digby.
1710. Sir Thomas Willoughby, of Wollaton, and Richard Newdigate, of Newark.
1711. Sir Thomas Willoughby, being called to the House of Peers, by the title of Baron Middleton of Middleton, in the county of Warwick; he was succeeded by the Honourable Brigadier-General Sutton.
1713. Brigadier-General Sutton and Richard Newdigate.
1714. (The first Parliament of George the First). Brigadier-General Sutton and the Honourable Conyers Darcy, who appear to have continued till
1723. When Brigadier-General Sutton and Sir Mathew Jenison were returned.
1727. Brigadier-General Sutton and the Honourable James Pelham.
1734. The same persons re-elected.
1737. Brigadier-General Sutton dying, he was succeeded by Lord William Manners.
1741. Lord William Manners and Job Staunton Charlton, of Staunton, were elected, and served in this and the ensuing Parliament.
1754. John Manners, the eldest son of Lord William, and Job Staunton Charlton.
1761. The latter retired, and John Manners and Thomas Thoroton were returned.
1768. John Manners and the Right Honourable John Shelley.
1774. George Sutton, the eldest son of Lord George Sutton and Major-General Henry Clinton.
1780. George Sutton gave place to his father, the Right Honourable Lord George Sutton, who, with Major-General, then Sir Henry, Clinton, Knight of the Bath, was returned.
1783. John Manners Sutton, the second son of Lord George, on the decease of his father, was elected.

1784. John Manners Sutton and the Right Honourable Constantine John Lord Mulgrave.
1790. John Manners Sutton and Lieutenant Colonel William Crosbie.
1796. John Manners Sutton declined in favour of his younger brother, Thomas Manners Sutton, who, with Colonel Mark Wood, was returned.
1797. Thomas Manners Sutton re-elected on vacancy, by accepting an office under the Crown.
1802. Thomas Manners Sutton re-elected on a similar occasion.
1802. At the general election Thomas Manners Sutton and Admiral Sir Charles Morris Pole.
1805. Thomas Manners Sutton vacated, and Henry Willoughby was elected.
1806. General Cotton and Henry Willoughby.
1812. General Cotton and Henry Willoughby.
1814. General Cotton being called to the House of Peers, by the title of Lord Cumbermere, George Hay Dawkins Pennant was elected.
1818. Henry Willoughby and General Sir William Henry Clinton, who continued until
1829, Mar. On resignation of General Clinton, Michael Thomas Sadler elected.
1830, Aug. H. Willoughby and M. T. Sadler.
1831, Feb. William Farnsworth Handley, elected *vice* Willoughby.
1831, May. W. F. Handley and Serjeant Wilde.
1832, Dec. William Ewart Gladstone and W. F. Handley.
1835, Jan. W. E. Gladstone and Thomas Wilde.
1837, Aug. W. E. Gladstone and Thomas Wilde. Mr. Wilde appointed Solicitor-General, 1840.
1840, Jan. Sir Thomas Wilde re-elected.
1841, June. W. E. Gladstone and Lord John Manners. Mr. Gladstone appointed Master of Mint in 1841.
1841, Sept. W. E. Gladstone. Mr. Gladstone appointed Colonial Secretary, 1846, and retires.
1846, Jan. John Stuart.
1847, Aug. J. H. Manners-Sutton and John Stuart.
1852, July. Granville E. Vernon and J. H. Manners-Sutton.
1857, Mar. Earl of Lincoln and John Handley.
1859, Apl. Grosvenor Hodgkinson and John Handley.
1865, July. G. Hodgkinson and Lord A. Pelham Clinton.
1868, Nov. G. Hodgkinson and Edward Denison. On decease of Mr. Denison in
1870, Mar. Samuel Boteler Bristowe, Q.C.
1874, Feb. Thomas Earp and S. B. Bristowe, Q.C.

APPENDIX.   331

ALDERMEN OF NEWARK,

From the first Incorporation of the Town by EDWARD VI., 1549,
Till the Alderman had the dignity of Mayor conferred upon him by CHARLES I., 1625.

Name	Year	Name	Year	Name	Year
Anthony Foster	1549	Christopher Stow	1575	William Parke	1601
William Phillipot	1550	Thomas Parker	1576	Edward Death	1602
William Riggs	1551	George Thexton	1577	Henry Webster	1603
Hugh Kelsterne	1552	Edward Kelsterne	1578	Robert Brignell	1604
Edward Sainton	1553	William Harrison	1579	Christopher Jenison	1605
Robert Howes	1554	Christopher Jenison	1580	Robert Webb	1606
Philip Robinson	1555	Edward Brown	1581	Peter Key	1607
John Corbridge	1556	John Death	1582	Edmund Metheringham	1608
Richard Leverton	1557	Thomas Bate	1583	John Twentyman	1609
William Leverit	1558	Anthony Haslam	1584	Bartholomew Martin	1610
Edward Kelsterne	1559	George Bridges	1585	Thomas Taylor	1611
John Brignell	1560	Edmund Metheringham	1586	John Brownlow	1612
John Key	1561	Nicholas Goddard	1587	Henry Webster	1613
Humphrey Taylor	1562	Thomas Cross	1588	John Noble	1614
William Leverit	1563	Thomas Herring	1589	Richard Burkitts	1615
William Robinson	1564	Brian Houlston	1590	Thomas Jenison	1616
William Blank	1565	William Harrison	1591	Robert Good	1617
Christopher Stow	1566	William Parke	1592	Christopher Haslam	1618
Edward Sainton	1567	Christopher Jenison	1593	Richard Herring	1619
Edward Kelsterne	1568	John Burton	1594	John Metheringham	1620
William Harrison	1569	William Standley	1595	Peter Smith	1621
William Standley	1570	Anthony Haslam	1596	John Jenison	1622
John Brignell	1571	Thomas Hartley	1597	Thomas Hobman	1623
Thomas Bate	1572	Edmund Metheringham	1598	John Brownlow	1624
George Bridges	1573	Thomas Hobman	1599	Henry Gill	1625
William Leverit	1574	Christopher Thompson	1600		

MAYORS OF NEWARK,

From their first Creation by CHARLES I., 1625.

Name	Elected in the Year	Name	Elected in the Year	Name	Elected in the Year
Henry Gill (Sworn July 12)	1625	Francis Fitzwilliams	1651	William Twentyman	1678
John Standish	1626	Jeffrey Ebdon	1652	William Hobman	1679
Henry Clifton	1627	Benjamin Wilson	1653	John Girton	1680
Thomas Jenison	1628	Matthew Jenison	1654	John Marris	1681
Christopher Wilson	1629	Christopher Wilson	1655	Richard Read	1682
Christopher Haslam	1630	Matthew Newham	1656	William Martin	1683
John Noble	1631	John Jenison	1657	William Martin	1684
Edward Standish	1632	William Martin	1658	William Rastall	1685
Peter Smith	1633	William Hobman	1659	George Birkbank	1686
Anthony Hobman	1634	Charles Dennis	1660	Robert Marris	1687
John Jenison	1635	Robert Atkinson	1661	Samuel Ellis (Elected Lady Day)	1688
Matthew Mercer	1636	Christopher Haslam	1662	Alexander Clarke	1688
Launcelot Thompson	1637	Richard Herring	1663	Isaac Sherwin	1689
Thomas Treece	1638	Leonard Jenison	1664	John Whalley	1690
John Johnson	1639	Hugh Treece	1665	William Twentyman	1691
John Standish	1640	Edward Newton	1666	Matthew Alvey	1692
Thomas Atkinson	1641	Robert Hoyes	1667	William Hobman	1693
Christopher Wilson	1642	William Brown	1668	Richard Rawson	1694
Thomas Arnold	1643	John Marris	1669	Richard Read	1695
Hercules Clay	1644	William Martin	1670	William Pocklinton	1696
Edward Standish (Jan. 1)	1645	William Basledine	1671	Edward Hobson	1697
Thomas Smith	1645	Robert Gregg	1672	William Martin	1698
William Baker	1646	George Birkbank	1673	Solomon Bettison	1699
Henry Camm	1647	Thomas Hodgson	1674	Robert Marris	1700
Launcelot Thompson	1648	Robert Morris	1675	William Snell	1701
William Watson	1649	Isaac Sherwin	1676	Timothy Ellis	1702
Robert Wilson	1650	Dennis Cooling	1677	John Cook	1703

APPENDIX.

MAYORS OF NEWARK—Continued.

Name	Elected in the Year	Name	Elected in the Year	Name	Elected in the Year
John Milnes	1704	John Twentyman	1763	Richard Fisher	1821
Matthew Alvey	1705	John Milnes	1764	John Hole	1822
Samuel Rastall	1706	Henry Milnes	1765	Charles Moor	1823
Thomas Lund	1707	Timothy Rastall	1766	James Dyson	1824
Samuel Peet	1708	Joseph Sikes	1767	William Hilton	1825
Robert Marris	1709	The Right Honourable the Earl of Lincoln	1768	George Hodgkinson	1826
John Herring	1710			James Prior Lacy	1827
Roger Pocklington	1711	Robt. Spragging (Elected Dec. 12)	1768	William Fillingham	1828
Solomon Dettison	1712	Samuel Twentyman	1769	William Readitt	1829
John Taylor	1713	Thomas Spragging	1770	J. J. Bigsby	1830
John Cook	1714	William Handley	1771	William Parker	1831
John Milnes	1715	Samuel Brooksby	1772	James Thorpe	1832
Thomas Clark	1716	Thomas Haslam	1773	P. R. Falkner	1833
Edward Moor	1717	Richard Eastland	1774	William Thompson jun.	1834
Samuel Rastall	1718	John Ridgill	1775	James Thorpe	1835
Henry Martin	1719	Henry Milnes	1776	Thomas Spragging Godfrey	1836
Christopher Buckley	1720	Robert Foster	1777		
Edward Eastland	1721	Samuel Sketchley	1778	Thomas Caparn	1837
Robert Marris	1722	William Martin	1779	Joseph Gilstrap	1838
John Herring	1723	Joseph Sikes	1780	Charles Ridge	1839
Benjamin Farnsworth	1724	David Stephenson	1781	Benjamin Nicholson	1840
Joseph Lund	1725	Samuel Twentyman	1782	John Clark	1841
Joseph Taylor	1726	Thomas Spragging	1783	Edward Little Bousfield	1842
William Hoyes	1727	William Handley	1784	Godfrey Tallents	1843
John Milnes	1728	Samuel Brooksby	1785	Joseph Branston	1844
Thomas Wilson	1729	John Godfrey	1786	James Snow	1845
Edward Smith	1730	George Lawrence	1787	George Hutton	1846
Samuel Rastall	1731	James Guthrie	1788	William Thomson	1847
Henry Martin	1732	Henry Milnes	1789	Robert Bishop	1848
Christopher Buckley	1733	William Jessop	1790	William Hall	1849
Joseph Lund (Sworn April 23)	1734	Samuel Sketchley	1791	William Hall	1850
Edward Eastland	1734	William Martin	1792	William Newzam Nicholson	1851
Robert Marris	1735	Thomas Bland	1793		
Thomas Haslam	1736	David Stephenson	1794	John Cooper	1852
Benjamin Farnsworth	1737	Robert Buck	1795	John Smith Caparn	1853
Joseph Lund	1738	Thomas Spragging	1796	William Ragsdale	1854
Francis Noble	1739	William Farmarie	1797	Henry Sutton	1855
William Hoyes	1740	John Godfrey	1798	George Hutton Riddell	1856
John Clough	1741	Charles Moor	1799	Edward Cooper	1857
John Pocklington	1742	George Lawrence	1800	Henry Branston	1858
Edward Smith	1743	James Guthrie	1801	Thomas Oldham	1859
Samuel Rastall	1744	John Youle	1802	James Holman Betts	1860
Thomas Killinger	1745	William Jessop	1803	Christopher Carter Footitt	1861
William Hoyes	1746	Samuel Sketchley	1804	Dr. Anders	1862
Edward Eastland	1747	Thomas Stansall	1805	Philip Handley	1863
Richard Harrison	1748	Thomas Bland	1806	John Gilbert	1864
Thomas Haslam	1749	William Parker	1807	Thomas Spragging Godfrey	1865
John Twentyman	1750	Robert Buck	1808	William H. Cubley	1866
Joseph Lund	1751	Richard Fisher	1809	John Cotham Bainbridge	1867
Francis Noble	1752	William Farmarie	1810	Richard Warwick	1868
William Wells	1753	Charles Moore	1811	Thomas Earp	1869
John Clough	1754	Edward Godfrey	1812	J. W. Smith	1870
Timothy Rastall	1755	James Dyson	1813	Henry Newbald	1871
Joseph Sikes	1756	William Hilton	1814	J. M'George	1872
Robert Spragging	1757	William Fillingham	1815	George Harvey	1873
Samuel Twentyman	1758	William Readitt	1816	E. M. H. Riddell	1874
Thomas Milnes	1759	Thomas Bland	1817	Henry Walton	1875
William Handley	1760	William Parker	1818	W. E. Tallents	1876
John Smith	1761	Thomas Stansall	1819	Becher Tidd Pratt	1877
Thomas Haslam	1762	Robert Buck	1820	Becher Tidd Pratt	1878

RECORDERS OF NEWARK.

Name	Year	Name	Year	Name	Year
John Wood, of Woodborough	1627	William Cartwright, of Normanton, near Southwell	1723	Job Charlton Brough, of Newark	1805
Gilbert Boun, of Normanton, near Southwell, Serjeant-at-Law	1645	John Heron, of Newark	1748	D'Ewes Coke	1806
		Robert Heron, of Newark	1753	John Balguy jun., of Nottingham	1811
Philip Laycock, of Woodborough	1654	Thomas Heron, of Newark	1754	James Fynes Clinton	1831
		Charles Mellish, of Blyth	1770	Nathaniel Richard Clarke	1833
William Rastall, of Newark	1680	Sir Richard Sutton, Bart., of Norwood Park	1777	James Fitzjames Stephen	1859
Robert Lord Lexington of Kelham	1686	Charles Mellish, on his return from abroad	1779	Samuel Boteler Bristowe, Jan.	1870
George Cartwright, of Ossington	1693	Thomas Manners Sutton, of Kelham	1794	John James Heath Saint (the present Recorder) April	1870

THE VICARS OF NEWARK.

Name	Year	Name	Year	Name	Year
Walter de Coddington	1301	John Buxton	1445	Simon Jacks	1612
William de Lincoln	1320	Nicholas Langton	1475	Edward Mason	1617
Galfridus de Wilford	1321	John Tristrop	1477	Samuel Keemol	1628
Francis Roslyn	1322	John Smythe	1479	John Moseley	1630
John de Leverton	1333	Edward Fowke	1521	Thomas White	16—
Thomas de Sikleston	1349	Sampson Lorde	152–	Richard Pearson	1666
Thomas de Westburgh	1359	Henry Lytherland	1532	Henry Smith	1668
Roger de Leverton	1361	Robert Chapman	154–	Ely Stansfield	1702
William de Vesse	1367	Christopher Sugden	1550	Bernard Wilson	1719
Roger de Leverton	1371	Nicholas Clayton	1573	Hugh Wade	1772
John de Seggefield	1375	William Smythe	1581	Charles Fynes	1776
John Sharp	1378	Lawrence Staunton	158–	Davies Pennell	1778
John Mare	1421	Edward Holden	1588	William Bartlett	1814
Thomas Marshe	1423	William Pell	1596	John Garret Bussell	1835
Robert Crossland	1425	Bryan Vincent	1597	Josiah Brown Pearson, LL.D., present vicar	1874
Nicholas Feriby	1425	Joseph Beck	1601		

INDEX.

ABERCROMBIE. A Courtier, p. 91.
Ad Pontem, now Farndon, 5.
Ædnoth. Bishop of Lincoln, 8.
Ael Tavum, the British name of N., 3.
Ætheric. Bishop of Lincoln, 8.
Alan de Caldwell's Daughter. Courtship of, 27.
Aldermen of Newark. List of, 331.
Aldermen of Newark. Atkinson, 165, 168; Baker, 138; Birkett. George, 197; Branston, 289; Brownlow. John, 100; Clifton. Henry, 100; Ellis. Timothy, 197; Forster. Anthony (1st), 65; Girton. John, 197; Haslam. Christopher, 100; Haslum. William, 197; Heron. Robert, 197; Hobman. Thomas, 101; Hobman. William, 197; Jenison. John, 100; Jenison. Thomas, 100; Right Hon. the Earl of Lincoln, 216; Martin. William, 197; Middlebrook. William, 100; Noble. John, 100; Outram. Robert, 101; Phyllypot. William, 301; Sikes. Joseph, 75; Smith. Peter, 100; Standish, 168; Standish. Gilbert, 197; Stanidge. John, 101; Sutton. Lord George, 216; Twentiman. William, 197; Webster. Henry, 90; Welby. William, 197; Wilson. Christopher, 101.
Aldermen appointed by James II., 197.
Alexander. Bishop of Lincoln, 9, 10, 174, 176.
Alexander. Bishop, builder of Newark Castle, 318.
Almaynes. The, 35.
Ambrose, 75.
Anderson. Edmund, 172.
Anderson. Edwin, 172.
Anderson. Francis, 172.
Anderson's *Hist. Commercial* quoted, 65.
Anderson. Stephen, 172.
Androys. Richard, obtains land at Newark, 63; possesses property at Newark, 63.
Anfield. Susanna, 200.
Anglo-Saxon Newark, 1, 3, 6.
Antoninus' *Iter*, sixth, cited, 3, 5.

Appleton Gate, 42, 91.
Architecture. of styles of, confounded, 5.
Arderne. John, eminent surgeon of N., 23.
Ashburnham's. Mr., account of the king's arrival, 158, 161.
Ashwell. John, first priest of Coddington Chauntry, 27.
Ashwell. Rutland, 74.
Aske, holds conference at Doncaster, 61; visits the king, 61; arrested, 61; drawn on hurdle at York, and hanged, 61.
Aske, takes command of rebels in Lincolnshire, and marches to York, 59; Pomfret Castle surrendered to, 60.
Askew. J., chauntry priest, 72.
Aslockton, birthplace of Cranmer, 64; rectory presented to Cranmer, 65.
Aslowby, 52.
Astley Hall, 89.
Atkins. Col., 168.
Atkinson. Alderman, 165, 168.
Atkinson. Nicholas, 181.
Atkinson. Thomas, mayor, 181, 183, 193.

BABTHORPE. Sir Nicholas, takes refuge in Pomfret Castle, 59; seized by Aske, 59.
Bagerley. Henry, 213.
Bailey's *Annals of Nottinghamshire* quoted, 21, 27, 31.
Baines. Francis, 75.
Baker. Alderman, 138; mayor, 162, 174.
Balderton (Baldertune), 8, 10, 57, 94, 128.
Balderton Gate Mission Rooms, Newark. *See* Streets.
Balderton. Lands in, left to Newark Church Chauntry, 28.
Balderton Road. *See* Streets.
Balderton. Roman antiquities found at, 5, 6.
Baldertune (*see* Balderton), 8.
Ballard. General, 117.
Balmes, Sir Bryan, 168.
Bank's *Dormant and Extinct Baronetage* quoted, 37.

Bardolf. Lord, with Lancastrian forces at N., 32.
Barmby, 52.
Barnby Gate, 232, 295.
Barnby Road. *See* Streets.
Barnebye, 8.
Barnet. Battle of, 32.
Barre Gate, 93.
Barton-on-Humber, 144.
Bathley, 97.
Bathley Grange, 97.
Baxter. Mr., cited, 3.
Beacon Hill, 128, 135.
Beaumont Cross, 18, 232, 323.
Beaumont Family, 18, 19.
Beck. Robert, 200.
Bede cited, 5.
Bedford. Captain, 172.
Bellasis. Lord, 151, 161, 164.
Bellasyse. Lord, Governor, 168, 195.
Bellasyse (Bellasis). Lord, reply to the summons to surrender, 156; order to surrender, 162.
Bellow. John, grant of land to, 63.
Bells of Newark Church, 206, 293-5.
Belvoir Castle, 116, 140, 143, 148.
Bencoinne. Captain Robert, 166.
Bentley. Stephen, chauntry priest, 72.
Beresford. John, of Eagle Hall, 104.
Berkshire. Earl of, 105, 183.
Besthorpe, 199, 201.
Beton. Colonel, 166.
Bettison Family. Ancient legend in possession of, 27.
Bever (Belvoir) Castle, 116.
Bevercotes. Sir Everard, 27.
Beverley. Sanctuary at, 43.
Birketts. Richard, 90.
Bishoppe. Thomas, 166.
Blackstone on Right of Sanctuary, 42.
Blackwell. Sir Thomas, 181.
Blyth on the old Great North Road, 6.
Bosome or Bozome Family, 37, 38, 39.
Boston. Chauntries at, 71.
Bovat. Definition of, 8.
Bowles. Sir Charles, 166.
Boylby, 52.
Bracebridge, 91.
Bradley. John, of North Muskham, 106.

INDEX.

Branston. Mr. H., purchases the Friary, 63.
Branston, Mr., alderman, 289.
Brant Broughton, 224.
Bray, Sir Edward, 27.
Braytoft, 40.
Breton, 75.
Brewer's *Historical Letters* cited, 5.
Brian's. T., deposition, 58.
Bridgford. East, the *Margidunum* of Antoninus, 5.
Bridges at Newark, Kelham, Muskham, and Nottingham, 6; Importance of, 6.
Briscoe. Mr. John Potter, his *Nottinghamshire Facts and Fictions* cited, 131; on early Newark printing, 233.
Bristowe. S. E., 263.
British antiquities found, 2, 6.
British fortification, 3.
Brodholm, 75.
Brooke, 75.
Brooke. Rev. Joshua, of Car-Colston, 10.
Brooke. Rev. Mr., 250, 251.
Brough, below Newark. The *Crococalanum* of Antoninus, 5.
Broughton. Sir T., killed at Stoke, 36; or drowned in the Trent, 36.
Brown. George, 272.
Brown. Robert, Receiver to Wolsey and Longland, 45; Benefactions of, 57.
Browne's *Britannia's Pastorals* quoted, 57.
Brownley. John, 90.
Brownlow. John, 100.
Broxholme. John, grant of land to, 63.
Buck. Dr., 234.
Bullar. Thomas, clerk of the peace, 101, 103.
Bunny. King's army in, 34.
Buonaparte. Threatened invasion of, 246.
Burdon Family, 38.
Bergh. Sir Thomas, joins Edward at Nottingham, 32.
Burghley, 148.
Burghley. Lord, 89, 99.
Burgundy. Duke of, assists Edward IV., 32.
Burnaby. Mr., on the Magnus estate, 52.
Burrell. Sir John, 168.
Burril. Thomas, murder of, 217.
Byron. Lady, 141.
Byron's connection with Newark, 257, 262.
Byron. Lord, 188.
Byron. Sir Richard, 120, 126, 140, 141, 171, 181.

CÆSAR. Sir Julius, 99.
Camden cited, 5, 10.
Candysche. Lincolnshire priest, 61.

Cantelupe. Sir W. de, a prisoner, 26.
Caparn. Robert, 272.
Carey Family. *See* Scarsdale.
Carleton. Colonel, 172.
Carleton. Sir Dudley, 91.
Carr. Sir Edward, 91.
Carrier. Dr. Benjamin, 90.
Cartwright. "Liefetenant" Thomas, 166.
Cartwright, Major, 120, 232.
Carucat. Definition of, 8.
Castle. Newark, 2, 3, 62; site of a Roman granary, 1; foundation of, 9; mint at, 9; surrendered, 11, 13, 15, 16; chapel in, 12; King John at, 14; Peter de la Mere at, 26; lease of, 92; dismantled, 174; description of, 175-9.
Castlegate, 2, 5, 62.
Catholic Emancipation. Newark and the, 263-264.
Cavalry. Dinner of the Newark, 257.
Cavendish. Colonel, 166.
Cavendish. General Charles, 119.
Caxton. Richards de Tuxford, 30.
Cecil. William, Earl of Exeter, 10, 89.
Cemetery Burial, by G. Milner, quoted, 4.
Chamberlain. Mr., 91.
Chambers'. Dr. Robert, *Book of Days* quoted, 24, 25.
Chapels, 314.
Chapel in the churchyard of N., 20.
Chapel of S.S. Philip and James, 12; St. John of Jerusalem, 12, 13.
Chapman's charity, 91.
Charles I., 100; and Sir Richard Willis, 325; charter of, referred to, 1; departure of, 153.
Charles II. petitions to, 186, 187, 188.
Charles II. grants a new charter, 188.
Charlotte. Princess, death of, 255.
Charlton. Job Staunton, 212.
Charters granted to Newark, Charles I., 1; of incorporation, 100; of Charles II., 188; of James II., 196.
Charters granted to Bishop Alexander, 175, 176.
Chastelyn. W., of London, 65.
Chauntries of Newark, 65-72; of Notts, 71, 72, 73.
Chaworth. Lord, 115, 181.
Chelintone, 8.
Cheney. J., 35.
Chesterfield. Duke of Clarence and Earl of Warwick at, 31.
Christ Church opened, 292.
Church. Chapel of Corpus Christi, 21; Fleming brass, 21, 22; reredos, 22; chauntry founded by William Saucimer, 28, 29;

endowed by first-fruits, 29; Prince Consort Memorial Window, 313; historical sketch of, 297-309; restoration of, 295; re-opening of, 295.
Church. Roman Catholic, erected in Parliament Street, 292.
Churches. Newark, *see* Newark.
Churchwardens. Lacy. Mr., 218; Ridgell. Mr., 218; Stevenson, Mr., 218; Sketchley. Mr., 219.
Clark. Alexander, 196.
Clarke. Thomas, mercer of Newark, 43.
Clarke. W. W., claims manor of Elston, 64.
Clay. Hercules, 135, 136, 137.
Clay's charity, 136.
Claypole, 10.
Clerk of the Peace. First, Thomas Bullar, 101.
Cleveland. John, Judge Advocate, 168, 169.
Clifton. Captain John, 166.
Clifton. Henry, 101.
Clifton. Major, 166.
Clifton. Sir Gervase, slain at Bosworth, 32, 73.
Clinton. General Sir Henry, 230.
Clinton. General Sir William Henry, 263, 265.
Clinton and Say. Lord, possesses Knesal, 62.
Clumber, 65.
Coach accidents in Newark, 253.
Cobb. Thomas, executed, 232.
Coddington, 57.
Coddington. Chauntry founded at, 27.
Coins found, 1, 2, 6, 7.
Cole. Lieut. and Captain Thomas, 166.
Cole MS. cited, 73.
Collect. Anglo Minorit, cited, 73.
Collingham. Gallows erected at, 17.
Collingwood's. Anthony, charities, 194.
Colours. Presentation of, 249.
Columboli. Thom. de Thorp, 30.
Constable. Henry, 10, 89.
Constable. Sir Philip, 168.
Constable. Sir Robert, 10; takes refuge at Pomfret Castle, 59; seiged by Aske, 59; executed, 61.
Convent in Newark. Bequest by Henry VII. to, 42.
Conway. Secretary, 99.
Cooke. Francis, 139.
Cooper. Sir Roger, 115, 118, 139, 181.
Corbet. Bishop, 99.
Corn Exchange. Opening of the, 295.
Corn Laws. Meeting in support of the repeal of the, 264.
Coroner. Brownley, John, 90.
Corporation. Insults to, 210.

INDEX.

Corporation Papers. Extracts from, 173.
Corporation plate. Sale of, 213.
Cotingtone, 8.
Cottonian MSS., 51.
Coude. John, 106.
Coventry. Chauntries at, 71.
Coventry. King's army in, 34.
Cracroft. Mr., 209.
Crane. Sir Richard, 129, 130.
Cranmer. Archbishop, a Notts man, his biography, 64.
Crayle. Daniel, 200.
Crecy. Midland bowmen at, 24.
Cressy Hall, 37, 40.
Cromwell. Colonel, 146.
Cromwell. John, 196.
Cromwell near Newark, 324.
Crophill Butler, 72.
Crosbie. Lieut.-Col. William, 234.
Cross. Beaumont, 18, 232 323.
Crosten. J., chauntry priest, 72.
Cubley. W. II., 289.

DABRIDGECOURT. John, 89.
Dabridgecourt. Christiana, 89.
Dabridgecourt. The Lanches, 89.
Dalaval. Mr., 209.
Dalison of Lincolnshire, 61.
Dallison. Sir Charles, 168.
Dallison. Sir Thomas, 128.
Dance of Death. *See* Newark Church.
Danes in Mercia, 5.
Danes ransacked Newark, 7.
Darcy. Colonel, 168.
Darcy. Lord, takes refuge in Pomfret Castle against rebels, 59; executed, 61.
Darley. Rob. de Thorp, 30.
Davenant. Sir William, 130.
Davencourt. Lord, 168.
David of Scotland confined at Nottingham, 24.
Dean. Dr., of York, 168.
Deincourt. Baron, 73.
Delalaunde. Sir T., 31.
De Montfort, 16, 17, 19.
Denison. E., M.P., death of, 314.
Dennett. J., of Newark, 30.
Derbyshire. Sutton Scarsdale, 73.
Devereux. Lady Penelope, 89.
Devon. River, 3.
Devonshire. Countess of, 89.
Deyncourt. Lord, occupies St. Augustine's, Newark, 63. (*See* 73.)
Diana, 89.
Dickens. Charles, Letter by, 310.
Digby. Lord, 127, 147.
Digby Sir John, 114, 115, 181, 188.
Dillon. Lord, 128.
Dimock. Rev. J. F., on chauntries, 70, 71.
Dives. Sir Lewis, 128.
Dodsworth. Roger, 89.
Dodsworth's MSS. quoted, 73.
Doncaster Lancastrians at, 31; Edward IV there, 31; Lord Shrewsbury and Duke of Norfolk at, 61; rebels leave Pomfret for Doncaster, 61; conference at, 61.
Doomsday Survey, 6, 8.
Douer. Lord Barinet, 167.
Drybridge, 2.
Dudley. Lady Robert, 89.
Dugdale cited, 37, 64.
Durant. Isabella, 9.
Durant. John, 19.
Dutch. Defeat of, commemorated, 246.
Dymock. Colonel, on the last siege, 169.
Dyson's Bequest, 76.

EARLES. Dr., 195.
Earthquake felt in Newark, 254.
Eastgate, 2.
Edge Hill, 114.
Edward the Confessor in Newark, 8.
Edward IV. (Duke of York), 30, 31; passed through Newark on his way to Doncaster, 31; returns to Nottingham, 32; proclaimed king, 32; marches to meet the rebels, 32; died, 32.
Edwinstowe Church, 21.
Edytha. Queen, in Newark, 8.
Egioke, Worcestershire, 73.
Eleanor. Queen, Crosses to, 18.
Election. Contest and petition, 235; under the new charter, 191, 192; experiences of Mr. Saville, 192, 193, 194; incidents of polling, 268; the number nine, 287-8.
Ellis' charity. Timothy, 205.
Elliss. Samuel, 197.
Elston, 10, 74.
Elston. Curious phenomenon at. 207.
Elston Manor claimed, 64.
Eltavona, the Roman name of Newark, 3.
Elvestone, 8.
Epperston, 74.
Ermine Street, 7.
Ersby. W., chauntry priest, 72.
Essex. Earl of, 139.
Euston. J., chauntry priest, 72.
Everton lordship. Enclosure of, 212.
Executions for rebellion, 61.
Exeter. Countesses of, 10, 89, 99.
Exeter. Earl and Duke of, 10, 32, 60, 61, 89, 105.
Eyre. Major-General, 168.
Eyre. Sir Gervas, 115, 181.
Eystcoyst. Chr. of Marcheland, 61.

FAIRFAX. General Lord, 115, 145.
Famine in Newark, 20.
Fanshaw. Sir Simon, 168.
Farendon (Farendune), 8.
Farendune, *see* Farendon.
Farmer. Dr., Chancellor of Lincoln, 168.
Farndon, the *Ad Pontem* of Antoninus, 5, 7.

Fedway. Sir Robert, 168.
Ferisby. Nicholas, vicar of Newark, 29.
Financial disputes, 181; panic, 263.
Fiskerton Ford. Retreat towards, 36.
Fledborough (formerly Flatburch), 8.
Fleming Family, 9, 21, 22, 23, 73.
Flintham, 99.
Floods. Great, 195, 293, 313, 314.
Flower. William, 90.
Folkingham, 52.
Food riots, 247.
Forster, Anthony, first alderman of Newark, 65.
Fosseway, 2, 5, 6, 7.
Foster's Bequest, 76.
Foster. Anthony, Widow of, 89.
Foster. Robert, 75; high sheriff, 218.
Foster. S., of Woodborough, 74, 75.
Fowdrey, Lancashire. Rebels landed at, 34.
France. Peace signed with, 252.
Free speech and its dangers, 104.
Free trade. Agitation about, 290.
Friars. Austin, confiscated property of the, 63.
Froude. J. A., cited, 47, 48, 58.
Fuller. Dr., 45, 196.
Fynes. Henry, 251.

GABRIEL, "Fader of the Observant Friars" at Newark, 73.
Gainsborough besieged, 119; mentioned, 138, 157.
Gardner. Captain, 128.
Gargrave. Lady Catherine, 183.
Garnett. H., 87.
Garnon, Hugonis, de Muskham, 30.
Garnon, Robert, de Muskham, 30.
Garnon. William, 208.
Gas. Newark lighted by, 292.
Gell. Sir John, 117.
Gentleman's Magazine quoted, 38, 39.
George III. Death of, 256.
George IV. Proclamation of, 256; death of, 271.
Geraldine. Capt. Lord, killed at Stoke, 36.
Gerard. Colonel Charles, 129.
Gerrard. Lord, 149.
Gibson cited, 5.
Gilbert de Gaunt seized Newark Castle, 12.
Gilbert. W., chauntry priest, 72.
Gilby. Colonel, 168.
Gill. Henry, 100.
Girton, 10, 199, 201.
Girton. John, 196.
Gladstone. W. Ewart, his representation of Newark in the House of Commons, 274; nominations and elections of, 274, 276, 282, 284, 289; dinner to, 285; personal sketch of, by Lord Albe-

2 X

INDEX.

marle, 284; criticism of, by Macaulay, 286.
Gloucester. Bishop Warburton of, 1.
Gloucester. Duke of, Castle seized by, 11.
Godfrey. E. S., presentation to, by the Red Club, 275.
Godfrey. Ensign E. S., 243.
Godiva, Countess, wife of Leofric, Earl of Mercia, 8.
Good. Robert, 90.
Gordon. Duke of, Death of, 265.
Graie. Colonel Henry, 153.
Graie. Colonel Theo., 153.
Grammar and Song Schools, Newark, founded and endowed, 52.
Granby. Marquis of, 215, 218.
Grandison. Lord, 128.
Grantham. Edward IV. at, 31; Chauntries at, 71; mentioned, 116, 144.
Gravesend, 74.
Grensham. Francis, 10.
Griesley. Sir Roger, 273.
Grym. Johan, 9.
Guilds in Newark, 53, 57, 65.
Gunthorpe given by Henry III. to Simon de Montford, 16.
Guthrie. Mr., Mayor, 234.

Hacker. Captain, 122, 140.
Halifax. Viscount, 191, 192.
Hall. Dr. Marshall, 310.
Hall (temp. Henry VIII.) quoted, 34.
Handley. Capt. William, 243.
Handley. John, 272.
Handley's charity, W. F., 205, 273.
Harby. Thomas, 97.
Harrington. Sir James, joins Edward in Nottingham, 32.
Harrington. Sir John, 74.
Hartley. Dr. David, 210, 211, 212.
Hartup. Sir Edward, 125, 127.
Haselam. Christopher, 90, 100.
Hawkes. Sam., 195.
Hawton. Land in, granted by Henry VIII., 63, 99.
Hawton Road, 314.
Hay. Lord, 91.
Hazelrigg. Staveley, 140.
Hazlitt. Mr. William Carew, 89.
Hearne. Colonel, 166.
Heath. Attorney-General, 100.
Hebbe. Daniel, 217.
Hebbe. William, execution and dissection of, 217.
Hedley. Yorks, 74.
Henderson. Sir John, 116.
Heneage at Louth, 58.
Hennings. Sir George, 168.
Henrietta. Queen, Visit of, to Newark, 118; letter of to the king, 118.
Henry. 31.
Henry III. King, and Newark Castle, 322.

Henry VII. marches to meet Simnel's troops, 32; Henry's adherents defeated at Barnet, 32. See also Richmond.
Henry VIII. and Cranmer, 64, 65.
Hering. Richard, 90.
Herne. Colonel, 168.
Herring. John, of Newark, numismatist, 2.
Hewson. Kathleen, 101.
Hewson. Richard, 101.
Hexham. Battle of, 31; sanctuary at, 43.
Heywood. Captain, 139.
Hilton. William, 293.
Hoare. Sir R. C., antiquary, cited, 4.
Hobard. Sir Miles, 130.
Hobman. John, 197.
Hobman. Thomas, 101.
Hobman. William, 196.
Hobson. Edward, 202.
Hodgkinson. George, 272.
Holbeach. H., Bp. of Lincoln, conveys Newark Manor and Castle to Crown, 65.
Holinshead's *Chronicles* cited, 35.
Holland. Edward IV. withdrew into, 32.
Holt. D., 236; trial of, 238.
Holton, 8.
Hopkins. R., chauntry priest, 72.
Hopton. Sir Ingram, 166.
Horncastle. Bishop's Chancellor murdered near, 59.
Horsley quoted, 3.
Hospital. St. Leonard's, Newark, 9, 10, 118.
Hostilities commenced, 114.
Howard. Colonel Thomas, 195.
Howard. Sir Thomas, 92.
Howe. Admiral Earl, 242.
Hubbard. Sir Michael, 125.
Hudson. G., 74.
Hugett. P., chauntry priest, 72.
Hugh, Bishop of Lincoln, 16.
Hull. Rebels at, 60.
Hull gates closed, 109.
Hume quoted, 1, 20, 64.
Hurst. Dr., 168.
Hussey. Lord, of Sleaford, quoted, 58; neglects to raise forces for the king, 59; executed, 61; estates at Kneesal, 62.
Hutchinson. Colonel, 74, 115, 117, 120, 125, 127, 153, 180, 182, 185, 186.
Hutchinson. Mr., 114.
Hutton. Captain Henry, 167.

Irlingham. Walter, prior of St. Katherine's, 29.
Illuminations in honour of peace being signed, 252.
Incorporation of Newark, 65, 100.
Ingram. Sir Thomas, 168.
Isabella. Queen, 89.
Issue Rolls entry, 26.

Jackson. Richard, 200.
Jackson. Robert, 253.
James I. and the countryman, 97.
Jenison Family. The, 63, 73, 90, 100, 202, 203, 204.
Jennings. Mr., 166.
Jesson. Mr., 234.
John. King, at Newark, 319, 320; sickness and death at Newark, 14; will of, 14, 15.
Johnson. John, 184, 200.

Kelham, 42.
Kelham. The king guarded at, 160.
Kelham Bridge, 6.
Kelham Hall, 310.
Kelom. J. de Kelom, 30.
Kelom. Robarti, de Newark, 30.
Key. Peter, 90.
Kingston Arms, 244.
Kingston. Earl of, 166.
Kirk Gate, 285.
Kildare. Earl of, and Simnel, 33.
Kilton, 65.
Kneesal granted to Lord Hussey, 62; and Lord Clinton and Say, 62; present owner, 62.
Knights Templars' Hospital founded, 12.

Lacy. Mr., 218.
Lacy's Charity, 206.
Lampin. Thomas, execution of, for forgery, 251.
Lancaster Herald. T. Mylnar, executed, 61.
Land and property. Transfers of, by Henry VIII., 62, 63.
Land of monasteries confiscated, 62, 63.
Land tenures. Curious, 64.
Langar, 146.
Langdale. Sir Marmaduke, 142, 145, 166.
Lascelles. Sir John, 105.
Lathom House, 139.
Lathom. Mr., 166.
Lawrence's charity. George, 246.
Lee. Thomas, 213.
Leef. Robert, 9.
Lecke. Colonel, 166.
Lecke Family, 37, 40, 73, 74, 75.
Lecke. Francis, 63, 78, 185, 195.
Lecke. Lady Mary, 99.
Lecke's charity. Lady Frances, 200.
Legend of St. Catherine's Well, Newark, 27, 28.
Legge. Major and Colonel, 128, 148.
Leicester, 34, 96, 145.
Lenthall. William, 183.
Lenton Priory. Henry III. and Prince Edward imprisoned at, 17.
Leofric, Earl of Mercia, possessed Newark Manor, 1, 8.
Leofric improved the castle, 9.
Lesley. David, 158, 165.
Letters Royal, 134, 170.

INDEX. 339

Leven. General, 159, 165.
Levett. James, 103.
Lexington. Lord, 168, 188, 197. See also Mr. Sutton.
Lilly. John, 97.
Lilly's charity, 97.
Lincoln, 59, 91, 138; bishops of, Ætheric, 8; Ædnoth, 8; Wulwi, 8; Remigius, 8; Alexander, 9, 10, 11; John Synwell, 9; Philip, 9, 11; Robert de Chesney, 12; Hugh, 16; Richard Fleming, 23; Longland, 45; Holbeach, 65; Castle seized, 12; Earl of, 33, 34, 35, 36, 216, 217. (See also Manvers, Earl, owner of Kneesal, 62. Newborough, Carleton, Moreland, Semperingham.) St. Catherine's Priory, 63; Stone Bow, 91; the George Inn, 91; Henry VII. at, 36; prisoners at, 36; the Spread Eagle Inn, 91.
Lindsey. Province of, 3; extent of, 3; meaning of name, 5.
Loads. Robert, of Cotham, 182.
Lombard Street, 2, 295, 314.
London Road, 314.
Long Bennington. Sir J. Markham attacks, 37.
Longdon Hall, 89.
Longland's (Bishop) palace plundered, 59.
Longstaffe. Mr. W. Hylton Dyer, cited, 57.
Loude. Sir J., bequeathed houses in Milnegate, 65.
Loughborough. King's army in, 34.
Loughborough. Lord, 127, 129.
Louth. Alarm-bell rung on visit of Heneage, 58; and the king, 60; chauntry at, 71.
Lowe. Capt. A. E. Lawson, on Lord Beaumont, 19; on the Leeke Family, 73; on the Markham Family, 40; on the Jenison Family, 202; on the Warburtons, 223; on the Sutton Family, 312.
Lovell. Lord, 34; at Stoke, 36; his death, 36, 37.
Lowther. Colonel, Governor of Pontefract, 166.
Lowthian. Lord, 158.
Loyalty. Sufferers for, 327.
Lucas. Sir Gervas, 140.
Lytherland. H., Vicar of Newark, joins the rebels at Lincoln, 62; goods seized, 62; "books of remembrance," 62; executed for high treason, 61.

MAGNUS charity, 53, 54, 55, 56.
Magnus. Rebus of, in Seassay Church, 57.
Magnus. Thomas, transfers his estates to Newark, 44; biography of, 44-57; takes refuge in Pomfret Castle, 59; seized by Aske, 59; and Queen Margaret, 124.

Malger held tolls, 12.
Manby, 172.
Mancefellde, 98.
Manchester. Clarence and Warwick, and the rebels at, 31, 32.
Manners. Lord, 251.
Manners. Lord John, election of (1841), 289.
Manners. Lord Robert, Death of, 209, 251.
Manners. Lord William, 209.
Manners. Sir George, 89.
Manners. Catherine, 89.
Mansfield, 71, 98, 139.
Markham Family, 37, 38, 39, 40, 41, 62, 63, 74, 104, 166.
Market-place. Mutiny in, 153.
Marris. John, 196.
Marsh. John, 10.
Marshe. T., 75.
Marshall. Lieut. R., 243.
Marshall. Mayor, 247.
Marston, Lincolnshire, 74.
Martin. Captain, 129.
Martin. William, 196.
Martin's charity. John, 189.
Martyn. Bartholomew, 90.
Mattersey, 52.
Maude. Corporal, 173.
Maurice. Prince, 148, 149.
Mayors of Newark. List of, 331-2.
Mayor appointed by James II., 197; Ellis. Samuel, 197; the first Henry Gill, 100; Guthrie, Mr., 234; The Right Hon. Earl of Lincoln, 217; Marshall, 247; Morris. Robert, 197; Snell. W., 75; Sikes. Jos., 75; Spragging. Thomas, 245; Sykes. J., 209; Launcelot. Thompson, 106. See 331-2.
Medralf. E., chauntry priest, 72.
Meering Family, 37, 38, 39.
Mercia. Earl of, possessed the Manor of Newark, 1, 7; gave Newark and Flatburch to Stow, 8.
Meldrum. Major, 140.
Meldrum. Sir John, 119, 125, 126, 129.
Melton Mowbray, 140, 142.
Metheringham, Edmund, 90.
Metheringham. John, 90.
Middlebrook. William, 101.
Middlegate, 9, 19, 75.
Middleton's, Lord, Estates. Sale of three of, 313-14.
Middleton. Thomas, Baron, possesses St. Augustine's Friary, 63. See also Willoughby.
Midgeley. Mr., 244.
Millgate, 28, 190.
Millington, John, 115.
Milne Gate, 20, 65, 94.
Milner. George, quoted, 4.
Minster. Lovel, Oxfordshire, Lord Lovel at, 36, 37.

Mint at the Castle, 9, 167.
Mirhill. Captaine, 167.
Mohidrip (? Medhop), 75.
Moleneux. Gervas, 90.
Monasteries. Suppression of, disturbances through, 58, 59; property of, how distributed, 62, 63.
Molyneux. Sir Francis, 202.
Mompesson. Rev. Mr., 185.
Money Panic. Meeting in Newark, 245.
Mong. Angl., 8.
Monk. General, 185.
Montague. Edward Wortley, 216.
Montague. Hon. Sydney, 216.
Montague. Lady Mary Wortley, 216.
Montaign. Master, 129.
Montgomery. Sir Thomas, joins Edward at Nottingham, 32.
Montreville. Mons. 158.
Monumenta Historica Britannica cited, 5.
Moore. Thomas, 217.
Moreby, a monk of Fountayns, executed, 61.
Mortimer's Cross, 31.
Mortmain Act, 9.
Moseley. Dr., vicar, 108.
Mossman. Kirby, 105.
Motchall, 93.
Moulton. W., chauntry priest, 72.
Mulgrave. Constantine, Lord, 231.
Municipal authority of Newark, 65.
Muskham Bridge, 6, 129, 130, 131.
Muskham. North, granted to Newstead, 21; mentioned, 76.
Mylnar. T., Lancaster Herald, executed, 61; his behaviour, 62.

NASHY, 145.
Naventby. John, King of Scotland, prisoner at Somerton Castle, 24.
Neal. Sir William, 129, 130.
Neile. Archbishop, 104.
Neille. Captain John, 31.
Neville. Gervase, 105.
Neville. Lord, takes refuge at Pomfret Castle, 59; seized by Aske, 59.
Neville. Sir James, 168.
Newark. Was it of Roman origin? 1; wall, 2; origin of name, 1, 5, 7; in Roman times, 1, 2, 3, 4, 5, 6, 7; its British, name, 3; its Roman name, 3; its Saxon name, 3; Episcopal see, 3; Saxons, 3; the Roman Eltavona, 3; destroyed by Scots and Picts, 3; of Celtic origin? 4; seat of Bishop of Lincoln, 6; held by Danes, 6; in Norman times, 6, 8; ransacked by Danes, 7; rebuilt by Edward the Confessor, 7; visited by Paulinus, 7; given to monastery of Stow, 8, 318; Wolsey at, 44; Scottish Army camps at, 47;

INDEX.

guilds, 53, 57, 65; Balderton Gate Mission, 57; Robert Brown's bequests to, 57; of Duke of Norfolk at, 60; confiscated land and property in and near, 62, 63; friars of Order of St. Augustine, 63, 64; Swan and Salmon Inn, 62; land in, granted by Henry VIII., 63; "Stocke," near, property in, 63; incorporation of, 65; municipal authority of, 65; Manor and Castle conveyed to Crown, 65; garrisoned for the king, 115; siege of, 116, 126, 142, 153, 226; Stock Library and Middleton Newsroom, 314. *See also* Grammar School, castle, church, vicars, mayors, aldermen, recorders, streets, etc.

Newark Castle. Thomas Adam, constable, 9; Wolsey at, 44; Castle Gate mentioned, 62.

Newark Church. An endowment of St. Catherine's Priory, 12; mentioned, 26; chancel erected, 41; choir stalls, 42; Dance of Death, 37, 38, 39, 40; Magnus' bequest to priests executing his obit, 53; memorials of the Markhams, 57; Lady Chapel, 58; Trinity Chapel, 58. *See also* Church.

Newark. Henry de, Dean and Archbishop of York, 20.

Newark. Lord, Address of, 110.

Newborough Monastery, Lincoln. Confiscated land of, 63.

Newcastle Family, 115, 118, 119, 123, 313.

Newdigate. Richard, 206.

Newspaper started. A Newark, 236.

Newtonn. Maior, 167.

Nicholas. Sir Edward, 113.

Noble. John, 90, 100.

Norfolk. Duke of, sent to assist Lord Shrewsbury, 60; at Newark, 60; at Doncaster, 61.

North Gate, 2, 9, 42, 75, 118, 174.

Norton. R., on discovery of ancient urns in Newark, 4.

Nottinggame, 98.

Nottingham. Trent Bridge at, 6; ransacked, 12; Bishop of St. Andrews a prisoner in castle, 20; David of Scotland prisoner at castle, 24; Peter de la Mare imprisoned in castle, 26; St. Anne's Well at, 27; castle, 30; Yorkists at, 30; Edward marches from, to meet rebels, 32; returns to Nottingham, 32; Edward IV. marches to, where he received aid, 32; Richard III. at, 32; marches to Bosworth Field, 32; king's prison at, 43; Lord Shrewsbury at, 59; passage at, fortified, 60; chauntries at, 70; expeditions against, 120, 122; Cavaliers in possession, 121; repulse of the second expedition, 123; free public libraries, 207, 233.

Odingsells. Emanuel, 74.

Oliver. Samuel, 245.

Ollerton on the old Great North Road, 6.

O'Neil. Lieut.-Col., 128.

Orde. Captain Anthony, 166.

Organ built in the church, 250.

Orme. W., of Elston, 74.

Osberton, 65.

Osmundthorpe. Newark, 42, 73.

Outram. Robert, 97, 101.

Owthorpe, 180, 186.

Oxford. Diana, Countess of, 102.

Oxford. Earl of, with Lancastrian forces at Newark, 32.

Oxford. King at, 157.

Page. Colonel, 145.

Palgrave. Sir John, 130.

Palmer, Mr., 115.

Palmer. Robert, 200.

Palmes. Sir Guy, of Ashwell, 74, 168.

Paman. Wm., 174.

Parchment making at Newark, 323.

Parish Lane, 185.

Parish registers. Extracts from, 190, 191.

Parliamentary representatives, 328.

Parliamentary representatives. List of, 330.

Parr. Sir W., joins Edward IV. at Nottingham, 32.

Parsons. Capt., 166.

Paston Letters quoted, 31.

Patent Rolls relating to Newark (temp. Edward III.), 26.

Paulinus. Missionary Bishop, 317.

Paulinus visits Newark and Southwell, 7.

Pavier. Lieut.-Col., 166.

Paxton. Mr., 245.

Paxton. William, 234.

Peace signed with Holland, 248.

Peck's *Annals* cited, 3.

Pelham. Captain, 166.

Percies join rebels, 59.

Perron. Cardinal du, 90.

Peter de la Mare, Speaker, confined for life, 26.

Peters. James, 208.

Philip. Bishop of Lincoln, 9.

Phillypot. William, 75, 76, 246, 301.

Philpot, 75.

Pierce. Dame Alice, 25, 26.

Pierrepont. Colonel, 120.

Pierrepont. Francis, 114.

Plague. The, 190.

Pocklington. Thomas, 27.

Pocock's *History of Gravesend*, 74.

Pomfret, 59, 60, 61.

Pontefract. Lord Shrewsbury marches to, 60.

Porter. Major-General, 127, 128.

Potter's Ditch, 2; Potter's Dike, 2.

Poyntz. General, 153, 154, 157.

Printing. Introduction into Newark, 233.

Priory of St. Catherine, near Lincoln, founded and endowed, 12, 63; Semperingham, 63.

Pryme. Abraham de la, 171, 200.

Provisions in 1801, 247.

Public-houses. The Talbot, 21; Saracen's Head, 21; White Hart, 21, 208; Dragon, 21; Swan and Salmon, 21, 762; White Hind, 244.

Puttenham, 89.

Races at Newark, 215.

Railway accident, 314.

Ramesden. W., receives lands, etc., 63.

Ramsey. Sir John, 166.

Ranby, 52.

Randall. Squire, 106.

Ratcliffe. King's army in, 34; "goode and true men" of, 34.

Rawson. Mr., 171.

Raynor. John, 202.

Read. Richard, 196.

Recorder. Gervas Moleneux, 90.

Recorders of Newark. List of, 333.

Reds. Procession of, 272.

Red Gutter; its origin, 36.

Reform Bill. Mr. Pitt's, 232.

Refuge. Places of, 323.

Regulations of the Town-Council, 207, 208.

Religious houses. *See* Monastery, Priory, Friars, etc.

Remigius. Bishop, 8.

Reniger. Samuel, 167.

Retirement of the Newark forces, 122.

Restoration. Rejoicings at the, 185.

Retford on the Great North Road, 6.

Reton, 65.

Review at Nottingham by the king, 111.

Rhodes. Joseph, 140, 141.

Rich. Lady, 89.

Richard III. ascended the throne, 32; at Nottingham, 32; slain, 32.

Richardson. Captain, 128.

Richmond assisted the king, 32; Earl of, at Shrewsbury, 32; ascended the throne as Henry VII., 32. *See also* Henry VII.

Ridgell. Mr., 218.

Riotous conduct in Newark, 244.

Risegate, 40.

Robbery of the parish church, 213.

Robert de Flintham, 19.

Robinson. J. C., on the Dance of Death, 38, 39.

Robsart. Amy, 89.

Rockett. Mr., 90.

Rogers. Capt. John, 166.

INDEX.

Roman antiquities found, 2, 3, 4, 5.
Roman Newark, 1, 2, 3, 4, 5, 6, 7.
Rooper. T., claims Manor of Elston, 64.
Roos. Lord, 89.
Roos. Thomas, Lord, of Orston, deprived of estates, 30.
Roses. Wars of the, Last of the. *See* Stoke, etc.
Rossiter. Colonel, 142, 153.
Rotherham. Edward IV. at, 32.
Rotul. Parl. cited, 34.
Royal Composition Papers. Extracts from, 183, 184.
Rufford granted to Sir J. Markham, 62; Abbey, 71.
Rupert. Prince, 126, 127, 140, 141, 142, 145, 148, 150, 152.
Russell. John, 196.
Rutland. Countess of, 99.
Rutland. Thomas, Earl of, 89.

SADLER'S. Mr., Maiden Speech, 269.
Sadler. Michael Thomas, 265, 271.
St. Anne's Well, Nottingham, 27.
St. Augustine Order of Friars, 63, 64.
St. Catherine's Chapel, Westhorpe, 27.
St. Catherine's Convent, near Lincoln, 41.
St. Catherine's Priory, 12.
St. Catherine's Well, Newark. Tradition as to the origin of, 27, 28.
St. Catherine's Well, Westhorpe, 27.
St. George. Richard, 90.
St. Leonard's Hospital, Newark, founded, 9; endowed, 10; *pas.* Stoke, 10, 23, 26.
Salisbury. Thomas, Bishop of, 176.
Saltpetre, 82.
Saltpetre man, 80.
Sanctuary. Right of, 42, 43.
Sandersonne. Captain Robert, 166.
Saucimer. Sir Guy, 27; William, 9, 28.
Saucimer. Matilda, 9.
Saunderson. Hon. Nicholas, 199.
Saunderson. Mr., 202.
Savage. Mr., 161.
Savile. Henry, 191, 192, 196, 200.
Savings' Bank, 314.
Saxon Chronicle quoted, 11.
Searsdale. Earl of, 63, 73.
Schools, 314.
Scofton, 65.
Scorvesley, 8.
Scotland. *See* Magnus.
Scotland. Discontent in, 107.
Scots and Picts destroyed Newark, 3.
Scots Commissioners' letter from Kelham to the Parliament, 159.
Scott. Mr. (afterwards Sir Gilbert G.), architect, 22.
Scirestone, 8.
Scrooby. Wolsey at, 44.
Seal of Newark, 77.
Selby. Peter, 251.

Sextons. List of, 295.
Shakerley. Ladye, 131.
Shakspeare quoted, 14.
Sheldon. Dr., 195.
Shelford, 21, 118, 166, 172.
Shelley. Right Hon. John, 216.
Sheriff. High, Sir John Digby, 114.
Sheriff. Sir Francis Thornhagh, 106.
Sherwin. Isaac, 196.
Sherwood Forest, 97.
Shelton. Hugh de, 19.
Shilton quoted, 18.
Ship money. Levying of, 105.
Shrewsbury, 32, 139.
Shrewsbury. Gilbert, Earl of, 98.
Shrewsbury. Lord, raises forces for the king, 59; at Nottingham and Newark, 59; marches to Pomfret, 60; assistance sent to, 60.
Sibthorpe. Magnus, resides at, 52.
Sidnacester, the Saxon name of Newark, 3; its position, 5.
Sieges of Newark, 116, 126, 142, 153. 326.
Sikes Family, 75.
Simnel. Lambert, claims to be Earl of Warwick, 32; at Dublin, 33; made prisoner at Stoke, 36; portrayed in Newark Church, 38. *See* also Stoke.
Simon. Richard, "a wily priest," 33.
Simpson. William, 244.
Skelton. W., chauntry priest, 72.
Sketchley. Mr., 219, 234.
Skroop. Sir Jarvis, 168.
Skrymshire, W., de Muskham, 30.
Sleaford Castle built, 9; in the king's hands, 11; John attacked with dysentery at, 14.
Sleeforth, 138.
Slingsby. Guildford, 116.
Sloane MSS. cited, 23.
Sloswick, 65.
Smith. Captain, 166.
Smith. Dr., cited, 5, 7.
Smith. Lieutenant, 140.
Smith. Peter, 100.
Smythe. Rev. J., Vicar of Newark, 42.
Snell. W., mayor, 75.
Snid or Snite River, 3.
Somerton Castle, Navenby. John, King of Scotland, imprisoned at, 24.
Southwell. Visited by Paulinus, 7; St. Mary's Church, 12; Lord's, Holy, and Lady's Wells, 27; origin of its name, 27; sanctuary at, 43; Wolsey at, 44; Queen Henrietta at, 119; arrival of the king at, 147, 159; Cromwell and his troops at, 180; General Monk and his troops at, 139, 144, 185, 247.
Spaldford, 8.
Spittal. The, 10, 88, 89, 128, 129, 165.

Spondon. J., de Newark, 30.
Spragging. Thomas, mayor, 245.
Standard. The raising of, 112.
Standish. Alderman, 168.
Standish. Edward, Maior, 174.
Stanhope. Colonel, 166.
Stanhope. Lady Anne, possesses Stoke Bardolph, 62.
Stanhope. Sir Richard, 74.
Stanidge. John, 101.
Stanley. Lord, 31.
State Papers cited, 47, 48.
Staunton. Anne, 195.
Staunton. Colonel William, 195.
Staunton. Johan de, 9.
Stephen seized castles, 11.
Stephens. Mrs., 211.
Stevenson. Mr., elected churchwarden, 218.
Stevenson. Mr. William, on Roman origin of Newark, 5, 6, 7.
Stoches, 8.
Stodman Street, 20, 236, 244.
Stoke, 94, 165.
Stoke Bardolph bestowed on Lady Stanhope, 62.
Stoke. Battle of, 33; its origin, 33; preparations for, 34, 35; description of the, 35; claimed, 64; loss of life at, 36; plague at, 166.
Stokum. Robert de, 9.
Stones' charity. Henry, 199.
Stow, the Sidnacester of the Saxons, 5.
Stow Monastery. Newark and Flatburch (Flodborough) given to, 8.
Stow. W., 35.
Stowe cited, 15.
Strafford. Sir Thomas Wentworth, Earl of, 97.
Streets of Newark. Appleton Gate, 42, 72, 91; Balderton Road, 271; Balkerton Gate, 19, 57; Barnby Gate, 19, 232, 295; Barnby Road, 314; Barr Gate, 93; Carter Gate, 20; Castle Gate, 2, 5, 20, 62; Coddington Lane, 20, 75; Cooke's Row, 20; Denholm Way, 20; Drybridge, 2; East Gate, 2; Ermine Street, 7; Fosseway, 2, 5, 6, 7; Hawton Road, 314; Kirk Gate, 285; Lombard Street, 2, 295, 314; London Road, 314; Middlegate, 9, 19, 75; Millgate, 28, 190; Milne Gate, 20, 65, 94; North Gate, 2, 9, 20, 42, 75, 118, 174; Parish Lane, 185; Parliament Street, 292; Pavement Street, 75; Potter's Ditch, 2; Red Gutter, 56; Sewsterne Lane, 7; The Spittal, 10, 88, 89, 128, 129, 165; Stodmere (Stodman) Street, 20, 236, 244.
Stukeley. Dr., Newark as a Roman city, 1, 2, 3; cited, 9, 18, 79; biographical sketch of, 215.
Sturtevant's charity. Mary, 216.

INDEX.

Sturtevant. William, 102.
Summer's charity. Thomas, 206.
Surtees Society. *See* Tonge.
Surtees Society Publications. Extract from, 171.
Sutton Family. Biographical sketch of, 310-12.
Sutton. John Manners, 231, 251.
Sutton. Lord George, 215, 216, 218, 230.
Sutton. Mr., 115, 181, 182. *See also* Lord Lexington.
Sutton. Richard, 206.
Sutton Scarsdale, Derbyshire, 73.
Sutton. Sir Charles Manners, 285.
Sutton. Sir Robert, 224.
Sutton. Sir W., 85.
Sutton. Thomas Manners, 245.
Swan and Salmon Inn, 62.
Swartz. Col. Martin, 35; killed at Stoke, 36.
Swift. Frances, 73.
Swineshead Abbey, John sick at, 14.
Sykes. Joseph, 209, 232.

Talbot. Gilbert, 35.
Talbot. The, 21.
Taylor. Brian, 98.
Taylor. Dr. Robert, sketch of, 214.
Theobald. Sir George, 104.
Therald de Burgenhall, Sheriff of Lincolnshire, brother-in-law to Leofric, 8.
Thesiger. Frederick, 287-8.
Thomlynson. Christopher, glover, of Newark, 43, 44.
Thompson. George, executed, 248.
Thompson. Joseph, 195.
Thompson. Launcelot, 97, 106.
Thornhagh. Colonel, 139.
Thornbagh. Sir Francis, 106.
Thornton. T., chauntry priest, 72.
Thorold. Sir W., 74.
Thoroton. Dr. Robert, referred to, 8, 10, 12, 73.
Thorpe claimed, 64.
Thurgarton priory, 21, 27, 72, 139.
Tilbury, 74.
Tillier. Colonel, 129, 130.
Tomlinson. James, 208.
Tonge's *Visitation of Yorkshire* quoted, 57.
Toplady. Alderman, 120.
Torneshay, 8.
Torre's *Collectanea* quoted, 21.
Town-clerk. Thomas Bullar, 103.
Town-hall built, 222.
Towton. Battle of, 31.
Trent bridges. The, 6, 121, 125, 138, 144.

Trent. River, navigation of, 1; Roman name, 3; baptism in, 7.
Trollope. Colonel, 168.
Trollope. Dr. Bishop, 174.
Truman. Henry, 195.
Tucker. Gertrude, 224.
Turberville. Captain Sir Troilus, 166.
Tuxford, 146.
Twentiman. John, 90.
Twentiman. William, 196.
Twentyman. Alderman John, 84, 88.
Twentyman. Captaine Edward, 167.
Twentyman. Mr., 115.

Valor Ecclesiasticus cited, 21, 70.
Vavasour. Richard, receives lands, etc., 65.
Vendour. John, of Newark, 26.
Vicars of Newark. List of, 333.
Victoria. Queen, proclamation of, 292.
Volunteer corps, 241, 242, 249.
Volunteer Infantry. Newark, colours presented to, 243; address to the king from, 245.
Vyner. Mrs. Anne, 74.

Walcotts, 52.
Walfild. Richardi, de Newerk, 30.
Walker. Sir Edward, 152.
Warburton. Bishop W., 1, 223-230.
Warburton Family. The, 327.
Warwick. Earl of, at Chesterfield, 31; at Manchester, 31, 32; assisted Henry to escape from the Tower, 32; in Warwickshire, 32, 113.
Washington. Captain Derey, 166.
Waterloo veteran. Death of a Newark, 253.
Waterworth. Dr., 28.
Webster. Henry, 90.
Welbeck Manor, 146, 147.
Welbourne, 217.
Wells. *See* St. Anne's, Nottingham; Southwell; Westhorpe.
Wellys. Sir Robert, 31.
Wesley. John, at Newark, 232.
Westhorpe. St. Catherine's Well at, 27.
Whalley. Colonel, 146.
Wharton. Captain William, 166.
Whatton Rectory presented to Cranmer, 64.
Wheeler. Major, 141.
White. Bishop, 198.
White. Captain, 117, 140.
White Hart, 208.
White Hind, 244.
White. Hugh, chauntry priest, 72.

White. J. de Colyngham, 30.
White. Thomas, 195.
White's charity. Bishop, 201.
White. Bishop, Library of, 201.
Whitecote. Lieut.-Col., 141.
Whitmore. Major Thomas, 166.
Whittington. Captain Luke, 195.
Widmerpoole. Mr., 180.
Wiggesley, 8.
Wild. Rev. J., 269.
Wilde. Serjeant Thomas (Solicitor-General), 266, 267, 271, 273, 284, 287.
Wilkie. John, 90.
Williamson. F., 169.
Williamson. Sir Thomas, 115, 181, 182, 188.
Willis' *Abbeys* cited, 73.
Willis. Sir Richard, appointed governor, 142, 146, 147, 151, 171.
Willoughby. Sir Francis, of Wollaton, 65. *See also* Middleton.
Willoughby. Henry, 251, 263, 271.
Willoughby. Lord, 125.
Willoughby-on-the-Wolds, the *Vernometum* of Antoninus, 5.
Willoughby. Sir Thomas, 206.
Willoughby. Mr., 231.
Willson. E. J., on the Fleming Brass, 22.
Wilson. Christopher, 101, 138.
Wilson. Dr. Barnard, 209, 217; biographical sketch of, 219, 220, 221; charity, 220.
Winthorpe, 189, 214.
Wirksworth, 74, 144.
Wise. W., chauntry priest, 72.
Witchrote. Captain William, 167.
Withrington. Lord, 174.
Wiverton House, 118.
Wolsey. Cardinal, at Newark, 44; at Southwell, 44; at Scrooby, 44; arrested for high treason, 44; at Leicester, 44.
Wood. Colonel Mark, 245.
Wood. John, 101.
Wood. Robert, 101.
Woodborough, 74.
Woodward. Hugh, 183.
Worham Eyrome, 92.
Worksop Rectory. Reversion of, 65.
Worsop Manor, 146.
Worthies. Warburton, W. (Bishop of Gloucester), 1.
Wright. John, 196.
Wulwi. Bishop of Lincoln, 8.
Wymunthorpe, 8.

York, 139; Edward IV. at, 31, 32; rebels refused admission to, 34.

LIST OF SUBSCRIBERS TO THIS VOLUME.

Those before whose names an asterisk is placed subscribed for the Special Edition, of which only One Hundred Copies will be issued.

ABBOTT, Mr. Thomas, Newark.
A. C. F., Newark.
Allott, C.E., Mr. C. S., Manchester.
Almond, Mr. R. P., Newark.
Anderson, Mr. John, Newark.
Armstrong, Mr. W. B., Newark.
Ashby, Dr. Alfred, Grantham.
Axtell, Mr. H., Southwell.

*BACON, Mr., Schools of Art, Newcastle and Stoke.
Bacon, Mr. T., Southwell.
Bagshaw, Mr. John, Mansfield.
Bailey, Mr. Edward, Collingham.
Bailey, Rev. A. W., Stoke.
Baines, Mr. C., Newark.
Baker, Mr., Newark.
Baker, Mr. W., Newark.
Bakewell, Mr. John, Balderton.
Ball, Mr. Thomas, Newark.
Barber, Mrs. S., Newark.
*Barfoot, Mr., Alderman, Leicester.
Barratt, Mr. G., Newark.
Bayliffe, Mr. R., Newark.
Beal, Rev. A. (formerly Newark).
Bealby, Mr. George, Collingham.
Beard, Mr. R. J., Newark.
Beardsley, Mr. F., Quorndon.
Bedford, Mr. Edward, Newark.
Beech, Mr., Newark.
Beech, Mr. James, Grantham.
Bell, Mr. J., Nottingham.
Belk, Mr. George, Nottingham.
Bennett, Mr. Edward, Newark.
Bennett, Mr. J. H., Collingham.
Bennett, Mr. W., Newark.
Bescoby, Mr. T., Retford.
Bilson, Mr. J., Newark.
Birch, Mr. George, Hampstead.
Bishop, Mr., Newark.
Bishop, Mr. R., Newark.
Blagg, Mrs., Langford.
Blyton, Mr. James, Newark.

Bocock, Mr. Charles, Newark.
Bousfield, Mr. E., Newark.
Bradley, Mr. T., Newark.
Bradley, Mr. T. N., Derby.
Bradshaw, Mr. Charles, Nottingham.
Bradshaw, Mr. Samuel, Pendleton.
Bramley, Mr. S., Mansfield.
Brammer, Mr. T., Newark.
*Branston, J.P., Mr. Alderman, Newark.
*Branston, J.P., Mr. Councillor J. G., Newark.
*Branston, Mr. George H., Newark.
Branston, Mr. H. H., London.
Branston, Mr. W. W., London.
Branston senior, Mrs., Newark.
Bristowe, Q.C., Mr. H. F., London.
Bristowe, Q.C., M.P., Mr. S. B., Twickenham.
Brodhurst, Mr. B., Newark.
Bromley, Sir Henry, Stoke.
Brookes, Mr. John, Southwell.
Brookes, Mr. Robert, Nottingham.
Brown, Mr. G., Newark.
Brown, Mr. Henry, Hull.
Brown, Mr. John, Newark.
*Brown, Mr. John Henry, Nottingham.
Brown, Mr. Thomas, Newark.
Bugg, Mr. Henry, Newark.
Bugg, Mr. Isaac, Newark.
Bull, Mr. A. E., Rolleston.
Bullen, Mr. John, Newark.
Burgess, Mr. J., Newark.
Burnby, Mrs., Bennington.
Bussell, Mr. Edwin A., Newark.
Bussell, Rev. F. V., Balderton.

CAFFERATA sen., Mrs., Newark.
Cane, Rev. T. C., Southwell.

Caparn, Mr. Councillor, J. S., Collingham.
Caparn, Mr. T. J., Farndon.
Capps, Mr. J. T., Newark.
*Castle, Mr. John, Newark.
Chamberlain, Mr. T., Kelham.
Chapman, Rev. W. Stacey, Newark.
Chappell, Mr. W., Tuxford.
Chawner, Mrs., Newark.
Cheetham, Mr. Thos., Newark.
Cherry, Mr. J. R., Newark.
Chettle, Mr. Thomas, Car-Colston.
Chew, Mr. George, Newark.
Clark, Mrs., Newark.
Clarke, Miss A., Newark.
Clarke, Mr. H., Newark.
Clarke, Mr. W. P., Newark.
Clinton, Rev. H. F., Cromwell.
Cockayne, Mr. B. H., Nottingham.
Collinson, Mr. S., Nottingham.
Cook, Mr. Robert, Wellingore.
Cooke, Mr. Thomas, Newark.
Cooling, Mr. W. J., Newark.
Cooper, Mr. H. G., Newark.
Cooper, Mr. R. H., Collingham.
Cooper, Mr. Thomas, Congleton.
Cosham, Mr. Thomas, Newark.
Cross, Mr. John, Newark.
Crossley, Mr. Councillor J., Newark.
Crowder, Mr. H., Newark.

DARCY, Mr. Robert, Newark.
Davis, Mr. Henry, Averham.
Davis, Mr. J. M., Newark.
Dent, Mr. John, Newark.
Derry, Mr. John, Newark.
Dixon, Mr. F., Newark.
Dixon, Mr. O., Newark.
Dodson, Mr., Rotherham.
Drabble, Mr. H. T., Newark.
Drabble, Mr. J. B., Winthorpe.

LIST OF SUBSCRIBERS.

Duke, Mr. W., Newark.
Dunn and Fry, Messrs., Nottingham.

*EARP, M.P., Mr. Thomas, Newark.
Edlin, Mr. Henry, Newark.
Edlin, Mrs. Jane, Newark.
Edwards, Mr. T., Newark.
Egglestone, Mrs., Newark.
Elam, Mr. John, Newark.
Elliot, Mr. F., Newark.
Else, Mr. Thomas, Newark.
Elson, Mr. Geo., Newark.
Esam, Mr. Geo., Normanton.
Eve, Mr. J., Collingham.
Ewen, Mr. J. E., Chester.
Eyre, Mr. Joseph, Balderton.
Eyre, Mr. Vincent, Newark.

FALKNER, Mr. E. S., Newark.
Falkner, Mr. P. R., Upton.
Ffytche, F.S.A., Mr. L. Lewis, Thorpe Hall, Elkington.
Field, Mr. S., Farnsfield.
Fillingham, Mr. B., Newark.
Finch-Hatton, Hon. M. E. G., Haverholme Priory.
Fisher, Mr. Edward, Sidmouth.
Fitzackerley, Mr. W., Newark.
Fletcher, Mr. C., Broomsgrove.
Fletcher, Mrs. W. O., Clapham.
Flinders, Mr. G., Newark.
Flowers, Mr. John, Newark.
*Forman, Mr. John, Nottingham.
Fox, Rev. John, Newark.
Francis, Mr. James, Kensington.
Freeth, Mr. G., Clifton.
Fretwell, Mr. Thomas, Newark.
Friend, Mr. H., Newark.

GABBITASS, Mr. J. G., Newark.
Gamble, Mr. G. H., Newark.
Gascoyne, Mr. George, Newark.
Gilbert, Mr. Henry, Barnby.
Gilbert, Mr. John, Birmingham.
Gilstrap, Mr. W., Fornham Park.
Gilstrap, Mrs., Winthorpe.
*Gladstone, Right Hon. W. E., Hawarden.
Glazebrooke, Mr. S., Newark.
Godber, Mr. S., Balderton.
Good, Miss. S., Newark.
Gould, Mr. Gilbert, Hartington.
Gould, Mrs. M., Newark.
Greaves, Mr. J. J., Preston.
Greenberry, Mr. G., Newark.

Greenhalgh, Mr. H. J., Mansfield.
Gregory, Mr. J., Newark.
Gresham, Mr. R. B., Newark.
Gretton, Mr. J., Newark.
Griffin, Mr. R., Newark.
Grocock, Mr. G., Newark.

HADFIELD, Mr. W. P., Newark.
Hall, Mr. Herbert, Newark.
Hall, Mr. John, Sibthorpe.
Hall, Mrs., Newark.
Hallowes, Mr. W. B., Newark.
Halls, Mr., Newark.
Halstead, Mr., Balderton.
Hankey, Mr. Douglas, Newark.
Hardy, Mr. W., Dudley.
Hardy, Mrs. A., Raithley Hall.
Harris, Mr. Joseph, Newark.
Harrison, Mr. H., Newark.
Harrison, Mr. W., Newark.
Harston, Mr. J. F., Newark.
Hart, Mr. George, Newark.
Hart, Mr. G. J., Collingham.
Harvey, Mr. Alderman, Newark.
Harvey, Mr. H., Collingham.
Harvey, Mr. John, Newark.
Hawkins, Mr. G., Newark.
Hayward, Mr., Langford.
Henderson, Mr. Thos., Newark.
Henry, Mr. Councillor R., Newark.
Heppenstall, Mr. Councillor C., Newark.
Heppenstall, Rev. F., Sedbergh.
Heymann, Mr. H., Nottingham.
Hibbs, Mr. W., Ollerton.
Hill, Mr. Samuel, Kelham.
Hindley, Mr. R. E., Newark.
Hitchin, Mr. W., Besthorpe.
Hodgkinson sen., J.P., Mr. G., Newark.
Hodgkinson junr., Mr. Grosvenor, Newark.
Hodgkinson, Mr. Robert, Newark.
Hole, Mr. James, Farndon.
*Hole, Rev. Canon, Caunton.
Holmes, Mr. G., Broughton.
Holmes, Mrs. Annie, Newark.
Hooks, Mr. D., Newark.
Hopewell, Mr. F. H., Newark.
Horncastle, Mr. H., Ollerton.
Horner, Mr. E., Newark.
Housin, Mrs., Fulbeck.
Howcroft, Mr. J., Newark.
Howitt, Mr. John, Newark.
Hoyes, Mr. Thomas, Hawton.

Huntsman, J.P., Mr. B., West Retford Hall.
Hurst, Mr. C. H., Newark.
Hurst, Mr. George, Newark.
Hurst, Mr. Hugh, Bromley.
Hurst, Mr. W., Newark.
Hutchinson sen., Mr.
Hutchinson, Mr. F. F., Newark.
Hutchinson, Mr. John, Newark.

*IRONMONGER, Mr. Councillor S., Newark.
Ironmonger, Miss, A., Newark.
Irving, M.D., Mr. Councillor, Newark.

JACKSON, Miss T. M., Hastings.
Jackson, Mr. Edward, Newark.
Jackson, Mr. Robert, Long Bennington.
James, F.S.A., Rev. T., Huddersfield.
James, Mr. Francis, Kensington.
Jenkinson, Mr., Newark.
Jenkinson jun., Mr., Newark.
Job, Mr. S., Newark.
Johnson, Mr. J., Newark.
Judge, Mr. C., Newark.
Jukes, Rev. J. G., Newark.

KELLY, Mr. W., Newark.
Kemp, Mr. E., Collingham.
Kent and Co., Messrs., London.
King, Mr. Jno., Leamington.
King, Mr. R. F. H., Newark.
Kirkby, Mr. R., Newark.
Kirkland, Mr. J. W., Southwell.
Knight jun., Mr. James, Newark.

LACY, Mr. William, Newark.
*Lammin, Mr. Henry, Newark.
Lane, Mr. Councillor C., Newark.
Lane, Mr. Walter, Newark.
Lawson, Mr. Isaac, Newark.
Lawton, Miss, Newark.
Lee, Mr. J. T., Winthorpe.
Leek, Mr. Richard, Southwell.
Levers, Mr. G. R., Winthorpe.
Leverton, Mr. John, Skegby.
Lighting, Mr., Newark.
Lilley, Mr. William, Newark.
Lineham, Mr. E., Wath-upon-Dearne.
*Lineham, Mr. F. R., Scarborough.
Lineham, Mr. John, Newark.
Loversidge, Mr. J. F., Newark.
*Lowe, F.S.A., Captain A. E. L., Highfield House.

LIST OF SUBSCRIBERS.

Lunn, Mr. A., Newark.
Luscomb, Mr. W. E., Collingham.
Lys, Mr. E. W., Newark.

MACKENZIE, Mr. Councillor T., Newark. —
M'Leod, Mr. J. W., Newark.
Maltby, Ven. Archdeacon, Farndon.
Manchester Free Library, Manchester.
*Manners-Sutton, J.P., Mr. J. H., Kelham Hall.
Manning, Mr. Alderman, Nottingham.
Manuel, Mr. B., Derby.
March, Mr. W., Newark.
Marsh, Mr. Thomas, Newark.
Marshall, Mr. Edward, Leicester.
Marshall, Mr. G. J., Newark.
Marshall, Mr. W., Newark.
Marsland, Mr. G. H., Newark.
Mather, Mr. W., Newark.
Matterson, Mr. R., Newark.
Matthews, Mrs., Newark.
*Massey, Mr. R. M., Kensington.
*May, Mr. Henry, Honolulu.
*Miller, Miss, Newark.
Mills, Mr. G. H., Newark.
Milthorp, Mr. E., Newark.
Mitchie, Mr. R., Leicester.
Morgan, Mr. Henry, Newark.
Morley, Mr. F. R., Leicester.
Morley, Mr. John, Leicester.
Morton, Dr. Thomas H., Sheffield.
Moss, Mr. W., Mansfield.
Moss, Mr. W., Newark.
Mounteney, Mr. B., Newark.

NEAL, Mr. James, Newark.
Nevile, Mr. E. H., Thorney.
Newark Constitutional Association.
Newark Mechanics' Institution.
Newark Stock Library.
Newbald, J.P., Mr. Alderman, Newark.
*Newton, Mr. William, Newark.
*Nicholson, J.P., Mr. Alderman, Newark.
*Nicholson, Mr. E. H., Newark.
Norris, Major G. G., Brinkley Castle.
Norris, Mr., Nottingham.
Nottingham Bromley House Library.
Nottingham Free Library.

Nottingham, the Town Council of (per Mr. Johnson). 6 Copies.

OATES, J.P., Mr. W. H. C., Langford Hall, Newark.
Oldham, Miss E. M., Balderton.
Oldham, Mr. E. E., Newark.
Oldham, Mr. John, Mansfield.
Oldham, J.P., Mr. Thomas, Newark.
Oldknow, Alderman Sir James, Mayor of Nottingham.
Osborne, Mrs., Balderton.
Ossington, the Viscountess, Ossington Hall, Newark.
*Ouvry, F.S.A., Mr. F., London.
Oxby, Mr. Thomas, Newark.

PALETHORPE, Mrs., Newark.
Palmer, Mr. Alfred E., Mansfield.
Parnell, Miss C., London.
Parnell, Rev. F., Godstone.
Parnham, Mr. T., Newark.
Parr, Mr. Samuel, Nottingham.
Paulson, Mr. William, Newark.
Pawson, Mr. John, Newark.
Payling, Mr. C., Newark.
Payling, Mr. E., Newark.
Pearson, Rev. Dr., Newark.
Pinder, Mr. Councillor T., Newark.
Place, Mrs. J., Nottingham.
Pocklington, Mr. F., Newark.
Postill, Mr. John, Newark.
*Pratt, Mr. Alderman B. T., Mayor of Newark.
*Pretty, Mr. T. C., Leeds.
Proctor, Mr. Harrison, Newark.

QUARITCH, Mr. B., London.
Quibell, Mr. W. O., Newark.

RADFORD, Mr. W., Newark.
Read, Mr. Alfred, Newark.
Reynolds, Mr. E., Tuxford.
Richardson, Mr. J. B., Newark.
Richmond, Mr. R. C., Collingham.
*Riddell, J.P., Mr. Councillor E. M. H., Carlton.
Ridge, Mr. C. J., Newark.
Ridge, Mr. John, Manchester.
Ridley, Mr., Liverpool.
Rippingale, Mr. W., Newark.
Robertson, Major, Widmerpool.
Robinson, Mr. G. H., Newark.
Rycroft, Mr. R., London.

SAINT, Mr. J. J. H., Recorder of Newark.
Saunders, Mr. Councillor, Newark.
Scrimshaw, Mr. J., Newark.
Scruton, Mr. P. D., Bennington.
Seels, Mr. G. H., Newark.
Seely, J.P., Colonel C., Sherwood Hall, Nottingham.
Sharpe, Mr. J. C., Newark.
Sharpe, Mr. S., Retford.
Shepherd, Mr. J., Newark.
*Sheppard, Mr. George, Newark.
Sheppard, Mrs., Newark.
Simmonds, Mr. E. T., Newark.
Simpson, Mrs. J. A., Newark.
Sims, Mr. J., Newark.
Sketchley, B.A., Mr. R. F., South Kensington Museum.
Slater, Mr. D., Newark.
Slater sen., Mr. W., Newark.
Slater jun., Mr. W., Newark.
Smith and Co., Messrs., bankers, Nottingham and elsewhere.
Smith, Mr. C., Barnby Villa.
Smith, Mr. Charles, Newark.
Smith, Mr. H. R., Newark.
Smith, Mr. J. F., Newark.
Smith, Mr. John, Newark.
Smith, Mr. Joseph, Newark.
Smith, Mr. J. W., Newark.
Smith jun., Mr. J. W., Newark.
Smith, Mr. W., Newark.
Smith, Mr. W. A., Newark.
Smith, Mrs. T., Newark.
Smith, Rev. E. W., Newark.
Smith-Woolley, Mr. T., Collingham.
Sneath, Mr. T. D., Newark.
Sorrell, Mr. Golding, Newark.
Speechley, Mr. H., Newark.
Spencer-Conyer, Mr. T., Hornsey Rise.
Spurrit, Mr. W. A., Camden Town.
Staley, Mr. J., Collingham.
Staniland, Mr. C., Newark.
Stephenson, Mr. G., Newark.
Stevens, Mr. W., Newark.
Stinson, Mr. R., Newark.
Stoakes, Mr. W. H., Newark.
Straw, Mr. R., Newark.
Strelley-Parker, Mr. R., Denby Old Hall.
Sugden, Mrs., Hexgreave Park.
Surgey, Mr. F., Kelham.
Symonds, Rev. H. G., Winthorpe.

2 Y

LIST OF SUBSCRIBERS.

TALBOT, Mr. W., Newark.
Tallents, J.P., Mr. Alderman, Newark.
Tallents, Mr. Godfrey, Newark.
Taylor, Mr. R. J., Newark.
Taylor, Mrs. H., Newark.
*Thorpe, Mr. James, Coddington.
Thorpe, Mr. Thomas, Newark.
Thrale, Mr. J. C., Newark.
Tinley, Mr. Edward, De Pue, Illinois, U.S.
Tinley, Mr. F. J., Southwell.
Tomlinson, Mr. E., Leicester.
Tomlinson, Mr. J. H., Newark.
Tomlinson, Mr. R. A., Sandbach.
Tomlinson, Mrs. W. H., Newark.
Torr, Mr. Charles Hawley, Nottingham.
Toule, Mr. J., Langford.
Turgoose, Mrs., Newark.
Turney, Mr. Sheriff, Nottingham.
Turton, Mr. E., Collingham.
Twidale, Mr., Thorpe.

UPTON, Captain R., Newark.

VASON, Mr. G., Newark.
Vaux, Mr., M.A., Balliol Coll., Oxford; and F.R.S., Sec. R.S.L., and R.A.S., London.
Veyret, Madame P. A., Paris.

WADDINGTON, Mr. C. F., Sheffield.
Walker, Mr. W., Newark.
*Walker, Sir A. B., Gateacre.
Wallis, Mr. G. H., Nottingham.
*Wallis, Mr. W., Newark.
*Walton, Mr. Councillor H., Newark.
Walton sen., Mr., Newark.
Wand, Mr. John, Leicester.
Ward, Miss, Winthorpe.
Warwick, Mr. G., Newark.
*Warwick, Mr. Huskinson, Easthorpe, Southwell.
*Warwick, Mr. J. F., Newark.
*Warwick, Mr. W. D., Newark.
*Warwick, Mrs., Newark.
Washington, Rev. R., Hawton.
Waterworth, Miss, Newark.
Watkin, Mrs., Newark.
Weaver, Mr. Councillor H., Newark.

Webb, Mr. A., Kelham.
Welch, Mr. W., Newark.
West, Mr. S. D., Newark.
White, Mr. Robert, Newark.
White, Mr. Robert, Worksop.
Whitelegge, Rev. Canon, Farnsfield.
Whittingham, Mr., Southwell.
Wigginton, Mr. H. B., Newark.
Wildsmith, Mr., Newark.
Wilkinson, Mr. J. T., Newark.
Wilkinson, Mr. Martin, Newark.
Wilkinson, Mr. W., Newark.
Williams, Mr. W. H., Newark.
Wills, Mr. H., Newark.
Wilson, Mr. Edward, Winthorpe.
Wilson, Mr. G., Derby.
Wilson, Mr. R. S., Tuxford.
Wilson, Mrs., Balderton.
Withers, Mr., Bourne.
Wood, Rev. A. W., S. Muskham.
Wood, Rev. W., Thorpe.
Woodcock, Mr. W. S., Newark.
Wright, Col. I. C., Stapleford.
Wright, Mr. John, Newark.
*Wright, Mrs. A., Southwell.
Wunch jun., Mr. E., Manchester.

NOTE.—*A number of Subscribers take more than one Volume each, and the names of others are omitted by request.*

www.ingramcontent.com/pod-product-compliance
Lightning Source LLC
Chambersburg PA
CBHW032044220426
43664CB00008B/859